Disaster Recovery

Disaster Recovery

BRENDA D. PHILLIPS, Ph.D.

CRC Press
Taylor & Francis Group

Boca Raton   London   New York

CRC Press is an imprint of the
Taylor & Francis Group, an **informa** business

AN AUERBACH BOOK

Auerbach Publications
Taylor & Francis Group
6000 Broken Sound Parkway NW, Suite 300
Boca Raton, FL 33487-2742

© 2009 by Taylor & Francis Group
Auerbach Publications is an imprint of Taylor & Francis Group, an Informa business

No claim to original U.S. Government works

Printed in the United States of America on acid-free paper
10 9 8 7 6 5 4 3 2 1

International Standard Book Number-13: 978-1-4200-7420-8 (Hardback)

Library of Congress Cataloging-in-Publication Data

Phillips, Brenda.
    Disaster recovery / Brenda Phillips.
       p. cm.
    Includes bibliographical references and index.
    ISBN 978-1-4200-7420-8 (hardcover : alk. paper)
    1. Emergency management--United States. 2. Disasters--United States. 3. Risk management--United States. 4. Hazard mitigation--United States. 5. Terrorism--United States--Prevention. 6. Disaster relief--United States--Planning. I. Title.

HV551.3.P49 2009
363.34'70973--dc22
                                            2009006920

Visit the Taylor & Francis Web site at
http://www.taylorandfrancis.com

and the Auerbach Web site at
http://www.auerbach-publications.com

This book is dedicated to the volunteers and staff, past, present and future, of the Mennonite Disaster Service.

Contents

SECTION I Understanding Disaster Recovery

SECTION II   Dimensions of Disaster Recovery

CHAPTER 5 — Environmental Recovery **133**

CHAPTER 6 — Historic and Cultural Resources. **159**

SECTION III Recovery Resources

Preface

This book is the result of many years of research, experience, and reflection on the part of many people. I am indebted to central scholars in the field of disaster research for sharing their time and knowledge with me. I thank particularly Dr. E. L. Quarantelli, cofounder of the Disaster Research Center, who first hired me as a graduate assistant while at The Ohio State University. Dr. David M. Neal was my graduate student colleague at the time and has been my husband for the past 22 years. As a continuing colleague in the field, he has given time, references, and suggestions—as well as lots of espresso—over the past 13 months while I wrote this book. Dr. William Anderson of the National Academies, formerly of the National Science Foundation (NSF), served as the program officer for my first NSF grant. I thank him for his faith and hope that this book serves as a useful guide to both students and those who work in the field of disaster recovery. I am indebted to the National Science Foundation for multiple grants that allowed me access to recovery locations. Many of those sites are included in this textbook as examples. For places that lack citations, the work is based on those NSF grants, which I hope produce additional societal benefits through this book.

This book is intended to be a guide through the laborious and often frustrating process of disaster recovery. There is no other stand-alone disaster recovery text or book like this, which made it particularly challenging to write. There is no formula or standardized content. There are no established concepts, and definitions vary from one author to another. Clearly, the field of emergency management remains an emerging discipline, especially in the area of recovery. To produce this book, I have addressed the key topics that arise repeatedly in a recovery setting. I have included what I have learned from the scholarly writings of my colleagues and from more than 25 years of my own research, volunteering, and consulting in the field. Time and space limit what I have been able to include. I look forward to readers' suggestions to include in a second edition.

I have tried to write this book in a realistic yet positive manner. Recovery can be massive and overwhelming but time and time again I have observed tremendous efforts to help those affected by disasters. I am warmed by the volunteers who dedicate months or years of their lives to helping others and believe that we are, as a nation, truly compassionate and caring people. The amount of time that public officials put into recovery is equally staggering, and I have seen colleagues work to the point of exhaustion repeatedly. The recovery period demonstrates the lengths to which people will stretch in order to be of service to people they do not even know. The faith-based organizations mentioned in this book particularly represent that spirit. They have been active at every single disaster I have studied, and I know they will be there, for whoever needs them, far into the future.

This book proved challenging because of the scant research that exists on the recovery period. I have tried to unearth and include as much information as possible. I value and appreciate the work of my colleagues in the disaster research field and hope that we continue to generate insights on the recovery process. If I have failed to include one of your contributions, I invite you to send it to me for the second edition. It is clear that recovery research, as well as changes to policy and practice, occur after the "big ones." Thus, readers will find a fair amount on September 11 and Hurricane Katrina, but I have also tried to include a range of geographic locations and jurisdictional sizes as examples.

Throughout this text, you will find an integration of several key themes. Rather than write a separate chapter on vulnerable populations, for example, I have integrated the topic into every chapter. People with disabilities, senior citizens, single parents, and others who face higher risk in a disaster should not be a separate chapter, they should be included in every way imaginable so as to generate an equitable, holistic recovery that leaves no one behind. A second theme is the importance of tying mitigation measures into every dimension of recovery. When we rebuild communities, we must do so in a way that fosters more disaster resilience to future events. We must take advantage of the opportunities that recovery provides. A third theme centers on maintaining environmental integrity. There are many ways in which we can rebuild so as to reduce future dependence on nonrenewable resources and to reduce our current impact on the Earth's assets. Future generations will thank us, and we can rest easier knowing that we have not harmed habitats or species during recovery efforts.

I acknowledge with deep appreciation the generosity of others who provided suggestions, photographs, permissions, figures, boxed content, and more. They include those acknowledged in the featured segments of each chapter (photos, figures, boxes, tables) as well as treasured colleagues and new friends who went above and beyond: Dr. Pam Jenkins of the University of New Orleans, who inspired me daily with her courage to survive and facilitate local recovery; Dr. Kathy Thomas for her input on the psychology chapter and dedication to those in trauma; Melvena Heisch of the Oklahoma State Historical Preservation Office, who taught me so much about the topic; Jenny Mincin, Elizabeth Davis, and Becky Hansen of EAD & Associates, LLC, who work daily to serve people with disabilities; Rev. Kris Peterson and Rev. Dick Krajeski, who embody the essence of community-based recovery; Dr. Elaine Enarson, the world's leading scholar-practitioner in gender and disaster; Jenna Campbell, who has led three mission teams (and is planning more) from First Presbyterian Church in Stillwater, Oklahoma to New Orleans; Sarah Norman-Black of the New Zealand Ministry of Civil Defence and Emergency Management; and valued colleagues who supported me throughout the effort, including Dr. Alice Fothergill (University of Vermont), Dr. Deb Thomas (University of Colorado-Denver), Dr. Lori Peek (Colorado State University), and Dr. Lynn Blinn-Pike (Indiana University-Purdue University) as well as Kevin King and the entire Mennonite Disaster Service office staff in Akron, Pennsylvania. The Interlibrary Loan Service at Oklahoma State University as well as librarians Steve Locy and Victor Baeza provided constant, near-daily help. I am also grateful to friends who listened to or supported me in various ways, including Glenn Jones, Sam Elkins, Dr. Jeanette Mendez (Oklahoma State), Dr. Tammy Mix (Oklahoma State), Connie Hunter, Ginger Sorrel, and every barista in Stillwater. I thank students I've worked with on many research projects relevant to this book and to my coprincipal investigators as well, including Dr. Dennis Wenger (a fellow Buckeye) and Dr. Tom Wikle (Oklahoma State University). I am grateful for your support and hard work. I hope that this book honors your efforts.

I also want to thank my editor Mark Listewnik, production coordinator Stephanie Morkert, and project editor Prudy Taylor Board of Taylor & Francis. Their constant support bolstered my efforts, and I thank them for their steadfast enthusiasm and consummate professionalism. I cannot imagine a better publishing experience. The staff of my department at Oklahoma State University provided support as well, including Vincent Burke, Pam Amos, Cindy Hutchinson, and Dr. James Scott.

Finally, I thank my parents, Frank and Mary Jane Phillips. My mother spent many days at my home cooking, cleaning, taking care of dogs and more so that I could write. My father remained patient and supportive throughout the entire time. I am looking forward to spending more time with my family now that this massive task is done.

I hope that each person reading this book finds the information useful and applicable. May you and your family be safe from harm, always.

About the Author

Brenda Phillips is a professor in the Fire and Emergency Management Program, an affiliated faculty member in the Gender and Women's Studies and the International Studies programs, and a senior researcher with the Center for the Study of Disasters and Extreme Events at Oklahoma State University. She recently coedited *Women and Disasters: From Theory to Practice* with Betty Hearn Morrow and has a forthcoming coedited book titled *Social Vulnerability* with Deborah Thomas, Alice Fothergill, and Lynn Blinn-Pike. She is a member of the Gender and Disaster Network and the International Research Committee on Disasters. Professor Phillips has conducted research on disaster recovery since 1982, beginning as a student of E. L. Quarantelli at The Ohio State University's Disaster Research Center. Her published research can be found in a variety of journals, including the *International Journal of Mass Emergencies and Disasters*; *Disaster Prevention*; *Disasters, Humanity and Society*; the *Journal of Emergency Management*; *Natural Hazards Review*; and *Environmental Hazards*. She has been funded multiple times by the National Science Foundation to study disaster recovery, particularly as it affects vulnerable populations. Dr. Phillips has been invited to teach, consult, or lecture in New Zealand, Australia, Germany, India, Costa Rica, Mexico, Canada, and the People's Republic of China. She is a graduate of Bluffton University (Ohio) and The Ohio State University.

Section I

Understanding Disaster Recovery

Chapter 1

Introduction

Learning Objectives

After reading this chapter, you should be able to:

- Describe the types of challenges likely to be faced during the disaster recovery process
- Describe the ways in which emergencies differ from disasters and why those definitions are relevant for a recovery context
- Explain why terminology matters in defining recovery
- Distinguish between a variety of terms typically used to mean recovery, including restoration, reconstruction, rehabilitation, and more
- Explain why recovery is best viewed as a process
- Distinguish between short-term and long-term recovery and identify activities common to both
- Understand the phase of recovery in the life cycle of comprehensive emergency management
- Identify linkages between recovery and the other phases of comprehensive emergency management, namely mitigation, preparedness, and response.

Introduction

This chapter provides an overview of various scenarios that you might encounter as a **recovery** manager, leader, survivor, or volunteer; outlines objectives for the book content; defines basic terms; and starts you on the recovery process.

This section provides an overview of **disaster** recovery scenarios that a recovery leader might face from three main types of hazards: natural, hazardous materials, and **terrorism** events. Three major events help us illustrate recovery challenges: Hurricane Katrina, the Oklahoma City bombing, and the *Exxon Valdez* oil spill in Alaska. As you read, imagine the challenges that might face you as the leader of each community's recovery efforts.

New Orleans, Louisiana

Certainly, images from Hurricane Katrina will remain with many of us for a lifetime. As we watched the Category 5 hurricane approach the Gulf Coast on August 29, 2005, it was clear that life might never be the same for those living in areas about to be impacted. Katrina brought a massive storm surge into portions of Louisiana and Mississippi, causing multiple failures in the levee system that had protected the area from flooding; devastating petrochemical industries; wreaking havoc on fishing communities; and tearing apart extensive sections of power, cell/telephone, water, and sewer lifelines crucial for community survival. More than 1300 persons lost their lives, and damage assessments revealed stark challenges for local, state, and federal leaders. In the City of New Orleans—a community of interconnected neighborhoods and home to 450,000 individuals—the numbers would stagger even experienced recovery managers.

- *Housing.* An estimated 515,249 homes sustained damage in Louisiana and another 200,384 in Mississippi, including single-family homes, apartment buildings, and public housing units (HUD 2006), demanding a massive **response** to hundreds of thousands who could not return home. One year after Katrina, approximately 114,000 evacuees had moved into temporary trailers, with tens of thousands more in rental apartments across dozens of U.S. states. Returning home continued to remain difficult, with rents having increased 46% (Brookings Institution 2008). Given that approximately 72% of the population had returned by 2008, much remains to be done. New Orleans's recovery will take many years, and the city will likely change dramatically. (For more detail, see Greater New Orleans Community Data Center 2007 and Brookings Institution 2008.) In the summer of 2008, 65,000 "blighted properties or empty lots" still existed in New Orleans (Brookings Institution 2008, 7).

- *Infrastructure and lifelines.* Katrina and the levee failures decimated key resources, including roads, bridges, ports, and utilities. One year after the storm, the Brookings Institution "Katrina Index" found that about half of the bus and streetcar routes were active, although only 17% of available buses were running, a critical need in an urban area where many do not drive (Brookings Institution 2007a). Two years after the storm, those numbers had not improved, with 19% of buses running, a number that remained consistent at the three-year mark as well (Brookings Institution 2007b, 2008). Companies had restored 41% of gas and 60% of electricity to prestorm customers. Nearly two years after the storm, the Brookings Institution "Katrina Index" (2007a) reported that "infrastructure indicators remain stalled this month. Thirty-six percent of the state-licensed hospitals in the region remain shuttered. Fourteen libraries remain closed across the five parishes. And only 58 out of 128 public schools have opened in New Orleans to date."
- *Economy.* The massive evacuation of the Louisiana parishes and the extensive damage meant that few employees could return. One year after Katrina, New Orleans had lost 190,000 workers, with major losses to key sectors. Health care and education lost 32,600 jobs, and Charity Hospital, a major resource for the poor, had closed. Schools and hospitals struggled to reopen; medical, dental, and optometry offices had lost their records and resources in addition to their staff. At the three-year mark, the majority of job losses continued to be in health, leisure, hospitality, local government, trade, transportation, and utilities (Brookings Institution 2008). Work remained challenging for many in New Orleans, in part due to the lack of child care. Orleans Parish had reopened 43% of the pre-Katrina child care centers, while adjacent St. Bernard Parish had reopened a total of 31% since the storm. The majority of the job losses occurred in specific sectors, with the greatest flooding including the Lower Ninth Ward and West Lake Forest (Brookings Institution 2008). Overall, about 81% of the pre-Katrina job base is back.
- *Environment.* Katrina represents one of the more challenging environmental disasters ever faced within the United States. Katrina's storm surge, strong winds, and subsequent levee failures caused massive spills across multiple parishes within Louisiana alone. The U.S. Environmental Protection Agency (EPA), contractors, and state and local environmental managers labored extensively to test and manage spills from literally millions of gallons of oil and hazardous materials, including "toxic and flammable chemicals, paint, pesticides and propane tanks," electrical waste, abandoned chemical containers, contaminated appliances, and extensive mold growth (GAO

2007, 5). EPA conducted testing of water, air, sediment, soil, and wastewater to determine habitability, potability, and toxicity levels. Often referred to as a potential "toxic brew" in the bowl-shaped city of New Orleans, environmental scientists had long expressed concern about whether the environment, let alone the city, could ever return to normal in such an event (Laska 2004). As the city began to repopulate, the U.S. Government Accountability Office (GAO) issued a report indicating that, although EPA had conducted extensive public education efforts, the agency had been unclear and inconsistent regarding recycling. To illustrate the complex challenges, all residents had to secure their refrigerators with duct tape and take them to the curb for recycling. Every bit of debris from every home had to be separated for appropriate disposal. In a city of nearly half a million people, with 80% of the area under water, everything had to be handled carefully to safeguard remaining environmental quality. However, GAO pointed to a lack of clarity in federal regulations regarding debris management plans and protocols as a particular problem. GAO indicated that the EPA had not sufficiently tested for potential asbestos contamination in areas undergoing demolition. Further, GAO noted that the EPA had not removed hazardous materials from national wildlife refuges expeditiously. In short, the extensive environmental problems caused by the disaster overwhelmed even federal capabilities, a situation compounded by a lack of preexisting legislation and funding.

- *Education.* Two years after Katrina, schools continued to be a problem in New Orleans. About 40% of the original number of students had returned by the two-year anniversary of the storm. Due to hurricane and flood damage, the slow repopulation, and a lack of teachers and school staff, fewer than half of the prestorm public and private school have reopened. School test results indicate that students have been affected by the storm's impact in other ways, as evidenced by falling scores in a statewide exam: "the number of eighth graders [in New Orleans] passing the LEAP exam fell from 64% pre-Katrina to 43%" (Brookings Institution 2007b). At the three-year mark, approximately 74% of the university population had returned. Dillard University, an historically black institution, suffered major damage in the flood; only 44% of the students were back by 2008.

The federal government, though criticized for its response and recovery efforts, had dedicated $109 billion to five states affected by Katrina one year after the storm. Half of that amount went to support families through temporary housing and related assistance, with the rest to restore infrastructure, manage debris, and address the critical levee situation (Brookings Institution

2006). While Katrina should not be considered a typical disaster by any standard (Quarantelli and Perry 2005), there are many lessons to be learned from what can happen when all sectors of a geographic area are devastated.

The Oklahoma City Bombing

On April 19, 1995, domestic terrorism brought the nation to a standstill. Just as the workday began to commence, a massive bomb detonated outside the Alfred P. Murrah Federal Building in Oklahoma City, bringing down a major section of the nine-story building full of workers and visitors. One hundred and sixty-eight persons died almost immediately, including several people in adjacent buildings. A day-care center, housed inside the Alfred P. Murrah Building, was destroyed. Nineteen infants and children died. Over 200 children lost a parent or were orphaned (Mallonee et al. 1996; Pfefferbaum, Call, and Sconzo 1999).

Fire, police, and ambulance services sent every available unit to the building. Area facilities treated 509 outpatients and hospitalized 83, many with significant and permanently disabling injuries. The building, simultaneously a disaster and a crime site, required careful attention in order to save lives and preserve evidence. First responders labored for days attempting to rescue the injured from very dangerous, shifting building parts. Medical staff made life-or-death decisions, often putting their own lives at risk to do so.

Voluntary organizations that traditionally respond to disasters faced an unusual recovery. Although some people faced displacement from businesses and homes, organizations that usually participate in rebuilding did not have their traditional work to do. This disaster, a foreshadowing of what the nation would face on September 11, 2001, demanded attention to the psychological aspects of recovery, a topic we will cover in detail in Chapter 10 (Social Psychological Recovery).

People in Oklahoma and across the nation have not forgotten those who died. The Oklahoma City National Memorial has been built on the site and is visited by hundreds of thousands of residents, tourists, and school-children every year. Visitors walk through one of two monolithic Gates of Time where the time of 9:01 a.m., the moment before, and 9:03 a.m., the moment after the attack, are held in place. Where the building used to stand, 168 chairs now bear silent witness to the lives that were lost (see Photo 1.1). On the Survivor Wall, 637 names of people who survived the attack are listed on pieces of granite. A 90-year-old American elm, which survived the bombing, represents the spirit of those left behind and is aptly named the Survivor Tree. During a 2007 ice storm, the state urban forestry officer worked with security guards and volunteers to shake ice and snow off branches of the Survivor Tree during a storm that destroyed

PHOTO 1.1   Chairs representing the 168 people who died in the Oklahoma City bombing. (Photo courtesy of the Oklahoma City National Memorial Museum. With Permission.)

or damaged thousands of trees across the state (Latzke 2007). A Rescuers' Orchard represents those who came in response and whose lives were forever changed as first responders to their fellow citizens. A piece of the fence used to surround the rubble now serves as a place where people leave mementos and remembrances.

Close to the anniversary of the attack, the Oklahoma City Memorial Marathon begins with 168 moments of silence. As runners traverse the 26.2-mile route, they surge past 168 banners, each representing someone killed that day, with thousands of runners wearing placards with the names of those lost. At the finish line, survivors and family members place medals around the necks of those who "Run to Remember." During the days that follow the event, numbered runners' bibs can be found tucked into the fence at the Oklahoma City National Memorial. In 2008, over 16,000 participants from all 50 states and four foreign nations ran the course, now among the largest marathons worldwide. Six thousand volunteers turned out to support the runners. Since its inception, the marathon has raised over $1 million for the National Memorial Museum. In the aftermath, remembering has become a healing part of the recovery and a symbolic and defiant demonstration against the power of terrorism.

Prince William Sound, Alaska

The *Exxon Valdez* oil spill along Alaska's coastline is usually referred to as the world's worst environmental disaster. The spill occurred in 1989 when a ship named the *Exxon Valdez*, attempting to avoid icebergs, ran aground outside of assigned shipping lanes in Prince William Sound. Although the state charged the captain with working while under the influence of alcohol, a jury declared him guilty of discharging oil, but not due to alcohol. The National Transportation Safety Board reported that other crew members and the Exxon Shipping Company failed to conduct maneuvers and supervision properly and that the U.S. Coast Guard did not provide an "effective vessel traffic system" (*Exxon Valdez* Oil Spill Trustee Council 2007).

The result? By most accounts, 11 million gallons of oil—or about 257,000 barrels—spilled into a pristine ecological area along the Alaska coastline, primarily in the rich fishing waters of Prince William Sound. The images that remain in the minds of those who were there or who watched via television recall oil-slick beaches, dying animals, exhausted workers, and a public concerned with lingering effects of the oil on their livelihood, health, and communities.

Over 10,000 workers, 1,000 boats, and 100 aircraft deployed to assist in the crisis along approximately 1300 miles of shoreline. As with other types of disasters, the type of damage varied. About 200 miles of shoreline sustained heavy to moderate oil spill; another 1,100 miles were touched with a light sheen. Overall, up to 9,000 miles of shoreline experienced some type of impact. Scientists concur that it is impossible to gauge the full effects of the spill (National Ocean Service 2005; Picou 1992). An estimated 250,000 seabirds died, along with 2,800 sea otters, 300 harbor seals, 17 gray whales, 14 sea lions, 22 orcas (killer whales), billions of salmon and herring eggs, and an unknown number of organisms important in the food chain and other parts of the environment.

The consequences of a hazardous-material event can be difficult to determine because so many conditions influence the possible outcomes. Determining the impact of a spill in Prince William Sound on commercial and recreational fishing, for example, proved difficult because those involved may have stopped their work and sport to help with the spill—thus altering the numbers of those involved from year to year (Carson and Haneman 1992). Economists have tried to estimate the price of replacing lost wildlife, although the challenge there is similar: How do you place a value on an animal? One estimate put a gull "replacement" at $167 and the more endangered peregrine falcon at $6,000. These estimates typically emanate from the animal's availability and the cost of raising one from young, but they do not reflect the aesthetic, spiritual, or environmental value.

Imagine, for example, the cost of replacing our national symbol, the American bald eagle, of which approximately 45,000 can be found throughout

Alaska (Brown 1992). Estimates suggest that 247 eagles died from the spill (Bowman, Schempf, and Hodges 1997). Many challenges occur when attempting to replace this historically endangered species. For example, it is not possible to capture and relocate an eagle because it will return to its original habitat to breed. Further, it is not possible to place chicks into the wild easily because of the lack of "surplus" chicks. The U.S. Fish and Wildlife Service has found that the costs of replacing an eagle are considerable:

- Each eagle costs $4,500 to raise a chick to a fledgling through using artificial nests.
- These chicks experience an 80% mortality rate.
- It takes five eagle chicks to raise one to adulthood.
- On average, the cost to raise five chicks to adulthood is $22,500.

The cost to "replace" 247 lost bald eagles would exceed $5.5 million. It is difficult to determine how well eagles have rebounded because prespill data are not available for comparison. However, one study indicates that the number of eagles had exceeded prespill levels by 1995—a trend found throughout Alaska, and perhaps more an indicator of the overall rebound of this endangered species than evidence that the species was not affected by the spill (Bowman, Schempf, and Hodges 1997). It is also worth keeping in mind that long-term effects on these magnificent birds may not be seen for multiple generations. Exxon claims to have spent $100,000 per eagle to save the birds that did not die.

The human impacts of an environmental spill also matter. Community impact of the oil spill varied based on geographic location and the socio-cultural nature of the community. Cordova, a small community of about 2,000, had become self-reliant on commercial fishing. The fisher people of the village possessed 44% of the area's herring fishery permits and 55% of the salmon fishery permits in Prince William Sound (Picou 1992). Because the community shares the benefits of their natural resources with each other, up to 90% of the residents depended heavily on their environment for food. The spill that contaminated the fishing area occurred two months before breeding season and closed the 1989 herring season to commercial fishing. Seven out of ten respondents in one study experienced work disruption, a number that would have brought any community to a standstill economically. Imagine 70% of those in your community not having work. Within Cordova, researchers observed social disruption and psychological stress for over 18 months following the accident (Picou 1992).

Twelve years later, some evidence came to light that the oil spill continued to have an impact (Short, Rice, and Lindeberg 2001). A survey conducted in 2001 indicated that about 20 acres of Prince William Sound shoreline still contained contaminated soil. Of 91 sampled locations, 58% included some level of contamination, usually a "lightly oiled" substance buried in the beach, with a noticeable odor and appearance.

Recovery challenges can be significant, complex, and daunting. And, although many recovery challenges span all types of hazards, it is worthwhile to look at how some disasters present unique challenges. In the next section, we examine the various types of hazards that may be faced following disaster events.

Types of Disasters

Those involved in recovery efforts will encounter three main types of disasters: **natural** events, **technological** events (hazardous materials and wastes), and terrorism. Although many of the issues described above will appear in all three types of disasters, there are some recovery challenges unique to each.

Natural Events

A variety of hazards, usually described as those caused through natural phenomena, can affect a community, including high winds, floods, and lightning. Problems occur when there is a misfit between the built environment, the natural systems in a given area, and when people inhabit such areas—by living in homes in floodplains, near earthquake faults, or close to areas at risk for wildfire (Mileti 1999). In this section, we look at the consequences of earthquakes, floods, hurricanes, tornados, and similar events that occur routinely in nature with very real human consequences.

According to the Federal Emergency Management Agency (FEMA), eight out of the top ten most expensive disasters in the United States were hurricanes, all of them occurring since 1998. The other two in the top ten include September 11 and the Northridge Earthquake. However, the most frequently occurring disasters between 2000 and 2007 were:

- 191 severe storms
- 62 floods
- 35 hurricanes
- 22 tornados

A good question for an emergency manager, then, is: should one prepare for a specific type of event, the most costly, or the most frequently occurring? The process of comprehensive emergency management (discussed later in this chapter) promotes an "all-hazards" approach, suggesting that by planning and preparing for one, it is possible to prepare and plan a recovery for most if not all types of hazards. After all, in a disaster situation, many of the issues will be the same: coordinating recovery efforts, housing the displaced, cleaning up debris, shoring up the economy, restoring environmental resources, and dealing with long-term psychological consequences. Let us look at the most common **natural disaster**s that might impact U.S. communities.

The National Hurricane Center (2007a, 2007b) indicates that three types of cyclones, which generate in the tropics, circulate counterclockwise. Hurricanes (minimum sustained winds of 75 mph), tropical storms (39–73 mph), and tropical depressions (38 mph or less) may generate high winds, heavy rainfall, strong waves, storm surges, and even tornados. Each type of cyclonic storm can cause considerable damage.

Tropical Storm Allison, for example, dumped 39.66 inches of rain on Houston, Texas, in 2001. When Allison ended, the Texas and Louisiana coasts had experienced significant flooding, 41 deaths, and $5 billion in damage—the worst tropical storm in U.S. history. On average, the U.S. experiences five coastal hurricanes annually; two will become major hurricanes. Damage may vary from projectiles that impale buildings and trees to extensive flooding of homes and buildings lasting for weeks. Because hurricanes can impact a broad area, restoring lifelines and infrastructure may require extensive outside resources, including removal of debris blocking transportation routes, airports, and railways.

Hurricanes are typically feared more than tropical storms or depressions, as they can vary in intensity and impact. Andrew, the third strongest hurricane in U.S. history, came ashore in southern Florida in 1992. Andrew claimed 23 lives and wrought $26.5 billion in costs to Florida and Louisiana. The National Hurricane Center relies on the Saffir-Simpson Scale to classify hurricanes, as seen in Table 1.1. Hurricane Katrina came ashore as a Category 5 and fell to a Category 4 level by the time it went past New Orleans and into Mississippi. The storm surge that pushed ashore led to much of the initial damage and caused levee breaks in New Orleans.

TABLE 1.1 Saffir-Simpson Hurricane Scale

Category and Winds	Types of Damage to Expect
1 (75–95 mph)	Damage can vary, but unsecured and manufactured housing may be at risk
2 (95–110 mph)	Manufactured housing will sustain damage; roof and other exterior damage to other types of homes; boats at risk, flooding likely
3 (111–130 mph)	Structures sustain damage; manufactured housing likely to be destroyed; trees blown down; inland and coastal flooding
4 (131–155 mph)	Small homes are destroyed; flooding more extensive; beaches may wash away
5 (155 mph and up)	Extensive damage likely; major flooding likely

Source: Adapted from National Hurricane Center (2007b).

Historically, coastal areas of the United States are at highest risk, although inland areas may also experience damage as winds move across inland areas. Hurricane Hugo, for example, destroyed major forest areas in the Carolinas in 1989. Hurricane Camille came ashore in Louisiana in 1969 but dumped up to 20 inches of rain in Virginia and West Virginia as it moved inland and across the United States.

Even within a specific type of natural hazard, such as a tornado, the damage can vary. Tornadic winds broke a wind gauge near Bridge Creek, Oklahoma, on May 3, 1999, when an F5 event exceeded 318 miles per hour. The massive event destroyed mile-wide swaths of rural areas, devastated a neighborhood in Midwest City (a suburb of Oklahoma City), and transformed Oklahoma's red clay landscape into a scene more like Mars. Wind speeds associated with tornados are analyzed using multiple indicators, such as degree of damage, resulting in these categories forming the Enhanced Fujita Scale, as seen in Table 1.2.

Higher wind speeds, coupled with other variables such as rotation, downburst strength, and type of structure in the tornado path, result in more significant damage. An EF1 that moves through a trailer home community could cause considerable damage, while a similar event going through an area of stronger, reinforced buildings may cause only minor damage. Within the United States, some areas of the country bear a heightened risk for tornado damage, namely areas of Texas, Oklahoma, and Kansas (see Photo 1.2) known as "tornado alley." However, tornados can happen elsewhere, as witnessed by the August 2007 EF2 that ripped up portions of Brooklyn, New York—the first tornado seen there since 1889. Recovery managers can expect to deal with massive debris, downed utility poles and electrical lines, missing traffic signs and lights, destroyed housing and businesses, damage to public facilities, disrupted social and medical services, injured livestock, damaged crops, and potentially traumatized residents.

Flooding can occur from various sources. Dams can break, sudden thunderstorms can overrun storm-water drainage systems, and hurricanes can dump amazing amounts of rainfall and push ashore storm surges of 20–40

TABLE 1.2 Enhanced Fujita Scale for Tornados

Enhanced Fujita Scale	Wind Speed (3-second gust)
EF0	65–85
EF1	86–109
EF2	110–137
EF3	138–167
EF4	168–199
EF5	200–235

Source: National Oceanic and Atmospheric Administration (2006) and Wind Science and Engineering Center (2006).

PHOTO 1.2 Damage from an EF5 in Greensburg, Kansas located in "Tornado Alley." (Photo by Andi Dube. Courtesy of the Mennonite Disaster Service. With Permission.)

feet high. Flooding represents the most common type of disaster to hit the United States, including flash flooding and river flooding. Central Texas is called "flash flood alley" because of the sudden and heavy rainfall that can occur. In 2001, up to 15 inches of rain fell in less than 6 hours in Austin, Texas, causing water to overflow creeks and storm-water drains. Nearly 700 buildings flooded (City of Austin 2007). Flooding can bring several challenges, notably removal of damaged items such as appliances and furniture. Buildings sustain additional problems as sheetrock, carpeting, doors, stairways, and porches swell with water and cause mold. Electrical, water, and wastewater systems may be destroyed or polluted. Flooded areas may be uninhabitable for some time, particularly for those with respiratory problems. Powerful river flooding can also take out bridges and roads.

Earthquakes happen when pressure builds up in rocks under the surface of the Earth. Rock shifts occur along a fracture, called a fault line, resulting in ground that shakes and can cause considerable damage (USGS 2007a). Seismologists measure earthquake size by gauging the magnitude, ground motion, and duration. Although the EF scale includes damage estimates, the Richter scale for earthquake magnitude does not. Rather, the Richter scale places earthquake magnitude by decimal points, with each whole number representing ten times in strength. Typically, people can feel a magnitude 4.5 earthquake and up. Whether or not a building has been constructed for seismic activity or is up to code can make the difference in whether a building comes down in a magnitude 6 or 7 earthquake.

The worst earthquake recorded, a 9.5, occurred near Chile in 1960, causing tsunami waves that claimed 1,655 lives. An offshore 9.1 earthquake in 2004, called the Indian Ocean Tsunami, set off massive waves that killed nearly 300,000 across over one dozen nations. The most deadly known earthquake happened in 1556 in China, when an earthquake with an estimated magnitude exceeding 8.0 killed 830,000 people. In the United States, the most expensive earthquake happened in Northridge, California, in 1994, and the largest magnitude event took place in Alaska in 1964 (USGS 2007b). We will discuss these latter two events in greater detail in upcoming chapters.

Terrorism

Although concern for terrorism represents a relatively recent issue within the United States, few can forget the reasons why. Terrorism can take two forms: domestic and international. The Oklahoma City bombing (see Photo 1.2), described earlier in this chapter, illustrates threats from within our borders and our own citizenry. Many readers will recall the anthrax attack as well, which appears now to be a domestic incident. The Atlanta Olympics bombings in 1996 occurred as the result of domestic terrorism. And, of course, this nation directly experienced international terrorism on September 11, 2001, when hijackers piloted airplanes into the World Trade Center and the Pentagon. Passengers on a United Airlines flight subverted an attack on the White House and the U.S. Capitol, dying in the heroic attempt when their plane crashed in Pennsylvania. A prior bombing at the World Trade Center occurred in 1993.

Attacks on Americans abroad should also be considered for the long-term effects they can have on individual families. Most of these attacks have targeted military or political symbols, such as the U.S. Barracks-Khobar Towers in Saudi Arabia that were destroyed by an exploding suicide truck bomb. There were also bombings at the U.S. embassies in Tanzania and Kenya in 1989 as well as a seaborne attack on the *U.S.S. Cole* in Yemen in 2000 (Rubin 2006). In this section, we will examine recovery challenges associated with terrorism.

The effects of terrorism can be particularly chilling and long lasting, as they represent deliberate, unexpected attacks on unsuspecting, innocent people. In the September 11 attacks alone, the final number of dead totaled nearly 3,000 from over 25 nations, among them aircraft passengers, civilians, flight crews, workers, members of the military, 50 police officers, and 319 firefighters. Approximately 6,408 human injuries and 600 animal wounds had been treated, and reports of up to 6,398 missing individuals had been placed. FEMA reported that 115,756 tons of debris had been removed to a landfill in New York by September 26. Debris-removal processes, described in Chapter 4, can prove even further damaging to human health.

By September 26, 2001, only 279 bodies had been recovered, an effort that turned into a DNA analysis lasting for years. Identifying the dead occurs for legal and societal reasons, including the effort to reduce the "mental anguish" of the survivors (Thompson 1991) and as an international human right (PAHO/WHO 2005). Body identification and retrieval of human remains is time consuming and costly, requiring expertise, training, and resources (Simpson and Stehr 2003). After September 11, two solutions emerged to identify missing persons. A formal "Patient Locator Service" used Web pages and search engines, resulting in 1.2 million hits within a week. The public generated the second solution, when bereaved relatives created missing-persons posters (Simpson and Stehr 2003). At the World Trade Center, a multistep process evolved: spotters would watch during backhoe operations, stopping if human remains were seen; a second examination of the debris occurred just before removal to the landfill. Once at the landfill, additional reviewers searched conveyor-belt debris for human remains. Forensic anthropologists confirmed the remains, which were then sent to the Disaster Mortuary Response Team (DMORT). DNA matching identified approximately half of the 20,000 human-remains samples; as of 2008, only 1,600 of the missing had been identified (Simpson and Stehr 2003; for updated numbers, see the 9/11 Research URL link in the Resource section at the end of this chapter). At least 10,000 human-remains samples have been frozen for future DNA analysis.

Long-term recovery needs emerged among the survivors, including treatment of horrific and permanent injuries; continual assessment of health-care needs, including those generated by asbestos and other concerns from working near the debris pile; and general mental-health needs. The American Red Cross, which received over $1 billion dollars in donations, established numerous forms of assistance, as did other nonprofit, faith-based, and governmental organizations. To illustrate the diversity of needs, the Red Cross issued its 48-page "Service Guide" in English, Spanish, and Chinese; FEMA produced general information flyers in several dozen languages. The American Red Cross established the Liberty Disaster Relief Fund to provide recovery grants to organizations assisting survivors. The grants targeted family members of those who died as well as persons who were injured, rescue and recovery workers, and those who lived in the area of the attack. The Red Cross programs provided financial assistance, health screenings, information and referrals, hotlines, job training and placement, mental health and wellness services, youth services, and substance-abuse treatment. The Red Cross alone sent 57,434 workers to help during the extended recovery period, of which 54,000 served on a volunteer basis.

In the aftermath of September 11, extensive debate occurred regarding how to best protect the nation from future attacks. Thus, the massive recovery period also generated new legislation, enhanced security, and the launch of the multiagency U.S. Department of Homeland Security, which subsumed FEMA. Such massive change can be anticipated in the aftermath of major events; it is necessary to anticipate that staff and citizenry will be taxed by these multiple burdens of recovering from the recent event as well as mitigating and preparing for the next.

Hazardous Materials and Wastes

FEMA tells us that a number of challenges face those concerned with hazardous materials, such as those resulting from chemical explosions, transportation spills, toxic waste sites, and even the problems generated by household paint, gasoline, and other common items strewn by tornados, floods, and other hazards. Because hazardous materials must be handled carefully, they represent potentially expensive and time-consuming recovery problems. Care must be taken to ensure that involved households, institutions, organizations, and industries are in compliance with handling hazardous materials and hazardous wastes in order to reduce the potential impact on the physical and human environment. EPA defines hazardous waste as "a waste with properties that make it dangerous or potentially harmful to human health or the environment … liquids, solids, contained gases, or sludge" (EPA 2007a).

FEMA estimates that 4.5 million facilities in the United States handle some type of potentially hazardous materials. Consider the range of those industries: from nuclear plants, oil refineries, and chemical manufacturers to the local nursery or dry-cleaning store (FEMA 2007). Problems may erupt at any phase of "production, storage, transportation, use or disposal" (FEMA 2007). Consider just the impact of transporting to and from those fixed sites along highways, pipelines, railways, and airways. It is easy to imagine the breadth and depth of the potential disaster that could occur when a truck spills or crashes, a train derails, or a pipeline fails.

A number of strategies have been designed to monitor and manage potential incidents arising from hazardous materials. In terms of disaster recovery, one of the most significant efforts is called the Superfund, which arose out of the Comprehensive Environmental Response, Compensation and Liability Act (CERCLA) that passed in 1980. Superfund was designed to clean up hazardous waste sites, many of which had been abandoned but were impacting local communities. The Environmental Protection Agency (EPA) was awarded authority to clean up sites or require those responsible for cleaning the site and reimbursing the government as needed. EPA has conducted analyses of tens of thousands of potential hazardous waste sites since 1980. One of the most familiar hazardous waste sites, which provided impetus for CERCLA, occurred in Love Canal in New York State.

From 1942 to 1952, Hooker Chemicals and Plastics put chemical wastes into a 16-acre landfill. In 1953, the landfill closed. Soon thereafter, a school and residential area with 200 homes were built nearby. In the 1960s, residents complained about odors. By the 1970s, a few studies showed chemicals were contaminating waterways, particularly Love Canal. To address the situation, the state bought out homes near the canal. President Carter declared an environmental emergency, resulting in the evacuation of nearly 1,000 families and designating a 350-acre area to be unsafe. Continual cleanup and monitoring occurred for a number of years. To contain the waste, a synthetic liner, clay cap, and barrier drainage system were put into place on 40 acres of the site. In 2004, EPA removed Love Canal from the Superfund National Priorities List. The original homes have been sold to new owners. Ten new apartment buildings have been built, and new industrial areas have been planned (EPA 2007b).

Recovery from technological disasters may take a very long time. Many issues and concerns remain unknown at present for specific kinds of technological hazards. For example, the multigenerational effects of spills on environmental resources, animal and plant life, and human populations are simply not well understood. Tools to mitigate technological hazards lag behind what we can do for natural hazards, such as building levees along waterways. For many technological disasters, such as oil spills, we depend on rules and regulations that operate at the federal level. Enforcement of those rules and regulations has varied over the years. Further, we do not appear to be sufficiently prepared for technological hazards at the national level, as "no government agencies, at any level, have plans for long-term recovery from technological hazards" (Mileti 1999, 213).

Environmental protection remains an important concern, one that will be infused through each chapter in this book. Although Chapter 5 focuses exclusively on environmental disasters, you will discover that each chapter features some type of environmentally friendly recovery action. Green rebuilding for homes and businesses, recycling debris generated by various hazards (yes, it is possible), and protecting our waterways and air and green spaces all emerge as important considerations for recovery efforts.

Now that we have illustrated the challenges of recovery and the types of hazards that could be faced, we turn to an examination of what terms are used in recovery and what they mean.

Definitions: Key Terms and Concepts

To launch a recovery process, all stakeholders must share a common understanding of what they expect to happen during recovery. Without a common set of assumptions, the recovery process may become fraught with conflict, disappointment, and disruptions. Clearly defining expectations, then, emerges as an important first task for any recovery manager. Thus, this section defines what we mean by *disaster* and *recovery* and places *recovery* within the four phases of the cycle of **comprehensive emergency management**.

Defining Disaster

Based on the above scenarios, it should be clear that disasters are more than common emergencies such as the traffic accidents, personal injuries, or house fires experienced by most communities. For these types of emergencies, first responders typically roll ambulances, squad cars, fire engines, and other resources.

For a disaster to occur, it must have a human impact that disrupts community functioning. In 1812, for example, an earthquake altered the course of the Mississippi River. However, because no one lived near the area, that event could not reasonably be considered a disaster—it lacked a human impact (Quarantelli 1988). Compare that event to the Mississippi River floods of 1993 and 2008, which caused widespread, extensive damage across multiple states, requiring massive evacuations and permanent relocations of thousands of homes and businesses.

In a disaster, local resources may become overwhelmed, requiring assistance from other jurisdictions, the state, or the assistance of the federal government. Disasters cause community functions to halt at least temporarily and, in some cases, for months or years. Disasters disrupt the social functioning of communities: People become displaced, schools and businesses close, hospitals bring in additional personnel and activate special emergency plans, and the critical infrastructure—power, water, transportation sectors—may be compromised (Quarantelli 1998a; Quarantelli and Perry 2005). Emergency managers, who have spent time laying a foundation to handle large-scale events, will now step in to guide the recovery by organizing and coordinating massive resources to meet widespread needs.

Comprehensive Emergency Management: Four Phases

In the late 1970s, the National Governor's Association (1978) designed a four-phase model to organize the activities of emergency managers. Known as the process of comprehensive emergency management, the "life cycle"

FIGURE 1.1   Life cycle of emergency management.

includes four phases of organized activities (see Figure 1.1). Typically, those four phases are referred to as **mitigation**, **preparedness**, **response**, and **recovery** (see Resources section for FEMA IS-1).

Designating four phases allows the emergency management community to organize key activities into functional, related areas. Each phase provides an array of strategies designed to result in safer communities. Although there is certainly overlap across the phases (Neal 1997), the following definitions describe each phase. Mitigation activities are designed to reduce the impact of disasters by introducing two main reduction measures. Structural mitigation activities include the built environment and typically include dams and levees to reduce flooding, seawalls to hold back storm surge, retrofitting buildings to withstand seismic activity, safe rooms to protect from tornados, and more. Preparedness activities typically include planning, educational efforts, coordination among key agencies, training, exercises, and inventorying assets that will be used during the response period. Both mitigation and preparedness phases are intended to enhance life safety and reduce the impact on people and property. Should those activities fail, varying degrees of response and recovery activities will be required. Response typically centers on efforts that promote life safety, such as deploying police, fire, and ambulance services;

conducting search and rescue; erecting barricades; securing unstable or dangerous sites; and initiating efforts to safeguard or repair utilities and key infrastructure like roads, bridges, ports, airports, and railways (FEMA IS-1).

Actions taken during the mitigation, preparedness, and response phases always influence recovery efforts. Should a community fail to engage in mitigation activities, it may face catastrophic destruction of the built environment with loss of life. Maintaining the integrity of a levee or a stormwater drainage system, for example, may mean that homes are not flooded, that businesses are not closed, and that community life may continue.

If preparedness efforts fail to include designing response and recovery plans, then officials will scramble to react, when a proactive set of activities could have avoided disaster-time stress and disruption. If a plan is in place prior to disaster, response efforts can proceed more smoothly and with forethought for the recovery process. For example, with adequate forethought, downed power lines can be replaced underground to mitigate future electrical disruptions. Communities with historic resources can set aside meaningful architectural and cultural resources during the response time in order to return the community to its familiar physical appearance.

In short, the prerecovery phases of mitigation, preparedness, and response set the stage for a smooth recovery and result in reduced costs to budgets and staff.

Defining the Recovery Phase

One of the most common desires heard after a disaster is to "return to normalcy." Media reports often feature individuals who declare their intent to "rebuild back, stronger than ever." But what is "normal"? Will a return to what was normal reduce future risks? If a community desires to rebuild stronger than ever, what does that mean? Will the economic reality mean that stronger is not affordable? Will political will and public support exist to ensure a stronger return?

What does it mean to recover? A variety of terms are often used synonymously to mean recovery, but in reality these may have different meanings to different people: rebuilding, **reconstruction, restoration, rehabilitation, restitution**, and recovery (Quarantelli 1998b).

In Chapter 13 you will work through the process of involving the public in envisioning a recovered community. Imagine the dialogue that might take place around the notion of what recovery means to people. Those interested in reconstruction may be only concerned with replacing the damaged building. Restoration may imply returning to similar conditions, including culturally, socially, and historically meaningful architecture. Others may feel that rehabilitation is important, which suggests that some type of improvement is required. It may also not be unusual in some types of events, such as terrorism or an industrial plant explosion, to hear the term *restitution* being used—the clear implication is that people have a legal claim for damages (Quarantelli 1998a).

Elected officials and emergency managers would be wise to choose their terms carefully rather than to allow the public to assume that rehabilitation or restoration is automatic when rebuilding may be the only economically feasible option. In situations where restitution emerges as a possibility, the recovery process may grow even more elongated and challenging—even to the point where the recovery effort itself becomes disrupted.

For the purposes of this book, the term *recovery* will generally be used, which typically means "putting a disaster-stricken community back together" (Mileti 1999, 229). The Federal Emergency Management Agency (FEMA) generally concurs, indicating that "recovery continues until all systems return to normal or better" (see FEMA IS-1, Toolkit, p. 1). In this book, though, you will find that mitigation serves as an important part of recovery in order to build more disaster-resilient communities.

Recovery as a Process

Today, most emergency managers and researchers view recovery as a process, defined as a series of stages, steps, and sequences that people, organizations, and communities move through at varying rates. The recovery process also typically involves two major subphases called short-term and long-term recovery. While each community may define the activities of the short-term and long-term phases slightly differently, depending on its perspectives and resources, some activities common to each phase can be identified.

FEMA (FEMA IS-1) defines short-term efforts as those that return "vital life support systems to minimum operating standards." **Short-term recovery** efforts usually include a transition from response activities to recovery efforts. Response activities focus on saving lives, including search and rescue; providing food, shelter, and clothing; and moving into activities that expedite the transition to long-term recovery. Key transitional activities usually center on managing donations and volunteers, conducting damage assessments, securing temporary housing, restoring lifelines, and clearing debris (NHRAIC 2005, 2–4).

FEMA's view of long-term recovery activities is that they "may continue for a number of years after a disaster. Their purpose is to return life to normal or improved levels." Long-term recovery activities serve as the primary focus of Part 2 in this book, and these include debris management, the environment, historical preservation, housing, businesses, critical infrastructure (roads, bridges, ports), lifelines (power, electricity, sewer), psychological recovery, and the public sector. The long-term recovery period can be viewed as an opportunity to foster improvements in the built environment in order to reduce the impact of future disasters. Such risk-reduction efforts, called mitigation, will be incorporated throughout the text. Ideally, effective mitigation efforts will reduce recovery needs and save money, lives, and property. The result of connecting mitigation to recovery is a more disaster-resilient community.

Each dimension of the recovery process addressed in this book can also be broken down into a series of stages. How people, organizations, and communities move through the phases may vary. Families, for example, move through a series of activities designed to return them to permanent housing (Bolin 1982). First, though, they may move through other stages, including living in a shelter, applying for aid, moving into temporary housing, acquiring resources, and reestablishing a household routine. Families with insurance and other financial resources may move through this process quickly, while others without the means to do so may face extended time in temporary units.

The nature of the hazard may also influence movement through the stages of recovery. Hazards that generate toxic conditions could mean that residents, business owners, and even government may need to stay away from the contaminated area until it is safe to return. When disasters overwhelm local and state capacities to respond and recover, a wide array of federal assistance can be accessed. That process begins with a request for a **presidential disaster declaration**.

Presidential Declarations

When local and state officials cannot meet the needs generated by the disaster, the federal government can assist. Consequently, local officials must understand how to access that aid and what conditions influence the type of aid that they can receive. In this section, we overview the process of requesting federal support; Chapter 15 describes a range of available programs.

The Stafford Act serves as the key piece of legislation that authorizes funding and outlines the boundaries of federal aid. This act allows the president of the United States to declare that a disaster exists and send aid to the states, the District of Columbia, Puerto Rico, the U.S. Virgin Islands, and American Samoa. FEMA can also provide assistance to the Marshall Islands, Micronesia, Guam, and the Northern Mariana Islands. In recent years, FEMA has provided considerable financial support to many of these areas (see Table 1.3). FEMA is only one of many federal agencies that support disaster recovery. (More on those federal partners will be covered in upcoming chapters and in Chapter 15 [Financing Recovery] on federal resources.)

TABLE 1.3   Most Expensive Presidential Disaster Declarations

Disaster	Year	FEMA Funding[a]
Hurricane Katrina (FL, LA, MS, AL)	2005	$29,318,576,948 [b]
September 11 WTC (NY, NJ, VA)	2001	$8,818,350,120
Northridge Earthquake (CA)	1994	$6,978,325,877
Hurricane Rita (TX, LA)	2005	$3,749,698,351
Hurricane Ivan (LA, AL, MS, FL, NC, GA, NJ, PA, WV, NY, TN)	2004	$2,431,034,355
Hurricane Georges (AL, FL, MS, PR, VI)	1998	$2,245,157,178
Hurricane Wilma (FL)	2005	$2,110,738,364
Hurricane Charley (FL, SC)	2004	$1,885,466,628
Hurricane Andrew (FL, LA)	1992	$1,813,594,813
Hurricane Frances (FL, NC, PA, OH, NY, GA, SC)	2004	$1,773,440,505

Source: Federal Emergency Management Agency, http://www.fema.gov/remember911/911_top10.shtm.

[a] Not adjusted for inflation.
[b] Final numbers expected to exceed this amount.

To obtain aid, the governor of the affected state must apply through one of ten regional FEMA offices. The request must be accompanied by a survey of the damages, which is called a preliminary damage assessment or PDA (more information can be found in Chapter 2). The PDA must demonstrate that damage exceeds local and state capacity to respond.

The governor and emergency managers must estimate the kinds of assistance required and the amount of financial impact. A FEMA team may verify the damage, although in some cases advance **emergency declaration**s can be made in order to preposition federal assets. States must verify that they can and will submit to the cost-sharing requirements of the Stafford Act and its programs. To illustrate, many funds for projects that replace or repair public facilities require that state and local governments pay for 25% of the total costs.

Two types of declarations can be secured. An emergency declaration can be secured for up to $5 million. Emergency support can be obtained to reduce loss of lives, prevent further damage to properties, or to mitigate damage to other geographic locations, such as river flooding that moves downstream. Major declarations, the second type, allow for a wider range of programs and financial assistance. In the remainder of this book, we will explore the various programs and partnerships available from the federal government under these declarations.

Summary

In this chapter, we learned that recovery is a multistage process through which people and organizations move at varying rates. Communities, no matter the kind of hazard or geographic location, will face similar challenges during recovery, including removing debris, rebuilding homes and businesses, repairing roads and bridges, restoring utilities, and managing recovery resources. Recovery efforts will also require attention to unique community features, including localized and regional matters that tie people to cultural, historical, and environmental resources.

To do so requires commitment from all levels of government and, as we shall see, from a broad array of voluntary organizations as well. The good news is that many civic-minded neighbors and professional emergency managers will be there as partners in the process. In the next chapter we will work through how that process might play out. Topics will include preliminary damage assessment as well as perspectives and strategies to frame recovery efforts. Chapter 2 lays a foundation for thinking about how best to proceed with a recovery effort.

This book invites you to learn about disaster recovery as a prospective partner in the recovery process. Whether you plan a professional career or intend to volunteer in a disaster context, this book will provide you with insights, ideas, and practical strategies for the major tasks to be done. If you live in a hazardous area, you and your household may be directly affected at some point in time. This book will give you an idea of where and how to start. Ideas contained herein should also give you some practical starting points to reduce your vulnerability, and that of others around you, to disasters. Take the content in this book to heart and use it to make a difference.

Study Guide

Summary Questions

1. What kinds of hazards exist? What are the differences between natural and technological hazards and acts of terrorism?
2. Review the different effects of natural and technological disasters as well as terrorism.
3. What are the differences between emergencies and disasters? How do scale, scope, and magnitude of an event influence the challenges of recovery?
4. How do you define recovery? Why does it matter? What are the differences among restoration, reconstruction, restitution, and rehabilitation?
5. What does it mean that recovery is a "process"?
6. What kinds of conditions influence a presidential disaster declaration?

Discussion Questions

1. What types of hazards are likely to face the community that you live in?
2. Where would you start to organize a recovery effort for the disasters described in this chapter?
3. Why is it best to think of recovery as a process?
4. What role do you see yourself playing in a recovery context?
5. How is the recovery going for Hurricane Katrina? Research the topic on the Internet at various federal, state, and local Web sites. What perspectives and views do you observe at each level?

Key Terms

Comprehensive emergency management
Disaster
Emergency declaration
Long-term recovery
Mitigation
Natural disaster
Preparedness
Presidential disaster declaration
Reconstruction
Recovery
Rehabilitation
Response
Restitution
Restoration
Short-term recovery
Technological disaster
Terrorism

References

Bolin, R. C. 1982. *Household and community recovery from disaster.* Boulder, CO: Institute for Behavioral Social Sciences.

Bowman, T. D., P. F. Schempf, and J. Hodges. 1997. Bald eagle population in Prince William Sound after the *Exxon Valdez* oil spill. *Journal of Wildlife Management* 61 (3): 962–967.

Brookings Institution. 2006. Special edition of the Katrina Index. Washington, DC: The Brookings Institution.

Brookings Institution. 2007a. Katrina Index. Greater New Orleans Community Data Center. www.gnocdc.org.

Brookings Institution. 2007b. The New Orleans Index: Second anniversary special edition. Greater New Orleans Community Data Center. www.gnocdc.org.

Brookings Institution. 2008. The New Orleans Index anniversary edition: Three years after Katrina. Greater New Orleans Community Data Center. http://www.gnocdc.org.

Brown, G. Jr. 1992. Replacement costs of birds and animals. http://www.evostc.state.ak.us/Publications/economic.cfm.

Carson, R. T., and W. Haneman. 1992. A preliminary economic analysis of recreational fishing losses related to the *Exxon Valdez* oil spill. http://www.evostc.state.ak.us/Publications/Downloadables/Economic/Econ_Fishing.pdf.

City of Austin. 2007. History of flooding in Austin. http://www.ci.austin.tx.us/watershed/floodhistory.htm.

EPA. 2007a. What is a Hazardous Waste? Environmental Protection Agency. http://www.epa.gov/epaoswer/osw/hazwaste.htm.

EPA. 2007b. EPA removes Love Canal from Superfund list. Environmental Protection Agency. http://www.epa.gov/superfund/accomp/news/lovecanal.htm.

EPA. 2007c. NPL Site Narrative for Times Beach Site. Environmental Protection Agency. http://www.epa.gov/superfund/sites/npl/nar833.htm.

Exxon Valdez Oil Spill Trustee Council. 2007. Frequently asked questions about the spill. http://www.evostc.state.ak.us/History/FAQ.cfm.

FEMA. No date. IS-1. Independent Study 1: Emergency Program Manager. Federal Emergency Management Agency. http://training.fema.gov/IS/crslist.asp.

FEMA. No date. Disaster Declarations. Federal Emergency Management Agency. http://www.fema.gov/media/fact_sheets/declarations.shtm.

FEMA. 2007. Hazardous materials. Federal Emergency Management Agency. http://www.fema.gov/hazard/hazmat/index.shtm.

GAO. 2007. Hurricane Katrina. GAO-07-651. Washington, DC: Government Accountability Office. http://www.gao.gov.

Greater New Orleans Community Data Center. 2007. Press release. www.gnocdc.org.

HUD. 2006. Current housing unit damage estimates: Hurricanes Katrina, Rita and Wilma. Department of Housing and Urban Development. http://www.dhs.gov/xlibrary/assets/GulfCoast_HousingDamageEstimates_021206.pdf.

Laska, S. 2004. What if Hurricane Ivan had not missed New Orleans? *Natural Hazards Observer* 29: 5–6.

Latzke, J. 2007. Saving Survivor Tree from storm. Associated Press as published in the *Stillwater News Press*, December 12, A9.

Mallonee, S., S. Shariat, G. Stennies, R. Waxweiler, D. Hogan, and F. Jordan. 1996. Physical injuries and fatalities resulting from the Oklahoma City bombing. *Journal of the American Medical Association* 276 (5): 382–287.

Mileti, D. 1999. *Disasters by design*. Washington, DC: Joseph Henry Press.

National Governor's Association. 1978. *Comprehensive emergency management*. Washington, DC: National Governor's Association.

National Hurricane Center. 2007a. Hurricane basics. http://www.nhc.noaa.gov/HAW2/english/basics.shtml.

National Hurricane Center. 2007b. Saffir-Simpson Hurricane Scale. http://www.nhc.noaa.gov/HAW2/english/basics/saffir_simpson.shtml.

National Oceanic and Atmospheric Administration Service. 2005. NOS Education, Discovery Stories. http://www.ocean service.noaa.gov/education/stories/oilymess/downloads/how_toxic.pdf.

Neal, D. 1997. Reconceptualizing the phases of disaster. *International Journal of Mass Emergencies and Disasters* 15 (2): 139–164.

NHRAIC (Natural Hazards Research and Applications Information Center). 2005. *Holistic disaster recovery.* Boulder, CO: Public Entity Risk Institute.

PAHO/WHO. 2005. Identifying cadavers following disasters: Why? Pan American Health Organization/World Health Organization. http://www.who.int/disasters/repo/6077.html.

Pfefferbaum, B., J. Call, and G. Sconzo. 1999. Mental health services for children in the first two years after the 1995 Oklahoma City terrorist bombing. *Psychiatric Services* 50 (7): 956–958.

Picou, J. S. 1992. Disruption and stress in an Alaskan fishing community: Initial and continued impacts of the *Exxon Valdez* spill. *Organization and Environment* 6 (3): 235–257.

Quarantelli, E. L. 1988. Disaster studies: An analysis of the social historical factors affecting the development of research in the area. *International Journal of Mass Emergencies and Disasters* 5: 285–310.

———. 1998a. The disaster recovery process: What we do and do not know from research. http://dspace.udel.edu:8080/dspace/handle/19716/309?mode=simple.

———, ed. 1998b. *What is a disaster?* London: Routledge.

Quarantelli, E. L., and R. Perry, eds. 2005. *What is a disaster?* Vol. 2. Philadelphia: Xlibris, International Research Committee on Disaster.

Rubin, C. 2006. Terrorism timeline. http://www.disaster-timeline.com/docs/TTL2007A-Apr15-secure.pdf.

Short, J., S. Rice, and M. Lindeberg. 2001. The *Exxon Valdez* oil spill: How much oil remains? Alaskan Fisheries Science Center. http://www.afsc.noaa.gov/Quarterly/jas2001/feature_jas01.htm.

Simpson, D., and S. Stehr. 2003. Victim management and identification after the World Trade Center collapse. In *Beyond September 11th: An account of post-disaster research,* ed. J. Monday, 109–120. Boulder, CO: University of Colorado.

Thompson, J. 1991. The management of body recovery after disasters. *Disaster Management* 3(4): 206–210.

USGS. 2007a. What causes earthquakes? U.S. Geological Survey. http://vulcan.wr.usgs.gov/Glossary/Seismicity/what_causes_earthquakes.html.

USGS. 2007b. The Richter Magnitude Scale. U.S. Geological Survey. http://earthquake.usgs.gov/learning/topics/richter.php.

Wind Science and Engineering Center. 2006. Recommendations for an Enhanced Fujita Scale. Lubbock: Texas Tech University.

Resources

- DNA Analysis for September 11. For updated numbers on DNA analysis, visit http://911research.wtc7.net/wtc/evidence/bodies.html.
- FEMA Independent Study Courses including FEMA IS-1, visit http://www.fema.gov. Select Training and then Independent Study Courses, which are free to U.S. citizens. Dozens of relevant courses are available including certification for a Professional Development Series.

- FEMA information on current disasters can be found at http://www.fema.gov.
- For free copies of academic research on disasters visit the Natural Hazards Center, University of Colorado at Boulder, at http://www.colorado.edu/hazards or the Disaster Research Center, University of Delaware, at http://www.udel.edu/DRC.
- National Memorial Museum website, Oklahoma City http://www.oklahomacitynationalmemorial.org/ and Memorial Marathon http://www.okcmarathon.com/
- Terrorism Timeline available at http://www.disaster-timeline.com/TTL2007A-Apr15-secure.pdf. Accessed July 21, 2008, (Rubin 2006).

Chapter **2**

Frameworks and Approaches to Disaster Recovery

Learning Objectives

After reading this chapter, you should be able to:

- Outline key ideas associated with major theoretical perspectives used in disaster recovery research
- Apply theories to disaster situations to explain potential and actual outcomes
- Use theories to identify the kinds of challenges that may affect recovery efforts
- Describe key challenges and barriers to the recovery process and preliminary strategies for succeeding with recovery efforts
- Explain how to conduct preliminary damage assessment and why this step is so crucial to the disaster recovery process
- Explain why recovery does not occur as a separate stage but, rather, should be linked to mitigation as a way to build more disaster-resilient communities

Introduction

This chapter focuses on ideas for understanding and generating the recovery process. First, we will start with two examples that illustrate the various issues associated with recovery. Next, we will move to theories that help us to explain and understand how communities may have ended up facing significant reconstruction. In short, theory will help us understand how a community arrived in its present situation.

Theories set the stage for understanding the challenges associated with recovery, particularly the kinds of barriers that you can expect to address as a community moves back toward "normal." We next take stock of what has happened in a disaster, through discussing a procedure called **preliminary damage assessment** (PDA). As mentioned in Chapter 1, PDA is the first step in acquiring outside resources, namely a presidential disaster declaration. In this chapter, we will learn how valuable the PDA can be to a variety of groups, and we will work through some examples of how it can be done.

Finally, we will turn to various perspectives on how to approach recovery. We will start with a popular approach, that recovery should be holistic. Part of a holistic approach emphasizes sustainable development to enhance the chances that communities will endure across time. **Sustainability** incorporates ideas that safeguard environmental assets and promotes the notion that we should rebuild in ways that enhance rather than deplete natural resources. The goal of a sustainable, **holistic recovery** is to ensure that all sectors and people enjoy an equitable chance to recover and to become more resilient in the face of future events. First, though, let us look at a recent event that helps us to understand the value of upcoming theories and perspectives.

The Indian Ocean Tsunami

On December 26, 2004, an earthquake of between 9.1 and 9.3 magnitude generated multiple tsunami waves that impacted at least 13 nations. Close to 300,000 people died. Of those deaths, approximately 80% were women and children; people with disabilities fared equally badly (Australian Council for International Development 2005; Oxfam 2005).

Gender mattered in the tsunami for social, economic, and cultural reasons. Women's work in coastal villages of India meant that women were gathered at the shore, waiting for the fishermen to return with the day's catch. Women would then process the fish and sell it at market, an economic activity they undertook to support their households. As the tsunami rolled ashore, women searched frantically for children and could not escape the powerful, 40-foot wall of water.

As the black water surged nearly one kilometer inward in Naggapattinam, India, women struggled to swim. Their clothing entangled their limbs as they sought to hold on to their children. Dense sand and debris swept along by the wave battered those struggling to survive. In the Batticola area of Sri Lanka, women and their children had gathered to bathe in the sea. Mortality numbers were high. And in Aceh Besar, Indonesia, male survivors outnumbered women nearly 4:1, the same ratios seen in Sri Lanka and India (Oxfam 2005). In short, the higher death rates can be attributed to the roles played by women, a lack of strength training for swimming and climbing trees, and traditional attire.

A disproportionate number of people with disabilities died as well. Numbers may rise in part because disabilities may prevent taking protective action. Another reason for the higher rates stems from emergency management organizations that do not address the specific needs of people with disabilities (Australian Council for International Development 2005). In one Indian care facility, over 90% of the children with disabilities died in the tsunami.

In Vailankanni, India (Photo 2.1), the tsunami crashed onto the shore and surged up a major commercial sector. Hundreds of businesses were destroyed. Along the coastline, the waters took thousands of homes among the fisher people's villages. Nestled less than a kilometer from the shore, the local hospital in Naggapattinam heard cries of "water, water" as their only warning. In an amazing effort, medical staff and family members carried nearly 300 patients up the stairs to safety. As they watched the water surge around the hospital compound, the staff slowly realized that they had saved everyone in the hospital. Medical staff then worked to the point of exhaustion to try and revive local villagers.

Do these patterns hold for other nations? What about other disasters? The answer is clearly no, as we witnessed after Hurricane Katrina (National Organization on Disability 2005). Thousands of Americans, lacking resources to evacuate, remained in place within their homes or congregate-care facilities. Few of us will forget the nursing home residents who drowned in their beds as the storm surge came ashore. And surely we recall the images of wheelchairs abandoned on the overpasses and bridges or scattered in the airport as evacuation flights ferried people away from New Orleans.

As the Oxfam (2005) report states, "Wherever they hit, pre-existing structures and social conditions determine that some members of the community will be less affected while others pay a higher price," a reality true not only abroad but at home as well. Such problems also linger into the recovery period. Consider these issues that arose after the tsunami and their reappearance along the U.S. Gulf Coast after Hurricane Katrina:

- Reports of domestic violence erupted in refugee centers after the tsunami and also arose in Louisiana, where all the protective shelters were destroyed.
- People with disabilities did not have accessible ramps, bathrooms, and other facilities in the tsunami relief camps. Katrina survivors filed a lawsuit (*Brou v. FEMA*) to ensure accessibility in the trailers that were provided for temporary housing.

PHOTO 2.1 Memorial for tsunami victims. (Photo by Brenda Phillips. With permission.)

- Both events destroyed livelihoods, particularly those associated with fishing and subsistence economies. Well-meaning donors sent the wrong kinds of boats to India and other nations. Along the U.S. Gulf Coast, fishing communities faced the loss of boats, homes, and socio-cultural networks that had helped them to survive economically.

Pressures to relocate have been resisted because of the problem of transferring fishing skills and resources and the potential loss of family and kin relationships.

- Power remained intermittent or nonexistent in significant sections of India and the Gulf Coast for up to several months.
- Local transportation routes were disrupted in both locations, as the tsunami or storm surge destroyed bridges and highways while claiming boats and other forms of transportation. Public transportation was slow to return, particularly in New Orleans.
- Economic development commenced almost immediately in both areas. Nongovernmental organizations provided means for Indian women to work on craft projects while the fishing industry regrouped. Small businesses reopened with the support of relief agencies. Along the Gulf Coast, businesses slowly reopened in the damaged areas, although some sectors, such as education, lagged behind significantly.
- Naggapattinam medical staff rebuilt the hospital further inland within one year with the help of relief agencies. Gulf Coast areas continue to wait for prestorm medical care to return, particularly affordable health-care options.

The process of disaster recovery occurs unevenly for different groups and populations. It is not possible to predict a specific sequence of steps or stages that people will move through during recovery. Nor is it possible to identify a timeline for that recovery. Through the application of theoretical frameworks, though, it is possible to understand why the problems develop and to identify areas of concern and populations that may face more difficult recoveries.

Theoretical Frameworks

The purpose of theory is to provide an explanation. Theory offers insight and understanding, often shedding light on why an event occurred or why a particular sector of the community experienced more damage. Disaster theorizing is yet in its early stages of development, with ideas borrowed from a variety of disciplines (Smith and Wenger 2006). In this section, we explore some of the more commonly used theories in the field and apply them to help us understand various recovery scenarios.

Systems Theory

Systems theory relies on the idea that several sectors, or systems, interact to produce a disaster event. For disasters, three systems emerge as important: the built, physical, and human systems (Mileti 1999; see Figure 2.1). A misfit of these three sectors will result in stronger possibilities for damage.

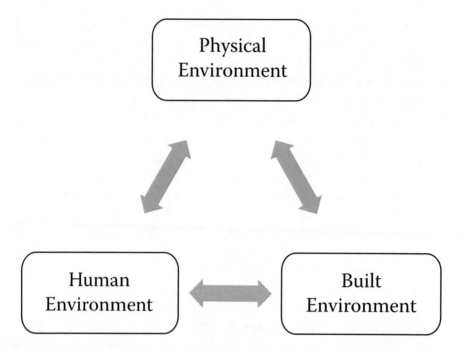

FIGURE 2.1 Systems theory. Disasters result from a misfit of the systems. Recovery needs are generated when hazards in the physical environment impinge upon the built environment with consequences for human survival and recovery. (Based on Mileti 1999.)

Physical systems include the various dimensions that arise naturally from our environment, including the atmosphere, where weather forms. The 2008 blizzard in Ohio that produced 20 inches of record snow in Columbus demonstrates one extreme of that weather system. If a community is not prepared for weather events, it may face disastrous consequences. Across many parts of Ohio, however, emergency management agencies have prepared for weather events including snowfall by preestablishing emergency routes, preplacing food among those who are homebound, and prepositioning road-clearing equipment. When the snow melts, another component of the physical environment called the *hydrosphere*, or water systems, may flood (Mileti 1999). If communities have allowed building in floodplains where extra water would otherwise go, there may be an impact on homes (the physical environment) and people (the human system).

Buildings, roads, bridges, ports, utilities, and other such structures comprise the constructed system or built environment (Mileti 1999). Recent disasters such as the 2007 Minneapolis I-35 bridge collapse demonstrate how dependent we are on our built environment. Beyond the loss of life, the bridge collapse caused significant traffic problems that required rerouting during reconstruction.

From a systems perspective, disasters occur when the connections among the natural, built, and human systems are disrupted. In 1811, an earthquake changed the course of the Mississippi River. The result on the built environment? Minimal impact. Few lived in the area at the time; consequently, the built environment suffered little damage (Quarantelli 1985). A similar event today on the New Madrid fault line could seriously damage major cities like St. Louis and Memphis. During the summer of 2008, an oil spill closed the Port of New Orleans at the mouth of the Mississippi River. As one of the nation's most critical ports, the closure stopped transportation of valuable cargo and the ferries that carried people and cars across the river. Determining the spill's impact on marshlands, animal life, water quality, and local fishing communities will take years of study. How we rebuild our physical environment to withstand such hazards matters. Equally important, we must connect the physical environment with the potential human and environmental impacts.

By now you probably understand that, without the presence of human beings, disasters will produce few challenges. Tropical storms will bring much-needed precipitation to rain forests. Earthquakes may produce uplift sufficient to generate extensive mountain chains over time. In the absence of homes and businesses along coastlines, hurricanes and tsunamis would lack much impact other than naturally generated topographical change.

Effects on the human system depend on a number of conditions. For example, it is clear that some populations face higher risks than others (Mileti 1999). Lower-income families may not be able to afford a built environment retrofitted or designed for seismic activity. They may have to live in inferior housing that cannot stand up to tornadic winds. For urban populations in general, a lack of public transportation and preplanned evacuation procedures may mean the difference between life and death. As we saw with Hurricane Katrina, many senior citizens and people with disabilities faced considerable challenges in escaping harm's way.

To summarize, systems theory says that disasters occur and recovery needs develop because of a misfit of three main systems: physical, built, and human. However, as we shall see in this book, the recovery period also offers an opportunity to rectify those misalignments and integrate a higher level of safety among systems.

Vulnerability Theory

Systems theory demonstrates that we cannot really engineer nature. Levees fail, dams burst, buildings topple, and bridges collapse despite our best efforts to prevent such damage. Within those structures, people live and work at significant risk. Vulnerability theorists would have us concentrate on human lives, with a particular concentration on those at highest risk and most vulnerable or susceptible to injury, death, economic disruption, and property loss. In short, **vulnerability theory** specifies that the social distribution of risk is not shared equally across all groups (Wisner 2001; Wisner et al. 2005; see Photo 2.2).

As seen in the Indian Ocean Tsunami example, it is clear that issues related to gender, disability, income level, and development status mean that some population segments bear disproportionate losses. Can the same be said of developed nations such as the United States? Indeed it can, as can be seen from Hurricane Katrina alone. Nearly 70% of the deaths caused from the levee failures occurred among the elderly, with a higher proportionate death rate among African Americans (Sharkey 2007).

By extension, vulnerability theory can be applied to the recovery period as well. Researchers have documented problems, for example, with relief policies and programs. After the Northridge earthquake in 1994, assistance programs were critiqued for exclusionary policies, which required "personal knowledge of federal programs, cultural and language skills, and physical location.... Local political culture compounded resource access problems for Latino disaster victims" (Bolin and Stanford 1999).

In a society long influenced by institutions that have hindered women's advancement economically and politically, it should not be surprising to find gendered recovery patterns too. Critics charge that recovery programs and

PHOTO 2.2   Marietta, GA, September 4, 2005 — Personnel from Amy and Air Force National Guard and Georgia Defense Force wait with wheelchairs and stretchers for evacuees from New Orleans and Hurricane Katrina. (Photo by George Armstrong/ FEMA News Photo.)

committees fail to include women's interests or contributions. Women tend to be those most likely to seek out and use relief programs, in an effort to tie their families to recovery assets. Women also appear more likely to serve as caretakers for diverse family members, including elders, children, and those with disabilities. In short, women link the family to recovery efforts (Enarson and Morrow 1998, 2000).

Vulnerability theory certainly specifies that some groups are at higher risk than others. Another dimension, though, points out that vulnerable populations bring resources to the table. However, emergency managers tend to underuse or not use their capacities at all (Wisner 2001). Community and advocacy groups, for example, represent important sources of information and links into a particular population. Imagine, for example, trying to link recovery efforts to people who are deaf without knowing American Sign Language or understanding the long and rich traditions associated with deaf culture.

Vulnerability theory directs those involved in recovery management to decentralize their recovery efforts, involve the community in solving problems, and integrate local knowledge for a better outcome. Equality of outcome is the final goal as well as coexistence with nature, rather than trying to engineer nature to serve human demands (Wisner 2001).

Sociopolitical-Ecology Theory

Systems theory outlines three interacting systems. **Sociopolitical-ecology theory** asks us to focus on interactions within a social system, particularly within the social systems comprising the human community (Peacock and Ragsdale 1997). From this perspective, disasters represent events that disrupt social system interaction. Those living within the social system work toward reestablishing their daily routines, trying to return to normalcy. Disasters overwhelm individual households, which require assistance from other parts of the social system to recover. Yet, competition erupts due to scarcity of resources or due to access limited by existing power relationships within the social system.

Competition occurs because of a lack of predisaster equities within the social system. Lower-income households, for example, may lack the income or insurance to rebuild. In a high-priced housing market, households will compete for the limited dwellings that remain. For communities that lack affordable housing, the winners and losers will be obvious: Lower-income households will double or triple up, be forced to relocate, or move into inferior or even less-safe housing. Small businesses, in contrast to chains or larger corporations, will lack the financial support to regroup and recover as well. Even predisaster community social service organizations may find that donations decline or go to disaster agencies. Thus those with whom the social service organizations interact (predisaster homeless, domestic violence survivors, people with disabilities, senior citizens) will then find themselves even further back in line for routine assistance.

The sociopolitical-ecology perspective suggests that competition may lead to conflict between actors and organizations within the social system. Recovery organizations, for example, tend to include the more powerful and influential members of a community, affording them decision-making power over the others in that same social system. Protests are likely to erupt, and the competition and conflict that arise from these differential power arrangements then "can result in delays, blockages, shortages and waste of limited resources within the field during critical recovery periods" (Peacock and Ragsdale 1997).

To summarize, the sociopolitical-ecology perspective predicts an uneven recovery process in which households will need support from other parts of the social system. Communities must therefore interact to provide that support and, ideally, to reduce the barriers that prevent individual household recovery: discrimination, poverty, exclusion, power dynamics, and even corruption, to name a few. Equitable participation and attention to the disparities experienced during recovery should lessen the uneven chance of returning home.

Feminist Theory

Feminist theory has only recently been connected to disaster practice, although considerable research examining how gender influences disaster experiences has evolved (Enarson and Phillips 2008). Feminist theory offers a wide variety of perspectives from which to examine problems that affect men and women differently, pointing out that women and children tend to be overimpacted by disasters. Each feminist theory offers varying explanations for the origins and outcomes of gender differentiation. Here, we examine three to illustrate the rich diversity of feminist thinking and its potential for understanding recovery challenges: liberal feminism, multiracial feminism, and feminist political ecology.

Liberal Feminism

Liberal feminism represents the strand perhaps most familiar because it targets gender discrimination located within social institutions. Court cases that seek restitution for lost wages represent one strategy used by liberal feminists to address inequities, for example. Within disasters, liberal feminists suggest that many barriers exist to increasing life safety for women and children. The remedy? Women should be involved in decision making regarding disaster policies and programs.

Researchers have documented gender bias in recovery organizations that fail to integrate women's perspectives (Enarson and Morrow 2000). It appears, for example, that domestic violence rates increase after disasters but that few, if any, disaster recovery organizations fund domestic violence programs. As another example, economic recovery programs typically do not address paid, home-based work such as secretarial, cyber-commuting, child care, sewing, and other work often lost to the disaster (Enarson 2001). Liberal feminists would offer inclusion as a key strategy, assuming that empowering women's voice and presence in the process would heighten attention to women's issues.

Multiracial Feminism

Multiracial feminists challenge the notion that "women" includes everyone. Noting that women's studies programs and mainstream feminist theorizing tend to represent the mainstream, multiracial feminism calls our attention to the status of culturally diverse women. Differences matter here, particularly when we understand the interaction of race, class, and gender when racist assumptions are made. For example, recovery workers have assumed at times that Latinas are migrant rather than long-term workers or that African-American women inherently share the same recovery situation across income levels (Enarson 2001). Cajun women living in a bayou fishing community report different recovery problems than women trying to rebuild in an urban context. The barriers to effective aid include language issues across generations, a need for recovery agencies to grasp the timing of various fishing seasons, the difficulties in navigating recovery programs without consistent access to utilities, the pressure of area developers to acquire land, and the unwillingness of organizations to send caseworkers and representatives into the marshlands to help women unable to reach land-based recovery offices easily. In short, multiracial feminism says that recovery managers cannot assume that all women are the same. Doing so distorts disaster practice; neglects needs that arise from an intersection of race, class, and gender; and results in differential household recovery.

Feminist Political Ecology

Feminist political ecology tries to integrate disaster recovery, gender issues, and environmental-justice issues. This perspective sensitizes us to how women rely on environmental knowledge to survive and how important it is to defend a land from destructive environmental practices. In many parts of the world, for example, women bear responsibility for stewardship of environmental resources, even for protection of floodplains, water supplies, and hillsides threatened by deforestation (leading to landslides when disaster strikes). Various studies over the past decades, beginning with Rachel Carson's 1962 call to environmental action over pesticide contamination, reveal that the bodies of women and children are at particular risk from environmental pollutants (Carson 1962). Thus, communities that suffer disasters because of environmental degradation—such as damage to the Louisiana coast that fails to stem a storm surge—would be well-advised to involve bayou women with histories of alerting the public to the escalating environmental damage. Those who live closest to and in concert with natural resources bear higher risk to their livelihoods, serve as early advocates for environmental conservation, and may be among those most willing to support green, sustainable approaches to recovery.

To summarize, feminist theory offers promising insights for disaster practice. Different theories point out alternative locations and solutions for recovery problems. Involving women from various backgrounds requires commitment from recovery organizations and emergency managers.

Emergent-Norm Theory

Considerable effort goes into producing plans for emergency and disaster response. Yet, recovery planning lags as a typical emergency management activity. Recovery, in contrast to the responses after disasters, can take years rather than days or weeks, cost considerably more in dollars, and involves far more staff, volunteers, and organizations. In terms of the life cycle of emergency management described in Chapter 1, recovery represents the least-thought-about phase, particularly at the local level. In short, recovery tends to be an ad hoc, emergent process. Emergence is defined as behavior or activities that newly appear in reaction to a disaster event. Interestingly, one might question whether such ad hoc processes are inherently good or bad.

Emergent-norm theory led disaster researchers to develop a related model called the Emergent Human Resources Model (EHRM). The EHRM explains that disasters tend to disable normal bureaucratic structures. As a consequence, it is likely that established procedures will not anticipate the full range of needs and issues that will arise. In addition, established procedures tend to reflect the people who created them and who may not understand the needs of all who are affected, for example, renters, students, people with disabilities, single-parent families, small business owners, culturally diverse groups, endangered species, and historic neighborhoods. Further, new types of disasters such as terrorism may generate unanticipated needs, for example, social psychological and long-term medical rehabilitation services. To respond to unmet, unanticipated, or newly appearing needs, relatively spontaneously generated actions and organizations will emerge (Dynes and Quarantelli 1968; Neal and Phillips 1995). These emergent entities are likely to model new or emergent norms (behaviors) and organizational structures.

Such was the case in Watsonville, California, after the 1989 Loma Prieta earthquake. Initially, Latino citizens charged that the city had not responded with sensitivity toward language or cultural needs. A Department of Justice investigation found that, although no overt discrimination had occurred, changes could be made. In response, the local American Red Cross hired a trilingual, tricultural specialist who later became a city emergency management coordinator. The Red Cross invited a local health organization, Salud Para La Gente, to participate in training and serve on its board. Salud responded by initiating its own internal disaster planning as well. The city also appointed an ombudsperson to reach out to the Latino community. In contrast to the protest march of a year earlier, the one-year anniversary of the earthquake showed a united community who marched together through the streets to city hall. Leading the way, a banner supported by local citizens read, *La tierra se movió y nuestros corazones se unieron* (The earth moved and our hearts united; we are now just beginning).

After Hurricane Andrew, a local recovery organization, We Will Rebuild, was charged with excluding women's interests. In response, an emergent organization that named itself Women Will Rebuild began to lobby for the interests of women and children. Their interests demonstrated unmet and unanticipated needs, including legal assistance; health and mental health services; temporary housing, particularly trailer life; recognition and accommodation of the circumstances of immigrant and migrant women; youth recreation; domestic violence issues; child care; and representation on the powerful We Will Rebuild committee. Women Will Rebuild secured some concessions, including representation on the executive committee of We Will Rebuild and the creation of two new committees: Families and Children, and Domestic Violence. Some funding was secured as well for teen pregnancy services, child care, and domestic violence programs and youth recreation (Enarson and Morrow 1998).

Emergent-norm theory suggests that existing bureaucratic structures—even those that are preplanned—may not anticipate fully the range of needs and services that will develop during the recovery process. New behaviors and organizational structures are likely to appear during the recovery period. Good planners, then, would be well advised to do several things. First, they should draw in underrepresented groups and populations to reduce the number of unmet needs. Second, they should anticipate that emergence will occur and decide early on how to use those newly appearing entities as resources rather than as foes.

Recap of Theoretical Frameworks

To summarize these theoretical perspectives, consider their similarities and differences. Systems theory looks at large-scale units that serve as subcomponents of an even larger system. Misfits among the systems result in disastrous consequences, particularly for the human environment. Vulnerability theory explains the disproportionate impact of disasters and identifies those who might be vulnerable as those with less power, economic clout, political position, or social privilege. Sociopolitical-ecology theory frames the problem as resulting from inequitable power relationships, with clear winners and losers. Feminist theory concentrates on the ways in which issues of gender, class, race, and income compromise the life safety and livelihoods of women and their children. Emergent-norm theory suggests that disaster recovery activities will occur without much preplanning. Taken as a whole, these theoretical perspectives help us to predict who is at risk and why those risks occur. Collectively, these theories point out the very human consequences of disaster recovery.

These theories also serve as guides to the kinds of activities that should be undertaken after disaster. Attention must be paid to balancing the effects of the various systems. By thinking in a holistic manner and integrating elements of the different system parts, we can build a stronger, more disaster-resilient whole. We must also pay attention to those at highest risk for a failed recovery and ensure that those most vulnerable and least powerful can participate in and share the benefits of a full recovery. We must understand that unmet needs will appear and be ready to handle them. Most importantly, these theories suggest that we must concentrate on preparing our communities and the households therein for disaster. If we build, or rebuild, with mitigation of future disasters in mind, we create a more disaster-resilient planet for our families and communities. For overviews of these theories, see Boxes 2.1 and 2.2.

Challenges of Recovery

As demonstrated in the earlier case studies and the issues revealed by the theoretical frameworks, recovery is a challenge. Each chapter in the remainder of this book lays out the challenges and offers research-based insights and practical strategies. Before starting on that journey, though, it is important to understand that recovery is not an easy or stepwise process.

As pointed out by a number of authors in *Holistic Disaster Recovery* (Natural Hazards Center 2005), recovery can be slowed by several obstacles. As demonstrated by the Indian Ocean Tsunami and certainly by Hurricane Katrina, the amount of damage matters. Catastrophic impact across a massive area means that the usual regional resources will not be available and that even federal resources may be taxed. Taking the time to mitigate any future risks may mean delays in rebuilding. It is not unusual, for example, for communities to put into place new codes, ordinances, and policies that govern the rebuilding process. Communities may also take advantage of a disaster to set aside floodplains and reduce wildfire threats. Systems theorists would applaud.

BOX 2.1   OVERVIEW OF KEY THEORETICAL IDEAS

Systems Theory

- Three systems matter: the built, natural, and human environments.
- These systems interact and share mutual dependencies.
- A misfit of these systems results in disaster.
- Opportunities during recovery include rectifying the misalignments, increasing the levels of safety, respecting the power and integrity of the environment, and creating more disaster-resilient built and human systems.

Vulnerability Theory

- It concentrates on people who face the highest risk to life safety, injuries, and property loss.
- It notes that risks are not shared equally.
- There are consequences of differential risks during the relief and recovery time periods.
- Recovery efforts should recognize that vulnerabilities cannot be rebuilt or reintegrated.
- Recovery represents a time to alter differential risks by attending to issues of income, development status, gender, race, income, and disability.
- People at risk also bring capacities to the recovery effort that should be recognized and integrated.

Sociopolitical-Ecology Theory

- Disasters disrupt social interactions.
- Interaction within the human system influences how people recover.
- People need resources to recover. Those resources are limited.
- Recovery time periods may see conflict and competition over scarce recovery resources.
- Powerful groups may prevent those with less power from accessing needed relief and recovery aid.
- Solutions include altering power arrangements so that discrimination, poverty, and corruption do not influence recovery outcomes.
- Participation of all people affected by disaster in the recovery process is essential.

Emergent-Norm Theory

- Disasters disable normal bureaucratic structures.
- New types of disasters such as terrorism or pandemics are likely to appear in the future, and bureaucratic structures will not be sufficiently prepared.

- New, unmet needs are likely to appear in a disaster recovery time period because of the above conditions.
- New structures, groups, and organizations will emerge to handle unmet needs.
- Recognize emergent structures as an asset for the recovery time period. Emergence points out areas for action and provides potential recovery assets among those involved in the emergent activities.

Source: Summarized from the references cited in this chapter section entitled Theoretical Frameworks.

BOX 2.2   FEMINIST PERSPECTIVES ON RECOVERY

Liberal Feminism and Disaster Recovery

- Identify the practical needs of women and children throughout the disaster event and how institutional arrangements can adapt to their needs: child care, protection from domestic violence, employment, housing access.
- Recruit and retain women staff in disaster recovery organizations, with particular attention paid to involving women from disaster-vulnerable populations and locations.
- Train and educate disaster recovery staff and volunteers in working with women of various educational, income, age, and disability levels.
- Target women-owned businesses and female-dominated nonprofits in business-recovery and economic-development programs.

Multiracial Feminist Theory and Disaster Recovery

- Involve organizations that empower women of color to participate in the recovery planning and implementation processes and pay them for their contributions.
- Build social networks between women's groups involving women of color in recovery activities, including funding initiatives and programs that pay for or reimburse staff and volunteer labor.
- Facilitate the active participation of women from underrepresented groups in disaster recovery planning.
- Target women leaders from diverse cultural groups for leadership positions in recovery staff and voluntary organizations.

Feminist Political Ecology and Disaster Recovery

- Involve women environmental leaders in planning mitigation activities for the full range of recovery needs in housing, environment, infrastructure, and businesses.

- Increase networking among disaster organizations and women involved in environmental-justice and sustainable-development organizations.
- Integrate women involved in local health and safety issues, including technological disasters and hazardous materials, for research on the long-term effects of these substances on women and children.

Source: Adapted from Enarson and Phillips (2008). Used with permission of the International Research Committee on Disasters.

Also important, government programs will funnel funding into an area, although such resources always come with rules and regulations that must be adhered to. Learning about these opportunities to fuel recovery takes time, especially if a community has not prepared for disaster in advance. While such resources certainly do not represent obstacles for the long term, working out issues related to damage, rebuilding procedures, and funding programs may delay recovery.

Such delays are not always appreciated by people eager for a return to normalcy. Government officials and recovery leaders will be wise to involve and inform the public so that they understand why delays occur, something that is always difficult when people are living in temporary settings with children, work demands, and an unfamiliar, even intimidating rebuilding process. As emergent-norm theory predicts, those involved in leading the community through recovery may need to take on new, unfamiliar roles. A public works director, for example, may be tasked with debris management. Local social workers may need to assist seniors displaced from assisted living facilities. The mayor and other officials will need to learn to "speak FEMA," as in learning the acronyms, programs, and limitations of what the federal government can do. The learning curve after disaster can be enormous and daunting. It may not be surprising that, for recovery leaders, the tasks feel completely overwhelming at times.

Consider, also, that the scenario discussed so far illustrates a community in which local leaders feel compelled to guide a recovery effort. The willingness of political, economic, and civic leaders to spend time, energy, and public funds on a recovery may vary from minimal to extensive. In a community beset with multiple kinds of problems, disaster recovery may need to compete with funding debates over other priorities: economic development, routine transportation construction, school issues, or public services such as police and fire. Communities that lack a strong tax base may need to make hard decisions about whether and how they can "return" and what "normal" might be like (Natural Hazards Center 2005).

Before you give up prior to finishing the rest of this book, though, take heart. Many communities have come back from disaster, some of them even stronger and more disaster-resistant than before. The remainder of this book outlines strategies based on prior research and actual cases for recoveries related to debris management, housing, the environment, historical and cultural preservation, the economy, and infrastructure. We start the process by examining the planning function in the next chapter, in a process that endorses participation by all key stakeholders, particularly the public. We also tend to the human side of recovery by understanding the impact that recovery can have on officials and staff involved in leading us through recovery as well as the social psychological impact of disaster on the broader public. We finish the book by looking at the resources necessary for full recovery: donations management, community involvement, voluntary organizations, and federal resources. The process begins by taking stock of what has happened in an effort called *damage assessment*.

Damage Assessment

When the winds and floodwaters subside and people emerge to look around, they inherently take stock of their surroundings. What's left? Who's hurt? Where do I start? Emergency managers, voluntary organizations, and government staff all take stock as well, in a process called damage assessment, literally a thorough inventory of the damages: lives lost and injuries; damage to various types of housing, schools, and businesses; and needed repairs for roads, bridges, airports, waterways, and railroads. Information about historical and cultural losses must be calculated. Damage to the environment must be assessed. As the figures add up, a picture of what the community faces and the kinds of help needed begins to emerge.

Emergency managers next summarize the damages in a report to the governor of their state, who then requests a presidential disaster declaration through FEMA (see Chapter 1). Without such a request, federal assistance cannot be awarded; FEMA staff will visually confirm the damages prior to making an award. Voluntary organizations also rely on damage assessments to determine how many volunteers to send, what skill sets they will need, and how long they will work in a community. Insurance companies will require damage assessments prior to writing out checks to policyholders and then use the information to gauge the impact on their companies. Thus, conducting a preliminary damage assessment is the first step on the path toward recovery.

Preliminary damage assessments can be made through several strategies of increasing sophistication. A simple, traditional approach to inventorying damage is called the *windshield survey* in which individuals drive through an area to count the numbers and types of homes and businesses impacted. A straightforward list can be created by designating the buildings as (1) destroyed, (2) with major damage, or (3) minimal damage. This visual method produces a quick list that estimates the range of damages. The obvious downside of a windshield survey is that a drive-by visual inspection can miss significant kinds of damage. A home or business that appears fine from the outside may harbor considerable structural and interior damage from an earthquake or nonvisible roof damage from a hailstorm. Thus, windshield surveys may underreport the damage in a community.

Door-to-door inspections by trained professionals can increase accuracy. Many communities lack a cadre of people sufficiently trained to perform this task. In areas with repetitive risks, such as earthquake-prone California, communities develop mutual aid agreements to bring in outside inspectors. These inspectors will examine properties for exterior, interior, and structural problems, resulting in a better understanding of the disaster impact and, hopefully, bringing about a stronger case for federal assistance. Even these inspections, though, can result in problems. After the 1989 Loma Prieta earthquake in California, some outside inspectors red-tagged buildings (see notice posted in New Orleans after Hurricane Katrina, Photo 2.3), defined as destroyed and unsafe to enter, that were not affected by the earthquake—these buildings were simply substandard dwellings. However, in an area of tight rental availability and high prices, such red tags meant that even more people became homeless. Thus, local knowledge coupled with outside expertise is the best way to manage door-to-door inspections.

PHOTO 2.3 Condemnation notice on house flooded during Hurricane Katrina. (Photo by Brenda Phillips. With permission.)

Specific conditions can affect assessment as well. Infrastructural damages to utilities, often underground, may be extremely difficult to assess. Drought conditions prior to the 1989 California earthquake meant that residents had to wait several years before the rains returned in order to complete an adequate assessment. And, although the levees in New Orleans have allegedly been repaired to their pre-Katrina strength, whether they can withstand additional impact remains to be seen.

More recent strategies for damage assessment incorporate satellite imagery. While still not available to most communities, satellite assessment can produce before-and-after images of damaged areas. Experts can identify zones of damage using this remote sensing technology and even detect the general degree of damage for the physical and built environment. Ideally, satellite imagery will then be supported through first-hand "ground truth" verification. As this tool becomes more advanced, it may produce rapid reconnaissance in less accessible areas. Rapid assessment can provide valuable information to organizations seeking to expedite response and plan resources necessary for recovery (Eguchi et al. 2003).

Nonstructural areas requiring damage assessment may prove difficult to calculate, and may require experts. Economic damage, for example, can be calculated in a variety of ways. Building damage is certainly one way to view the impact. However, estimation of losses demands additional information. For example, how long will a business experience downtime during which it cannot produce goods or provide services? What about displacement costs while being relocated temporarily? And what about the impact on staff who may have lost their homes and cannot return quickly to work locations?

Some industries may prove even more challenging to assess. Hurricanes Katrina and Rita, for example, slammed the commercial and recreational fishing industries of Louisiana, Alabama, and Mississippi. Documenting the losses required examination of commercial revenue records, licensing data, vessel sales data, storm surge modeling, and field-based observations (Caffey et al. 2007). Louisiana, suffering from a double hurricane impact (Katrina and Rita) along coastal areas, experienced considerable losses in its fisheries. Experts estimate that of the $98 million in fisheries losses across the three states, Louisiana alone suffered 60% of the total costs (Caffey et al. 2007).

To summarize, recovery starts with damage assessment so that communities, officials, and organizations can know where to begin and how to scale their efforts. The damage-assessment process provides evidence to qualify for a potential presidential disaster declaration. With or without such aid, a community must now initiate its predisaster recovery plan or launch a postdisaster planning effort.

We next explore various approaches to the recovery process before turning to the pre- and postdisaster recovery planning effort that will be described in Chapter 3.

A Sustainable, Holistic Approach to Recovery

Once the damage has been assessed, it is time to decide how to approach the recovery process. Ideally, approaches and planning will have been conducted prior to disaster (see Chapter 3), but more often than not, recovery occurs as an ad hoc, emergent process. Contemporary perspectives on how recovery should commence center on several ideas that are described in the remainder of this chapter. A more comprehensive discussion on each dimension of a sustainable recovery, on which this brief overview is based, can be read in *Holistic Disaster Recovery*, a publication of the Natural Hazards Center (2005).

Sustainability has become a popular concept driving recovery planning. Six principles define sustainability: consensus-building through **participatory recovery** processes; ensuring for **quality of life**, **economic vitality**, **equity**, and **environmental quality**; and mitigating to ensure **disaster resilience** (Natural Hazards Center 2005). Let us examine each one in turn.

Participatory Process

For a community to recover fully requires the participation of many people and organizations. As theories described earlier in this chapter demonstrate, the diversity of those participants matters. The processes required to facilitate adequate discussion, foster understanding, and move toward meaningful outcomes for the majority of those affected thus require commitment from local leaders. Participatory processes that involve the stakeholders, those who are affected by the disaster and the recovery process outcomes, mean that as many people as possible will have been informed about and been allowed to participate in decision making that affects their lives. Participatory processes, as will be described later in Chapter 13, should result in building consensus or agreement around the recovery. A community may face a variety of decisions:

- Whether to rebuild in a particular location or accept a federal buyout
- Whether a community should take the time to redesign transportation
- How much money to put toward residential versus economic development
- Whether sustainable features like solar power and other energy-efficient features should be required
- Whether taxes should be raised to strengthen roads and bridges
- Whether to require mitigation measures such as safe rooms in trailer parks

Involving the public means that a wider array of concerns can be raised, that the public will ultimately be more likely to support the decisions, and that the community will reflect its unique and diverse character.

Quality of Life

What makes daily life enjoyable for you in your community? Is it the interactions you have with your neighbors? The sports and recreation opportunities? Freedom from crime, high taxes, or harsh climates? Perhaps your children, siblings, or nieces and nephews like their schools, hopefully as much as you appreciate your university, college, or alma mater. For some, living in a unique cultural context or area rich with historical character makes for a pleasant living environment. Quality of life means different things for different people; ultimately, local people need to decide what is meaningful to them (Natural Hazards Center 2005).

Participatory processes can help reveal what people want to retain or move toward. Communities engaged in recovery efforts that intend to survive into future years attend to quality-of-life issues. Although pressures to rebuild may feel far more powerful than ensuring for something as intrinsic and self-satisfying as quality-of-life issues, incorporating these concerns and retaining the nature of the community help people remain tied to a place. Place attachment, as will be described in Chapter 5, is part of our unique identities. We know where we are and who we are because, in part, of where we live and how we feel about that location. The places where we live matter to us.

Economic Vitality

People have to make a living. Communities depend on economic enterprises to provide products and services that we need, from car sales and gasoline to food, dry cleaning, fitness centers, coffee shops, educational opportunities, corporate work environments, factory products, and essential support services like housekeeping, child care, health care, office support, and more. An economy that will survive and rebound from disaster is likely to have been successful prior to the event; yet, with foresight, a disaster recovery process that integrates economic interests can help people recover lost income and launch recoveries. Economies that rebound also generate needed tax and sales revenues to help with public sector recovery (Natural Hazards Center 2005).

The full range of economic enterprises must be considered, from home-based and small businesses to large corporations. Each type of business will experience different effects from the disaster. Each business will move through varying stages, from temporary disruption to long-term dislocation. And each economic enterprise will have varying amounts of resources to withstand the impact. Smart communities recognize this diversity and design recovery processes that build on local strengths, support those at highest risk, and ensure continued economic diversity into the future.

Social and Intergenerational Equity

The ultimate goal of a sustainable recovery is to enable everyone to have an equal chance of recovery. Yet, as pointed out by the theories described earlier in this chapter, not everyone gets the same opportunity to rebound. Social, economic, and political circumstances interfere with recovery. Historic patterns of discrimination, for example, mean that some populations may have been segregated into particular areas of a geographic location (Cutter 2005), usually areas with a higher potential for flooding, seismic impact, or other hazards effects.

Social conditions also come into play when some populations have been marginalized from the political process. In the example described earlier of bayou women, their voices were simply not heard by those in politically powerful positions, despite their early warnings of environmental damage (erosion of coastal wetlands) that would later result in the devastating storm surge from Hurricane Katrina. For those living in the poorest neighborhoods along the Gulf Coast, the hurricane still means that they cannot afford to come home. Because they now live in temporary locations in far-away cities, many find it difficult to participate in recovery decisions that will affect their lives and families forever.

The pressures to rebuild may mean that those with a stake in the outcome will not be included. Persons in authority positions, for example, may not even realize that they are excluding vitally necessary perspectives from persons with cognitive, mobility, or sensory disabilities, or the concerns of senior citizens or people working in home-based economic enterprises. Designing a sustainable community demands the full participation of all the stakeholders to ensure an equitable conclusion.

Environmental Quality

Systems theory demands understanding that a misfit of the natural, built, and human environments will result in damage to one or more systems. The feminist ecology approach described earlier directs attention to how we live in relation to our natural environment, with particular concern for the human system in which women and children from diverse cultures may experience environmental effects differently. Postdisaster recovery offers opportunities to protect natural resources and even change how we impact our environment. For example, debris management may allow us to sort and recycle debris for appropriate uses (see Chapter 4).

We may also decide to set aside land for open space, turning flood-prone areas into parks. Perhaps a locally endangered species can be preserved through new efforts that restore natural habitat and reintroduce native plants more resistant to local climate extremes. We can also build features into residential and business sectors such as solar power and other green features. New developments might feature increased green space, permeable surfaces, and tree cover to reduce stormwater runoff. Entire ecosystems may even be carefully safeguarded by limiting use and impact. Restoration actions could not only improve those ecosystems, but also increase the natural protections they offer through restoring sand dunes, removing invasive species that undermine local plant and animal species, and replenishing wetlands that break storm surges. Environmental protection and conservation efforts represent valuable and key dimensions of recovery, topics that will be addressed in more detail in Chapter 5.

Disaster Resilience

By the time you finish reading this chapter, you may be convinced that you never want to go through the trauma of disaster recovery. There is simply a lot that has to be done to recover, and the effort may consume households, organizations, and government for years. The good news is that you can reduce the impact of future disasters by incorporating **mitigation** measures into disaster recovery efforts. By taking the time to identify appropriate ways to reduce future risks, you can help your community to develop greater disaster resilience.

There are two main forms of disaster mitigation: **structural mitigation** and **nonstructural mitigation**. Structural mitigation includes the built environment, such as levees, dams, safe rooms, hurricane clamps on roofs, elevated buildings, retrofitted interiors (extra steel rebar, for example, in earthquake areas), and hardened exteriors. New codes and ordinances written after disaster can increase the presence of these features. Nonstructural mitigation measures can also include insurance, warning systems (especially to those at highest risk), educational programs, and planning. Disaster mitigation measures will be incorporated throughout each chapter of this book, so be alert to look for opportunities to increase your household's or community's resilience to local hazards.

Problems with a Sustainable Approach

As Dr. Eve Passerini has discovered in her research, implementing sustainable approaches remains difficult. She studied three separate locations: (1) Pattonsburg, Missouri, which was damaged in the 1993 Midwest floods; (2) Jordan Commons, Florida, a community that Habitat for Humanity planned after Hurricane Andrew; and (3) two Czech Republic communities affected by 1996 flooding. Despite eager and enthusiastic support for the ideas of sustainability, many efforts ultimately failed. Communities eager to recover rejected some ideas or, overwhelmed by the extent of the effort, accomplished basic rebuilding rather than integrating sustainable designs into their reconstruction. Organizations that promoted and supported sustainable projects lost funding or dissolved.

Dr. Passerini found that two major reasons accounted for the lack of success in sustainable projects: structural and cultural barriers. As one example of a structural barrier, consider that the United States favors nonrenewable, subsidized energies including coal, gas, oil, and nuclear sources. Further, we live in a car culture, and millions commute to work every day. Are we ready for alternative fuel cars on a nationwide basis? Or for public transportation across large states like Texas?

Culturally, we may not be ready for changes in visual design. One community, for example, rejected an energy-efficient geodesic school building design as inconsistent with local preferences. Perhaps most important, Dr. Passerini found that change was unlikely when ideas came in from outside of a community; in short, a "message of sustainability does not easily take root in communities" (Passerini 1998). Another study discovered that, despite a local community's enthusiasm to rebuild sustainably with energy-efficient designs, funding could not be secured to complete all the desired projects (Childers and Phillips 2002).

Overall, we are not yet sure if any single approach to disaster recovery truly works, particularly those that urge sustainability (Passerini 2000). We may be at the early stages of sustainability taking root, but it is clear that significant hurdles must be overcome. Structural and cultural barriers, coupled with insufficient funding, remain as considerable barriers to sustainable recovery.

Summary

In this chapter we examined various theories and perspectives that helped us to understand the impact of disasters and the challenges of disaster recovery. Several theories pointed out that disasters affect different populations and places in different ways. Recovery efforts must accordingly understand that people will move through the recovery process at different rates. Good recovery managers recognize these differences and design recovery processes that do not leave people behind as the recovery ensues.

Disaster recovery challenges will vary from one area to another as well. However, because few areas plan for recovery, it is likely that local leaders, organizations, and agencies will be taxed to manage the numerous and significant tasks of rebuilding. Further, rebuilding cannot simply return a community to what it was before. Sustainability approaches emphasize the goal of an improved community that is far more disaster resilient. Leadership to promote sustainable and equitable outcomes will be necessary as the various pressures to rebuild lives mounts. Involving stakeholders in the decision-making process fosters greater understanding and support for mitigation efforts and results in a higher quality of life.

In Chapter 3 we will look at both pre- and postdisaster recovery planning and outline strategies for recovery managers, voluntary agencies, elected officials, and emergency managers. Decreasing the impact of disasters on future generations is well worth the effort.

Study Guide

Summary Questions

1. Explain the key points of each main theory given in this chapter: systems theory, sociopolitical-ecology theory, feminist theory, vulnerability theory, and emergent-norm theory.
2. Describe and summarize the typical techniques used for damage assessment. Of what value is the information generated by damage assessment?
3. What are key elements of a holistic approach to recovery?
4. What are the benefits of a sustainable approach? What are some of the challenges?

Discussion Questions

1. Using any of the theories from this chapter, identify the types of challenges that you might expect to discover in a disaster recovery scenario.
2. If you were to rebuild your community from a devastating disaster, what changes would you make in your community? Given that many authors suggest that recovery offers a window of opportunity, what might you do differently this time around?
3. By using the key principles for a holistic recovery, identify areas of concern in your community for a disaster recovery effort. What issues might be present for those areas?
4. Sustainability has been promoted as an exciting and long-term approach for disaster recovery. Yet, studies have uncovered considerable challenges in implementing sustainable approaches. How might your community respond to new energy-efficient designs and other options for sustainable recovery?

Key Terms

Disaster resilience
Economic vitality
Emergent-norm theory
Environmental quality
Equity
Feminist theory
Holistic recovery
Mitigation
    Nonstructural mitigation
    Structural mitigation
Participatory recovery
Preliminary damage assessment (PDA)
Quality of life
Sociopolitical-ecology theory
Sustainability
Systems theory
Vulnerability theory

References

Australian Council for International Development. 2005. Tsunami and people with disabilities: summary issues for consideration. http://www.acfid.asn.au/.../docs_issues/docs_disability-and-development/tsunami_disability_issues.pdf.

Bolin, R., and L. Stanford. 1999. Constructing vulnerability in the first world: The Northridge earthquake in Southern California, 1994. In *The angry earth: Disasters in anthropological perspective*, ed. A. Oliver-Smith and S. Hoffman. New York: Routledge.

Caffey, R., R. Kazmierczak Jr., H. Diop, and W. Keithly Jr. 2007. Estimating the economic damage of Hurricanes Katrina and Rita on commercial and recreational fishing industries. In *American Agricultural Economics Association Annual Meeting*, Portland, OR.

Carson, R. 1962. *Silent spring*. Boston: Houghton Mifflin.

Chang, S. E., and A. Falit-Baiamonte. 2002. Disaster Vulnerability of Businesses in the 2001 Nisqually Earthquake. *Environmental Hazards* 4:59–71.

Childers, C., and B. Phillips. 2002. Sustainable development or transformative development: Arkadelphia, Arkansas, after the tornado. Boulder, CO: Natural Hazards Research and Applications Information Center.

Cutter, S. 2005. The geography of social vulnerability: Race, class and catastrophe. http://understandingkatrina.ssrc.org/.

Dynes, R., and E. L. Quarantelli. 1968. Group behavior under stress: A required convergence of organizational and collective behavior perspectives. *Sociology and Social Research* 52: 416–429.

Eguchi, R., C. Huyck, B. Adams, B. Mansouri, B. Houshmand, and M. Shinozuka. 2003. Resilient disaster response: Using remote sensing technologies for post-earthquake damage detection. Buffalo, NY: Multidisciplinary Earthquake Engineering Research Center.

Enarson, E., and B. Morrow. 1998. Women will rebuild Miami: A case study of feminist response to disaster. In *The gendered terrain of disaster: Through women's eyes*, ed. E. Enarson and B. H. Morrow. Miami: Laboratory for Social and Behavioral Research, Florida International University.

Enarson, Elaine. 2001. What Women Do: Gendered labor in the Red River Valley flood. *Environmental Hazards* 3:1–18.

———. 2000. A gendered perspective: Voices of women. In *Hurricane Andrew*, ed. W. Peacock, B. H. Morrow, and H. Gladwin. Miami: International Hurricane Center.

Enarson, E., and B. Phillips. 2008. Invitation to a new feminist disaster sociology: Integrating feminist theory and methods. In *Women and disasters: From theory to practice*, ed. B. D. Phillips and B. H. Morrow. Philadelphia: Xlibris, International Research Committee on Disasters.

Hancock, B. 2005. *Riding with the Blue Moth*. Champaign, IL: Sports Publishing L.L.C.

Mileti, D. 1999. *Disasters by design*. Washington, DC: Joseph Henry Press.

Mitchell, L. 2003. Guidelines for Emergency Managers Working With Culturally and Linguistically Diverse Communities. *Australian Journal of Emergency Management* 18 (1):13–24.

National Organization on Disability. 2005. Report on Special Needs Assessment of Katrina Evacuees (SNAKE) Project. http://www.nod.org.

Natural Hazards Center. 2005. *Holistic disaster recovery: Ideas for building local sustainability after a natural disaster*. 2nd ed. Boulder, CO: Natural Hazards Center.

Neal, D., and B. Phillips. 1995. Effective emergency management: Reconsidering the bureaucratic approach. *Disasters: The Journal of Disaster Studies and Management* 19 (4): 327–337.

Oxfam. 2005. The tsunami's impact on women. http://www.oxfam.org.uk/what_we_do/ issues/conflict_disasters/downloads/bn_tsunami_women.pdf.

Passerini, E. 1998. Sustainability and sociology. *The American Sociologist* 29 (3): 59–70.

———. 2000. Disasters as agents of social change. *Natural Hazards Review* 1 (2): 67–72.

Peacock, W., and A. K. Ragsdale. 1997. Social systems, ecological networks, and disasters: Toward a socio-political ecology of disasters. In *Hurricane Andrew: Ethnicity, gender and the sociology of disasters*, ed. W. G. Peacock, B. H. Morrow, and H. Gladwin. London: Routledge.

Pennebaker, James. 1997. *Opening Up*. NY: Guildford Press.

Quarantelli, E. L. 1985. What is disaster? The need for clarification in definition and conceptualization in research. In *Disasters and mental health selected contemporary perspectives*, ed. B. Sowder. Washington, DC: U.S. Government Printing Office.

Sharkey, P. 2007. Survival and death in New Orleans: An empirical look at the human impact of Katrina. *Journal of Black Studies* 37 (4): 482–501.

Smith, G., and D. Wenger. 2006. Sustainable disaster recovery: Operationalizing an existing agenda. In *Handbook of disaster research*, ed. H. Rodriguez, E. L. Quarantelli, and R. Dynes. New York: Springer.

Webb, G., K. Tierney, and J. Dahlhamer. 2000. Businesses and Disasters: empirical patterns and unanswered questions. *Natural Hazards Review* 1 (3):83–90.

Wisner, B. 2001. Development of vulnerability analysis, edited by E. Enarson. Emmittsburg, MD: Federal Emergency Management Association Higher Education Project.

Wisner, B., P. Blaikie, T. Cannon, and I. Davis. 2005. *At risk*. 2nd ed. London: Routledge.

Resources

- Brou vs. FEMA settlement, go to http://www.fema.gov/pdf/library/ brou_fema.pdf. Accessed July 28, 2008.
- Damage Assessment Forms and Procedures, City of Los Angeles, http://www.lacity.org/emd/epdp2a3b.htm. Accessed July 1, 2008.
  - Gender and Disaster Network, http://www.gdnonline.org. Accessed July 28, 2008.
- Holistic Disaster Recovery, visit http://www.colorado.edu/hazards. Be sure to select the link to the 2001 version of the book for a free downloadable copy.
  - RADIX, http://www.radixonline.org/. Accessed July 28, 2008.
- Theoretical position papers that reflect vulnerability, socio-political and feminist perspectives can be found at these websites:

Chapter 3

Disaster Recovery Planning

Learning Objectives

After reading this chapter, you should be able to:

- Explain the value of predisaster recovery planning
- Describe key principles of an effective planning process
- Outline the main elements of a pre- or postdisaster recovery plan
- Understand why planning is considered to be a process
- Identify a list of stakeholders that should participate in the recovery-planning process
- Name the key federal partners and other organizations available to support recovery efforts and planning
- Illustrate reasons why recovery planning should be linked to other phases, particularly mitigation

Introduction

In 1997, the twin communities of Grand Forks, North Dakota, and East Grand Forks, Minnesota, suffered massive damage to the entire area. Whole neighborhoods were lost to flooding, and the historic downtown of Grand Forks suffered additional damage when a massive fire broke out. Ten years later, a rebuilt community learned lessons clearly relevant to this chapter:

"Successful disaster management results from good advance planning, training and partnership building, ongoing communication and the ability to work through issues as a team" (Grand Forks 2007).

Though not the best time to commence recovery **planning**, the postdisaster time period is when most recovery planning occurs. Recovery feels massive in the aftermath, with officials facing competing priorities and cumbersome bureaucratic processes. Meanwhile, frustrated homeowners want to return to normal and businesses experience extensive disruptions. Communities face staggering amounts of debris to manage. Volunteers clamor to assist. Yet, without a plan, there is no clear vision of where to start. This chapter demonstrates the need for predisaster recovery planning and recognizes that postdisaster recovery planning is more likely.

First, we begin by discussing key principles and processes that underlie planning. Next, we consider various roles and responsibilities that must be taken on to launch recovery. We then move on to **predisaster planning** and **postdisaster planning** efforts. Throughout the planning sections, we address mitigation opportunities as a means for using recovery to build a more disaster-resilient community.

Getting Started with Planning

Long-term community recovery planning is "the process of establishing a community-based, postdisaster vision and identifying projects and project funding strategies best suited to achieve that vision, and employing a mechanism to implement those projects" (FEMA 2005).

A process that provides opportunities for robust participation tends to be more successful (Beierle and Cayford 2002). Successful processes that engage the public feature effective communication, involve motivated **stakeholders** through active participation, and provide an open forum where people can exchange views (Beierle and Cayford 2002). Involving a wide set of stakeholders, defined as those most likely to be affected by the process, increases the potential to create a plan benefiting all with vested interests. Let us examine several of these important public-involvement elements, starting with basic ideas for the context of recovery planning.

Planning Principles

To start, consider the term *long-term community recovery*. What does that mean and imply? For FEMA, the notion of *long term* implies efforts to "re-establish a healthy, functioning community that will sustain itself over time" (FEMA 2005). Doing so means rebuilding so that the community is stronger, better, and with greater **disaster resilience**, i.e., able to withstand the hazards that continually threaten an area. Retrofitting buildings for future earthquakes, disallowing building in a floodplain, and strengthening local building codes, **ordinances**, and inspections to withstand assaults by local hazards represent a few options.

Key Principles

FEMA (2005) recommends that communities use these key planning principles:

- Empower locals to drive the recovery process. All recovery is local, and area residents must be involved to ensure an effective recovery design.
- Involve the public. Without support from the public, a recovery effort is likely to languish or fail.
- Incorporate projects designed to foster recovery. Projects must stem from what local people believe are the most important efforts. Local priorities drive recovery.
- Include mitigation efforts to build disaster-resilient communities. Without mitigation measures, a recovery effort may ultimately fail when the next disaster occurs.
- Build partnerships among local, state, and federal partners. Recovery starts locally but typically requires input, funding, and support from state and federal partners.

Experts concur that these general guiding principles help ensure that recovery projects reflect local character and build resistance to recurring hazards. To guarantee that these principles are followed requires effective leadership, which may come from both expected and unexpected sources (Krajeski and Peterson 2008; Quarantelli 1997). Leaders must include elected officials and established community leaders. Grass-roots leaders can also make significant, insightful, and supportive contributions. These principles represent the spirit and intent of this chapter. The principles will be addressed more fully in Chapter 11 (Public-Sector Recovery), Chapter 13 (Community Resources), and Chapter 14 (Volunteer Organizations).

Leadership

People possess varying leadership skills. Some may excel in moving a group through the decision-making process, while others thrive during project-implementation stages. Some may burn out from the exhaustion of the effort, and others will step up. Building a hardy core of dedicated and potential leaders serves the planning process well. Effective recovery planning requires involving individuals with varying leadership skills who can plan out, engage, and sustain a community-based recovery planning effort.

Thus, leaders should reflect the broad characteristics of the community and possess specific leadership abilities.

Several types of leadership skills are necessary. First, leaders should enjoy broadly based community confidence and support. Involving individuals with abilities to communicate and connect across generational differences, cultural diversity, genders, languages, and within the disability community is key. A good leader is well versed in multiple ways to communicate, including face-to-face conversations as well as group settings. The ability to use e-mail and Web sites and skill to work with the media are also highly ranked talents. The ability to communicate across demographic and technological divides inspires a higher degree of credibility and trust among those who need to participate in the planning process.

Second, an effective leader bases recovery planning on collaboration and consensus building in order to heighten stakeholder buy-in. Committing to a collaborative process requires understanding that such an effort takes time, patience, and expertise. Leaders may need to convene the planning group themselves or, if funds become available, select and hire an experienced facilitator (see Box 3.1).

Third, leaders must work diligently to coordinate meetings. Doing so requires scheduling capabilities and an understanding of people's time constraints. Holding a meeting every Monday night at 7 p.m., for example, means that parents must leave early to put children to bed and that people doing shift work cannot participate. It may be necessary to hold public meetings in auditoriums, over cable television, in chat rooms or other electronic forums, or through Internet video streaming. A good leader understands that diverse means must be used to invite the fullest possible range of participation from across the community.

It may be a good idea to invite several persons to share leadership responsibilities. Indeed, it is difficult to find a single person who is the most effective communicator, the best coordinator, and the top media spokesperson. Several types of leaders may be needed, including those who are task oriented, to keep the process on track. Leaders who inspire others to participate in the process should be on the planning team too. Thus, a joint leadership team may be the best strategy, and this can also serve as a form of contingency planning if one leader cannot be present due to illness or other responsibilities.

Coordination and Communication

Efforts must be made to coordinate the planning process, including the involvement of individuals and organizations (Quarantelli 1997). Coordination means more than providing information about what is happening. Coordination means that all stakeholders are informed about and allowed to participate in the process. Doing so requires considerable effort

BOX 3.1 HIRING A RECOVERY CONSULTANT

Your community's recovery is important. Recovery planning will affect area homes, businesses, infrastructure, environmental resources, historic and cultural character, and more, perhaps permanently. How you rebuild may minimize future impacts as well. Thus, if a community opts to hire a consultant, it should select one who has:

- A degree in emergency management, hazards planning, or disaster research
- Extensive experience in disaster recovery in other communities (Consultants without experience in multiple kinds of disasters should not be considered.)
- A strong record of conducting community-based planning
- Prior clients that can provide a strong recommendation
- A proven track record of following through from the start to the finish
- Reasonable fees (Securing bids from multiple consultants is a good idea.)
- A focus on process and an understanding of how recovery moves through stages
- A holistic outlook that incorporates all dimensions of recovery planning
- A patient demeanor
- An ability to communicate with a variety of stakeholders
- A strong, experienced team in place to back up and support the consultant
- A concern for how recovery planning affects all populations
- Experience in linking recovery planning with mitigation efforts
- An exceptional understanding of federal programs and regulations that influence recovery efforts
- A sound network among professionals who may be brought in or consulted to enhance the recovery-planning process
- A willingness to do the homework required to understand local context
- A commitment to involving the community in a meaningful capacity
- An understanding of a participatory process
- Facilitation skills

Source: **Courtesy of Brenda Phillips**

to identify, involve, and keep representatives connected to the planning process. Communication among those involved in recovery planning is paramount, which may necessitate multiple, redundant efforts across various media. Further, coordination means that a good leader works to help each stakeholder believe that he or she is an important contributor.

Communication goes beyond the members of a recovery planning team, though. The larger public needs and deserves to know what is discussed within their community both before and after a disaster. Communication efforts can be made through media outlets, Web sites, door hangers, public meetings, and local organizations (more on this will be discussed in Chapter 13—Community Resources). Because the public wants and needs to return home and restart their lives, they will be eager to get accurate information. Establishing an information center, a recovery planning kiosk or office, and a Web site can help to share accurate information. Inclusion of a rumor-control feature is always a good idea as well (FEMA 2005; Natural Hazards Center 2001; Schwab et al. 1998).

To summarize, the recovery-planning process must be local, inclusive, and open to the public (see Box 3.2). The transparency of the planning process builds confidence among the public that the participating partners are accountable to the broader community of stakeholders (Norman 2004). Connecting the planning process to those whose lives will be affected now and for the long term matters because "recovery cannot succeed if the aims, priorities and processes do not have community support" (Norman 2004). Effective leaders understand these basic principles.

BOX 3.2 BENEFITS OF LONG-TERM COMMUNITY RECOVERY PLANNING

- Brings stakeholders together in a process that promotes coordination, communication and cooperation
- Links local planners to state and federal officials with critical resources and experience
- Provides for a fuller, more comprehensive or "holistic" recovery that links components together, such as the impact of rebuilding on the environment
- Allows for vision and focus to emerge from the interaction process
- Provides an opportunity to link recovery to mitigation, resulting in a more disaster-resilient community
- Fosters partnerships between existing and emerging stakeholders and those with resources; brings new partners into the recovery-planning process
- Enables the local community to have a say in how they imagine the future for themselves, their children, and grandchildren

Source: FEMA (2005)

Planning as a Process

The FEMA perspective, and one endorsed by experts, is that planning involves the entire community (FEMA 2005; Quarantelli 1997; Schwab et al. 1998). A process implies a series of steps or stages that a community will move through prior to actually rebuilding or taking major action. Those steps are (FEMA 2005):

1. Assess the need for a recovery plan
2. Choose a leader and decide where to start
3. Identify sources of outside assistance
4. Inform the community through a public-information effort
5. Build consensus around the recovery vision and plan
6. Work through the issues and recognize opportunities
7. Develop a vision of a more disaster-resilient community
8. Specify and prioritize recovery projects
9. Write the plan, pulling all the elements together into a comprehensive whole
10. Identify project leaders
11. Locate funding streams and sources for the projects
12. Operationalize the plan and put it into action
13. Review projects regularly and update the plan at periodic intervals

The process starts with a "big picture" view: What type of recovery plan do we need? It may be that the tornado damaged only the downtown, so that a focus on economic recovery and area infrastructure could be sufficient. Or, the hurricane may have devastated a wide area with considerable damage across all sectors. The scale and scope of the planning constitute the first decisions to be made. Leaders then launch a recovery effort by involving and informing the public from the earliest stages. FEMA and recovery experts concur that taking the time to build agreement around what needs to be done leads to greater understanding and community support. By involving the community, it is possible to flesh out what issues might occur and to identify ways that the community could be improved. FEMA also recommends that recovery plans integrate mitigation to reduce the impacts of future disasters. Doing so requires identification of a comprehensive plan that details specific projects. Once the projects are identified, it is time to divide up the tasks, secure funding and launch the recovery effort. Seeing it through is the final step.

Sustaining the community through the planning stages will require dedicated team work. After the 1989 Loma Prieta earthquake, the City of Santa Cruz convened a planning group called Vision Santa Cruz (Wilson 1991). The team worked diligently through hundreds of meetings, many involving public input, to redesign the downtown and other damaged areas (for more detail, see Chapter 11—Public-Sector Recovery). Vision Santa Cruz eventually spun off committees and subgroups for various aspects of the recovery effort.

Because the recovery may go on for years, planning fatigue may set in, coupled with the daily chores of individual household recoveries that face some participants. Local officials leading the recovery while handling their own returns to routine and simultaneously moving the community through other dimensions of recovery, may find the burden immense. Burnout among recovery leaders and participants is to be expected, and putting a team into place with sufficient support and with the ability to integrate new members can help to sustain the process. By integrating the community, a recovery effort has a ready pool of replacement members to sustain the effort.

Stakeholders and Participants

In his book on collaborative leadership, David Chrislip says that when planners involve key stakeholders, the process can generate "constructive engagement, a carefully considered rationale for its recommendations, and strong leaders within the group that help facilitate its work" (Chrislip 2002). Who are those key stakeholders and participants?

Different sources advocate a potentially wide array of participants. FEMA's self-help recovery-planning book (FEMA 2005) recommends inviting a range of public officials, city staff, and local representatives, including public works, public information staff, planners, emergency managers, business owners, local builders, neighborhood association leaders, health sector participants, voluntary agency representatives, and environmental groups. Authors of *Planning for Post-Disaster Recovery and Reconstruction*, published by the American Planning Association (Schwab et al. 1998) also suggest including the city or county attorney, public utilities, staff responsible for codes and zoning, school officials, community relations staff, first responders, and accounting personnel. The general character of the community also matters, so invitees should include people who represent historic preservation interests, tourism, recreational and professional sports, education, and local populations.

Community Involvement and Inclusiveness

Beyond these initial lists, it is important to ensure that the planning team also mirrors the demographic makeup of the community, particularly those who will be affected the most. Too often, we forget to include some persons.

Single parents may face a particularly difficult time participating, unless the planning team provides child care or a means through which the parent can join in, such as Web-based participation. The Americans with Disabilities Act (ADA) requires that meeting locations and event processes be accessible. When designing public information materials, including Web sites, planning leaders must ensure access for people with visual limitations. American Sign Language should be provided at live meetings, and closed captioning should be available for television or video streaming. Senior citizens may not want to attend evening meetings, so providing alternative locations and times brings their perspectives into the process. Likewise, new immigrants to the area may need particularly sensitive outreach to welcome them as contributors to the community recovery process. Communities with histories of exclusion and segregation will need to work even harder to convince marginalized sectors that they are welcome. Lower-income families or those lacking formal education may need encouragement to feel sufficiently empowered to participate in a process that might seem intimidating.

What is the value of bringing a wide range of stakeholders into the planning process? It's simple. When we include a broader and more diverse range of people, we ensure that the solutions brought forward are more realistic, fit with the local realities of people who live in our communities, and result in more support for the plan. Seniors and people with disabilities may offer insights for elder-friendly transportation systems and housing. Single parents can reveal needs for safe rooms in rental apartments and trailer courts. New immigrants may bring fresh perspectives from their home countries.

It is also important to bring a wide set of stakeholders into the process early on. As Louise Mitchell (2003, 14) writes about Australian mitigation planning processes, "It is important that groups are not left out of the disaster-reduction process. People who are marginalized in the early stages are marginalized later." Inviting wider participation builds upon an inherently democratic process that leads to "civic action in the broader interests of the community" (Chrislip 2002). Participation makes collaboration possible, defined as a "mutually beneficial relationship between two or more parties to achieve common goals by sharing responsibility, authority and accountability for achieving results" (Chrislip 2002). Collaboration is an investment that can return dividends for recovery planning.

Federal and State Partners

Finally, as FEMA (2005) suggests, efforts to liaise and consult with other sources of support will be needed. Various state and federal agencies can offer support, resources, insights, and experience. As FEMA correctly points out, "You can't do this alone." The **National Response Framework** Emergency Support Function (ESF) #14, Long-Term Community

Recovery, includes a wide set of potential partners for consultation, as listed in Box 3.3.

ESF #14 provides technical support that may be especially useful to communities lacking experience with recovery planning. FEMA has also provided funds in previous disasters to hire consulting firms to help local communities design recovery plans. FEMA can also provide technical support and coordination, as depicted in Box 3.4.

After the 1994 Northridge earthquake, unique programs to rebuild multifamily housing emerged from state and federal partnerships. The joint partnerships resulted in securing extensive funding that launched a difficult recovery process in what was then the most expensive disaster in U.S. history. Each chapter in this book includes examples of such partnerships, so be sure to note how local, state, and federal coalitions can be built for each dimension of disaster recovery.

Recovery Planning

Two kinds of recovery planning can occur. We will look first at two options for recovery planning: (1) the benefits of pre-event recovery planning and (2) the option of linking recovery planning to other local planning efforts. Following these sections, we will examine short-term and long-term recovery planning. Because the identified elements for short- and long-term recovery planning are similar, both pre- and postevent plans should incorporate the elements listed in those sections. Key elements are reviewed in separate sections and then developed more fully in the chapters that follow. The remainder of this book is thus designed to outline the substantive content that should be considered for recovery planning.

Pre-Event Recovery Planning

The City of Los Angeles, facing significant risks from an earthquake hazard, has led the way in predisaster recovery planning. Facing a 60% probability of a 7.5-magnitude earthquake within the next 30 years, Los Angeles first commenced its recovery-planning efforts in 1987. A multiagency team including both academic expertise and city staff experience created working groups to design pre-event and postevent plans (City of Los Angeles 1994). Los Angeles assumed that long-term recovery could exceed ten years.

The city's forward-thinking efforts included extensive consideration of mitigation strategies as well as management procedures for specific needs. The plan outlined specific short-term and long-term tasks. Short-term efforts included "damage assessment, debris removal, temporary relocation

BOX 3.3   FEDERAL AND NATIONAL PARTNERS FOR LONG-TERM COMMUNITY RECOVERY

The National Response Framework includes functional areas called Emergency Support Functions (ESFs). Each ESF focuses attention on specific tasks that must be done. ESF #14 currently focuses on recovery functions. Each ESF has a lead agency, a set of primary agencies, and a broad cadre of support agencies that may include nonprofit organizations. For ESF #14, those units currently include:

ESF Coordinator:

Department of Homeland Security/Federal Emergency Management Agency

Primary Agencies:

Department of Agriculture
Department of Homeland Security
Department of Housing and Urban Development
Small Business Administration

Support Agencies:

Department of Commerce
Department of Defense
Department of Energy
Department of Health and Human Services
Department of the Interior
Department of Labor
Department of Transportation
Department of the Treasury
Environmental Protection Agency
Corporation for National and Community Service
Delta Regional Authority
American Red Cross
National Voluntary Organizations Active in Disaster

Source: FEMA National Response Framework ESF #14
http://www.fema.gov/emergency/nrf/mainindex.htm

Note: A link to ESF #14 agency capabilities can be found in the Resources section at the end of this chapter.

of residents and businesses, immediate restoration of services, immediate abatement of extreme structural hazards and repair of homes, stores and industrial facilities" (City of Los Angeles 1994). Long-term considerations addressed damage to buildings, reestablishing city functioning, repair of

BOX 3.4   FEDERAL SUPPORT FOR RECOVERY PLANNING

The 2008 revision of the National Response Framework specified that ESF #14, Long-Term Recovery Planning, could provide pre-event and postevent technical support and coordination mechanisms that direct agencies to:

- Work with state, tribal, and local governments; NGOs; and private-sector organizations to support long-term recovery planning for highly impacted communities.
- Link recovery planning to sound risk-reduction practices to encourage a more viable recovery.
- Strategically apply subject-matter expertise to help communities recover from disasters.
- Coordinate development of national long-term recovery strategies and plans in coordination with other relevant federal departments and agencies that have independent authorities and responsibilities for addressing key issues regarding catastrophic incidents. These may include accessible housing (incident and permanent), large displacements of individuals including those with special needs, contaminated debris management, decontamination and environmental restoration, restoration of public facilities and infrastructure, and restoration of the agricultural sector.
- Gather information from federal departments and agencies and state, tribal, and local governments to assess the impacts and needs.
- Convene interagency meetings to develop an incident-specific federal action plan delineating specific agency participation to support specific community recovery and mitigation activities and to avoid duplication of assistance to recipients.
- Facilitate sharing of information among agencies and ESFs and coordinate early resolution of issues and the timely delivery of federal assistance.
- Coordinate identification of appropriate federal programs to support implementation of long-term community recovery plans under current authorities and funding. This process identifies programs, waivers, funding levels, requests for additional authorities, and possible new legislation needed to address identified program gaps.
- Provide technical assistance such as impact analyses, economic revitalization, and recovery-planning support.
- Coordinate with ESF #6 (Mass Care, Emergency Assistance, Housing, and Human Services), ESF #8 (Public Health and Medical Services), and the state(s) to identify long-term recovery needs of special needs populations and incorporate these into recovery strategies.
- Coordinate with ESF #3 (Public Works and Engineering), ESF #10 (Oil and Hazardous Materials Response), and the state(s) to identify long-term environmental restoration issues.

- Coordinate with animal welfare and agricultural stakeholders and service providers in long-term community recovery efforts.
- Coordinate implementation of the recommendations for long-term community recovery with the appropriate federal departments and agencies if the recommendations include program waivers, supplemental funding requests, and/or legislative initiatives.
- Facilitate recovery decision making across ESFs and increases awareness of communities' existing development and hazard mitigation plans.

Source: FEMA National Response Framework ESF #14
http://www.fema.gov/emergency/nrf/mainindex.htm

Note: A link to ESF #14 agency capabilities can be found in the Resources section at the end of this chapter.

damaged utilities and infrastructure, and additional attention to mitigation and **land-use planning**.

Los Angeles held a workshop in 1988 to focus on five key issue areas: organization and authority under the plan; rehabilitation of residential, commercial, and industrial areas; restoration of public-sector services; economic recovery; and land-use planning. The city identified lead and support agencies for each task area comparable to how the National Response Framework eventually came to be organized. A subsequent workshop convened planners to add two additional sections to the plan: psychological rehabilitation and vital records (City of Los Angeles 1994).

Proving that a plan is a living document that should be revisited, Los Angeles again reviewed and revised its plan after the 1989 Loma Prieta earthquake. The revised plan added new functional areas, including interjurisdictional issues, traffic mitigation, and public information plans. Separate subsections of the plan spelled out expectations for each department pre- and postevent. For example, the Cultural Affairs Department was tasked with reviewing design criteria for postevent repairs and historic preservation concerns. The Environmental Affairs Department entered into efforts to map "significant ecological areas" for protection during extreme events and to create plans for disseminating public health and environmental advisories. The Housing Department was charged with designing regulations to protect renters. Housing staff also took on responsibility to create a Housing Task Force by building pre-event partnerships with the U.S. Department of Housing and Urban Development (HUD), FEMA, and the Small Business Administration (City of Los Angeles 1994).

Linking to Other Types of Planning

Many communities undergo **comprehensive planning** to anticipate future needs, manage residential construction, and encourage economic development. For example, the City of Denton, Texas, convened a wide set of stakeholders in the late 1990s to devise the Denton Plan, which is now being implemented (see link in the Resources section of this chapter). Several sections of the plan relate to recovery planning, particularly intentions to set aside and not build in floodplain areas. Such restrictions on land use serve as guides for recovery planning. Thus, linking efforts ensures consistency across both comprehensive and recovery plans. It may even be possible to integrate recovery planning into comprehensive planning, in essence using one process instead of two, thereby ensuring a greater integration of vision as well as use of local funds and staff time (FEMA 2005; Natural Hazards Center 2001; Schwab et al. 1998).

The federal government also requires, through the Disaster Mitigation Act of 2000, that all jurisdictions must have a mitigation plan in place prior to receipt of postdisaster hazard-mitigation funds (for example, the Hazard Mitigation Grants Program; see Chapter 15—Financing Recovery). So, if a community intends to use the postrecovery period as an opportunity to mitigate future risks, it must have conducted **hazard-mitigation planning**. FEMA provides an extensive set of materials to guide a community through mitigation planning (see Resources section at the end of this chapter). Such efforts can serve as a lead-in for recovery planning, as the mitigation planning process requires analysis of local hazards and mapping of physically and socially vulnerable areas. Knowing where your community faces the highest risks before an event allows for recovery planning that targets directly the areas most likely to bear damage.

Working in the pre-event recovery time also allows for greater consideration of postevent options. You will have time to research energy-efficient designs, for example, and to specify changes to bridges, roads, and utilities after an event. Elected officials will be able to design emergency ordinances that can be updated and passed quickly to expedite processes such as debris management and permitting processes for rebuilding. (For examples of these, see Schwab et al. 1998.) In short, pre-event planning allows for a fuller, faster, more meaningful recovery plan. And, of course, pre-event planning means that you have the benefit of working in a less stressful environment.

Short-Term Recovery Planning

No standard yet exists for what should go into either a pre- or postevent recovery plan. However, most plans lean toward a functional approach that separates tasks into short-term and long-term recovery. We will look at examples of both next. First, though, it is important to think about the life cycle of emergency management. The response period is beginning to end with a transition to recovery. Handling the two phases may exhaust local resources. As Professor David Neal from the Center for the Study of Disasters and Extreme Events at Oklahoma State University observed after a tornado in Lancaster, Texas, "Disaster managers must consider response and recovery issues simultaneously, i.e., as they attempt to coordinate initial response activities, they must also begin formulating a strategy to handle existing and developing recovery issues" (Neal 2004, 51). The community now begins to transition to recovery issues. The line between those two phases is never clear and can require varying times to handle different kinds of hazards. The magnitude of a disaster can also delay recovery efforts. Communities may need to wait for floodwaters to subside or a hazardous material to be handled safely. Several tasks are usually undertaken in the transition from response to recovery, which is our next topic.

Emergency Measures

As mentioned in Chapter 2, the first task to initiate recovery is damage assessment. Pre-event planning efforts can research and design damage-assessment procedures, train staff in how to conduct such inventories, and prepare a local emergency management agency to expedite state and federal assistance. By incorporating mapping (such as geographic information systems, for example) into the damage-assessment process, areas requiring debris removal and prioritization for short-term recovery efforts can be identified. Because damage assessment to the public roads, bridges, overpasses, and even utilities may take some time (see Chapter 9—Infrastructure and Lifelines), it is important to integrate recovery of each into both short-term and long-term planning.

Short-term recovery may include debris removal, including both emergency road clearance and more-extended planning for residential, storm-related, or other types of debris removal. It is likely that debris removal will move into the long-term recovery period and may go on for several years. If debris cannot be removed, it can impact future events. For example, the ice storm that hit Oklahoma in December 2007 left debris in rural areas. Heavy rain in April 2008 moved tree limbs and vegetation into creeks and rivers. Debris that piled up caused a bridge failure.

Short-term recovery may also include restoration of utilities, a task that took up to one month after Hurricane Andrew hit southern Florida in 1992. And, although utility companies bear responsibility for such restoration, clear lines of communication and partnerships between local jurisdictions and utilities make the process far speedier. For example, restoration of utilities for essential services such as hospitals, assisted-living facilities, and homes with people dependent on oxygen support must be expedited. By building partnerships with utility companies, lives can be saved and the recovery can begin.

Preplanned Ordinances

In the first few weeks after a disaster, a community may need to pass emergency ordinances that guide how work is to be done (Schwab et al. 1998). A pre-event plan can develop sample ordinances prior to impact, thus saving time and expediting the recovery effort. Emergency ordinances may include:

- Legal procedures for removal of debris on roadways and for access to private property when warranted
- Legal authority for the creation and powers of a recovery task force (Schwab et al. 1998)
- Links to comprehensive planning regarding rebuilding in floodplains and other hazardous areas
- Means for protecting and safeguarding historic and cultural resources
- Procedures for a residential permitting process to jump-start the rebuilding process
- Maps for new zoning, including consideration of any new zoning designations, such as residential, commercial, and industrial areas
- Changes to how land is or may be used, including setbacks to allow for sidewalks or easements to place utilities underground
- Special "overlay" districts that create conditions for particular uses, such as a wildland/urban interface (such as after wildfire) or to protect coastal areas (Schwab et al. 1998)
- Preservation of environmental areas, especially wetlands and other sensitive areas
- Rebuilding regulations that require a certain percentage of new construction to fall within local affordability guidelines

A short-term recovery-plan section should also include a public information and communications strategy to keep residents, business owners, and others knowledgeable about what is happening. In Chapter 4, for example, we will learn about public-information efforts surrounding debris management because the public must participate in and support such efforts. Postdisaster communications can be prewritten in multiple languages and accessible formats so as to maximize the number of people who can be kept informed. Internet Web pages can be predesigned as well, archived, and then pulled up for immediate use.

Gathering Resources for Long-Term Recovery

People love to help. Consequently, recovery planning should involve donations (see Chapter 12) and volunteer management (see Chapter 14). Coordinating these resources toward their best use and establishing contact lists for volunteers to help with the long-term recovery lays a foundation to rebuild. Working with voluntary organizations prior to disaster, including spelling out how coordination and communication would occur during a recovery effort, is helpful as well. The National Voluntary Organizations Active in Disaster (NVOAD) is a well-established network of voluntary and faith-based agencies that provide labor, materials, and more (see Resources section). Thus, state and local VOAD units should be invited to participate in the recovery planning. Knowing each other's capabilities before disaster can smooth out implementation of any pre- or postdisaster operations. Local communities may want to preselect an organizational form through which to coordinate. As described in Chapter 14, the organizational form might evolve as a long-term recovery committee, a locally led interfaith effort, or a more-specific unmet needs committee.

Long-Term Recovery Planning

In this section we examine the typical elements of a pre- or postdisaster recovery plan. In the first section, we look at forward-thinking strategies for housing recovery. After housing, we move on to examine business, environmental, historical, cultural, infrastructural, psychological, and public-sector recovery. Each section features ideas that will be expanded further in upcoming chapters.

Housing

Disaster recovery plans for the permanent-housing sector should commence with an overview of the housing situation before and after the disaster. By looking at the situation before the disaster, it may be possible to identify issues and areas of concern. For example, it may become apparent that some areas of the community require attention because of vacant lots, thereby directing postdisaster planners to infill those areas with new housing. As another example, the predisaster community may lack sufficient affordable housing. The postdisaster housing context allows a community to make affordable housing a priority. In short, the housing-recovery planning process starts with a picture of the community's past and designs a renewed, even reinvigorated, residential sector.

New visions of a rebuilt housing sector emanate from design principles that a community comes to embrace through the visioning and consensus-building process. The **visioning process** is defined as a series of meetings through which the stakeholders state their dreams and goals for the rebuilt community.

Postdisaster scenarios may also provide an opportunity for incorporating comprehensive planning. Communities could redesign neighborhoods and incorporate new amenities like sidewalks, underground utilities, greenways, or dog parks. In short, the housing reconstruction process should be embraced as an opportunity.

Starting points for those principles might come from the principles of sustainability within a holistic framework (see Chapter 2). Communities may want to consider some of the following (Natural Hazards Center 2001):

- *Mitigation.* Communities should research and integrate measures that will create more disaster-resistant housing to withstand the most common hazards. Homes should incorporate features that provide safety to residents, especially for rapid-onset events. Safe rooms in tornado areas (see Photo 3.1), hurricane clamps for roofs in areas of high winds, and exterior elements (shingles, siding) that increase fire-resistance serve as some examples.
- *Environmental quality.* Homes can be designed to increase their energy efficiency, thereby reducing the overall burden on nonrenewable

PHOTO 3.1 This tornado shelter at the Iowa State Fairgrounds outside Des Moines can provide safety to 400. (Photo Iowa Homeland Security and Emergency Management Division/FEMA News Photo.)

resources. Green rebuilding introduces environmentally friendly designs such as solar panels, native plant landscaping that requires minimal water (called *xeriscaping*), and recycled building materials. More ideas on energy-efficient windows, insulation, and lighting can be found in Chapter 7 (Housing). Beyond the individual house, the design of the neighborhood should be considered as well. A community may want to encourage higher density in some areas so as to increase open space. Doing so would reduce the amount of stormwater runoff (see Chapter 5 for more on this).

- *Quality of life.* What kind of neighborhood do you like to live in? Perhaps you like the activity of a downtown area, or the quiet of a suburban locale. Some may feel more comfortable surrounded by nature, while others prefer a walkable community with public transportation. Knowing what physical environments people prefer leads to residential design consistent with how people want to live. Incorporating quality-of-life issues helps identify areas that connect to housing, such as transportation arteries, parks and open space, and streetscapes.

- *Social and intergenerational equity.* This principle ensures that people from all cultural groups, abilities, income levels, and ages enjoy access to postdisaster housing and do not experience displacement as a result of the housing reconstruction vision and process. People who lived in the area before have a right to return home. Reconstruction decisions, though, have the potential to displace people. For example, disallowing trailer parks means that lower-income families may have to leave permanently. Thus, housing recovery plans will need to include a range of both temporary and permanent housing. Planners could develop a Web-based system that inventories available post-disaster rental units (homes and apartments). Planners should also pre-identify locations where temporary units such as trailers, mobile homes, or other forms of manufactured housing can be placed. If there are significant numbers of individuals living in congregate settings—group homes and residential schools, low-income hotels (including those for seniors), assisted living facilities, or nursing homes—it is wise to preplan alternatives.

- *Participatory recovery process.* The **holistic recovery** process discussed in Chapter 2 requires public involvement. By bringing in a wide range of participants, planners can identify a wider range of concerns and solutions. With broadly based community involvement, issues of social and intergenerational equity may surface as well, as can ideas to avoid population losses. In addition to residents, builders and developers involved in reconstruction or new construction should be invited to the planning table to learn about and contribute to the community's vision. Suggestions for **participatory recovery** processes are incorporated throughout the text, particularly in Chapter 13 (Community Resources).

- *Economic vitality.* People need to live close to where they work. Linking residential recovery to transportation arteries and places of employment allows people to return. Further, linking residential and economic sectors more closely reduces air pollution, gasoline costs, and traffic congestion. It is also important to remember the range of places where people work, including in their own homes. Rebuilding may also provide an opportunity to rezone areas so that businesses such as banks, dry cleaners, cafes, and gas stations can locate closer to residential areas.

- *Thinking holistically.* It is important to think holistically when rebuilding. Care must be taken to think through the possible effects of rebuilding, including negative and positive consequences. By connecting housing to other dimensions of the recovery, it is possible to enhance quality of life, offer positive environmental benefits, support local businesses, and revitalize a devastated community. Being comprehensive with a recovery-planning effort pays dividends retrievable at a future time.

A wise community also tackles the difficult issues as well. Some communities may find that vital records were destroyed by the disaster, meaning that property lines and ownership could be contested. Procedures to deal with this dilemma, such as land surveys and even mediation planning, will be needed. Demolition of damaged housing units, both private and public, is painful for all. Legal regulations govern when a city can "take" land or engage in demolition. Due process must be followed so that everyone's rights are considered. Public housing, though, falls outside the control of the residents.

After Hurricane Katrina and the levee failures in New Orleans, public housing was demolished through an agreement among the city, state, and federal HUD offices amid tremendous outcry and protest. Replacement housing is expected to be "mixed income use" which means that neighbors will come from varying income levels. Such an approach has been popular among planners as a way to integrate communities more successfully and to bridge economic divides among people. However, protestors say that such an approach will lead to permanent displacement of poor residents and benefit those with higher incomes. Clearly, this is the type of situation that should be discussed pre-event to reduce discontent and address equity issues.

Other issues that may arise include the historical and cultural character of a neighborhood. Homes that have such value should be preserved, and a

community may need to specify how the rebuilding will occur so as to mitigate future hazards while maintaining the historic character of the homes.
Retaining such features helps people maintain a sense of connection to the
history and heritage of the area. In New Orleans, the new musician's village
reflects the colorful heritage of this city and incorporates mitigation features
(see Photo 3.2).

Because the housing stock represents the largest portion of any community, it is a good idea to create a housing task force. Members will need to
represent the full population in all its diversity as well as the various partners that may be involved in the rebuilding, such as builders, developers,
and voluntary organizations. After the 1989 earthquake, Santa Cruz created a housing task force that included subcommittees on temporary and
permanent housing. By involving local leaders and citizens, the city devised
creative solutions for both needs. This issue will be discussed in Chapter 7.

Business

The economic sector provides necessary goods and services, jobs, and sales
tax revenue. Thus, it is important to include all those with economic interests in any planning effort. As we will see in Chapter 8, the full set of businesses must be considered for recovery planning, including home-based and

PHOTO 3.2 The new Musicians' Village built through volunteer labor in New
Orleans features elevations to mitigate flood risk and preserve historic architecture characteristic of New Orleans. The village recognizes the importance of
connecting culture, work and housing during recovery efforts. (Photo by Brenda
Phillips. With permission.)

cyber-commuting businesses as well as small businesses and the corporate and industrial sectors.

As with housing, both temporary and permanent recovery need to be considered. Many businesses may be able to survive displacement and downtime by relocating to temporary quarters. Larger chains and franchises will often relocate local businesses into mobile homes or other manufactured housing close to the original site. Pharmacy chains did so after Hurricane Andrew, thus providing an important and urgently needed service. Even businesses not directly damaged are likely to be affected by the loss of customers.

In Santa Cruz, local businesses relocated into dome-shaped "Phoenix pavilions," so named after the mythical phoenix that rises from the ashes to be reborn. These pavilions opened between the October 17 earthquake and Christmas, allowing for both local businesses and tax revenues to rebound. Another local business relocated a few blocks away and produced coffee cups that read "Santa Cruz Book Tent." Because of subsurface damage to utilities and other infrastructure, parts of the downtown remained closed for several years. By providing temporary relocation, many businesses were able to return eventually to their original locations.

Another option may be for businesses to partner with others. Newspapers, for example, often use the printing facilities of an adjacent media partner while they wait to return to their facilities. The Internet also provides temporary options for some businesses by relocating their services into cyberspace. Home-based businesses may need particular attention, as they tend to fall through the cracks of most economic recovery efforts. Home-based consulting, repair work, insurance, hair care, child care, and ironing and sewing services may keep a home-based business alive and provide desperately needed household income.

Communities can help businesses recover by designating a business recovery task force that includes all economic interests. Preexisting organizations, such as the Black or Hispanic Chamber of Commerce or the Business and Professional Women's Association, may be able to provide leadership and resources for convening meetings and moving forward. As we will learn in Chapter 8 (Business Recovery), some businesses fare better than others. Generally, the smaller the business or the fewer resources it has, the less likely it is to survive (Webb, Tierney, and Dahlhamer 2000).

A connection between task force members and local officials should be encouraged to facilitate communication and coordination. Officials need to understand issues that may emerge within the business community, such as the loss of parking spaces, the impact of street closures, or the loss of pedestrian traffic (Chang and Falit-Baiamonte 2002). Businesses need to stay connected to what officials are doing, including consideration of special sales taxes to generate postdisaster income, establishment of new transportation routing, or creation of a special district to stimulate economic growth.

Rebuilding rates for businesses can vary. Those that share connected space, such as a strip mall or city block, may need to relocate for longer periods of time while the shared space is rebuilt. Thus, as with housing, it is wise to pre-identify rental locations or suitable areas for placement of temporary units. Larger buildings can also take years to rebuild if they were seriously damaged. Ideally, businesses will incorporate mitigation measures and environmentally friendly construction practices into their recovery efforts, which may take extra time to research in a postdisaster context.

The return of tax revenues to the locally damaged area will be welcome as well. New Orleans, a major port city and popular tourist destination, has taken years to recoup tax revenues from Hurricane Katrina. The Brookings Institution and the Greater New Orleans Community Data Center have gathered data on sales tax revenues. As can be seen in Table 3.1, Katrina dramatically impacted all but motor vehicle sales. Because so many people had to replace damaged, flooded, or destroyed vehicles, motor vehicle sales rebounded first after Katrina. General sales have returned, though not to prestorm levels. Hotel and motel revenues have not yet fully rebounded, a startling and significant loss in an economy where convention business and tourism provided thousands of jobs as well as millions in tax revenues.

In addition to the financial impact, vital business records may be lost. Paper and electronic files hold information related to personnel, taxes, inventory, vendors, and customers. Loss of such resources, including computing systems, can stagger even the strongest businesses. Thus, predisaster business continuity plans must include backups for vital records. Postdisaster, rapid access to those resources can hasten business resumption.

Certainly, an element of business recovery planning must include strategies to keep people safe (in a predisaster plan) or to enhance safety through postdisaster mitigation. Both customers and employees should be kept in mind. The massive loss of life on September 11 revealed how critical it is to conduct emergency evacuation planning and to exercise those plans. Workplaces that plan for disaster and introduce mitigation measures into the workplace can increase safety for both employees and customers. Safe

TABLE 3.1 Pre- and Post-Hurricane Katrina Sales Tax Revenue in New Orleans

Month and Year	General Sales	Hotel and Motel	Motor Vehicle	Total Tax Revenues
January 2005 (pre-Katrina)	$12,095,836	$642,046	$824,388	$13,562,270
September 2005 (post-Katrina)	$ 120,007	$143,481	$860,071	$ 1,123,559
September 2006	$ 7,840,364	$391,791	$974,215	$ 9,206,371
September 2007	$ 9,138,572	$375,279	$954,383	$10,468,234

Source: Greater New Orleans Community Data Center and the Brookings Institute. With permission.

rooms for tornados, elevated areas to avoid flooding, warning devices including those for informing people who are blind or deaf, and other measures can truly mean the difference between life and death for employees and customers. Employees may also face the loss of their homes. Thus, businesses will need to plan for temporary or permanent replacement of personnel.

Finally, in keeping with the principles of sustainability, businesses as well as residences can "think green." Postdisaster rebuilding provides opportunities to address environmental concerns. For example, a large-scale business may want to reduce its water consumption with low-flow toilets and other water conservation measures such as xeriscaping. Electrical fixtures can be changed to use low-energy fluorescent lights. Heating, cooling, and boiler systems can also be upgraded to higher efficiency units (Smart Energy Design Assistance Center 2006). Recycled materials can be used for everything from insulation to parking lots. Businesses can also reduce storm-water runoff by incorporating green space. Use of green materials, such as flooring made from natural products with fewer chemicals, may not only be good for the environment but also for employees and customers.

Environmental Resources

An argument could be made that some areas and populations benefit from what might otherwise be seen as a disaster. For example, a fire that damages part of a national park also allows for some seeds to be released. Fires across some prairie areas replenish the ecosystem as well. But many hazards are either initiated by or worsened by human encroachment such as wildfire, or decimation of natural barriers such as coastal wetlands. Thus it is our ethical responsibility to serve as good stewards of the environment and to protect and preserve what is damaged or threatened by disasters.

Environmental recovery planning may start with existing predisaster assessments that list and locate threatened or endangered flora and fauna. By developing pre-event partnerships, rapid action to protect these elements and to contain further damage can be implemented. A full range of hazards appropriate to the local context must be considered. Areas that include major transportation arteries like rivers, ports, and highways require coordination to manage hazardous-materials disasters. But natural disasters pose threats as well. For example, in areas of heavy rainfall, damage can be caused to riparian areas, defined as riverbank habitats, when embankments slide or erode.

As we will see in Chapter 5, a number of partners will be required for environmental recovery. Thus, planners might want to invite representatives knowledgeable in water, ground, air, wildlife, and vegetation issues. Depending on the area, those with expertise in forest ecosystems, hazardous materials, mountain habitat, and coastal concerns should be considered. Academics, scientists, parks employees, and environmental advocates can provide input. And, because of the potential for hazards to affect environmental conditions downstream or downwind, other jurisdictions and levels from local through state and federal representatives may need to be included.

Strategies to protect the environment rely heavily on existing statutes, laws, and ordinances. Consequently, input from those with expertise in environmental law should be consulted. Those working on environmental planning must either include those who understand these rules and regulations, or they must educate themselves so as to avoid violations. Beyond these preexisting conditions, planners can offer new ordinances that direct local jurisdictions to protect natural resources. Ordinances can set aside environmentally sensitive lands, disallow encroachment on an endangered species habitat, and limit routing for hazardous cargo.

Postdisaster programming may include efforts to rescue and restore. In past disasters, such efforts have featured (for more detail, see Chapter 5):

- Volunteer organizations that rescue injured animals, such as after oil spills along shorelines and waterways or in areas damaged by wildfire
- Tree planting to restore landscaping and forest areas due to hurricanes or wildfire
- Shoring up riverbanks damaged by rapidly flowing floods that provide access to water and food for area wildlife
- Conducting a census of threatened and endangered species to determine the impact of the disaster on their populations and habitats
- Setting aside areas used by endangered species to preserve their presence
- Assessing contamination of ground, water, and air after spills and other hazards prior to the return of humans to their homes and communities
- Initiating long-term studies of the effects of certain hazards, such as airborne contaminants from fire, chemical releases, or terrorism on humans as well as various parts of the ecosystem

Finally, environmental recovery planning must include mitigation measures designed to safeguard environmental resources. Such efforts could range from educational programs to the generation of cross-organizational partnerships as well as set-asides of sensitive areas (Natural Hazards Center 2001).

Historic and Cultural Resources

All communities include people who care tremendously about historic and cultural properties. Most counties or parishes have local historical associations, and many host locations where locally relevant collections can be viewed by the public. Cultural groups and clubs often put together annual events to celebrate ethnic heritage or promote cultural diversity. State historical preservation offices provide expertise on legal, architectural, and historic matters. Both before and immediately after disaster, these prospective partners can be consulted to establish prevention, response, and recovery efforts that safeguard historic and cultural treasures, provide labor, and salvage the unique character of the community.

Because people tend to focus more on getting back into a normal routine for their families, historic and cultural heritage may be overlooked. However, opportunities to save the unique character can be identified and made part of the recovery effort. In Lancaster, Texas (see link in the Resources section of this chapter), for example, prison labor was used to salvage bricks to restore the damaged historic downtown. National Parks officials have conducted planning efforts to provide rapid movement of museum exhibits when floodwaters threaten Harper's Ferry in Virginia. Priceless paintings and other artwork were lost in the terrorist attack of September 11, but others were uncovered and saved through careful retrieval. Our national, local, and cultural heritage is at risk without pre- and postdisaster recovery planning.

Mitigation measures must be thoroughly researched for impacts on historic and cultural resources. For example, although putting on a stronger, better, and more disaster-resistant roof and siding may seem like a good idea, doing so could easily undermine the historic character of the structure. Relocation of properties could remove them from their historic context. Elevations might prove more context-appropriate but are expensive and can harm the structural integrity of a building. Diverting waterways that overflow in historic areas could cause problems for environmentally sensitive areas. The challenges can be significant, but it is possible to hang on to the distinctive areas that mean something to us personally and collectively.

FEMA assisted Milton, Massachusetts, in conducting a thorough assessment of its options after repetitive flooding continued to threaten historic downtown and neighborhood areas. A variety of options had to be examined and presented to the community prior to determining the best combination of cost, historic preservation, and disaster-resistant features (more on this in Chapter 6).

Infrastructure

Many states and counties have, in recent decades, conducted assessments of their public utilities and key infrastructure, including bridges and highways. As the American Society for Civil Engineers (ASCE) summarizes in its *Report Card on the Nation's Infrastructure* (2005, with an update for 2008; see Resources section for link to report), the nation has earned a grade of D overall.

Unfortunately, infrastructure repairs are so expensive that sometimes it may be a long time before they can be undertaken, let alone mitigated.

For example, ASCE estimates that it would take $1.6 trillion for the nation's infrastructure to be rated as "good." Such expenditures would likely have to occur through funding established by Congress in order to improve railroads, aviation facilities, bridges, dams, levees, waterways, and more. A number of legislative acts remain pending before Congress.

While we wait for funding, the infrastructure continues to be a problem. Annual repairs and operating costs of poorly maintained roads costs $67 billion across the nation. Disasters can cause further damage. In 2007, the Army Corps of Engineers estimated that 150 levees might fail in future flooding due to poor maintenance (see ASCE link in Resources section). ASCE estimated in 2007 that, of 599,893 bridges, 25.59% remained "structurally deficient or obsolete."

The public infrastructure is situated between local needs and federal capacity to fund significant and continuing failures. What can be done is to start with the known problems and anticipate failure points. Planning can identify ways to reroute traffic and ensure the steady flow of the public as well as commercial activity. Government can also prioritize preexisting needs and ask the public to pass special taxes or approve funding alternatives. After disaster, care must be taken to strengthen the infrastructure so that it is not just rebuilt to its prior capacity, but to resist future hazards. Mitigation opportunities might include locating utilities underground in areas with high wind hazards, strengthening levees to higher levels for locations that experience flooding, and updating the stormwater drainage system (FEMA 2005; Natural Hazards Center 2001; Schwab et al. 1998).

Social and Psychological Recovery

If you remember systems theory from Chapter 2, both the built environment and the human systems are affected by disaster. When a household is impacted by disaster, the burden of recovery can be immense. When an entire community is disrupted, normal support systems may not be there—your neighbors, friends, and family may be temporarily relocated somewhere else. The people who normally help you cope with life's adversities may be feeling the effects as well. And, although mental health needs usually do not increase dramatically after most disasters, a variety of social and psychological needs may arise that require planning attention.

It is possible to identify areas of concern for social and psychological recovery. First, some groups tend to fare worse after disaster than others, particularly those at lower income levels. Such groups are more likely to access and use social services such as health care, public transportation, unemployment assistance, and other services. Loss of those services can be critical. Some hazards, such as pandemics that isolate people or rapid-onset events that prevent evacuation or necessitate sheltering in place, may be more difficult. Some groups may experience higher death and injury rates.

People who experience the deaths of those around them, injury, or property loss may be more susceptible to psychological trauma that requires professional support. While in most cases posttraumatic stress disorder (PTSD) is relatively rare, circumstances may increase rates such as complete loss of the community, long-term displacement from social networks, and proximity to physical trauma affecting individuals and those around them.

Planning for psychological recovery can commence at several levels. First, involve properly credentialed and professional counselors. Second, generate a list of providers and plans for trauma counseling. Training these providers in postdisaster or mass emergency counseling represents a third leg in the process, and may need to involve those who connect to populations at risk. Schoolteachers, child-care workers, home health-care providers, disability organization representatives, senior-citizen-center staff, first responders, and others can recognize warning signals of potential problems. For example, Dr. James Pennebaker of the University of Texas at Austin has found that about six weeks after a disaster people stop talking about the effects of the event. At the same time, psychosomatic symptoms, defined as internalized physical consequences of the psychological trauma, begin to surface, including headaches, backaches, and head colds (Pennebaker 1997). Observing these and other signals can alert trained professionals that someone may be in need of assistance.

Finally, developing a plan to deliver appropriate kinds of services needs to be undertaken. As we will read in Chapter 10, various efforts have been used successfully. After September 11, for example, the American Red Cross offered multiple kinds of counseling programs in varying languages. School professionals in Oklahoma City provided long-term support to dozens of school sites after the domestic terrorist attack. Counseling may need to range from play therapy for children to intense debriefing and critical incident stress management for professional emergency managers, first responders, and other public officials. Further, counseling should be culturally sensitive, as people respond based on how their culture teaches them to express (or not) the feelings associated with loss and tragedy.

Counseling should be viewed as a positive opportunity to put an experience into perspective, learn to manage the consequences, and find a path to move forward. Many communities plan for a one-year anniversary event. Commemorations range from private meetings held among those directly affected to public occasions that remember those who were lost and recognize the progress that has been made.

In 2001, Oklahoma State University lost ten members of its basketball team and staff in a plane crash. In his book, *Riding with the Blue Moth*, author Bill Hancock speaks of working through the depression associated with losing his son, Will, in the accident (Hancock and Nantz 2006). Hancock nicknamed the depression as a "blue moth" that accompanied him as he rode a bicycle across the United States during his time of mourning and recovery. His message, using fitness to combat trauma, inspired the creation of an annual running event called *Remember the Ten* in Stillwater, Oklahoma. The race drew over 1,300 participants in its second year. By recognizing, acknowledging, working through, and finally writing about the trauma associated with tragedy, Hancock inspired others to confront the psychological challenges associated with healing from trauma.

Public-Sector Recovery

City and county offices, as well as supportive social and other services provided by local and state authorities, are also vulnerable to disaster. After September 11, contingency plans allowed for a rapid relocation of New York City's emergency operations center. Building so that public services can rebound quickly means that the broader community can begin to recover. Thus, attending to restoration of key public services should be a priority. At the same time, care needs to be taken to understand that public servants and public employees may have also been affected by the disaster. Just as they struggle to help the community rebuild, they struggle to reclaim their losses as well.

Disaster recovery is not the time when the public sector wants to learn on the job. Thus, recovery planning means that all relevant departments must become involved in setting out a clear understanding of tasks, how they might be accomplished under conditions ranging from a minor emergency to a major catastrophe, a division of labor for who does what, and a set of mutual aid agreements with other jurisdictions to provide support. For example, conducting damage assessment is an immediate task that has to be done even if roads are blocked. Aerial reconnaissance and satellite imagery can be used, but these require specialized skills and knowledge. Thus, training staff on the full set of tasks that needs to be done under beleaguered circumstances emerges as a primary planning focus.

Training staff locally on what they need to do, how their work may change in a disaster context, and where they might be relocated to support critical services is only the start. Because disasters bring public staff into contact with new people, programs, procedures, and policies, public personnel must be trained on how to maximize these resources. FEMA, for example, provides considerable support to areas designated as a presidentially declared disaster. Local officials and staff must understand the opportunities and limitations of FEMA programs in order to help their community. Records that account for expenditures must be carefully kept. Contracts with companies that provide services, such as debris removal, must be carefully monitored to ensure compliance. Specific hazards, such as a chemical release, will bring city or county employees into contact with the Environmental Protection Agency and probably other state agencies. In an area hard hit, voluntary organizations represent an important resource, so the community needs to be ready to work with and manage potentially massive numbers of volunteers, where they will stay, and what kinds of projects they may work on.

As described in Chapter 11, the public sector will have to address a number of elements in their share of the recovery plan:

- Just as with housing and businesses, the public sector may need to consider downtime and displacement. Just how long might it take to relocate into a temporary facility? How long will employees work in a displaced setting? In New Orleans, for example, police and fire staff continued to work in temporary trailers three years after the hurricane.
- What vital records must be backed up for government and related services to continue? Locations that provide backup for computer records and hard copies, such as property records that may date back before computers, must be secured.
- What types of emergency ordinances, such as road clearance, must be written and passed?
- How will government temporarily replace employees unable to work because of injury or property loss at their own homes? What kinds of employee-support programs need to be arranged? How will employee turnover be handled?
- What federal regulations must be adhered to in order to avoid damage to the environment and local fines?
- What kinds of mutual aid agreements should we develop before disaster strikes?
- What happens if the event occurs during an election time? How will the political process be affected and implemented to ensure a continuation of the democratic process?
- How will government communicate with people to inform them of everything from sorting debris to obtaining a permit to rebuild?
- What kinds of emergency accounting procedures need to be established to ensure that the community complies with FEMA requirements to obtain reimbursement?

And, of course, mitigation measures should be undertaken to strengthen the public sector against future losses. By preplanning, areas of potential loss can be identified, such as moving records and key personnel out of below-ground areas susceptible to flooding. Facilities can be "hardened" with stronger, even bullet-resistant windows. Barricades can be placed in front of buildings suspected of being terrorist targets. If the local government has a written mitigation plan, the area may be eligible for significant assistance with mitigation of public facilities. The public sector must serve as a model for what should be done in the broader community.

Summary

Ideally, communities will develop recovery plans before disaster strikes. In most locations, though, postdisaster recovery planning is more likely. Plans should address both short-term and long-term needs. Where possible, recovery planning should connect to comprehensive plans and land-use planning. Elements of recovery plans should address housing, which comprises the bulk of any area's building inventory. Economic recovery must be considered as well so that people can return to work. Rebuilding must also take place without seriously damaging local environmental resources. Care should be taken to salvage the unique historic and cultural character of the community. Recovery efforts across all sectors must connect to the infrastructure, as disaster represents an opportunity to strengthen area infrastructure and reduce future risks to bridges, railways, ports, water supplies, and utilities. The public sector bears the responsibility to lead the effort, support and involve the public, and drive the recovery toward a successful conclusion.

The remainder of this text addresses each of these planning concerns in more detail. In the next chapter, we start with a short-term recovery need that may extend well into the long-term period. Debris management must be undertaken quickly, but also correctly, to minimize damage to the environment, allow the community to launch rebuilding, and safeguard health effects from improperly managed debris.

Study Guide

Summary Questions

1. What are the benefits of pre-event recovery planning?
2. List and explain the basic principles used for recovery planning.
3. Why is recovery planning considered to be a process? What kinds of stages or steps can be anticipated to expedite recovery planning?
4. What leadership qualities should be present in those facilitating the recovery-planning effort?
5. Which groups of persons are considered to be central stakeholders in a recovery-planning process? Why is each group so important to a recovery-planning effort?
6. Why are partners necessary beyond the local level? Who are the essential state and federal recovery partners that might contribute to recovery planning?

7. Why is it important to link mitigation efforts to recovery planning? What should be done with mitigation planning before disaster as opposed to after disaster?
8. What are the key planning elements of a recovery plan?

Discussion Questions

1. In looking around your community, which stakeholders should be present at the recovery-planning table?
2. What might you do differently in your community after a disaster? Change transportation routing? Add more affordable housing? Act to revitalize specific economic sectors?
3. What environmental, historical, and cultural resources exist in your community and what should be done to safeguard those treasures both before and after disaster? How could you incorporate such efforts into recovery planning?
4. Consider the range of potential recovery leaders in your community. First, think about the types of leaders present and which types you might want to include, such as an elected official, a public employee, or a local community leader. Second, try and identify particularly appropriate individuals to lead the recovery. Why would these persons be effective leaders?
5. What are some common means for convening the broader public to address something that affects the entire community? Is there a specific city office that conducts outreach? Or, does each department try to inform and involve the public? How do they do so?
6. Does your community have a recovery plan? If yes, is it pre- or post-disaster? If not, why not?

Key Terms

Comprehensive planning
Disaster resilience
Hazard-mitigation planning
Holistic recovery
Land-use planning
National Response Framework
Ordinance
Participatory recovery
Planning
Postdisaster planning
Predisaster planning

Stakeholders
Visioning process

References

Beierle, T., and J. Cayford. 2002. *Democracy in Practice: Public participation in environmental decisions*. Washington, D.C.: Resources for the Future.

Chrislip, D. 2002. *The collaborative leadership fieldbook*. New York: John Wiley.

City of Los Angeles. 1994. Recovery and reconstruction plan: City of Los Angeles. Los Angeles: Emergency Operations Organization.

FEMA. 2005. Long-term community recovery planning process: a self-help guide. Washington D.C.: Federal Emergency Management Agency.

Grand Forks. 2007. Lessons learned. http://www.grandforksgov.com/Flood/Lesson_Learned.pdf. Accessed January 27, 2009.

Krajeski, R., and K. Peterson. 2008. But she is a woman and this is a man's job. In *Women and disasters: From theory to practice*, ed. B. D. Phillips and B. H. Morrow. United States: Xlibris and International Research Committee on Disasters.

Mitchell, L. 2003. Guidelines for Emergency Managers Working With Culturally and Linguistically Diverse Communities. *Australian Journal of Emergency Management* 18.

Natural Hazards Center. 2001. *Holistic disaster recovery*. Boulder, CO: Public Entity Risk Institute.

Neal, D. M. 2004. Transition from response to recovery after the Lancaster, TX, tornado: An empirical description. *Journal of Emergency Management* 2 (1): 47–51.

Norman, S. 2004. Focus on recovery: A holistic framework for recovery. Paper presented at New Zealand Recovery Symposium, Napier, New Zealand.

Pennebaker, J. 1997. *Opening Up*. NY: Guildford Press.

Quarantelli, E. L. 1997. Ten criteria for evaluating the management of community disasters. *Disasters* 21 (1): 39–56.

Schwab, J., K. C. Topping, C. C. Eadie, R. E. Deyle, and R. A. Smith. 1998. *Planning for post-disaster recovery and reconstruction*. Washington, DC: FEMA/American Planning Association.

Smart Energy Design Assistance Center. 2006. Disaster recovery for small business, fact sheet 1. Urbana-Champaign: University of Illinois at Urbana-Champaign.

Wilson, R. C. 1991. *The Loma Prieta earthquake: What one city learned*. Washington, DC: International City Management Association.

Resources

- American Society of Civil Engineers, Report Card for the Nation's Infrastructure, http://www.asce.org/reportcard/2005/index.cfm.
- Arkadelphia, Arkansas illustrative recovery plan, http://www.camiros.com/areasofpractice/communityplan/disaster/arkadelphia/illustrative_recovery.html.
- Center for the Study of Disasters and Extreme Events, Oklahoma State University, http://csdee.okstate.edu.

- Denton, Texas Comprehensive Plan, http://www.cityofdenton.com/pages/dentonplan.cfm.
- DHS/FEMA National Response Framework Emergency Support Function (ESF) #14 Recovery. Links to documents and tools, http://www.fema.gov/pdf/emergency/nrf/nrf-esf-14.pdf. A list of agencies that support long-term recovery planning can be found toward this end of this pdf.
- FEMA Mitigation Planning materials and documents, http://www.fema.gov/plan/mitplanning/index.shtm.
- Lafayette, Louisiana recovery web site, http://www.lafayettela.gov/LARecoveryReferences.asp, an exceptional set of resources for planning recovery, including the consideration of people with disabilities.
- Lancaster, Texas Historic Preservation Committee, http://www.lancaster-tx.com/index.php?option=com_content&task=view&id=149&Itemid=448. Accessed May 2008.
- Los Angeles Recovery and Reconstruction Plan, http://www.lacity.org/emd/pdf/eompp/divplans/r&r%20annex%20plan.pdf.
- National Voluntary Organizations Active in Disaster (NVOAD), guidelines for long-term recovery planning and committees can be found at http://www.nvoad.org.
- Princeville, North Carolina information, http://www.seeingblack.com/x040901/princeville.shtml.
- Remember the Ten Run, http://www.remembertheten.com.

Section II

Dimensions of Disaster Recovery

Chapter 4

Debris Management

Learning Objectives

After reading this chapter, you should be able to:

- Describe the types of debris generated by various hazards
- Outline a debris-management plan
- Identify resources at the state and federal levels for debris management
- Explain the debris-management cycle and the phases of debris management
- Recommend the kinds of persons appropriate for a debris-management team
- Estimate debris amounts that need to be managed
- Name legal issues related to debris management
- Discuss the pros and cons of various debris-removal strategies
- List health and safety concerns associated with debris-removal processes
- Categorize different kinds of legal issues, federal contracts, and monitoring procedures
- Describe procedures for temporary and permanent debris-removal sites
- Develop basic elements of a public-education plan for debris removal

Introduction

Debris removal is a crucial action to take after disasters. Ambulances cannot reach the injured if roads are blocked. Likewise, utility companies need to reach power stations and deal with downed power lines. Red Cross workers must open shelters and bring in food with their emergency response vehicles. Thus, debris-removal crews must move quickly to help. Emergency debris-removal work occurs first, usually when crews—and even emergent citizen groups—move debris to the side of the road. Debris-removal work then symbolizes, both literally and in reality, key efforts to jump-start the recovery process.

Debris-management teams and work crews rank among the least recognized but most important partners in the disaster recovery process. Their efforts can reduce the impact of debris on area **landfills**, prevent environmental contamination, spur household and commercial rebuilding, restore aesthetic appeal to a damaged neighborhood, and even expedite investigation of criminal activities in a terrorist attack. This chapter walks you through the issues, challenges, and opportunities unique to **debris management** and encourages you to think through how to plan for such circumstances.

Remember the different hazards discussed in Chapter 1, and then turn your mind toward what those events would leave behind: the mud and muck from a flood, charred homes from wildfire, and downed power lines from tornados. Debris could be scattered over hundreds of miles. This chapter provides an overview of debris generated by specific hazards. The section concludes with a consideration of why it is important to manage disaster-generated debris quickly and appropriately.

Hurricane Hugo

In September 1989, Hurricane Hugo, a strong Category 4 storm (National Hurricane Center, no date), reached the Carolinas. Inland winds generated damage in excess of $7 billion dollars in North and South Carolina. Woody, vegetative debris from Carolina forests covered massive areas. In Mecklenburg County and Charlotte, North Carolina, the EPA estimated that 400,000 tons of green waste awaited disposal (EPA 1995).

Charlotte faced a particular problem, one increasingly common across the United States. Area landfills had an anticipated lifespan of 2.5 years normal use beyond the hurricane. The EPA estimated that moving woody debris to the landfill would have cost two years of its lifespan. A crisis loomed, then, for where to take garbage from nondisaster events. Further complicating debris-disposal options, local officials sought alternatives to burning because of concerns with air quality and ozone pollution (Steuteville 1992a).

To respond to the disaster as well as the air pollution and landfill-space crisis, Charlotte identified as many potential debris locations as possible, eventually setting up seven sites across 100 acres of private and public space. The city used landfills, space at the airport, and even vacant property to set up debris-management operations. Residents and four different contractors took trees and other woody vegetation to the sites, where ten tub **grinders** (explained later in this chapter) mulched limbs. Contractors cut up firewood. The City gave the mulch and firewood to citizens free of charge, an effective effort to reduce and recycle the debris. Debris-removal operations took 17 months to handle at a cost of $7 million (Steuteville 1992a; EPA 1995).

September 11

Various kinds of pressures will erupt to push debris removal forward as quickly as possible. However, rapid removal can also generate problems in both the short term and the long term. Consider, for example, the enormous effort required to remove the debris from the World Trade Center after September 11 (see Box 4.1). The location was simultaneously a smoldering and dangerous pile, a crime scene, a location for search and rescue, and an area for retrieving human remains. The debris-removal process became a logistically complex, physically challenging, and emotional process for all involved.

We are still attempting to determine the long-term effects of September 11, an effort that will likely continue for some time. Studies suggest that both short- and long-term health problems may have developed due to inhalation of debris matter from the World Trade Center (Lin et al. 2005; Landrigan et al. 2004; CDC 2002; Szema et al. 2004; Trout et al. 2002). The attack generated a number of potential respiratory irritants, including particulate matter, smoke, asbestos, metals, organic compounds, and dust. Each phase of the debris-management process presented new problems. In the first 12 hours after the attack, airborne matter proved the most health threatening. During the following two weeks, fires, smoke, settling dust, particulates, and diesel exhaust increased airborne hazards. Fires continued through December at the site, accompanied by diesel exhaust, gases, and particulates (Landrigan et al. 2004).

The dust prompted concern when it seeped into people's homes, sometimes up to several inches thick. One year after the attack, researchers looked at asthma symptoms within the dense residential area around the World Trade Center and compared them with a group of residents outside of the affected area. These symptoms consistently occurred among those living in the affected area (Lin et al. 2005):

- Eye and nose irritation or burning
- Nasal and sinus congestion

BOX 4.1   WORLD TRADE CENTER DEBRIS

The Government Accountability Office reported a number of challenges associated with debris after September 11:

- "The September 11, 2001, terrorist attacks on the World Trade Center turned Lower Manhattan into a disaster site on a scale the nation had never experienced. The World Trade Center was a complex of seven buildings on 16 acres surrounding a 5-acre plaza. The twin towers were at the center of the complex. Each tower had 110 floors, with approximately 43,200 square feet on each floor. As the towers collapsed, the area was blanketed in a mixture of building debris and combustible materials that coated building exteriors and streets, as well as the interiors of apartments and offices, with dust. This complex mixture gave rise to another major concern: that thousands of residents and workers in the area would now be exposed to known hazards in the air and in the dust, such as asbestos, lead, glass fibers, and pulverized concrete" (GAO 2007, 1).
- "There are an estimated 330 office buildings in Lower Manhattan below Canal Street and roughly 900 residential buildings with approximately 20,000 apartments. In 2002, after initial efforts by the city of New York to advise New York residents how to clean the World Trade Center dust in their homes, FEMA and EPA entered into an interagency agreement to address indoor spaces affected by the disaster. While EPA has responded to hazardous material releases for decades, the WTC disaster was the first large-scale emergency for which EPA provided testing and cleanup in indoor spaces. WTC dust is a fine mixture of materials that resulted from the collapse and subsequent burning of the twin towers and includes pulverized concrete, asbestos, and glass fibers. WTC dust entered homes and offices through open windows, was tracked in, or was picked up by air-conditioning system intakes" (GAO 2007, 8–9).
- "EPA reported it was unable to develop a method for distinguishing between normal urban dust and WTC dust; therefore, the agency reported it could not assess the extent of WTC contamination and had no basis for expanding the cleanup effort" (GAO 2007, 5).

Source: GAO (2007)

- Hoarse throat or throat irritation
- Recurring headaches

In addition, people in the study reported more unplanned medical visits and use of respiratory medications than the comparison group. These symptoms occurred and persisted after September 11. The potential for further injury was present. For example, post-inhalation injury that produces asthma is called reactive airways dysfunction syndrome or RADS

(Nemery 2003). Specific groups experienced debris-related problems. Sore throats and bronchial problems were especially persistent among firefighters (Fagan et al. 2003; Landrigan et al. 2004), a problem that became known as the "World Trade Center cough" (Landrigan et al. 2004). Truck drivers and other debris workers reported the cough, increased phlegm, and a new "wheeze" (Landrigan et al. 2004).

Workers cleaning up nearby buildings were assessed through a New York mobile medical screening project. These workers were primarily Hispanic day laborers who did not speak English, did not have health insurance, and had not received training to work with hazardous materials. Most were not given personal protective equipment. The subjects of the study reported irritated airways, headaches, fatigue, dizziness, and problems sleeping. These symptoms remained even after they stopped working in the contaminated buildings (Malievskaya, Rosenberg, and Markowitz 2002).

Concern also developed for expectant mothers. Assessing pregnancy risks is challenging, as there are so many factors that influence fetus development. Nevertheless, the few studies done after September 11 suggest an increased chance of lower birth weights or shortened pregnancies (Landrigan et al. 2004). These results suggest that debris management is more than the removal of destroyed buildings; it is a critical part of the process of managing public health across the community.

The General Accountability Office (GAO 2007) reported that health concerns from working at Ground Zero have lingered. On September 11, 2007, as the names of the deceased were read aloud at a memorial service, the 2,974th name was added: an individual who worked four blocks away had died, apparently from lung disease believed to be associated with the dust from the World Trade Center.

In summary, debris management needs to be planned in advance and managed carefully to ensure that first responders can get in to save lives, people can return home to begin the recovery process, businesses can get back on track, and employees can earn paychecks. Debris management also helps psychologically by restoring aesthetic qualities to a devastated scene. Debris-management teams can anticipate that they will experience pressures to handle debris in a way that moves the recovery along. However, they must carry out their work in a way that does not compromise people's health and safety or damage the environment. In the next section, we examine problems generated by various hazards so that debris-management planners can anticipate the types of issues that they will face.

Hazard-Specific Debris Problems

This section first reviews the types of debris that can be anticipated, followed by types of materials generated in hazard-specific events. Carefully working through each type of debris and hazard can enhance debris-management planning efforts.

Debris can be categorized into matter produced directly and indirectly by the event, and as material that results during response and recovery (Solis et al. 1995). Disasters produce debris directly through destroying buildings, fences, trees, landscaping, playgrounds, and more. Planners should expect to remove matter that deteriorates, sometimes quickly, including dead animals and livestock. Other directly generated debris includes shrubs, trees, and leaves. Environmental materials may include soil, sediment, mud, rocks, and sand. The levee failures in New Orleans, for example, pushed massive sand boils up under the levees and into homes. Removing damaged buildings required first handling tons of the displaced sand (ASCE 2005). Construction and household debris (bricks, carpet, furniture, plastic, glass, metals, tiles, piping, flooring, lamps), white goods (appliances, furnaces, hot water heaters), vehicles (cars, trucks, boats), personal items, electronic waste (computers, televisions, telephones, printers), and hazardous wastes (industrial, commercial, and residential, including chemicals and batteries) complete the list of debris possibilities directly created in a disaster (Solis et al. 1995; Lauter 2006).

An example of indirectly generated debris occurs when refrigerators cannot be opened and food rots (Lauter 2006). After Hurricane Katrina, officials advised the public that the best strategy to deal with food that had rotted inside refrigerators was to seal them with duct tape and take them to the curb. This being New Orleans, many residents then decorated their refrigerators with slogans, political commentary, and messages of hope (see Photo 4.1). Well-intentioned donation drives can also leave piles of items to deal with. After Hurricane Andrew, donors dropped clothing off in front of libraries and businesses, assuming that someone would come by and use it. In the heat, humidity, and nearly daily rainfall of southern Florida, clothing rotted and contributed to a powerful stench.

Finally, debris can result from the aftermath of the disaster itself. People without food, water, and shelter will congregate in new locations and use resources like bottled water, ready-to-eat meals, canned food, and fast food. These activities produce "leftovers" that debris-management teams deal with (Solis et al. 1995). All of this occurs on top of what the disaster can do! In the next sections, we will look at hazard-specific types of debris.

Floods

As can be seen in Table 4.1, different hazards create various types of debris problems. Floods can occur as slowly or rapidly moving events. Each generates unique problems. Rapidly moving events push water along, picking up and rolling debris (branches, signs, boxes, even vehicles) into masses that

PHOTO 4.1   Flooding along the Gulf Coast after Hurricane Katrina meant that affected homeowners had to seal their refrigerators with duct tape to isolate putrefied food. Residents then took their appliances to the curb. Debris-removal teams removed the food and freon before recycling the appliances. Local residents of New Orleans often decorated their refrigerators with messages. (Photo by Brenda Phillips. With permission.)

stack up against bridges. The result is bridge failure. Moving water is dangerous, as people who try to drive cars through water at a depth of even a few inches have found out when their cars are picked up by the water flow. Flood waters also seep into wood construction, soaking interior sheetrock, furniture, and carpeting. All of this must be removed. Soaked items that remain must be treated to avoid mold growth. The mud and sediment that remains becomes a debris-management challenge as well because it must be removed too. Landslides can occur if significant amounts of mud and sediment remain.

Tornados

A tornado can occur in a range of conditions as described in Chapter 1. Even relatively low-level events such as an EF1 can cause significant damage to mobile homes or campgrounds. A major tornado outbreak, such as the one experienced on May 3, 1999, across the state of Oklahoma, can be devastating. The Oklahoma tornados destroyed over 5000 cars; killed livestock;

TABLE 4.1 Hazard-Specific Debris

Type of Hazard	Type of Debris to Expect
Flood	High waters or high-speed flow can cause significant damage. Debris to be managed will include mud, sediment, construction and demolition (C&D), appliances, tires, hazardous waste, etc.
Tornado	Power, wind speed, and storm width can vary the debris field, which will include buildings, roofing materials, cars, utility poles, traffic lights, homes, agricultural damage, roofs, mobile homes/metal, and vegetation.
Hurricane	Coastal damage can be significant due to storm surge and associated flooding. Inland winds can generate enormous amounts of debris as well. Debris to expect includes sediment, trees, vegetation, personal property, construction, household items, and livestock carcasses.
Earthquake	Seismic activity can collapse residential buildings and infrastructure; fires and explosions can cause additional damage. Debris to be expected includes road and bridge materials, buildings, household and personal property, downed power lines, broken water pipes, and sediment from landslides.
Wildfire	Fires generated naturally may produce beneficial results; wildfires that affect urban areas can produce massive amounts of charred wood, ash, dead trees, and potentially mud and sediment from landslides due to denuded vegetation and loss of ground cover.
Hazardous materials	Hazardous materials can vary considerably in their amounts and toxicity. Debris removal must consider safety for the public and workers, determine the type of contamination and its effects on the environment, and develop appropriate identification, separation, removal, neutralization, interment, incineration, or other strategies for final disposal.
Terrorism	Terrorism can produce significant amounts of debris, depending on the type of attack, including buildings, vehicles, and hazardous materials. Debris management must be coordinated with appropriate policing and investigative agencies prior to and during the removal process.

Source: FEMA IS-632, Debris Management, www.fema.gov; EPA (1995).

damaged thousands of homes, schools, and churches; ripped out traffic signs; and downed utility poles. High winds and rain left the familiar red clay dirt of Oklahoma on every building, road, and remaining tree in its path. Although the temptation to clean mud, dirt, and other sediment from structures and roads through water dispersion methods may be tempting, such massive runoff can further impede the local stormwater drainage system. Thus, in addition to the anticipated construction and demolition (C&D) debris, care must be taken to deal with other deposits from high-velocity wind events.

Hurricanes

After Hurricane Iniki damaged the Hawaiian county of Kauai in 1992, officials faced three types of hurricane-related debris. First, they needed to deal with items and vegetation scattered over a wide area. Second, they needed to handle debris generated when residents and businesses cleaned up their properties and began demolition. Third, vegetation cleanup continued simultaneously with debris from reconstruction (Friesen, Harder, and Rifer 1994). Hurricanes are notorious for creating massive vegetation loss, although forward-thinking planners can use the materials to their economic advantage, as we will see in an upcoming section.

Earthquakes

Although we may think of earthquakes as shaking events, the type of movement can vary. Additional hazards can erupt, including landslides, fires and explosions, and flooding from burst water pipes (EPA 1995). Because seismic activity influences both the aboveground built environment and any infrastructure located in the ground, it may take time to conduct damage assessments to determine total losses—and ultimately the amount of debris. For example, the city of Watsonville, California, continued to hold classes in its high school for a year after the 1989 Loma Prieta earthquake until it determined that the building had to be demolished. Although most debris removal had occurred by then, a new task with extensive amounts of C&D loomed. Meanwhile, in nearby Santa Cruz, underground utility lines in the downtown sector had to be replaced, involving reconstruction and rerouting of traffic for years after the event. In the hillsides of the city, a drought had been going on, delaying the rebuilding process until the stability of mountainous slopes could be determined. With some hazards, it may take a while to manage completely the full amount of resulting debris.

Wildfires

Fires that affect human populations char household and personal property. Fires also deposit large amounts of ash and sediment and can generate landslides. The Oakland Hills "firestorm" of 1991 occurred when 65-mile-per-hour winds, high temperatures, and drought conditions produced conditions ripe for wildfire. A single ember from a previously contained "hot spot" erupted into flame fueled by freeze-damaged Monterey pines and oil-laden, highly explosive eucalyptus trees. What became one of the worst firestorms in U.S. history claimed 25 lives and injured 150. The debris from this event included 2843 destroyed homes across 1520 acres (Parker 1991). Postfire hazards can cause additional problems. When fires sweep through watershed areas, heavy rains can generate dangerous stream channel flows (Spittler 2005). Such was the case in 1980 after a fire in San Bernardino, California, when channel sediment destroyed or damaged 41 homes (Boyle 1982). Thus, postwildfire debris management must address not only the charred remnants of people's lives, but also the potential threat of sedimentary runoff.

Hazardous Materials

In both natural and hazardous-materials disasters, care must be taken to manage hazardous waste. Households contain chemicals, paints, pesticides, and other items that have to be separated for proper disposal. In the rush to return to normal, contractors and residents may not separate items immediately, requiring public education efforts and additional work crews to separate materials (EPA 1995). Hazardous waste, such as freon, must be taken from refrigerators carefully and disposed of properly. Food and waterborne diarrheal illnesses can result from animal and human waste, which can also promote the spread of hepatitis, parasites, and leptospirosis. Contamination from animal waste can disseminate coliforms (NC DHHS n.d.). North Carolina faced such a problem after Hurricane Dennis caused massive flooding. The eastern part of the state had as many as 9 million hogs. Extensive ponds with hog excrement flooded. Estimates vary, but as few as 28,000 to possibly several hundred thousand hogs perished. The USDA's Natural Resource Conservation Service assisted with animal disposal methods, which included burial, composting, and incineration. An emergency conservation program assessed streams for wastewater contamination (NRCS 1999).

Terrorism

The events of September 11 in New York City, Washington, D.C., and Pennsylvania—coupled with domestic attacks on Oklahoma City and through anthrax contamination in the mail—have increased our awareness of how debris management must be included for long-term recovery after terrorist attacks. The World Trade Center attack produced over 1.5 million tons of mixed construction debris (Swan 2002). The attack destroyed seven buildings, including the North and South Towers of the World Trade Center, which collapsed onto the Custom House and damaged the Tishman Center. Other damaged buildings included the Marriott Hotel, the World Financial Center, the Verizon Building, and the Bankers Trust Building. Over 3,000 vehicles were destroyed. Dust up to several inches deep covered Manhattan and infiltrated homes and buildings for blocks (Swan 2002). As described earlier in this chapter, debris management must be coupled with great sensitivity for the human impact. Debris teams must also collaborate with investigative agencies collecting evidence.

Problems Specific to Debris

A number of problems have been revealed in the previous examples, scenarios, and tables. Consideration of these problems specific to debris management emerges as a prerequisite for any planning effort.

Landfills

As Hurricanes Iniki and Hugo demonstrated, large-scale events can spawn massive amounts of debris. The question is, where should we put it? Many of us simply place our garbage at the curb for removal, not thinking about where it goes. Or, we drop off our recyclables and think little of how it is moved, managed, and transformed. Three million cubic yards of debris generated by Hurricane Iniki on top of normal operations and capacities to staff, transport, sort, sell, and dispose of the waste materials can overwhelm local resources. In Kauai, for example, the only landfill offered less than four years' capacity prior to Hurricane Iniki. The hurricane created seven years' worth of "normal" refuse (Friesen, Harder, and Rifer 1994, 37). The best option in such circumstances is to separate, reduce, **reuse**, recycle, sell, and otherwise downsize the materials in what can be a time-consuming enterprise.

Geography

As Hurricane Iniki further demonstrates, location matters. Kauai is an island location, and transporting debris off-island was expensive and logistically challenging (Friesen, Harder, and Rifer 1994). Geographic locations also influence the type of debris that might be generated (Solis et al. 1995). Coastal and tropical communities hit by hurricanes, for example, are likely to face challenges with sand and leafy vegetation. Urban areas that experience ice storms will deal with fallen tree limbs, downed utility lines, and inaccessible roads. Rural locations may discover that high winds have removed valuable topsoil, complicating local agricultural production. Communities with significant industrial facilities, such as the oil and petroleum plants in Texas and Louisiana, may need to manage hazardous spills.

To think through the ways in which geography influences debris management, look around your community. You may discover that the uniqueness of the economy, the historic character of the residential sector, and the type of environmental riches found locally spell out the postdisaster debris challenges.

Work Crews and Safety

Media reports usually focus on the numbers of those killed and injured by the event, forgetting to acknowledge the postdisaster risks. Working with downed power lines, operating heavy machinery and chain saws, and being around potentially hazardous materials can cause health and safety issues for work crews and the general public. Because debris-removal crews may stay on-scene for some time, supervisors should understand the fatigue that comes with this work. The stress that culminates from such conditions, coupled with being away from home in what may be temporary and uncomfortable accommodations, should be thought through as well, particularly in scheduling work shifts, overtime, and time off (Solis et al. 1995). Injury prevention depends on these considerations.

Health and safety concerns should include protection from nails, glass, sharp metals, splintered wood, chemicals, asbestos, household wastes, biowastes, and more (Solis et al. 1995). To ensure that workers and the public remain safe, debris-management plans should include detailed procedures on how to educate those at risk on hazards and how to respond appropriately. Workers should be trained in the proper use of personal protective equipment and given frequent breaks, particularly in conditions of heat, humidity, extreme cold, and long hours. Supervisors should monitor compliance with safety procedures and intervene to correct situations where safety regulations are not being followed. Care should be taken in all areas of debris operations, from pickup to temporary storage to permanent disposal as well as sorting, use of heavy equipment, and working with debris that may contain asbestos or biohazards (FEMA 2007). Additional suggestions can be found in Box 4.2.

The Human Dimension

As you read this section, look around or reflect on what you have in your home or office. Items are not easily replaced, particularly those that represent emotional or symbolic attachments. Disasters destroy, bury, displace, and transport personal possessions, sometimes over long distances. With forethought, debris-management planning can help people retrieve meaningful items: photographs, a grandmother's china, rings, important papers and documents, antiques, or a wedding dress.

Imagine the cost to replace items in general. FEMA (IS-632) calculates losses for a 2000-square-foot house damaged in a two-foot flood this way:

- A 2000-square-foot home without basement × $77 square foot × 50% structural loss = $77,000
- Assume that 35% of the contents were lost = $53,900
- The grand total of $77,000 + $53,900 = $130,900 loss

BOX 4.2 WORKER SAFETY AND HEALTH CONSIDERATIONS

The Centers for Disease Control recommends a number of procedures to heighten disaster site safety relevant for debris-removal operations:

- Assign key personnel and alternates responsible for site safety.
- Describe risks associated with each operation conducted.
- Confirm that personnel are adequately trained to perform jobs.
- Assign a key person to handle volunteers.
- Describe the protective clothing and equipment to be worn by personnel during site operations.
- Describe site-specific medical surveillance requirements.
- Describe needed air monitoring, personnel monitoring, and environmental sampling.
- Describe actions to be taken to mitigate existing hazards (e.g., containment) to make work environments less hazardous.
- Define site control measures (e.g., secure the area) and include a site map.
- Establish decontamination procedures for personnel and equipment.

Public education campaigns, discussed later in this chapter, would be wise to integrate similar messages about public handling of debris into their outreach materials.

Source: CDC (2008)

The 1989 Loma Prieta earthquake brought buildings down in the Marina District of San Francisco. Fortunately, the anticipated fires did not reach most residential areas, thus presenting the possibility of retrieving lost items. Bulldozers moved into the debris pile, and then slowly pulled back. Residents moved forward carefully to examine and pull out what they could. They set items inside a barricaded ring for owners to claim. Out at the landfill, volunteer crews and staff from garbage companies and public works crews kept their eyes open for such things as rings and tried to match items to owners (Brickner 1994).

On a more serious level, debris management must also be concerned with events caused by terrorism. Before debris management can begin, and during the removal process itself, care must be taken to preserve evidence and to identify and safeguard human remains. At The World Trade Center, a multistep process evolved: spotters would watch during backhoe operations, stopping if human remains were seen; a second examination of the debris occurred just before removal to the landfill. Once at the landfill, additional reviewers searched debris moving along conveyor belts for human remains. Forensic anthropologists confirmed the remains that were then sent to the Disaster

Mortuary Response Team. DNA matching identified approximately half of the 20,000 recovered samples of human remains (Simpson and Stehr 2003).

Understanding the human losses associated with debris management can make the difficult process of planning for and dealing with the generated materials more meaningful. Removing the visible symbols of destruction can be psychologically restorative to those affected and potentially move them toward rebuilding and recovering. Returning lost possessions can bring hope and comfort and, ultimately, enable people to move through the grief connected to deep loss.

Debris Estimation

How much debris can a community anticipate? During the immediate response period, local emergency management agencies usually conduct preliminary damage assessments (see Chapter 3) to estimate losses and apply for state and federal assistance. Local staff members in public works, stormwater drainage, waste, and wastewater can help in the damage estimation process. Such information helps the local community develop contracts for removal, assess resources needed, identify locations for temporary storage and permanent disposal, and designate work teams to start what could be a long-term and arduous process.

Several ways to estimate debris can be used. Traditional methods rely on formulas developed by the U.S. Army Corps of Engineers. Depending on estimation skills and the ability to "see" through debris piles (which may contain voids), those estimations can vary—but they serve as a standard starting point. Emerging strategies to conduct debris estimation include aerial and satellite imagery.

Quantitative estimates are usually calculated in cubic yards or tons. For example, a debris pile is usually calculated by length times width times height divided by 27 to equal the estimated cubic yards (Swan 2000). As part of the quantification, estimation crews have to identify location and debris type (FEMA IS-632; see Table 4.2). Mapping, including the integration of geographic information systems (GIS), to locate and prioritize removal is useful (EPA 1995); GIS can map out debris areas in residential areas, schools, business sectors, and critical infrastructure (FEMA IS-632).

Let us consider the challenges associated with a particular type of hazard, a major hurricane. The U.S. Army Corps of Engineers (USACE, see FEMA IS-632) identifies two broad categories for events such as a hurricane, although these categories also represent the types of debris anticipated from other events as well. These two categories are clean woody debris and mixed **construction and demolition debris** (C&D). If a public education campaign has been launched as part of the debris-management plan (see upcoming sections in this chapter), then the public should immediately sort

TABLE 4.2 Debris-Pile Calculations

Debris Type	Calculations
One-story building	L′ × W′ × H′ / 27 = _____ cy × 0.33 = _____ cy (the 0.33 estimates the open air space within the home)
Mobile homes	Single wide = 290 cy (calculated as a solid cube and a total loss) Double wide = 450 cy (calculated as a solid cube and a total loss)
Personal property	Flooded home without a basement = 25–30 cy Flooded home with a basement = 45–50 cy
Trees	15 trees, 8 inches in diameter = average of 40 cy 8′–10′ root = takes one flatbed trailer to move
Vegetative cover (for additional square footage of houses, see FEMA IS-632, Job Aid 9580.1)	1600-square-foot house with no vegetative cover = 98 cy For light cover, 98 cy × 1.1 For medium cover, 98 cy × 1.3 For heavy cover, 98 cy × 1.5

Source: Federal Emergency Management Administration, FEMA Independent Study 632.

debris into these two types. While emergency road clearance is absolutely necessary, cleanup crews, contractors, and residents must be immediately advised to develop separate piles and not push more onto the roadside piles. Communities that do not do so face longer debris-recovery time periods and additional, often extensive, efforts to separate materials.

For events such as hurricanes, the U.S. Army Corps of Engineers (USACE) estimates that 30% of the piles will contain clean, woody debris that can be mulched, recycled, or reused. The remaining 70% C&D will include (see FEMA IS-632):

- 42% burnable items that require sorting
- 5% soil
- 15% metals
- 38% landfill material

For a total of 7 million cubic yards (cy) of debris, 2.1 million cy would thus be clean, woody debris, and 4.9 million cy would be mixed C&D. To deal with the C&D material:

- 2,058,000 million cy can be burned
- 245,000 cy can be potentially reused as soil if properly handled
- 735,000 cy of metal can potentially be salvaged and sold to scrap-metal dealers
- 1,862,000 cy can be sent to landfills

Given the aforementioned problems with landfill capacity and the costs of managing debris, calculating debris-pile content to devise a management strategy can result in reduced effects on work crews, landfills, and the environment, and it can also generate funds to pay for debris removal. Given the financial and human impact of a lingering recovery, the effort is well worth it.

Debris-Management Planning

As encouraged in Chapter 3 (Disaster Recovery Planning), advance efforts to identify and address the logistical challenges of debris removal can expedite a community's recovery process. The debris-management planning and operations cycle can be described in four stages: normal operations, increased readiness, response, and recovery (Swan 2000).

Normal operations represent the optimal time period to conduct planning. Local planners should look for and encourage a variety of partners to join the planning process, as more perspectives bring a wider view of options, encourage partnerships, provide more realistic assessments of what can be done, and encourage pre-event communications (Swan 2000). In short, face-to-face interaction among all key partners makes for a more effective postevent recovery. Identification of temporary storage and permanent disposal sites should occur during normal operations, as well as designing appropriate types of contracts (described later in this chapter) and procedures to monitor contracts (Swan 2000). Further, this time period can serve as an opportunity to spur local **recycling**, **reduction**, and reuse efforts.

During increased readiness, an event may be imminent or a hazard season may be about to start, such as the start of tornado season on March 1 or hurricane season on June 1. Staff should be further identified and trained, including those responsible for generating contracts, ensuring that federal accounting regulations are adhered to, and launching public education campaigns. During this time, planners can review and update plans, contact key partners, and train work staff. The full array of partners from local through federal should be contacted, with an updating of phone numbers and other contact information.

The response phase usually involves public works and sanitation crews clearing roadways for search and rescue work. Debris-management teams should work closely with those conducting damage assessments. Contracts must be initiated and carefully reviewed. Interaction between local and state agencies and, in the case of a presidentially declared disaster, various federal agencies is initiated (Swan 2000). This time period lays the foundation for expedited, careful, and appropriate removal. An urge to return to normalcy can be anticipated; thus communities that plan for debris removal will ensure that their communities move into the recovery phase in a realistic, environmentally safe, and humanistic manner.

Recovery time periods may go on for some time, even years. These time periods can take a toll on work staff; thus careful management of and appreciation for the human resources involved is necessary. As one planner in Sandusky, Ohio, said after a major storm, "We did everything wrong." By trying to remove debris quickly and without a plan, an even "greater mess" was created (Steuteville 1992b). Planning, then, emerges as the single best strategy for debris management.

The Planning Team and Process

Debris-management planning starts with identifying the local, regional, and state partners that need to be involved in the process. The team may consist of more players than you think because of the many challenges that can arise in a particularly large disaster. Local departments of public/street works, stormwater drainage, waste and wastewater management, utility companies, fleet management (gas, maintenance of vehicles), landfill operators, engineers, environmental specialists, recycling coordinators and operators, and even public education specialists, elected officials, accountants, and legal experts will need to either be centrally involved or included in operations training.

Once the key members of the local debris-management team are in place, planning can commence. The next tasks involve assessing local issues and capacities, writing a plan, and training those likely to become involved in debris operations. Box 4.3 details some of the general tasks recommended for debris-management plans. Developing an organizational chart to show the lines of communication and levels of authority will be useful. Care should be taken to keep and update a list of contact information for each key person. A debris manager and deputy managers should be designated to guide the planning team and coordinate actual operations. Once the plan is written, a training schedule should be developed to apprise each person of operational procedures and ensure that a smooth transition can occur when disaster strikes (FEMA IS-632).

Local teams should identify the full range of potential regional, state, and federal partners that may become involved, and then develop a plan to expand their team to include these key members. At the regional and state level, it will be necessary to identify agencies and organizations with key resources, including recycling and waste expertise, available landfill space, extra vehicles and personnel, and expertise in funding debris operations. Through mutual aid agreements, these partners can be brought in to help with local operations. And, because disasters cross jurisdictions, working across political and legal boundaries from the start will improve operational coordination and collaboration. Additional information on the federal role can be found later in this chapter.

BOX 4.3   KEY ELEMENTS FOR DEBRIS-MANAGEMENT PLANNING

- Debris-management team
  - Organizational chart
    - Members, agencies, and roles (local)
    - Expansion to include regional and state (mutual aid)
    - Expansion to include federal partners (FEMA, USACE, EPA)
  - Contact information (updated regularly)
  - Regular schedule of training
- Hazard identification and debris types
- Damage-assessment process
- Debris-estimation procedures
- Capacity assessment
  - Linking to existing efforts
    - Recycling programs
    - Solid-waste management planning
  - Landfills, temporary sites
    - Environmental impact
  - Reduction strategies
    - Reduce, reuse, recycle, incineration
  - Transportation assets
- Environmental issues
  - Hazardous materials
  - Household hazardous waste
  - Air, water, soil
  - Erosion
- Historical issues
- Phase I: initial response
  - Road clearance
  - Public education
- Phase II: recovery
  - Working with FEMA and the National Response Plan (ESF-3)
  - Temporary sites
  - Permanent disposal
  - Contract monitoring
- End of operations
  - Site closure
  - Environmental assessment and restoration
  - Financial compensation
- Annexes
  - Mapping
  - Public information plan (media and citizens)
  - Mutual aid agreements
  - Health and safety procedures
  - Accounting procedures

- Prewritten ordinances
- Draft contracts
  - Time and materials
- Legal matters
  - Right of entry
  - Hold harmless
  - Levels of authority
  - Condemnations
- Post-event evaluation
  - Timeline for debriefing and revisions to the plan

Sources: FEMA (2007); Solis et al. (1995); FEMA (IS-632); EPA (1995)

Legal Issues

Section 504 of the Stafford Act specifies that the federal government can provide assistance during times of emergency. However, there are certain legal issues that need to be considered. For example, if you are an absent homeowner or renter, would you want someone coming into your home to remove items without your knowledge or approval? Residents must move their debris to the curbside for pickup. Homeowners and renters must work with their insurance agents to obtain any allowable funds to cover debris removal, demolition, and clearing a foundation slab. These items are not always covered by insurance.

In some circumstances, such as when public health, public safety, or economic recovery is threatened, officials may remove debris from your property. In situations where owners lack insurance coverage and cannot pay for removal costs, legal condemnation can occur. First, local municipalities have to secure what are called "right of entry" or "hold harmless" agreements. Care must be taken to ensure, as well, that local historic and cultural treasures are not damaged in such a removal. FEMA can provide assistance with these procedures.

Debris-Reduction Methods

Recall the previous debris-estimation section, where the USACE broke hurricane debris down into two categories of woody debris and mixed C&D. Based on their example of 7 million cubic yards of mixed C&D, burning will reduce volume by 95%. Chipping and grinding can reduce woody debris by 4:1 or about 75% (FEMA IS-632). What options are there to reduce debris in an environmentally friendly manner?

Recycling

We are fortunate to be living in a time when recycling has become commonplace in many communities. Municipalities often sponsor periodic hazardous-waste disposal days for paint, pesticides, and other household disposables (see Photos 4.2 and 4.3). This existing culture of recycling can be used to reduce the amount of materials that go to temporary sites and permanent landfills. The environmental impact is obvious, but the economic benefits are important as well. After Northridge, FEMA paid for a debris-recycling program. During a one-month period, the average fee for the recycling facility was $21.55 per ton, in contrast to $24.92 per ton at other disposal facilities. Indirect costs for recycling were also lower, including transportation and staff time (EPA 1995). A surprising amount of debris can be recycled, as seen in Table 4.3.

Incineration

Debris can also be reduced through burning. Uncontrolled, open-air incineration does not allow for environmental control and is not usually recommended. Imagine the potential impact on local air quality, especially for

PHOTO 4.2 Many communities hold a household hazardous-waste recycling day. Encouraging these activities reduces potential hazardous debris that can be strewn by a disaster. (Photo by Brenda Phillips. With permission.)

PHOTO 4.3   Households can hold a variety of potentially hazardous materials. (Photo by Don Bishop. With permission.)

children and adults with breathing problems such as asthma or chronic obstructive pulmonary disease. Similarly, uncontrolled burning may spark wildfires. If incineration is used, it should be limited to woody, vegetative debris. Consider how long it would take to extinguish a debris pile that contained tires, fuels, or other potentially explosive materials (FEMA 2007, 44).

A feasible option is to use controlled, open-air incineration. Such burning of clean, woody debris produces minimal damage to the environment, but it should be limited to less urban areas. The ash by-product can be used as a soil supplement in agricultural production (FEMA 2007, 44). Controlled incineration includes two methods: air-curtain pit incineration and portable air-curtain incineration.

An air-curtain incineration procedure involves digging a pit and installing a blower unit. The blower feeds air to the fire and traps smoke and small particles. Incineration can burn up to 25 tons per hour if proper controls and construction methods are followed. Portable **air-curtain incinerators** use a premanufactured pit rather than one dug on site. Careful environmental controls, when followed, reduce the impact on the public. Thus incineration represents an effective reduction strategy that can spare landfill capacity and offer a cost-effective solution. Environmental controls can be set for smoke density, explosion prevention, and hazardous materials release

TABLE 4.3 Recycling Opportunities after Disaster

Debris Material	Opportunity	Used after:
Mud, sand, dirt	Screened and shaken, and assessed for potential toxicity, can be used for topsoil in agricultural production or residential areas, or as landfill cover	Missouri floods, 1993
Shingles	Ground up, can be used for resurfacing asphalt roads	Hurricane Iniki, 1992
Metals from mobile homes, porches, vehicles	Sort using electromagnets and sell to scrap dealers.	Missouri floods, 1993
White goods (appliances)	Sell to scrap dealers	Missouri floods, 1993
Building materials	Sell or give away to restore centers: vinyl siding, windows, cabinets, insulation, appliances, furniture, electrical cables, studs, etc.	Missouri floods, 1993
Trees, limbs	Make into mulch, compost, firewood, charcoal, and boiler fuel; distribute to residences, parks, businesses, paper mills, schools, companies using boilers	Hurricane Andrew, 1992 Hurricane Hugo, 1989 Hurricane Iniki, 1992 Hurricane Mitch, 1998 Loma Prieta earthquake, 1989
Historic elements	Set aside for use on rebuilt buildings	Lancaster, TX, tornado, 1994 Loma Prieta earthquake, 1989
Concrete and road materials	Reuse as a road base or for coastal reclamation as allowed by environmental laws	Kobe earthquake, 1995

Source: EPA (1995); FEMA (2007); Brickner (1994); Hayashi and Katsumi (1996).

or contamination (FEMA 2007). Locating the pits requires care as well. You can imagine what would happen if the incineration caused a debris fire at a temporary site with tons of debris across 100 acres.

Grinding and Chipping

Woody, vegetative debris can be reduced through various grinding and chipping methods. Grinding and chipping can reduce at a 4:1 volume ratio, meaning that four cubic yards can be reduced to one cubic yard. While this reduction is not as effective as incineration, the reuse of clean debris through grinding and chipping can be beneficial economically and environmentally. Local communities can sell the mulch and wood chips or offer them to public schools, health-care facilities, and agricultural areas. In areas where topsoil has been removed by a natural hazard, such reuse can help restore topsoil and keep plants and crops moist (FEMA 2007, 47).

Grinders are used to handle large amounts of debris, but they do require a large area to stockpile the resulting mulch. In previous disasters, though, the mulch has proven quite popular with residents, landscapers, and others eager to restore an aesthetic quality to their damaged properties. Thus, although the mulch may quickly pile up, having a plan in place to disperse the mulch may be a good idea. **Chippers** are used to chop up brush from downed limbs and trees. Doing so allows the mulch to be used locally and reduces transportation costs (FEMA 2007, 48).

After Hurricane Iniki, officials worked with FEMA and expert consultants to identify options for reducing, reusing, and recycling debris. In Kauai County, debris-management teams separated green waste for mulch, sold wood to a sugar plantation for use in its boiler system, sold scrap metal to a metals market, established a reuse center for building materials, and ground asphalt shingles up for use as road base (Friesen, Harder, and Rifer 1994).

Reuse

Residents and municipality leaders may want to think creatively about how to reuse materials. Many communities now include "re-stores" that recycle doors, windows, cupboards, cabinets, hinges, doorknobs, and other construction materials. Imagine what a forward-thinking community could do with a demolition crew of scout troops to reduce the effects on the local landfill, reuse materials for a good cause, and help residents start their rebuilding process. Many voluntary organizations may also come to help with the rebuilding after a disaster. Some of these organizations may set up operations for years, and they are prime candidates for refurbishing and using abandoned tables, chairs, and other furniture in their temporary lodgings.

After the 1993 Midwest floods, Lincoln County in Missouri brought in county crews to retrieve siding, windows, shingles, insulation, cabinets, rafters, decks, and more from destroyed homes. Demolition contractors were then allowed to sell or donate these items. Scrap dealers were allowed to take appliances (EPA 1995). After Hurricane Andrew, Louisiana State University used a grinder borrowed from a local paper mill to process downed trees. After reducing the woody material, LSU used the mulch to cover tree roots on campus (Steuteville 1992b).

Planning for the Action Stages

Debris operations are launched in two stages: initial response and recovery. The first stage, initial response, starts during the emergency response time period and aids with life-saving activities. The second stage, recovery, moves the community through reconstruction.

Phase I: Initial Response

In the immediate aftermath, debris-management operations can and will save lives and expedite the community's recovery. During Phase I, FEMA (2007) specifies the priority of emergency roadway debris clearance. Think about the impact of a major disaster on your hometown—which roads would need to be cleared first? Certainly the highest priority should go to major arteries, particularly those that allow for travel by ambulances, fire trucks, and police cars. Roads into government offices should take priority next so that officials and employees can access resources and lead the response and recovery. Roads into neighborhoods need to be cleared as well as routes leading into key businesses like pharmacies, medical supply companies, and grocery stores. Areas with congregate populations—assisted-living facilities, state schools, and nursing homes—should also get priority.

Emergency road clearance typically involves pushing debris to the roadside into nonseparated piles. Such actions can be misleading to the public, who may now think that a roadside is where they should move their household debris. The existence of a rapid public-education campaign can help in avoiding this response (see upcoming section) and ultimately reduce the costs of hiring contractors to separate items for proper disposal. Local municipalities may want to offer a "time and materials" contract to move debris quickly by bringing in outside equipment and labor. Such contracts are limited to 70 hours of work and can be awarded to noncity companies, such as local construction firms (FEMA 2007). When roadsides are relatively clear, debris operations can move into the next stage of the recovery.

Phase II: Recovery and Operations

As a society, we have a tendency to take solid-waste management for granted until there is a problem picking up garbage or until the local landfill reaches capacity. The crews who remove our waste often work out of our sight, while we are asleep or at work. We may not realize how important they are to preserving our environmental integrity through proper disposal, nor do we stop to think about the conditions that these crews work under—in high heat and humidity or extreme cold. Yet, these crews represent the advance guard in recovery operations by removing what the disaster has torn apart and disposing of it in a way that safeguards our personal and collective health.

During the long-term recovery operations, local officials need to continue to educate the public about curbside separation, and to work with contractors to sort items appropriately. FEMA recommends that locals monitor contractor activities, in part to keep costs down. For example, after the 1999 tornados in Oklahoma, red mud covered everything. As mud dries, it may become necessary to water it down to prevent contaminating the area, contributing to breathing problems, or eroding the topsoil. However, water increases the weight of a debris pile, as do dirt and sand. Because contractors are paid by the weight of the load on a truck, water can significantly increase the cost to local and federal agencies. Contractors are also carefully monitored to ensure that they separate the debris as instructed and that separated items are sent to the proper facilities for incineration, scrap-metal sorting, plastics recycling, and other appropriate reduction measures (FEMA 2007).

Two types of contracts can be used during Phase II: unit-price and lump-sum contracts. The unit-price contract is awarded when the amount and type of debris remain uncertain, thus allowing for the amount and type of work to be adjusted. However, strict accounting procedures must be conducted to verify the actual amounts that are hauled and discarded. Lump-sum contracts can be offered as well. These contracts spell out a fixed price for a fixed amount of work to be undertaken. Lump-sum contracts can be awarded for area or pass methods. The area methods specify a geographic area where the contractor goes through once to pick up debris. The pass method would hire the contractor to pass through a community once a week for three weeks for a fixed fee. As with other contracts, loads and disposal must be carefully monitored and inspected for separation, contamination, and even fraud.

Working with FEMA and the National Response Plan (ESF-3)

In presidentially declared disasters, FEMA may offer assistance through its Public Assistance Program (see Chapter 1 for the definition of a presidentially declared disaster—and the resultant federal response—and Chapter 15 for FEMA's Public Assistance Program). In some circumstances, the National Response Framework (NRF, see Chapter 3) may be activated. When this occurs, Emergency Support Function 3 (ESF-3), "Public Works," provides support to affected jurisdictions. The U.S. Army Corps of Engineers serves as the lead agency for ESF-3, supported by the fuller set of FEMA officials and related agencies working as partners under the National Response Plan (NRP).

Under ESF-3, FEMA can provide considerable assistance. Personnel who can support local and state authorities include:

- The Public Assistance Officer (PAO) and a deputy PAO for debris form a Debris Coordinating Committee to work with the State PAO and local officials.

- The deputy PAO manages debris assignments, which are usually termed "missions."
- A debris advisor provides expertise and advice to the Debris Coordinating Committee and Deputy PAO for debris. The debris advisor also works with the U.S. Army Corps of Engineers.
- A debris specialist helps applicants to work through the application, paperwork, and related requirement procedures.
- Other personnel may include an attorney, a public information officer, and environmental officers. Technical contractors may provide even more-specific support (FEMA 2007).

Missions may be awarded to remove debris from roadways and take it to temporary or permanent disposal sites, to support monitoring of contractors, and to demolish damaged structures. States request these missions when they are unable to handle the debris situation (FEMA 2007).

FEMA and other agencies can provide considerable support and expertise when local and state officials lack resources to manage the debris and especially when a debris-management plan has not been completed. However, municipalities must be extremely careful to follow federal regulations and procedures to develop contracts, sites, and accounting procedures to ensure reimbursement. FEMA can provide for up to 75% of the costs of debris removal, which can save local taxpayers a lot of money.

Temporary Sites

Temporary sites must be developed, monitored, and maintained so that debris can be effectively reduced and separated. Without a temporary site plan in place, recovery efforts will lag, resulting in potentially significant logistical and environmental problems (Friesen, Harder, and Rifer 1994). Kauai staff dealing with Hurricane Iniki debris had to shut down temporary sites in order to train staff more effectively. Some efforts took time to put into place, including a means for monitoring debris, managing odors, and reducing water runoff that could cause environmental contamination.

Temporary debris-storage sites need to be assessed for their potential environmental impact. Ideally, the temporary site will not contaminate water, soil, or air during operations. Think about the types of debris mentioned in the first part of this chapter. How would you prepare a site to receive these materials? FEMA (2007) suggests that temporary sites may need liners to be placed so that ash, hazardous waste, and fuels do not seep into the ground and local watershed. Efforts need to be made to prevent or reduce effects from hazardous spills. See Box 4.4 for criteria to establish temporary debris-storage and -reduction sites (TDSR).

> ## BOX 4.4 TEMPORARY DEBRIS STORAGE AND REDUCTION SITES (TDSR) CRITERIA
>
> - Site ownership
>   - Public or private lands? How long are they available? Is there a cost?
> - Site size
>   - One hundred acres per one million cubic yards of debris are required. Is the site large enough to allow for sorting, ingress/egress, monitoring, storage, and reduction methods?
> - Site location
>   - Can equipment be moved in, out of, and around the site easily? Is the site close to good transportation routes? Is there a potential for groundwater or wetlands contamination? What is the environmental condition before use? Are there any threatened or endangered species or sensitive ecosystems? Has the site been assessed for historic or archaeological sites? Will site use have an impact on area residences and businesses?
>
> *Source:* FEMA (2007)

The temporary site also has to be in a convenient location, but one that does not increase traffic congestion. Remember, the roads may be blocked or closed after disaster! Likewise, temporary sites should be away from residential areas to avoid noxious fumes and their potential impact on persons with breathing problems. Vehicles also need to be able to move easily through the site so that inspections, monitoring, and dumping can proceed without delays. Temporary sites mean exactly that as well: they are temporary. Debris must be "constantly flowing" to keep the reduction efforts underway and to move remaining debris to area landfills (FEMA 2007). Once operations have ended, another environmental assessment needs to be prepared to determine any effects from contamination and to specify correct remedial actions that can be taken. State and federal environmental protection agencies should be partners in this process. Ideally, the site will return to its predebris operational status.

Hurricane Andrew in 1992 quickly overwhelmed local recycling centers. Metro-Dade County then used parks as neighborhood staging areas for residential recycling of the countless downed trees and limbs. Together, they mulched half a million tons of wood waste that was then used on other parks, agricultural areas (a foundation for the area's economy), and residential properties (EPA 1995). By using their plan's debris-management strategy and educating the public, the county reduced the impact on landfills—a good outcome considering the annual threat of hurricanes in this part of the nation.

Permanent Sites—Landfills

Existing landfills across the United States include those that accept municipal solid waste, bioreactor waste, construction and demolition debris, and industrial waste (EPA 2007). Although **landfill** capacity is available nationwide, specific areas report problems with the lifespans of their landfills (EPA 2006). The total number of landfills appears to have declined in recent years, but 30 states are adding landfill capacity (Simmons et al. 2006). Disasters can claim that life span overnight. Thus, careful use of permanent landfills has to be ensured so that we do not shortchange ourselves for routine solid-waste disposal. Generation of municipal solid waste increases annually, and evidence suggests that the per-person amount of waste generation has risen over the past several decades (EPA 2006).

Close to 3,500 communities offer yard trimmings composting programs, and recycling recovered 79 million tons of municipal solid waste in 2005 (EPA 2006). Recycling and other reduction programs across the United States have made a difference—an effort that you can participate in by encouraging recycling in your home and community. By 2005, curbside recycling programs had developed in 8,550 communities across the nation (EPA 2006), although some states have reduced their programs (Simmons et al. 2006).

Use of existing landfills must be undertaken with great care. First, pre-identification can map out locations for disposal of particular items. Second, coordination with solid-waste managers can streamline debris removal and disposal processes. Careful oversight will be required to ensure that soil and groundwater contamination does not occur in permanent landfills. Third, extraordinary efforts may need to be taken to reduce, reuse, incinerate, and recycle materials, as described earlier in this chapter.

For terrorism events, care must be taken to assist other agencies involved in investigation and criminal prosecution. The September 11 attack on New York City destroyed Building 7, which had included the NYC Office of Emergency Management and an FBI office. On-site debris removal required careful excavation and examination for weapons, ammunition, and evidence from prior cases. As debris-removal teams moved materials from Ground Zero (Photo 4.4) to the Fresh Kills landfill on Staten Island, FBI agents worked through the debris by hand. Once at the landfill, front-loader operators spread the debris onto a large area for examination. FBI agents and police officers then searched the scene using rakes or by hand. Following this procedure, a bucket-loader operator took the material to another area, where work crews used shaker screens to find further items, including human remains and personal items (Swan 2002). Overall, debris was sorted and examined between four and six times, through 1.5 million tons of material. Debris management thus required collaboration of the FBI, first responders (fire and police), contractors, and city officials. Particular care was taken to

PHOTO 4.4   By March 2002, more than 1.4 million tons of debris had been removed from the area around Ground Zero in New York City. (Photo by Larry Lerner/FEMA News Photo. With permission.)

observe, retrieve, and identify human remains. The Smithsonian National Museum of American History has immortalized retrieved items in an exhibit, such as a calculator, an identification badge, a door from a NYC fire truck, a piece of an airplane, and various documents. (The exhibit can also be viewed online at http://americanhistory.si.edu/september11/.)

Public Education Campaigns

By educating the public about disaster debris, we can reduce materials placed into landfills and raise cash to offset costs (Friesen, Harder, and Rifer 1994). Involving the public requires a preplanned educational program that starts, ideally, even before the disaster strikes. Citizens should know where to find information about debris management. The community's Web site is a good place to start teaching citizens to separate out flammable and nonflammable debris as well as recyclable household hazardous waste. The media can prepare public information messages, send reporters to cover debris sites, and encourage residents to participate. Media coverage can reach many people quickly, relieving the burden on the debris-management team.

Other public education strategies can include door-to-door information distribution. Working with neighborhood associations, schools, libraries, disaster assistance locations, places of worship, grocery stores, and restaurants can also aid information dissemination. Think also about the types of information that will be needed: debris pick-up schedules, separation and disposal procedures, what to do with hazardous waste, how to identify debris workers, where to get more information, and how to report illegal dumping. Residents who are elderly or disabled will need to know where and how to access public assistance (FEMA 2007). After the Northridge earthquake, officials set up a multilingual phone bank with operators who spoke English, Spanish, and Korean (EPA 1995).

Citizens may also worry about city entry onto their property and their rights regarding such entry, how condemnations and demolitions may be handled by the city, and which agencies to contact regarding concerns. They may wonder, "Who are those people in the haz-mat suits, and what are they doing in my garbage? Is something in there that could hurt me?" A public education campaign that outlines procedures, identifies personnel and removal times, and spells out citizen rights and responsibilities is necessary. Debris-management planning invites citizens to be part of an environmentally friendly debris-removal effort.

Hurricane Katrina

The challenges described in this chapter for debris management became evident after Hurricane Katrina. In August 2008, the U.S. Government Accountability Office released a report indicating that "nearly 3 years later, the New Orleans area still faces significant debris management issues and challenges." By July 2008, FEMA estimated that it had provided funding for 16,900 home demolitions, while another 6,100 awaited demolition. Total debris estimation in the New Orleans area alone surpassed 100 million cubic yards, or twice that of Hurricane Andrew (GAO 2008). Debris removal was so massive that restrictions were eased for disposition of some materials. Nonetheless, the Louisiana Department of Environmental Quality issued over 100 enforcement actions for violations. Approximately half involved solid waste, hazardous waste, or water contamination. Among the actionable violations were the presence of unauthorized waste at C&D sites, including tires, medical waste, and creosote telephone poles; failure to cover waste with soil as required; failure to meet effluent limitations; and inadequate supervision at the landfill sites. Air-quality violations included failures to manage asbestos-containing materials. Efforts to manage the debris, control illegal dumping, monitor disposal sites, and move the recovery forward will continue for years.

Summary

This chapter provides an overview of the debris-management planning process, which includes preplanning for debris scenarios, particularly those for specific hazards. Additional steps in the debris-management process include emergency response to remove roadway debris for lifesaving efforts. In the recovery stage, debris-management teams work to reduce the amount of debris through various reduction efforts, including recycling, reuse, and incineration. Local jurisdictions should plan debris management carefully, following federal regulations to safeguard the environment, save funds, and protect worker safety. Temporary sites for debris must be set up, monitored for compliance with federal regulations, and then returned to a predisaster state. Permanent sites should be used at minimal levels to reduce overall effects on local landfills. A public education effort will have to be launched to ensure that the public participates in separating and reducing debris from households, particularly hazardous household waste.

Debris-management teams pave the way for the recovery. Until the debris is removed, residents cannot rebuild and businesses cannot reopen. Debris management represents the single most important action that can safeguard environmental resources. Debris-management teams thus launch the disaster recovery effort. In the next chapter, we will see how important their actions are as we discuss disasters and environmental recovery.

Study Guide

Summary Questions

1. What kinds of debris can various disasters generate?
2. Describe the kinds of problems that can be expected during the debris-management process.
3. How can different kinds of debris be estimated? For example, how much debris might a one-story building or a mobile home generate in a massive tornado?
4. What key stages must be involved in a debris-management planning process?
5. How can debris be reduced?
6. What are the differences in how temporary and permanent debris sites are managed?
7. How can the federal government assist local municipalities with debris removal?

Discussion Questions

1. In thinking about the most common hazards that have impacted your community, what types of debris should you expect to see after an event?
2. What do you see as the different debris challenges created by natural materials, hazardous materials, and terrorism events?

3. What kinds of additional hazards can occur if debris is not managed correctly? Think about flash flooding, environmental contamination, and diseases.
4. Are there any existing programs in your community for recycling, reduction, and reuse? Look beyond the local recycling bins and search for businesses that grind mulch, salvage scrap metal, and reuse building materials.
5. How many years will it take to fill up the local landfill? What would happen if an event generated five years worth of debris overnight?
6. Look at a listing of city offices. Can you identify potential partners in a debris-management planning process such as public works, stormwater management, and waste and wastewater management?
7. Does your community have a debris-management plan? What would you recommend as design elements of such a plan or to refine an existing plan?
8. What strategies would work best in your community to educate the public both before and after a debris-generating event?

Key Terms

Air-curtain incinerator
Chipper
Construction and demolition debris (C&D)
Debris
Debris management
Debris-management team
Grinder
Landfill
Recycling
Reduction
Reuse

References

American Society of Civil Engineers. 2005. Report Card for America's Infrastructure. Washington D.C.: American Society of Civil Engineers.

Brickner, R. 1994. How to manage disaster debris. *C&D Debris Recycling* April: 8–13.

Boyle, G. 1982. Erosion from burned watersheds in San Bernardino National Forest. In *Proceedings of the symposium on dynamics and management of Mediterranean-type ecosystems*, ed. C. E. Conrad and W. C. Oechel, 409–410. USDA Forest Service Report PSW-58.

CDC. 2002. Self-reported increase in asthma severity after the September 11 attacks on the World Trade Center—Manhattan, New York, 2001. *Morbidity and Mortality Weekly Report* 51: 781–784.

CDC. 2008. Suggested guidance for supervisors at disaster rescue sites: Site safety checklist. Centers for Disease Control. http://www.cdc.gov/niosh/emhaz2.html#checklist.

EPA.1995. *Planning for disaster debris*. Washington, DC: U.S. Environmental Protection Agency.

EPA. 2006. *Municipal solid waste in the United States: 2005 facts and figures*. Washington, DC: U.S. Environmental Protection Agency. www.epa.gov/osw/nonhaz/municipal/pubs/mswcharo5.pdf.

EPA. 2007. Solid waste landfills. Washington, DC: U.S. Environmental Protection Agency. www.epa.gov/epaoswer/non-hw/muncpl/landfill/sw_landfill.htm.

Fagan, J., S. Galea, J. Ahern, S. Bonner, and D. Vlahov. 2003. Relationship of self-reported asthma severity and urgent health care utilization to psychological sequelae of the September 11, 2001 terrorist attacks on the World Trade Center among New York City area residents. *Psychosomatic Medicine* 65: 993–996. http://www.psychosomatic-medicine.org/cgi/content/abstract/65/6/993/.

FEMA. 2007. FEMA 325. Washington, DC: Federal Emergency Management Agency. http://www.fema.gov/government/grant/pa/demagde.shtm.

FEMA. 2008. Understanding your risks: Identifying hazards and estimating losses. FEMA 386-2. Washington, DC: Federal Emergency Management Agency.

FEMA. n.d. Independent study 632: Debris operations. FEMA IS-632. Washington, DC: Federal Emergency Management Agency. http://training.fema.gov/IS/crslist.asp.

Friesen, G., J. Harder, and W. Rifer. 1994. Closing the loop after the storm. *Resource Recycling* 37–44.

GAO. 2007. World Trade Center: EPA's most recent test and clean program raises concerns that need to be addressed to better prepare for indoor contamination following disasters. GAO-07-1091. Washington, DC: General Accountability Office.

GAO. 2008. Hurricane Katrina: Continuing debris removal and disposal issues. GAO-08-985R. Washington, DC: General Accountability Office.

Hayashi, H., and T. Katsumi. 1996. Generation and management of disaster waste. *Soils and Foundations* January: 349–358.

Landrigan, P., P. J. Lioy, G. Thurston, G. Berkowitz, L..C. Chen, S. N. Chillrud, S. H. Gavett, P. G. Georgopoulos, A. S. Geyh, S. Levin, F. Perera, S. M. Rappaport, C. Small, and NIEHS World Trade Center Working Group. 2004. Health and environmental consequences of the World Trade Center disaster. *Environmental Health Perspectives* 112 (6): 731–739. http://www.ehponline.org/members/2004/6702/6702.html.

Lauter, L. 2006. *Disaster debris removal after Hurricane Katrina*. Washington, DC: Congressional Research Service.

Lauter, L. 2006. Disaster debris removal after Hurricane Katrina: Status and associated issues. Washington D.C.: CRC Report for Congress.

Lin, S., S. Lin, J. Reibman, J. A. Bowers, S.-A. Hwang, A. Hoerning, M. I. Gomez, and E. F. Fitzgerald. 2005. Respiratory symptoms and other health effects among residents living near the World Trade Center. *American Journal of Epidemiology* 162 (6): 499–507. http://aje.oxfordjournals.org/cgi/content/full/162/6/499/.

Malievskaya, E., N. Rosenberg, and S. Markowitz. 2002. Assessing the health of immigrant workers near Ground Zero: Preliminary results of the World Trade Center Day Laborer Medical Monitoring Project. *American Journal of Industrial Medicine* 42 (6): 548–549. http://www3.interscience.wiley.com/journal/100520074/abstract?CRETRY=1&SRETRY=0.

National Hurricane Center. n.d. Hurricane Hugo. http://www.nhc.noaa.gov/HAW2/english/history.shtml#hugo.

Nemery, B. 2003. Reactive fallout of World Trade Center dust. *American Journal of Respiratory and Critical Care Medicine* 168: 2–3.

NC DHHS. n.d. Public health and flood waters. North Carolina Department of Health and Human Services. www.dhhs.state.nc.us/docs/floodfaqs.htm.

NRCS. 1999. EWP aids livestock disposal. USDA/Natural Resources Conservation Service. http://www.nrcs.usda.gov/news/thisweek/1999/991203.html.

Parker, D. 1991. Response to the Oakland-Berkeley Hills conflagration. San Francisco Fire Department. www.sfmuseum.org/oakfire/contents.html.

Simmons, P., N. Goldstein, S. M. Kaufman, N. J. Themelis, and J. Thompson, Jr. 2006. The state of garbage in America. *BioCycle* 47 (4): 26.

Simpson, D., and S. Stehr. 2003. Victim management and identification after the World Trade Center collapse. In *Beyond September 11th: An account of post-disaster research*, ed. J. Monday, 109–120. Boulder, CO: University of Colorado.

Solis, G., H. Hightower, J. Sussex, J. Kawaguchi. 1995. Disaster debris management. Report for Emergency Preparedness Canada. University of British Columbia.

Spittler, T. 2005. California fires, floods and landslides. Presented at the Disaster Resistant California Conference. ftp://ftp.consrv.ca.gov/pub/dmg/thp/documents/memorandas/Landslides%202005.pdf.

Steuteville, R. 1992a. Hugo sets an example. *BioCycle* 33 (10): 33.

Steuteville, R. 1992b. Recycling after the storm. *BioCycle* 33, 10: 30–33.

Swan, Robert C. 2000. Debris management planning for the 21st century. *Natural Hazards Review* 1/4: 222–225.

Swan, R. 2002. Overview of the nation's worst debris-generating disaster (World Trade Center). *Environmental Practice* 4 (2): 67–69.

Szema, A. M., M. Khedkar, P. F. Maloney, P. A. Takach, M. S. Nickels, H. Patel, F. Modugno, A. Y. Tso, and D. H. Lin. 2004. Clinical deterioration in pediatric asthmatic patients after September 11, 2001. *Journal of Allergy and Clinical Immunology* 113: 420–426.

Trout, D., A. Nimgade, C. Mueller, R. Hall, and G. S. Earnest. 2002. Health effects and occupational exposures among office workers near the World Trade Center disaster. *Journal of Occupational and Environmental Medicine* 44 (7): 601–605.

Resources

- EPA information on landfills can be found at http://www.epa.gov/osw/nonhaz/municipal/landfill/sw_pubs.htm. Accessed January 26, 2009.

- FEMA offers a free course at their website on debris management. To obtain a copy of the CD-ROM materials, visit http://training.fema.gov/IS/crslist.asp for Independent Study-632. Accessed July 28, 2008.

- North Carolina Division of Waste Management at http://wastenot.enr.state.nc.us/SWHOME/emergen.htm. Accessed July 28, 2008.

- U.S. Army Corps of Engineers information on disaster assistance including debris removal can be found at http://www.usace.army. mil/. Accessed July 28, 2008.

Chapter 5

Environmental Recovery

Learning Objectives

After reading this chapter, you should be able to:

- Describe various types of environmental damage that can occur in the context of natural, technological, and terrorist disasters
- Identify a range of strategies for providing for environmental recovery
- Discuss why people value and appreciate environmental resources and why resource protection can mitigate future risks
- Explain the value of environmentally friendly recovery strategies
- Link environmental recovery to a holistic strategy around housing, transportation, business, and infrastructural recovery

Introduction

Most of us take pleasure in and value our **environmental resources**. It is likely that most people reading this book recycle, participate in outdoor activities, or enjoy the thrill of seeing a secluded waterfall or a new species of bird. Parents socialize their children to appreciate the world around them by identifying plants and animals, going for walks, looking for butterflies, visiting zoos, planting flowers, caring for pets, and providing winter food for birds and other animals. It is frightening, then, to think that the world we love could be endangered through our own actions, and it is equally reassuring to know that, if we safeguard planet Earth, it can return that safety to us during times of disasters.

Maintaining and even enhancing environmental integrity matters. The environment has historically served as a natural buffer to disasters. Coastal marshes and wetlands can stem a strong storm surge. Sand dunes, which may be destroyed during development, can break waves and function as habitat for local wildlife. The quality of human life can also be determined by our relationship to the environment. Many species exist with a chain of life, dependent on the resources contained within a particular ecosystem. Species thus serve as bio-indicators, or markers, of changes to the quality of local life. Frogs that are born with extra or missing limbs or, indeed, the complete disappearance of an amphibian species (Phillips 1995) suggest that significant climatic changes or environmental contamination may be occurring locally. Working in concert with nature to preserve the environment can work to enhance local quality of life for wildlife, plant life, and humans as well.

There are several ways to think about environmental recovery as we work through this chapter.

First, we can damage our environmental resources through our own actions, such as oil spills in pristine waterways, chemical contamination of soils and groundwater, or poor management of our own waste.

Second, even after disasters, our actions matter. As seen in Chapter 4 (Debris Management), the choices we make about how to handle debris can contaminate or protect the environment. Thus, disaster recovery management makes a difference to environmental recovery.

Third, the damage we have already done can worsen disaster impact. For example, Hurricane Katrina pushed into the southern Louisiana parishes and overwhelmed the levee system. It was clear that pre-Katrina, human-induced damage to coastal wetlands wiped out natural protections that could have stemmed the storm surge.

Fourth, the choices that we make can undermine the integrity of animal and plant habitats, including the ranges of endangered species.

Fifth, environmental recovery provides an opportunity to protect, conserve, and even restore environmental resources.

This chapter thus examines each of these dimensions by considering why the environment matters, the types of environmental resources that must be secured, strategies and approaches for doing so, and opportunities to make a difference at the personal through federal levels. In this chapter, you will learn that you can be part of the solution even if disaster has not yet struck your community.

A wide range of environmental contexts can be affected by disaster. By now, you will probably have read several other chapters that reveal this problem. Floods carry away critical soil and sand. How we handle debris can affect local air quality. Water sources can be contaminated by poor storm-water runoff management, and certainly many jurisdictions are concerned about terrorist attacks on local water supplies. Contamination of waterways, lakes, fishing habitats, and the ground can mean that entire communities may have to change their way of life or relocate completely. Species can be wiped out by how we manage recovery, such as eliminating critical areas such as riparian corridors along creeks and rivers. Restoration or protection of plants (particularly native species) can mean that the full chain of life from insects to reptiles to birds can remain. An established or replenished tree canopy can increase energy efficiency, reduce our dependence on power sources, and provide aesthetic qualities to neighborhoods. As we move through this chapter, consider each example and scenario as it may apply to your community, and think creatively about what to do before disaster as well as after to safeguard our environment.

This chapter examines the environmental resources that can be threatened by disaster and explores what we can do during recovery to salvage, restore, and replenish those community riches. In the next section, we explore a disaster case in Missouri that reveals how critical the environment is to us and how our actions can influence its viability. Next, we turn to a flood event that demonstrates a systems perspective. In this Nevada flood case, we will see how threats to environmental resources can also affect human systems, in this case cultural and historical resources of Native American burial sites.

Times Beach, Missouri

Times Beach, Missouri, just 20 miles southwest of St. Louis, surpassed Love Canal (see Chapter 1) in terms of contamination. In the early 1970s, the city hired a contractor to spray oil on unpaved roads in an effort to manage dust. Unfortunately, the oil contained dioxin. EPA took samples in late 1982, coinciding with the time when the nearby Meramec River flooded Times Beach. EPA analysis found dioxin levels to be "less than 1 part per billion to 127 parts per billion," but significant enough for the Centers for Disease Control (CDC) to recommend that the population should leave.

Additional studies led the EPA to provide $33 million of its Superfund for clean-up of uncontrolled hazardous materials sites to buy homes and relocate the entire population of 2,800 residents (EPA 2007). FEMA supported the relocation effort, and all residents had found new homes by 1986.

Cleanup procedures continued until 1997, and a state park opened on the site in 1999. A significant level of effort went into the cleanup, including (EPA 2007):

- Installation of spur levees to control water speed during floods and minimize erosion from contaminated soils
- Elevation of the Missouri River levee as part of the spur project
- Excavation and extensive thermal treatments of contaminated soil
- Removal and disposal of both contaminated and noncontaminated structures
- On-site incineration for dioxin-contaminated wastes
- Disposal of ash in an appropriate on-site facility

In addition, the on-site incineration facility treated over 265,000 tons of contaminated wastes from an additional 27 eastern Missouri dioxin sites. Imagine the number of agencies, organizations, and citizen groups involved in this level of cleanup from a hazardous waste site. Local, state, and federal government had to work closely and carefully together for 15 years to manage the cleanup, relocate the citizens, identify the full scope of the dioxin contamination in the state, and restore the area to viability. Fifteen years is a long time to recover.

Stillwater, Nevada

After an extensive drought period that occurred in the 1970s, an area in northern Nevada experienced higher-than-usual rainfall in the early 1980s (Baldrica 1998). In one of those difficult decisions that must be made, officials chose to allow a natural dike to be overrun in order to save area homes. Waters inundated an area called the Carson Sink, home to the Stillwater Marsh. Such wetlands serve as important natural nesting, resting, and feeding areas for birds. The flooding led to extensive die-off of marsh vegetation, which of course destroyed nesting areas as well. In addition to environmental matters, the event also influenced historical and cultural resources. (We will read more about these topics in Chapter 6.)

Systems theory (see Chapter 2) tells us that the physical and human environments are connected. The Stillwater Marsh is also a National Register District that includes prehistoric sites loaded with Native American treasures such as arrowheads, campsites, and tools (Baldrica 1998). It took until 1986 for the floodwaters to ebb, but as they did, federal employees from the U.S. Fish and Wildlife Service notified the State Historic Preservation Office that human bones and related artifacts of daily life had been revealed. State and federal officials faced a number of challenges, such as funding an effort to safeguard and retrieve these archaeological finds, battling the damage caused by exposure to wind and weather, preventing thievery, and coping with problems arising from access to the site. The State of Nevada put together an effort from several state and local agencies and used volunteers to cover or retrieve artifacts. In 1987, federal partners hired an on-site archaeologist and consulting firm to conduct excavations and help manage the site. New dikes were put up around archaeological sites, and nesting sites were built to accommodate returning wildlife.

Because the Stillwater site contained human remains, U.S. Fish and Wildlife officials and Nevada State Museum staff worked with Paiute and Shoshone tribal leaders to bury the remains in an underground crypt (Baldrica 1998; Dansie 1999). Since the floods, the U.S. Congress has passed Public Law 101-601, which provides for the protection of Native American remains and any objects that may have been placed within the burial site. When remains are discovered, federal authorities must notify Native American tribes possibly connected with the deceased. Section 3 of the law directs that such remains must go to a descendant of the deceased or, if that cannot be determined, to the tribe on whose lands the remains were discovered (National Park Service 2007). Respect for the remains of Native Americans stirs strong sentiments. Imagine the graves of your family member being disrupted and how traumatic that would be. For Native American tribes, the issue is embedded within a history of abuse of their rights. Federal law now protects the rights of the deceased and those who seek to honor the dead. Environmental recovery efforts must consider not only the legal dimensions on this issue, but the ethical and humanitarian dimensions of a tribe's ancestry and culture.

Approaches to Environmental Recovery

Four approaches to environmental recovery can be used to plan a strategy after disaster. These approaches include working through a set of principles that foster **sustainability**, providing for a holistic recovery, encouraging **environmental conservation** by rebuilding "green," and mitigating future risks.

Sustainability

A number of perspectives can be used to think about environmental recovery. A first starting point, influenced by the efforts of geographer Gilbert F. White, stems from the work of Dennis Mileti, Mary Fran Myers, and others at the Natural Hazards Research and Applications Information Center (NHRAIC) at the University of Colorado-Boulder (Mileti et al. 1995; Mileti 1999; see Box 5.1). In their work, they suggest that we must approach environmental issues in light of making our planet *sustainable*. To be sustainable means that we should think through decisions that ultimately safeguard environmental resources for future generations. To be truly sustainable, though, we must think through additional issues.

BOX 5.1   PRINCIPLES OF THINKING SUSTAINABLY

During the 1990s, the Natural Hazards Research and Applications Information Center (NHRAIC) at the University of Colorado-Boulder convened 100 experts in the field of disasters, including researchers and emergency managers. They conducted a thorough assessment of research to date, culminating in an overview book by NHRAIC director Dr. Dennis Mileti named *Disasters by Design*. In that book, Dr. Mileti said that sustainability "means that a locality can tolerate—and overcome—damage, diminished productivity, and reduced quality of life from an extreme event without significant outside assistance" (Mileti 1999, 4). The challenge to creating a sustainable local environment means that we must make a commitment to several key principles.

"Maintaining and enhancing environmental quality" falls at the top of list, meaning that we should make a commitment to not overburden our ecosystem; rather, we should live closer in concert with what our ecosystem can provide without undermining its resources (Mileti 1999, 5). Further, we must make a commitment to local quality of life. Though each community may define quality of life differently, many of us would choose environmental protection in order to enjoy everything from our backyards to national parks and reserves. A third principle urges us to build a resilient local capacity, particularly designing mitigation actions that work in concert with nature rather than against it. One tool for doing so includes land-use planning that would deny intrusion into environmentally sensitive areas such as wetlands and floodplains. We must also "recognize that vibrant local economies are essential" (Mileti 1999, 6).

Suggestions later in this text introduce ideas of rebuilding businesses with "green" capacities as one strategy toward sustainable local economies. Green rebuilding involves efforts to use recycled materials, introduce solar energy, and employ other means to reduce impact on the environment. As part of ensuring that our local communities remain sustainable, we must also attend to the challenges faced by vulnerable populations such as the elderly, racial and ethnic minorities, and the poor. Too often, toxic sites have unduly impacted already marginalized populations. Environmental recovery must incorporate principles of *environmental justice* (Bullard 1990), so that recovery measures enhance rather than undermine equity.

For example, each community will face difficult challenges as it tries to do its best with scarce resources, including limitations on political will and economic capabilities. Each community will have to decide where to place the line between acceptable and unacceptable risk. Is it economically reasonable to replenish the beach or more practical to deny building permits near the beach, particularly for structures that impinge on nesting grounds and other habitats? In states where tourism provides paychecks, tax revenues, and recreational opportunities, these decisions are difficult.

A related dimension of a sustainability perspective concerns the impact on various human populations (Mileti 1999). How can we ensure that the ways in which we manage the environment and disaster recovery do not worsen preexisting vulnerabilities? If we pass ordinances that protect floodplains or approve federal acquisitions of properties, will we displace the low-income families that tend to live in such areas? Or, if we divert the flow of water, will it impact negatively on fisheries and related industries downstream, with implications not only for animal life, but for economic livelihoods? As another example, if we choose to incinerate disaster debris from demolished houses, what will the impact be on air quality, not to mention on those with asthma or chronic obstructive pulmonary disease?

Holistic Environmental Recovery

In the book *Holistic Disaster Recovery* (NHRAIC 2001), local officials are urged to think about a second approach, holistic recovery, by incorporating environmental quality into all dimensions of recovery. Those working on rebuilding homes may want to "rebuild green" in order to increase energy efficiency, use recycled materials, and decrease their impact on the environment.

To reduce air pollution and provide a means of transportation for low-income, elderly, and other people without access to an automobile, recovery planners may want to design new public transportation systems that use alternative fuels and encourage people to use mass transit. New ways of working that decrease the impact of commuting can also be considered, such as wiring a city completely for Internet access and encouraging employers to offer cyber-commuting as a work option. Communities may also want to take advantage of opportunities to protect floodplains or areas with destroyed buildings by converting them to parks, trails, and other prospects for recreation, or even encourage ecotourism as a way to create recreational opportunities, protect local environmental resources, and sponsor new jobs.

As inspired by *Holistic Disaster Recovery*, a community may find creative ways to integrate environmental recovery into other dimensions:

- After a disaster, job loss may range from temporary to permanent. Consider how to involve those who are experiencing disrupted incomes in the recovery effort: restoration of coastal areas, debris management, public environmental education, and rebuilding efforts.
- Use the recovery as an opportunity to alter stormwater management. Damaged roads can be redesigned to incorporate new drainage systems that divert runoff, filter silt that might otherwise clog storm drains, and ultimately improve local water quality.

- Pass ordinances that require builders to comply with limits on sediment erosion and runoff while also preserving habitat. Require fencing around sites to reduce the loss of bare soil during construction. Require efforts to protect existing trees from removal or damage caused during construction.
- Identify heritage trees that have lived for 100 years or have special historic significance. Establish a tree-protection program for these environmental resources.
- Reward green building of homes and businesses with tax incentives, grants, and citywide programs such as construction information fairs.
- Reinvigorate the local economy by creating, saving, or restoring historic, cultural, archaeological, or tourism sites, ultimately resulting in new jobs, businesses, and other opportunities.
- Provide for recreational opportunities by setting aside open space or by participating in federal acquisition buyouts or federally funded trails-construction programs.
- Involve the public through volunteerism, such as tree plantings, habitat restoration, creation of certified wildscapes on private and public properties, and educational programs in local schools.

Rebuilding Green

A third principle that resonates with each of the prior approaches, either implicitly or explicitly, is the idea of rebuilding in environmentally friendly ways. Commonly referred to as "rebuilding green," this approach has struggled to be implemented in communitywide ways. In one community, though, **rebuilding green** may emerge as a model for an entirely new way of recovery.

On May 4, 2007, a massive EF5 tornado destroyed Greensburg, Kansas (National Weather Service 2007). The tornado, estimated at 1.7 miles wide and 205 miles per hour, obliterated 95% of Greensburg, claiming the lives of 10 residents and injuring an additional 13 (*Kiowa County Signal* 2007). In a town of approximately 1,400 (U.S. Census 2006), such an impact would be nearly unbearable—but Greensburg responded with courage and an eye toward the future. Taking a cue from its name, Greensburg determined that it would attempt to rebuild green, the first town in the United States to try to do so in such a complete manner.

What is a "green idea"? Going green means different things to different communities, which embrace the idea as they understand it and as it is feasible locally. For some, going green may mean implementing a basic recycling program. For others, going green may mean engaging in aggressive strategies to set aside wildlife habitats, reduce all kinds of pollution, and require particular rebuilding to reduce water consumption, save energy, and reuse building materials.

After the F5 tornado destroyed most of Greensburg, the mayor announced the town was "going green" for its recovery. The town's recovery plan, supported by the Kansas Office of the Governor and FEMA, includes a key guiding principle: to be "a community that recognizes the importance of the natural environment and balances the need for growth and economic development with the maintenance and improvement of the government" (Greensburg 2007). As stated in its recovery plan Greensburg is attempting to:

- Put a framework into place to see the project through to its end. Area residents have created Greensburg GreenTown as a Web-based source for information (www.greensburggreentown.org).
- Certify builders using the U.S. Green Building Council's guidelines. The council is a coalition that certifies buildings at different levels according to environmentally conscious standards, some of which can be seen later in this chapter and throughout the text.
- Encourage green rebuilding practices and materials that reduce water use; support the use of recycled materials; promote energy efficiency; and decrease the use of chemicals, paints, and glues that emit toxic fumes. Doing so decreases energy bills, conserves energy for future generations, reduces air pollution, and minimizes forest consumption.
- Harness local energy for local use and the creation of new businesses. In a nod to the wind that took the town, Greensburg hopes to develop wind farms along with other locally appropriate uses of agricultural waste and landfill methane to produce alternative fuels. Other proposed solutions include using solar power to produce electricity for parks, signs, parking lots, and even to heat swimming pools.
- Promote restorative landscaping that uses native and drought-tolerant trees and plants, which ultimately use less water once established.
- Increase walking paths and trails for recreational opportunities and to reduce use of vehicles that consume gasoline and emit air pollution.

Greensburg is fighting back by going green! The town has created a non-profit organization to help support green initiatives, invited vendors to demonstrate the virtues of a natural-gas car, offered a green-building teleclass, and excited business owners about green options. Indeed, a portable sawmill company came to town to turn destroyed trees into useable lumber (Greensburg 2007). In addition, a model-homes project is building 12 "state-of-the-art green homes" as showcases and to encourage ecotourism by using the buildings for education and lodging.

Clearly, Greensburg sees opportunity amidst the devastation. The community's emphasis on rebuilding green demonstrates the promise provided by a holistic approach as well. The natural resources of the environment are linked to housing and economic development across the entire population. Greensburg intends to return stronger and more disaster-resilient than ever (see Box 5.2)

BOX 5.2   ZERO-ENERGY HOMES

If you have not yet paid an energy bill for your apartment or home, you may not realize how much it can take away from your paycheck. Prices of oil, gas, and electricity have steadily risen. With global climate changes occurring as well, we can anticipate that energy costs to heat and cool our homes will continue to increase. For those with low incomes, such as senior citizens living on social security checks or single-parent families, energy costs can consume money that is desperately needed for food, medicines, and other survival needs. After disaster, the opportunity exists to build homes that require less energy and, ultimately, translate into environmental savings of precious earth resources as well. As the Appalachian State University (ASU) Energy Center says (Tait 2007), zero-energy homes are part of a green building trend that "is a smart move for companies to embrace both ethically and economically."

A zero-energy home is defined as one that will "combine a high degree of energy efficiency with the on-site production of renewable energy." In short, your home would produce the same energy as it would require, resulting in a "zero" balance (Tait 2007, 1). To do so, you would design the home to be energy-efficient and integrate systems that provide energy. Using lower or zero energy reduces our overall demand on the Earth's resources, which defines our **ecological footprint**. (Numerous Web sites can be found easily on the Internet to calculate your ecological footprint.) By rebuilding greener, we not only help our communities recover, but build back our planet's defenses against human impact.

How might you rebuild such a home? One option is "passive solar orientation" which, according to ASU, puts 70% of the windows facing within "20 degrees of due south" (Tait 2007, 3) to capture sunlight—which is then redistributed through various "thermal masses" such as the concrete slab foundation or even a water storage tank. Your family can do other things to increase its energy efficiency. One option would be to incorporate solar water heating into your home and to purchase energy-efficient appliances, windows, and other home items (NAHB Research Center 2006). You can even try that now, by examining your home to search for ways to increase insulation, caulk leaky windows, and purchase energy-efficient lights.

In New Orleans, an organization called "Make it Right" is rebuilding green by using energy-efficient means. Their efforts include rooftop solar thermal installations to reduce energy costs by up to 90%. In the hot and humid environment of the Louisiana coast, this effort will truly make a difference. For the latest on their efforts, visit http://www.makeitrightnola.org/.

Sources: Tait (2007) and NAHB Research Center (2006)

Strategies and Tools for Environmental Recovery

As with other recovery dimensions like housing, businesses, and critical infrastructure, the recovery time period can present opportunities to conserve, restore, and protect environmental resources, with clear implications for the areas of concern mentioned earlier: air, land, water, animal and human species, and hazards reduction. In this section, we examine some strategies and tools that do just that. Strategies describe general approaches to what we would like to do, while tools represent actual means of implementing the strategy.

Environmental Protection

Environmental protection, defined as actions taken through legal means, requires us to act to ensure that species and their habitat survive and even thrive. Disasters represent natural events that would occur regardless of human presence. However, human choices about disaster-recovery management can threaten the existence and survival of species at risk. Working in concert with nature, though, can result in an effective solution that reduces risks for humans and animals in their coshared ecosystems.

An example can be found in Arizona, where the town of Kearny faced a dilemma when floodwaters inundated its wastewater treatment plant and a town park along the Gila River watershed (FEMA 2005). The dilemma centered on where and how to relocate the town's plant outside of the floodplain. The dilemma arose because the recovery areas included habitat used by an endangered species. The southwestern willow flycatcher had been enjoying the riparian habitat of the Gila River as a breeding site, in an area fed by the treatment plant's evaporation ponds. Their original habitat had been decimated due to the invasion of another species: human beings. Preserving the second largest breeding site in Arizona for this bird became imperative. FEMA provided a key tool through its hazards-mitigation grants and public assistance programs to fund a solution (details in Chapter 15—Financing Recovery). Working with FEMA and the U.S. Fish and Wildlife Service, Kearny built a new treatment plant that provided for water to flow from the new plant into the wetlands, thereby ensuring a habitat for the endangered flycatcher.

Another strategy includes protecting greenways, which also allows for safeguarding floodplains. This can be done by establishing regulations that prevent building or, when disaster strikes, not permitting rebuilding. At present, FEMA holds federal responsibility for permitting building in floodplains.

After disaster, cities can pass ordinances disallowing rebuilding. In certain circumstances of repetitive risk, they may qualify for federal acquisition funds that help homeowners to relocate. Because low-income, minority, and elderly populations are most likely to reside in such areas, relocation may represent a risk to the loss of important social networks and cultural ties. More on this subject will be discussed in later chapters. For now, it is enough to emphasize that the idea of maintaining, creating, or safeguarding greenways represents a good general strategy.

Community leaders may become convinced of the potential of greenways when they learn that they can enhance property owners' home and land values, which generates new tax funds (Platt 2000). Greenways naturally allow for activities such as walking, hiking, biking, and bird watching. Such pathways also allow for animals to travel through even urban areas in a safe, protected, and species-appropriate habitat. The city of Houston, Texas, accomplished this when it turned 19 miles of the repetitively flooding Sims Bayou into a greenway. The problem was solved with the assistance of the U.S. Army Corps of Engineers, which widened the bayou using materials that allowed natural vegetation to grow. Additional tree and shrub cover restored the riparian habitat as well (Platt 2000).

Stormwater runoff also poses a challenge across the United States. Heavy rains in some areas, such as when Tropical Storm Allison dumped 37 inches of rain on Houston, Texas, over a five-day period (National Weather Service 2001), can erode soil, carry sediment and debris into the stormwater drainage system, clog those systems, and carry chemicals and noxious substances into the watershed. Flash flooding can result, as can water pollution that affects the local supply of drinking water.

Other pollutants pose possible future disasters to local water supplies. An EPA study in 2008 discovered that a number of pharmaceutical by-products had entered the water supplies in 24 major metropolitan areas, affecting potentially 41 million Americans (Donn, Mendoza, and Pritchard 2008). Although the amounts are currently small, follow-up studies will be necessary. The drugs, including antibiotics, anticonvulsants, mood stabilizers, and sex hormones, enter through human waste, but they can also move into the water supply when people flush medicines. Prescriptions, vitamins, and other medicines should be disposed of properly through local hazardous waste disposal programs.

Before a disaster, communities can develop far-sighted stormwater draining systems—most commonly in areas of new development. In older areas, drainage problems may have been addressed through a patching system. The occurrence of a disaster could be an opportunity for a complete makeover to mitigate future effects. Some tools that can be used include development ordinances that minimize the use of nonpermeable surfaces. When a development includes extensive concrete or asphalt surfaces, stormwater picks up car oils and other chemicals as it moves through the drainage system toward the watershed.

Obviously, an environmentally friendly solution is to increase open space in new developments, possibly by limiting the number of units or by increasing population density in multifamily units, smaller homes, or multistory buildings. A trade-off thus occurs when buildings are located in more closely connected areas, leaving some portion of the development area as open and green space. With practices discussed elsewhere in this chapter, such as incorporating native plants and increasing tree cover, a new development can actually help absorb stormwater runoff and represent a green development strategy (NHRAIC 2001).

Communities may also opt to establish stormwater treatment wetlands, "small, constructed ecosystems designed to enhance storm-water quality that has suffered as a result of urbanization and development" (White and Meyers 1997). Such wetlands can be set up as detention ponds, which, though sounding unpleasant, can be environmentally friendly and aesthetically pleasing. Native plant vegetation in a wetland reduces the flow of water, removes sediments that carry harmful pollutants, and invites wildlife (Wallace 1998). Although such wetlands have to be carefully constructed, the payoff may be worth it. A study by White and Meyers (1997) discovered that up to 90% of pollutants may be reduced, depending on wetlands construction and storm intensity. Residents in Cedar Rapids, Iowa, report that wetlands along the Cedar River have improved their drinking water through the removal of nitrates (Wallace 1998).

Environmental Conservation

The term *conservation* implies taking action to ensure that a habitat, species, or resource will not be reduced, touched, or damaged by human encroachment, use, or maltreatment. After a disaster, opportunities exist to do just that by setting aside lands that historically flood or have been seriously damaged by earthquakes, landslides, wildfire, or other disasters.

Easements provide one tool for environmental conservation (NHRAIC 2001). An easement occurs when property owners and another party, such as a state park system, agree to limit development and activities on that land. Owners may receive tax incentives or payments in exchange for such use and may then use the funds to improve other areas of their property—a win for the environment, the homeowner, and the broader public. The Nature Conservancy, a proactive environmental foundation dedicated to environmental conservation, identifies several benefits of easements, including protecting water and land, preserving habitat, keeping local areas unique, creating a buffer between public and private lands, and creating ecotourism (Nature Conservancy 2007).

Perhaps even more ideal would be land acquisition, where lands could be bought simply for the purpose of conservation of environmental resources or to create a new area where people might enjoy low-impact activities. For example, the Tall Grass Prairie in Pawhuska, Oklahoma—while not the result of a disaster—provides a model where purchased land created a tourism opportunity and restored a now-thriving herd of several thousand buffalo to the area.

Further south, a determined group of local homeowners in Denton, Texas, worked with city parks and recreation officials to purchase floodplain land and establish a nature preserve right in the heart of the community's most rapidly growing sector. Cross Timbers Park, a name that reflects the rapidly vanishing Cross Timbers Forest ecosystem, opened in 2002. The park provides nature trails, a teaching gazebo for children's environmental education activities, and more importantly, a safe place for old-growth trees and indigenous species like the Texas horny lizard. Given that Texas is home to 540 species of birds, 1,200 species of animals, and at least 2,220 plants unique to the north central Texas area, establishment of Cross Timbers Park proved to be far sighted (Pierson 2007). The Cross Timbers Park Project partnered homeowners, park officials, donors, schools, the local master naturalists' organization, and the Lady Bird Johnson Wildflower Center. The park was consistent with comprehensive plan efforts to prevent development in local floodplains. Since park establishment, the city has worked to minimize riparian (riverbank) erosion (see Photo 5.1).

The city of Garland, Texas, hired an organization named American Forests to examine benefits provided by the local tree canopy (see Box 5.3). Although the urban area of Garland enjoys less-than-average tree cover, American Forests found significant payoffs. In particular, tree roots absorb stormwater runoff, which subsequently reduces impact on stormwater drainage and containment systems and minimizes the loss of soil carried off by water. Reducing runoff also prevents leaves and other debris from clogging storm drains, which, if unchecked, can lead to localized flooding. Trees also provide beneficial effects for local air quality and save on energy bills, estimated at $2.5 million in annual savings (*Civil Engineering News* 2000). Imagine what an above-average tree canopy—or a replaced tree cover—could do for local savings, including your own home's energy bill. Several tools can ensure that the tree canopy remains intact either before or after disaster. For example, communities may pass ordinances that protect old-growth trees and forests, regulations that require developers to preserve trees, and restrictions that place fencing around trees and other environmental areas to protect them from bulldozers and other large vehicles during the recovery efforts.

Environmental Restoration

To restore something means to return it to its original state or as close as possible. To do so may mean organizing clean-up crews or even more massive

2006/11/28

PHOTO 5.1 **Efforts to manage soil erosion in a floodplain along Cross Timbers Park, Denton, Texas. (Photo courtesy of the city of Denton, Texas. With permission.)**

efforts to stabilize or repair an area. **Environmental restoration** may be very hard to accomplish given the extensive damage we have caused to date. The evidence is easy to find after Hurricane Katrina, although the concern had been in place for years.

A few months before Hurricane Katrina, sociologist Shirley Laska, director of the Center for Hazards Assessment, Research and Technology at the University of New Orleans, foretold the devastation. Due to a series of circumstances, particularly environmental devastation to the formerly rich coastal resources, a major hurricane was predicted to send storm surge into the parishes below New Orleans. Because coastal marshlands had been devastated by redirected waters, sediment, and pollution, their formerly natural ability to break the storm surge would mean that levees in the great city of New Orleans would be compromised. A particular program stemmed from a controversial channel constructed in 1965 to connect the Gulf of Mexico to the city to help ships avoid the sometimes difficult Mississippi River (Laska 2006). Known as MRGO (Mississippi River Gulf Outlet), the channel systemically dumped heavy saline water into the coastal areas, killing a swamp forest that served as a natural storm-surge barrier.

Laska (2004) told us that half a million people would not be able to evacuate due to a lack of transportation or because they were elderly, had

BOX 5.3 TREE CANOPY BENEFITS

Trees make a difference to a community. By taking action to regreen the community by restoring the forest, local officials, homeowners, and volunteers can provide a variety of benefits to a recovering locale (Burban and Andresen 1994):

- Provide psychological value by offering a place to relax at home, the local park, or even at a restored or newly created arboretum
- Increase economic value, as the presence of trees increases a home's market value and decreases energy costs
- Help reduce future disaster events by absorbing stormwater and reducing runoff of sediments caused by flooding
- Support the local climate by shading homes and cooling the air
- Enhance environmental integrity by offering places for wildlife to live, eat, and raise their young
- Offer educational opportunities by providing a place to teach children about environmental resources (Burban and Andresen 1994) (The Cross Timbers Park in Denton, Texas—discussed in this chapter—offers one such example.)

disabilities, or were living in situations where they had to assist homebound family members. A massive rescue effort would be necessary. Hurricane Katrina pushed a massive storm surge toward the city and into MRGO. The surge overwhelmed the Industrial Canal (as well as other places that were affected). As you well know, 80% of the city flooded, and approximately 1,500 people died. In New Orleans, at least 450,000 people experienced displacement, many permanently, the worst diaspora since the Dust Bowl storms of the 1930s (NOAA 2005). It is clear, as Dr. Laska (2004) points out, that "we must overcome our urge to control nature." The EPA continues to monitor the area for contamination from hazardous spills during the flooding (see Photo 5.2).

Coastal restoration necessary to protect the U.S. Gulf Coast may seem overwhelming given the magnitude and cost, but families and neighborhoods can do something in their own area to participate. Think about it; the environmental movement's motto is "Think globally, act locally," which means that, after disaster, even an individual can participate in environmental restoration. One simple fix is to create a backyard wildlife habitat to ensure that local species enjoy food, water, and nesting areas. The National Wildlife Federation provides guidelines and a certification program that can single out your property—whether an apartment or a massive ranch—as meeting the needs of local wildlife. If we start in our own backyards and link our efforts to others, we promote environmental values that ultimately help to resist decimation of larger areas.

PHOTO 5.2 **The EPA hazardous-waste collection site in Cameron, Louisiana. Hazardous wastes must be separated and stored prior to proper disposal. (Photo by Robert Kaufmann/FEMA News Photo. With permission.)**

For those owning property, further steps can be taken to reestablish what was probably there before the neighborhood: an ecosystem for local plant, mammal, and avian life. Landscaping after disaster provides such an opportunity. A strategy for such an effort would be to replace the lost "layers" of an ecosystem. Animals, reptiles, insects, and birds require different layers to move about, hide, and nest from ground to tree canopy. A local landscaping effort can include restoration of native grasses and flowers, shrubs, vines, and small and large trees (see Box 5.3). The local environmental conditions should be taken into consideration. In the south and west, for example, heat and drought conditions mean that plant selection is crucial. Selection of local, native, or indigenous plants means that they are more likely to survive temperature extremes and to provide the kinds of food that local animals prefer to eat. This practice is called **xeriscaping**, which means that we landscape using low-water and heat-resistant plants. Doing so reduces water consumption and runoff.

Schools can participate as well to involve and educate children about the importance of environmentally friendly disaster recovery. Understanding animal migration can become part of the local recovery strategy too. Something as simple as a school butterfly garden promotes environmental understanding. Butterflies and birds migrate in particular patterns and at specific times of year. Creating friendly pathways for them to travel not only serves the environment, but returns pleasing aesthetic qualities to the locally devastated landscape. Some communities may even capitalize on this kind of restoration to promote ecotourism. Imagine, for example, developing ecotours of the Gulf Coast wetlands to visibly explain their importance. Revenues from tourist dollars could be put toward restoring these precious areas and increasing life safety from storm surges. If we think locally, we can have a broader impact. The remaining sections in this chapter promote environmentally friendly rebuilding strategies. By rebuilding and recovering in greener ways, we can make a difference now and for future generations.

Environmental Partners

The environment touches all our lives in many ways. It is not surprising that a number of agencies, organizations, and community groups hold a vested interest in what happens to the environment after disaster. We are also fortunate, at this point in time, to be in a place where people often seek to act in environmentally responsible ways to safeguard our environment. As work by Dr. Laska pointed out earlier, this can only be good for the environment and, ultimately, good for human survival as well. This section looks at two sets of potential partners for environmental recovery: federal agencies and environmental action groups.

Federal Partners

The federal government includes a wide array of agencies that can participate in environmental recovery. The Environmental Protection Agency, along with FEMA, represents an obvious partner. But others participate as well, as we have seen elsewhere in this chapter, including the U.S. Fish and Wildlife Service in the Department of the Interior and the National Park Service. In this section, we look at the key federal partners: FEMA and EPA.

Several pieces of legislation guide federal action and decision making when environmental matters become part of a disaster recovery operation. For example, the **National Environmental Policy Act** (NEPA) requires that federal partners participate in a particular process when environmental matters arise. Part of NEPA mandates that the President's Council on Environmental Quality (CEQ) establish regulations. CEQ then requires that FEMA, as a federal agency, must set up appropriate regulations (FEMA 2007). As noted earlier with the Gila River watershed project in Kearny, Arizona, FEMA must make an environmental impact assessment before it can act. If there is any major impact on the environment, FEMA in concert with others must determine options and present those alternatives to the public for its input.

FEMA will likely take two courses of action (Rossman 1994). The first is to perform an environmental assessment to see what could happen as a result of the action that is proposed and to identify alternatives. If there may be an impact, FEMA must file a **notice of intent** to conduct an **environmental impact statement** (EIS) to determine whether the proposed action will change current land-use planning, affect many people, be controversial, unduly affect air or water quality, cause a threat to the public, result in an undue cumulative impact, or is similar to any previous FEMA actions that required an EIS.

Of interest to us later in Chapter 6, FEMA must also prepare an EIS if the action could impact a property on the National Register of Historic Places. FEMA must do an EIS if it determines that the action might affect "wildlife populations and their habitats, important natural resources, floodplains, wetlands, estuaries, beaches, dunes, unstable soils, steep slopes, aquifer recharge areas, or delicate or rare ecosystems, including endangered species" (FEMA 2007).

Working with federal partners requires an understanding of the laws, regulations, and processes that govern how they can act, which may help us to understand why federal response seems slow in some cases. For environmental recovery, taking time to consider the full impact and to involve the public seems like a good idea.

Another major act is CERCLA, the **Comprehensive Environmental Response, Compensation, and Liability Act** that was passed in 1980 and amended in 1986 by the Superfund Amendments and Reauthorization Act (Rossman 1994). Federal agencies or state and local government can raise concern about a site, such as the Times Beach, Missouri, example described earlier in this chapter. **Superfund** allows for a tax to be collected in order to deal with hazardous waste. Management of Superfund projects is handled by the Office of Solid Waste and Emergency Response (OSWER), which is part of EPA.

CERCLA (as does NEPA) outlines a process in which EPA and others identify sites that may contain environmental hazards and, through a public involvement process, move the site toward a **remedy** (Rossman 1994). The public involvement process starts with a Notice of Intent regarding an environmental action. Through a process called **scoping**, EPA and others initiate informal meetings to integrate a broad array of interested parties in the decision-making process. EPA will draft an EIS, solicit responses during a public comment period, and write a final EIS. A decision will be made regarding the actual or potential site, and EPA will negotiate and implement a cleanup remedy. As of October 2007, EPA had placed 1,245 sites on the **National Priority List**, with an additional 66 proposed for listing. Is there a hazardous site where you live? To find out, visit the EPA "Where You Live" map at http://www.epa.gov/superfund/sites/npl/where.htm. For information about basic steps to take before returning home to an area with a hazardous-materials incident (see Box 5.4).

Environmental Action Partners

A complete discussion of all the partners interested in supporting environmental recovery would be impossible. From long-established environmentally friendly organizations to recent entertainment stars starting or supporting green rebuilding, the good news is that there is a lot of help for environmentally friendly community recovery.

Environmental action groups like the Sierra Club and the Nature Conservancy offer experience, networks, ideas, resources, and organizational depth to help with environmental recovery. Organizations like these have national, state, and local chapters with persons vitally interested in providing expertise, volunteer time, and hope to communities impacted by disaster. As one example, the Delta Chapter of the Sierra Club in Louisiana has advocated shutting down MRGO, the Mississippi River Gulf Outlet described earlier. In agreement with scientists who forecast the storm-surge effects due to wetlands loss, this environmental organization seeks closure

---

BOX 5.4   FEMA RECOMMENDATIONS FOR A HAZARDOUS-MATERIALS INCIDENT

The following are FEMA guidelines for the period following a hazardous-materials incident:

- Return home only when authorities say it is safe. Open windows and vents and turn on fans to provide ventilation.
- Act quickly if you have come into contact with or have been exposed to hazardous chemicals. Do the following:
- Follow decontamination instructions from local authorities. You may be advised to take a thorough shower, or you may be advised to stay away from water and follow another procedure.
- Seek medical treatment for unusual symptoms as soon as possible.
- Place exposed clothing and shoes in tightly sealed containers. Do not allow them to contact other materials. Call local authorities to find out about proper disposal.
- Advise everyone who comes into contact with you that you may have been exposed to a toxic substance.
- Find out from local authorities how to clean up your land and property.
- Report any lingering vapors or other hazards to your local emergency services office.

Source: FEMA, http://www.fema.gov/hazard/hazmat/hz_after.shtm.

of MRGO in order to restore the Louisiana coast's original abilities to reduce storm surges, prevent saltwater intrusion, preserve and restore wetlands, and enhance the local quality of life for the people, plants, and wildlife struggling to survive (Delta Chapter 2007).

In recent years, various organizations and groups have emerged to work with animals at risk during and after disaster. Spurred on by the horrific damage from the *Exxon Valdez* oil spill (see Chapter 1), universities, environmental groups, and local volunteers have become increasingly organized and ready to spring into action. Consider the example of the 2007 San Francisco oil spill, which injured thousands of birds. At the University of California, Davis, faculty, staff, and students activated their Oiled Wildlife Care Network (see Photo 5.3) to bring in 25 participating organizations across 12 facilities to rescue and rehabilitate animals. By coupling response with research, UC-Davis became a leader in finding a way to save animals at risk.

Finally, never underestimate the value of contributions from unusual partners. You will learn in Chapter 6 about damage to an historic property, Andrew Jackson's Hermitage. When a tornado damaged the trees, an interesting array of partners stepped in to help. One of the more distinctive efforts came from the Gibson Company, which created unique guitars made from the downed, historic trees, many of which had been planted by President Jackson himself. Called "Old Hickory" in memory of the president's nickname, these guitars sustained a sense of history, recycled wood

PHOTO 5.3 Oiled Wildlife Care Network director Michael Ziccardi helps Will Meadows release a rehabilitated surf scoter in Tomales Bay, California. (Photo by Paul Meadows. With permission.)

that might otherwise have gone to landfills, and created cultural relics. We will turn to historical preservation issues in Chapter 6.

Summary

A variety of disasters can have an impact on our environment. Natural disasters can cause massive flooding and runoff that erodes riparian areas and depletes topsoil. Acts of terrorism can threaten water sources. Hazardous materials can contaminate residential areas as well as environmentally sensitive habitats.

Environmental recovery must take place in ways that promote sustainable approaches, incorporate holistic perspectives, and rely on green rebuilding. A number of strategies and tools can be used for environmental recovery. Environmental protection measures rely on existing or newly developed rules, regulations, and policies that must be adhered to. The consequences of disregarding these measures can be significant for the environment.

Conservation efforts typically focus on protecting environmentally sensitive areas. Disaster recovery can be used as an opportunity to rezone such areas and protect wetlands, floodplains, and human habitats. Environmental restoration can bring back areas, such as coastal wetlands, to protect humans from future events, serve wildlife and environmental resources, and restore the balance between the physical and human environment. A number of partners can participate in environmental recovery. Residents can promote green rebuilding, recycling, and responsible disposal of hazardous materials. Families can develop environmentally friendly landscapes and encourage schools to teach children about the environment. Federal partners, including FEMA and EPA, can provide advice, funding, and other support before and during environmental recovery. Environmental advocacy organizations can also participate by providing programs, volunteers, resources, and support for effective recovery strategies.

In the next chapter, we will examine historical and cultural resources. Coupled with environmental resources, they represent assets that remain at risk without human protection. We must be good stewards of all.

Study Guide

Summary Questions

1. How do natural disasters, hazardous-materials/technological disasters, and terrorist acts impact the environment?
2. Describe sustainable and holistic approaches to environmental recovery.
3. What is green recovery? How can it benefit the environment?

4. What are the differences between environmental protection, conservation, and restoration?
5. What are the basic expectations in circumstances where CERCLA or NEPA are used?
6. How can federal partners be of assistance during environmental recovery?
7. In what ways can environmental advocacy groups be helpful during environmental recovery?

Discussion Questions

1. Are there currently any environmental initiatives going on in your community? What are they? Who is involved?
2. What are your community's regulations regarding development? Are there guidelines about detention ponds, stormwater drainage, permeable surfaces, or density?
3. What would you do to replace environmental features such as trees and landscaping at your home in a disaster? Can you identify such environmental resources in your community, perhaps at a local park or arboretum?
4. What kinds of hazardous-materials recycling programs exist in your community? How many of your friends and family know about or participate in these locations and events?
5. What is your opinion on the MRGO controversy?
6. Which kinds of environmental advocacy groups are in your area, and what are their issues?

Key Terms

Comprehensive Environmental Response, Compensation, and Liability Act (CERCLA)
Ecological footprint
Environmental conservation
Environmental impact statement
Environmental justice
Environmental protection
Environmental resources
Environmental restoration
National Environmental Policy Act (NEPA)
National Priority List
Notice of intent
Rebuilding green
Remedy

Scoping
Superfund
Sustainability
Xeriscaping

References

Baldrica, A. 1998. Flood case study: Stillwater, Nevada. In *Disaster Management Programs for Historic Sites*, eds. Dirk Spennemann & David Look, 139–142. San Francisco: Association for Preservation Technology.

Bullard, R. D. 1990. *Dumping in Dixie: Race, class, and environmental quality*. Boulder, CO: Westview.

Burban, L. L., and J. W. Andresen. 1994. Storms over the urban forest. http://www.na.fs.fed.us/spfo/pubs/uf/sotuf/intro/intro.htm.

Civil Engineering News. 2000. Texas city relies on tree canopy to reduce runoff. *Civil Engineering* 70 (10): 18.

Dansie, A. 1999. International implications of the impact of repatriation in Nevada museums. *Society for American Archaeology Bulletin* 17 (3). http://www.saa.org/Publications/saabulletin/17-3/index.html.

Delta Chapter. 2007. Katrina response: Update on the plan to close the MRGO. http://louisiana.sierraclub.org/katrina.asp.

Donn, J., M. Mendoza, and J. Pritchard. AP Probe Finds Drugs in Drinking Water. Associated Press. March 9, 2008.

EPA. 2007. Superfund. http://www.epa.gov/superfund/index.htm.

FEMA. 2005. New treatment facility accommodates endangered species. http://www.fema.gov/ehp/gila.shtm.

FEMA. 2007. National Environmental Policy Act (NEPA). http://www.fema.gov/plan/ehp/ehplaws/nepa.shtm. Accessed September 1, 2008.

Greensburg. 2007. Long-term recovery plan. Greensburg and Kiowa County, Kansas. http://www.greensburgks.org.

Kiowa County Signal. 2007. Tornado death toll in Kansas town hits 10. http://www.kiowacountysignal.com/homepage/x2127956704.

Laska, S. 2004. What if Hurricane Ivan had not missed New Orleans? *Natural Hazards Observer*. http://www.colorado.edu/hazards/o/archives/2004/nov04/nov04.pdf.

———. 2006. Respect for nature as cornerstone to community resiliency: The view from Katrina "Ground Zero." *Natural Hazards Observer* 31 (2). http://www.colorado.edu/hazards/o/archives/2006/nov06/nov06e.html.

Mileti, Dennis, J.D. Darlington, E. Passerini, B. C.Forrest, M. F. Myers. 1995. Toward an integration of natural hazards and sustainability. *The Environmental Professional*, vol. 17 (2): 117–126.

Mileti, D. 1999. *Disasters by design*. Washington, DC: Joseph Henry Press.

NAHB Research Center. 2006. The potential impact of zero energy homes. http://www.toolbase.org/PDF/CaseStudies/ZEHPotentialImpact.pdf.

National Park Service. 2007. National American Graves Protection and Repatriation Act. http://www.nps.gov/history/nagpra/MANDATES/25USC3001etseq.htm.

National Weather Service. 2001. Tropical Storm Allison floods: June 5–9, 2001. http://www.srh.noaa.gov/hgx/projects/allison01.htm.

National Weather Service. 2007. Tornadoes, rain, hammer Central Plains. http://www.noaanews.noaa.gov/stories2007/s2855.htm.

Nature Conservancy. 2007. How we work: Conservation methods. http://www.nature.org/aboutus/howwework/conservationmethods/privatelands/conservationeasements/.

NHRAIC. 2001. *Holistic disaster recovery*. Boulder, CO: Natural Hazards Center.

NOAA. 2005. Hurricane Katrina: A climatological perspective (preliminary report). Technical report 2005-01. National Oceanic and Atmospheric Administration. http://www.ncdc.noaa.gov/oa/reports/tech-report-200501z.pdf.

Phillips, K. 1995. *Tracking the vanishing species: An ecological mystery*. New York: Penguin Books.

Pierson, D. 2007. Biodiversity in North Central Texas. http://www.nhnct.org/urban/biod.html.

Platt, K. 2000. Going green. *Planning* 66 (8): 18–21.

Rossman, E. 1994. Social organization of risk: Public involvement in federal environmental planning. *Industrial Organization and Environmental Crisis Quarterly* 8 (3). http://oae.sagepub.com/cgi/content/abstract/8/3/191.

Tait, A. 2007. Zero energy homes. Appalachian State University Energy Center. http://www.healthybuilthomes.org/docs/Zero_energy_homes_report%20ASU.pdf.

U.S. Census. 2006. Fact sheet: Greensburg, Kansas. http://www.census.gov/servlet/SAFFPopulation?_event=ChangeGeoContext&geo_id=16000US2028675&_geoContext=$_street=&_county=Greensburg%2C+ks&_cityTown=Greensburg%2C+ks&_state=&_zip=&_lang=en&_see=on&ActiveGeoDiv=&_useEV=&pctxt=fph&pgsl=010&_submenuId=population_0&ds_name=null&_ci_nbr=null&qr_name-null&reg=null%3Anull&_keyword=&_industry=.

Wallace, S. D. 1998. Putting wetlands to work. *Civil Engineering* 68 (7): 57–59.

White, K. D., and A. L. Meyers. 1997. Above par storm-water management. *Civil Engineering* 67 (7): 50–51.

Resources

- Backyard wildlife habitat programs, go to The National Wildlife Federation's website at http://www.nwf.org/backyard/
- Cross timbers forest eco-system, see http://www.nhnct.org/urban/biod.html and http://www.uark.edu/misc/xtimber/index.html
- Greensburg, KS tornado damage can be viewed at, http://www.kansas.com/static/slides/050507tornadoaerials/
- Kearny, Arizona information can be seen at http://www.townofkearny.com/about.html
- Personal responsibility, visit http://www.epa.gov/cleanup/whatyoucando.htm

Chapter 6

Historic and Cultural Resources

Learning Objectives

After reading this chapter, you should be able to:

- Explain the value and meaning of historic places, properties, and cultural resources
- Define the criteria for recognition as a historic property
- Understand the economic value of historic and cultural resources
- Outline basic plans that can be put into place to protect historic and cultural resources before disaster
- Describe how various communities have recovered historic and cultural resources after disaster
- Identify several funding sources for recovery efforts
- List steps and actions important to disaster recovery and mitigation planning
- Demonstrate an understanding of the value of mitigation strategies for historic and cultural resources

Introduction

What do you like the most about your hometown, or perhaps your university or alma mater? Where do you like to go on vacation? When you get there, do you wander through an **historic district** to eat and shop? Perhaps you visit an art museum? Where do you take your vacation pictures—in front of a famous site like Times Square in New York City or the Lincoln Memorial in Washington, DC? As you drive closer to these destinations, do they seem familiar, perhaps even raising a level of excitement as you draw closer? Is there something about the character of the buildings, the layout of the downtown, or the look of your neighborhood that evokes nostalgia or a sense of belonging? If so, it is because of a combination of things: the physical structures that exist, the meanings that we attach to these places, and the roles that they play in our sense of cultural heritage. Historic and culturally meaningful locations tie us to the past, to a sense of identity—of who we are, the people who came before us, and the legacy that we intend to leave.

What happens when disaster strikes these locations? In the rush to recover, there is a risk of losing the unique characteristics of these meaningful locations. This chapter looks at the value of historic and **cultural resources** and examines the challenges and strategies associated with preserving our heritage. In the next few subsections, we will look at several scenarios that demonstrate the potential impacts of disasters on historic and cultural resources and what we can do to mitigate the damage.

The St. George Hotel, Santa Cruz, California

In 1894, a massive fire swept through downtown Santa Cruz, California, devastating the fledgling coastal town and decimating the local Chinatown area. However, Santa Cruz residents rebuilt their downtown with spirit and flair. One of the most imposing buildings to be built was the Hotel St. George, named after the mythical St. George, slayer of the fire-breathing dragon. The hotel, built by Anson Hotaling, boasted elegant and opulent appointments: a marble staircase, lavish bathtubs, Italian mosaic floors, custom carpeting, oil paintings, and a latticework courtyard. Hotaling added grandeur to the dining rooms with art nouveau features and commissioned murals.

Hotaling's son remodeled the St. George in 1912, adding commercial Italianate qualities along with a Tudor lobby, tile-roofed towers, iron balconies, and stucco relief. Throughout the 1930s, the St. George staff hosted grand-hotel conventions, treating many people to their first elevator ride. The rise of beach tourism, however, led to a decline in the use of the St. George, which ultimately became an option for low-income residents. The 1960s brought a renaissance and increased tourism. In the 1960s, the St. George hosted part of the psychedelic culture in its "Catalyst" room while the downtown turned into a thriving outdoor mall. The large, impressive structure enjoyed social, historic, and economic value over the near-century of its existence. As a massive structure facing both sides of a city block, the

St. George sat as an imposing feature of downtown Santa Cruz (California Preservation Foundation 1990).

On October 17, 1989, at 5:04 p.m., St. George residents heard a low rumble and then felt an intense 7.1-magnitude earthquake. The so-called Loma Prieta quake damaged 175 historic buildings in Santa Cruz, 16% of the county's historic buildings (ARG 1990). The Pacific Garden Mall, a district in the National Historic Register, suffered a direct hit from the earthquake. The earthquake dealt severe damage to one-third of all downtown buildings. Of these downtown structures, 16 or 59% were contributing resources to the National Register Historic District. Of all buildings listed or eligible for the **National Register of Historic Places**, the earthquake demolished 52%, and the city red-tagged another 16%, including the St. George (ARG 1990). Thus, saving socially and historically significant buildings became a cause for several community groups. Estimates for the construction of a new, equivalent hotel reached $6 million, several million dollars beyond repair estimates.

Competing interests over the future of the hotel focused on sentiment and historic preservation vis-à-vis economic interests and revitalization of the downtown. In another sense, razing the St. George represented hanging onto part of the pre-earthquake Santa Cruz versus moving on, almost as if a community death had occurred and people felt the need to cling or proceed with their lives. "Friends of the St. George," an emergent community organization, moved to save the formerly grand hotel. Preservationists alleged the city "wrongfully claimed emergency exemptions to environmental laws safeguarding historic buildings" (Bergstrom 1990). The Historic Preservation Commission held hearings on the St. George, with opposing sides (engineers and owner) stating the building needed to be razed. FEMA leaned toward repair, and the **State Historic Preservation Office** opined that "the hotel is economically repairable" (Barab 1990).

In the late summer of 1990, the city issued a demolition permit to the owner. Preservationists went to district court. City attorneys argued that the city could not reopen Pacific Avenue and that merchants could not get on with business until the hotel came down (Bergstrom 1990).

Neither side came to define the ultimate end of the St. George. Nearly one year after the earthquake, someone set fire to the venerable hotel. Local and state firefighters determined the fire to be arson, with six separate fires set by an individual later determined to be a transient with no local ties to community groups or organizations. The fire removed the decision from community hands, and the city razed the building. As demolition ensued, crews salvaged identifiable exterior components of the hotel to be included in a rebuilt structure mirroring the original architecture. The hotel reopened on the Pacific Garden Mall a few years later. Efforts to save the appearance of the St. George and reintegrate it into the rebuilt downtown worked well with a holistic perspective: to integrate historic preservation, disaster recovery, and economic development. Today, the Pacific Garden Mall is thriving, and the St. George is part of the postdisaster renaissance (for another example, see Box 6.1).

The Importance of Historic Places

In one sense, a **place** is just a physical location. Yet, places are "environmental contexts with real consequences for people" (Hummon 1986, 35). Places are important because they give us a sense of identity (Hummon 1986, 34). In a larger sense, places create a basis for community identity and shared heritage.

Defining "Place"

We develop perspectives on places that locate us socially and physically. Hummon (1986, 1990) suggests that we develop ties to places such as orientational ties, or knowing one's way around. There are other kinds of place ties as well. Place role ties mean knowing how to act; communal ties link us to family; and value ties reflect places we consider desirable or undesirable to live. A disaster, such as an earthquake, commands both a physical and social relocation, a renegotiation of a sense of place, and a renegotiation of community identity. Disasters threaten more than physical structures and, because these structures and places mean something to us, they threaten our own sense of identity, our links to our ancestors, and the fabric of our lives that we want

---

BOX 6.1   MONTEZUMA, GEORGIA

Although the challenges may seem intimidating, postdisaster historic and cultural recovery efforts also present opportunities. In 1994, Tropical Storm Alberto caused a 500-year flood event across Georgia. The state worked with FEMA and others to assess damages and design appropriate recovery treatments. In the town of Montezuma, population 4,500, floodwaters inundated the entire downtown, of which 45 buildings qualified as a National Register Historic District (Barksdale 1998). Floodwaters damaged the buildings' structural integrity as well as their historic brick features. Over the years, though, owners had put up nonhistoric aluminum fronts. The disaster thus represented an opportunity to remove those nonhistoric fronts to reveal the original brick character. With thorough assistance from the National Trust for Historic Preservation and the Georgia Trust, the little town of Montezuma capitalized on an opportunity to build on its history and encourage "heritage tourism" (Barksdale 1998), an effort that serves as a central downtown development plan to this day. (For more, see the Web site in the resources section of this chapter.)

to pass on to children and grandchildren (Phillips 1996). Losing places takes something away from us. Is there something more than the meaningfulness of a place for our identities? From an economic point of view, the answer is yes.

The Economic Importance of Historic Places

Historic dimensions of our communities also provide economic benefits (FEMA 2005a). In Virginia, every $1 million spent in rehabilitating historic properties produces 15 construction jobs and 14 additional support jobs. Tourists to historic Virginia sites spend three to four nights on average and $497 per trip, a dependable revenue! In Florida, historic preservation brought in 123,000 jobs in 2000. Tourists spent $3.7 billion visiting historic sites, which generated $317 million in income and $657 million in state and local tax revenue. Historic properties and sites stabilize our economy and must be recovered after disaster for more than just their local heritage.

For example, Andrew Jackson's home near Nashville, called the Hermitage, suffered serious damage after a 1998 tornado. It was not the house that was so badly damaged; rather, the losses came from 2,000 trees taken down by the tornado—some planted by President Jackson himself in 1838. Removing them would require thought and consideration, as they had fallen across beautifully landscaped lawns visited annually by thousands of tourists.

To manage the destruction, crews would have to avoid using heavy machinery to prevent damage to landscaped areas. As suggested in Chapter 4 (Debris Management), crews mulched tree limbs and cut trunks into sections for removal. Some trees remained in place despite their damage, as evidence of the 1998 tornado, an historic event itself. Conservators worked with a forest certification program to recycle historic wood. The Gibson Guitar Corporation made limited-edition guitars called "Old Hickory" from salvaged woods. Profits were returned to the Hermitage for restoration purposes. A tree-replacement program used native Tennessee trees (Adams 1999).

Interestingly, the damage also revealed new artifacts and sites of potential significance. Archaeologists examined each area to locate and retrieve artifacts, uncovering a previously unknown area of blacksmithing. Though disaster harmed this historic site, it also revealed new treasures for the site.

Look around your neighborhood and imagine it without landscaping and trees. Storm survivors often comment on the loss of this aesthetic element of their hometowns, which serve as orientation markers, provide shade in the heat of the day, and often represent a family or civic activity that has grown, literally, in their hearts. Communities may go to great lengths to save historic trees. The Survivor Tree at the Oklahoma City National Memorial represents recovery from the bombing. During a 2007 ice storm, volunteers worked diligently to save it. In the spring of 2008, schoolchildren planted saplings grown from Survivor Tree grafts.

How do we know whether something qualifies as an **historic property** or a cultural resource? Although debate still lingers over definitions and limitations, it is important to understand some of the boundaries for what is considered worth saving. We turn to this topic next.

What Qualifies as a Historic Property and a Cultural Resource?

Historic and cultural resources are often defined similarly. FEMA (2005a) defines *historic properties* as "any prehistoric or historic district, site, building, structure, or object included in, or eligible for inclusion in, the National Register of Historic Places maintained by the Secretary of the Interior." The National Register specifies criteria that include (see Web-site links in Resources section at end of chapter):

- Significance to American history that may include architecture, archaeology, landscapes, engineering, and culture in districts, sites, buildings, structures, and objects
- Reflections of contributions to American history or the lives of significant persons
- Characteristics associated with a time period or type of construction or art
- Items or locations that might reveal information about prehistory or history
- A documented existence of at least 50 years

Cultural resources are usually defined in terms of being tangible or intangible items. The tangible items include the built environment, such as buildings, monuments, and art. Think about the library that you use to borrow books, study, or conduct research—the building is a tangible collection of intangible treasures, namely, knowledge amassed by a people situated within a given cultural context. Symbolically, these ties to the past suggest that a future can be built again (Spennemann and Graham 2007).

The things that we cannot physically experience are intangibles, like language, folkways, and skills (Spennemann and Graham 2007). It may be difficult to imagine disaster damage to the intangibles, but think about a coastal bayou community that has been repeatedly flooded. As it becomes more and more difficult to rebuild and return, the way of life created by a mix of Cajun, Native American, and/or Vietnamese American fishing communities can be undermined. In many such Gulf Coast communities, only the elders speak Cajun French while their grandchildren speak only English. As the younger generations leave for other opportunities and safer locations, the chance to retain a unique, culturally based way of life disappears. Both tangible and intangible cultural resources are difficult to restore once they are seriously damaged; if destroyed, they are considered irreplaceable.

The North Carolina State Historic Preservation Office and its North Carolina Department of Cultural Resources (2007) follows the definition: "A property is considered historic if it is listed in or eligible for listing in the National Register of Historic Places." You might be surprised how many such places are listed or eligible in your state. In North Carolina alone, 45,000 such properties are listed in the National Register either as stand-alone buildings or as part of its 375 historic districts. An additional 4,700 properties are eligible for possible inclusion. Imagine the damage a major hurricane could cause to these historic treasures and the effort it would take to retain this state's unique architectural character. In a disaster, it is important to consider not only those on a list, but those also deemed eligible for potential inclusion. In addition to the threat caused by disasters to historic and cultural resources, hazardous events can also undermine or reveal additional resources. Hurricanes, floods, and other events can topple trees, revealing new artifacts, building foundations, and even burial grounds (North Carolina Department of Public Resources 2007; Baldrica 1998). Care must be taken, then, to protect and preserve both the existing historic and cultural resources and those newly revealed by disaster. Let us turn next to how disaster circumstances affect historic and cultural resource preservation.

Challenges and Opportunities after Disaster

Historic and cultural preservationists argue that a major threat to such treasures comes from *a rush to recover*, to return a community to normal. In efforts to protect lives, remove debris, and launch a recovery process, historic structures may be condemned, demolished, or swept away (Kariotis 1998). Thus, the first weeks after a disaster represent both a threat to historic structures as well as an opportunity to save and restore what remains (Donaldson 1998).

Care must also be taken to ensure that inspectors and those not familiar with local history are informed about the value of various resources. Full consideration should be given to how historic structures might be saved, even those with serious structural damage (Donaldson 1998). A rush to demolish buildings rather than shore up, stabilize, fence off, or otherwise protect may cause unnecessary losses. Thus, damage-assessment teams (see Chapter 2) should include persons familiar with historic buildings, such as a preservation architect or engineer, who know older construction methods and can recommend ways to salvage damaged structures (Donaldson 1998).

Preservationists recommend avoiding changes to historic buildings, which may result in loss of their historic integrity. Imagine, for example, an item that you may have collected as a child, or even as an adult (Siekkinen 1998). Although some items in your collection may have been loved so much they are worn or torn, others may have been treasured in pristine condition, perhaps still in their original packaging, like a collectible doll or a rare baseball card. For collectors, original condition matters, and the same is true for historic and cultural resources. People who buy baseball cards describe them as in "mint" or "near mint" condition, where a bent corner, a fingerprint, or other seemingly slight damage can reduce the card's value; for truly rare cards, it can mean a purchase price in the thousands of dollars. A push toward recovery may mean that otherwise salvageable structures might be lost or damaged further, even through mitigation measures to make the building stronger.

Different kinds of hazards can also present challenges. The main threat to cultural heritage in Tucson, Arizona, is high wind or fire, often leading to the loss of roofs (Kimmelman 1998). In response to this local hazard, the city of Tucson has written standards for what materials can be used to replace roofs in historic districts. One property owner in the historic El Libre National Register Historic District of Tucson replaced a lost roof and brought it up to code with stronger beams, all under the guidance of state historic preservationists: everyone won (Kimmelman 1998).

As another example, the Los Encinos State Historic Park suffered damages after the 1994 Northridge earthquake, despite retrofitting by earthquake bracing and tying conducted five years earlier (Winter 1998). Postearthquake efforts sought to repair the building with minimal alteration, but it proved difficult to secure funding, as repairs exceeded $1 million. A combination of federal funding with money carved out of an existing state budget brought in the funds needed for restoration. Federal partners and other strategies can reduce the impact of disasters and save historic and cultural resources. This is our next topic.

Resources for Historic and Cultural Preservation

Two key resources can be useful in protecting and saving historic and cultural treasures. These include developing a plan of action and knowing where to turn when disaster does strike.

Predisaster Response and Recovery Planning

Atlanta's Fox Theatre experienced a very bad fire in 1996 that led staff to assess and identify new strategies to protect this Georgia Landmark Museum

Building, a **historic landmark** structure that is also on the National Register of Historic Places (Martin and King 2000). During restoration, they created a new archives space with a sprinkler system, rolling compact storage, and steel cabinets. They also developed an extensive photograph catalog documenting the location and status of furniture and other features unique to the "Fox." They are ready should disaster strike again.

Without a doubt, preplanning for disaster remains the single most valuable activity that communities can do to protect historic and cultural heritage. Specific steps that can be taken include first understanding the role of local ordinances and statutes that may affect what you can do postdisaster. Properties that represent or house resources should be assessed for items that can be used in an event, including smoke and fire detectors, fire extinguishers, and alarm systems. Second, planners can create a database listing historic properties that should be protected, including information on the location and description of the resource. Be sure to make hard and electronic backup copies of the list. Buildings or museum artifacts could be ranked according to their importance. Third, planners can specify guidelines for what to do in an actual event, including prioritizing structures and items and outlining specific activities that should be done to protect items.

It would also be good to think through who should serve on a response and recovery team for an historic structure. Certainly, owners and staff should be involved in any planned action and trained on how to preserve, move, and store items and objects (Roy 2001). A historic recovery team may also require engineers, historic preservation architects, librarians who understand the impact of climate on rare documents, and people who can physically move items out of harm's way. Perhaps a set of volunteers or museum docents could serve as the team core. Consideration should be given to whether to stabilize buildings and store artifacts on site or move them. If items should be moved, a plan must be developed for how, where, and when to do so. Imagine that a hurricane is two days away but you have a chance to move Native American artifacts out of the storm surge area. Who should be involved in the process? Would exposure to the air deteriorate items further? Should they be moved up and out of the estimated height of the storm surge but remain in the building? These kinds of difficult choices require expertise.

A written plan should include building maps, locations of artifacts, assessment and accumulation of equipment needed for protection or an evacuation, and a division of labor for who does what in an emergency. Historic artifacts may also require special treatment, too, such as a backup generator to keep the climate suitable for rare books and ancient relics. A list of vendors that can provide emergency supplies should be included as well (Eck 2000; Estes 2000).

A good example comes from a national historic park. Repetitive flooding of the Potomac and Shenandoah Rivers near Harper's Ferry, West Virginia, led park staff to design quick response measures to lessen the postdisaster recovery challenges (Noble 2001). Their plan features these elements:

- Listing which artifacts are saved first in a building evacuation plan and also indicate which items can remain in place if there is a flood
- Identifying "no storage" areas in the basements that flood
- Putting flood hatches into the floors of some buildings (Staff members open the hatches after floodwaters diminish. The muck then goes into the basement, where it is pumped out.)
- Replacing wooden doors that swell during floods with water-resistant woods
- Placing specialized tools in convenient locations to use for dismantling exhibits and removal to a safer location
- Locating computer cables for interactive exhibits above anticipated high water levels
- Training staff to implement the plan
- Creating a list during evacuation of where artifacts are taken for later retrieval

Harper's Ferry links us to a brave and courageous past, when John Brown and others launched a resistance to slavery and lost their lives in the attempt. African-American writers like Frederick Douglass and W. E. B. DuBois made Harper's Ferry the site of intellectual movements and speeches that invigorated the thinking of people for generations. It is good to know that our National Park Service has taken steps to protect this location and its treasures from floods. For more information, see the links in the Resource section at the end of this chapter. Next, we turn from planning to the people who can make a difference for historic and cultural resources after disaster.

Human Resources within State or Tribal Areas

State Historic Preservation Offices (SHPO) and **Tribal Historic Preservation Offices** (THPO) can be helpful in providing an inventory of historic locations and can reach out to owners, caretakers, and others to educate them about means for saving locations. Let us turn first to an example of a SHPO that helped with recovery under the most challenging of circumstances. Then, we turn next to the events of September 11th.

The Oklahoma City Bombing

Few of us probably realize that damage occurred to historic and cultural resources in the Oklahoma City bombing. Downtown Oklahoma City began to grow in the 1890s after the land run of 1889. Building activity commenced quickly with "an army of businessmen hastily erecting hotels, lumber yards, saloons, and retail outlets" (Blackburn, Henderson, and Thurman 1980; Smelker 1995). Five major railroads spurred growth, and by 1900 Oklahoma City had become the regional leader in processing and shipping cotton. A building boom took place from 1898 to 1906, with brick and stone buildings replacing the hastily built wooden structures. New structures in the warehouse district featured the Romanesque revival style, with "large arched windows on the lower floor with pairs of groupings on the upper floors" that can still be seen today (Blackburn, Henderson, and Thurman 1980, 12).

A second building boom soon increased the number of two- and three-story businesses located in what would eventually become the capital city. From 1919 to 1931, a third boom brought unique landmarks to the area such as the ten-story Skirvin Building, first opened in 1911 and now one of the Historic Hotels of America, as recognized by the National Trust for Historic Preservation. By 1995, downtown Oklahoma City included a recognizable set of structures with historic architecture and meaningful context. The bombing of the Murrah Federal Building rocked structures up to 30 miles away, including the offices of one of the agencies responsible for safeguarding our history, the Oklahoma State Historic Preservation Office (SHPO).

In 1995, SHPO offices were housed in the Journal Record Building. Originally called the India (Masonic) Temple Shrine, the building was built in 1923 through the joint efforts of 16 Masonic lodges. The architecture featured "simplified Classical Revival" with an "unadorned façade utilizing Ionic columns and capitals on the upper floors and a plain frieze at the top" (American Institute of Architects 1989, 30). In its early days, the building housed a grand hall where 1920s-era residents enjoyed traveling troupes, musicals, and concerts. During the Depression, the Masons lost the building, which was then sold at auction. Despite the removal of Masonic symbols, the building retains its historic and cultural importance. In the 1970s, the Journal Record Publishing Company used the building to publish legal and job printing. The building also housed governmental agencies and political offices.

Damage assessments of the bombing characterized the Journal Record Building, located just north of the Murrah Federal Building, with "unsafe severe external and internal structural damage" (Oklahoma State Preservation Office 1995). Debris flew through the air, causing injuries to SHPO staff, some of whom were hospitalized. The SHPO offices sustained heavy damage, and because it was also a crime scene, staff lost access to offices and important records needed to preserve the damaged downtown (see Photos 6.1 and 6.2). Staff relocated to a temporary site and eventually moved into offices in the Oklahoma History Center across from the state capitol (Oklahoma Historical Society 1995). Despite the damage and

PHOTO 6.1   View of Oklahoma City bombing damage. (Courtesy of the Oklahoma State Historic Preservation Office. With permission.)

PHOTO 6.2 Interior damage to the State Historic Preservation Office, Oklahoma City. (Courtesy of the Oklahoma State Historic Preservation Office. With permission.)

injuries, SHPO staff quickly conducted damage assessment in the affected area (Osborne 1998, 2000).

The Oklahoma SHPO worked with several partners, including the National Park Service, the National Trust, the American Institute of Architects, FEMA, and volunteer architects and engineers. Damage assessment began with a chart provided by the General Service Administration. Conducting damage assessment, the usual first step to launch disaster recovery, was particularly challenging given that the entire area was a crime scene controlled by the FBI.

Given that national attention focused on the Murrah Federal Building, you might be surprised to learn that 73 National Register listed or eligible buildings were included in the area where damage occurred, most commonly window damage, but also misaligned roofs that had been picked up by the blast as well as damage to masonry, interior partitions, and floor connections. Sprinkler systems that were set off by the blast saturated portions of buildings and later caused problems with mold. Damage assessment teams found damage up to 30 miles away to civic, religious, business, and commercial buildings (Osborne 1998, see Photo 6.3).

Oklahoma prioritized 19 locations and one historic district for repairs (American Institute of Architects 1995). The SHPO gave information to building owners and, along with federal agencies, offered technical assistance. The National Park Service provided a $40,000 planning grant. The SHPO extended the funds to historic churches and to the city for survey

PHOTO 6.3 Interior of a local church damaged by the Oklahoma City bombing. (Courtesy of the Oklahoma State Historic Preservation Office. With permission.)

purposes. The grants were also used to support a National Register nomination for the Automobile Alley Historic District along with development of a preservation plan and design guidelines for the district. Many property owners used tax incentives to reduce rebuilding costs (Osborne 2000). In this case, preserving the past symbolized resistance to terrorism and represents how such efforts link a historic past to collective resilience (Spennemann and Graham 2007).

September 11

September 11 claimed cultural resources representing some of the world's most revered treasures. When the towers came down, the world lost art by Picasso, Lichtenstein, Rodin, Calder, Miro, and others. Artifacts from an eighteenth-century African burial ground were housed in the World Trade Center as well. Exterior facades of art deco buildings and historic cathedrals suffered damage. Falling debris crushed the 35-foot-high Church of St. Nicholas, which housed relics of St. Nicholas and St. Katherine. Inventory lists for art, photographs, and artifacts were lost as well, a crucial resource that was needed to estimate losses (Heritage Preservation 2002). At the Pentagon, rare collections of military art were destroyed, along with extensive materials in the library.

As shown in Chapter 4, debris management can make a difference. Through the careful removal of rubble, some cultural resources resurfaced. At the site of the World Trade Center, artifact boxes from the African burial ground were found as well as part of a famous Calder mobile. Preservation staff worked to clean dust and other materials from artworks. Crews used chemically treated sponges to clean historic grave markers and monuments. At the Pentagon, freeze-drying of boxes saved about 99% of the book collection (Heritage Preservation 2002).

Working with Federal Agencies for Historic and Cultural Preservation

Other ways to assist property owners require the support of local, state, and even federal partners. Communities can help property owners by providing informational brochures on how to preplan or salvage and preserve after disaster (see links in Resources section). Government can also provide incentives, such as tax credits to reward those who retrofit. Government may also offer property tax relief, and insurance providers can be encouraged to reduce premiums for those who mitigate potential damage to historic properties (Look and Spenneman 2000).

The **National Historic Preservation Act** (NHPA) of 1966, as amended in the year 2000, says that before any federal agency takes action it must consider how the action would affect historic properties (FEMA 2007a). Section 106 of the NHPA requires FEMA and other federal agencies to consider how their actions may affect historic properties and to consult with the Advisory Council on Historic Preservation. The Section 106 process stipulates that the federal agencies must consult the SHPOs, THPOs and other tribes, and the public as they carry out their responsibilities under the NHPA. The goal is to avoid, minimize, or mitigate adverse effects to historic properties. Typically, FEMA works with the SHPO and THPO to identify and assess historic properties. If adverse effects can be identified, FEMA and the SHPO/THPO work together to develop preservation strategies (FEMA 2007a, see Box 6.2).

FEMA can provide assistance if damage occurs in a major disaster and if the damaged collections or objects hold "significant cultural value." FEMA policy relies on definitions from professional organizations to define what they can fund. For example, a collection may be considered significant because of its value as a reference material or by having importance as an artistic, historic, scientific, educational, or socially important object (FEMA 2007b). A FEMA preservation officer will work with state officials to identify appropriate methods to stabilize and restore damages to at least a minimal level. To illustrate, damage to a painting might require treatment to restore its aesthetic value, although damage to a display might simply require shoring up so that it can be put back in view (FEMA 2007b). And after a tornado tore through Richland, Georgia, in 2007, FEMA helped save the Harmony Primitive Baptist Church, originally built in 1839. FEMA assisted the state of Georgia with other buildings by making architectural sketches and salvaging portions of historic buildings for museum collections (FEMA 2007c).

The **Heritage Emergency National Task Force** was formed in 1995 as a partnership of 41 federal agencies and historic preservation organizations (Quarantelli 2003). The goals of the Heritage Emergency National Task Force (2008) are to:

- Help cultural heritage institutions and sites be better prepared for emergencies and obtain needed resources when disaster strikes
- Encourage the incorporation of cultural and historic assets into disaster planning and mitigation efforts at all levels of government
- Facilitate a more effective and coordinated response to all kinds of emergencies, including catastrophic events
- Assist the public in recovering treasured heirlooms damaged by disasters

Most recently, the Advisory Council on Historic Preservation convened the Preserve America Summit to outline recommendations. The council's 11 key priorities included "dealing with the unexpected" to preserve historic properties. Specific activities included integrating "historic preservation,

BOX 6.2   THE NATIONAL HISTORIC PRESERVATION ACT AND DISASTER RECOVERY

Before disaster recovery can commence, the National Historic Preservation Act, Section 106, requires federal agencies to analyze how their initiatives, called *undertakings*, might influence historic and cultural resources. This means that FEMA and others working with them must look at archaeological and historic properties that are either (1) listed on or (2) eligible for the National Register of Historic Places. Circumstances under which Section 106 applies include "alteration, rehabilitation, removal or demolition, or any other modification," all of which become likely options in a disaster context (Oklahoma State Historic Preservation Office 2002, 2004). Standards established by the secretary of the interior apply in order to retain the historic character of the property.

To illustrate, FEMA, the Oklahoma State Historic Preservation Office, the Oklahoma Archaeological Survey, and the Oklahoma Department of Civil Emergency Management entered into an agreement regarding any undertaking. The key part of the agreement reads: "FEMA will not approve funding of any Undertaking until it is reviewed pursuant to this Agreement." FEMA's Preservation Officer carries responsibility for ensuring that contractors meet qualifications established by the secretary of the interior. The contractors must be expert professionals for the archaeological and architectural/historic survey work, research, and planning, including development of plans and specifications for rehabilitation or carrying out archaeological salvage operations.

The agreement also "acknowledges that Tribes possess special expertise related to properties that possess tribal religious and cultural significance, and FEMA may utilize this expertise in determining if any such properties are eligible for the National Register." In a state like Oklahoma, where records reveal historic and cultural ties to 37 tribes (for example, the Osage, Quapaw, Choctaw, Chickasaw, Cherokee, Creek, Seminole, Apache, and Cheyenne), recognizing tribal legacies and expertise matters.

FEMA and the SHPO consult to determine which properties in the area are "eligible" for the National Register. Through this consultation, they reach consensus on the eligibility of properties not already listed in the National Register. Formal listing in the National Register is a separate process from that of the evaluation that takes place under Section 106.

Review must then occur prior to any undertaking. This partnership results in a higher chance that historic and cultural resources will not be lost in the rush to return to normal, an outcome that occurs too frequently after disaster.

Source: Information courtesy of the Oklahoma State Historical Preservation Office.

archaeological, and cultural resources into state, tribal, and local mitigation strategies resources." The council encouraged local and state agencies to develop mitigation, response, and recovery strategies as part of area disaster planning (Advisory Council on Historic Preservation 2007). Clearly, state and federal partners have worked diligently to preserve historic resources. What have you done in your own home?

Saving Your Family's Treasures

Think about the items that make your home special, or that matter to your parents or grandparents. Is it the photograph album that you would save as you dashed out the door from a rapidly approaching wildfire? Or perhaps it is a special memento from a trip to another country, something that represents what you appreciated about its culture? Maybe your family enjoys living in a home with an architectural style unique to the 1930s or 1960s. Would you like to keep that special character after a tornado? You may want to think through what you can do before, during, and after disaster to protect your personal treasures.

The Heritage Emergency National Task Force provides useful suggestions on its Web site for families, organizations, and others interested in protecting and preserving cultural resources. (For more details, see the links below for the Heritage Emergency National Task Force and the Georgia Historic Preservation Division.)

Before disaster
- Develop an inventory of what you have for insurance purposes and store the list in an out-of-state location or in cyberspace. Take photos and videos of your valuables and store them in a safety deposit box or with a friend out of state. (Photos and videos can also be saved in digital form on CD, DVD, or flash drive and stored physically or in cyberspace.) Put rare documents like birth certificates, military papers, a family genealogy, and social security cards into the safety deposit box as well, and send copies to that out-of-state friend. Be sure that the bank is located out of a floodplain and has its own emergency response plan in place to protect your items.
- Develop a plan of action for what you would protect in instances where you have advance warning, such as a hurricane or flood. Could you move the grandfather clock or the family piano? Should you have a "go box" into which you would quickly throw the graduation and wedding photos?
- What can you do to mitigate the impact of disaster on structures and landscaping? Can you retrofit the building in earthquake

country? Put on additional roof clamps? Arrange to secure ply-wood over an architecturally unique window?

After disaster:

- If you followed the above instructions, contact your out-of-state friend. If you were unable to preplan, follow the remaining suggestions and visit the Web sites listed below.
- Protect yourself and your family by wearing masks, using protective gloves and clothing, and limiting access to the site.
- Go to the site as soon as possible, before items are exposed to further damage from debris, dust, wind, and rain.
- Remove items carefully. Check with a professional before cleaning items, particularly if dust, soot, or ash covers them. Removing such debris can actually damage the item further.
- Check with an insurance agent to see what your coverage provides.
- Photographs can be restored through careful techniques. Select the photographs most meaningful and in the best condition and contact a professional photographer for advice. In some states, postdisaster programs may be offered to help families with this. Contact your state historic preservation officer and the state office of emergency management.
- For further ideas, visit the Heritage Emergency National Task Force Web site at http://www.heritagepreservation.org, and read through drying-out strategies for floods at the Georgia Historic Preservation Division Web site, http://hpd.dnr.state.ga.us/assets/documents/flood_rebuilding_communities.pdf.
- Develop a mitigation plan for future events in your home.

Building Mitigation into Historic and Cultural Resource Recovery

Communities that face continual threats from disaster may wish to follow the example of Milton, Pennsylvania, which worked with federal partners to address its local hazards. After centuries of repetitive flooding, FEMA helped Milton to identify options for its historic business sector and neighborhoods. Through a public-involvement process, Milton sorted out options for its historic structures. Debate centered on the cost as well as the effect of the mitigation option on the structure.

Milton's options were not clear cut, and there were pros and cons for each strategy. FEMA can offer to purchase properties in floodplains as part of its Federal Acquisitions Program. However, such properties are then destroyed, which is not the way to go with historic resources. Relocation can be an option, although it also carries the possibility of damaging structural integrity while moving a building from its historic location. Elevation can also be an option to raise the building above an anticipated flood level. Beyond the buildings, Milton also considered structural-diversion improvements and stream-channel modifications that would change the direction of the river but potentially also damage historic neighborhoods (FEMA 2002). How might you integrate mitigation initiatives into your community's recovery plan for historic properties and cultural resources? Let us examine FEMA's recommendations and resources.

FEMA's Mitigation Strategy for Historic Properties and Cultural Resources

FEMA (2005a) provides an extensive set of guides and worksheets in its series of mitigation planning guides. The sixth guide focuses on mitigation for historic properties and cultural resources and outlines a four-step process that a community can work through. As described next, the four-step process involves developing a planning team and community support, conducting a risk assessment, and creating a mitigation plan followed by both implementing and monitoring the plan.

Step One

The first mitigation step involves assessing community support, developing a team, and engaging the public. How much does the public know and understand about local historic and cultural resources? Perhaps the first step, then, is to ensure that the public learns about locally meaningful places and artifacts. It is easy to use events to increase understanding, such as holding costume contests on locally historic days, integrating historic lessons into parade floats, or hosting field trips for children, senior citizens, and college students. Newspapers and other media can be used for special columns, stories, and photos of the past that remind people of local heritage (FEMA 2005a).

Officials may need to be educated about their roles as guardians of historic legacies. Because elected officials may change after elections, it may be a good idea to provide educational overviews of national, state, and local laws, policies, and programs for which officials hold responsibility.

The next part of step one is to build a team of people interested in leading mitigation efforts. FEMA recommends considering:

- Preservation architects and historic preservation planners
- Professional and amateur archaeologists
- University faculty and staff, as well as library and museum staff from the area
- Representatives from historic neighborhood associations

- Historic societies
- Tribal representatives
- Elected officials and community leaders

Once the team has been put together, it is time to identify the risks that face historic and cultural resources. Because this text focuses on the disaster recovery period, it is likely that a hazard is already well known. However, it is beneficial to conduct further inquiry, which happens in step two.

Step Two

In the second major step, a planning team assesses the risk. Several substeps can be undertaken. For example, the first action should be to conduct a complete inventory of historic and cultural resources, usually through a survey that documents the items both visually and descriptively. It is a good idea to try and determine the value of the resources so as to estimate potential losses, although replacement of priceless items may be difficult to assess.

A next action is to research past disasters, a task that this group is likely to enjoy, as it allows them to delve into local history. Talking with older residents, diving into archives and records, and laying out a timeline of the type and extent of prior damages will reveal what other risks exist besides the present disaster. By mapping the risks vis-à-vis the locations of resources, the planning team can then identify locations of concern. The planning team, with the community's support, must prioritize which properties it will address, as it is likely that funds will not cover all mitigation options (FEMA 2005a).

Step Three

Identifying mitigation options occurs during the third major step. As seen in Figure 6.1, FEMA identifies five main types of possible mitigation actions (FEMA 2005a). The first set of options focuses on prevention. By following

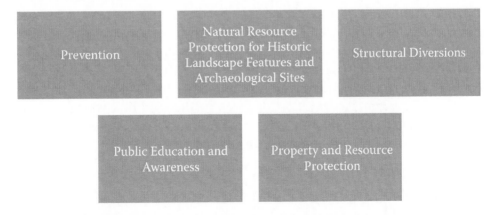

FIGURE 6.1 Mitigation actions for historic properties and cultural resources. Based on FEMA 2005a.

or upgrading local relations, historic items can be protected. Codes that prohibit building in floodplains, preserve open space, and manage stormwater all represent protective measures. After a disaster, local communities may decide to strengthen these regulations, and it is wise for historic-preservation enthusiasts to support such changes.

Property and resource protection measures encourage basic property improvements, including elevations, relocations, retrofitting for seismic activity, or reinforcing older structures to resist hazards. Areas that bear risk of terrorist activity can benefit from increased security access, improved perimeter lighting, and even integration of blast-resistant walls and windows.

Structural diversions, while possibly not aesthetically appealing, may further protect locations at risk. Erecting barriers and barricades may prevent access by terrorists or floodwaters. Seawalls and levees may also deter potential damage from flooding, which is the nation's most frequently occurring hazard. However, it is important to remember that these measures serve as deterrents rather than as assured protection (FEMA 2005a).

Protection of natural resources may seem like it fits into Chapter 5 (Environmental Recovery), with its emphasis on gardens, rivers, and wetlands. But such areas also represent historic locations or landscapes where tribes lived or dinosaurs lie buried. These locations may serve as recreational opportunities for **heritage tourism** trips. By mitigating disasters in these areas, we can retain their economic and cultural value to our communities. Thus, managing vegetation, invasive plants and species, and reducing erosion and flooding can lessen the impact of disasters in future events.

Step Four

Public education and awareness represent a fourth mitigation step. By reading this chapter, you already know more about cultural and historic resources than most of the people in your community. By passing on this information, you can become part of the local mitigation strategy. Starting at home is always an option, and by working to ensure that your family's treasures are safe from harm, you raise awareness further. By assisting your community's recovery and mitigation efforts involving historic and cultural resources, you can take the effort one step further and link your family to your community. The planning team could use someone like you to educate the public about the value and meaning of its work.

Funding Mitigation and Recovery Work

A number of funding sources may be used for the work described here. While few sources specifically offer disaster funding, a number of federal agencies and national organizations include it as an option in their grant programs (FEMA 2005b). For example, the National Center for Preservation Technology and Training provides grants up to $40,000 to protect cultural resources against natural disasters. The National Historic Publications and Records Commission offers funds for disaster planning and training. Emergency grants can be obtained from the National Endowment for the Arts and the National Endowment for the Humanities.

FEMA's Public Assistance Program may provide money for eligible costs. The FEMA Museum Eligibility Policy allows funding for nonprofit museums, which have as their primary purpose saving "artistic, historic and scientific" collections of value to the public. FEMA's Collections and Individual Objects Policy specifies that such collections must be of "exceptionally significant value" (FEMA 2005b).

Summary

In this chapter, we learned that houses, businesses, roads, and bridges are not the only valuable assets in a community. Historic and cultural resources matter to people as well. Because these resources represent meaningful places, ties to the past, and legacies to pass on, it is important to preserve what we can both before and after a disaster strikes. FEMA (2005a) defines *historic properties* as "any prehistoric or historic district, site, building, structure, or object included in, or eligible for inclusion in, the National Register of Historic Places maintained by the Secretary of the Interior." *Cultural resources* are usually thought of as artifacts and traditions that people produce specific to their way of life.

A number of challenges exist in preserving historic and cultural resources, including a rush to recover, integrating experts into the recovery team, and avoiding changes to historic locations. Strategies include pre- and postdisaster response and recovery planning. A number of federal and state partners exist to help. Many have worked out preexisting arrangements for postdisaster recovery efforts. By knowing about these partners and resources, it is possible to help retain the essence of a given location and what it means to the residents and, indeed, the rest of the nation.

You can start at home by safeguarding your own family's heritage as described in this chapter. By doing so, you lay a foundation to avoid some of the emotional losses that occur when a house is destroyed or severely damaged. In the next chapter, we will learn about housing recovery and the challenges associated with rebuilding. By addressing the recovery of historic and cultural resources in disaster recovery efforts, a return to normal will not result in loss of places that offer identity, roots, and meaningful ties.

Study Guide

Summary Questions

1. Why are historic places, properties, and landscapes important to people?
2. What kinds of economic values can be associated with historic and cultural resources?
3. What are the differences between historic properties and cultural resources?
4. Identify three key challenges to maintaining historic integrity of properties after a disaster.
5. What is the value of predisaster planning for recovery of historic and cultural resources?
6. Which organizations or agencies can be counted on at the state and national levels to assist with historic and cultural resource recovery efforts?
7. Describe the steps in the mitigation planning process for historic and cultural resources.

Discussion Questions

1. For those of you on a university campus, walk around and see what statues, awards, rare books, and building elements you can spot. How important are they to the character of where you live and to the legacy of your institution? How do they symbolize who you are, and what efforts might you take to ensure they will still be there to show to your grandchildren?
2. Restoration, preservation, or salvage? Which strategy would you have chosen for the St. George Hotel? Take different sides of the debate: the engineers, owners, historic preservationists, downtown business owners, or local community residents who enjoy the Pacific Garden Mall. What is your perspective about what to do with the damaged structure after the earthquake and then after the fire?
3. Review the information on the Hermitage and the destruction of 2,000 trees. What would you do to replace environmental features such as trees and landscaping at your home in such an event? Can you identify such environmental riches in your community, perhaps at a local park or arboretum? Look also at the historic buildings and other structures in your hometown. How does the physical environment relate to those structures? Should a preservation plan be put into place to salvage and restore environmental resources of historic locations prior to disaster?

4. Imagine that you are the mayor or a city council member in your hometown. Now imagine that your hometown depends on tourism to historic sites for generation of local tax dollars. What are your key responsibilities before and after a disaster?

5. How should you start to safeguard your personal or family treasures? What can you do to help preserve items meaningful to you, your parents, or your grandparents?

Key Terms

Cultural resource
Heritage Emergency National Task Force
Historic district
Heritage tourism
Historic landmark
Historic property
National Historic Preservation Act
National Register of Historic Places
Place
State Historic Preservation Office
Tribal Historic Preservation Office

References

Adams, C. 1999. Recovering from a devastating tornado at Andrew Jackson's Hermitage: A case study. *APT Bulletin* 30 (1): 43–49.

Advisory Council on Historic Preservation. 2007. The Preserve America Summit: Charting a future course for the National Historic Preservation Program. Washington, DC: Advisory Council on Historic Preservation. http://www.preserveamerica.gov/docs/Summit_Report_full_LR.pdf.

American Institute of Architects. 1989. *Great Buildings Ahead*. Oklahoma City: Oklahoma City Community Foundation, Inc.

American Institute of Architects. 1989. *Great buildings ahead*. Oklahoma City, OK: American Institute of Architects, Central Oklahoma Chapter, and the Metropolitan Library System.

Baldrica, A. M. 1998. Flood case study: Stillwater, Nevada. In *Disaster management programs for historic sites*, ed. D. H. R. Spennemann and D. W. Look, 139–142. San Francisco and Albury, New South Wales, Australia: Association for Presentation Technology and The Johnstone Centre, Charles Sturt University. http://marshall.csu.edu.au/DigiBooks/DisManSFO/DisManSFO.html.

Barab, P. 1990 Save the St. George from the mall dragons. *Santa Cruz Sentinel*, June 17, 1990. P. 1.

Barksdale, D. 1998. Disaster recovery response to Tropical Storm Alberto. In *Disaster management programs for historic sites*, ed. D. H. R. Spennemann and D. W. Look, 133–138. San Francisco and Albury, New South Wales, Australia: Association for Presentation Technology and The Johnstone Centre, Charles Sturt University. http://marshall.csu.edu.au/DigiBooks/DisManSFO/DisManSFO.html.

Bergstrom, M. 1990. Hotel checks out: demolition finally begins on St. George. *Santa Cruz Sentinel*. October 23, 1990. P. 1.

Blackburn, B. L., A. Henderson, and M. Thurman. 1980. *The physical legacy: Buildings of Oklahoma County 1889 to 1931*. Oklahoma City: Southwest Heritage Press, Oklahoma County Historical Society.

California Preservation Foundation. 1990. *History at risk: Loma Prieta seismic safety and historic buildings*. Oakland: California Preservation Foundation.

Donaldson, M. W. 1998. The first ten days: Emergency response and protection strategies for the preservation of historic structures. In *Disaster management programs for historic sites*, ed. D. H. R. Spennemann and D. W. Look, 25–30. San Francisco and Albury, New South Wales, Australia: Association for Presentation Technology and The Johnstone Centre, Charles Sturt University. http://marshall.csu.edu.au/DigiBooks/DisManSFO/DisManSFO.html.

Eck, C. R. 2000. Earth, wind, fire and water: Historic preservation planning in Miami-Dade County, Florida. *Cultural Resources Management* 23 (6): 11–13.

Estes, J. 2000. Disaster Preparedness: Are you ready? Cultural Resource Management 23 (6): 11–13.

FEMA. 2002. Looking to the future. Washington, DC: FEMA.

FEMA. 2005a. Integrating historic property and cultural resource considerations into hazard mitigation planning. FEMA 386-6. Washington, DC: FEMA. http://www.fema.gov/pdf/fima/386-6_Front%20Matter.pdf.

FEMA. 2005b. Before and after disaster: Federal funding for cultural institutions. FEMA 533. http://www.heritagepreservation.org/PDFS/Disaster.pdf.

FEMA. 2007a. National Historic Preservation Act (NHPA), 1996 as amended (2000). http://www.fema.gov/plan/ehp/ehplaws/nhpa.shtm.

FEMA. 2007b. Collection and individual object eligibility. Disaster Assistance Policy 9524.6. http://www.fema.gov/government/grant/pa/9524_6.shtm.

FEMA. 2007c. FEMA helps preserve historic treasures. http://www.fema.gov/news/release.fema?id=35990.

Foard, M. 1996. *After the flood: Rehabilitating historic resources*. Atlanta: Georgia Department of Natural Resources, Historic Preservation Division. http://hpd.dnr.state.ga.us/assets/documents/1996_after_the_flood_complete_rev.pdf.

Heritage Emergency National Task Force. 2008. History of the task force. http://www.heritagepreservation.org/programs/tfhist.htm.

Heritage Preservation. 2002. *Cataclysm and challenge: Impact of September 11, 2001, on our nation's cultural heritage*. United States: Heritage Preservation.

Hummon, D. M. 1986. Place identities: Localities of the self. In *Purposes in built form and culture research*, ed. J. W. Carswell and D. Saile, 34–37. Proceedings of the 1986 International Conference on Built Form and Culture Research. Lawrence: University of Kansas Press.

Hummon, D. M. 1990. *Commonplaces: Community ideology and identity in American culture*. Albany, NY: SUNY Press.

Kariotis, J. 1998. The tendency to demolish repairable structures in the name of "life safety." In *Disaster management programs for historic sites*, ed. D. H. R. Spennemann and D. W. Look, 55–60. San Francisco and Albury, New South Wales, Australia: Association for Presentation Technology and The Johnstone Centre, Charles Sturt University. http://marshall.csu.edu.au/DigiBooks/DisManSFO/DisManSFO.html.

Kimmelman, A. 1998. Cultural heritage and disaster management in Tucson, Arizona. In *Disaster management programs for historic sites*, ed. D. H. R. Spennemann and D. W. Look, 31–38. San Francisco and Albury, New South Wales, Australia: Association for Presentation Technology and The Johnstone Centre, Charles Sturt University. http://marshall.csu.edu.au/DigiBooks/DisManSFO/DisManSFO.html.

Look, D. W., and D. H. R. Spennemann. 2000. Disaster management for cultural properties. *Cultural Resources Management* 23 (6): 3–5.

Martin, C., and L. King. 2000. A lesson well learned: New methods of disaster preparation for Atlanta's Fox Theatre. *Cultural Resource Management* 23 (6): 17–19.

Noble, B. J. 2001. "Lord willing n' the creek don't rise": Flood sustainability at Harpers Ferry National Historical Park. *Cultural Resource Management* 24 (8): 16–18.

North Carolina Department of Public Resources. 2007. Attention: Owners of historic or older properties affected by a natural disaster. http://www.hpo.dcr.state.nc.us/flyer.htm.

Oklahoma Historical Society. 1995. *Preservation Oklahoma News* 1 (4): 2.

Oklahoma State Historic Preservation Office. 1995. Historic buildings affected by the bombing at the Alfred P. Murrah Federal Building. Unpublished report of Damage-Assessment Team.

Oklahoma State Historic Preservation Office. 2002. Fact sheet 10: Frequently asked questions about Section 106 Review. Oklahoma City: Oklahoma Historic Society.

Oklahoma State Historic Preservation Office. 2004. *Review and compliance manual Section 106 process*. Oklahoma City: Oklahoma Historic Society.

Osborne, E. 1998. Disaster response for the Oklahoma City bombing. In *Disaster management programs for historic sites*, ed. D. H. R. Spennemann and D. W. Look, 145–148. San Francisco and Albury, New South Wales, Australia: Association for Presentation Technology and The Johnstone Centre, Charles Sturt University. http://marshall.csu.edu.au/DigiBooks/DisManSFO/DisManSFO.html.

Osborne, E. 2000. Terrorist attack: Disaster response for the Oklahoma City bombing. *Cultural Resource Management* 23 (6): 44–48.

Phillips, B. D. 1996. Homelessness and the social construction of places: The Loma Prieta earthquake. *Humanity and Society* 19 (4): 94–101.

Quarantelli, E. L. 2003. The protection of cultural properties: The neglected social science perspective and other questions and issues that ought to be considered. Preliminary paper 325. University of Delaware, Disaster Research Center.

Roy, C. 2001. Disaster recovery: Developing a plan. *Cultural Resource Management* 24 (8): 13–15.

Smelker, C. 1995. *History of Downtown Oklahoma City*. Unpublished manuscript.

Spennemann, D., and K. Graham. 2007. The importance of heritage preservation in natural disaster situations. *International Journal of Risk Assessment and Management* 7 (6–7): 993–1001.

Winter, T. A. 1998. Impact of the Northridge earthquake on the Garnier Building, Los Encinos State Historic Park. In *Disaster management programs for historic sites*, ed. D. H. R. Spennemann and D. W. Look, 99–110. San Francisco and Albury, New South Wales, Australia: Association for Presentation Technology and The Johnstone Centre, Charles Sturt University. http://marshall.csu.edu.au/DigiBooks/DisManSFO/DisManSFO.html.

Resources

- Criteria for the National Register can be found at: www.nationalregisterofhistoricplaces.com. Accessed August 4, 2008.
- Funding sources, see FEMA guide #533, Before and After Disaster: Federal Funding for Cultural Institutions which can be accessed at www.heritagepreservation.org/PDFS/Disaster.pdf. Accessed August 4, 2008.
- Harper's Ferry, West Virginia (People, Stories, Collections) http://www.nps.gov/hafe/historyculture/index.htm. Accessed August 4, 2008.
- Historic Skirvin Hotel in Oklahoma City photos and information, visit http://www.historichotels.org/hotel/Skirvin_Hilton
- Hurricane Katrina, visit FEMA's page on the subject at http://www.fema.gov/hazard/hurricane/2005katrina/hp_resources.shtm. Accessed August 4, 2008.
- Montezuma, Georgia Downtown Development Authority http://www.montezuma-ga.org/dda/default.htm. Accessed August 4, 2008.
- National Register of Historic Places. What is historic in your hometown? Visit this website to look:http://www.nationalregisterofhistoricplaces.com/
- Salvaging family treasures after fire, see http://www.heritagepreservation.org/PROGRAMS/TFsoot.HTM. Accessed August 4, 2008.
- Tribal Historic Preservation Office website, http://www.achp.gov/thpo.html. Accessed August 4, 2008.

Chapter **7**

Housing

Learning Objectives

After reading this chapter, you should be able to:

- Outline the various steps that displaced residents go through as they find temporary and permanent housing
- List the steps involved in securing federal assistance for temporary and permanent housing
- Identify the general challenges of housing recovery
- Make clear the limitations of various models for housing recovery
- Discuss the pros and cons of various temporary housing options
- Describe challenges faced by renters and homeowners in securing permanent housing
- Explain the value of a professional case-management process to assist displaced residents
- Understand the benefits and challenges associated with permanent relocation
- Present the various roles played by local, state, and federal government during housing recovery
- Discuss the ways in which voluntary organizations assist with the housing reconstruction process
- Link mitigation to housing recovery

Introduction

We see the devastation on television, grateful that it is not our house this time. Yet, with a seemingly indomitable spirit, the victims turn to the camera and vow "we will rebuild." A few days onward, this latest disaster slips out of the news and away from our minds. But those individuals, numbering in the hundreds of thousands in the case of Hurricane Katrina, stay amid the rubble, sorting through memories, trying to get aid, and realizing that going home will require more than spirit. Having a home matters economically as well. Residences represent nearly 70% of all structures in a community, the single largest investment of most American families (Comerio 1998a). In this chapter, we examine the steps involved in securing **permanent housing** after a disaster.

The lucky ones are those with insurance sufficient to cover their losses. However, many people will not have carried or been able to afford enough insurance to recover. If you live in a "bullseye" area frequently visited by storms, earthquakes, or wildfire, doesn't it seem logical to purchase such insurance? Isn't it the responsibility of the individual to do so?

Yet, insurance can be expensive. When people earn low wages, work part-time, or are unable to work, they will not be able to afford coverage. Renters may find themselves in even more of a bind when their apartment building is damaged and the owner cannot afford to make repairs. Rebuilding a large apartment building can take years. If local apartments are expensive to rent and if availability is low, you may not be able to stay where you work, have family and friends, and prefer to live. For those affected by massive flooding or other events that destroy an entire community, it may be years before residents can return home.

The City of New Orleans, with an original pre-Katrina census of over 450,000 is only 72% repopulated as of 2008, three years after the storm. The 2008 population numbers represent only a slight increase since 2007 (Brookings Institution and GNOCDC 2008). Locals there question, "who's back?" It appears that the population in New Orleans is different—higher-income households returned first, and low-income neighborhoods still may have only a single homeowner back on a block. To demonstrate, consider that in June 2008, 52% of "active residences" were "located in largely unflooded planning districts" (Brookings Institution and GNOCDC 2008, 19). Further, new demographics have changed the cultural character of the city, and several hundred thousand persons remain displaced across the nation, unable to return home or to initiate rebuilding from so far away.

In short, it is not so easy to go home again. To do so requires considerable individual household effort, coupled with support from local, state, and federal government and, often, voluntary organizations dedicated to those who fall through the cracks of government assistance.

In this chapter, we will examine the challenges associated with housing recovery and focus on the means by which people return home. This chapter takes a realistic look at how difficult it can be and at the extent to which all levels of government and voluntary organizations must become involved. As University of California-Berkeley researcher Mary Comerio (1997, 176) reports, "Housing is the single greatest component of all losses in terms of economic value and in terms of buildings damaged."

When you lose your home to disaster, you have a couple of choices. You can find a rental, stay somewhere temporarily, or move away permanently. Local conditions may influence your options. Despite what you really want, your preferred choice may not be what you get. In the next section, we examine several disaster housing recovery scenarios. Each represents a particular housing challenge that must be faced as well as challenges universal in all disasters. We turn first to the case of the 1994 Northridge earthquake that damaged an urban area with multifamily buildings: Where would renters go while owners rebuilt? Our second case presents a small community that chose not to leave and outlines some of the reasons for staying. Last, we turn to the devastating flood that inundated most of Grand Forks, North Dakota, and East Grand Forks, Minnesota.

Northridge, California

Urban areas may present unique challenges, depending on how the hazard affects the area's housing construction. Further, local conditions may influence the housing recovery process. In 1994, such a set of factors came together when a 6.8-magnitude earthquake struck Northridge in southern California. Most of the damage occurred in 15 San Fernando Valley neighborhoods. (Comerio 1996, 1998, 1997).

Northridge represents the first major earthquake to affect a large urban area since 1933. By any standard, the impact was significant. Insurance companies estimated they lost $12.5 billion. Los Angeles County placed yellow or red tags on 7,000 single-family homes and 27,000 multifamily buildings. Multifamily apartment buildings represented 84% of the damaged homes. Although most families were able to relocate quickly into nearby available rental housing, the effort to restore the multifamily housing would take years (Comerio 1998; Comerio, Landis and Rofé 1994).

Southern California was experiencing an economic recession at the time. With few apartment owners having purchased expensive earthquake insurance premiums, the stage was set for a long-term housing reconstruction nightmare. In this area, apartment buildings were often owned by multiple partners. But because of the recession, the owners (now lacking renters) faced limited cash income and had to rely on personal finances for expensive repairs. Most owners could not qualify for the traditional **Small**

Business Administration (SBA) loans available after disaster. California voters also declined to support a tax increase for reconstruction (Comerio 1998a). FEMA typically provides funds for single-family housing but not for multifamily units. With multifamily apartment buildings taking such a hit, and with no federal programs in place for this circumstance, damaged areas soon came to be called "ghost towns." As the buildings emptied, new problems developed with criminal activity and vandalism (Comerio 1998a; Bolin and Stanford 1998). Perhaps fortunately, though, 1994 was an election year, and political support for reconstruction prompted some unique efforts (Wu and Lindell 2004).

Funding for multifamily reconstruction developed from several sources. To deal with the security problems, FEMA paid for security guards and perimeter fencing and paid to board up buildings and drain pools. The city of Northridge received $321 million in Housing and Urban Development (HUD) Supplemental Disaster Relief Funds for area housing. HUD also advanced funds from its Community Development Block Grants (CDBG) and HOME Investment Partnership Funds. The city of Los Angeles also put together several programs, including $10,641,000 in funding for single and multifamily housing. Private lenders offered forgiveness on some mortgages. Los Angeles provided loans for 12,000 units that would not otherwise have received assistance. By 1997, three-fourths of the units were repaired (Comerio 1998a).

Despite this unusually high level of effort to restore multifamily housing, a number of renters "fell through the cracks" of the assistance efforts, as we will find nearly always occurs in disasters. As one renter said, "I was not wearing my hearing aids that morning, of course, it was 4:31 in the morning. When my foot hit the floor, my bare feet felt every piece of glass that had broken. My husband was out of town, I was alone and extremely scared; my husband is profoundly deaf, no one even told him there had been an earthquake. I went to FEMA there was no interpreter. Someone later suggested I call my congress woman. Almost nine months passed before I got my FEMA check." When people fall through the cracks, many voluntary organizations step up to assist. Up to 160,000 area residents received help from approximately 450 voluntary organizations.

Princeville, North Carolina[1]

In 1999, seven major rain events, including two hurricanes, destroyed most of Princeville, North Carolina. FEMA offered to relocate residents via what is known as a **buyout**. In an interesting and controversial decision, the town's elected officials voted 3–2 to decline the offer. Although some individuals accepted the offer, most stayed, an interesting choice, as Princeville has flooded dozens of times in its history. What would cause people to want to stay in a location like this? The answer lies in Princeville's history and heritage.

Locals first named the area Freedom Hill when Union troops told local slaves that the Civil War had ended. These new citizens established the first town incorporated by African Americans (Brown 2001; U.S. Department of State 2003). Freedom Hill later became "Princeville in honor of a resident who led the community through a flood in the 1880s" (Hicks 2001). People and their ancestors have lived in Princeville for generations, and the land represents something very meaningful to them.

As we might find in many rural locations, housing conditions had declined over time. In 1974, the North Carolina Department of Natural and Economic Resources categorized 45.5% of Princeville's housing as deteriorating and an additional 38.6% as unsafe. The local average household income at the time of the 1999 flooding was $15,916, in part because 51% of households were elderly women living on social security, with limited means for recovery.

Many Princeville residents felt strongly about their community's legacy. Their heritage includes extensive stands against racism, defending the town's right to self-determination, battles against segregation and economic deprivation, and of course coping with the continual threat of flooding. Princeville also represents a heroic place in our nation's history: "to be absolute owners of the soil, to be allowed to build upon their own lands cabins, however humble, in which they should enjoy the sacred privileges of a home, was more than they had ever dared to pray for" (The Freedman's Bureau as quoted in Mobley 1981, 2). In Princeville, former slaves could afford land, establish homes, raise families, and enjoy a life where they were collectively safer against threats of violence. As the generations unfolded, people took care of each other. They built a community together, standing firm against all threats to their right to exist. In 1976, the Edgecombe County Bicentennial Commission recognized that legacy of determination:

> In the midst of two of the most destructive floods of 1924 and 1940, there were a few diehards who refused to leave their homes or businesses. They took refuge on the second floor of the Grade School and imported their food by a motor boat. It was these die-hards with other local citizens who returned that kept Princeville alive. They too envisioned their forefathers' dream— they wanted a unique town; unique because it would be a town of Blacks governed by Blacks.

To help the rebuilding process, local elected officials and the Congressional Black Caucus lobbied for aid. The President's Council on the Future of Princeville was created to "help this city that occupies such a significant place in our history." The council later recognized that:

The legacy of Princeville is one of survivorship.... The people of Princeville are very proud of their heritage and their ability to overcome adversity. Their decision to stay was a courageous one, and the Federal Government can provide Princeville with the opportunity to preserve its place in American history while rebuilding a better, safer, and more disaster resistant community.

An extensive set of voluntary, community, and civic organizations sent volunteer teams to help Princeville rebuild. To reduce the chance of further risks, the levee was strengthened to withstand a similar flood, and drainage ditches were cleared of tree roots and brush. Volunteers built homes 3–5 feet higher in elevation (see Photo 7.1). Most people in Princeville returned home.

The Red River Flood

In 1997, a series of winter blizzards with heavy snowfall caused spring flooding in Grand Forks, North Dakota (population 52,000), and East Grand Forks, Minnesota (population 9,000); the collective area that was affected is referred to as Grand Forks. On April 18, officials evacuated neighborhoods along the Red River as sirens sounded. Levee failures and overtopping poured water across 1.7 million acres, including the entire downtown commercial sector (Fothergill 2004). All public schools sustained major

PHOTO 7.1 Home elevation in Princeville, North Carolina. (Photo by Brenda Phillips. With permission.)

damage. Almost everyone had water damage to their homes and livelihoods (Fothergill 2004).

On April 19, fire broke out downtown and damaged three city blocks. The floodwaters prevented the fire department from fighting the fire, so airborne firefighters were dispatched to pour chemicals into the inferno. On April 21, the Red River crested at a record 54.35 feet, well beyond the 28-foot flood stage and several feet over the levees. It took a month before the Red River finally fell below flood stage (City of Grand Forks 2007a). Ninety percent of the city flooded at a cost of $1 billion, one of the worst natural disasters in U.S. history (FEMA 2007b). Approximately 1,000 homes had to be demolished, including entire neighborhoods (Fothergill 2004).

The disaster revealed the complexity of coming back for many populations, a situation not unique to Grand Forks. For example, locals reported that death rates among the elderly seemed to increase in the years following the flood. Suicide rates among younger residents also reportedly increased. Domestic violence may have increased, but certainly services decreased with so many service providers and protection authorities now facing displacement themselves (Fothergill 2004). As we find in other disasters, gender distinctions—coupled with age, income, and cultural divisions—made the recovery challenging. Single mothers, representing one in ten households, found it difficult to secure affordable housing. Latina women reported feeling excluded, encountering some racial hostility while seeking agency assistance and housing. Woman-owned businesses suffered because the flood destroyed in-home livelihoods such as typing, child care, salons, and bookkeeping. Without child care, other women had to step out of paid employment; some found new work in disaster-relief agencies. Older women delayed retirements in order to survive economically (Enarson 2001).

Yet, Grand Forks rebounded. Ten years later, residents looked back to realize they had produced considerable new construction, including 985 individual homes, 594 townhouses, and 1,328 multifamily units (City of Grand Forks 2007b). How did they rebuild Grand Forks housing? Doing so required strong leadership and joint partnerships among local, state, and federal entities. During the rebuilding, FEMA provided $9.8 million for travel trailers and mobile homes to 787 displaced residents, and poured $73 million into **individual assistance**, including $44.8 million in housing for 21,846 applicants in Grand Forks County (FEMA 2002). The National Flood Insurance Program (NFIP) paid $75 million in claims to the city.

The state relied on an extensive set of agencies to help with the recovery. The North Dakota Department of Human Services partnered with others, such as the Red Cross, to help those formerly in nursing homes or receiving home-based care (North Dakota Emergency Services 2007). The Bank of North Dakota, the only state-owned bank, offered lines of credit to the Department of Emergency Management, the city of Grand Forks, and the

University of North Dakota. The state's Housing Financing Agency focused on **temporary housing** and financing permanent-housing recovery. What you read here only represents a small portion of the state and federal effort.

To safeguard the community's future, the city bought homes in flood-prone areas and established new earthen berms and concrete floodwalls (City of Grand Forks 2007b). FEMA, the state of North Dakota, and HUD offered funding for mitigation projects that included buyouts totaling $40 million in order to relocate 850 properties outside of the floodplains (FEMA 2002). Enhanced flood-control projects strengthened levees and repaired or built pumping stations and stormwater drainage systems (sewers, ditches).

Did it work? In April 2006, Grand Forks watched as the fifth-highest flood in its history caused no damage (FEMA 2007a). Ten years after the flood, the city's population had returned to higher levels than before the flood. An industrial park had brought in 2,000 new jobs. The downtown and its historic structures were restored, along with new housing options across the city. "It is the people who make recovery happen—citizens, business own-ers, elected officials, government partners, volunteers, disaster relief workers and politicians" (FEMA 2007b).

Challenges and Problems

A wide range of challenges awaits those involved with housing recovery efforts. First, the nature of the hazard may require different approaches. After the 1989 Loma Prieta earthquake, for example, a prequake drought condition delayed rebuilding in the more mountainous areas. Officials waited until the rains returned to determine slope stability before awarding rebuilding permits, a time period that lasted for several years. As an extreme example, Superfund sites that involve hazardous materials or toxic waste (described further in Chapter 5, Environmental Recovery) may mean per-manent evacuations and **relocations** of entire communities. And, though post-Katrina rebuilding has been launched along the Gulf Coast, a poten-tially "toxic brew" from chemicals, pesticides, oils, and other contaminants in the storm surge and flood raises questions about whether rebuilding should occur in some areas.

Local real estate conditions will influence rebuilding too. Low vacancy rates mean units are simply not available. A lack of affordable rental housing may mean temporarily living in trailers, doubling or tripling the number of people in a home, or leaving the area. Postdisaster prices may also escalate for area housing, meaning that low-income families will struggle. As seen in the scenarios above, the type of housing also matters. Single-family homes that have been insured will return more quickly. The cost to rebuild repre-sents yet another challenge. A house built in 1940 with a paid-off mortgage of $15,000 may now cost $100,000—or more in some areas—to rebuild.

For those living in congregate settings, such as nursing homes, assisted-living centers, or group homes, a range of partnering agencies may have to provide temporary and permanent solutions. Responding agencies may not have thought through how to assist particular populations, such as households with a family member who has a disability. Providing sufficient numbers of accessible temporary trailers remains problematic to this day. Large or multigenerational families may need more space to stay together, although postdisaster housing often downsizes due to the costs of rebuilding.

Geographic areas can influence options too, such as in areas like New York City or the West Coast, where prices of rentals and homes remain out of reach for many. The state of the economy can influence rebuilding, such as the regional recession that influenced the Northridge recovery. Ties to places matter as well, and can influence decisions to stay or leave. Historic preservation provides us with a meaningful connection to our past and serves as a reason to rebuild.

Though we may think that the government will step in to provide assistance, even these roles are influenced by some considerations. First, a disaster must meet the criteria for a presidential disaster declaration so that assistance becomes available. For example, ice storms, which may disrupt power and bring down thousands of trees on homes, may not qualify for all types of federal assistance. Federal funding occurs within legislated boundaries that influences what homeowners, renters, and municipalities can receive. However, FEMA and the Small Business Administration (SBA) do provide considerable resources through grants and loans for repairs and rebuilding, particularly to homeowners (see Figure 7.1).

The arrival of recovery organizations, donations, and volunteers also matters. In larger-scale disasters, it is not unusual for many voluntary, civic, and **faith-based organizations** to arrive and help with the rebuilding. In a catastrophic context like Katrina, those resources will be stretched to their breaking point. Organizations will still face other disasters at the same time, leaving some communities unassisted. Generally, though, the arrival of these volunteers means that those who would face difficulty rebuilding—especially single parents, seniors, people with disabilities, low-income families, and others—may have a chance to go home.

Approaches to Housing Recovery

In this section, we will explore various strategies for rebuilding a damaged residential sector. First, we will start with general overviews of how recoveries might be fueled. Next, we will explore rebuilding philosophies consistent with those described in Chapter 2. Finally, we will explore efforts that rebuild with an eye to the future.

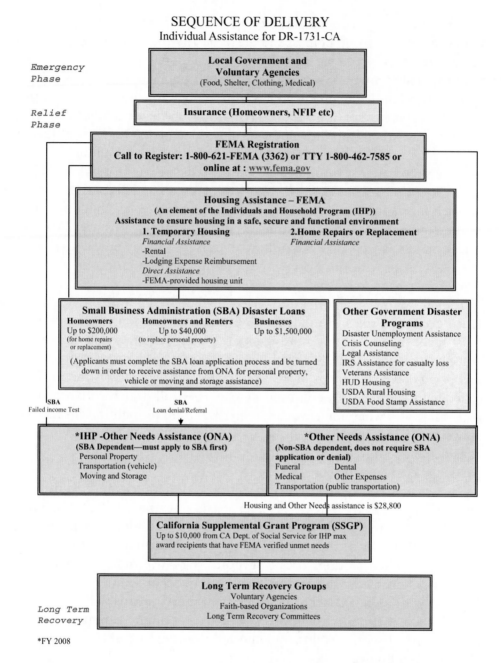

SEQUENCE OF DELIVERY
Individual Assistance for DR-1731-CA

Emergency Phase

Local Government and Voluntary Agencies
(Food, Shelter, Clothing, Medical)

Relief Phase

Insurance (Homeowners, NFIP etc)

FEMA Registration
Call to Register: 1-800-621-FEMA (3362) or TTY 1-800-462-7585 or online at : www.fema.gov

Housing Assistance – FEMA
(An element of the Individuals and Household Program (IHP))
Assistance to ensure housing in a safe, secure and functional environment

1. Temporary Housing
Financial Assistance
-Rental
-Lodging Expense Reimbursement
Direct Assistance
-FEMA-provided housing unit

2.Home Repairs or Replacement
Financial Assistance

Small Business Administration (SBA) Disaster Loans

Homeowners	Homeowners and Renters	Businesses
Up to $200,000 (for home repairs or replacement)	Up to $40,000 (to replace personal property)	Up to $1,500,000

(Applicants must complete the SBA loan application process and be turned down in order to receive assistance from ONA for personal property, vehicle or moving and storage assistance)

Other Government Disaster Programs
Disaster Unemployment Assistance
Crisis Counseling
Legal Assistance
IRS Assistance for casualty loss
Veterans Assistance
HUD Housing
USDA Rural Housing
USDA Food Stamp Assistance

SBA Failed income Test

SBA Loan denial/Referral

*IHP -Other Needs Assistance (ONA)
(SBA Dependent—must apply to SBA first)
Personal Property
Transportation (vehicle)
Moving and Storage

*Other Needs Assistance (ONA)
(Non-SBA dependent, does not require SBA application or denial)
Funeral   Dental
Medical   Other Expenses
Transportation (public transportation)

Housing and Other Needs assistance is $28,800

California Supplemental Grant Program (SSGP)
Up to $10,000 from CA Dept. of Social Service for IHP max award recipients that have FEMA verified unmet needs

Long Term Recovery Groups
Voluntary Agencies
Faith-based Organizations
Long Term Recovery Committees

Long Term Recovery

*FY 2008

FIGURE 7.1 Sequence of aid delivery, California wildfires. (From FEMA.)

Recovery Models

In her book *Disaster Hits Home*, Professor Mary C. Comerio (1998a) describes four general **recovery models** for urban disasters:

Redevelopment model
Capital-infusion model

Limited-intervention model

Market model

In the **redevelopment model**, national-level agencies will lead and fund the recovery. The redevelopment model has been used where urban areas have been completely destroyed, such as the 1976 Tangshan, China, earthquake that killed at least 242,000 and destroyed 90% of a major urban area. Following up 28 years later, Professor Ken Mitchell (2004, 49) of Rutgers University described the Tangshan recovery as one that "now bids for inclusion among the world's more advanced urban areas." How did such a transformation occur? The central government devised a master plan and began rebuilding systematically. Physical infrastructure received top priority, and then prototype buildings adhered to strong mitigation standards. Soon after, housing received top priority in order to provide shelter to hundreds of thousands. The central government devoted 60% of annual reconstruction to housing (Mitchell 2004, 52).

A second model, the **capital-infusion model**, brings in outside aid through government or voluntary-organization assistance (Comerio 1998). This model is most common in developing nations, where relief organizations assist with housing and economic development activities. Massive relief efforts occurred after the Indian Ocean tsunami, when dozens of nations and relief organizations set up villages, offered economic development packages to restore local businesses, and assisted with rebuilding schools and hospitals. Thirteen nations suffered losses from the tsunami; dozens of nations contributed capital to provide relief.

Comerio's third model is the **limited-intervention model**. In this approach, insurance provides relief funds along with some government assistance. As Professor Comerio reports, and as we shall see shortly in the section on permanent housing, this model "tends to favor creditworthy home owners over poor or financially strapped home owners, and it completely overlooks all rental housing" (Comerio 1998a, 127). In short, the limited-intervention model assumes that individuals can afford to assume responsibility for the majority of their losses and will act to do so.

The final model is the **market model**, where the "real estate market will sort out the winners and losers" (Comerio 1998a, 127). This model means that you will have to rebound from the disaster on your own, without grants or loans from the national government. This model can result in considerable displacement of those affected by the disaster.

In the United States, the limited-intervention model best depicts housing recovery strategies. Both personal responsibility and broader support must take place for people to return home. Taking on personal responsibility is difficult though, for example, when senior citizens survive on monthly social security checks. The "winners" are those with sufficient economic means to rebuild or relocate. For those who would otherwise fall through the cracks, voluntary agencies and faith-based organizations (FBOs) step in. But the truth is that many people will face permanent displacement from homes, neighborhoods, and important social and religious support networks.

Holistic Recovery for Housing

As described in Chapter 2, a holistic approach to recovery means that all dimensions affecting the continued well-being of the community are considered. Holistic recovery requires that we consider fully all the elements that make a place worth living in: a vibrant economy, environmental quality, an equal chance for all to return home, a locally meaningful quality of life, a recovery process that includes and involves all stakeholders, and a rebuilt community that resists future disasters (NHRAIC 2005). What does this mean for housing recovery? At a minimum, a holistic recovery (NHRAIC 2005) suggests that housing recovery efforts should:

- Ensure that people of all generations, incomes, and educational levels have a place in the rebuilt community by providing housing that is not only affordable but accessible.
- Rebuild a diverse set of residential settings, including rentals, single, and multifamily dwellings as well as congregate-care locations and group homes.
- Avoid further damaging the natural environment by carefully managing debris and rebuilding materials (more on this in Chapter 4, Debris Management).
- Recognize and honor what makes the community a meaningful place to live, including cultural and historical elements (more on this in Chapter 5, Environmental Recovery, and Chapter 6, Historic and Cultural Resources). Increase the amount of green space in a community and safeguard places that are environmentally sensitive. Help restore the natural environment by replacing lost trees with native plants, flowers, and grasses that attract and retain local wildlife.
- Support efforts to build a more resilient economy by connecting housing to places of employment, perhaps through cyber-commuting, and other innovative solutions (more on this in Chapter 8, Business Recovery).
- Connect to public transportation so that people can return to work with less impact on environmental elements, including air pollution, perhaps by constructing pedestrian and biking pathways (more on this in Chapter 9, Infrastructure and Lifelines). Work effectively with the repaired infrastructure, including utilities, perhaps considering such options as underground location of utilities.

- Revise codes and ordinances to protect floodplains and upgrade stormwater drainage systems.

Mitigating Future Risks

If you have been through a disaster devastating enough to take your home, you obviously do not want to go through it again. But given the high risks that exist in many locations, is it realistic to rebuild? Mitigation implies engaging in activities that reduce risks, an "essential component of recovery because the best way to reduce the cost of post-earthquake rebuilding is through reduction of damages" (Comerio 1997, 177).

Two **mitigation options** exist. **Structural mitigation** means to incorporate built-in features that reduce risks. For example, in an area with high winds, it would be wise to include features that strengthen roofs, windows, and doors. After Hurricane Hugo damaged the U.S. Virgin Islands in 1989 (FEMA 2007c), a new mitigation code required hurricane roof clips, anchoring systems, and shutters. Public education, a **nonstructural mitigation** measure, served to explain to inspectors and homeowners how the new code could help make the islands a safer place to live. After Hurricane Katrina, voluntary organizations elevated homes under construction to avoid future storm surges (see Photo 3.2 in Chapter 3, which shows reconstructed homes in the Musicians' Village in New Orleans).

The federal government currently requires that communities must have mitigation plans in place prior to disaster. Some municipalities have been able to do so, but much of that work remains underway. The consequence is that those involved in rebuilding must aggressively pursue and support efforts that reduce future risks. Doing so means that, if a community has a mitigation plan in place, new codes, ordinances, and other safety measures will need to be followed. Regardless, it is advisable to engage in rebuilding that reduces future risks relative to the hazards that arise.

To illustrate, consider these "best practices" reported on the FEMA Web site. (or further detail, see http://www.fema.gov/plan/prevent/bestpractices/index.shtm.) Consider the mix of funding, partnerships, and imagination that bolstered safer living environments:

- In Lawrence County, Ohio, flooding threatened to repeatedly damage homes. With support from the Ohio Emergency Management Agency and FEMA, homeowners elevated their properties 3 feet to avoid future risks.
- In Los Angeles County, a planned development called Southern Oaks includes a 200-foot-wide greenbelt, designed specifically to provide a perimeter from wildfires. In the 2003 fires, the greenbelt gave firefighters a stronger chance to save homes. Because of the additional

earthquake hazard, builders bolted homes onto high-tension foundation slabs.

- Twisters that tear through the heart of the nation will meet resistance in Shawnee, Kansas. City code now requires that all multifamily developments must have tornado safe rooms built to FEMA-approved specifications.
- Historic Victorian homes in Ferndale, California, have been provided additional mitigation against repetitive flooding. A FEMA Hazard Mitigation Grant increased the size of the creek in some places and restored some natural areas to aid in water flow. The California Department of Transportation provided funding for drainage improvements.

Homeowners, renters, elected officials, and those involved with reconstruction should incorporate mitigation features into new construction. Municipalities should be encouraged to revise codes and ordinances that determine the level of future safety for their citizens. The best time for such changes to be made typically occurs right after disaster, when support is highest. Known as the "window of opportunity," now is the time to build in disaster-resistant features to protect future generations.

Types and Definitions of Disaster Housing

As hinted at earlier, it takes time to transition from a place of devastation into a rebuilt home. Most households move through a series of stages, although certainly not at the same pace. Some households are able to skip some stages and go straight from displacement into permanent housing while others require time to get resources into place and rebuild their homes. E. L. Quarantelli, the cofounder of the Disaster Research Center now at the University of Delaware, describes these stages as a four-fold process. People who are displaced after a disaster move from **emergency shelter** to **temporary shelter**, into temporary housing, and finally into permanent housing (see Figure 7.2).

Emergency and Temporary Shelter

What distinguishes each phase of the process? During the emergency shelter phase, people tend to find shelter that typically lasts less than 24 hours (Quarantelli 1982). Such shelter could be a car, a tent, or even a location where others gather, such as a school, or—as we saw with Hurricane Katrina—overpasses, areas of high ground, rooftops, or the convention center in New Orleans. Emergency sheltering does not provide any amenities such as food,

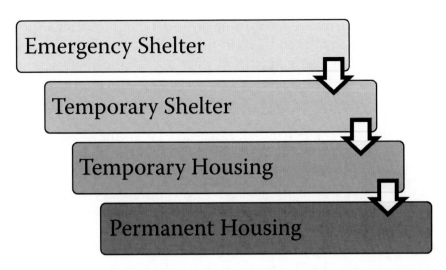

FIGURE 7.2 Sequence of return to housing. (Based on Quarantelli 1982. With permission.)

water, or clothing, and sometimes it does not even provide a roof over one's head.

Temporary shelter is distinguished by several factors. Usually some organizations in the community preplan a facility with food, water, bathrooms, sleeping areas, and security from the disaster. In the United States, the American Red Cross operates shelters under a congressional mandate. However, it is also common for local organizations to open facilities for displaced residents. Typically, only about 20% of all evacuees go to such shelters, with most preferring instead to stay with family, friends, or in hotels—at least until funds run out (Tierney, Lindell, and Perry 2001). Most shelters close within days, although in some circumstances they may remain open for months. After Hurricane Katrina, governmental and voluntary organizations established additional types of temporary shelter, including previously closed military bases, convention centers, recreational facilities, campgrounds, cruise ships, and hotels. Over 1,000 shelter locations opened across dozens of states, providing respite to over 1 million evacuees. Shelters remained open for months.

Temporary Housing

This chapter is mostly concerned with the latter two phases of housing recovery: temporary and permanent housing, which extend into the long-term recovery period. Temporary housing is characterized by reestablishing a household routine, including cooking, laundry, sleeping in private rather than public quarters, and living in a place that allows for travel to work and school (Quarantelli 1982). As with sheltering, not all households may accept temporary housing offered by assisting organizations, preferring instead to stay with families and friends, even if doubled or tripled up in cramped spaces. Income can also influence whether one uses temporary housing, with higher-income households appearing less likely to accept or even apply for aid (Quarantelli 1982).

Forms of temporary housing can vary, depending on local conditions such as availability of rental units, open spaces for mobile homes and travel trailers, and larger facilities that can accommodate people from places like nursing homes. The cost is also a factor. The price of a one-bedroom rental unit can vary dramatically across the United States from a few hundred dollars to several thousand. In the event of a massive disaster, where the entire community is destroyed, such as the EF5 tornado that destroyed Greensburg, Kansas, extensive efforts may be required to provide temporary housing. For a catastrophic event like Hurricane Katrina, the task of offering temporary housing requires months of creative planning, financing, and implementation, with significant expenditures from the federal, state, and local governments.

After a presidentially declared disaster, FEMA can provide funds and resources from its Individual Assistance Program (sometimes referred to as the Individual and Household Program) for temporary housing. In the following subsections, we will review three types of temporary housing used most commonly: rental units, trailers, and congregate-care facilities.

Rental Units

The best temporary housing solution at the local level is usually rental of apartments, homes, and, if necessary, trailers. Local rentals help stimulate the economy after a disaster by bringing in a new revenue source in the form of FEMA rental payments. Another boost to the local economy comes when residents remain in their community, shop locally, and support businesses where friends, family, and neighbors need to return to work. Local rentals also mean that children can stay in the same school system and parents can return to work. Being able to rent locally also keeps traumatized survivors connected to supportive social, religious, and cultural networks that help them through the ordeal of recovery (Turner et al. 2007).

Typically, FEMA or state and local governments will work with other agencies, including the local public housing office, charitable organizations, landlords, and realtors to compile lists of available rental units. After the 2007 California wildfires, HUD allowed prospective landlords and property owners to list units in its Internet-based National Housing Locator System. Nearly 26,600 available units were identified within weeks, with 22,000 of them within a 300-mile radius of San Diego County (HUD 2007). Newly homeless families could search by city, area code, price range, accessibility for people with disabilities and seniors, number of bedrooms and bathrooms, and whether the landlord could accept HUD housing vouchers (see www.socialserve.com). HUD also offers a regular voucher program, usually referred to as Section 8 and also called the Housing Choice Voucher Program. Vouchers must be put toward approved public housing. Families in that program prior to disaster can relocate across the United States using the vouchers (HUD 2008a).

Ideally, all displaced families will be able to find space that can accommodate the size of their family and its specific needs, including care of children, the elderly, and persons with disabilities. Many locations, however, lack affordable housing, rental availability, or units for persons with disabilities. Some rental units and even trailer parks may limit the size and number of pets, whom most people view as members of the family. Service animals, of course, must be accommodated in accordance with the Americans with Disabilities Act. Sometimes unique solutions must be developed.

As one example, in Santa Cruz after the 1989 Loma Prieta earthquake, high rents and limited availability meant few options for low-income families. To meet the need, local leaders established a Motel Voucher Program. Families could stay in local motels that allowed for cooking, thus providing a way to reestablish most household routines. More recently, the Lutheran Episcopal Services in Mississippi (LESM) worked with the Realtor Relief Fund in Mississippi to help renters after Hurricane Katrina. LESM provided disaster assistance to small landlords to help them qualify for matching funds to repair and rehabilitate rental property. To qualify, landlords had to commit to renting at pre-Katrina levels and to rebuilding affordable rental units. The approach was based on a holistic philosophy: help small, low-income landlords become self-sufficient; return affordable rental units to the market; keep workers close to their jobs; help the local economy; and stabilize communities.

Mobile Homes and Travel Trailers

Visualize a major urban area such as New York City, Los Angeles, Atlanta, or Detroit. Urban living means that homes often lack a sizable yard or even a driveway or garage. Where would you put travel trailers or mobile homes? That was exactly the problem in New Orleans, where FEMA was hard-pressed to locate areas large enough to accommodate this form of temporary housing. To handle the massive demand, FEMA created trailer parks across Louisiana, including fairgrounds and other open spaces. Within New Orleans, FEMA used parking lots next to postal offices and other public locations. To deal with the small yards, FEMA perched small travel trailers on tiny yards. The first trailers went into Louisiana in December 2005, and as of June 2008, 16,059 remained in place across the state (Brookings Institution 2008).

Trailers are not considered ideal temporary housing solutions by most everyone. Governmental officials considering trailer placement need to deal with a wide variety of problems. First, trailers are best placed in existing trailer parks with utilities and amenities like trash pickup, laundry, local transportation, and a place for children to play safely. The reality is that few communities have such open pads available to receive trailers. Consequently, officials face the challenge of creating a trailer-park site as rapidly as possible to move people out of temporary shelters. Doing so requires establishing the infrastructure for the site, including the aforementioned utilities as well as roads, driveways, and trailer pad sites.

Trailers must then be moved from storage or be purchased; checked for code compliance, safety, and health issues; and renovated if necessary. FEMA must then assign families to an appropriate trailer location that is close to work and schools, and ideally nearby kin and other social networks that can support them during the recovery. Utilities must be turned on, and families have to move in, all of which can take considerable time and expense. It is probably no surprise that trailers are often viewed as a last resort.

Trailer residents also report that they dislike the living experience—akin to camping out with your family for months or years at a time. Both mobile homes and trailers reportedly escalate family stress and increase the potential for conflict. After the Buffalo Creek flood in West Virginia in 1972, the haphazard placement of people into trailers without regard for prior social networks and neighborhoods increased family dysfunction (Erikson 1978). Perhaps it is not surprising to discover that trailer residents often refer to themselves as "spam in a can."

Living in a new and especially in an unfamiliar location requires people to reorient their routines, including buying groceries, doing laundry, obtaining health care, traveling to school and work, and finding transportation or new routes to those sites. Other problems may crop up too. FEMA faced a significant problem after Hurricane Katrina when formaldehyde was discovered in some trailers. In some instances, FEMA allowed residents with health concerns to temporarily relocate to hotels and motels. The final problems with trailers and trailer parks include moving residents into alternative housing, waiting until the home is rebuilt, closing down the trailer park, restoring the site to its original state, and transporting the trailers back to a storage site to await the next disaster.

Congregate-Care Facilities

After the 1989 Loma Prieta earthquake, local officials sought creative solutions to provide housing for residents displaced from three single-room occupancy (SRO) hotels in downtown Santa Cruz. Such SROs provided an affordable place to live for many in an area of high rents and limited availability. SRO residents ranged from low-income and nearly homeless individuals to seniors and people with cognitive disabilities. FEMA provided funding to reopen a closed nursing home. Many of the displaced found a home there, cared for by local social workers and staff experienced in providing an appropriate environment. The SROs eventually reopened about two years later, showing that such creative, locally inspired, and governmentally funded partnerships may be needed.

Large-scale facilities may be necessary for a number of populations besides people living in low-income hotels. State schools and other settings for people with cognitive disabilities represent another category for potential congregate temporary housing. And of course, nursing homes, rehabilitation units, and assisted-living centers are not immune to disaster. Ideally, congregate populations would be relocated collectively along with their caretakers, health-care staff, and social services staff to maintain continuity of care, but often this is not logistically possible. Key personnel, for example, may have lost their own homes or cannot get to a new place of work.

Clearly, there are problems with temporary housing of all kinds. In 2008 and early 2009, FEMA created a **National Disaster Housing Plan** and a **National Disaster Housing Strategy** in response to problems stemming from Hurricane Katrina and other events. Details can be viewed in Box 7.1.

BOX 7.1 NATIONAL DISASTER HOUSING STRATEGY AND PLAN

In June 2008, FEMA released its National Disaster Housing Plan, and in January 2009 it offered a National Disaster Housing Strategy plan. The National Disaster Plan is designed to provide interim housing (referred to as temporary housing in this chapter). To do so, FEMA's prioritized approach is:

1. Maximize available housing resources. Steps will include:
   - Reducing further damage to homes by installing tarps on roofs
   - Offering up to $28,800 in grants for repairs
   - Providing rental assistance funding
   - Identifying vacancies of rental property
   - Authorizing temporary hotel-motel funding as transitional shelter
   - Providing funding to other states hosting displaced residents
2. Use traditional forms of interim housing. Efforts will include:
   - Providing manufactured housing on private property, existing pads or a new site (last resort)
   - Conducting pre-placement interviews (PPIs) with victims to determine length of interim stay
   - Identifying pad locations and negotiate leases
   - Identifying private properties for placement, including mobile home parks or other locations

- Transporting mobile homes and trailers to affected area quickly
- Accelerating production of new manufactured housing
- Testing all temporary housing units for formaldehyde

3. Employ innovative forms of interim housing. Those forms may involve:
   - Identification of eligible households for alternative housing units
   - Considering placement of "Katrina Cottages," which are small, quickly placed pilot units currently being assessed
   - Work with HUD to look for multifamily apartment rehabilitation projects under a current pilot program
   - Authorize permanent housing construction where interim housing is not available or not cost effective

To maximize support and outreach to disaster victims, FEMA plans to:

- Assign additional staff to register victims for assistance
- Accelerate housing inspections
- Increase public communications to victims

Each state will be asked to establish and lead a Housing Solutions Task Force to bring together state and federal agencies, voluntary organizations, and private-sector partners in a planning effort. FEMA encourages including disability organizations and advocacy groups to help serve people with special needs or with literacy or language issues.

These plan elements will be further developed in a National Disaster Housing Strategy.

Source: FEMA 2009 Disaster Housing Strategy. http://www.fema.gov/pdf/media/2009/ndhs_pdf.

Once families have entered into and begin moving through the temporary housing stage, they face the daunting task of finding permanent housing including rebuilding. We turn to this phase next.

Permanent Housing

The remainder of this chapter will deal with permanent housing, including the many challenges and problems associated with housing recovery; the approaches that can be used to regenerate lost residential stock; the perspectives of individuals, government officials, and voluntary organizations involved in the permanent housing phase; and the resources required to rebuild. Permanent housing is defined as a home from which the originally displaced person or family will not have to move again as a result of the original disaster (Quarantelli 1982). Moving displaced families from shelters to permanent housing can be time consuming, frustrating, and exhausting.

Few local officials are prepared for the job (Quarantelli 1982), as assisting residents with housing is only one task among the many others that arise: debris management, donations and voluntary management, infrastructure and utilities restoration, environmental recovery, historical and cultural retention, business-sector rebuilding, and maintenance of public-sector services. In general, three options exist for residents: move into rental facilities, rebuild or purchase a new home, or move away permanently.

Renters

Residents can reach the permanent-housing stage most quickly if they can secure rental units, an option most appropriate for those who rented predisaster. As with the temporary-housing phase, officials and organizations may assist renters in moving quickly to permanent rental housing by developing lists of available units and distributing them to those who are displaced. A number of charitable disaster organizations may be able to provide assistance with a first month's rent and a deposit. Other experienced disaster organizations like the American Red Cross and Salvation Army may provide vouchers to purchase necessary household items, basic furniture, and essential appliances or may be able to pass on such items if they were donated and are in good shape (see Chapter 12, which addresses the challenges associated with such donations).

Low-income families could face a more extended time before reaching permanent housing, depending on the availability of affordable units. Families who live in public projects or units funded by HUD (Phillips 1998) may need to wait until new units are authorized by HUD. After the 2005 Gulf Coast hurricanes, FEMA and HUD collaborated on the Disaster Housing Assistance Program (DHAP) that provided rental housing assistance coupled with **case management**. The latter dimension focused on having public housing agencies assist renters/clients with a range of services, including job training, financial education, and other services. DHAP provided a means to assist families with moving out of the temporary FEMA trailers and into rental units (HUD 2008b).

Homeowners

Depending on one's income level, insurance, amount of damage, and understanding of the (re)building process, getting back to permanent housing can occur quickly or it can take years. For those with minimal damage, adequate insurance, and some savings, it may be fairly easy to either stay in one's home during repairs or use insurance funds for a short-term stay elsewhere. At the other end of the continuum, those with major damage may face considerable time away from home. Think about the steps that have to be undertaken before that happens:

- Debris must be sorted, piled, and removed, including hazardous materials like household and vehicular chemicals, pesticides, and painting supplies.
- Insurance and/or federal and state funds for rebuilding must be secured. Insurance companies can deliver a check within days, or there could be delays ranging from weeks to years. For example, an insurance company may determine that the damage is either flooding or wind that is not covered, a situation that often ends up in court. Insurance companies may face business foreclosure in a large-scale event and may not be able to fulfill their obligations. Companies may also experience difficulty in accessing closed-off areas to determine damage.
- If insurance money is not available, homeowners will need to secure grants or loans for rebuilding.
  - FEMA provides grants and loans to homeowners through four main types of housing needs. A homeowner may secure funds for temporary housing, repair to make the home "safe, sanitary and functional," replacement costs not covered by insurance, and permanent home construction (FEMA 2008). The process requires the homeowner to apply through the Small Business Administration (for a typical example, refer back to Figure 7.1). Based on income, the homeowner will either receive a loan (maximum of $200,000) or be rejected and referred to individual assistance programs for a grant. The maximum grant in 2008 was $28,800. Since it is nearly impossible to rebuild a home anywhere in the United States for $28,800, most families will then apply to any state funds that may become available and to local groups such as the Long-Term Recovery Committee or the **Unmet Needs** Committee (see Chapter 14, Voluntary Organizations, for additional detail).
  - Homeowners must go through a FEMA inspection to verify property damage.
  - Homeowners (and renters) may also qualify for other assistance, including room furnishings, appliances, educational materials including computers and school books, tools used for a job, cleanup items, damage to a vehicle, and moving and storage expenses. FEMA defines "housing needs" to include structural parts of the home, components including windows and cabinets, sewage and water systems, heating and cooling systems, and utilities and costs related to securing and reconnecting trailers (FEMA 2008).
- Delays with insurance and processing aid requests can take a minimum of one month until the homeowner knows that he or she will

receive rebuilding funds. However, delays of up to months—even years, with court cases—may result.

- For a single-family home or small condo unit, the building site must be cleared and prepared. A concrete slab may need to be removed and repoured, or a new housing footprint may need to be laid out. In some areas without adequate replacement insurance, it may simply not be affordable to rebuild to the same size as before.

- Blueprints for a new home must be designed and approved.

- Building permits and a building contractor, as well as subcontractors for such things as plumbing, electrical work, and framing, must be secured. These tasks depend on others, including city officials who may implement new codes to enhance safety (such as roofing restrictions), updates to ordinances (such as how far the house is set back from the street), or new ideas for the rebuilt community (for example, to incorporate sidewalks, open space, or underground utilities). A shortage of available contractors and subcontractors may delay rebuilding.

- If you have completed the prior steps, you can now begin the rebuilding process. That is, if you can secure the necessary building supplies. In past disasters, it has been difficult to purchase sheetrock for the interior walls of the home, as well as windows and roofing materials. After Hurricane Katrina, those involved in rebuilding their homes would go to the local building supplies store that week to see what was in. If doors had been shipped, they bought and stored doors or waited for the next shipment.

- If you are one of the persons lacking sufficient insurance and if you qualified for the FEMA grant, you may now have $28,800 to rebuild your home. Many of the elderly living on social security—who own their homes outright, but cannot afford sufficient insurance coverage (or perhaps any at all)—now find themselves in a bind. Low-income families now face a seemingly insurmountable road back home. Several options may appear to provide additional help:

  - The state you live in may choose to offer funds for rebuilding. After the 2007 California wildfires, the State Supplemental Grant Program of the California Department of Social Services issued grants to those who received the maximum FEMA award (FEMA 2007a). The state provided grants of up to $10,000 for repairs, temporary housing expenses, and personal property.

  - At this point you may now have $38,800, still not enough to rebuild nearly anywhere, particularly in areas with higher costs of living. Even if you paid $25,000 originally for your home during the 1940s or 1950s, the cost of rebuilding that same home today could soar well over $100,000. How will you make up the difference?

- Most communities establish a Long Term Recovery Committee or Unmet Needs Committee that connects to clients through social service providers. Case managers will usually sit with a family and establish a plan for getting them back home. The case manager will present that case to the committee, and voluntary organizations will offer assistance to that family. As detailed in Chapter 14 (Voluntary Organizations), many faith-based and civic organizations will either provide specific resources or services (like shingles and roofers) or take on an entire home and rebuild it for a family. Voluntary labor is the only way that thousands of people return home (see Photo 7.2).
- As you move through the rebuilding process, it is necessary to have each major portion of the home approved by city inspectors. These inspectors ensure that the home complies with local codes, which are designed to ensure your safety and address design standards for the community, including historic elements.
- Congratulations! You may now purchase new furniture and appliances or request them through voluntary organizations that have gathered such donations. It is time to move back home.

PHOTO 7.2 Voluntary housing labor, New Orleans. (Photo courtesy of First Presbyterian Church, Stillwater, OK. With permission.)

If you grew weary reading through the process, imagine staying in a travel trailer, hotel room, or with family while rebuilding. You may be living out of suitcases, unable to cook the kinds of food that you want, and traveling out of your way to take children to now-distant schools or to your own worksite. You are trying to stay on top of the rebuilding; to schedule contractors, subcontractors, and inspectors; to deal with the FEMA and insurance paperwork; and to remain optimistic that you will get home again. You are away from neighbors and social support networks and, if this is a catastrophic event like Katrina, you may be away from your own family. Indeed, many households had to live apart for years after Katrina, with the majority of the family renting in cities like Houston, Jackson, or Atlanta while one family member stayed in the damaged area guiding the rebuilding and trying to hold on to a job.

For some families, it may seem like the easier route is to accept a permanent relocation, especially if they live in a repetitively dangerous area that continually floods. However, as we will see next, such permanent relocations will have both advantages and disadvantages.

Permanent Relocations

In the United States, federal funds can be used by states to acquire homes (usually in floodplains) in order to voluntarily and permanently relocate residents out of floodplains and other dangerous areas. These acquisitions, also known as buyouts, have been used increasingly since the 1990s as a way to mitigate disaster risks. From a governmental perspective, relocation results in reduced expenses for future disasters, a form of cost effectiveness. The Office of the Inspector General defines cost effectiveness using OMB guidelines for benefit-cost analysis. Benefit-cost analyses for buyouts are based on "an estimate of damages and losses before mitigation; an estimate of damages after mitigation; an estimate of the frequency and severity of the hazard causing damages, that is the risk (such as floods) and the economic factors of the analysis (such as the mitigation project's useful lifetime, which is usually 30 years)" (FEMA 2001, 26–27). The government uses buyouts as a means to decrease rapidly increasing disaster-related costs and losses (National Wildlife Federation 1998; Mileti 1999).

The largest buyout occurred in Missouri after the Midwest Floods of 1993 (National Wildlife Federation 1998). Missouri governor Mel Carnahan established the buyout program using funds from FEMA and the Community Development Block Grant program (SEMA 1994). Fifty-seven communities in Missouri participated in the program, an effort labeled a great "success" primarily because subsequent flooding resulted in dramatically reduced presidential disaster declarations and costs to the government.

The Missouri Buyout Program cost FEMA $100 million overall, with $54.9 million dedicated to acquiring 4,800 properties. As seen in Figure 7.3,

Arnold, Missouri	1993 Flood	1995 Flood	2002 Flood
Sandbagging sites	60	3	0
Public Assistance	$1,436,277	$71,414	$0
Individual Assistance Applications	52	26	1

FIGURE 7.3 Missouri buyout data. (Adapted from FEMA 2002.)

success was measurable in Arnold, Missouri, where buyouts dramatically reduced costs from repeat floods (FEMA 2002; FEMA/DHS 2003).

Resistance to Relocations

Relocations may not always be viewed with enthusiasm by residents. After relocations in Prairie du Chien, Wisconsin, Rivera (1993) observed that "a community and a way of life was lost. The people who lived by the river, and made their lives along the river were swept away without a trace. Their history has almost been completely eliminated." Officials also observed this in Belham, North Carolina, where elevations proved more appropriate: "The reason the town was built in this location was because of the water. Many residents enjoy fishing and crabbing and boating and they will not relocate. People who live here aren't going anywhere" (Tibbetts 1999, 7).

As described in Chapter 5 (Environmental Recovery) and Chapter 6 (Historic and Cultural Resources), places are important to people because we embed ourselves into the fabric of a geographic location that has meaning for our individual and collective identities (Hummon 1998, 1990; Altman and Low 1992; Brown and Perkins 1992; Rubinstein and Parmelee 1992; Phillips 1998). Homes in particular provide "financial security, sentimental experiences, social relationships, and memories; and a cultural symbol that expresses stability, comfort, and identity" (Cheng, Kruger, and Daniels 2003, 89). In short, we have memories tied to places (Lavin and Agatstein 1984). The places where we live also help people to form stronger community bonds and a sense of commitment to a larger set of common goals (Brown and Perkins 1992; Proshansky, Fabian and Kaminoff 1983; Rapoport 1982b, 1982a). People forced to leave desirable locations may find it difficult to connect to a new place, including finding work that may have been tied to the previous locale.

Massive and continual disruption to those ties, such as when an entire community's social fabric is disrupted, may lead to significant personal and familial dysfunction (Erikson 1978). In an Australian study, Handmer (1985, 7) noted "high identification with community and place are also associated with resistance to relocation as is community identification itself." In short, when we experience displacement, we lose a critical resource (Phillips 1995).

Relocations that occur against the wishes of residents may result in considerable social and psychological disruption, adding to the stress experienced by disaster victims (for more, see Chapter 10, Social Psychological Recovery). This may be especially true for those required to leave the community permanently. Families with strong coping skills fare better, especially those that are able to "redefine the meaning of material possessions, immerse themselves in recovery activities and develop new understandings of what is important in life" (Riad and Norris 1996, 179). Relocation may be particularly challenging in some contexts, such as in locations where there are higher numbers of seniors or where, like the example with Princeville, there are strong cultural ties to places. Older residents may be more motivated to resist acquisition (Handmer 1985). Understanding how culture influences resistance to leaving a place, even a repetitively dangerous location, may enable us to understand why people will not leave and how best to make an offer to acquire properties.

Relocations that have occurred in the context of urban renewal advocate the importance of relocating the *entire* community and its way of life in order to preserve the social, cultural, environmental and psychological ties that enable people to survive and even thrive (Vaske and Kobrin 2001). For relocations to work, it appears that it is important to preserve "important primary social relationships and social support networks" found in families, neighborhoods, and the broader community (Rohe and Mouw 1991, 57). To do so requires a commitment from across the spectrum of organizations and agencies involved in housing recovery.

The Role of Local Government

Within the local government, a variety of expected and sometimes new roles must be played to launch the housing recovery. Initially, removing debris from roadways, yards, and homes requires effort from sanitation and street crews. Under a disaster, FEMA can pay for up to 75% of the costs of debris removal, which can take months to years. Local government will also need to convene a planning group if a recovery plan is not already in place (and as described in Chapter 3, most communities lack such guidance). Planning groups should include a housing task force that will look at and make a series of recommendations for rebuilding. That task force should include wide representation from across the community and consider all kinds of housing types (single family, multifamily, affordable housing) and look for creative ways to "rebuild smart" and retain the original population of the community (see Box 7.2).

Local government will also need to consider whether to change or keep existing ordinances. Disaster does represent an opportunity to make things different, even better. Change, though, may require concerted effort to

> **BOX 7.2 EQUITABLE HOUSING RECOVERY: LEARNING FROM WATSONVILLE, CALIFORNIA**
>
> As a means to assist renters and low-income homeowners, the city of Watsonville, California, passed an ordinance that 25% of all new postquake housing must be affordable. Watsonville went one step further and provided grants from $20,000 to $50,000 for people unable to secure loans. Overall, Watsonville committed $1 million to the recovery of low-income housing. Such action remains unusual in postdisaster reconstruction, but it is certainly sorely needed (Comerio 1998b). The American Planning Association (2004) describes affordable housing as a national crisis, with increasing numbers unable to secure adequate housing. In such situations, families may have to accept housing that is less than safe, including buildings not retrofitted for earthquakes, mobile homes that cannot withstand significant tornados, or homes that were built in or near floodplains. When disaster strikes and lower-rent housing takes a disproportionate hit, renters face a difficult journey home.

educate the public on the available options and why they represent sound ideas. Local government will have to balance an urge to "return to normal" and rebuild as quickly as possible vis-à-vis incorporating mitigation measures, rebuilding green, and ensuring a holistic recovery. Quickly convening a planning group with wide representation from across the community and working to build a consensus is key. Ideally, this kind of work will have taken place prior to the disaster so that new ideas can be acted upon and integrated into the reconstruction process as rapidly as possible.

Many communities opt to put new ordinances and codes into place after disaster, which will affect the rebuilding process. Some communities may now require hurricane roof clips or disallow wood-shake shingles with a reduced fire tolerance. In areas of wildfire, new guidelines may require a 3-foot "no vegetation" zone around a house perimeter as well as use of hardy native plants, driveways, and walkways that deter the approach of fire (Firewise 2008).

Local government will also oversee the process of issuing rebuilding permits. For most communities, that process can begin when debris removal is near an end. New ordinances and codes may delay the permitting process, as can decision making regarding the hazard itself. In areas of repetitive flooding, for example, communities may delay permitting until decisions are reached about relocations or elevations. Government is also responsible for ensuring that new construction follows existing and new codes. It does so through inspections on new construction, particularly the electrical, plumbing, and other central features of a home. Though it may seem bureaucratic, such a paperwork inspection process ensures that a homeowner enjoys a higher degree of safety with a newly built structure.

Without a doubt, though, the most significant role of local government concerns working with the public, state, and federal governments as well as volunteer organizations. Patience with exhausted and frustrated residents, and a commitment to helping them cope with the many layers of government, bureaucracy, and unfamiliar procedures will serve local leaders well. Convening and leading the recovery task force is only the first step of many that must be taken. Involving the public with proper notification, involvement, and decision making will produce a more accepted set of procedures for recovery. Although it is not possible to please everyone all of the time, a process to involve the public (see more in Chapter 13) is an absolute necessity.

Local governments may exhaust their staff through the seemingly relentless course of meetings and other activities required to get their communities back to normal. In Chapter 11, we will examine the impact of the disaster process on city staff. The good news is that there are partners out there willing to support a community that may be going through its first or its worst disaster event in local history.

The Role of the State

The role of the state may vary, depending on its resources, from providing direct funding to advocating for residential construction to serving as a liaison or pass-through for federal resources. The state plays a critical role in documenting the damages through a preliminary damage assessment. The governor then submits the damages, along with a request for a presidential disaster declaration, to FEMA. When the president grants the request and FEMA arrives, the state may function as a liaison to the local areas that were impacted, easing the transition of the federal partner into the affected areas. The state can also assist the federal partner by explaining local context, including political, economic, and demographic considerations that affect the recovery.

As described earlier in the scenarios, both California and North Dakota provided funding through state programs to help homeowners and those invested in multifamily housing. States may also direct agency resources to trouble spots, for example, in providing staff to investigate problems with insurance agencies, to encourage banks to initiate forgiveness on mortgage payments, and to protect consumers from unscrupulous contractors. Under federal guidelines, local and state funds must pay for 25% of the damages, while the federal partner pays 75%. Such amounts could run into millions of dollars, and into the billions for larger events.

State governments must serve as a liaison with other recovery partners. After the 2008 tornados in Tennessee, HUD worked with the state to streamline programs and expedite the use of CDBG and HOME funds (Federal block grant for affordable housing) for those affected by the disaster. States may also play an important role in working with donations offered to disaster victims by managing or working with appropriate agencies to organize and distribute donations. The state may provide resources so that voluntary agencies can get together and assess need. The state, as a lead entity for the interests of its citizens, may provide key leadership—often unseen—that serves as the glue that binds the levels of government together in a functioning housing recovery system.

The Role of the Federal Government

You have probably heard both praise for and critiques of the federal government's role in housing recovery (GAO 2007). Financially, FEMA and other agencies put significant amounts of money into the hands of homeowners, business owners, and others involved in putting communities back together again. Is it enough? Some might argue that the nature of our governmental system means that we all share responsibility in putting our lives back in order again. As a homeowner or a renter, it is certainly wise (though not always possible) to carry insurance sufficient to recover from disasters. In reality, insurance policies against some hazards are simply unaffordable for many. To help those in need, the federal government follows guidelines established by the Stafford Act and related programs. New programs may also be initiated for specific disasters, but in reality, all levels of government have some kind of limitation on what they can offer to the local and state government and to individual residents.

Upon approval of the presidential disaster declaration, FEMA may accept applications from homeowners for its Individual Assistance Program. As explained earlier in this chapter, there are two types of main aid for housing-related damages: grants and loans. Ideally, these loans will be supplemented with state and local funds along with a resident's insurance policy. In short, it will probably be necessary to pull together funds from multiple sources to rebuild, and our federal government is one of the key players in that funding.

FEMA may also set up a **Disaster Recovery Center** (DRC) where residents and local organizations can speak with representatives about housing assistance and rental information. The DRC is usually designed as a one-stop shopping center where information from all kinds of agencies can be provided. FEMA will also establish a 1-800 telephone number where applicants can submit information prior to approval and will maintain a Web site for online applications as well.

To ensure that compliance with federal rules is followed, FEMA sends out inspectors to verify the damage. Officials from the agency may also conduct an audit to ensure that funds dispersed were spent on actual damages. Homeowners may qualify for up to $200,000 in low-interest loans from the

Small Business Administration. Both homeowners and renters may obtain a loan up to $40,000 for personal property and vehicles damaged by the event.

When major disasters strike, the federal government may set up a **joint field office** and implement the National Response Framework. Housing matters fall under several functional areas, but for persons unable to begin rebuilding without additional financial assistance and volunteer labor, Emergency Support Function #6 (ESF #6), Mass Care, provides a location where interested organizations can initially convene and assess their potential role. While this type of federal housing support is not usually visible to the public, it plays a significant role. By providing a location and means for initial assessment, FEMA allows for the emergence and coordination of voluntary organizations willing to assist those otherwise unable to return home due to limited funds.

Returning home may not be as easy for some as for others. For people with disabilities, the return home may be one of those longer journeys. Disability may intersect with other life circumstances as well. For example, disabilities increase as people age. Senior citizens may face tighter budgets too, and not be able to qualify for loans. The journey starts with accessing aid and, as the quote earlier from the Northridge earthquake survivor demonstrates, access and information are not always quickly available. The National Organization on Disability recognizes three main forms of disabilities of concern to us here: mobility, cognitive, and sensory disabilities.

Temporary shelters are required by law to accept people with disabilities, including their service animals, but in reality some shelters have turned some away or referred them to "special needs" shelters, which is a violation of the Americans with Disabilities Act (ADA). Even temporary FEMA trailers have come under fire. One year after Katrina, a class-action lawsuit titled *Brou v. FEMA* resulted in a settlement for people with disabilities. The plaintiffs had filed suit when they were given inaccessible trailers that did not include ramps and wider doorways for wheelchairs, accessible bathrooms (bathrooms are typically very confining in a travel trailer), and lower kitchen counters and appliances (Fitzmaurice 2006; see Photo 7.3).

Think about the challenges of returning home. First, roads and walkways must be passable so that those with mobility disabilities can pass through to their homes. Both inside and outside of the home, items that were tossed about by the disaster must be removed. Assistive devices that were lost must be replaced, such as telecommunications equipment, motorized equipment and weather radios that alert people who are deaf. And, though mitigation remains the most important new feature in a home to reduce future risks, mitigation must be thought through for its effects on someone with a disability. Elevations make sense in flood-prone areas, but such elevations must be accessible.

An individual with a cognitive disability (such as Alzheimer's, a stroke survivor, an individual with autism) and his or her family may require

PHOTO 7.3   Reviewing a FEMA trailer for accessibility. (Photo by Patsy Lynch/ FEMA News Photo.)

guidance to apply for assistance and to design a supportive home environment. Someone with a sensory disability, including blindness, will benefit from learning how to renavigate his or her home and neighborhood.

Although many voluntary organizations care about circumstances such as those mentioned here, they may not have the expertise or experience to step up as fully as needed. Local and state organizations should be invited in to participate, including departments of rehabilitation, Veterans' Administration offices, disability advocates, and particularly the disability community itself. Integrating these partners early on into housing recovery planning represents the single best strategy to ensure that everyone gets to return home. The federal government has established several important initiatives to address the disaster needs of people with disabilities, such as elements of the National Disaster Housing Strategy described earlier in Box 7.1. In the coming years, students of emergency management should follow these initiatives as they develop further, including efforts by the National Council on Disability, the Federal Highway Administration, the Department of Justice, and the Department of Homeland Security.

Voluntary Organizations

Without a doubt, many thousands of families could never return home without the support of voluntary organizations such as the Mennonite Disaster

Service, Lutheran Disaster Relief, Habitat for Humanity, civic clubs like the Lions, and university students who volunteer their spring break time. In this section, we will look at the key roles played by voluntary organizations, including addressing unmet needs, assisting with case management, repairing and rebuilding homes, and assisting families with replenishing household goods.

Unmet Needs

In most disasters, a Long-Term Recovery Committee (LTRC) forms at the local level, usually with support and participation of outside organizations. Sometimes, the LTRC spins off an Unmet Needs Committee (UNC), or voluntary organizations establish a stand-alone UNC. An interfaith effort may emerge as well. The purpose of these committees is to identify needs that have not been addressed through insurance or governmental aid. As noted earlier, a family may secure the maximum FEMA grant but still lack the funds or knowledge for reconstructing their home.

During a committee meeting, a case manager (described next) will present the situation of a client family and identify specific needs that remain unmet. Voluntary organizations will then offer assistance with repairs, portions of a rebuilding project, resources, or may even take on an entire home to rebuild. A home may be rebuilt with the assistance of volunteer roofers from Presbyterian Disaster Assistance, building supplies from a Seventh-Day Adventist-managed multiagency warehouse, electrical work from volunteers in a trade union, sheetrock crews from Lutheran Disaster Relief, and painters from a group of university students. A skilled and experienced voluntary organization may even take on the entire rebuild from start to finish, rolling in volunteer crews from all over the country. Organizational leaders will work closely with the family whose home is being rebuilt, being sure to use insurance and FEMA money appropriately and then to supplement with labor and supplies as needed.

Construction crews require a number of skilled individuals to manage a project from start to finish. Architectural renderings must be completed prior to construction and then be approved through the local permitting process. Disasters may delay permitting, especially when local government changes building codes and ordinances. Similarly, the local government may take the disaster as an opportunity to update neighborhoods to new standards by incorporating sidewalks or underground utilities. A skilled construction leader must be engaged to see the project through from start to finish, and that person must understand many dimensions of building: electrical wiring, plumbing, pouring concrete foundations, framing the structure, roof construction, and more. Finding such an individual to coordinate this on a volunteer basis, often for months at a time, can be challenging.

Next, voluntary organizations must roll in individuals skilled enough to do specialized labor such as the wiring, plumbing, and heating and air conditioning systems. Others can be trained prior to or on the job, including installing drywall and shingles and doing basic work like plumbing and even flooring. Cabinetry work, hanging doors, putting in windows, and other more challenging work may mean scheduling work crews carefully so that the traditional one-week volunteer comes at the right time. More on these dimensions can be found in Chapter 14 (Voluntary Organizations).

Case Management

If you have never been through a disaster or have never built a home, the entire process may be quite confusing and even overwhelming. Many decisions must be made, and care has to be taken to ensure that building occurs within what local codes and ordinances require. For families facing the intimidating task of doing this work in a postdisaster context, assistance may be needed. Increasingly, communities seeking to help their residents have turned to a case-management process where disaster victims become clients in a system that ensures that their needs are met and that the family moves through the rebuilding process with adequate support.

To accomplish case management, a recovery committee may hire and train people to manage client cases. Where locals are overwhelmed, an outside organization may send in volunteers to assist, or they may conduct their own casework when they work on a family's home.

Disaster victims require appropriate and professional support. The profession of social work requires that the case-management process transpire through careful consideration of the steps that a client must go through and the resources that are required. The process should be followed by those working with professional standards who are accountable to both the client as well as the supervising agency. Until recently, managing individual clients and their families in disasters was often done through locally generated processes. After Hurricane Katrina, a faith-based effort emerged to professionalize the case-management process. The United Methodist Committee on Relief (UMCOR) led this effort by establishing Katrina Aid Today, a national case-management consortium. UMCOR's leadership designed a multistage process involving these steps (Earl 2007):

- *Engagement.* Clients in need enter through an intake process, where potential clients are assessed. Once determined eligible for services, the local agency opens a file and assigns a case manager.
- *Assessment.* The case manager assigned to the client listens to the history and current situation, and then works with the client to visualize what recovery would look like. Part of that process involves assessing the client's financial resources, barriers to recovery, available

resources, and time constraints. The case manager can check with FEMA and other agencies on the client's status. UMCOR, through Katrina Aid Today, provides a variety of tools for this, including a "Disaster Recovery Case Manager's Tool Kit" containing such items as assessment forms and release-of-information forms.

- *Recovery planning.* Once the client has been assessed, the case manager works with the client to establish a recovery plan. Action steps are identified and responsibilities are assigned. The plan moves the client through the recovery process.

- *Implementation and advocacy.* In this stage, the plan is initiated. The case manager may support the client through identifying resources and presenting the client's situation to the Unmet Needs Committee or other recovery organization. Case managers help to ensure that clients move toward recovery, do not duplicate services or benefits, and qualify for available resources.

- *Monitoring.* As the client makes progress through recovery, case managers reassess the action steps, identifying new barriers or stall points. Understandably, the disaster recovery process is difficult, and case managers can help to ease that process.

- *Closure and evaluation.* The final steps involve closing a client file either because the recovery action plan has been completed, because the client wishes to close the file, or because the client may transfer out of the process. Evaluation by the client, the case manager, and the agency supervisor then occurs.

UMCOR has led an important national effort to ensure professional standards and accountability for the case-management process. Their decades-long experience as a disaster voluntary organization has resulted in an absolutely critical contribution to disaster recovery for those affected. See Table 7.1 for a problem-solving checklist.

Summary

This chapter described how people, organizations, and government officials work through the housing recovery process. Steps involved in housing recovery include moving people from emergency or temporary shelter into temporary housing and, ultimately, permanent housing. Temporary housing may involve motels, trailers or mobile homes, temporary congregate facilities, or rental units. Permanent housing may take some time to secure or rebuild, especially in catastrophic events. Four housing recovery models may be followed, although the limited-intervention model is the one most common in the United States. Limited intervention occurs when insurance funds are combined with government assistance. For low-income

TABLE 7.1 Problem-Solving Checklist For Case-Managers

NEEDS	Potential Resources
❑ **HOUSING** • Relocating to less expensive housing, security deposits, • relocating to stable housing, • property taxes, • arrears related to disaster, • home repairs	FEMA Subsidized housing, bank loans, family loans, board of social services, housing assistance program
❑ **UTILITIES** • Heat, gas, phone, electricity, water, cable	L.I.H.E.A.P. Energy assistance LifeLine
❑ **NUTRITION** • Food, education	Food certificates, local food banks, Food stamps, WIC, Local hospital, community nursing
❑ **CHILD CARE**	Local religious institution Volunteers, after school programs
❑ **CONCRETE NEEDS** • Clothing, furniture, appliances	Salvation Army
❑ **EDUCATION**	
❑ **EMPLOYMENT**	
❑ **HEALTH / MEDICAL**	Hospital assistance program, Medicaid/Medicare Visiting nurse agencies, parish nursing, PAAD
❑ **IMMIGRATION ISSUES**	
❑ **INCOME ASSISTANCE**	Board of social services, unemployment compensation, disability (social security), workers' compensation
❑ **LANGUAGE /INTERPRETER**	International Institute
❑ **LEGAL SERVICES**	Legal aid, local law school
❑ **FINANCIAL SERVICES**	Credit counseling, bankruptcy, financial planning association
❑ **SENIOR SERVICES**	Area Office on Aging
❑ **TRANSPORTATION** • Public transportation, car repair, auto insurance	
❑ **VOLUNTEER ASSISTANCE**	
❑ **WELL-BEING** • Mental health, spiritual needs	

UMCOR-Katrina Aid Today   Version 02.17.06

Source: United Methodist Committee on Relief (UMCOR) and Katrina Aid Today. Available at http://www.katrinaaidtoday.org. With permission.

households, additional assistance may be necessary from a combination of governmental agencies and voluntary organizations. Local government typically bears responsibility for creating a rebuilding plan. That plan usually includes new, stronger building codes and ordinances and a permitting process. State government serves the role of providing funding and being a liaison to the federal government. Federal agencies can provide tremendous amounts of funds, programs, and technical advice. A number of voluntary and faith-based organizations may arrive to assist with rebuilding and reestablishing households. Those organizations often link to clients through a case-management process that is becoming increasingly formal and professionalized.

To afford to rebuild and to move toward recovery requires that people regain their economic livelihoods and that governments generate and use tax revenues. In the next chapter we will examine business-sector recovery and how it links to other dimensions of the housing recovery process. Strategies and ideas for green rebuilding are included in Chapter 8. Future chapters look at how local government addresses housing and other parts of the recovery process (Chapter 11). In Chapter 12 we look at how donations must be gathered and used for recovery, including housing. Chapter 14 looks comprehensively at how voluntary organizations assist with recovery, particularly housing.

Study Guide

Summary Questions

1. What four stages are involved as people move from shelter into permanent housing? How is each stage different?
2. Explain the differences between the four models of housing recovery. What are the limitations of each?
3. List and explain the challenges associated with housing recovery.
4. What would you expect to have to do as a renter affected by disaster?
5. What steps would you move through as a homeowner trying to rebuild?
6. What are some ways that mitigation has been built into disaster housing recovery?
7. What are the various roles of local, state, and federal government in housing recovery?
8. How do voluntary organizations provide support during housing recovery?
9. What are the basic steps in a case-management process?

Discussion Questions

1. Would a model other than limited intervention work as a housing-recovery strategy in the United States?
2. Look around at your community. What is the rental market like? Are there issues with availability or affordability? What would happen if your community lost 10% of its rental housing?
3. Examine the housing costs in your community. What is the range? Assume that you have just gone through a disaster that has taken over 1,000 homes with a variety of housing prices. How will those different homeowners be affected? What will their recovery experience be like?
4. Take on the perspective of one of the following and describe what you would do to fulfill your obligations in housing recovery: mayor, city council member, religious clergy, case manager, governor, FEMA official.
5. Go to the FEMA Web site and check its individual assistance page (currently at www.fema.gov, click on Disaster Assistance). What would it be like for you to apply for assistance? Does the process make sense to you?
6. Visit the **National Voluntary Organizations Active in Disaster** Web site (currently at www.nvoad.org). What kinds of organizations provide what kinds of assistance?
7. Why should there be a professionalized case-management process for displaced disaster survivors?

Key Terms

Buyout
Case management
Disaster Recovery Center (DRC)
Emergency shelter
Faith-based organization (FBO)
Individual assistance
Joint field office (FEMA)
Mitigation options
  Nonstructural mitigation
  Structural mitigation
National Disaster Housing Plan
National Disaster Housing Strategy
Permanent housing
Recovery models
  Capital-infusion model

Limited-intervention model
Market model
Redevelopment model
Relocation and buyout
Small Business Administration (SBA)
Temporary housing
Temporary shelter
Unmet needs

References

Altman, Irwin, and Setha Low, eds. 1992. Place attachment. New York: Plenum Press.

American Planning Association. 2004. Affordable housing crisis: The silent killer. http://www.planning.org/affordablereader/domesticpolicy/apr04.htm. Accessed August 2008.

Bolin, R. C., and L. Stanford. 1998. The Northridge Earthquake: Community-based approaches to unmet recovery needs. *Disasters* 22 (1): 21–38.

Brookings Institution and GNOCDC. 2008. Anniversary edition: Three years after Katrina. Greater New Orleans Community Data Center. http://www.gnocdc.org.

Brown, B., and D. Perkins. 1992. Disruptions in place attachment. In *Place attachment*, ed. I. Altman and S. Low. New York: Plenum Press.

Brown, F. 2001. The destruction of Princeville, the nation's oldest black-governed community. EarthAfrica News Service. http://www.seeingblack.com/x040901/princeville.shtml. Accessed February 20, 2003.

Cheng, A., L. Kruger, and S. Daniels. 2003. "Place" as an integrating concept in natural resource politics: Propositions for a social science research agenda. *Society and Natural Resources* 16: 87–104.

City of Grand Forks. 2007a. Flood timeline. http://www.grandforksgov.com/Flood/Timeline.pdf.

———. 2007b. Rebuilding. http://grandforksgov.com/Flood/Rebuilding.pdf.

Comerio, M. 1996. *The impact of housing losses in the Northridge earthquake: Recovery and reconstruction issues.* Berkeley: Institute of Urban and Regional Development, University of California-Berkeley.

———. 1997. Housing issues after disasters. *Journal of Contingencies and Crisis Management* 5: 166–178.

———. 1998a. *Disaster hits home: New policy for urban housing recovery.* Berkeley: University of California Press.

———. 1998b. Hazards mitigation and housing recovery—Watsonville and San Francisco one year later. In *National report to Congress on the Loma Prieta earthquake*, D29–D34. Washington, DC: U.S. Geological Survey.

Comerio, M., J. Landis, and Y. Rofé. 1994. *Post-disaster residential rebuilding.* Berkeley: Institute of Urban and Regional Development, University of California-Berkeley.

Earl, C. 2007. Case management. Available at http://www.katrinaaidtoday.org/casekey.cfm, accessed January 26, 2009.

Enarson, E. 2001. What women do: Gendered labor in the Red River Valley flood. *Environmental Hazards* 3: 1–18.

Erikson, E. H. 1978. *Everything in its path.* New York: Simon and Schuster.

FEMA. 2001. Buyouts: Hurricane Floyd and other issues relating to FEMA's hazard mitigation grant program. Washington, DC: Federal Emergency Management Agency, Office of Inspector General, Inspections Division.

FEMA. 2002. Success stories from the Missouri buyout program. http://www.fema.gov/mitigationbp/bestPracticeDetailPDF.do?mitssId=845.

FEMA. 2007a. State grant program gives funds to California wildfire victims. http://www.fema.gov/news/newsrelease.fema?id=41790.

FEMA. 2007b. Grand Forks flood. http://www.fema.gov/hazard/archive/grandforks/contents.shtm.

FEMA. 2007c. Building better: New building code and power upgrade, U.S. Virgin Islands. http://www.fema.gov/mitigationbp/brief.do?mitssId=950.

FEMA. 2008. Disaster assistance available from FEMA. http://www.fema.gov/assistance/process/assistance.shtm.

FEMA/DHS. 2003. The 1993 Great Midwest Flood: Voices 10 years later. Washington, DC: Federal Emergency Management Agency/Department of Homeland Security.

Firewise. 2008. Practical Firewise information. http://www.firewise.org/usa/fw_practices.htm.

Fitzmaurice, S. 2006. Katrina disability information, FEMA lawsuit. http://www.katrinadisability.info.

Fothergill, A. 2004. *Heads above water: Gender, class and family in the Grand Forks flood.* Albany: State University of New York Press.

GAO. 2007. Disaster assistance: Better planning needed for housing victims of catastrophic disasters. Washington, DC: Government Accountability Office.

Handmer, J. 1985. *Local reaction to acquisition: An Australian study.* Boulder, CO: Natural Hazards Research and Applications Information Center.

Hicks, G. 2001. Princeville: Intimate grounds. http://sai.cup.edu/caltimes/inside/mar01/1intimate.html.

Hirayama, Y. 2000. Collapse and reconstruction: Housing recovery policy in Kobe after the Hanshin great earthquake. *Housing Studies* 15: 111–128.

HUD. 2007. HUD encourages California landlords to place listings in the National Housing Locator to help those in fire area. News release, Oct. 30, 2007. Housing and Urban Development. http://www.hud.gov/news/release.cfm?content=pr07-164.cfm.

HUD. 2008a. Disaster Housing Assistance Program (DHAP). Housing and Urban Development. http://www.hud.gov/news/dhap.cfm.

HUD. 2008b. Disaster Voucher Program (DVP). Housing and Urban Development. http://www.hud.gov/offices/pih/publications/dvp.cfm.

Hummon, D. 1986. Place identities: Localities of the self. In *Purposes in built form and culture research*, ed. D. Carswell and D. Saile, 34–37. Proceedings of the 1986 International Conference on Built Form and Culture Research. Lawrence: University of Kansas Press.

Hummon, D. 1990. *Commonplaces: Community ideology and identity in American culture.* New York: SUNY Press.

Hummon, D. 1992. Community attachment: Local sentiment and sense of place. In *Place attachment*, ed. I. Altman and S. Low. New York: Plenum Press.

Lavin, M. W., and F. Agatstein. 1984. Personal identity and the imagery of place: Psychological issues and literary themes. *Journal of Mental Imagery* 8: 51–66.

Mitchell, J. K. 2004. Reconceiving recovery. In *New Zealand Recovery Symposium proceedings*, ed. S. Norman, 47–68. Wellington, NZ: Ministry of Civil Defence and Emergency Management.

Mobley, J. 1981. *Princeville: A black town in North Carolina, 1865–1981*. Raleigh: North Carolina Department of Cultural Resources.

National Wildlife Federation. 1998. *Higher ground: A report on voluntary property buyouts in the nation's floodplains*. Vienna, VA: National Wildlife Federation.

NHRAIC. 2005. *Holistic disaster recovery*. Boulder, CO: Natural Hazards Research and Applications Information Center.

North Dakota Emergency Services. 2007. North Dakota response to the 1997 disasters. http://www.fema.gov/pdf/hazard/archive/grandforks/report.pdf.

Parker, R. S. 2000. Single-family housing. In *Managing disaster risks in emerging economies*, ed. A. Kreimer and M. Arnold, 80–84. Washington, DC: World Bank.

Phillips, B. D. 1993. Cultural diversity in disaster. *International Journal of Mass Emergencies* 11: 99–110.

———. 1996. Homelessness and the social construction of places: The Loma Prieta earthquake. *Humanity and Society* 19 (4): 94–101.

———. 1998. Housing low income and minority groups after Loma Prieta: Some policy considerations. In *National report to Congress on the Loma Prieta earthquake*. Washington, DC: U.S. Geological Survey.

Proshansky, H. M., A. K. Fabian, and R. Kaminoff. 1983. Place identity. *Journal of Mental Imagery* 8: 51–66.

Quarantelli, E. L. 1982. Sheltering and housing after major community disasters: Case studies and general observations. Newark: Disaster Research Center, University of Delaware.

Rapoport, A. 1982a. Identity and environment. In *Housing and identity*, ed. J. S. Duncan, 6–35. New York: Holmes and Meier.

———. 1982b. *The meaning of the built environment*. Beverly Hills, CA: Sage.

Riad, J. K., and F. H. Norris. 1996. The influence of relocation on the environmental, social and psychological stress experienced by disaster victims. *Environment and Behavior* 28 (2): 163–182.

Rivera, J. C. 1993. Moving off the floodplain. Paper presented at the West Lakes Regional Meeting, Association of American Geographers, Milwaukee, WI.

Rohe, W. M., and S. Mouw. 1991. The politics of relocation: The moving of the Crest Street Community. *Journal of the American Planning Association* 57 (1): 57–68.

Rubenstein, R., and P. Parmelee. 1992. Attachment to place and the representation of the life course by the elderly. In *Place attachment*, ed. I. Altman and S. Low. New York: Plenum Press.

SEMA. 1994. The response, recovery and lessons learned from the Missouri floods of 1993 and 1994. Paper presented at the Missouri Emergency Preparedness Assn./State Emergency Management Agency 1994 Spring Conference.

Tibbetts, J. 1999. Raising up and moving out. *America's Hurricane Threat* 2 (1): 1–12.

Tierney, K., M. Lindell, and R. Perry. 2001. *Facing the unexpected*. Washington, DC: Joseph Henry Press.

Turner, M., B. Williams, G. Kates, S. Popkin, and C. Rabenhorst. 2007. *Affordable rental housing in healthy communities: Rebuilding after Hurricanes Katrina and Rita*. Washington, DC: The Urban Institute.

U.S. Department of State. 2003. Statement by the president on preservation of Princeville, North Carolina. http://usinfo.state.gov/usa/blackhis/pville.htm. Accessed August 1, 2008.

Vaske, J., and K. Kobrin. 2001. Place attachment and environmentally responsible behavior. *The Journal of Environmental Education* 32: 16–21.

Weiss, N. E. 2006. Rebuilding housing after Hurricane Katrina. Washington, DC: Congressional Research Service.

Wu, J. Y., and M. Lindell. 2004. Housing reconstruction after two major earthquakes: The 1994 Northridge earthquake in the United States and the 1999 Chi-Chi earthquake in Taiwan. *Disasters* 28: 63–81.

Resources

- FEMA Applying for Assistance, http://www.fema.gov/assistance/index.shtm
- FEMA Individual Assistance Center, https://www.disasteraid.fema.gov/IAC/home.jsp
- FEMA Online Disaster Portal, http://www.fema.gov/about/programs/daip/
- FEMA Recover and Rebuild, http://www.fema.gov/rebuild/index.shtm
- FEMA Travel Trailer FAQ's, http://www.fema.gov/assistance/dafaq.shtm#travel
- FEMA Travel Trailers, http://www.fema.gov/assistance/trailer.shtm
- FEMA, Rebuilding Smarter, http://www.fema.gov/rebuild/smart_strong.shtm
- Grand Forks, visit http://www.grandforksgov.com/gfgov/home.nsf/Pages/Facts-at-a-Glance and http://www.grandforksgov.com/gfgov/home.nsf/Pages/Flood%20Anniversary. For FEMA documents on Grand Forks, visit http://www.fema.gov/hazard/archive/grandforks/contents.shtm
- Greater New Orleans Community Data Center (Brookings Institution Reports), http://www.gnocdc.org
- Gulf Coast Recovery Office/FEMA, Individual Assistance http://www.fema.gov/hazard/hurricane/2005katrina/weekly_ia.shtm
- Housing and Urban Development HOME information, http://www.hud.gov/offices/cpd/affordablehousing/programs/home/index.cfm
- Hurricane Katrina, State of Louisiana The Road Home Program, www.road2LA.org
- Operation Fresh Start, Soldiers Grove, Wisconsin (and video), http://www.wisn.com/video/13935075/detail.html and http://freshstart.ncat.org/case/soldiers.htm

Endnote

1. I am grateful to Patricia Stukes for contributing to field work and insights generated for this section. The observations and comments, though, are those of the author and do not necessarily reflect the views of others.

Chapter 8

Business Recovery

Learning Objectives

After reading this chapter, you should be able to:

- Understand the conditions that influence business recovery
- Identify the full range of businesses that are impacted and the varying needs that they may have
- Explain the purposes of business-continuity planning
- Define and estimate displacement and downtime for businesses affected by disaster
- Recognize that disasters both directly and indirectly affect businesses, and that even businesses not directly impacted can sustain losses
- Explain steps and activities involved in business-recovery planning
- Describe strategies for business resumption after disaster
- Provide alternative, ecofriendly "green" rebuilding solutions for businesses of all sizes and types
- Discuss various federal programs that assist businesses affected by disasters

Introduction

To understand the widespread impact of disasters on businesses, think through the types of places where you go to secure various goods and services. First, you wake up and dress for the day wearing clothes purchased locally. Next, you drive or take a vehicle to work or school using gasoline bought in the neighborhood. Along the way, you go through a drive-through for coffee and breakfast, then arrive at work where you may be an employee or business owner. During the day, you will use, interact with, or visit restaurants, dry cleaners, bookstores, fitness centers, beauty salons, grocery stores, or farmers' markets. To do your job or operate your business will require the delivery of office supplies, parts, and packages. You will also need insurance coverage and basic utilities. Your business or workplace may be frequented by pedestrians, or by those who drive or cyber-commute. Disruptions to any of the means by which they arrive at your business can be costly.

Or, perhaps you work out of your home providing day care, consulting, catering, Internet-based services, ironing, repairs, sewing, or other home-based enterprises. Loss of any of these goods and services may undermine your ability to pay rent, purchase food, provide for your family, or survive economically. Depending on your savings and resources, a disaster may mean depleting your savings and starting completely over while simultaneously rebuilding a home damaged by a storm.

Local government officials will become concerned that economic disruption will cause people to move out of the community. Considerable tax revenues and even entire industries may be lost. In summary, it is not surprising that local leaders often convene around an economy damaged by disaster, even making it a priority above other recovery concerns. In the next section, we will look at several scenarios to understand the impact of disasters on businesses and the challenges that result.

The Northridge Earthquake

The U.S. Federal Emergency Management Agency (FEMA) places the 1994 Northridge earthquake (Los Angeles, California) as the second costliest disaster in U.S. history, with economic damage totaled at $25 billion. As an example of the types of damage that can be caused by a disaster, and by this earthquake in particular, consider how those affected by the local economy fared when 617 businesses experienced closures.

Well over half of the businesses affected lost electricity, and close to half lost telephone service. Temporary closures occurred when teams moved in to conduct structural assessments. Businesses also remained closed to replace inventory, replenish supplies, and repair damages. As a result of these kinds of disruptions, 40% of businesses noticed a reduction in the number of customers (Tierney 1996). The average amount of damage across the business sector came in at $156,273.

Rippling effects from business closures also affected employees. One in ten Northridge businesses could not afford to pay their employees. Lack of income obviously hindered the abilities of business owners and employees to pay rents, mortgages, and other bills; to feed and clothe their families; and to repair damages to their own homes (Tierney 1996). Even when businesses stayed open, road closures and housing disruption meant that employees could not travel to work. Indeed, 60% of businesses reported that employees had trouble getting to work.

September 11, 2001 in New York City

Without doubt, September 11, 2001, stands out as an unprecedented assault targeted specifically on U.S. businesses. The effects were considerable. Fatalities among the businesses, first responders, emergency management community, and visitors in the World Trade Center and surrounding area surpassed 3000 lives. The economic impact was tremendous, with a total cost of lost earnings due to lives lost, property damage, cleanup, and restoration listed at between $33 to $36 billion (Bram, Orr, and Rapaport 2002). Measuring economic losses may seem cold in the context of lives lost, but those losses affect people in very personal ways. For example, one study estimates that approximately $7.8 billion were lost in earnings of those killed— funds that would have accumulated during a normal lifespan, supporting family members and the broader community through purchases of homes, groceries, clothes, and other goods and services (Bram, Orr, and Rapaport 2002).

Effects of the attack also cost short-term earnings, affecting specific industries. As might be expected, the attack impacted the air transportation industry, with as many as 11,000 jobs lost (Bram, Orr, and Rapaport 2002). The hotel and restaurant industry suffered a drop-off in tourism, with the hotel industry losing 6,000 jobs and the restaurant sector reporting 9,000 lost jobs. The restaurant industry recovered within a few months, but the air transportation industry took longer; between $3.6 to $6.4 billion in lost wages have been estimated (Bram, Orr, and Rapaport 2002).

National attention naturally focused on the World Trade Center and the two towers that collapsed. However, significant collateral damage occurred in the area. To illustrate the impact, consider that nearly 30 million square feet of commercial office space was lost. Fourteen million square feet had been located in the World Trade Center, but an additional 15 million in retail and office space was destroyed nearby. Contents lost in the World Trade Center totaled another $5.2 billion. (See more on this in Chapter 6, Historic and Cultural Resources, which notes the priceless artifacts that were lost.) Add in the impact on the infrastructure, with a destroyed sub-way tunnel and Port Authority train station as well as massive damage to a utility switching facility and substations, and the time needed to recover increases (Bram, Orr, and Rapaport 2002).

As devastating as the impact was, researchers have also noted that businesses played pivotal roles in the response to the attack (McEntire, Robinson, and Weber 2003). The city's Emergency Operations Center had been located in the World Trade Center and was relocated in 24 hours through the help of various manufacturers and utility companies (Kendra and Wachtendorf 2002; McEntire, Robinson, and Weber 2003). A convention center housed search and rescue teams; news reporters disseminated information; and cell phone repair vehicles streamed in to reestablish communications, enabling affected businesses to accept credit cards and resume business operations. Insurance companies paid funds out to generate recovery. Private companies assisted with funeral services, provided counseling, and identified the remains of those killed (Kendra and Wachtendorf 2002; McEntire, Robinson, and Weber 2003). In short, the impact on the business sector was overwhelming; yet, the business community stepped up to support emergency response and long-term recovery as well.

Conditions That Influence Business Recovery

What influences whether and how businesses recover? The question is not easily answered, particularly given the limited research that has been undertaken on this question. Furthermore, it is difficult to disentangle the effects of a disaster from other conditions, such as whether a business would have failed anyway or whether an owner might have opted to change professions or to retire. Ultimately, it is difficult to determine whether the pre- or postdisaster regional economy was the cause of business closures (Tierney 2006; Webb, Tierney, and Dahlhamer 2000). In this section, we look at the research that has been done on business recovery and see what conditions might influence a postdisaster recovery.

Preparedness

It would seem almost self-evident that preparedness efforts would translate into a faster or better recovery. However, research suggests that preparedness may not be sufficient. One study examined businesses subjected to flooding (Des Moines, Iowa) and earthquake (Northridge, California). By using a checklist of typical preparedness measures, researchers discovered that most businesses engaged in minimal preparedness activities (Webb, Tierney, and Dahlhamer 2000).

What kinds of activities? Interestingly, businesses were more likely to conduct basic efforts such as pulling together first-aid supplies or teaching first aid to employees. Only 5% of the businesses studied in the Northridge area had planned for relocation, which can be exceedingly expensive. Other preparedness measures such as planning, buying generators, or implementing mitigation measures were quite unlikely to be undertaken (Dahlhamer and Tierney 1998; Webb, Tierney, and Dahlhamer 2000).

Business-Continuity Planning

Given the importance of preparedness, it probably seems startling that so few businesses conduct efforts that preserve the integrity of their enterprises and protect employees. **Business-continuity planning** addresses and reduces the risks that face the business and its most valued assets, the employees. Morgan Stanley Dean Witter prepared carefully prior to September 11 in part by conducting evacuation drills in the World Trade Center. Every employee survived the 1993 bombing, and of the 2,700 total employees, six died in the September 11 attack (Laye 2002).

The field of emergency management provides guidelines for preparing communities and households that can be applied to businesses. Business-continuity planning commences when a planning team is assembled to lead the enterprise through key planning steps.

A first step involves identifying the risks that a company would face. Local emergency managers may be able to provide general risk assessments from routine hazards; specific industries will need to examine internal threats, such as the risk of a major explosion at a chemical plant. John Laye, author of *Avoiding Disaster*, recommends that the next step involve a business-impact analysis to identify the kinds of disruptions that may occur and their impact on the functioning of the business. Laye recommends that businesses separate critical functions and establish priorities for business resumption.

Three strategies can be used (Laye 2002). First, continuous operations such as those necessary to a bank may require immediate resumption of computing functions. This is usually accomplished through establishing a backup facility prior to disaster. A second strategy involves rapid restoration of business functions within a few days after the disaster. A third strategy, full-fledged recovery, may take some time, depending on the impact on the business, damage to the surrounding area, and the company's assets. By prioritizing key functions and preidentifying strategies to provide for continuous operations or rapid restoration, it may be possible for a company to survive. We will read further on this topic in an upcoming section on FEMA's recommendations for business-recovery planning.

Business Size and Type

The businesses most likely to prepare at higher levels tend to be larger businesses with resources to do so (Webb, Tierney, and Dahlhamer 2000) or industries required legally to prepare, such as chemical companies or nuclear plants (Tierney 2006). Larger businesses also tend to fare better when attempting to recover from disasters as well, for the same reason: they have resources they can fall back on, including insurance, funds, and employees who specialize in risk management (Webb, Tierney, and Dahlhamer 2000), a characteristic that seems to be more true of private firms (Dahlhamer and D'Souza 1997). Larger businesses may also be part of a larger chain of stores or restaurants and can pull from those locations to replace damaged contents or even borrow employees.

The type of business may also matter in recovery. Some businesses are more likely to prepare, particularly those involved in finance, real estate, and insurance, as studies have found in the Northridge and Memphis areas (Webb, Tierney, and Dahlhamer 2000). Smaller businesses seem to be more likely to not survive. By examining related research on nondisaster business failures, it is clear that small businesses are more likely to be owned by women and minorities (Tierney 2006). Small businesses owned by African Americans experience higher failure rates outside of disaster; about 40% of these businesses are owned by African-American women (Tierney 2006). It is likely that these kinds of businesses will experience higher risk in times of disaster.

Owning versus Renting a Business

Do you own or rent your home? Chances are, if you rent your home, you understand that your options to mitigate various hazards may depend on your landlord's willingness to do so. Businesses that rent face the same dilemma and appear to be more at risk for failure (Chang and Falit-Baiamonte 2002). Further, stores that rent in an area with a key anchor store that draws in customers face higher risks should that anchor store fail or be damaged (Tierney 2006). One strategic step that a rental business can take is to insure its contents against loss. By establishing a relocation plan in order to reduce **downtime**, a rental location can rebuild more quickly. A preestablished plan that anticipates how to contact and lure back lost customers is also recommended. Finally, a **rainy-day fund** to cover the costs of **displacement**, moving, and reestablishing in a new location is a good idea.

Magnitude of the Impact

Does the size, magnitude, or intensity of the disaster matter to a business now facing recovery? The answer seems to be both yes and no. For the

Northridge earthquake, the intensity of the earthquake was related to recovery. As you might expect, areas that shook at a higher intensity sustained more serious damage—but not only to the business. Higher intensity shaking affected utilities, lifelines, pedestrian and customer traffic, and transportation (Tierney 1996, 2006). Thus, even without direct damage, businesses may be affected, as it may be impossible to receive supplies, deliver goods, or produce services. The hit that the business experienced, coupled with the impact on the regional capacity to recover, will influence how well the business can regroup and resume operations.

Magnitude of the impact also relies on local land-use planning, building codes, and other mitigation measures (Tierney 2006). A magnitude 7.1 earthquake in California will cause less damage because of the stricter, long-term mitigation efforts of local and state jurisdictions. The May 2008 earthquake in the People's Republic of China (PRC) that claimed well over 50,000 lives was a magnitude 7.9. Because the temblor struck in more rural and older areas lacking in structural mitigation efforts, a profound loss of life occurred along with the destruction of factories, businesses, schools, and industries that provided income to millions of people. Massive infrastructure disruption occurred as well, including collapsed bridges, blocked or destroyed roads, and up to 400 dams that sustained significant damage. Economic restoration to the area will take decades.

Infrastructural Damage

Does it matter if you sustain direct damages? Here, the answer is clearly no. As seen with the earthquake in Sichuan Province, PRC, all bridges leading into the damaged area were destroyed, and rescue crews could not reach the injured and trapped because the earthquake heavily damaged or blocked 70% of the roads. Efforts to restart economic opportunities so that people can earn money, feed their families, secure health care, and rebuild their lives will be extremely difficult.

Damage to the infrastructure, which includes transportation arteries, ports, airports, rail lines, and public conveyances and to lifelines such as water, power, gas, sewer, and phone/cell coverage disrupts all businesses, with or without damages. The 1993 Midwest floods affected nine states in a record event. The infrastructural impact was profound. The Mississippi River, the single largest waterway transporting cargo in the United States, closed due to damage to bridges, ports, and connected transportation arteries, including highways and railways (Tierney, Nigg, and Dahlhamer 1996).

Businesses reported substantial losses; those in Des Moines, Iowa, totaled approximately $200–$500 million alone (Tierney, Nigg, and Dahlhamer 1996). Median structural damage was $10,000 but went as high as $2.5

million to a single business; only one-quarter had flood insurance (Tierney, Nigg, and Dahlhamer 1996). In a survey conducted by the Disaster Research Center at the University of Delaware, businesses ranked these lifelines in order of need: electricity, telephone, sewer/wastewater, natural gas, and water (Dahlamer and Tierney 1998; Dahlhamer and D'Souza 1997; Tierney 1996, 2006; Tierney, Nigg, and Dahlhamer 1996; Webb, Tierney, and Dahlhamer 2000). The implications for government and utility industries are clear: get these resources back up and operating as quickly as possible to avoid negative economic consequences.

Indirect Effects

Indirect effects occur when a disaster produces business disruption but not direct damage. Some examples of indirect effects that have an impact on both businesses and consumers include:

- Businesses could not operate in Manhattan after September 11, when security efforts prohibited entry by residents and tourists (Tierney 2006).
- Coffee prices increased after the Port of New Orleans, the leading port in the nation for caffeine lovers, was closed due to Hurricane Katrina.
- Businesses lost access to supplies and resources—a "downstream" problem that can affect all kinds of businesses (Tierney 2006), such as increased gasoline prices—after Hurricane Katrina reduced production in the petroleum industry.
- Food prices increased due to agricultural damage that includes not only crop production, but also farm equipment; the 1993 Midwest floods caused $6–$10 billion in such agricultural damages (Tierney, Nigg, and Dahlhamer 1996).
- Lost work can be an issue for **home-based businesses**. In the 1997 flood at Grand Forks, North Dakota, businesses incurring such losses included tailoring, ironing, day care, and beauty care, all of which were owned by women (Enarson 2001).

From these few examples, it is easy to understand that a business might not sustain a direct hit but still experience business interruption or failure. As noted above, infrastructure is often the key condition that influences indirect effects. In Des Moines, Iowa, 80% of the businesses surveyed did not have water, 40% experienced sewer disruption, 35% lost electricity, and 23% went without telephone services. Businesses reported an average of 12 days without these services (Dahlhamer and Tierney 1998; Dahlhamer and D'Souza 1997; Tierney 1996, 2006; Tierney, Nigg, and Dahlhamer 1996;

Webb, Tierney, and Dahlhamer 2000). In short, flooding was not the major cause of business closures; rather, business operations could not resume because of indirect effects.

Experience

It would also seem intuitive that businesses with prior experience in disasters would be more likely to prepare and thus more likely to recover. However, such may not be the case. Prior experience did not expedite recovery for businesses after the 1989 Santa Cruz, California, earthquake or the 1992 Hurricane Andrew in Homestead, Florida. Does experience prompt preparedness that helps you in the next disaster? Again, that may not be the case based on a couple of studies. To illustrate, only businesses that had prepared in advance *and* subsequently experienced disruption from the Northridge earthquake increased their preparedness as a result of the experience (Webb, Tierney, and Dahlhamer 2000). Though the picture is not clear, it may be that businesses pour energies into recovery and then move on, either out of resources or otherwise unable to mitigate and prepare for the next event, even if they want to do so.

Location

Realtors are famous for saying that "location, location, location" is what matters most in selling a house. The same can be said to be true of business locations. Businesses located in desirable areas gain attention and customer loyalty. In Seattle, Washington, two of those locations include the Pioneer Square and SoDo (South of Downtown) areas. In 2001, a 6.8-magnitude earthquake struck deep underground and became the most expensive disaster to hit the area (Chang and Falit-Baiamonte 2002). Researchers conducted a survey of locally affected businesses to determine their experiences.

As we learned previously, even businesses not directly damaged could sustain losses. In Seattle's Nisqually earthquake, nearly 70% of the businesses not directly damaged experienced considerable losses (Chang and Falit-Baiamonte 2002). Problems stemmed from several factors. First, negative media attention may have deterred customers. Second, area repairs and accessibility problems may have discouraged customers, reducing foot traffic in the area (Chang and Falit-Baiamonte 2002). Third, in Pioneer Square and SoDo, customers turned to competitors for goods and services, undermining further the viability of local businesses (Chang and Falit-Baiamonte 2002).

The Good News

At this point, it may be hard to believe that business recovery can occur after a disaster, but it can and it does. Indeed, most businesses appear to recover from disaster. For example, 37% of businesses surveyed in the Santa Cruz area actually reported increases in their business after the 1989 earthquake (Webb, Tierney, and Dahlhamer 2000). Some industries may experience growth related to the recovery, such as postdisaster construction. Other firms, including those that deal with storm debris, will secure contracts that bring in income (Tierney 2006; Webb, Tierney, and Dahlhamer 2000). Exceptions tend to come from businesses that were on a downward spiral prior to the disaster.

Challenges during the Recovery Period

What can you expect during the disaster recovery period? As seen in Box 8.1, losses can be estimated prior to impact or calculated postimpact using the formula presented. Losses are related to the type of hazard that the business confronts. FEMA provides loss estimation tables for several kinds of hazards in their mitigation planning book series; in this scenario, we will use the flood figures (FEMA 2001).

Total loss calculation must include consideration of the structure, its contents, and the use and function of the structure. First, structural loss needs to take into consideration the replacement value of the structure. Buildings can sustain damage from minimal amounts to complete losses. In the flood-loss scenario that FEMA proposes, the structural replacement value is multiplied by the percentage of damage to calculate total structural loss. The next step in calculating losses includes listing the replacement value of the contents multiplied by the percentage of damage. The third step is to determine losses related to structure use and function. First, FEMA recommends determining the average daily operating budget and then multiplying that amount by the estimated downtime, or time spent out of the facility. Add in the displacement cost per day times the displacement time, and a figure representing the total structure use and function loss can be determined. To do so, the total losses for structure, contents, and use/function are added together.

In the three scenarios seen in Box 8.1, consider that only a minimal amount of damage (and days of downtime) has been calculated. Obviously, losses sustained from complete destruction could mean that a hospital facility could take years to rebuild and might never return; tourism from an historic location might not generate dependable revenue for local taxes and employees; municipalities would certainly not be able to rebuild a sewage treatment plant without governmental aid. These examples serve as

BOX 8.1   LOSS ESTIMATION AND CALCULATION

To calculate losses, FEMA recommends considering several steps. In Step 1, you identify the cost of replacing the structure times the percent of damage that it sustained. This results in an overall estimation of the loss to the structure. In Step 2, you consider how much it costs to replace the lost contents for the entire structure multiplied by the percentage of damage to those contents. This estimates the total loss of contents. Step 3 examines downtime and displacement in order to calculate the loss of the structure and its function. In Step 4, all three previous steps are totaled to estimate the total potential loss.

1. Structural replacement value × percent damage = loss to structure
2. Replacement value of contents × percent damage = loss of contents
3. Average daily operating budget × functional downtime + displacement cost per day × displacement time in a temporary facility = structure use and function loss
4. Structure loss + content loss + function loss = total loss

To illustrate the FEMA formula, consider the losses that could be sustained to several different types of facilities in a flood hazard:

- A hospital:
  - Structural replacement $2,500,000 × 5% damage = $125,000
  - Contents loss $3,750,000 × 7.5% damage = $281,250
  - Structure use and function loss $2,055 daily operating budget × NO downtime + $2,500 displacement cost per day × NO displacement time = $0
  - $125,000 + $281,250 = $406,250 in total losses
- An historic lighthouse:
  - Structural replacement $1,500,000 × 18% damage = $270,000
  - Contents loss $50,000 × 27% damage = $13,500
  - Structure use and function loss $2,191 daily operating budget × 7 downtime days + $500 displacement cost per day × 2 displacement days in a temporary facility = $16,337
  - $270,000 + $13,500 + $16,337 = $299,837 in total losses
- Sewage treatment plant:
  - Structural replacement $2,500,000 × 13% damage = $270,000
  - Contents loss $2,500,000 × 19.5% damage = $487,500
  - Structure use and function loss $82,191 average daily operating budget × 3 days functional downtime + $200,000 displacement cost per day × 3 displacement time days in temporary facility = $846,573
  - $270,000 + $487,500 + $846,573 = $1,604,073

Source: Federal Emergency Management Agency, 2001, Understanding Your Risks: Identifying Hazards and Estimating Losses, FEMA 386-2.

motivation to conduct and implement predisaster mitigation measures and to initiate business-continuity planning. Without doing so, businesses face an increased likelihood of postdisaster failure.

Businesses and industries that hope to demonstrate resiliency engage in loss estimation and mitigation planning to reduce the effects of disasters. Businesses that do not build internal resiliency face recovery challenges that include downtime, displacement, relocation, and disruption to employees—and that is all before the rebuilding can begin. In this section, we examine each element separately then turn to reconstruction strategies for the economic sector.

Downtime and Effects

Educational institutions represent large-scale industries that employ thousands of individuals with related benefits for surrounding communities. In the 1990s, the University of California-Berkeley (UCB) worked with FEMA administrator James Lee Witt to create a loss-estimation program (Comerio 2000). Together, they established five parts to the effort: (1) hazard analysis, (2) loss estimation, (3) economic impact, (4) creation of a national model, and (5) creation of a long-term funding program model, the Disaster-Resistant University Initiative. UCB served as the pilot site for the first three steps. First, Professor Mary Comerio led efforts to assess the area's earthquake hazard. Assessment required examination of microzonation soil maps and estimates of ground shaking for occasional, rare (7.0 magnitude), and very rare (7.5 magnitude) events.

The primary focus of UCB's efforts, besides life safety, focused on downtime that could devastate university and adjacent community economies. Downtime is defined as the time period when a business cannot function due to the impact of the disaster. That impact can be experienced directly through damage to facilities and resources, or indirectly when area transportation access is disrupted or when damage to residential sectors prevents employees from working.

To estimate downtime, Comerio looked at the location and condition of campus infrastructure, including building use such as for classes, laboratories, offices, libraries, or special events. A rare earthquake event was estimated to cause up to two years of downtime before the university could resume a normal schedule. In a very rare event, the campus would have to close for an entire year, and four years would elapse before a return to normal operations. That same very rare event would impact not only the university, but three counties as well, affecting 8,900 jobs, $680 million in personal income, and $861 million in sales. A U.S. Geological Survey working group estimated the odds of two in three that the Bay

Area would experience a magnitude 7 (rare) or larger earthquake by the year 2020 (http://pubs.usgs.gov/fs/1999/fs151-99/).

Comerio's study served as a wake-up call for the university, which established a 20-year timeline and a $1-billion budget. UCB focused mitigation efforts on buildings representing a significant loss of external research dollars that would be needed to help the university survive and to continue scientific inquiry of benefit to the larger society. By 2006, UCB had spent over $650 million on seismic retrofits and contents retrofits. A risk analysis showed it had reduced life safety risk to nearly zero in retrofitted buildings and had cut both estimated financial losses and downtime in half (Comerio 2008).

Displacement and Relocation

Few companies appear to plan for relocation during the time when their businesses are not able to operate in original locations (Dahlhamer and Tierney 1998). Yet the ability to reestablish production, service delivery, and other functions in an alternative location could potentially save a business. Relocation may be very difficult if a business has not planned for such a contingency. Large-scale operations may not be able to acquire sufficient space; smaller businesses may not be able to find a comparable location with the necessary customer base. Home-based businesses may lose important resources as well as customers. Many home-based businesses, particularly those operated by women, appear to fare poorly in disasters (Enarson 2001).

As can be seen in Table 8.1, downtime from a hazard can be significant. What can be done, then, to help with temporary relocation of businesses? Large chains, such as major drug stores, have been able to relocate successfully into temporary trailers. After Hurricane Andrew, for example, pharmacies moved into mobile homes for the duration of the rebuilding. In 1989 after the Loma Prieta earthquake, small stores in Watsonville, California, operated from mobile homes and generated sales sufficient to stay alive during a multiyear rebuilding.

That same 1989 Loma Prieta earthquake nearly destroyed the downtown Santa Cruz Pacific Garden Mall, which hosted unique and locally beloved stores. The mall's businesses represented 20% of the city's sales tax revenue,

TABLE 8.1 Flood Displacement Times

Flood Level	Displacement Time
1 foot	134 days
2 feet	230 days
3 or more feet	365 days

Source: FEMA 2001.

which needed to be replaced as quickly as possible (Wilson 1991). Santa Cruz used several unique efforts to host downtown businesses temporarily. In one extremely supportive example, community residents worked side by side with owners of a local bookshop to move store contents several blocks away into a temporary site. Bookshop owners responded with humor to the relocation by creating new coffee cups that marked out the words "Santa Cruz Bookshop" with "Santa Cruz Book Tent." The bookstore survived its displacement and returned to the rebuilt downtown.

A few streets away from the badly damaged Santa Cruz downtown, city officials worked with business owners to erect aluminum-sided buildings in parking lots adjacent to the downtown. Named the "Phoenix Pavilions" after the legendary bird that rose from the ashes, the structures went up within five weeks. The pavilions housed downsized versions of local stores, similar to booths used in open-air or antique markets. Customers returned and supported local merchants more than anticipated (Wilson 1991). Repairs to the downtown took several years to complete, and damage to infrastructure, including underground water and sewage lines, extended for several years more. Without the Phoenix Pavilions, the downtown would have lost far more businesses and revenues vital to support the city's budget.

September 11 represents an even larger scale of event. The destruction of the World Trade Center towers meant that 20 million square feet of office space was lost. To imagine this, consider that the area would be approximately "the size of Atlanta's central business district" (McEntire, Robinson, and Weber 2003). And, bear in mind that not only the businesses destroyed in the towers had to relocate, but so too did many nearby buildings that suffered either direct or indirect damages. Several strategies were used. Some businesses moved into hotel rooms (McEntire, Robinson, and Weber 2003), a means also used by New Orleans's area universities after Hurricane Katrina. Some businesses moved to nearby areas in New York and New Jersey. In the supportive spirit common after disaster, even former competitors provided space. Other businesses moved into available rental space and used data stored on backup computers, a predisaster business-continuity strategy (McEntire, Robinson, and Weber 2003).

To summarize, few businesses plan for relocation whether it is temporary or permanent. Businesses most likely to survive appear to have preplanned an effort to salvage key documents necessary for business operations to continue. Businesses that enjoy community support and can regroup quickly enough, stay close to their original location, and provide locally needed goods and services also appear to be more likely to survive. However, it is clear that relocation is a vulnerable time for businesses primarily because of a lack of forethought. Relocation may not even be possible if critical employees cannot get to work at the new location.

Impact on Employees

There are several issues to discuss when we think about employees. First, there is the impact of a disaster on employees who are at work. Second, employees must face challenges associated with personal losses of homes and possessions. It is possible that a disaster may undermine a business not through impact on the facility or office, but by destroying the homes of local employees. Third, if downtime continues, employees may need to find other work. Fourth, relocation may mean that employees cannot commute to the new location, and employers lose these valued personnel.

However, there is good news to consider in this section. Employees at work have a tendency to step up and help out, even to the point of endangering their own lives, to save others in peril.

Employers also have an ethical responsibility to protect employees at work. Some federal and state laws mandate specific responsibilities to protect employees from harmful chemicals or fires, for example. Yet, as we observed in the section above, few businesses engage in general preparedness efforts for disaster unless they have sufficient resources to do so, leaning instead toward provision of first-aid kits and related training. This places employees and businesses at risk. It is thus imperative that businesses develop pre- and postdisaster plans to support their human resources.

For example, employees may need support through the recovery. Employers that put training time into an employee face the loss of a valued asset. Similarly, employees who may have lost their own homes now need their income sources more than ever. However, businesses will have to balance their own needs vis-à-vis those of employees who may need flexible hours and days in order to manage their personal recovery. Employees may also face longer or more arduous commutes due to transportation damage or to disruptions to public transportation; three years after Hurricane Katrina, for example, only 60% of the bus routes were functional. Living in a temporary location may also add commuting time, expenses, and stress.

Employers thus may want to prepare a contingency plan that helps employees during a disaster recovery time. Suggestions might include:

- Preidentify temporary housing close to the work location for key employees.
- Offer **cyber-commuting** to employees who can work at a distance.
- Offer flexible times and days for work.
- Suggest job sharing among those affected by the disaster, including temporarily moving to part-time status.
- Establish a key contact in human resources to aid the employee with benefits, particularly if the employee has an injured family member.

- Bring in a credentialed counselor to provide support to employees in distress or arrange for a list of such counselors to be distributed among employees (for more, see Chapter 10, Social Psychological Recovery).
- Fund a child-care program so that parents can work and manage their own household recovery.
- If the business has been damaged, schedule a grand reopening and invite past employees.
- Assign a human-resources manager or other manager to check in regularly with employees who lost their homes. Identify specific stressful points and provide information on benefits that may be helpful to them.
- If employees have been injured while on the job, schedule a team of managers to check on that person daily for his or her specific needs.
- If employees or customers have been killed, schedule a formal memorial service and place a memorial plaque in the business; assign a team of managers to work with the affected families through the next year; hold a one-year memorial service (see Chapter 10); schedule additional disaster training and exercises in their honor to build employee capacity; invite surviving family members back for special events.
- Recognize and reward the heroism of specific employees who made a difference on the day of the disaster and during the business recovery.
- Identify employees who may face higher risks, such as janitors working alone at night or early in the morning and unable to access warning information; lower-waged employees who will face additional trials in recovering lost housing; and employees working at home who may have lost key resources to continue doing so (Phillips 2005).
- Update the business-contingency plan on a regular basis at least once a year. Consider new elements to strengthen the plan (Phillips 2005): Cross-train employees in several jobs.
- Integrate disaster training into specific events held during the year, such as the anniversary of the business opening, or Administrative Professionals' Day, Bring Your Daughter to Work Day, or even Boss's Day.
- Put safety information on the company Web site and post on information kiosks.
- Upgrade safety features, including those that provide warnings and other critical information to employees with disabilities. (For suggestions, visit the Job Accommodation Network at http://www.jan.wvu.edu/.)
- Increase insurance coverage and establish an emergency relief fund for the business and its employees.

Role Abandonment

It is commonly believed that people, particularly first responders and others, may abandon their roles in the face of disaster. This is a myth (Dynes 1987). And, it is a mythical behavior not only for those we can count on most in disasters, who put their lives on the line daily, but for employees in general. As one study noted, hotel employees provided critical first aid and prevented further injuries after the collapse of a Hyatt Regency skywalk in 1981 (McEntire, Robinson, and Weber 2003). A fire in a Kentucky supper club that killed 150 would have claimed more lives without employee intervention. When flames broke out, wait staff notified patrons and led them to safety when they could have evacuated immediately and not placed their own lives at risk (Johnson 1988). When the attack on the Twin Towers occurred, staff tapped as floor emergency coordinators directed fellow employees to safety, carried people with disabilities or injuries down the staircases, and even stayed behind to try and save others, losing their lives in the process. People can and will behave heroically and altruistically in the most dire of situations.

In short, employees can generally be counted on to stay on the job and to assist others that have been injured. Businesses that recognize this valuable trait in their staff can use this as the basis for preparedness planning and drills. Companies that provide such efforts, including training, can build a cadre of individuals who know exactly what to do when disasters strike. As described in the section above, employers can draft their personnel into preparedness initiatives, consequently increasing employee safety, the ability of the business to protect customers present at the time of disaster, and the chance the business will survive with its workforce intact and ready to mobilize for recovery.

Strategies for Business Recovery

Given the above scenarios and explanations, business recovery will emerge as an uphill battle, but not one without opportunities and options. Clearly, local leadership and a willingness to build partnerships make a difference. Communities with strong business partnerships, such as those established through chambers of commerce or professional associations, can build on these networks to launch recovery efforts. Initial efforts must be taken to reduce potential losses, followed by an overall strategy designed to aid not only individual businesses, but areas of economic enterprise and industry as well. In this section, we examine strategies that have been used in previous events as sources of inspiration.

Loss-Containment Process

Loss containment is defined as a set of measures taken to "reduce the costs associated with disaster impacts" (Dahlhamer and Tierney 1998) that may include emergency response measures such as sandbags or firebreaks, suctioning water out of buildings, moving contents to more secure locations, or even rapid restoration of key lifelines. Efforts to apply savings or to secure loans from other sources may also reduce losses.

It has not been unusual for entire areas to experience massive disruption, leading to extraordinary efforts to stabilize those locations. The Red River Valley flood, for example, inundated the downtown. As if that were not bad enough, fire broke out that prompted aerial firefighting to try and minimize related losses. The Loma Prieta earthquake badly damaged downtown areas in both Santa Cruz and Watsonville. A tornado in Lancaster, Texas, devastated the historic downtown square. As a sign of resilience, though, local merchants erected handmade signs in Lancaster. A travel agency put up one that read "Welcome to Oz" and invited customers to take a vacation from the event. Across the downtown square, another business owner put up a sign that read "Warm fuzzies available." After Hurricane Andrew slammed into southern Dade County, Florida, a hotel that experienced downtime placed a giant band-aid on the side of the building. People and businesses can and do rise to the occasion.

Each community also stepped up collectively to aid the business sector. For example, Santa Cruz officials launched a public-relations campaign to advertise businesses that remained open. Efforts included putting up banners along routes leading to area beaches. At the downtown Pacific Garden Mall, the town set out signs identifying open businesses throughout the years of reconstruction. To lure people to the downtown, artists placed life-sized cutouts of people waiting in line to see a movie. A few blocks away, a fenced-off area featured the "Plywood People's Plaza," including an oversized teddy bear painted by local children. Officials tied plastic sheeting containing children's earthquake poetry along several blocks of temporary fencing. Santa Cruz made the downtown a destination point despite the damage, which brought people back to functioning businesses and into the Phoenix Pavilions. Returning a customer base is often a first step in loss containment, and Santa Cruz responded creatively and effectively.

Business-Recovery Planning

Business-continuity planning as described earlier represents efforts to ensure continuity of operations with an emphasis on key records. Recovery planning spans additional areas. As described in Chapter 3 (Disaster Recovery

Planning), the first step is to convene a recovery-planning group. Some communities may incorporate business-recovery planning into their overall recovery-planning effort or might establish a separate committee to focus solely on economic interests. Regardless, economic recovery must be tied into the overall effort to maximize the ultimate result.

FEMA recommends four levels of business-recovery planning (see Figure 8.1; a checklist is available at http://www.fema.gov/business/bc.shtm):

- Level 1: Executive awareness and authority
  The business-recovery team first determines whether the business-recovery plan (BRP) has been developed or updated within the last six months.
- Level 2: Plan development and documentation
  The BRP is examined to see whether it includes these key sections:
    - Incident management, including designation of responsible employees for specific functions
    - A section on emergency response
    - A section on recovery efforts and restoration
    - Plans for conducting an exercise to test the plan
    - A plan for maintaining the BRP
    - A contact list of those responsible for recovery functions, with a log to ensure that the list is updated frequently to provide correct contact information
    - An assessment of the hardware, software, and support equipment necessary to recover the business and its functions
    - An offsite location for temporary business resumption with appropriate data backups and storage

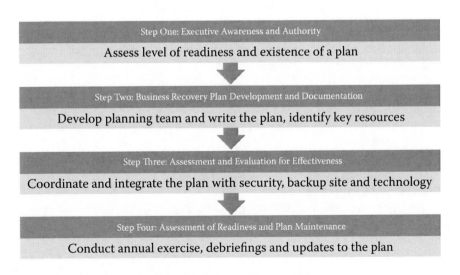

FIGURE 8.1 Business-recovery planning. (From FEMA.)

  – A training plan for teaching responsibilities to the team
  – An exercise schedule to test the plan
- Level 3: Management and recovery team assessment and evaluation for effectiveness
  The team must approve the document and ensure that it is coordinated with security procedures.
  Management ensures that training, exercises, debriefing, and corrections to deficiencies are made.
  Changes in hardware, software, key equipment, and security procedures are integrated into the plan within 30 days of those changes.
- Level 4: Management and recovery team assessment of readiness and plan maintenance
  The team conducts an annual exercise, reviews the results, and addresses deficiencies in training and the BRP.

To ensure a comprehensive and effective recovery, the full range of community needs must be integrated so that a sustainable community emerges and proves resilient beyond the next disaster (Monday 2005). As seen in Box 8.2, businesses must be (re)located close to workforces. Employees must have access to adequate and affordable housing as well as to public transportation to work. Rebuilding cannot further undermine environmental resources and should enhance environmental quality. Infrastructural repairs must be expedited simultaneously with mitigation measures that foster resilience. For example, businesses should follow and support efforts to bury power lines and improve stormwater drainage.

BOX 8.2   RECOVERY STRATEGIES FOR ECONOMIC SUSTAINABILITY

How can damage beyond the economic sector be repaired to enhance economic sustainability? In *Holistic Disaster Recovery*, a number of recovery strategies can be implemented (Monday 2005):

- Damaged transportation facilities:
  - Rebuild to enhance capacity. Increase the ability to bring people into a business district and to move goods in and out of a community.
  - Rebuild to improve functionality. Create a different circulation pattern or create and/or expand transit.
- Damaged public facilities:
  - Rebuild to transform/expand school facilities in support of economic strategies.

- Upgrade public spaces to support economic revitalization. Create new sidewalks and street furniture and plant street trees to create a downtown "civic living room."
- Locate new public uses into a damaged area. Establish a community center for displaced families and others.
- Rebuild a port facility with state-of-the-art characteristics resulting in greater capacity, reduced energy consumption, restoration of environmental features, enhanced pollution controls, and disaster-resilient design.
- Damaged utilities:
  - Create new infrastructure that supports economic growth while incorporating sustainable features. Rebuild a damaged telecommunications system for increased capacity; establish stormwater systems where none existed; increase capacities of water, wastewater, or power facilities to meet future economic needs.
- Environmental damage:
  - Restore damaged environmental features in ways that support other economic goals. Consider adding improved public pedestrian access along the coastline to encourage tourism while repairing coastal erosion damage.
  - Integrate natural features into business district recovery. Upgrade damaged river levees with improved walkway connections and linkages with a downtown commercial area.
  - Establish new tourism opportunities based on interest in understanding natural systems. Set up an "earthquake park."
- Establish memorials or tributes in new greenbelt areas.

For additional suggestions, see Chapter 5 in *Holistic Disaster Recovery* (Monday 2005).

Source: Excerpted and reprinted courtesy of the Natural Hazards Research and Applications Information Center and the Public Entity Risk Institute.

District Overlays

Most communities require specific zoning for business and residential areas. Zoning dictates the kind of business activities that can take place. For example, a zone designation may specify that retail but not industrial sites can be developed. Overlay districts provide for additional regulations. Environmentally friendly regulations, for example, might offer habitat protection or limit redevelopment in an area of seismic activity (Schwab et al. 1998). Design elements might be included that integrate the overall look of a community, enhancing aesthetic qualities for customers. Mitigation features that elevate businesses, increase the use of sprinkler systems, include fire-resistant roofs, and offer safe rooms can be added as well. The **district overlay** provides a window of opportunity to enhance the business sector.

As described in a book published by FEMA and the American Planning Association (Schwab et al. 1998), overlay districts can develop in several ways. Arkadelphia, Arkansas, for example, created an overlay district that emphasized affordable housing, clustered development, parking, and shared facilities (Schwab et al. 1998). The Arkadelphia 2025 Commission, the community's main planning body, worked with FEMA consultants and University of Arkansas design students and faculty to develop ideas that would feature the unique character of the town, thus drawing both customers and tourists back into the area damaged heavily by an F4 tornado. Embedded in the overall recovery plan, the downtown vision linked well to a reinvigorated traffic circulation pattern and to efforts that encouraged the arrival of new businesses.

Environmentally, special overlay regulations might require the inclusion of bike paths and racks. Further, regulations might specify that trees either be protected or reintroduced. (Remember from Chapter 5 that tree canopy reduces stormwater runoff and decreases energy consumption in the summer heat.) Design elements might be included to encourage pedestrian traffic, such as wider sidewalks, benches, and outdoor gathering places. Additional features that serve as child-friendly elements (lower-height water fountains) or that encourage shopping by people with disabilities can be included too. To summarize, district overlays provide a tool for revisiting the zoning and codes of a damaged area and for introducing more modern, holistic design elements.

Revitalization

Disasters provide opportunities. Areas that have been hoping or planning to revitalize their commercial sectors can use disaster recovery as a time frame to do so. Downtown revitalization requires that those involved incorporate elements that attract and retain customers and clients. Those elements may include mixed use that includes residential and business locations. Santa Cruz did so with its downtown and also made such locations affordable for many residents. By retaining its single-room-occupancy hotels, many senior citizens were able to return to the downtown that they loved. In keeping with a holistic recovery perspective, the effort promoted intergenerational equity as well. Other elements could rely on local character, such as using environmental features like a river area to build trails or destination spots (Monday 2005). Other communities have featured their local history by building in elements that recall the past, such as reproduction town clocks, murals, gazebos for summer concerts, and the like.

The Santa Cruz vision called for a three-story limit on most structures, mandated the retention of the historic downtown character, and improved traffic circulation (Wilson 1991). Santa Cruz also decided on elements that would keep the downtown consistent with what community aesthetics demanded. This meant that the downtown included design elements to bring back the grand character of the town originally built before 1900. The St. George Hotel, for example, retained architectural elements that brought the façade back to its original look (see Chapter 6 for more details).

The National Trust for Historic Preservation (NTHP) provides information and resources for such postdisaster revitalization. For example, the NTHP offers the Main Street Four-Point Approach™ to revitalize older business areas (National Trust for Historic Preservation 2008). The Main Street approach moves a community through consideration of overall design, how to economically restructure and promote its downtown, and how to organize. The town of Paso Robles, California, had just started a Main Street program when struck by a 2002 earthquake. The community used funding from the Main Street and Community Development Block Grant programs to retrofit buildings for seismic activity, retain the historic elements of the downtown, and regenerate its economy (Monday 2005).

Rebuilding Green

Environmentally friendly features can be linked to business recovery. Streetscaping that restores damaged trees helps reduce stormwater runoff, provides beneficial effects for air quality, and promotes a pleasing, aesthetic quality to a business. Rebuilding "green" can also represent a feature that reduces costs to the business overall and promotes a more sustainable local environment. Green recovery can also take advantage of local natural resources by incorporating them into the recovery. The small, historic town of Princeville, North Carolina, for example, developed a heritage trail that linked the Tar River to historic features in the community, including its former town hall and the local church. The trail, supported and funded by a number of state and federal partners, featured walking paths and birding information. As a means to recognize the historic character of the first town incorporated by African Americans, Princeville led the way in pushing for a green recovery.

Businesses from large to small can take advantage of advances in green rebuilding to incorporate new features into their rebuilding efforts. As seen in Box 8.3, the Smart Energy Design Assistance Center at the University of Illinois at Urbana–Champaign offers very practical suggestions.

BOX 8.3   GREEN RECOVERY FOR SMALL BUSINESSES

Using the principles of sustainability and environmental quality in this book, small businesses can plan to rebuild green by using ideas suggested by the University of Illinois at Urbana–Champaign's Smart Energy Design Assistance Center (www.sedac.org). Ideas recommended by SEDAC include:

- For structural damages:
  - Upgrade insulation with R-13 minimum insulation in the walls and R-38 minimum in the attics
  - Install more-energy-efficient windows, ideally low-E with a U-value of less than 0.35
  - Use ENERGY STAR® high-reflectance roofing material
  - Seal the building the reduce air infiltration
- To upgrade lighting:
  - Use compact fluorescent lights
  - Use high-efficiency T8 fluorescent lights with electronic ballasts
  - Install occupancy sensors
  - Install bilevel switching
  - Consider daylighting
  - Use LED exit signs
- For repair or replacement of HVAC systems:
  - Verify the size of system necessary and consider an upgrade; bigger is not necessarily better
  - Replace older systems with new, high-efficiency units that offer sealed combustion boilers/furnaces (90% or better) and air conditioners with a SEER of 13 or greater
  - Install high-efficiency rooftop units
  - Use a system that includes exhaust-air heat recovery if applicable
  - Seal existing ductwork
  - Install a geothermal heat pump if applicable
  - Install programmable zone thermostats
  - Control ventilation based on occupancy
- For office equipment:
  - Replace damaged computers with energy-saving features like flat-screen monitors and laptops
  - Research other office equipment for more energy-efficient options
- For facilities open to the public, such as hotels, motels, or restaurants, consider:
  - Low-flow faucet aerators, shower heads, and 1.6-gpf toilets
  - Low-flow commercial faucet sprayers
  - Demand-controlled kitchen exhaust

- High-efficiency motors
- Instantaneous water heaters
- Vending machine energy controls

For more information and ideas, visit www.sedac.org and www.energystar.gov.

Source: Fact Sheet 1 by the Smart Energy Design Assistance Center, University of Illinois at Urbana–Champaign. With permission.

Funding Business Recovery

From reading Chapter 7 (Housing), you might anticipate that the federal government will provide considerable assistance to businesses seeking to recover. Though considerable resources, funds, and expertise have certainly been poured into economic recovery, researchers find that the external aid is not as directly linked to recovery as you might assume. From a study of the Northridge earthquake, researchers discovered that those who accepted federal assistance actually had lowered chances of recovery (Dahlhamer and Tierney 1998; Dahlhamer and D'Souza 1997; Tierney 1996, 2006; Tierney, Nigg, and Dahlhamer 1996; Webb, Tierney, and Dahlhamer 2000).

Why would federal assistance, which should be a source of recovery aid, actually result in a reduced chance of recovery? Based on the Northridge earthquake survey, those who accepted the aid also had the most severe damage. Federal assistance to businesses does not include grants, only loans. Although the loans are offered at very low interest rates, the loans may actually place more of an economic burden on already beleaguered businesses (Dahlhamer and Tierney 1998). A related problem may stem from the nature of the loans, which are designed to help with immediate operations (see EIDL loans in the following subsection) or long-term recovery. These types of loans cannot change problems that stem from losing customers or from regional economic downturns (Tierney 2006). In short, many businesses rely on savings, including retirement funds, to preserve their livelihood (Webb, Tierney, and Dahlhamer 2000). Next, we examine some of the possible sources of funding for business recovery.

The U.S. Small Business Administration

The **Small Business Administration** (SBA, see Photo 8.1) offers **physical disaster loans** to businesses of all sizes. Up to $1.5 million can be secured to repair or replace the property, equipment, inventory, and fixtures. Funds of up to 20% in additional money can be obtained as well to mitigate future

PHOTO 8.1   U.S. Small Business Administration specialists answer questions at a FEMA Disaster Recovery Center in El Reno, Oklahoma. (Photo by Marvin Nauman/ FEMA News Photo. With permission.)

disasters. Interest rates of up to 4% are guaranteed, with a repayment of no more than 30 years, depending on the capacity of the business to repay the loan. If the business or nonprofit has credit available elsewhere, the interest rate can go up to 8%. Funds cannot be used to expand or upgrade a business "unless required by local building codes." Funds can be used to refinance a mortgage if the business does not have credit elsewhere and has sustained uninsured damages. Collateral to secure the loans is required to the extent possible; a second or third mortgage can be used as such (for more information, visit http://www.sba.gov).

An **Economic Injury Disaster Loan** (EIDL) from the SBA can provide up to $1.5 million dollars at an interest rate not to exceed 4% for a term of up to 30 years. EIDL loans are not intended to cover physical damage; rather, these SBA funds are intended to provide funds to cover operating expenses until the business recovers. For example, after tropical storms Lili and Isidore, SBA gave out 130 EIDL loans totaling $1,100,500 to provide "working capital" for businesses that sustained income losses. Further, the money can be used for accounts payable or to make payments on short-term notes.

Some conditions apply; for example, the business must hold flood hazard insurance if located in a repetitive flood area (www.fema.gov). The program is limited to small businesses and agricultural cooperatives, but not farmers or ranchers. Eligible businesses must be in a situation where they cannot recover using their own resources and need governmental assistance.

The National Trust's Main Street Program

The National Trust's Main Street programs mentioned earlier give back their investment in time of disaster. After Hurricanes Katrina and Rita, Main Street communities offered support and help to downtowns in Mississippi and Louisiana. For example, the Downtown Beloit (Wisconsin) Association selected Biloxi, Mississippi, as its partner. Within a month after Hurricane Katrina, the "Beloit to Biloxi" initiative raised money through a concert, gallery openings, farmer's market, and more. An Eagle River, Wisconsin, Main Street effort raised over $30,000 in funds for the American Red Cross through an auction supported by over 100 local businesses (Lawniczak 2008). Through the National Trust and the outreach of concerned business communities, the spirits of businesses affected by disaster can be elevated along with their potential for recovery.

Help from Recovery Organizations

A number of business types may fall through the cracks of existing assistance or fail to qualify for loans. After Hurricane Katrina, a number of voluntary organizations offered assistance to such businesses. For example, The Mennonite Economic Development Associates (MEDA), in partnership with funding from the Mennonite Disaster Service, created a "Back to Business" program for the Gulf Coast, including Louisiana, Mississippi, and Alabama. MEDA offered investment capital and financial and consulting support to local organizations that provide small loans, sometimes called **micro-loans**, to owners of small-scale businesses. In particular, MEDA focused on businesses owned by people of color, women, and low-income individuals. Their goal was to build capacity of these local partners by:

- Providing services of a staff member working in New Orleans
- Investing capital in a credit union to expand its ability to make loans to small business owners
- Working with local partners to establish microbusiness development programs in underserved communities
- Investigating ways to help specific businesses, such as the fishing industry, to link to more-profitable markets

MEDA has partnered with others to assist individuals developing businesses that provide child care, hair care, massage therapy, painting, construction, photography, and shrimp fishing. By identifying those at risk for business loss, MEDA and its partners have prevented considerable loss of income and helped the Gulf Coast to maintain a culturally and economically diversified set of communities.

Disaster-Resilient Businesses

As noted throughout this text, mitigation measures can make a difference. Businesses may be most compelled to add mitigation measures in the disaster recovery time period if sufficient funds remain available. FEMA recommends a number of basic steps keyed to specific hazards:

Protect your business from all natural hazards
- Protect business records and inventory
- Install a generator for emergency power

Protect your property from an earthquake
- Anchor large equipment properly
- Anchor tall bookcases and file cabinets
- Anchor and brace propane tanks and gas cylinders
- Bolt sill plates to foundation
- Brace cripple walls
- Install latches on drawers and cabinet doors
- Mount framed pictures and mirrors securely
- Restrain desktop computers and appliances
- Use flexible connections on gas and water lines

Protect your property from fire
- Deal with vegetation and combustible materials
- Replace roofing with fire-resistant materials

Protect your property from flooding
- Build with flood-damage-resistant materials
- Dry-floodproof your building
- Add waterproof veneer to exterior walls
- Raise electrical-system components
- Anchor fuel tanks
- Raise or floodproof HVAC equipment
- Install sewer-backflow valves
- Protect wells from contamination by flooding

Protect your property from high winds
- Maintain EIFS (exterior insulation and finish systems) walls
- Protect windows and doors with covers
- Reinforce double-entry doors
- Reinforce or replace garage doors
- Remove trees and potential wind-borne missiles
- Secure metal siding and metal roofs

- Secure built-up and single-ply roofs
- Secure composition-shingle roofs
- Brace gable-end roof framing

Additional details are available at the FEMA Web site, including downloadable pdf files on how to install a generator or protect business records. See http://www.fema.gov/plan/prevent/howto/index.shtm.

Summary

In this chapter, we learned that businesses can be impacted by disasters either through direct damages or indirectly through related disruptions. Although advance preparedness seems like a good idea for businesses, the truth is that preparedness tends to focus on acquiring first aid kits or teaching first aid. Larger businesses are more likely to be ready for disaster because they usually dedicate more resources to preparedness. The magnitude and scope of the impact can influence recovery too, in part because of how area infrastructure is affected. Location matters as well, as business sectors that lose pedestrian traffic, parking, or rental spaces are more likely to experience a difficult recovery.

To prepare for a disaster, businesses should calculate probable losses to their structure and contents. Downtime should be considered as well, which is defined as the length of time that a business cannot operate. Displacement costs should be factored in too, including moving to a new location and reestablishing services. Businesses should examine the impact of disasters on employees and consider ways to temporarily replace those affected by the disaster. Further, businesses need to assist employees or customers injured in the business. Business-recovery planning can spur resumption of local enterprises. Loss-containment measures may reduce the impact. Local government and supporting groups can act to lure customers back to the damaged area, even during rebuilding efforts.

Recovery also represents an opportune time for new ideas. District overlays may enhance the business-sector appearance and functionality. New features can be integrated into the business and economic sector, including green features such as streetscapes and energy-efficient elements. Businesses may face difficulty securing external aid due to the limits on funds available. The U.S. Small Business Administration offers two types of loans to businesses. The National Trust's Main Street Program has also funded disaster recovery efforts. Voluntary organizations may step up to assist those unable to secure business-recovery loans.

It is clear that business recovery depends on many things, particularly the availability of key infrastructure such as roads, bridges, and transportation systems that bring in customers and employees and allow for delivery of goods and services. Utilities provide lifelines to businesses through electricity, water, sewer, and gas services. Without these, even undamaged businesses can fail. We turn to the topic of infrastructure and utilities in the next chapter.

Study Guide

Summary Questions

1. What can businesses expect in the aftermath of a disaster? What kinds of direct and indirect losses might be experienced?
2. What main conditions influence business preparedness?
3. How are losses estimated for businesses including structure and contents losses?
4. What is the difference between displacement and downtime?
5. How might loss-containment measures make a difference in business recovery?
6. Describe the main four steps and related activities in FEMA's business-recovery planning strategy.
7. How can energy-efficient design be integrated into business recovery?
8. What is the value of mitigation measures for business recovery?

Discussion Questions

1. What kinds of businesses exist in your community? Be thorough and look at major industries, small businesses, and home-based enterprises.
2. Assume that a major disaster has gone through the downtown or a key area in your community. How might you rethink that location for traffic flow, parking, and streetscaping to lure customers back?
3. In your community, which organizations, agencies, and groups would be central to helping the business sector to recover? Who should be involved in such an effort?
4. If you work inside or outside of the home (or if a family member does), how prepared is that business for disaster? What recommendations can you offer to reduce risk and help plan for recovery? What can businesses do to retain valuable employees after a disaster?
5. What might a new district overlay look like in an area where you live? How would you like to see an economic area in your community be reconceptualized after disaster?

Key Terms

Business-continuity planning
Cyber-commuting
Displacement
District overlay
Downtime
Economic Injury Disaster Loan (EIDL)
Home-based business
Micro-loans
Physical Disaster Loan
Rainy-day fund
U.S. Small Business Administration (SBA)

References

Bram, J., J. Orr, and C. Rapaport. 2002. Measuring the effects of the September 11 attack on New York City. *Economic Policy Review* 8 (2): 5–20.

Chang, S. E., and A. Falit-Baiamonte. 2002. Disaster vulnerability of businesses in the 2001 Nisqually earthquake. *Environmental Hazards* 4: 59–71.

Comerio, M. C. 2000. The economic benefits of a disaster-resistant university. Berkeley: University of California–Berkeley.

Comerio, M. C. 2008. Personal communication with author.

Dahlhamer, J. M., and M. J. D'Souza. 1997. Determinants of business disaster preparedness. *International Journal of Mass Emergencies and Disasters* 15 (2): 265–283.

Dahlhamer, J., and K. Tierney. 1998. Rebounding from disruptive events. *Sociological Spectrum* 18: 121–141.

Dynes, R. R. 1987. The concept of role in disaster research. In *Sociology of disasters*, ed. R. R. Dynes, B. De Marchi, and C. Pelanda. Milan, Italy: Franco Angeli.

Enarson, E. 2001. What women do: Gendered labor in the Red River Valley flood. *Environmental Hazards* 3: 1–18.

FEMA. 2001. *Understanding your risks.* Washington, DC: Federal Emergency Management Agency.

Johnson, N. 1988. Fire in a crowded theater: A descriptive investigation of the emergence of panic. *International Journal of Mass Emergencies and Disasters* 6 (1): 7–26.

Kendra, J. M., and T. Wachtendorf. 2002. Creativity in emergency response to the World Trade Center disaster. In *Beyond September 11*, ed. J. Monday. Boulder, CO: Natural Hazards Research and Applications Information Center.

Lawniczak, J. 2007. Main street helping main street: the Wisconsin Story. Washington D.C.: National Main Street Center, National Trust for Historic Preservation.

Laye, J. 2002. *Avoiding disaster: How to keep your business going when catastrophe strikes.* Hoboken, NJ: John Wiley.

McEntire, D., R. Robinson, and R. Weber. 2003. Business responses to the World Trade Center disaster: A study of corporate roles, functions, and interaction with the public sector. In *Beyond September 11th*, ed. J. Monday. Boulder, CO: Natural Hazards Research and Applications Information Center.

Monday, J., ed. 2005. *Holistic disaster recovery*. Boulder, CO: Natural Hazards Research and Applications Information Center.

National Trust for Historic Preservation. 2008. What is the Main Street approach to commercial district revitalization? http://www.mainstreet.org/content.aspx?page=3&section=2.

Phillips, B. 2005. Gender and disasters: Workplace disaster preparedness. *Journal of Employee Assistance* 35 (2): 25–27.

Schwab, J., K. C. Topping, C. C. Eadie, R. E. Deyle, and R. A. Smith. 1998. *Planning for post-disaster recovery and reconstruction*. Washington, DC: FEMA.

Tierney, K. 1996. Business impacts of the Northridge earthquake. Newark: University of Delaware Disaster Research Center.

———. 2006. Businesses and disasters: Vulnerability, impacts, and recovery. In *Handbook of disaster research*, ed. H. Rodriguez, E. L. Quarantelli, and R. R. Dynes. New York: Springer.

Tierney, K., J. Nigg, and J. Dahlhamer. 1996. The impact of the 1993 Midwest floods: Business vulnerability and disruption in Des Moines. In *Cities and disaster: North American studies in emergency management*, ed. R. T. Sylves and W. L. Waugh. Springfield, MO: Charles C. Thomas.

Webb, G., K. Tierney, and J. Dahlhamer. 2000. Businesses and disasters: Empirical patterns and unanswered questions. *Natural Hazards Review* 1 (3): 83–90.

Wilson, R. 1991. *The Loma Prieta earthquake: What one city learned*. Washington, DC: International City Management Association.

Resources

- Basic supplies for businesses, see Appendix C (pages 38-41 in Avoiding Disaster (Laye 2002).
- Business Continuity Planning Association, http://www.bcpa.org/
- Business continuity planning for non-profits, visit http://nonprofit risk.org/tools/business-continuity/intro/1.htm.
- FEMA Business Recovery page at http://www.fema.gov/business/guide/index.shtm).
- Main Street USA, http://www.mainstreet.org, "Coping with Disaster" http://www.mainstreet.org/MediaLibrary/MSN_2002_10_Coping WithDisaster.pdf.
- Small Business Administration, Disaster Recovery Plan, http://www.sba.gov/idc/groups/public/documents/sba_homepage/serv_da_disastr_revcovery_plan.pdf
- University of California-Berkeley initiative information can be found at http://peer.berkeley.edu/publications/peer_reports/reports_2006/reports_2006.html.

Chapter **9**

Infrastructure and Lifelines

Learning Objectives

After reading this chapter, you should be able to:

- Understand the predisaster state of the nation's infrastructure and lifelines
- Identify the various impacts that disaster can have on the current infrastructure and utilities
- Describe the social impacts of disruption of infrastructure and utilities
- Understand the procedures that typically move damages of infrastructure and utilities toward a state of restoration
- Specify holistic strategies for rebuilding damaged infrastructure and utilities so as to enhance the overall recovery
- Outline mitigation options for communities to consider for repairs to infrastructure and utilities

Introduction

The 1964 Alaskan earthquake, which lasted for an unusually long three minutes, rocked numerous towns, including large cities like Anchorage and smaller more remote areas in Kenai. A significant portion of downtown Anchorage collapsed, including commercial stores, an apartment building, and several schools. Decades later, uplift from the earthquake can still be seen in parts of Anchorage, including an earthquake park.

Earthquakes can generate additional hazards; such was the case in the 1964 Alaska event, which caused landslides and tsunamis (Sokolowski n.d.). A large landslide in Anchorage caused damage to water, gas, sewage, telephone, and power sources. A tsunami rolled over the coastline, damaging ports, fishing communities, and waterways (U.S. Geological Survey 2007). Described in many reports as the "Great Alaskan Earthquake," the event demonstrates the power of a disaster to disrupt not only homes and businesses, but the **infrastructure** and utilities that facilitate response and expedite recovery.

It may seem that bridges, airports, waterways, and the like represent the interests of engineers rather than the general reader like yourself. However, infrastructure and utilities demand our attention because we depend on them, often taking them for granted until they fail and we experience inconveniences.

How does our nation fare in terms of predisaster infrastructure? As one of the largest and most powerful nations worldwide, you might be surprised to discover that, in the opinion of a number of experts, our infrastructure is in trouble. The American Society of Civil Engineers (ASCE) issues a "Report Card for America's Infrastructure." In its most recent report published in 2005, the ASCE gave our nation an overall grade of D. ASCE identified troubles with roads, solid waste, transit facilities, wastewater, aviation, bridges, dams, water, energy, waterways, railways, and more. Problems stem from a lack of necessary repairs and updates, insufficient funding, and inadequate attention from policy makers (ASCE 2005). Let us review a few areas of concern.

ASCE found that 27% of the nation's 590,750 bridges could be rated structurally deficient or functionally obsolete. Although the good news is that the percentage of bridges in those categories had dropped slightly in prior years, the cost to eliminate such deficiencies is a staggering $9.4 billion per year for 20 years. The next time you drive over a bridge in your area, notice any posted restrictions. In order to increase safety, officials may have limited the vehicle size or weight or the traffic volume allowed on the bridge.

The ASCE report card also showed that roads are costing us billions of dollars in lost time due to traffic congestion and increased accidents. According to the Federal Highway Administration, one-third of our roads are considered "poor, mediocre or fair" (ASCE 2005). Traffic congestion continues to increase as our population grows, especially in urban areas. The good news is that federal and state funding exists for roads and is being used to improve conditions. How else might we reduce the impact of traffic on our roads system? Public transit, which can serve as a means of reducing congestion, wear and tear on the roads, air pollution, and personal gasoline costs, merited a D+ on the ASCE report card. ASCE reported that transit use increased 21% between 1993 and 2002. The Federal Transit Authority indicates that urban bus conditions are somewhat improved, although the average state of train cars has declined. In rural areas, about half of the transit options are beyond a normal life span (ASCE 2005).

To better understand the impact of disasters on our infrastructure, and how the infrastructure might fare in a disaster, we will next examine two scenarios. The first case is the 2007 Minneapolis I-35 bridge collapse. Our second case is the massive 2003 power failure. A third example describing the Mississippi River floods of 2008 can be found in Box 9.1.

BOX 9.1   THE 2008 MISSISSIPPI RIVER FLOODS

Disasters further undermine infrastructure in need of repair and damage areas that were in good shape. The Mississippi River floods of 2008 caused significant problems with roads and bridges in several states. As one example of how repairs occur, the U.S. Department of Transportation gave $1 million for emergency road and bridge repair to the state of Iowa. The funding strengthened the federal–state partnership required to initiate recovery:

> "We're making this down payment so repairs can start immediately and communities can receive the assistance they need without further delay," Secretary Peters said. "The people of Iowa need to know that everything will be done to restore the state's damaged highways and bridges quickly."

> "As Governor, I am committed to doing whatever I can to return life to normal for Iowans, and this funding will help us do just that," said Iowa Governor Chet Culver. "I want to thank the U.S. Department of Transportation for making this commitment to Iowa's transportation recovery efforts. Together, with the help and cooperation of everyone on the local, state and federal levels, I am confident that we will rebuild our state—even better and stronger than before."

> Secretary Peters said the $1 million quick release was intended to help Iowa address repairs that need immediate attention to restore essential traffic in eastern portions of the state until a full assessment of the damage is completed.

> The Secretary added that the Department would continue to work with officials from Iowa and other Midwestern states as they evaluate the extent of road damage caused by the floods. She said more resources will likely be made available based on those evaluations.

> The Federal Highway Administration's emergency relief program provides funds to states for the repair or reconstruction of federal-aid highways damaged by natural disasters or catastrophic events. The program typically works on a reimbursable basis.

Source: Federal Highway Administration, http://www.fhwa.dot.gov/pressroom/dot0886.htm

Minneapolis I-35W Bridge Collapse

Minneapolis, Minnesota, experienced catastrophic failure of a key bridge on the I-35W highway during the evening rush hour on August 1, 2007 (see Photo 9.1). Bridge construction began in 1964, and the bridge was opened for public use in 1967. Approximately 140,000 private vehicles crossed the bridge daily as well as nearly 5,000 commercial vehicles. Traffic traversed via four lanes in each direction. The bridge was constructed as a deck steel-truss bridge, which has a normal life span of about 50 years. By 2007, the bridge had been in service for 40 years (Minnesota Department of Transportation 2007; NTSB 2008).

The state inspected the bridge in 2006 and labeled it as poor, with "corrosion at some areas where the paint system has deteriorated, poor weld details in the steel truss members and flood beams, bearings that are not moving as they were designed to move, and existing fatigue crack repairs to the truss cross beam and approach spans" (Minnesota Department of Transportation 2007, 2). The state had repaired some cracks in the approach spans. Further, the state had conducted multiple tests indicating that the deck truss should not experience fatigue cracking. Before the collapse, weld cracks were not detected (Minnesota Department of Transportation 2007). A November 2008 report indicated that gusset plates, which strengthen

PHOTO 9.1   The Minneapolis, Minnesota, bridge collapse. (Photo by Todd Swain/ FEMA News Photo.)

joists, failed (CNN news report Nov. 15, 2008). Thirteen deaths occurred, with an additional 145 injured, including several dozen children on a school bus.

The 2003 Cascading Power Failure

In August 2003, a power failure disrupted service to eight states. Called a "cascading failure," the event occurred when critical plants and lines experienced transmission instability and went offline. The incident began at about noon, when instability led to three power plants and transmission lines going offline in Ohio and Michigan. Going offline led to further instability at the regional level. Between 2 and 3 p.m., four large transmission lines tripped, and at 4:10 p.m., many additional plants and lines tripped in Ohio and Michigan. At 4:11 p.m., the cascading failures began across the city of New York, causing tens of thousands of people to walk home. The event extended into other areas of New England and parts of Canada (U.S. GAO 2003).

Ultimately, the largest blackout in U.S. history touched 50 million people, closed businesses, stopped transportation, shut down gasoline stations, prevented parents from reaching children in day care or at home alone, disrupted cell phones and 9-1-1 communications, and compromised the life safety of people with disabilities (U.S. GAO 2003; ASCE 2005). As the ASCE notes: "Air and ground transportation systems shut down, trapping people far from home; drinking water systems and sewage processing plants stopped operating, manufacturing was disrupted and some emergency communications systems stopped functioning. The lost productivity and revenue have been estimated in the billions of dollars" (ASCE 2005).

Although the blackout demonstrates what can happen when a power failure serves as the disaster event, think also of disasters that cut off electricity such as ice storms, hurricanes, and tornados. **Utility** companies swarmed areas affected by Hurricane Katrina for months, bringing in crews from across the United States to repair severely damaged electrical equipment. New Orleans remained darkened for months, with power returning slowly to neighborhoods and even more slowly to individual homes and businesses. Other services dependent on electricity lagged even further behind, such as temporary housing like FEMA trailers, not to mention amenities like cable television, Internet service, health and medical services, and more. Home construction could not commence until dependable energy sources returned to power construction tools. Businesses could not reopen in the absence of even minimal infrastructural support. Clearly, human systems rely on dependable infrastructure and utility services.

The Social Impacts of Infrastructural and Utility Damage

By now, it is easy to understand how important infrastructure and utilities are to individuals, families, and communities. Systems theory (see Chapter 2) demonstrates how the built environment connects to the human system. Alarm clocks powered by electricity wake us up in the morning, followed by gas-heated showers and clean water piped directly into our houses at our command. Coffee jolts us awake, through caffeine that arrived via water-based ports and airports and then transported to our locale via highways and bridges. At work or school, we log on to the Internet, usually through high-speed lines or wireless connections. During the day, we call friends, send photos and text messages, and assume that our cell phones will work just about anywhere. To find out what is going on during the day, we may tap into radio or television stations that also transmit weather images from various radar installations. At an individual level, it is easy to see the impact of infrastructure and utility availability for our daily routines. In a disaster context, the problems can be far more serious.

Daily Life

Should we have a traffic accident, we assume that 9-1-1 will work, speeding resources to our aid. Medical facilities depend heavily on utilities and infrastructure; most have backup generators, although an alarming number are located below ground level, as was the case in several New Orleans hospitals. People dependent on power supplies include those using oxygen on a regular basis as well as individuals who use power for durable medical equipment such as scooters or motorized wheelchairs.

Systems theory predicts that disasters disrupting one component of a system can profoundly affect other systems. Consequently, disruptions to the infrastructure suggest serious consequences for human systems. As our urban areas have grown, we have become "increasingly dependent upon infrastructure transmission and distribution networks for … transportation, energy, communications, water supply, and wastewater collection and treatment" (Zimmerman 2001, 97). Such rapid growth tends to increase disruptions in part because of the interdependence and connectivity of the systems. **Interconnectedness**, defined as a "formal linkage between two different systems" tends to occur when newer systems tie into older infrastructure components (Zimmerman 2001, 99). Such disruptions are experienced as "street congestion, electric power blackouts, and outages of communications systems" and have become somewhat unpredictable (Zimmerman 2001, 98).

Disaster Context

Loss of infrastructure and utilities in a disaster context can be significant. For example, disruptions to telephone, cellular, or Internet service can have dramatic impacts. Hurricane Katrina took out cellular capacities in Louisiana for many customers. First responders, emergency workers, volunteer organizations, and local residents were unable to communicate well, or sometimes at all, because of the disruptions. Text messaging worked fairly well after a week, but cell service did not return for some time. To contact others, it was often necessary to use a phone-tree system by calling someone you could reach who would then pass on the message or drive out of the affected area completely to relay the message. Attempting to provide relief proved very difficult without this key communication tool.

Families that were separated before or during the evacuation could not easily locate each other. To deal with the disrupted communications, shelters placed residents' names on Internet-based lists and searched other shelter lists to find and reunite family members. Organizations like Traveler's Aid and Angel Flight used airport infrastructure to reconnect those who were separated. Media outlets and child protective service organizations used Internet and televised appeals to find lost children. But, could we expect such challenges outside of a catastrophic context like Hurricane Katrina?

Professor Joanne Nigg from the Disaster Research Center at the University of Delaware examined indirect economic effects should an earthquake damage utilities in Memphis, Tennessee. Memphis is an area that could potentially be affected by a major event along the New Madrid fault. In her study, businesses estimated how long they could operate without specific utilities. Electricity emerged as the key concern for businesses that would be unable to function without power. Lack of telephone service would disrupt operations quickly as well, followed by water, wastewater treatment, and lastly natural gas (Nigg 1995). Business and professional services would probably close the fastest, followed by manufacturing and construction, wholesale and retail businesses, and then by offices supporting finance, insurance, and real estate. Bearing in mind that these results reflect businesses that might not even sustain direct damage, only disruption, it is easy to see the broader impacts of utility failures in disasters (Nigg 1995). In the next section, we look at the impacts of disasters more closely for specific elements of infrastructure and utilities.

The Impacts of Disaster on Infrastructure and Utilities

What might happen to the infrastructure and utilities in our communities and states should disaster strike? The ASCE (2009) report includes a breakdown of the top three infrastructure concerns for each state in the United States as well as the District of Columbia. It is clear that each state experiences considerable challenges, although the top three concerns may vary. In Florida, with a strong tourist economy and increasing population, roads and mass transit lead the list of top concerns. Illinois identifies its roads as a problem, where 17% of the state's bridges are also ranked "structurally deficient or functionally obsolete" (ASCE 2009). North Carolina ranks 34% of its major roads as poor or mediocre. According to the ASCE, the nation is already in trouble even before disaster strikes. Let us look at some key infrastructure elements and utilities to understand better what can happen in disasters.

Roads

Those of us who live in areas with ice and snow understand the impact of severe weather on our roads through the potholes our cars hit. Floodwaters can damage roads as well by destabilizing roadsides or undermining the area beneath the road surface. Earthquakes push roadways up, buckling them and creating uplift that makes travel more treacherous. Hazardous materials spills can shut down roads for some time to allow proper cleanup; runoff can further damage nearby areas.

Transportation arteries matter to us, and any disruption can seriously impact our lives. Transportation planners note that disasters require evacuations, search and rescue, delivery of critical assets, and may even require quarantine, blockades, or other measures to limit the spread of a hazardous material or biological, radiological, or chemical agents used by a terrorist (Litman 2006). Indeed, losing transportation capacities can cause considerable societal disruption beyond the physical impact on the road (Chang 2003).

We rely on transportation systems to an extent that we might not imagine. For example, a single highway lane serves about 2,000 maximum vehicles per hour or 600 buses. However, an evacuation may reduce that number as people tow trailers, campers, boats, or other vehicles to safeguard these items as well as livestock and other personal property. Under these conditions, it is reasonable to assume that highway carrying capacity drops to 1,000 vehicles per hour. Litman (2006) suggests that if each vehicle carries 2.5 passengers, a four-lane highway can lead about 10,000 people to safety each hour, assuming that no accidents or gasoline shortfalls occur. In a city of 1 million people with two four-lane highways, the time required to evacuate everyone would total 50 hours (Litman 2006).

Certain disasters do not allow time for evacuation. For example, a hurricane approaching the coast of Texas would demand that people on Galveston

Island evacuate using their one bridge prior to the approach of storm surge. The call to evacuate the island must occur at least 48 hours prior to that surge, which means evacuating people when the predicted landfall areas remain uncertain. Hurricane Rita, which approached the Houston area above Galveston Island, launched a massive evacuation far beyond what officials called for. It appears that at least 3 million people in the area, rather than the expected maximum of 1.2 million, left after seeing what Katrina did to Louisiana and Mississippi. As a consequence, extensive traffic congestion—100 miles long in some areas—led to people running out of gasoline and gas stations without fuel (Litman 2006). People could not get to work, open or assist in shelters, or reach their own families. In the event's biggest tragedy, a bus carrying nursing-home residents caught fire, and 24 patients perished on the gridlocked highway.

Public Transit

Depending on where you live, public transportation may be a routine way to move about your community. Subways, bus routes, and rail transport can all be disrupted in disasters, with significant consequences for our ability to travel to school or work, deliver and retrieve children from day care, buy groceries, visit family in the hospital, or enjoy recreational opportunities. Since September 11, concern has arisen over the vulnerability of such "soft targets." A nuclear, chemical, or biological release in such a public transit system could easily and quickly spread deadly consequences throughout a large area. The sarin chemical gas attack on the Tokyo Metro caused the deaths of a dozen people. Initiated as an act of domestic terrorism, well over 1,000 people were affected. London's metro system, called the Underground, fared worse in 2005 when suicide bombers set off three explosions. Over 50 people died and nearly 1,000 sustained injuries.

It seems clear that the heaviest impact yet observed from a natural hazard on a public transit system occurred in New Orleans as a result of Hurricane Katrina. As an urban area with a low-income and working-class population heavily dependent on public transportation, the public transit system was essential. Before the storm and levee failure, more than 70,000 people rode a total of 368 operational buses on a daily basis in the city of New Orleans (Brookings Institution and GNOCDC 2008). However, public bus transportation has been very slow to return. Within 12 months after the flood, only 69 of the buses, 19% of the original fleet, had returned to operation, serving a total of 21,519 daily riders. One year later, ridership had declined some to 19,744, although two additional buses had come into operation. By early 2008, the number of operational buses remained at 69 total vehicles. Ridership had increased to only 25,022.

Bridges

Bridges fail in all kinds of scenarios. Clearly, the national need to update bridges to current design standards represents a stand-alone concern. Disasters result when bridges collapse due to structural failure, such as the Minnesota bridge collapse, or are damaged due to other causes. Earthquakes, for example, occur in varying magnitudes and as the result of differing ground motion. Estimations for a possible large-magnitude New Madrid earthquake that could affect the St. Louis area are startling. In a study using FEMA's HAZUS-MH software that assesses risks and supports mitigation planning, researchers calculated damage and losses for bridges if a 7.7-magnitude earthquake were to occur (Luna, Hoffman, and Lawrence 2008). Though the event is considered a low probability, the consequences are high, with "564 bridges with a probability of at least 50% moderate damage" (Luna, Hoffman, and Lawrence 2008, 10). The cost? At least $864 million in repairs. The **indirect losses** including business disruption would add even more to that amount. As one comparison, the actual earthquake that occurred in Northridge cost $7–9.5 billion in indirect losses (Enke, Tirasirichai, and Luna 2008).

Infrastructure is often interrelated, and damage to one part can result in serious consequences to another. In 1993, for example, a barge struck a bridge near Mobile, Alabama, when the operator failed to see the structure due to heavy fog. The accident occurred about 2:45 a.m. Approximately five minutes later, a passenger train traveling at a high rate of speed struck the damaged tracks on the bridge and derailed. A fuel car ruptured, causing a massive fire. Forty-seven people died from either drowning or burns (Tolchin 1993). To summarize, the risks associated with bridge collapse stem from structural failures, damage due to the impact of natural hazards and terrorist attack, and the interconnectedness of the infrastructure.

Levees and Dams

Dams, which provide a water supply, recreational opportunities like boating and fishing, and waterways for transportation of public goods, also represent both a means for and a concern about public safety. Dams can hold back heavy rains and prevent floods. However, dam failures have claimed thousands of lives. In 2008, despite the heroic efforts of local citizens, dozens of dams failed along the Mississippi River, inundating communities, businesses, and homes. As of July 2008, the flooding had claimed 24 lives. The ASCE has graded the nation's dams as a D with concerns. Approximately 95% of the nation's dams are maintained at the state level, which is where the problem tends to exist. **High-hazard dams** are defined as those whose failure would risk life and cause property damage. Texas, for example, has 857 such locations; Pennsylvania lists 725; New Jersey reports 583; and New Hampshire's high-hazard dams total 357 (ASCE 2005).

Costs to monitor, maintain, and repair dams are as high as $10.1 billion per year just for dams that ASCE deems "critical." Policy makers have addressed the problem through the National Dam Safety and Security Act of 2002, which, though enhancing state safety programs, failed to provide funding for repairs (ASCE 2005). As you might expect, the number of unsafe dams continues to increase.

Ports and Airports

In 1985, an earthquake struck Mexico City, Mexico, damaging the airport and preventing both passenger travel and rescue assistance for some time. Hurricane Katrina disrupted transportation into and out of the Port of New Orleans, one of the nation's busiest container ports and the entry to extensive Mississippi River travel. Because waterways offer a less expensive way to route cargo, losing both a port and waterway access can be costly. Similarly, the New Orleans airport, which served as an operations center for rescue flights into and out of the area, took considerable time to recover from the hurricane. Louis Armstrong Airport served 443,809 passengers in June 2005, a number that fell to 18,966 in September 2005 just after the storm and levee failures. By March 2006, the number had risen to 246,598, but the airport has not yet reached its prestorm capacity.

Both direct and indirect losses occur as a result of such an impact. **Direct losses** are the easiest to calculate and can be defined as the financial impact lost as a consequence of the loss of the infrastructure. A direct loss for an airport, for example, would include passenger fares and the personal cost of lost wages. Damage to the airport from the storm as well as the use of the facility for medical triage and rescue flights also adds up.

Indirect losses can be defined as those that arise outside of the infrastructure but are related to the disruption of a key piece of the infrastructure. The impact on a tourist economy that relies on an airport, for example, has been considerable. Hotels have not regained lost revenues, which include taxes paid into the local governmental budget. Restaurants and their staff cannot return without a customer base. In the months that followed Hurricane Katrina, for example, the famous Café Du Monde in the French Quarter closed before 10 p.m. on weekends. When the people cannot come back, rebuilding can take an extensive period of time. The repopulation of the city has stalled, which causes the unfortunate cyclical effect of reducing demand for infrastructure like the bus system mentioned earlier.

There can be a more positive effect of disasters, though. September 11 led to some upgrades in the port assets. For example, in Florida, Port Everglades received $44 million to improve security, including "access control, closed circuit television installation, security operations center construction, perimeter security, identification badge center, and waterside security" (ASCE 2005). Airport security also changed dramatically after September 11. The Transportation Security Administration (TSA) has established careful procedures to reduce the potential for hijackings, explosions, or other risks. Many of us have experienced the TSA regulations as we stand in line to be screened, x-rayed, and searched for possible weapons or devices. Currently, TSA requires us to carry fluids and gels in a clear quart-size bag for examination and to submit our government-issued identification card for scrutiny. Onboard, new doors bar entry to the cockpit, and an air marshal may be on board to protect us further. Regulations change when new risks are revealed, and TSA regulations are subject to daily changes.

Communications

How important is your cell phone to you? How frequently do you call or text? Cellular use has increased at a rate more rapid than adoption of the Internet. In 2002, both cellular and landline users totaled approximately 1 billion. Just four years later, however, there were twice as many cell owners as landline users (Comer and Wikle 2007). In short, the rapid adoption of the cell phone has led many of us to change how, when, and where we can communicate either personal conversations or business activities. The loss of cell phones would have a significant impact on our daily lives and the ways in which our families and businesses function.

The 2001 attack on the World Trade Center destroyed three cellular sites but affected a total of 173. To restore communications, Verizon brought in 55 mobile cell towers to the area. In disasters, cell phone usage tends to escalate rapidly. The problem is that key offices and personnel cannot then communicate effectively, including first responders and emergency managers. In response, cell providers blocked up to 92% of calls, although they managed to restore most usage capacity within a few hours and total usage within one week (Condello 2001; Zimmerman 2003).

Wireless resources do more than enable us to talk or text. The Wireless Emergency Response Team attempted to find survivors in the World Trade Center rubble by trying to detect wireless devices. To do so, they used "cell registration patterns, radio emissions from wireless devices of persons trapped in the debris, and database look-up services to track potentially trapped victims" (Zimmerman 2003, 246–247). The team was able to do so in part by drawing on the resources of other offices and companies, which were made available because of preexisting relationships of the parties involved.

Water and Sewer

The city of Waveland, Mississippi, needed to establish multiple phases for restoration of water and sewer service after Hurricane Katrina. St. Bernard Parish, Louisiana, lost two water-treatment facilities, six sewage-treatment plants, and 89 out of 92 pumping stations (FEMA 2005). In Orleans Parish, 44,300 catch basins and 8 million linear feet of drain lines were clogged. Humans cannot survive without water, and the recovery of these critical facilities took months, with thousands of outside workers and agencies sending assistance and funding.

Electricity and Gas

We are dependent on electricity. Without this critical lifeline, we cannot heat or cool our homes, operate computers, read at night, run a business, cook for our families, or hold school. People who rely on power for oxygen, durable medical equipment, and kidney dialysis face threats to life without electricity or generators. Hospitals and nursing homes struggle to provide basic care without power sources. The U.S. electric power grid, however, requires considerable upgrading (ASCE 2005), which represents both a problem in disasters and an opportunity should we decide to prioritize power during the recovery effort.

The 1989 Loma Prieta earthquake caused over 1,000 natural gas pipeline leaks (Eguchi and Seligson 1994). Repairs to the distribution system in San Francisco's Marina District took one month at a cost of $17 million. At least $7 million in costs could have been reduced through better consumer action. Customers, fearing fires from leaks, turned off their gas. Nearly 1,200 employees were needed to relight the gas pilot lights in 156,355 homes. Electrical utilities had to deal with damage to transmission facilities at a cost of $19 million. Power was restored fairly quickly, however, because of the utility company's ability to bypass "damaged equipment and [operate] with reduced levels of circuit protection" (Eguchi and Seligson 1994, 142).

In Waveland, Mississippi, FEMA provided $6 million to repair the gas lines, and the city requested an additional $1 million for underground damage. In New Orleans, recovery to individual households lagged. One year after the storm, only 41% of the prestorm customers had gas service. About 60% of the prestorm electricity had been restored to residences (Brookings Institution 2006).

Damage Assessment

As with other dimensions of recovery, the first step is damage assessment (see Photo 9.2). Emergency management agencies and inspectors may work with

PHOTO 9.2   A preliminary damage assessment team looks at damage caused to a bridge by three storms in West Virginia during 2008. Debris from the storms caused the bridge damage. (Photo by Robert Kaufmann/FEMA News Photo.)

affected utility companies to conduct their own assessment of state-supervised roads, bridges, and dams. Debris removal (discussed in Chapter 4) is the first assessment that needs to be taken. Ice storms, for example, will take down power lines, which need to be removed carefully so as to reduce any further potential for damage or injury to workers. Downed limbs and other debris picked up during floods will also stack up behind obstacles, causing water force to build up and potentially destroy bridges. Thus, identifying debris locations and prioritizing areas for removal serves as a first step in launching recovery efforts (see Box 9.2). Removing such debris requires careful coordination and planning with multiple local and state departments and utility companies. Planning how to remove debris and how to stage repair crews requires communication among those partners in order to expedite recovery.

Protective measures may also need to be taken. The public may need to be further protected from harm, for example, by erecting barricades to prevent entry on dangerous roads and bridges. Public notice may need to be issued if water facilities have sustained damage (such as a pipeline break) and local drinking supplies have been compromised. To be safe, for example, officials may choose to issue notices requiring residents to boil water prior to drinking or cooking. Most agencies suggest boiling water strongly for at least two minutes to kill bacteria. Some may suggest adding purification tablets or other measures.

BOX 9.2   GETTING THE POWER BACK ON

How do you know when your power will come back on after a disaster? Most companies attend to outages by prioritizing emergencies. Depending on where you are, power is likely to be returned to you in this order:

- Utility employees will attend to downed power lines first in order to reduce the risk of further injuries from live wires.
- Locations that care for the injured and ill will likely be next on the list, including fire stations, police, hospitals, nursing homes, and shelters.
- Utilities will then identify locations where they can quickly restore the largest number of customers.
- Individual homes and businesses will come last if they have not been restored by the previous efforts.

Ultimately, in deciding how recovery should ensue, we must decide on what kinds of risks we are willing to accept, what kinds of funds we are willing to spend, and what types of behavioral changes we are willing to undertake. For example, is it possible to encourage Americans to change their transportation behavior and use mass transit? In 2008, rising gasoline prices increased such behavior, which may indicate what truly motivates behavioral change: the cost to our bank accounts. The same financial concerns extend to infrastructure and utility recovery. How much are we willing to increase our taxes and utility payments to reduce future risks to our power, communications, and water sources or to our roads, bridges, and ports? Costs for some changes can be relatively minimal compared with repeated years of damage, suggesting that a cost–benefit analysis can reveal considerable savings.

However, it may simply not be feasible to do so due to local, regional, or even national economic circumstances. After the Oklahoma ice storms of 2008, the costs were deemed too much to bury utility lines underground. The Oklahoma Corporation Commission estimated the cost at $57.5 million. In comparison, the costs of the storm included 29 deaths and power losses to 600,000 homes and businesses for up to a month. Alternatives to underground burial include vegetation management, burial of new lines, smart-grid installations that reroute power around downed lines and transformers, and encouraging backup generator use (Oklahoma Corporation Commission 2008).

Another dimension of damage assessment examines the human impact. Most communities, through emergency planning procedures, should have already preidentified locations and populations most at risk, such as individuals dependent on oxygen at home, congregate care facilities including nursing homes, hospitals, and other facilities dependent on power, water, gas, and access to transportation. However, it may also be true that a number of jurisdictions have not taken their response and recovery planning to this level, particularly regarding individuals living at home—the population may simply be too large to do so, or the jurisdiction may not have the resources. Regardless, rapid identification must be made of people and locations at risk due to the infrastructure or utility disruptions. Doing so allows for the recovery partners to prioritize locations for debris removal and restoration.

As an example, the 1998 ice storm that hit Canada produced five times the ice of any previous storm, reaching 100 mm or nearly four inches of ice. The area slowly ground to a halt. Hundreds of power and telephone lines came down. Traffic slowed, as did public transit. Ultimately, one in five Canadians lost power for up to three weeks. Although most did not go to public shelters, officials urged senior citizens to do so out of concern they could die of hypothermia during the extreme event. First responders conducted door-to-door contact to find those in need who could not be reached with phone lines down. When the event ended, 10% of Ottawa's trees were destroyed and another 70% had sustained damage. With Ottawa serving as the capital city, the impact was tremendous. To launch recovery, the nation sent its largest peacetime deployment of military personnel along with massive numbers of power and phone workers from outside the area (Scanlon 1999).

Final steps in the damage assessment process may include assessment of business disruption and identification of key locations that require support and prioritization (for example, home health agencies, grocery stores, and pharmacies). Other locations may be assessed, depending on priority. For example, public buildings could be assessed for damage and prioritization as well as parks and recreation facilities that may serve as shelters, distribution centers, and information locations. Officials may also determine whether those businesses and facilities require further assistance to recover and integrate them into the recovery plan. An assessment may also be made to determine the impacts should area businesses not reopen as a result of damage or nonrepairs to the area's infrastructure and utilities. (For help with funding those efforts, see Box 9.3.)

BOX 9.3 FEMA'S PUBLIC ASSISTANCE PROGRAM

Where does the financial aid for infrastructure and utility restoration come from? The federal government has provided extensive aid in prior disasters. (For a description of federal resources, see Chapter 15, Financing Recovery.) FEMA's Public Assistance (PA) Program offers "repair, replacement, or restoration of disaster-damaged, publicly owned facilities and the facilities of certain Private Non-Profit (PNP) organizations. The PA Program also encourages protection of these damaged facilities from future events by providing assistance for hazard mitigation measures during the recovery process." FEMA pays up to 75% of the cost of repairs to a public facility such as a water-treatment plant, with the state and local government making up the remaining 25%. To qualify for PA funds, the state must conduct a preliminary damage assessment to allow the governor to request a presidential disaster declaration (PDD). Once issued, the PDD allows for FEMA personnel to meet with state and local officials for a kickoff meeting. During that session, a public-assistance coordinator will describe the application process and the types of allowable projects.

FEMA allows for repairs to roads, bridges, auxiliary structures, lighting, and signage.

- FEMA allows road repairs to include:
  - Surfaces
  - Bases
  - Shoulders
  - Ditches
  - Drainage structures
  - Low water crossings
- FEMA permits the following repairs to bridges:
  - Decking and pavement
  - Piers
  - Girders
  - Abutments
  - Slope protection
  - Approaches
- Repairs to water-control facilities may be conducted on:
  - Dams and reservoirs
  - Levees
  - Lined and unlined engineered drainage channels
  - Canals
  - Aqueducts
  - Sediment basins
  - Shore-protective devices
  - Irrigation facilities
  - Pumping facilities
- Utilities can be repaired as well:
  - Water-treatment plants and delivery systems
  - Power generation and distribution facilities, including natural-gas systems, wind turbines, generators, substations, and power lines
  - Sewage-collection systems and treatment plants
- Communications

Funds can be made available for mass-transit systems as well.

Source: FEMA Public Assistance Guide, www.fema.gov

Infrastructure and Utility Recovery

Dr. Stephanie Chang at the University of Washington studied the 1995 earthquake in Kobe, Japan. The important port city of 1.5 million people sustained incredible damage from a 7.2-magnitude earthquake (Chang 2001, 2003). Over 4,500 people died, and 130,000 buildings sustained damage. Highway superstructures, bridges, and roads collapsed, and the railway service did not return for eight months. Reconstruction at the port took until 1997.

Dr. Chang emphasizes the idea of **accessibility**, which is defined as "the ease with which land-use activities such as employment opportunities can be reached from a location by using [in this case] a transportation system" (Chang 2003, 1052). In short, we need to move about to take care of families, return to work, and launch both personal and community efforts. Transportation systems enable us to do that. Decision making about repairs to a transportation system, then, must take into consideration how repairs can aid those living in the area. In Kobe, some areas of the city experienced slower repairs to their transportation access points and routes, which resulted in "spatial disparities in disaster recovery that continued for years after the earthquake" (Chang 2003, 1059; 2001).

Could such an event happen here? Chang estimated the effects of a significant earthquake in Seattle. Her analysis suggested that 106 bridges could close due to the damage (Chang 2001). How might recovery decisions affect the abilities of some neighborhoods to recover as well? It is not hard to imagine that a similar Kobe pattern may occur in New Orleans. With only a portion of the original bus routes open, it is even more difficult for low-income households and families to return home.

However, because disasters represent opportunities, the postdisaster time period can serve as a way to implement new transportation systems, redesign transportation arteries to enhance movement, and launch or expedite public transit systems. Ideally, any restoration efforts will move people more effectively to and from work or school and cause minimal environmental impact.

As described early in this chapter, the nation's infrastructure requires attention outside the context of disasters as well as during and after such an event. Efforts to restore the infrastructure must understand that repairs need to be integrated holistically with other reconstruction efforts. For example:

- Reconstruction can encourage public transportation, walkways, bike paths, and other strategies to reduce traffic congestion and related impacts on roads and bridges (ASCE 2005).
- Businesses can offer employees flex-time, shared jobs, and even cyber-commuting to reduce impact on the nation's infrastructure (ASCE 2005).

- Utilities can take the opportunity to bury power lines, upgrade systems, and adhere to the latest engineering designs to make their facilities and services more resilient to disaster.
- Land-use planners can reassess the locations of public facilities and identify locations that relocate key assets like water treatment plants out of harm's way.
- Social scientists and engineers can work together to design recoveries that permit equitable restoration of neighborhoods and businesses so that low-income neighborhoods are not lost and employees important to the local economy can continue to work.
- Recovery initiatives can incorporate the latest research into rebuilding efforts, such as seismic resistance, blast performance, and security improvements.

Mitigating Future Risks

After the Loma Prieta earthquake in 1989, the National Research Council and the U.S. Geological Survey convened experts in a national symposium. Among the practical lessons gleaned from the event, experts noted that efforts to mitigate the risk "paid off" (National Research Council 1994). It was also equally clear that where mitigation measures, such as steel reinforcement, had not taken place, both the public and private owners paid a price. In what could have been a far worse outcome, the National Research Council observed that the earthquake caused 4,000 landslides. Because a drought had been ongoing for some time in the area, the consequences of the landslides were less than expected. However, the event served as a warning to engage in mitigation measures and land-use planning.

Many mitigation efforts are hazard specific (see Table 9.1). Floods, for example, require structural mitigation measures that include elevations, dams, and levees. Earthquake hazards dictate that officials must pay attention to unreinforced masonry, which can fall easily and injure or kill, by introducing new building codes that retrofit high-risk buildings. Similarly, bracing furniture, bookcases, and cupboards inside a home can reduce the chance that items will fall onto residents. Hurricanes threats can be reduced through shuttering a home, passing codes that deny building permits in storm surge areas, or requiring that key wetlands be conserved to stem flood risks. Ice storms and high-wind events can also bring down power lines, suggesting that a recovery period can be used to bury such lines and reduce the chance of a repeat event. To accomplish mitigation measures, though, requires that the public work through a decision-making process that specifies the line of acceptable risk (Mileti 1999).

What other solutions are there for reducing the effects of disasters on our infrastructure and utilities and enhancing an ability to rebound from an event

TABLE 9.1   Mitigation Measures for Specific Hazards

Hazard[a]	Structural Mitigation Measure	Nonstructural Mitigation Measure
Terrorist attack (bombing)	Hardening of the facility Blast-resistant exteriors Security perimete Blast-resistant windows	Preparedness initiatives Securing high-risk areas such as parking lots Checking IDs and minimizing access
Flooding	Dams Levees Elevations Remove debris from waterways	Flood insurance Land-use planning to reduce building in floodplains
Tornado	Safe rooms Tie-downs Impact-resistant films	Codes that mandate safe rooms, congregate shelter facilities, and require adequate insurance
Hurricane	Elevations Shutters Roof anchoring Tie-downs	Land-use planning to protect environmentally sensitive areas, including wetlands and dunes
Hazardous-materials spill	Containment systems	Transportation routing Monitoring compliance with existing laws
Wildfire	Fire-resistant roofs Sprinkler systems Fire- and smoke-detection systems	Protection of the urban–rural interface Control of vegetation around buildings Public education

Source: FEMA Mitigation Guide 386-7.

Note: As noted throughout this chapter, both structural (built) and nonstructural (codes, ordinances, insurance) mitigation measures can be used to build a more disaster-resilient built environment. This table demonstrates some options for hazard-specific mitigation measures that can be introduced during the recovery period.

[a] For a full listing of suggestions on other types of hazards, see FEMA Mitigation Guide 386-7, pp. 3–4.

(see Table 9.2)? Professor Rae Zimmerman, who studied the impact of the World Trade Center attack on public infrastructure, describes **flexibility** as a key tool (Zimmerman 2003). This idea promotes flexibility in both "physical configurations" and "social institutions," suggesting that interconnected system parts must demonstrate **resilience**, robustness, and adaptability.

Flexibility includes several features such as establishing alternative routes to deliver infrastructure capacity to customers or users. You might think of this as similar to a highway detour of sorts. Zimmerman suggests that the increasing prevalence of wireless connectivity for the Internet demonstrates an alternative route.

A second key component of flexibility depends on how well human systems manage assets for infrastructure recovery, such as the workers,

TABLE 9.2   Mitigation Measures for Infrastructure and Utilities

Area of Concern	Structural Mitigation Measure	Nonstructural Mitigation Measure
Roads, highways	Maintenance Annual inspections Closures	Alternative-routing contingency plan Expansion or development of public transit options
Bridges	Blast-performance research Debris management	Annual inspections Expert assessments Adequate funding
Ports and airports	Bomb-detection technology Radar and warning systems Air and water traffic control	Alternative-routing contingency plan Security procedures
Communications	Redundant systems	Partnerships Flexible, interoperable systems able to communicate across organizations
Power and gas outages	Utility lines placed underground Older breakers replaced Subsystems updated Surge protection	Prioritization of locations for those at highest risk, including medically dependent populations Inspections Education of the public about gas leaks
Water	"Smart" shutoff valves that activate automatically in a hazard Security systems to prevent intentional contamination	Mutual-aid agreement with surrounding jurisdictions to supply water Education of the public about water safety protocols
Sewer and wastewater	Stormwater drainage systems Preservation of open space	Recycling and hazardous-waste-reduction programs

Sources: National Research Council 1994; Department of Homeland Security, http://www.dhs.gov/xprevprot/programs/gc_1189168948944.shtm.

transportation vehicles, supplies, and other resources necessary for the recovery effort. A third component involves informing customers and users about what is going on with the infrastructural failure and what options exist while repairs are being conducted. Utility companies, for example, usually feature Web sites that graphically depict current power outages and their strategy for restoring energy.

Interestingly, Zimmerman implicitly suggests that two of three key components rely on how humans manage the situation, ideally through preparedness, prepositioning of assets (such as salt or sand prior to a snowstorm or sandbags before a flood), and effective management. Flexibility, though, is not necessarily the ultimate solution because, as Zimmerman (2003, 244) points out, rapid transfers such as from one water line to another can also lead to "catastrophic failure across all of these systems if they are affected at the same time."

The efforts of the Wireless Emergency Response Team described earlier in this chapter demonstrate flexibility, particularly through using preestablished relationships and resources. Efforts such as these suggest an emerging means for enhancing flexibility when disasters damage normal systems (Zimmerman 2003). The mission of the Wireless Emergency Response Team is (http://www.wert-help.org/pages/vision.php):

- Leading advanced wireless expertise, technology and infrastructure support for search and rescue operations in national crises
- Conducting focused research and reporting key learnings to industry, government and the public
- Providing emergency guidance for 9-1-1 centers, law enforcement, wireless service providers and family members

Although recovery from damage to the infrastructure and utilities seems to rely heavily on the expertise of engineers and construction companies, we must also attend to the social dimensions of how we manage those efforts. By strengthening institutions and organizations that handle infrastructure and utility recovery, we build flexibility and resilience to disaster. Ways to do so include knowledge resources, relational resources, and a capacity to mobilize (Pinera and Reed 2007). Knowledge resources rely on "technical, managerial and financial knowledge," in short, on how well prepared and trained the staff and managers are prior to an event (Pinera and Reed 2007, 408). Relational resources include links between, for example, a utility company and its customers as well as those who interact with the entity, such as officials, emergency managers, and other governmental agencies or departments that rely on its services.

Thus, although the infrastructure and utilities may constitute the built environment, by using a systems theory perspective and understanding linkages between other components, particularly human systems, it is possible to enhance a more resilient response to disaster, thereby decreasing recovery time not only for the built environment, but for impacted neighborhoods, communities, agencies, and the like. As experts noted at a post-September 11 conference, there was good news about the ability of lifelines to demonstrate resiliency, but there were also lessons for those living outside the New York City context (MCEER 2002, 3): "Many of the service providers in New York (e.g., Consolidated Edison, Verizon, MTA) possessed sufficient excess capacity in people, equipment and other resources to provide an effective and relatively rapid restoration of services. Less robust systems, or infrastructure systems in less highly resilient cities, would likely not have fared as well."

Planning and Preparedness

Efforts to reduce the impacts of disasters must involve a wide array of partners in the planning and preparedness stages. In studying the potential effects of an earthquake on lifelines in the Memphis area, Professor Joanne Nigg noted that a key strategy is for "communities to incorporate lifeline service providers into their disaster response and recovery planning.... Emergency management officials and leaders in the business community must become more active." In short, preparing our communities for the impacts of disasters on infrastructure and utilities is a "collective problem" that requires recovery managers to work across sectors and with all potentially affected users (Nigg 1995, 57).

Transportation planners encourage the development of resilience, defined as a "system's ability to accommodate variable and unexpected conditions without catastrophic failure" (Litman 2006, 14). Resilience includes diverse and redundant options that operate within the system, such as alternative routes coupled with preplanned evacuation strategies. For a recovery time period, the notion of resilience suggests preidentification of roads, bridges, highways, and routes susceptible to failure in specific events. A far-reaching advance roads construction and rehabilitation program that enhances the potential of transportation arteries to resist damage is a good step. A plan of how to reroute traffic so as to expedite vehicular movement postdisaster is necessary as well. Litman (2006) also suggests that communities create transportation systems that offer multiple routes out of and into an area, including roads, railways, waterways, and other viable routes.

Summary

The state of our infrastructure is, according to the American Society of Civil Engineers, in serious trouble. (The latest ASCE Report Card on the State of American Critical Infrastructure was issued in 2009 as this book was in press. The grades include: aviation, D; bridges, C; dams, D; drinking water, D-; energy, D+; hazardous waste, D; levees, D-; inland waterways, D-; rail, C-; roads, D-; solid waste, C+; transit, D; and wastewater, D-.) Because of existing problems with roads, bridges, dams, ports, and other key assets, it is likely that disaster could have a significant impact. Because we rely on our infrastructure to such an extent, we must plan and prepare for disruptions caused by disasters. Such events could result from the effects of a hurricane storm surge that tears out railroads, water-treatment facilities, and highways or that could occur when an infrastructure element fails, such as a major bridge collapse. Significant related damage can occur due to infrastructural failure, including disruption to area businesses, health care, government, and residential sectors. Rapid restoration is often key to preserving life safety and property. Both short- and long-term strategies for recovery of infrastructure and utilities are likely. Utilities appear most likely to rebound first. Infrastructural repair may take years to complete, as it takes time to acquire funding, bid out contracts, and commence repairs or initiate completely new construction.

The recovery time offers a chance to build in disaster resiliency to the built environment. In addition to structural mitigation measures, it is also important to build resilience in human systems that manage infrastructure and utility disruption. Flexibility within the built environment and the social institutions that manage such disruptions can enhance recovery. Because these systems are interconnected, they must demonstrate resilience, robustness, and adaptability (Zimmerman 2003). Infrastructure and utility damage are collective problems in which we all share (Nigg 1995).

Study Guide

Summary Questions

1. Describe the various components that are considered critical infrastructure and lifelines and why they are important to prioritize after disaster.
2. What are the impacts of disruption to critical infrastructure and lifelines for various populations, particularly the elderly and people with disabilities?
3. Describe the key first steps that must be taken to understand the impacts of damages to the infrastructure and utilities.
4. Define flexibility and what it means for both the built environment and human systems.
5. Why is interconnectedness important for recovery of infrastructural and utility damage?

Discussion Questions

1. The American Society of Civil Engineers (ASCE) report referenced in this chapter contains state-by-state reports that are currently available at www.asce.org/reportcard. Look up your state and identify the three top concerns where you live. Should a disaster strike, what failures or problems could you expect? Research the topic further and see if the state has any efforts underway to address current deficiencies.
2. What are you willing to do to reduce impact on an already beleaguered road system? Do you walk, bike, or drive to work? If you drive, do you carpool? What kinds of public transit options exist near you, including bike paths, buses, rail systems, and other options?

3. What should you do if you hear there is a "boil water" notice? Contact your local water-treatment plant or visit its Web site for further information. If your area does not offer that information, use an Internet search engine to find similar information.

4. Look up the state emergency management agency where you live. Does it have an approved mitigation plan listed on its Web site? If there is a list of partners, see if there are connections to infrastructure and utilities.

5. What is the name of the utility company that supplies power to your home, school, or workplace? Visit its Web site and look for information on how it handles utility disruptions.

6. What are the worst roads in your county or parish? How did they get into this state? What local plans exist to repair this key piece of infrastructure?

7. How is stormwater managed in your locale? Are there areas where water routinely collects? Why is that so? Can you find areas that need attention, such as drains or ditches that are clogged? Does the city or county have a plan for upgrading the stormwater system?

Key Terms

Accessibility
Direct losses
Flexibility
High-hazard dam
Indirect losses
Infrastructure
Interconnectedness
Resilience
Utility

References

ASCE. 2005. *Report card for America's infrastructure*. Washington, DC: American Society of Civil Engineers.

ASCE. 2009. Report Card for America's Infrastructure. Washington, DC: ASCE, January 2009, at http://www.asce.org.reportcard/2009/index.html.

Brookings Institution. 2006. Special edition of the Katrina Index: A one year review of key indicators of recovery in post-storm New Orleans. Washington, DC: The Brookings Institution.

Brookings Institution and GNOCDC. 2008. The New Orleans Index. New Orleans, LA: Greater New Orleans Community Data Center.

Chang, S. E. 2001. Structural change in urban economies: Recovery and long-term impacts in the 1995 Kobe earthquake. *The Kokumin Keizai Zasshi* 183 (1): 47–66.

Chang, S. E. 2003. Transportation planning for disasters: An accessibility approach. *Environment and Planning A* 35: 1051–1072.

CNN. NTSB design flaw led to Minnesota bridge collapse. Nov. 15, 2008. www.CNN.com/2008/US/11/14/bridge.collapse?index.html.

Comer, J., and T. A. Wikle. 2007. Worldwide diffusion of the cellular telephone, 1995–2005. *The Professional Geographer* 60 (2): 1–18.

Condello, K. 2001. Wireless industry: Impact and recovery efforts summary report. Paper presented at the Cellular Telecommunications and Internet Association Conference, Washington, DC.

Eguchi, R. T., and H. A. Seligson. 1994. Lifeline perspective. In *Practical lessons from the Loma Prieta earthquake*, ed. Committee for the Symposium on Practical Lessons from the Loma Prieta Earthquake, 135–164. Washington, DC: The National Academy Press.

Enke, D. L., C. Tirasirichai, and R. Luna. 2008. Estimation of earthquake loss due to bridge damage in the St. Louis metropolitan area, II: Indirect losses. *Natural Hazards Review* 9 (1): 2–19.

FEMA. 2005. Public works rebuilding. Federal Emergency Management Agency, Gulf Coast Recovery Office. http://www.fema.gov/hazard/hurricane/2005katrina/works.shtm.

Litman, T. 2006. Lessons from Katrina and Rita: What major disasters can teach transportation planners. *Journal of Transportation Engineering* 132 (1): 11–18.

Luna, R., D. Hoffman, and W. T. Lawrence. 2008. Estimation of earthquake loss due to bridge damage in the St. Louis metropolitan area, I: Direct losses. *Natural Hazards Review* 9 (1): 1–11.

MCEER. 2002. *Proceedings of the MCEER Workshop on Lessons from the World Trade Center Terrorist Attack: Management of complex civil emergencies and terrorism-resistant civil engineering design*. Multidisciplinary Center for Earthquake Engineering Research Workshop, New York City.

Mileti, D. 1999. *Disasters by design*. Washington, DC: Joseph Henry Press.

Minnesota Department of Transportation. 2007. Interstate 35W Mississippi River Bridge, Minneapolis Fact Sheet, August 6, 2007. Minneapolis: Minnesota Department of Transportation.

National Research Council. 1994. *Practical lessons from the Loma Prieta earthquake*. Washington, DC: National Academy Press.

NTSB. 2008. Safety recommendation. Washington, DC: National Transportation Safety Board.

Nigg, J. M. 1995. Business disruption due to earthquake-induced lifeline interruption. Preliminary paper 220. Newark, DE: Disaster Research Center.

Oklahoma Corporation Commission. 2008. Inquiry into undergrounding electrical utilities in the state of Oklahoma. Oklahoma City: Oklahoma Corporation Commission.

Pinera, J.-F., and R. A. Reed. 2007. Maximizing aid benefits after urban disasters through partnerships with local water sector utilities. *Disaster Prevention and Management* 16 (3): 401–411.

Scanlon, J. 1999. Emergent groups in established frameworks: Ottawa Carleton's response to the 1998 ice disaster. *Journal of Contingencies and Crisis Management* 7 (1): 30–37.

Sokolowski, T. J. n.d. Great Alaskan earthquake and tsunamis of 1964. NOAA report. http://wcatwc.arh.noaa.gov/64quake.htm.

Tolchin, M. 1993. Report revises times in train wreck. *New York Times*, October 8. http://query.nytimes.com/gst/fullpage.html?res=9F0CE5D8173BF93BA35753C1A965958260

U.S. GAO. 2003. Electricity restructuring: 2003 blackout identifies crisis and opportunity for the electricity sector. Washington, DC: U.S. Government Accountability Office.

U.S. Geological Survey. 2007. Large earthquakes in the United States and the world. http://neic.usgs.gov/neis/eq_depot/usa/1964_03_28.html.

Zimmerman, R. 2003. Public infrastructure service flexibility for response and recovery in the attacks at the World Trade Center, September 11, 2001. In *Beyond September 11th*, ed. J. Monday, 241–267. Boulder, CO:, Natural Hazards Center.

Resources

- American Society of Civil Engineers, visit http://content.asce.org/history/index.html.
- America's Report Card on Infrastructure. The latest ASCE Report Card on the state of American Critical Infrastructure (2009) was issued as this book was in press. Copies can be found at this website: http://www.asce.org/reportcard/2009/index.html.
- FEMA's Public Assistance Program, take IS-630 Public Assistance, a free course available at http://training.fema.gov/IS/crslist.asp.
- Minnesota Bridge Collapse, go to the Minnesota Department of Transportation website at http://www.dot.state.mn.us/i35wbridge/index.html
- Public transit information and updates, visit the Federal Transit Authority at http://www.fta.dot.gov/
- Transportation Security Administration at http://www.tsa.gov/.
- Wireless Emergency Response Team, see http://www.wert-help.org/pages/aboutwert.php. The report on the World Trade Center can be found at http://www.wert-help.org/pages/reports.php.

Chapter 10

Social Psychological Recovery

Learning Objectives

After reading this chapter, you should be able to:

- Identify the kinds of social psychological reactions and concerns that may arise in the context of various kinds of disasters: natural, technological, or terroristic
- Discuss impacts on various populations that may bear disproportionate risks for social psychological trauma
- List and explain the various factors that may influence how people experience potentially traumatic events
- Understand the implications of social psychological research for designing therapeutic interventions
- Appreciate the need for professional therapies and appropriate credentialing of those involved in social psychological recovery efforts
- Describe strategies for providing therapeutic relief for various populations and for different kinds of social psychological needs

Introduction

Popular images of disaster victims describe them as panicked, unable to function, and at a loss in the face of widespread destruction. Cameras zoom in on a distraught individual and our hearts go out to the person seemingly in **trauma**. Yet, these images represent stereotypes and mythical depictions of how most people actually respond to disaster (Tierney, Lindell, and Perry 2001). In most circumstances, people tend to respond to disasters the way they respond to nondisaster crises. And, predisaster conditions matter. If people had serious psychological issues before disaster, those problems are likely to continue afterwards. The "good news" about disaster, then, is that, most of the time, most of us will be able to step up and face difficult circumstances.

Will we find the situation stressful? Probably. Will we find ways to cope? Most of the time, yes. Will there be people who face significant trauma as a result of the event? Certainly. Are those most at risk predictable? Researchers are beginning to hone in on that answer. As we work through the next examples, think about the circumstances of the event and how it might have impacted those at risk. Was this a "typical" disaster or one that represented unusually disruptive circumstances? What conditions influenced how people responded? And, how did the caring community that surrounds those people respond? How might we create and participate in recovery programs that make a difference after disaster and even reduce potential or actual trauma? This chapter addresses these topics.

September 11

Most of the people reading this text will remember September 11, 2001, very clearly. At first we puzzled over why a plane could have hit the World Trade Center and wondered if it was a rare accident. Even more watched as the second large plane impacted and realized that this was terrorism, a deliberate attack on our nation. Tens of thousands of people traveling on planes unexpectedly landed in unfamiliar locations as the ground-stop commenced. We heard next of the Pentagon being attacked and then of the plane that went down in Pennsylvania. Rumors spread, with concerns raised over potential car bombs in the Capitol and other critical locations. We watched the towers fall, knowing that thousands of people were still inside, including hundreds of firefighters, police, and medical staff.

As the days ensued, we watched and we participated in putting up posters of the missing, joining candlelight vigils, attending worship services, and asking who could have perpetrated this massacre. Thousands of children lost a parent that day. Many became widowed instantly. Pets waited at home for beloved owners who never returned. We bought out every U.S. flag in the nation and placed them everywhere, uniting as one through a collective trauma, unable to do much else but look on and feel the shock and pain. And we felt anger, fury at the perpetrators, and frustration at our inability to reach those responsible and bring them to justice. Some acted out their rage in attacks on Muslims, who feared for their lives at times (Peek 2003). A full range of emotions surfaced across the nation, from traditional expressions of grief to outright retaliation.

September 11 certainly set the stage for traumatic response to a disaster event. Psychologists tell us that such massive events with extensive loss of life are more likely to lead to personal trauma. For those most directly affected through personal injury or death of a loved one, trauma is likely to worsen (Norris, Friedman, and Watson 2002; Norris et al. 2002). Dozens of organizations worked to set up post-September 11 recovery programs, including personal counseling, group **therapy**, **residential care**, and long-term follow-up. Specific programs targeted seniors, children, and families.

Most people responded normally by expressing feelings of anger, grief and frustration, reactions understandable given the context of the event. Moreover, expressing emotional reactions helps us to process our experiences both individually and collectively. Indeed, in the aftermath of September 11, collective emotional expressions surfaced across the nation: public service announcements of people from far away proclaiming "I am a New Yorker"; communal rituals that promoted healing, including memorials and moments of silence; family and friends that called, e-mailed, and connected across the distances, sending cards and banners to complete strangers; and tremendous outpourings of donated funds, resources, and volunteer time. Americans responded with compassion, working collectively through the pain of the event to comfort complete strangers. In a word, those affected by the attack responded with **resilience**.

Three Mile Island

In 1979, an accident at the Three Mile Island (TMI) nuclear plant in Harrisburg, Pennsylvania, prompted concerns for some time among residents. According to the U.S. Nuclear Regulatory Commission, the accident occurred due to a failure in a secondary, nonnuclear area. In response, the reactor shut down in the nuclear portion of the plant. A relief valve then opened and subsequently failed to close as anticipated. Cooling water came out of the open valve and caused overheating in the core of the reactor. Misleading signals from the valve provided confusing information. Plant operators took actions that "made conditions worse," and the nuclear fuel overheated. Zirconium cladding that holds the nuclear fuel pellets ruptured, and fuel pellets began to melt, leading to a severe "core meltdown, the most dangerous kind of nuclear accident." Potentially serious releases of radiation could have occurred. The U.S. Nuclear Regulatory Commission later indicated that average radiation levels emitted per person were less than that of a chest x-ray; a maximum dose of radiation, though, could have been far worse (U.S. Nuclear Regulatory Commission n.d.).

At the time, though, area residents went through what came to be called an ambiguous event filled with uncertainty. The governor recommended that pregnant women and preschool children evacuate within a five-mile radius of the plant. The plant was not reentered for over a year. Multiple health and psychological studies took place after TMI, the worst such accident of its kind in U.S. history. Further, a number of new rules and regulations were passed to afford greater standards and protections for plants, workers, and the public. Evacuation studies were initiated, and TMI came to represent a benchmark in emergency protection for technological incidents.

As you might expect, those living in closest proximity to TMI reported higher psychological distress, including **depression**, stress, and **anxiety**. Concerns included potential exposure to radiation that might cause cancer. People who lost trust in experts expressed higher anxiety and depression. Those who reported being "resigned" to a restart as something they could not change also experienced symptoms. However, although psychological symptoms were higher among those affected by the TMI accident and restart, their symptoms were overall lower than those of a comparison group of patients in a mental health outpatient clinic (Prince-Embury and Rooney 1988). Clearly, actions taken by officials did make a difference, as those who felt that they could trust officials reported fewer symptoms; credibility issues of utility officials persisted long after the accident (Davidson, Baum, and Collins 1982).

Psychological Impacts of Disasters

As the above scenarios demonstrate, disasters can generate some psychological impacts. But how serious are the symptoms? How concerned should we be? What can we do, both before and after disasters, to rebound from the impact? Professor Fran H. Norris, a faculty member in the Department of Psychiatry at Dartmouth Medical School, has published extensively on the topic of mental health and disasters. Along with colleagues, she conducted an analysis of 160 study samples that included 60,000 disaster victims. From those studies, Dr. Norris and her colleagues observed several types of outcomes from disasters.

Most studies found a broad range of symptoms from stress to the more serious **posttraumatic stress disorder** (PTSD). PTSD occurs as a result of trauma and leads to symptoms and reactions that impair one's abilities to function fully in personal and professional circumstances. PTSD is usually associated with some form of reexperiencing the trauma through, for example, painful recall or flashbacks. Most studies that examined PTSD in a disaster context found that rates varied from low to high and that it was usually impacted by specific conditions, such as the severity of the event (more on this later).

Across the 160 studies, depression emerged as the next most common symptom after disaster, although disaster victims also reported higher than usual levels of anxiety (Norris, Friedman, and Watson 2002; Norris et al. 2002). There are several forms of depression and anxiety. Both conditions may be thought of as occurring along a continuum from mild to severe. Anxiety, which includes PTSD, could include phobias or panic attacks. Symptoms might include trouble sleeping, difficulty in concentrating, or even physical sensations like shortness of breath, chest pain, or dizziness (Hamida and Malone 2004). Depression is a mood disorder, and there are various kinds that can be clinically diagnosed. Symptoms might include sadness, sleeplessness, and feelings of guilt, lack of energy, or difficulty concentrating (Tesar 2002). Anxiety disorders tend to be characterized by excessive worry or fear, whereas depression tends to be characterized by a sense of hopelessness or helplessness. PTSD, other forms of anxiety, and all forms of depression should be diagnosed by a professional clinician.

Posttraumatic stress disorder has been studied extensively, although further research is warranted (Brewin, Andrews, and Valentine 2000). What is clear is that going through a disaster is not necessarily enough to predict that someone will develop PTSD. Other factors appear to include preexisting trauma as well as education, gender, race, ethnicity, and severity of exposure. Studies report varying levels of PTSD, suggesting that we need more research. In short, we cannot assume that PTSD will develop automatically. At present, rates of PTSD following disaster remain fairly low for most kinds of disasters (Norris et al. 2002), but this certainly should be on a list of potential concerns following an event.

Other studies have found health problems and concerns to be present among disaster victims at levels higher than nondisaster victims. The most commonly reported problem was trouble sleeping (Norris, Friedman, and Watson 2002; Norris et al. 2002). You might expect that people would turn to increased use of alcohol, drugs, and smoking. However, such increased behaviors were not as common except for people who already experienced problems associated with alcohol. Patients and respondents in the studies also reported stress that came from difficult personal relationships and newly generated family problems, such as conflict. Other studies have reported increases in domestic violence after disaster, although such numbers remain difficult to pin down (see Box 10.1).

Interestingly, studies by Norris and her colleagues revealed a decrease in specific resources that would normally help people to recover. Subjects reported that they experienced losses in social support, feelings of connections to others, belief that you can control what happens around you, optimism, perceived control, and a feeling that you can do something about the situation (Norris, Friedman, and Watson 2002; Norris et al. 2002). Such social supports are crucial to retain and depend on after disasters. Our

BOX 10.1 VIOLENCE AGAINST WOMEN IN DISASTER

Domestic violence is a social fact contributing to the vulnerability of women to disaster. Women in violent relationships are a vulnerable population less visibly at risk than poor women, refugees, single mothers, widows, and senior or disabled women. Indeed, violence against women in intimate relations crosses these and other social lines, impacting an estimated one in four women in the United States and Canada, and as many as 60% in parts of Africa, Latin America, and Asia.[1]

Violence against women is likely to be present after as well as before a disaster, but does it increase? Barriers to reporting multiply in the aftermath of widespread damage, but some indicators suggest that violence does increase, although the data are very limited:

- Sexual and domestic violence are often identified as issues for women refugees in temporary camps.[2]
- Some field reports of social impacts include abuse, as in this account of an Australian flood: "Human relations were laid bare and the strengths and weaknesses in relationships came more sharply into focus. Thus, socially isolated women became more isolated, domestic violence increased, and the core of relationships with family, friends and spouses were exposed."[3] Increased violence was also noted in field reports from the Philippines after the Mt. Pinatubo eruption.[4]
- The national Canadian press reported domestic violence increasing during the massive 1998 ice storm in Quebec and Ontario. A Montreal Urban Community Police Chief reported that one in four calls he had received the past week came from women about abuse. Crisis calls were not up at the local shelter, but the hot line had been closed by the storm for two days.[5]
- The director of a Santa Cruz battered women's shelter reported that requests for temporary restraining orders rose 50% after the Loma Prieta quake. Observing that housing shortages were restricting women's ability to leave violent relationships, she urged that "when the community considers replacement housing issues, battered women should not be overlooked."[6] Five months after the earthquake, a United Way survey of over 300 service providers ranked "protective services for women, children, and elderly" sixth among 41 community services most unavailable to residents.[7] Reported sexual assault also rose by 300%.[8]
- A quarter (25%) of all community leaders responding to an open-ended question about the effects of the *Exxon Valdez* oil spill on family problems cited "increase in domestic violence" first, in contrast to increased child neglect (4%) and elder abuse (4%). Asked whether spouse abuse increased after the spill, 64% agreed; they also reported increased child physical abuse (39%), child sexual abuse (31%), elder abuse (11%), and rape (21%).[9]

- Following the Missouri floods of 1993, the average state turn-away rate at shelters rose 111% over the preceding year. An existing federal grant was modified to increase funding to 35 flood-affected programs in an innovative disaster recovery grant targeting both substance abuse and domestic violence. The final report notes that these programs eventually sheltered 400% more flood-impacted women and children than anticipated.[10]
- After Hurricane Andrew in Miami, spousal abuse calls to the local community helpline increased by 50%,[11] and over one-third of 1,400 surveyed residents reported that someone in their home had lost verbal or physical control in the two months since the hurricane.[12]
- A survey of U.S. and Canadian domestic violence programs reported increased service demand as long as six months to a year later in the 13 most severely impacted programs. In Grand Forks, North Dakota, requests for temporary protection orders rose by 18% over the preceding year, and counseling with ongoing clients rose 59% (July 1996–July 1997).[13]
- Police reports of domestic violence in the seven months after Mt. St. Helens erupted increased by 46% over the same period the year earlier.[14]
- After Hurricane Mitch, 27% of female survivors (and 21% of male survivors) in Nicaragua told surveyors that woman battering had "increased in the wake of the hurricane in the families of the community." Among community leaders (68% of whom were men), 30% of those interviewed reported increased battery as did 42% of the mayors (46 men and 2 women) who were interviewed.[15]
- Conflicting data are reported by journalists contacting selected shelters about the possible impacts of September 11, 2001. In some communities very far from Ground Zero physically, shelters reported receiving increased calls for help, although in other cases shelters reported reduced case loads as families reunited. National Public Radio reported that increased calls for help were made to the Loveland, Colorado, crisis center in the weeks immediately following.[16]
- Both domestic violence and sexual assault were widely reported to increase in the aftermath of the 2004 Indian Ocean tsunami. Examples from Sri Lanka cited by researchers include women battered because they resisted their husbands' sale of their jewelry or disputed their use of tsunami relief funds and mothers blamed by fathers for the deaths of their children. One nongovernmental organization (NGO) reported a three-fold increase in cases brought to them following the tsunami.[17]
- Four New Orleans shelters and two nonresidential programs were closed by Hurricane Katrina in 2005, and advocates reported that "women are being battered by their partners in the emergency

shelters." In the first four months after the U.S. Gulf Coast hurricanes, 38 rape cases were reported to women's services, which
initiated documentation projects to capture sexual assaults of
disaster-displaced women.[18]

Source: **Dr. Elaine Enarson. With permission.**

friends and family can provide considerable resources to help us cope with
and recover from the event. As Norris et al. (2002, 17) indicated, "Social
resources appear to be more vulnerable than psychological resources to the
impact of disaster."

So, how concerned should we be about the effects of disasters? Norris
and her colleagues evaluated the results of the 160 studies and the 60,000
victims. Approximately 11% of the studies reported minimal impairment,
meaning that stress and associated symptoms were "transient" or relatively
short-lived. Just over half (51%) of the studies could be characterized as
finding moderate impairment or stress that was "prolonged." In most cases,
symptoms went away within one year, as found with studies of events like
Hurricane Hugo and Three Mile Island.

It is important to note that the worst consequences of disasters originated from the most severe events, particularly those involving mass
violence. Disasters that generated more serious symptoms included
major events like Hurricane Andrew, the *Exxon Valdez* accident, and
the Oklahoma City bombing. Further, a number of the studies reporting more severe impairments took place in developing nations after massive events and in conditions with few resources to aid recovery (Norris,
Friedman, and Watson 2002; Norris et al. 2002). In studies with higher
impacts, it was also clear that loss of social resources was correlated with
an increase in the symptoms of mental duress. Perhaps even more important, how we function before disaster typically predicts the state of our
mental health afterward (Norris, Friedman, and Watson 2002; Norris et
al. 2002).

We turn next to more-specific details on how disasters might affect people
on the basis of who they are and where they are situated in their life circumstances. For example, does age make a difference in how disasters affect us?
What about gender? Does occupation make a difference? Let us see.

Age

Does age influence how we respond to disaster? Will age offer some kind of
protective effects, or does it get harder to cope as we age? Much concern has
been expressed about the effects of disasters on children. Generally, we are still

not completely sure how disasters affect the smallest children, but it appears that the youngest may be easiest to comfort. Children of school age may be more affected (Norris, Friedman, and Watson 2002; Norris et al. 2002).

The impacts of major events have been studied for their effects on children, particularly September 11, Hurricane Katrina, and Hurricane Andrew. One study of September 11 found that parents reported 10% of all New York City (NYC) children received some type of counseling (Fairbrother et al. 2004). Most (44%) were counseled in school settings, while just over one-third (36%) went to mental health professionals, psychiatrists, psychologists, or other counselors. About 20% received spiritual care or other kinds of support.

Approximately 18%, or nearly one in every five NYC children in one study, experienced some kind of posttraumatic stress symptom. Of particular concern, though, only 27% of the children with very severe reactions received any kind of counseling services. What influences whether children receive services? It turns out that parents are very influential. If parents experience higher rates of distress, they are more likely to see that their children also receive counseling (Fairbrother et al. 2004).

How about those of us in the middle stages of life? Evidence shows that middle-aged survivors tend to get a lot of support from social resources but give even more (Norris, Friedman, and Watson 2002; Norris et al. 2002). As caretakers of children and often for the elderly, it may not be surprising to learn that this group of people shoulders responsibilities for others beyond themselves.

Evidence suggests that age may offer some kind of buffering, somewhat like the inoculation effect of a flu shot. For example, some age differences were found after the Three Mile Island (TMI) event. Older residents reported less distress and were also less likely to have taken protective actions (Prince-Embury and Rooney 1988, 1990). Older residents at TMI reportedly used a more emotion-focused coping style, although such a strategy did not necessarily decrease their stress. As researchers suggest, "The significance of the event becomes relative to a lifetime of circumstances experienced by the individual" (Prince-Embury and Rooney 1988, 779). The inoculation hypothesis means that older people bring a lifetime of experiences to the disaster and rely on coping strategies they have learned along life's journey as a means to deal with the current event (Norris, Friedman, and Watson 2002a; Norris et al. 2002).

Relationships

There is a fair amount of evidence that being married or in a committed relationship matters. Partnered couples, for example, report fewer health problems, probably because they look out for and take care of each other. However, at TMI, researchers discovered that married people were more likely to report psychological symptoms (Cleary and Houts 1984), which may be related to proximity to the event and concern over the effects on family members. Such persons were also more likely to take protective actions, which suggests they felt more concern overall as well.

Being a parent apparently makes recovery more stressful, probably understandable among those who worry about the welfare of their family and reactions of their children. Living in temporary shelter or temporary housing is not easy, nor is reestablishing a household routine in an unfamiliar location. Yet it is important that parents learn and use effective coping strategies, as their distress also predicts if children will report distress (Norris, Friedman, and Watson 2002; Norris et al. 2002). In general, children appear to respond similarly to how their parents and adult role models behave. Without a framework to understand the chaos and change that surrounds them in disaster, they look to adults to determine how they should respond. Younger children mimic behaviors they see; thus, responding with resilience and optimism can benefit your children as well as yourself.

Gender

Gender may make a difference for those affected by disasters. Studies suggest that gender may increase the likelihood of stress and PTSD (Norris, Friedman, and Watson 2002; Norris et al. 2002). However, others contend that gender influences the types of impacts that are experienced as well as the resources available for coping. Seen this way, reports of increased rates of psychological symptoms among women and girls may reflect more the nature of an unequal society rather than a greater propensity for psychological symptoms.

Many societies, for example, socialize females to respond emotionally, which may reflect a healthy way to surface emotional reactions. Women also tend to be among those who handle the aid requests for the family or conduct casework for those affected. Women also historically bear a disproportionate responsibility for child and elder care, appear more likely to lose their home-based work, and experience higher levels of domestic violence after disaster. Thus, studies that measure if someone cries, experiences anxiety, or feels overwhelmed may reflect more the way in which society structures gender roles.

Studies examining PTSD across a variety of contexts, including disaster, indicate that gender may or may not be a risk factor for PTSD. Other factors may lead women to report problems or prior ordeals, particularly childhood trauma (Brewin, Andrews, and Valentine 2000). In short, it is important to plan for gender-related psychological symptoms but not to assume that such may occur.

Gender also makes a difference with men, too. Men are socialized typically to be the strong member of the family, even the hero. Men appear to be less likely to heed warnings or take protective action. After Hurricane Mitch, researchers found that men had higher death rates because they stayed behind to try and salvage the family's resources. As indicated earlier, exposure to injury and disaster severity can increase symptoms of mental duress. After disasters, men are more likely than women to use alcohol, also a behavior typically associated with masculinity and an accepted norm within male-dominated cultures (Norris, Friedman, and Watson 2002; Norris et al. 2002). Thus, gendered effects of disasters on mental health are not exclusively associated with women.

Race and Ethnicity

Ethnic groups may experience higher levels of symptoms, though the cause may not be related to their cultural background. Six studies of younger victims revealed that minority youth experienced higher symptoms compared with majority youth in four of the cases (Norris, Friedman, and Watson 2002; Norris et al. 2002). Culture may also influence how we respond to disaster, with some cultural values leading us to be either more or less expressive.

Some analysts also feel that race and ethnicity masks the real cause, which stems from being historically marginalized. Social and historical factors such as underemployment, racism, and being vigilant against violent attacks may explain why Hispanics and African Americans experienced higher PTSD rates after Hurricane Andrew (Perilla, Norris, and Lavizzo 2002). Being forced to endure housing segregation, job discrimination, and lack of educational opportunities has meant that minority groups bear disproportionate risk in disasters. Due largely to discrimination and the lower incomes that result, minority groups have historically been relegated to poorer, substandard housing in floodplains or lacking in mitigation measures, such as retrofitting for earthquake hazards (Cutter 2005). Adverse effects on mental health are believed to be higher because of a higher likelihood of being exposed to disaster. Living in areas of higher risk or in housing that fails to protect increases such exposure.

Occupation

Does the kind of work that we do in a disaster context result in a decline in mental health? What levels of concern should we have about first responders, rescue and recovery workers, social workers, and volunteers? Rescue and recovery workers appear to respond fairly well to the trauma they experience, most probably because of the training they have received, which allows them to anticipate disaster circumstances. Professionals appear to go through the experience better than volunteers (Dyregrov, Kristoffersen, and Gjestad 1996).

Although our neighbors are often the first ones to pull us out of the house damaged by a disaster, first responders (police, fire, medical personnel) usually arrive on-scene rapidly. What happens to these types of professionals in disaster contexts—something beyond the usual fire or traffic accident? Several studies of Oklahoma City firefighters who responded to the bombing discovered relatively low levels of psychological symptoms. PTSD, for example, was found in 13% (or 24) of 181 firefighters who rescued the injured or recovered the dead in perilous conditions. An argument could be made that firefighters train and work in a culture that demands emotional toughness, thus keeping PTSD rates low. However, it could also be argued that an unexpected, horrific event in one's homeland would produce more severe responses. Consistent with other studies, researchers found that those who had to handle the remains of the children were more likely to experience PTSD (North et al. 2002).

Specific kinds of events and circumstances, though, may cause difficulties. A common thread running through most studies of rescue-and-recovery workers reveals that traumas involving children are particularly difficult. The loss of innocence, the trauma to a young body, and empathy with the victim all appear to influence mental health. Further, working with the families of the deceased also produces some degree of symptoms (Norris, Friedman, and Watson 2002; Norris et al. 2002).

After September 11, social workers trying to aid those who were traumatized reported "secondary traumatic stress" (STS). STS occurs when social workers or similar professionals begin to experience the emotions and symptoms of their clients (Pulido 2007). Most such professionals had not been trained on what to expect, how to help, or what to do with their own symptoms—which often showed up a year after the event, when sessions with clients had already ended. Emotional reactions ranged from anger to irritability and even flashbacks based on client descriptions. Dealing with the pain felt by the children was especially difficult. The lack of professional support and programs for these affected professionals certainly did not help (Pulido 2007).

Compassion fatigue, defined as a "reduced capacity or interest in being empathic," results from working with people who have experienced trauma. This condition appears to include **secondary trauma** and potentially the effects of job burnout (Boscarino, Figley, and Adams 2004). In another study of social workers in New York City, compassion fatigue after September 11 was associated with how much these professionals were exposed to the trauma as well as the degree of social support they experienced and the work environment.

Exposure to the attack may make a difference in volunteer workers. One study discovered that volunteers from outside of New York City with previous disaster experience fared better than volunteers from the New York area. Consistent with other studies, previous traumas, personal unmet needs, and substance abuse were found to increase rates of PTSD. Age tended to reduce those effects, as did previous disaster experience and living with a partner (Bocanegra, Brickman, and O'Sullivan 2004). Volunteers reported that only 39% had any type of training for the emotional aspects of their work. Box 10.2 shows the types of concerns they reported and the behaviors they reported as a result of their experience. As you read through the data, remember that volunteers often drop their own lives, leave families, and volunteer in temporary, often uncomfortable settings. Few experience any kind of connection to mental health services (Adams 2007).

BOX 10.2   THE IMPACT OF SEPTEMBER 11 ON VOLUNTEERS

What types of volunteer work did people provide after September 11? What did they worry about while volunteering, and how did they respond to those concerns? In a study published in the *International Journal of Mass Emergencies and Disasters* (www.ijmed.org), researchers tracked the work performance, concerns, and behaviors of 163 volunteers.

- Volunteers performed these types of work:
  - 94% provided information and referrals to relevant services
  - 85% assessed financial needs
  - 85% assessed other service needs
  - 77% escorted clients to service providers
  - 63% provided other concrete assistance to clients
  - 34% provided counseling
  - 29% wrote and distributed checks
  - 26% served as interpreters
- Concerns among the volunteers included:
  - 56% one's own safety
  - 55% family's safety
  - 45% prejudice or discrimination
  - 39% own emotional well-being
  - 39% emotional well-being of a loved one
  - 37% flying
  - 31% air quality
  - 29% getting a job
  - 24% safety and security concerns
  - 18% keeping a job
  - 11% war and global security
- Behavior changes included:
  - 57% more time in activities they enjoy
  - 33% eat more or eat less
  - 30% began or increased physical exercise
  - 29% began or increased religious/spiritual activities
  - 14% began or increased yoga/relaxation
  - 12% began or increased alcohol use

- 10% began or increased tobacco use
- 4% began or increased use of prescription drugs

Source: de Bocanegra, Brickman, and O'Sullivan (2004). (With permission from the *International Journal of Mass Emergencies and Disasters* and courtesy of the International Research Committee on Disasters.)

Collective Loss

Very little is known about the effects of **collective loss**, where an entire community is destroyed, lives are lost, and former neighbors and social networks disperse. What is suspected, though, is that the loss of community seriously undermines peoples' abilities to cope with trauma. Because social resources are so important to psychological well-being, the experience of a disaster wiping out a neighborhood or the larger community constitutes a major personal loss.

The first study to look at such loss was conducted in a small mining town called Buffalo Creek, West Virginia. In 1972, 132 million gallons of debris-filled water burst through a weakened dam and flooded a mountain hollow. Those who survived the early-morning event scrambled through windows and up the mountainsides. They watched as their homes and loved ones were taken by the water, powerful enough to uproot railroad lines. The federal government then established trailer camps, where people found temporary homes, but not always near the familiar neighbors who would normally provide comfort and solace. The recovery effort has been described by some as worsening the effects of the flood by taking away crucial social resources necessary for survival. Lawsuits followed, blaming the coal company for the damages and losses. The conditions for significant trauma were present, including loss of loved ones, friends, family, worship location, jobs, and social networks. Other contributing factors to trauma were the extent of personal injuries, the fact that the disaster was human-caused, and the severity of the impact on postdisaster life. Studies reported higher-than-usual levels of alcohol and drug abuse, divorce, and problems with children (Erikson 1976).

Imagine, then, the trauma potentially induced by the Hurricane Katrina evacuation. Three years later, residents of the Gulf Coast still lived in cities far away from the friends, family, clergy, social services, health care, familiar routines, culture, music, and food that makes a place truly home. Initial reports suggest that, particularly among the displaced residents of New Orleans, stress is high, with the potential for serious traumatic responses (Coker et al. 2006). Rates of mental illness have increased as have reports of domestic violence, suicides, and homicides (Jenkins and Phillips 2008). The loss of community—particularly in a place like New Orleans, with its distinctive neighborhoods, community groups, grassroots organizations, and unique culture and history—is keenly experienced. The population of New Orleans remains far below its original numbers, and parts of the city, such as the Lower Ninth Ward, lag far behind in rebuilding and returning. Given these conditions, the collective losses experienced suggest a potential for continued trauma for the displaced evacuees.

In other situations, specific populations may experience higher risks during the recovery. However, it remains difficult to pin down whether the disaster caused that risk or added to the risk that already existed predisaster. Social workers, for example, have observed higher rates of deaths among elderly survivors. As one social worker said in Biloxi, Mississippi, after Katrina, "I seem to be going to a lot more funerals." The same was true after the Loma Prieta earthquake, when social workers specializing in the elderly noted a similar pattern. Though these anecdotal accounts may appear to contradict other findings reported in this chapter, there seems to be a common element. Most of these elderly lived in socially isolated circumstances, connected to the community through professional caseworkers rather than through family. Until additional studies accumulate, it seems advisable to define strategies that engage those living alone or far away from family and friends.

Factors Influencing Social Psychological Recovery

Does the type of disaster matter? How might specific hazards influence the recovery process? In this section we look at those questions and consider other factors that influence social psychological recovery postdisaster. For example, friends and family matter—a lot. Going through a protracted and difficult recovery also influences our reactions. The magnitude and scope of the disaster can impact us. A related concern stems from the number of fatalities and our exposure to the deceased. Preexisting trauma also makes a difference. First, we look at the question of disaster types.

Natural versus Technological Disasters and Terrorism

Does the type of disaster affect psychological reactions? It appears that disasters caused by human error or intent may have a stronger psychological impact. The goal of terrorism is to inspire fear and anxiety. The uncertainty of an attack, coupled with the suddenness of an event, unsettles many of us. Levees that fail despite our best engineering, employee errors that result in nuclear accidents, and similar events demand accountability. Anger erupts; people point fingers in blame and seek out those culpable.

With terrorism, such as the anthrax attack in 2006, there is often no clear culprit. Technological failures often result in lawsuits, which can take years to resolve. It usually takes up to a year to determine the cause of an airplane crash. Massive violent outbreaks, especially those in which the murderers take their own lives, leave difficult-to-resolve questions.

Meanwhile, those affected are left to deal with how to handle the very human impacts when lives and homes are lost and family members sustain injuries. Medical costs mount; frustration and stress build; and it becomes difficult to move on without an explanation for why something happened. The explosion of Pan Am Flight 103 over Lockerbie, Scotland, in 1988 represents such an event. A terrorist-placed bomb on the airplane sent fiery debris into a local housing unit. Several people died on the ground; others were trapped; and many saw traumatized bodies. Psychiatric assessments found higher-than-expected levels of depression and PTSD, particularly among the elderly (Livingston et al. 1992).

Natural disasters may also produce similar consequences. Research on such events suggests that those who believe humans are responsible for a flood, for example, may view the event as similar to one of technological origin. If humans are believed responsible, and that someone or some agency should have prevented the situation, then **blaming** may erupt (Blocker and Sherkat 1992). Usually, the most visible agencies in disasters receive blame for what seems to be going wrong. Historically, those agencies have included FEMA and the Red Cross, whether the problems originated with these agencies or not.

What is important to bear in mind is that blaming ultimately does not serve the individual well psychologically. Rather, psychologists advise us to bring a positive outlook to the situation; to surround ourselves with strong sources of social support; and to look for healthy, effective means for coping. Ultimately, these approaches produce a stronger path toward recovery (see Box 10.3).

BOX 10.3   COPING WITH AND REBOUNDING FROM DISASTER

From what we have learned so far in the numerous studies of disasters and mental health, it appears clear that people in any occupation touched by disaster could benefit from:

- Strong social support from family members, friends, and colleagues
- Staying or becoming healthy and fit
- Addressing prior traumas to build stronger coping strategies
- Prior training for what to expect should disaster happen
- Working within their occupation when disaster strikes

- Affiliating with an organization that provides appropriate preassignment training on what to expect
- Particularly strong training and support programs for child-care workers, educators, health-care workers, and others involved in working with children
- Ensuring that workers who come into contact with injured or deceased children receive debriefing and referral to counseling as needed
- Long-term support for those closest to the disaster, especially in disasters of severe magnitude and those that involve injuries and fatalities
- Monitoring the impact of workload on employees (or yourself) and including respite time to avoid burnout, avoidance, or other dysfunctional responses
- Avoiding misuse of alcohol or cigarettes
- Continuing to monitor for symptoms for years after an event, especially one of significant magnitude or one that involved deaths
- Monitoring the potential for an increase in domestic violence and providing resources to community organizations seeking to serve those at risk

Nature of the Recovery Process

The nature of the recovery process may also produce conditions that increase or exacerbate mental health issues. For many families, especially in a tight housing market, multiple moves may be necessary before finally securing either temporary or permanent housing. It could be years before a family can return to a familiar location; meanwhile, children must attend new schools, make new friends, and adapt to new ways in a new environment. Parents will take on multiple burdens, coping with the effects of the disaster on their children, trying to understand and access aid, dealing with a possible job loss, rebuilding a damaged or destroyed home, and worrying about financial matters. The process of moving through a FEMA application, which is explained in Chapter 7 (Housing), requires patience and persistence. Working through the local permitting process to rebuild a house is equally challenging. Are you familiar with how to build a house? How to find a contractor and make the right choices? Do you have the skills or time to put in effort or sweat equity on your own home? What if you or family members are recovering from a disaster-related injury? A family member with additional challenges—limited literacy, shift work, or personal illness—may feel the stresses continue to mount.

Think about the stress of living in a temporary trailer. FEMA prefers to relocate people in apartments and rental homes, but the reality is that many communities construct mobile-home parks or allow trailers to be placed on available lots. Living in small trailers cannot be easy, with barely enough space to turn around, let alone cook, play with children, do homework, pay the bills, manage the laundry, and maneuver through other parts of daily life. Yet tens of thousands of Americans have been doing so since the 2005 hurricanes.

The financial impact can be significant as well. As described in Chapter 8 (Business Recovery), smaller, woman-owned, minority-owned, and home-based businesses tend to fail at higher rates. Lacking sufficient resources to survive displacement and downtime, the financial impact on the business owner and his or her family can be severe. To keep going, many business owners tap into their savings, including retirement accounts. Facing the loss of one's livelihood, coupled with depletion of financial resources, can be taxing on one's spirit and energies.

Social Networks

Social resources appear to "mediate or buffer" the effects of disasters (Cleary and Houts 1984). Our friends and family help us to cope with the impact of a distressing event. Without their support, we may experience higher rates of stress, anxiety, depression, and even PTSD. We may find it difficult to cope with the effects of the disaster. With their help and support, though, we may find that the road seems less difficult, that the burdens are easier to bear, and that recovery is possible. As described later in this chapter, developing and nurturing positive and supportive relationships makes a difference in how we respond to and recover from disaster.

Magnitude and Scope of the Disaster

Studies of PTSD have one clear finding in common: The magnitude and scope of the disaster make a difference. Individuals with higher or prolonged exposure have higher PTSD rates. Those who experience the most severe disasters have been diagnosed with more severe trauma. For example, shelter evacuees from Hurricane Katrina spoke to researchers about seeing the bodies of neighbors in the water and of having loved ones perish on the bridges and overpasses from lack of medical care or water. People rescued from rooftops desperately tried to save those who slipped away into the waters in Mississippi and Louisiana (Blinn-Pike, Phillips, and Reeves 2006; Coker et al. 2006). Such individuals fall among those most at risk for PTSD and should be assessed in shelters. Follow-up therapies, designed specifically for these circumstances, should be incorporated into recovery plans.

Mass Fatalities and Missing Persons

In events that involve deaths, people will experience distress. Those believed to be most at risk include first responders, body handlers from morgues and mortuaries, funeral directors, and those most closely associated with having to handle the bodies of those who have been lost. Evidence suggests that stress may also accumulate from having to work with distraught family members, lack of social service support, or exposure to the bodies of children (Phillips et al. 2008; Taylor and Frazer 1981b; Ursano and McCarroll 1990).

Massive events with significant numbers of deaths may cause stress and pain stemming from identification of the dead. Bodies must be identified to claim insurance and to reduce "mental anguish" (Blanshan and Quarantelli 1981; Thompson 1991). Identification may prove very difficult in particular hazards. After Hurricane Katrina, a separate morgue was set up specifically to process and identify fatalities; efforts slowed because of a need to ascertain cause of death due to pending charges and lawsuits. After the Indian Ocean tsunami, Thai officials faced delays in processing DNA due to sweltering heat, inconsistencies in data-collection procedures, and jurisdictional challenges. In some nations, foreign nationals had to be exhumed later for identification (Scanlon 2006). In the case of the September 11 attacks in New York City, only about half of the 20,000 human samples have been identified through DNA analysis, although extensive efforts continue (Simpson and Stehr 2003).

It is hard to wait for the final disposition of a loved one's remains. The situation is similar to the pain experienced by families of military members still missing in action. The ambiguity of the circumstances makes it difficult to address emotional responses and to move on with the requirements of daily life and survival. Families unable to confirm deaths or still awaiting the remains of loved ones should be afforded memorial services and counseling as needed.

Those tasked with handling the dead during a mass-fatality event must be carefully selected. The stresses associated with this task may be reduced through training, adequate supervision, and **debriefing** (Phillips et al. 2008; Taylor and Frazer 1981a, 1981b; Taylor 1983, 1989; Thompson 1991). Family support for those involved in handling the dead is also recommended (Davidson 1989).

Preexisting Conditions and Traumas

One of the clear indicators that someone may experience an increase in psychological symptoms or face the potential to experience PTSD is a personal history of preexisting conditions and traumas. Psychologists have clearly observed that if a prior trauma has not been processed through professional counseling, the present disaster may cause problems. Likewise, preexisting mental-health conditions, such as depression or anxiety, may be worsened by disaster. While such an outcome is not a certainty, the presence of such preexisting conditions should serve as an indicator that trauma may develop. Coupled with other factors such as the magnitude of the impact, socioeconomic challenges, lack of social resources, and loss of community links, trauma is more likely to occur.

What we should learn from this chapter, then, is to strengthen ourselves to build resilience to trauma. A second and equally important lesson is to develop strong social support networks and to participate in providing those resources to others both before and after disaster. What we do before an event to make ourselves and our friends and family more resilient to disasters can positively influence not only how we experience the disaster, but how we can manage other, nondisaster events as well. In short, personal resilience and strong interpersonal relationships can make a difference during disaster recovery.

Building Resilience to Disaster Trauma

We should anticipate a wide range of reactions to disaster. At the same time, we should also be confident that most of us will respond well to disaster and the related traumas. Still, information is power. You will be better prepared to work through the recovery period if you understand (a) the factors that can lead to adverse psychological symptoms and (b) what you—as a survivor, volunteer, or professional—can do to be more resilient in the face of disaster.

Resilience to Disaster

Recent studies of resilience, defined as an ability to "maintain relatively stable, healthy, levels of psychological and physical functioning" (Bonanno 2004, 21) demonstrate that gender, age, and race and/or ethnicity may make a difference. Women appear to be less resilient, although the reasons are not clear. In the context of recovery, women tend to shoulder much of the responsibility for helping multiple generations through the experience. The additive effect of such circumstances has yet to be assessed. The effect of race and ethnicity is not clear, although some PTSD studies have found higher rates among some minorities. As noted before, though, such studies typically do not address the effects of socioeconomic status, which may be stronger than race and ethnicity (Bonanno et al. 2007).

Older persons appear to have higher levels of resilience than younger persons, especially those in their middle years. Avoidance of substance abuse also appears to boost resilience. The absence of other life traumas, both before and after the event, indicates the likelihood of better mental health. Screening for such traumas may reveal the presence of (or the potential for) difficulties in the event of disaster (Bonanno 2004; Bonanno et al. 2007).

Before Disaster Strikes

Before disaster occurs in our communities, we can do a number of things to build resilience and provide valuable resources to ourselves, our coworkers or employees, and our community.

Get Information

Information about disasters can come from many sources and in many forms. Numerous organizations—from FEMA to the American Red Cross to faith-based organizations—now offer brochures, Web pages, and courses that can be taken online, in Red Cross chapters, or in places of worship. The first step is to find out what kinds of disasters are likely to impact the area. Is the risk from a natural, technological, or terrorism event? Second, what kinds of steps must be undertaken to prepare a household or workplace? Are there particular populations at higher risk in those locations, such as children, people with disabilities, pets or service animals, or senior citizens? What additional information is necessary to inform yourself and these populations about the risks they may face? Specific organizations offer considerable information online, including the Agency on Aging (www.aoa.gov), the National Organization on Disability (www.nod.org), the National Council on Disability (www.ncd.gov), and the Humane Society of the United States (www.hsus.org). Information has been described as "power," and in the present context, it means empowering individuals to face their risks. By doing so we take positive, proactive steps to reduce worries and mitigate the impacts that might occur.

Get Training

Most of us will remember some type of training that we experienced as children for a particular hazard: fire drills, tornado evacuations, or sheltering for an earthquake. Training makes a difference and prepares us to react appropriately. Training can be obtained online or through in-person classes with reputable, experienced organizations. You can also join units that help prepare for disasters such as a Red Cross disaster action team or a community emergency response team. Most communities offer opportunities to volunteer in such a capacity that allows for even greater depth of training. The first responder on a disaster scene is usually a family member or neighbor who pulls victims from a burning building or collapsed structure. To reduce the severity of that exposure, training can make a difference.

Also of relevance to this chapter, consider taking sessions or training that promotes positive mental health. Stress management workshops offer one route. They are offered routinely by human-resources offices, mental-health **outreach** units, places of worship, and medical care facilities. Therapy can also provide benefits and should be viewed as a positive means of restoring lost energy or concentration and increasing personal wellness. Both individual and group therapies can be used, including sessions with counselors specifically trained to work with disaster personnel and survivors. As the recovery lingers and the tasks become more tiresome, therapy may be a very beneficial way to maintain energy, focus, and commitment. As discussed later, other routine means of stress reduction can also help, including fitness work, yoga classes, and vacation.

School Programs

There are multiple means available to teach children about disasters. Providing information and training—from tornado drills to dealing with mass violence, for example—can save lives. Educating children on disasters can also help them to understand behaviors that can reduce uncertainty during an event. When children know what to do, it is likely that their postevent trauma can be reduced. There are several reliable organizations that provide substantial and helpful resources:

- The American Red Cross has developed Masters of Disaster kits for use in school systems; kits are also available for family use. These age-appropriate materials can be incorporated into existing science curricula (e.g., earth sciences) and have been reviewed by professional educators for use from kindergarten through eighth grade. For more information, see http://www.redcross.org/disaster/masters/.
- FEMA offers a special page for children, called the "FEMA for Kids" Web page. Materials provide fun activities for parents and children, including ideas for helping children to prepare a pet-readiness kit. Linked pages offer content for parents and teachers. For more information, see http://www.fema.gov/kids.
- "Project Heartland," described later in this chapter, reached out to schoolchildren affected by the Oklahoma City bombing and by the anniversary of the event.

Personal Fitness

Researchers have suggested that exercise can help survivors, caseworkers, and emergency responders to cope with the effects of a disaster (Armstrong, O'Callahan, and Marmar 1991). Exercise helps to reduce stress, promote fitness, and boost energy needed to get through disaster recovery time periods. Time spent in exercise can also provide opportunities for contemplation and reconciliation.

In his book *Riding with the Blue Moth*, author Bill Hancock recounts his bicycle trip across the United States while working through the pain of losing his son. His family's loss occurred when ten men associated with the Oklahoma State University basketball team died in a plane crash on January

27, 2001. Hancock named the pain the "blue moth," which accompanied him on his cross-country ride, appearing at various times even as he learned how to go on (Hancock 2005). His effort inspired the "Remember the Ten" 5K and 10K races now held annually in Stillwater, Oklahoma. The races and Hancock's ride reveal that fitness can offer a useful means for working through a trauma and turning the journey into a tool for healing a broader community. The races raise money for the Oklahoma State University counseling center, which generates continuing support for those affected by the accident (see link in Resources section).

Exercise and fitness programs can be introduced into a community through various means. Local faculty members, gyms, and personal trainers might become involved in leading walks, yoga classes, or giving talks. Scouting groups and other organizations could promote hiking and camping activities. Schools and worship centers could invite people to attend fitness festivals and other fun events. Senior centers can bring in residents for chair-based exercise. Or, a community could raise money and awareness through sponsoring races, softball leagues, or soccer tournaments.

Volunteer

Volunteering may also help prepare you and your organization for serving effectively in a disaster situation and for surviving a disaster recovery. In general, volunteer work has been found to increase personal well-being by increasing "happiness, life satisfaction, self-esteem, sense of control over life, physical health" (Thoits and Hewitt 2001, 115). Joining such work through voluntary associations can help link you to pre- or postdisaster work. Faith-based groups often provide a means through which you can enact your personal beliefs. Both options link prospective volunteers to networks of people socially committed to making a difference in a disaster context. The value of volunteering and being part of an effort that improves the community appears to provide positive benefits for many people. Volunteering simply makes us feel better by decreasing psychological distress and depression, and can improve overall mental health (see Photo 10.1).

Care must be taken to include those who might lack the means to participate by finding a way for volunteers to join in, such as offering carpooling or suggesting home-based work like stuffing envelopes, writing letters, or maintaining Web sites. People with disabilities should never be overlooked either, as they can bring valuable insights and connections to the process. After Hurricane Katrina, for example, students and staff at a school for the deaf cleared debris, disseminated information, provided sign language in shelters, and reconnected people who were deaf to their families. Teenagers, who might otherwise turn to inappropriate means for coping, can be drawn in as well for debris clearance, landscaping, child care, and reconstruction work. For additional options see Chapter 14 (Voluntary Organizations).

PHOTO 10.1 Volunteers from a Presbyterian Disaster Assistance mission team offer volunteer labor and a prayer shawl to a New Orleans resident. (Photo by Larry Caldwell, First Presbyterian Church, Stillwater, Oklahoma. With permission.)

Social Resources

After the Oklahoma City bombing, firefighters reported that their "most common coping method was turning to friends or relatives" (North et al. 2002, 174). To be sure, social resources can affect how we respond to disaster and how well we recover from exposure to any trauma. To increase resiliency, consider:

- Building strong networks among families and friends. In the absence of family support, develop positive interpersonal relationships with others.
- Ensuring that workplaces become or remain places of support by working at effective relationships with coworkers and supervisors.
- Joining groups that offer social support, such as places of worship, support groups, and civic organizations especially after relocating due to a disaster.
- Building strong and positive mental health for yourself and your family. Focus on working together as a team to face adversity, and practice that skill to build competence when smaller events arise.
- Developing a family disaster plan and taking the family through a basic first-aid course.

- Practicing a family disaster plan from exiting a burning building to evacuating before a large event to sheltering in place for a rapid-onset event.
- Protecting family members from domestic violence that occurs after disaster.

Social Psychological Recovery

In this section, we look at barriers to accessing psychological recovery and recommend ways to break through such obstacles. The section also outlines programs and ideas that can be used in a recovery context to restore, safeguard, or promote positive mental health.

Barriers to Accessing Assistance

Assistance to people in disaster recovery contexts can take several forms. Red Cross workers offer mental-health services through shelters and out-reach teams. Faith-based volunteers, just through their presence, often give someone a person who will listen to him or her. Counseling and therapy can range from limited interventions and assessments to long-term individual or residential care. A number of barriers, though, may prevent people from accessing the assistance they need.

Asking for help with emotional or psychological trauma may be difficult for some people to do. Mental-health issues have, unfortunately, been stigmatized in this country, causing people to avoid or refuse help. Many of us are socialized to be strong and independent, and asking for or seeking help seems like an admission of failure. Others may not understand or recognize that counselors use therapies and treatments that have worked for thousands of people. The experience and expertise of those involved in providing such assistance far outweighs our own experience; thus seeking out properly credentialed and trained professionals to help us through difficult circumstances makes sense. If you broke your leg, would you set it yourself?

An additional barrier to therapy stems from lack of income to cover expenses associated with mental-health assistance. After disaster, though, the Red Cross and many faith-based organizations establish programs. The American Red Cross provides properly credentialed mental-health outreach workers in most disasters. Lutheran Disaster Services offers Camp Noah for children affected by disaster. COPS (Concerns of Police Survivors) also brings children into camps for play, counseling, and to simply be among other children who have lost a loved one serving on that "thin blue line." Other organizations may be willing to provide pro bono or income-based services. Caseworkers assigned to those affected by disaster should be prepared to link clients to resources. Further information can be found at the end of this chapter.

Therapy provides many benefits, particularly helping people to work with and learn to manage difficult circumstances in their lives. By encouraging our friends and families, as well as ourselves, to take advantage of programs offered after disaster, we can help to initiate healing. Being supportive of those who need or seek out assistance can make a difference. By encouraging those who may be suffering to view therapy, counseling, or outreach as a positive step, we may be able to help another person on his or her journey toward recovery.

Outreach

Organizations that provide assistance tend to offer relatively short-lived programs. However, evidence suggests that programs need to be offered for some time after a disaster, especially those of large magnitude. The September 11 attacks represent an example of this. Project Liberty, created by the New York State Office of Mental Health, offered crisis counseling and referral to those affected. An examination of service provision found that people who lost family members represented 40% of the counseling visits, a number that declined to 5% within five months. However, rates for uniformed personnel increased after one year (Covell et al. 2006). Experts suggest that such programs should be offered for a while, with outreach to particular groups that may access assistance at varying rates and times during the course of recovery.

The Stafford Act allows for services, including the Crisis Counseling Assistance and Training Program. Funds from FEMA and others make it possible to conduct outreach, public education, and counseling as well as referrals through professionals, schools, worship locations, and workplaces (Elrod, Hamblen, and Norris 2006). States must submit applications for these funds. In establishing programs, state directors have noted particular challenges in reaching new immigrants, seniors, migrants, undocumented workers, homeless persons, and those who are mentally ill. People who have lived in the community are usually the best to conduct outreach. Training of those outreach workers is crucial for them to be able to connect with affected populations, especially those who may be socially disconnected from the larger community. Experts agree that such outreach and mental-health efforts should be a part of any recovery plan prior to disaster (Elrod, Hamblen, and Norris 2006).

School Programs

After September 11, approximately 25% of children living in the area of the World Trade Center received counseling, compared with 10% of children living across New York City; more than half of that counseling occurred in a school environment (Fairbrother et al. 2004). Multiple school-related personnel participated, including teachers, school psychologists, and counselors.

Teachers and educational staff have long-term, almost daily contact with children. Naturally, then, schools represent an appropriate location for establishing and offering services. The Oklahoma Department of Mental Health and Substance Abuse established Project Heartland about a month after the bombing to provide crisis counseling to school children and affected families. Six schools, including one damaged by the bombing and one that evacuated students and staff members, were located within five miles or less from the site of the bombing. Yet, massive media coverage meant that schoolchildren across the state experienced potentially traumatic exposure.

Project Heartland accordingly offered services to 66,000 students in both public and private schools. The largest program included consultation, education, training, system support, and treatment team meetings (Pfefferbaum, Call, and Sconzo 1999). Additional services brought advocacy, support interventions, parent meetings, educational publications, and a range of individual, group, and family counseling to those affected. Counselors formed groups to deal with the loss, organized training sessions for teachers and staff about how to recognize signs of trauma and grief, and identified stressor points, including the anniversary of the event. Concern continued that avoidance of dealing with the trauma, a common reaction, could continue to interfere with a return to social well-being and disrupt school performance. Those concerns escalated in the third year after the attack, when the media provided extensive coverage of the criminal trials associated with the attack (Pfefferbaum, Call, and Sconzo 1999). Project Heartland provided skills and resources to teachers and staff members to deal with the long-term impact.

Critical-Incident Stress Management

Critical-incident stress management (CISM) covers a number of treatments and interventions that can be used immediately and in long-term counseling and therapies. The most well-known, and debated, approach is called critical-incident stress debriefing (CISD), which we turn to next. Following the section on CISD, we examine a few other strategies for working with traumatized populations, including support groups, spiritual care, and community remembrances.

Critical-Incident Stress Debriefing

Critical-incident stress debriefing (CISD) is intended for use where people have been exposed to an acute situation. CISD was originally designed for first responders. CISD walks those affected through seven stages within one to two days after the event. A credentialed professional is required to lead the effort, which involves creating a supportive environment so that people can talk openly. Additional phases involve describing the incident, sharing thoughts and feelings, noting psychological responses, and learning about normal reactions. The final phase allows for referrals to other professionals, if necessary (Armstrong, O'Callahan, and Marmar 1991).

In 1991, a gunman entered the Luby's Cafeteria in Killeen, Texas, where he shot 55 people. Emergency medical workers responded to the site, where they faced life-and-death triage decisions among people they knew, including neighbors, friends, and community leaders. Psychology professor Dr. Sharon Jenkins studied the effects of the massacre on these workers. Her work found that, in the days following the event, 28% reported anxiety and worry, 22% expressed anger and hostility, and 19% experienced sleep disturbances (Jenkins 1998). To cope, 94% sought out coworkers and 50% went to professional counselors. As Jenkins (1998, 193) observed, "Workers also reported feeling helped by others and by participating in CISD, which some saw as a way of helping their coworkers. Postemergency intervention involving mutual support may be especially effective for this population." The gunman died as well, which meant that answers for why the incident occurred would not be answered. Jenkins recommended that CISD and other techniques could be particularly useful "for emergencies that challenge beliefs about human nature of interpretations of justice."

Other Types of Debriefing

CISD may not work in all contexts. For example, after the Loma Prieta earthquake, the American Red Cross offered debriefing for its volunteers and staff working in urban shelters where numerous challenges had surfaced (Armstrong, O'Callahan, and Marmar 1991). Caseworkers seeking to aid survivors were, within a month, "exhausted" from the accumulation of chronic rather than acute conditions, bureaucratic entanglements, negative publicity, changing policies, fears of aftershocks, and more (Armstrong, O'Callahan, and Marmar 1991, 584). A modification of CISD was used, where Red Cross volunteers and staff were able to discuss the situation, understand feelings and responses, and identify productive coping strategies. Volunteers also felt guilty at taking breaks. By going through the debriefing, volunteers learned to take the recommended work breaks to improve their mental health and ability to help others (Armstrong, O'Callahan, and Marmar 1991).

Debriefing has been critiqued as well. In Australia, researchers studied how stress debriefing helped the recovery of 195 emergency service personnel (Kenardy et al. 1996). The study found no differences between those who received stress debriefing versus those who did not in terms of their rate of recovery. A counterargument posed by the researchers is that stress debriefing "may be working and preventing those who were debriefed from getting worse" (Kenardy et al. 1996, 47). Others counter that CISD in particular has not been studied sufficiently and that the program applies specifically to first-responder groups.

Support Groups

Support groups for various concerns of life are common across communities, including those associated with Alzheimer's disease, cancer, grief, and diabetes. After disaster, support groups may appear among affected survivors or as the result of specific programming. After September 11 and Hurricane Katrina, for example, people met in groups to work through trauma issues. By meeting with others who understand what you have been through, you can feel less alone. Talking with others also helps to recognize that some responses are normal and affords an opportunity to identify useful coping mechanisms.

Ideally, support groups will be facilitated by a professional with experience in the areas of concern. An example of a professional organization that provides support through structured group activities is COPS, Concerns of Police Survivors (see link in Resources section). COPS responds to the families of officers killed in the line of duty. Programs include annual conferences, a walk-a-thon in Washington, DC, camps for children, debriefings for fellow officers, counseling, scholarships, and teen programs. Retreats are also available for the full range of people affected: parents, spouses, siblings, adult children, and in-laws. Finally, because the loss of an officer occurs on the job, COPS supports family members and coworkers through criminal trials. COPS represents a model for serving comprehensively the entire community affected by a traumatic loss.

Spiritual Care

In times of disaster, the faith-based community truly steps up into a familiar role for clergy and religious leaders. Faith helps people transition through major events in life, both happy and sad, including funerals, weddings, and births. Numerous faith-based disaster organizations provide spiritual care to stricken communities. (For additional details, see related links in the Resources section of this chapter.):

- Church World Services has led efforts to outline a code of conduct for those involved in providing disaster spiritual care. Their criteria emphasize respect for people from all walks of life and all faiths, being honest and fair to all affected, respecting the values of local faiths and populations, and coordinating with other active organizations. Church World Services also lists what disaster survivors should expect from spiritual care, including confidentiality, a comforting presence, care appropriate within one's faith tradition, and that no harm should come from the interaction.

- The United Methodist Committee on Relief provides information on its Web site as part of its program titled Spiritual Care in Disaster Response. Resources include information on basic trauma reactions, the phases of mental health response to disaster, and guidelines for seeking professional counseling.
- The Lutheran Disaster Response trains and certifies individuals for its Chaplain Network and then sends its clergy out to affected areas. Lutheran Disaster Response also offers an online devotional guide for disaster recovery as well as information useful to volunteers who will spend time with survivors.

Community Memorials

Social resources matter before and after disaster strikes. Connecting and reconnecting those social resources can occur through various means. Impromptu memorials often spring up at disaster sites, where people leave flowers, teddy bears, medals, and other mementos to share in the connected loss (Eyre 2006). Candlelight vigils and prayer services are common in the days and weeks that follow an event. In Greenville, South Carolina, community members created a luminary labyrinth to remember those who died in the September 11 attacks. People walked the illuminated path as they contemplated the event, remembered those who were lost, and collectively shared a quiet grief.

It is not unusual that people rely on anniversaries of events to bring together those who were injured physically, psychologically, and socially, to remember, reflect, and honor those lost. Anniversaries also serve as markers of time that allow us to recognize how far we have come with rebuilding not only homes, but families, neighborhoods, and communities. The American Red Cross, in concert with several airlines, brought families to the World Trade Center, Pentagon, and Shanksville, Pennsylvania, to remember the one-year anniversary of September 11. In the United States, the Family Assistance Act requires airlines to bring families to the one-year anniversary of a plane crash (Eyre 2006). Memorials continue to the present day. On September 11, 2008, families gathered again in all three locations. The Pentagon dedicated its memorial on that day and opened it to the public, while work continues on a memorial in New York City (see Photo 10.2).

Anniversaries can take various forms. Those who were together during an event may gather together again, either privately or publicly. Private occasions may be as simple as being together at the time and day of the disaster or gathering those affected for a meal or meeting. Public occasions vary more widely. People in Cardington, Ohio, recognized the one-year

PHOTO 10.2 The Pentagon Memorial was dedicated on September 11, 2008. A Bell of Honor was rung as each name was read. The memorial includes benches designed with the names of 184 lost, including 59 people aboard American Airlines Flight 775 and 125 within the Pentagon. (Photo by Cherie Cullen, U.S. Department of Defense.)

anniversary of the 1982 tornado with a community-wide remembrance service and a song written specially for the occasion. The 1989 Loma Prieta earthquake inspired multiple ways to honor those who were lost. Santa Cruz efforts ranged from heartfelt notes placed at locations of loss to a public ceremony that included a traditional favorite song, "This Land is Your Land." Politicians made speeches, the Red Cross handed out balloons, and people gathered at the town clock that had stopped precisely at the time of the earthquake. In nearby Watsonville, volunteer organizations held a house blessing that marked a Hispanic family's return to permanent housing (Phillips and Hutchins-Ephraim 1992). A few years later, Homestead, Florida, marked the one-year event of Hurricane Andrew with the building of a new home in 24 hours and grand reopenings of area businesses. After each anniversary of the Oklahoma City bombing, those who run in the memorial marathon event tuck their runner's bibs into the survivor fence.

More formal memorials often follow. Plaques are common ways to memorialize the names of those who were lost. In Watsonville, the community and city funded a fountain in front of city hall. Painted tiles surround the fountain and tell the story of the community coming together across cultural divides to rebuild shattered lives. In short, disaster anniversaries provide an opportunity to formally move the community toward recovery and to allow for "collective remembering" (Eyre 2006; Forrest 1993; Phillips and Hutchins-Ephraim 1992). Memorializing has entered the Internet also, with antiterrorism messages and opportunities for survivors to tell their stories (Eyre 2006).

Anniversary events and memorials may promote healing by bringing people together, assuring those who survived that their loved ones will not be forgotten, and creating locations and times where collective remembering and gathering can take place. As described in Box 10.4 and seen in Photos 10.3 and 10.4, the creation of the memorial can be just as transformative and inspirational.

BOX 10.4   CREATING THE BLUFFTON UNIVERSITY BASEBALL TEAM MEMORIAL

On March 2, 2007, a charter bus carrying members of the Bluffton University, Ohio, baseball team went off an overpass in Atlanta, Georgia, while en route to their spring training in Florida. Five members of the team perished as well as the bus driver and his wife; others continue to work at long-term rehabilitation of their injuries. Since the day of the crash, Bluffton's students, faculty, and families have built on the strength and faith of their community to promote healing. During the first week, the university held prayer and candlelight vigils and a public memorial service. Internet pages were dedicated to those who were lost and, as a nation watched, the team took the field to play out the rest of their season as a way to honor the teammates and friends they lost.

In the year that followed, conversations took place over how to best honor the team. University President James M. Harder spoke with faculty member and artist Gregg Luginbuhl, a 1971 Bluffton graduate, about plans for a Circle of Remembrance with a unique centerpiece. After reflecting on this challenge during his own daughter's soccer game, he was inspired to propose an interactive bronze casting that would include the team:

> A home plate has five sides. A home plate looks like a house. The phrase "touching home" has layers of meaning. I had defined a concept that I was excited about, and that seemed to have the potential to contribute to a healing process. Sometimes I doubted that the players would be interested in the idea. But I was re-energized on a December evening when players and coaches gathered to make their mark. Baseball is a game for hands—hands which hold the bat and ball, hands which send signals, hands which congratulate. I invited players to make a hand print that represented their experience of the bus accident. I asked them to limit words and numbers, since the hands themselves would communicate more universally. I think we will never forget gathering around the mound, considering the mark and its placement and watching as others made their lasting impressions in the clay.

In the end, "home" in this work references a run-scoring achievement, individual homes and families, Bluffton University as a home for its students and our heavenly home. Players' marks show support for each other, unity, perseverance, and love for each other and for the game that they have all played together.

Five footprints, taken from the actual cleats of Zachary, David, Scott, Cody and Tyler represent their many achievements and ultimate success, as well as the impact that they each have had on all of our lives. I ask all who visit this site to think of rounding the bases as a metaphor for our work, for our lives and especially for our spiritual journeys. Through individual achievement, a hit or a walk, we get on base. We make judgments, decisions and take risks (maybe steal a base), but, by and large, we survive or progress with the help of our coaches and teammates. Sometimes we make it home and celebrate the journey—knowing the joy of our contribution to the team. And then we try to get on base again. "Touching Home" is an end to a journey. And a beginning.

Source: Bluffton 5 (Spring 2008) With permission.

(Bluffton *is a magazine for Bluffton University's alumni and friends. For more information on Bluffton University and its baseball team, please visit http://www.bluffton.edu.*)

Summary

What people need most, before and after disaster, is to build strong, effective, interpersonal networks among family and friends. Such social resources will enable healing and recovery after disaster and support those affected through difficult days. Similar to the grief that you might experience with the loss of a loved one, disaster recovery requires time and a willingness to work through associated challenges. Those seeking to help friends through recovery can provide a warm hug, a listening ear, or a shoulder to lean on. Employers wanting to support affected workers can provide professional debriefing, clinical resources, flex time, and more. Community and faith-based organizations can offer respite care, child care, and adult day care as well as rebuilding and reconstruction, financial support, and spiritual care to support parishioners and the broader community through the recovery period. What is common to all—whether family, friends, employees, or community members—is that emotional and psychological recovery from disaster depends on the compassion and commitment of concerned others.

PHOTO 10.3 The creation of the Bluffton University bronze sculpture. (Photo by Gregg Luginbuhl. With permission.)

Study Guide

Summary Questions

1. Distinguish between normal reactions to disaster and traumatic impact and those reactions that may require intervention, support services, or therapy.

2. What variations in social psychological responses to disaster may occur among the populations present in your community? Think here about the differential impacts that research suggests may occur based on age, gender, ethnicity, and socioeconomic status.

3. Identify and describe the various individual, situational, contextual, and locational conditions that may influence social psychological recovery needs.

4. What are some typical postdisaster psychology services and programs that have been used in previous disasters? Would these work in your community? Are these programs already available where you live?

5. What barriers prevent people from accessing postdisaster therapies? Discuss the role of stigma, income, and other factors that may prevent people from accessing the aid they need to recover fully.

PHOTO 10.4 The Bluffton University memorial and team field. (Photo by Kelli Cardinal. With permission.)

6. What kinds of intervention programs and efforts have been attempted in a postdisaster setting?

Discussion Questions

1. What should an emergency management agency, aid agency, or professional psychological association do before a disaster to credential and train volunteers who can assist in social psychology services?
2. What kinds of information services could you preestablish before a disaster strikes? Where might you want to place those resources? Should they be developed for specific concerns and populations? How so?
3. How could you encourage people who are experiencing trauma to use and benefit from therapeutic services and programs in your community after disaster?
4. Where can you find professionals and trained volunteers able to help you or your community after a disaster?
5. What are the first three things you should do after a disaster strikes regarding social psychological recovery? What needs may exist or emerge during the long-term recovery period?

Key Terms

Anxiety
Blaming
Collective loss
Compassion fatigue
Debriefing
Depression
Outreach
Posttraumatic stress disorder (PTSD)
Residential care
Resilience
Secondary trauma
Therapy
Trauma

References

Adams, L. M. 2007. Mental health needs of disaster volunteers: A plea for awareness. *Perspectives in Psychiatric Care* 43 (1): 52–54.

Armstrong, K., W. O'Callahan, and C. R. Marmar. 1991. Debriefing Red Cross disaster personnel: The multiple stressor debriefing model. *Journal of Traumatic Stress* 4: 581–593.

Blanshan, S., and E. L. Quarantelli. 1981. From dead body to person: The handling of fatal mass casualties in disaster. *Victimology* 6: 275–287.

Blinn-Pike, L., B. D. Phillips, and P. Reeves. 2006. Shelter life after Katrina: A visual analysis of evacuee perspectives. *International Journal of Mass Emergencies and Disasters* 24: 303–330.

Blocker, T. J., and D. E. Sherkat. 1992. In the eyes of the beholder. *Organization and Environment* 6: 153–166.

Bocanegra, H. T. d., E. Brickman, and C. O'Sullivan. 2004. Vicarious trauma in aid workers following the World Trade Center attack in 2001. *International Journal of Mass Emergencies and Disasters* 22 (1): 35–55.

Bonanno, G. A. 2004. Loss, trauma, and human resilience. *American Psychologist* 59: 20–28.

Bonanno, G. A., S. Galea, A. Bucciarelli, and D. Vlahov. 2007. What predicts psychological resilience after disaster? The role of demographics, resources, and life stress. *Journal of Consulting and Clinical Psychology* 75: 671–682.

Boscarino, J. A., C. R. Figley, and R. E. Adams. 2004. Compassion fatigue following the September 11 terrorist attack: A study of secondary trauma among New York City social workers. *International Journal of Emergency Mental Health* 6 (2): 1–10. http://mailer.fsu.edu/~cfigley/Tests/documents/IJEMH_6_2.pdf.

Brewin, C. R., B. Andrews, and J. D. Valentine. 2000. Meta-analysis of risk factors for post-traumatic stress disorder in trauma-exposed adults. *Journal of Consulting and Clinical Psychology* 68: 748–766.

Cleary, P. D., and P. S. Houts. 1984. Psychological impacts of the Three Mile Island accident. *Journal of Human Stress* 10 (1): 28–34.

Coker, A. L., J. S. Hanks, K. S. Eggleston, J. Risser, P. G. Tee, K. J. Chronister, C. L. Troisi, R. Arafat, and L. Franzini. 2006. Social and mental health needs assessment of Katrina evacuees. *Disaster Management and Response* 4 (3): 88–94.

Covell, N. H., S. A. Donahue, G. Allen, J. J. Foster, C. J. Felton, and S. M. Essock. 2006. Use of Project Liberty counseling services over time by individuals in various risk categories. *Psychiatric Services* 57: 1268–1270.

Cutter, S. 2005. The geography of disaster: Race, class and Katrina. Social Science Research Council 2005. http://understandingkatrina.ssrc.org/.

Davidson, A. D. 1989. Air disaster: Coping with stress. *Police Stress* 1 (2): 20–22.

Davidson, L. M., A. Baum, and D. L. Collins. 1982. Stress and control-related problems at Three Mile Island. *Journal of Applied Social Psychology* 12: 349–359.

Dyregrov, A., J. Kristoffersen, and R. Gjestad. 1996. Voluntary and professional disaster workers. Journal of Traumatic Stress 9/3: 541–555.

Elrod, C. L., J. L. Hamblen, and F. H. Norris. 2006. Challenges in implementing disaster mental health programs: State program directors' perspectives. *The ANNALS of the American Academy of Political and Social Science* 604: 152–170.

Erikson, K. 1976. *Everything in its path*. New York: Simon and Schuster.

Eyre, A. 2006. Remembering: Community commemoration after disaster. In *Handbook of disaster research*, ed. H. Rodriguez, E. L. Quarantelli, and R. R. Dynes, 441–455. New York: Springer.

Fairbrother, G., J. Stuber, S. Galea, B. Pfefferbaum, and A. R. Fleischman. 2004. Unmet need for counseling services by children in New York City after the September 11th attacks on the World Trade Center: Implications for pediatricians. *Pediatrics* 113: 1367–1374.

Forrest, T. 1993. Disaster anniversary: A social reconstruction of time. *Sociological Inquiry* 63: 444–456.

Hamida, T., and D. Malone. 2004. Anxiety disorders. http://www.clevelandclinicmeded. com/medicalpubs/diseasemanagement/psychiatry/anxiety/anxiety.htm.

Hancock, B. 2005. *Riding with the blue moth*. Champaign, IL: Sports Publishing LLC.

Jenkins, P., and B. D. Phillips. 2008. Battered women, catastrophe, and the context of safety after Hurricane Katrina. *NWSA Journal*. Forthcoming.

Jenkins, S. 1998. Emergency medical workers' mass shooting incident stress and psychological reactions. *International Journal of Mass Emergencies and Disasters* 16: 181–197.

Kenardy, J. A., R. A. Webster, T. J. Lewin, V. J. Carr, P. L. Hazell, and G. L. Carter. 1996. Stress debriefing and patterns of recovery following a natural disaster. *Journal of Traumatic Stress* 9: 37–49.

Livingston, H. M., M. G. Livingston, D. N. Brooks, and W. W. McKinlay. 1992. Elderly survivors of the Lockerbie air disaster. *International Journal of Geriatric Psychiatry* 7: 725–729.

Norris, F. H., M. J. Friedman, and P. J. Watson. 2002. 60,000 disaster victims speak: Part 2, Summary and implications of the disaster mental health research. *Psychiatry* 65: 240–260.

Norris, F. H., M. J. Friedman, P. J. Watson, C. M. Byrne, E. Diaz, and K. Kaniasty. 2002. 60,000 disaster victims speak: Part 1, An empirical review of the empirical literature, 1981–2001. *Psychiatry* 65: 207–239.

North, C. S., L. Tivis, J. C. McMillen, B. Pfefferbaum, J. Cox, E. L. Spitznagel, K. Bunch, J. Schorr, and E. M. Smith. 2002. Coping, functioning, and adjustment of rescue workers after the Oklahoma City bombing. *Journal of Traumatic Stress* 15: 171–175.

Peek, L. 2003. Reactions and responses: Muslim students' experiences on New York City campuses post-9/11. *Journal of Muslim Minority Affairs* 23: 271–283.

Perilla, J. L., F. H. Norris, and E. A. Lavizzo. 2002. Ethnicity, culture and disaster: Identifying and explaining ethnic differences in PTSD 6 months after Hurricane Andrew. *Journal of Social and Cultural Psychology* 21: 20–45.

Pfefferbaum, B., J. A. Call, and G. M. Sconzo. 1999. Mental health services for children in the first two years after the 1995 Oklahoma City terrorist bombing. *Psychiatric Services* 50: 956–958.

Phillips, B. D., and M. Hutchins-Ephraim. 1992. Looking back: The Loma Prieta earthquake one-year anniversary. Paper presented at Southwestern Sociological Association meeting, Austin, TX.

Phillips, B. D., D. M. Neal, T. Wikle, A. Subanthore, and S. Hyrapiet. 2008. Mass fatality management after the Indian Ocean tsunami. *Disaster Prevention and Management*. 17/5: 681–697.

Prince-Embury, S., and J. F. Rooney. 1988. Psychological symptoms of residents in the aftermath of the Three Mile Island accident and restart. *Journal of Social Psychology* 128: 779–790.

———. 1990. Life stage differences in resident coping with the restart of the Three Mile Island Nuclear Generating Facility. *Journal of Social Psychology* 130: 771–779.

Pulido, M. L. 2007. In their words: Secondary traumatic stress in social workers responding to the 9/11 terrorist attacks in New York City. *Social Work* 52: 279–281.

Scanlon, J. 2006. Dealing with the tsunami dead: Unprecedented international cooperation. *The Australian Journal of Emergency Management* 21 (2): 57–61.

Simpson, D., and S. Stehr. 2003. Victim management and identification in the World Trade Center collapse. In *Beyond September 11th*, ed. J. Monday, 109–120. Boulder, CO: Natural Hazards Center.

Taylor, A. J. W. 1983. Dealing with death. *Australian Funeral Director* : 31–33.

———. 1989. Grief counseling from the mortuary. *New Zealand Medical Journal* 102: 562–564.

Taylor, A. J., and A. G. Frazer. 1981a. Psychological sequelae of Operation Overdue following the DC-10 air crash in Antarctica. Wellington, New Zealand: Victoria University of Wellington.

Taylor, A. J. W., and A. G. Frazer. 1981b. The stress of post-disaster body handling and victim identification work. *Journal of Human Stress* 8: 4–12.

Tesar, G. 2002. Depression and other mood disorders. http://www.clevelandclinic-meded.com/medicalpubs/diseasemanagement/psychiatry/depression/depression.htm#definition.

Thoits, P. A., and L. N. Hewitt. 2001. Volunteer work and well-being. *Journal of Health and Social Behavior* 41 (2): 115–131.

Thompson, J. 1991. The management of body recovery after disasters. *Disaster Management* 3 (4): 206–210.

Tierney, K. J., M. Lindell, and R. Perry. 2001. *Facing the unexpected*. Washington, DC: Joseph Henry Press, National Academies.

Ursano, R. J., and J. E. McCarroll. 1990. The nature of a traumatic stressor: Handling dead bodies. *The Journal of Nervous and Mental Disease* 178 (6): 396–398.

U.S. Nuclear Regulatory Commission. n.d. Fact sheet on the Three Mile Island accident. http://www.nrc.gov/reading-rm/doc-collections/fact-sheets/3mile-isle.html.

Resources

- American Psychological Association; Graduate Programs in Disaster Mental Health, http://gradpsych.apags.org/jan08/postgrad.html; APA assistance in disasters, http://www.apa.org/topics/topicdisasters.html
- Camp NOAH, Lutheran Disaster Services, http://www.lssmn.org/disasterresponse/campnoah/default.htm
- Church World Services, http://www.cwserp.org/files/uploads/72SpiritualCare.pdf
- Disaster Chaplaincy, http://www.disasterchaplaincy.org/
- Domestic Violence Resources can be found at the Gender and Disaster Network, www.gdnonline.org.
- FEMA for Kids, http://www.fema.gov/KIDS
- International Critical Stress Incident Foundation, http://www.icisf.org/

- Internet sources of memorials: We Are Not Afraid http://www. werenotafraid.com; Tsunami Stories, http://www.tsunamistories. net
- Lutheran Disaster Care, http://www.ldr.org/care/
- National COPS (Concerns of Police Survivors), http://www.nationalcops.org/
- National Voluntary Organizations Active in Disaster Spiritual Care Links, http://www.nvoad.org/articles/ESCCchapterB.pdf
- New York City September 11 Health Registry and Programs for those affected, can be viewed at http://www.nyc.gov/html/doh/wtc/html/employees/treatment.shtml
- New York Disaster Interfaith Services, http://www.nydis.org/downloads/Tips_SpiritualCare.pdf. Accessed June 15, 2008.
- Red Cross Emotional Support Program, 2005 Hurricanes http://www.a2care.org/about_the_program.html
- Red Cross, September 11 overview of programs, http://www.redcross.org/press/disaster/ds_pr/020905report.html
- Riding with the Blue Moth, http://www.ridingwiththebluemoth. com/pages/8/index.htm; Remember the Ten races, http://www. remembertheten.com
- United Methodist Committee on Relief, http://new.gbgm-umc.org/UMCOR/getconnected/resources/spiritualcare/
- United States Nuclear Regulatory Commission Fact Sheet and Diagram, Three Mile Island http://www.nrc.gov/reading-rm/doc-collections/fact-sheets/3mile-isle.html

Endnotes

1. United Nations Social Statistics and Indicators, *The World's Women: 1995 Trends* (New York: United Nations, 1995).
2. League of Red Cross and Red Crescent Societies, *Working with Women in Emergency Relief and Rehabilitation Programmes* (Field Studies Paper 2, Geneva, Switzerland, 1991).
3. Narelle Dobson, "From under the Mud-Pack: Women and the Charleville Floods." *Australian Journal of Emergency Management* 9, no. 2 (1994): 11–13.
4. Zenaida Delica, "Women and Children during Disaster: Vulnerabilities and Capacities," in *The Gendered Terrain of Disaster*, ed. Elaine Enarson and Betty Hearn Morrow (Westport, CT: Greenwood, 1998).
5. *Globe and Mail*, January 14, 1998, A6.
6. United Way of Santa Cruz County, *A Post-Earthquake Community Needs Assessment for Santa Cruz County* (Aptos, CA: United Way of Santa Cruz County, 1990), 201. See also, Jennifer Wilson, Brenda Phillips, and David Neal, "Domestic Violence after Disaster," in *The Gendered Terrain of Disaster*, ed. Elaine Enarson and Betty Hearn Morrow (Westport, CT: Greenwood, 1998).

7. United Way of Santa Cruz County, *A Post-Earthquake Community Needs Assessment for Santa Cruz County* (Aptos, CA: United Way of Santa Cruz County, 1990), 25.

8. Commission for the Prevention of Violence against Women. 1989. "Violence against Women in the Aftermath of the October 17, 1989 Earthquake: A Report to the Mayor and City Council of the City of Santa Cruz" (Santa Cruz, CA).

9. Sharon Araji, "The Exxon-Valdez Oil Spill: Social, Economic, and Psychological Impacts on Homer," unpublished final report to the community of Homer (Anchorage: University of Alaska, Department of Sociology, 1992).

10. Victoria Godina and Colleen Coble, "The Missouri Model: The Efficacy of Funding Domestic Violence Programs as Long-Term Disaster Recovery," final evaluation report, December 1995 (Jefferson City: The Missouri Coalition Against Domestic Violence, 1995).

11. Gigi Laudisio, "Disaster Aftermath: Redefining Response—Hurricane Andrew's Impact on I & R," *Alliance of Information and Referral Systems* 15 (1993): 13–32.

12. Centers for Disease Control, "Post-Hurricane Andrew Assessment of Health Care Needs and Access to Health Care in Dade County, Florida," EPI-AID 93-09 (Miami: Florida Department of Health and Rehabilitative Services, 1992).

13. Elaine Enarson, *Responding to Domestic Violence and Disaster: Guidelines for Women's Services and Disaster Practitioners* (Vancouver: BC Institute Against Family Violence, 1997).

14. Paul Adams and Gerald Adams, "Mount Saint Helen's Ashfall: Evidence for a Disaster Stress Reaction," *American Psychologist* 39 (1984): 252–260.

15. CIETinternational, "Social Audit for Emergency and Reconstruction, Phase 1—April," study conducted by CCER (Managua, Nicaragua: Coordinadora Civil para la Emergencia y la Reconstrucción, 1999), www.ccer-nic.org/doc/htm.

16. "Shelters Have Empty Beds: Abused Women Stay Home," *New York Times*, October 21, 2001.

17. Sarah Fischer, "Gender Based Violence in Sri Lanka in the Aftermath of the 2004 Tsunami Crisis," Chapter 4, 2005, http://www.gdnonline.org/resources/fisher-post-tsuami-gbv-srilanka.doc.

18. Reported by Lin Chew and Kavita Ramdas in the Global Fund for Women report "Caught in the Storm: The Impact of Natural Disasters on Women," December 2005, http://www.globalfundforwomen.org/work/programs/natural-disasters.html.

Chapter 11

Public-Sector Recovery

Learning Objectives

After reading this chapter, you should be able to:

- Understand the challenges that face local public officials managing disasters
- Explain different perspectives on how to manage recovery
- Identify the various roles of local government in managing disasters
- Name various challenges that arise for public officials managing recovery
- Discuss how officials can facilitate recovery efforts through responsible leadership
- Demonstrate the value of including elected officials and governmental staff in the recovery process
- Discern resources and opportunities for local government during the recovery process
- Describe the ways in which local government fits into and influences all dimensions of disaster recovery

Introduction

It is difficult enough to imagine your neighborhood in ruins and to think through how and where you, as an individual, would start to rebuild. For public officials and staff, the process of facing the damage is so much broader. They must think of their own homes as well as devastation across commercial and industrial sectors, bridges and roads, utilities, and residences. Beyond the built environment, they must also be concerned with preserving the unique character of the city to retain its population. Local environmental qualities must be salvaged or improved. Massive amounts of debris must be managed to hasten the recovery process. Local officials will have to convene hundreds of recovery meetings, work with state and federal partners, and satisfy a public eager to return home.

Government officials and staff must step up to lead the recovery, probably facing unfamiliar tasks in a crisis situation. Leaders within your city must learn and adapt to state and federal regulations. They have to secure and be accountable for funds, donations, and volunteers. When recovery stalls or efforts fail, they will face the wrath of the public and potential loss of office. Consequently, leaders must promote an optimistic view and maintain forward momentum. In helping the community through the painful elements of recovery, they must attend to their own psychological well-being and that of governmental staff. The burden of recovery can be immense.

Leading a community through a recovery can also provide opportunities, too. Government now has the chance to address problems identified through earlier comprehensive planning. The chance to make homes and businesses more disaster-resilient now exists. People overlooked previously can now be included in the planning process, increasing civic participation across the community. As the governmental leaders in Greensburg, Kansas, did, elected and appointed leaders must convene the public and work across many levels of government to recover (see Photo 11.1).

In short, governmental leaders must weigh and face the challenges while remaining positive about the opportunities that recovery can bring. As former FEMA director James Lee Witt wrote in his book *Stronger in the Broken Places* (Witt and Morgan 2002, 223–224), recovery is "a chance to lay new foundations and support beams that can weather the next disaster better. It's a chance to decide if there's a way to get out of the way of that disaster altogether. It's a chance ..."

In the next section, we will look at how one community did that and then examine two different approaches to recovery **leadership** and management: the emergent-norm versus the bureaucratic approaches. This chapter thus reviews governmental roles for recovery. Readers will find additional useful information in Chapter 3 (Disaster Recovery Planning) and Chapter 15 (Financing Recovery).

PHOTO 11.1   Mayor John Janssen (in the orange shirt) holds a meeting with recovery planners and FEMA personnel. Greensburg, Kansas, is planning a community to be more energy efficient. (Photo by Leif Skoogfors/FEMA News Photo.)

Santa Cruz, California

In what has become a classic work on local government response to disaster, Santa Cruz city manager Richard C. Wilson described his city's experience after the 1989 Loma Prieta earthquake (Wilson 1991). In his book, *The Loma Prieta Earthquake: What One City Learned*, Wilson indicated that the first recovery concern is fiscal responsibility. FEMA can provide considerable support to local governments affected by disaster. However, FEMA also requires financial accountability as well as a 25% match to any federal assistance. Thus, in the midst of trying to move from response to recovery, helping city staff survive their own personal damage, negotiating contracts, managing massive tasks such as debris removal and demolitions, city staff and officials must also safeguard the community's financial well-being. Although FEMA provides guidelines and assistance in interpreting those guidelines, Wilson (1991, 50) notes that a local leader will "simply have to exercise your best judgment in approving expenditures."

Hard decisions must also be made, including tearing down historic landmarks. Rapid cost–benefit analysis of such landmarks must be made, and officials will have to live with the consequences of their decisions. Further, during a time when facts are needed, officials in Santa Cruz often had to rely on estimates, sometimes waiting up to a year to unearth all the relevant information. For example, estimating losses was difficult because infrastructural and underground utilities took time to assess. Yet, FEMA applications had to be generated to secure funds, and decisions had to be made.

From the Santa Cruz perspective then, recovery involves two stages (Wilson 1991, 55–56). The first is "immediate efforts to help the community continue to function as an economic entity." As described in Chapter 8, Santa Cruz set up pavilions for the displaced downtown businesses. The effort, successful within a few months, helped restore economic resources for both the short and the long term. Santa Cruz and Santa Cruz County also passed "Measure E" that allowed a half-cent sales tax within the county to support earthquake recovery, which allowed short-term rebuilding to begin.

The second phase involves addressing the long-term concerns. City officials worked with the Santa Cruz Downtown Association to launch "Vision Santa Cruz," an extensive planning effort that worked by consensus to create a plan, streetscape, and design for the rebuilt downtown. Santa Cruz hired a redevelopment professional to lead the effort. City Manager Wilson worked with state officials to design legislature allowing the city to expand its redevelopment activities.

Wilson writes that local government will know how to use routine economic development tools. However, disaster may provide a wider range of tools, and local leaders must "seize their opportunities" (Wilson 1991, 61). Tremendous efforts went into leading the area through the disaster toward recovery. Today, the unique downtown Santa Cruz Pacific Garden Mall has been rebuilt through careful design that emulates its original historic character. Community members continue to enjoy their beloved downtown. To see the restored Pacific Garden Mall with the bookstores, coffee shops, restaurants, movie theater, and unique shops inspires other communities to tackle the difficult tasks of local leadership. (Photographs of Santa Cruz can be viewed at the city's Web site, http://www.ci.santa-cruz.ca.us/.) Santa Cruz and city leaders stepped up, designed creative solutions to the earthquake damage, and worked closely with the community. Their success serves as an example of how local government can make it work despite considerable challenges. We will revisit the Santa Cruz story throughout this chapter.

Approaches to Governmental Leadership

In Chapter 2 we discussed several theoretical approaches to disaster recovery. One of those theories, the **emergent-norm theory**, stands in contrast to more formalized, bureaucratic ways for government to respond, a perspective we turn to next.

Ideally, bureaucratic procedures allow governmental offices to treat everyone the same, thus promoting a streamlined, equitable process. Routine, established rules and regulations seemingly offer a sense of order and logic, a pathway through which people move toward recovery.

Those vested with **bureaucratic authority**, which arises out of the established system, have the power to compel others to move through a set of rules and regulations. Critics argue that doing so frustrates people who feel they are nothing more than a number or a file. Further, each household experiencing recovery will face unique challenges. One homeowner may have secured sufficient insurance, while a neighbor could not afford to do so. Down the street, renters may face eviction in a tight market with high prices. New immigrants may not understand how the aid system works. Another household could require temporary housing that is accessible for wheelchairs only to discover that it is not available (see Box 11.1). As we will learn in Chapter 14, a number of organizations will come forward to help those who "fall through the cracks" of aid programs. Historically, most of those efforts have included emergent programs or organizational structures.

BOX 11.1   *BROU V. FEMA*

In a lawsuit filed after Hurricane Katrina, survivors complained that FEMA and the Department of Homeland Security had not provided sufficient numbers of accessible trailers for people with disabilities. Further complaints included a lack of ramps for wheelchairs as well as inaccessible bathrooms and kitchens. The lawsuit indicates that many people with disabilities had not received accommodations and were waiting in hotels and other temporary locations. As of February 2006, six months after the hurricane, FEMA had provided 34,808 trailers, of which 417 or 1% met accessibility guidelines.

The settlement provided a toll-free number for local residents to call. In March 2007, the Advocacy Center in New Orleans, Louisiana, received its third report from FEMA. Of the 2,553 people with disabilities that called the number, 1,400 needed accommodations, and 1,260 had received such units. An additional 256 needed modifications to their housing units, of which 243 had received such renovations.

Sources: FEMA. 2006. *Brou v. FEMA* settlement. http://www.fema.gov/pdf/library/brou_fema.pdf

Advocacy Center, 2007, Update on FEMA lawsuit, http://www.advocacyla.org/news/fema.php

---

The idea of emergence has led to the **Emergent Human Resources Model** (EHRM). This model emphasizes a flexible, problem-solving approach to disasters. The EHRM assumes that disasters disrupt routines but do not undermine the capacities of individuals or institutions to manage them (Dynes and Quarantelli 1968; Neal and Phillips 1995). Disasters tend to be decentralized events that require government to respond similarly (Tierney,

Lindell, and Perry 2001). EHRM suggests that government should focus on solving problems rather than enforcing existing rules and regulations. Indeed, as described in Chapter 13, a pluralistic decision-making process leads to the best recovery outcomes (Dynes 1993). Rebuilding will require that people must move through a process that involves adherence to procedures, codes, and ordinances. However, most disasters compel city staff and officials to review and revise those rules and regulations. Accordingly, flexibility can result in a more disaster-resilient built environment. By monitoring how a city process affects those rebuilding, it may be possible to adapt the system to be more effective.

Former FEMA director James Lee Witt took office after Hurricane Andrew. People were still living in tent cities a year after the 1992 event. Witt wrote, "My task as director was clear: to slash red tape and redefine how the federal government responds to crises in its citizens' lives" (Witt and Morgan 2002, 4). To change governmental bureaucracy, Witt listened to people: at FEMA headquarters, in their devastated homes, and at public meetings. What he learned underscores decades of research: that disasters tend to disable bureaucracies. Witt's comments suggest that government leaders need to humanize the disaster recovery process, treat residents (who are neighbors, friends, people we know from work or worship) as people facing the worst times of their lives, and handle each person's case as if he or she were family.

What might the emergent-norm theory and EHRM model suggest for government's role in disaster recovery? Here are some possibilities:

- A decentralized, pluralistic recovery framework involves and integrates all sectors and residents in recovery planning. For example, the business and residential sectors are equally important and should each receive fair attention. Low-income renters should be as involved as insured homeowners in established developments.
- Business as usual may not work. Designing new, flexible approaches to debris management, housing recovery, and economic development should be considered.
- Debris management can establish programs to recycle mulch in city parks.
- Housing recovery could feature occupational-specific locations, such as an artist's village.
- Cyber-commuting could be enhanced through a communitywide wireless network.
- The predisaster permitting process for rebuilding may not work fast enough. Staff should be sensitized to listen to how homeowners and landlords are experiencing that process. Specific staff should be appointed as liaisons to disaster organizations helping with rebuilding.

- Staff should be tasked with identifying how and where the existing system is failing. A recovery team should be asked to specify solutions.
- Opportunities to design mitigation features into rebuilding should be identified and offered as incentives during the rebuilding process.
- The recovery process may take years. New problems may be uncovered as time unfolds. Government planning could develop a team that specifically tackles newly discovered issues.

Postdisaster recovery challenges mean that governments will have to be flexible, creative, and adaptive. By doing so, they can take advantage of new insights and generate a recovery that can be more forward-thinking and result in a stronger, more disaster-resilient community. Disaster leadership is the ultimate responsibility of government.

Roles of Government

Georgia State University political science professor William Waugh (2000, 3) writes that "emergency management is the quintessential governmental role." By this, Dr. Waugh means that governments were first formed to provide broader support to citizens than what they could muster individually or as households. Early volunteer fire brigades represent one such example. Further, disaster management is typically handled at the local level, a role that has been particularly challenging since cities began to form (Wolensky and Wolensky 1990). In a disaster-recovery scenario, "It is local government's responsibility to … make effective use of the resources that may be provided from the outside, and to make the decisions that will determine the course of events" (Wilson 1991, 11).

Various sections in this book have emphasized the importance of the public sector in leading and supporting recovery efforts. From volunteer and donations management to debris removal and the rebuilding of homes, businesses, and infrastructure, it is clear that government ultimately must step up and coordinate recovery efforts. This chapter looks at recovery from the internal perspective of local government. First, we examine various roles played by local government in launching recovery (beyond those discussed in other chapters).

The Governmental Context

Local government historically has experienced less power and influence than state or federal government. Local government also tends to lack critical disaster resources, particularly in areas that are rural, have fewer hazards, or cannot afford to employ a professional emergency manager with appropriate staff. The number and qualifications of emergency management staff will vary considerably across various jurisdictions. In many areas, a limited number of staff may need to suffice due to budget limitations. In larger areas, more staff may be affordable. Most jurisdictions, however, report a general lack of sufficient personnel. FEMA has recommended one emergency management professional per each 100,000 residents, although it is unlikely that most jurisdictions can afford to do so. In large areas such as New York City, for example, a staff of 100 serves a city of 9 million (Edwards and Goodrich 2007). High-level emergency management positions may also be filled with political appointees rather than with professional, experienced emergency managers. While emergency managers represent an important resource to tap into during recovery, local government may find that emergency management offices lack personnel, resources, and expertise. Because most emergency management agencies concentrate on phases other than recovery, it is likely that a broadly based recovery committee will have to provide leadership—although emergency managers should never be excluded. Rather, emergency management should play a critical role (more on this later in this chapter). Such a situation may be exacerbated by conditions at the federal and state levels.

Wolensky and Wolensky (1990) write that federal reorganizations have caused confusion and uncertainty at the state and local levels. FEMA, for example, has been reorganized or reinvented multiple times since its inception in the 1970s. After September 11, FEMA was subsumed under the Department of Homeland Security along with dozens of other agencies. Funding, programs, and priorities changed, and FEMA lost its cabinet-level position. As one example of the changes since then, the National Incident Management System (NIMS) now requires that the Incident Command System (ICS) be used (see link in Resources section). Because NIMS and ICS are so new, training has yet to reach into all levels of government at the depth and breadth required for efficient use of the system (Neal and Webb 2006). When one level of government uses a given system, miscommunication and confusion can result. Similarly, Hurricane Katrina demanded unusual and new levels of recovery programming that may or may not be available for subsequent disasters.

An emphasis on response and terrorism developed in DHS after September 11 as well. Nationally, though, floods are the most common disasters to strike a community. Hurricane Katrina prompted renewed attention to natural hazards as well as to mitigation and recovery. In recent years, a broader, all-hazards approach has reappeared in federal and state policies and programs. Such changes are experienced locally as a pendulum that swings from one extreme to another, fostering unevenness across disaster management. Because local leadership changes through the election system, a loss of knowledge about disaster policies and programs may impede the most effective disaster recovery. It is necessary then for public officials to monitor changes at the state and federal levels to be sure that they can secure necessary resources for their communities.

Other forces may influence the local government experience of disaster as well. For example, although recovery planning calls for mitigation measures, implementing them may be difficult. Land-use planning that emphasizes preservation of floodplains, for example, has been challenging (Wolensky and Wolensky 1990). The private sector, particularly developers, may oppose new regulations. Because the private sector may hold more resources and power than elected officials and staff, their interests may prevail. Further, because recovery tends to prompt new, unmet needs, locally emergent groups may pressure local government to adopt particular actions. The postdisaster recovery process for elected officials and staff, then, may become a particularly thorny place to work.

Further, elected officials may be relatively new to disaster management and will have to learn quickly should a disaster strike. Typically, they will rely on staff with expertise in the area, although many municipalities may lack that expertise as well. In short, disaster recovery in many locales may be a learning experience conducted under the most challenging of conditions. Nonetheless, local government possesses a particular kind of authority called **legal-rational authority**. Authority means that someone can exercise power over another. Legal-rational authority is the type of power that is given to public officials through virtue of being elected to office. That power is exercised through recovery leadership.

Leadership

The public places its confidence in those elected to provide leadership in times of crisis. Sometimes the recovery goes well, but quite often there are stumbling points for any community. Residents may become disgruntled and look to the entity believed most responsible. Although it may be easy to point fingers at local government as the problem for why the recovery is not going well, the situation is more complicated (Wolensky and Wolensky 1990). Still, the public holds elected officials accountable for what happens locally. The conundrum, then, is how to preserve the public trust in the face of shifting priorities at state and federal levels. Effective local government in a disaster context requires "leaders who can utilize existing resources and mobilize new ones" (Wolensky and Wolensky 1990, 716.). Leaders may come from unexpected places inside government, and "the employee who stepped up to the plate can be placed in charge of a new project" (Witt and Morgan 2002, 223). Good governmental leaders look deeply within their staff, colleagues and commission members for the people most able to see the community through the recovery.

Local government will need more than legal-rational authority to prompt recovery. Often, the task requires other kinds of leadership and authority as well. In mitigation planning, it is often necessary for a "champion" to shoulder the challenge of speaking for mitigation. The same is true for recovery, particularly because this stage in the life cycle of emergency management may require steadfast devotion to a lengthy and difficult journey. Champions often possess another type of authority, called **charismatic authority**. Charisma is a quality often difficult to define, but it is generally described as a quality that pulls others toward a common goal. Charismatic individuals may possess a gift of communicating well, or drawing others to them and promoting a cause. Reverend Martin Luther King, Jr., for example, was often described as possessing charismatic authority. Charismatic leaders can be found among elected officials, certainly, but also within the community. A well-known religious leader or community activist may be able to rally others around the recovery effort. Trusted figures including educators, neighborhood association presidents, and physicians may be tapped to lead the recovery effort together. And, certainly, governmental leaders should keep an eye open for the grass-roots leader to emerge as well, someone connected to the reality that people are experiencing who can speak for and interact with those across various communities (see more on this in Chapter 13). By connecting with the community, it may be able to generate more support, thereby driving forward the recovery effort.

Political Will

Why do recoveries sometimes languish? Why aren't there sufficient mitigation measures already in place to protect the public? Why is it that few jurisdictions develop recovery plans? The answer is complex and requires consideration of several conditions. It may be that a locale does not have the economic resources to complete the task. Or, it could be that local hazards have not been assessed adequately. Perhaps the emergency management staff remains understaffed, underutilized, or unrecognized. Elected leaders may have other items on their agendas. The public may think "it won't happen here" or underestimate the probability that it could. When disasters do strike, the public nearly always clamors for a return to normal, and local officials feel pressured to tackle immediate needs like housing, business reestablishment, and restoration of lost tax revenues. It is up to elected officials, government staff, and recovery leaders to "protect the health, safety, and welfare of the community from the desires, power, and influence of those who promote short-sighted solutions. They need to foster personal and community responsibility for recovery decisions that will affect their community for years to come" (Natural Hazards Center 2005, 2–7). In short, leaders must exert their influence by influencing the community to recover as fully and as completely as possible. They "must develop and create a will that is infectious," a situation that is often referred to as **political will** (Natural Hazards Center 2005, 2–7).

The development of political will means that leaders have pledged themselves to the recovery plan and intend to see it through. Those who possess political will examine issues and options, make difficult decisions, provide funding, keep recovery teams and residents focused on the process, and move everyone toward collective, positive outcomes (Natural Hazards Center 2005, 2–8). Government can do so by:

- Distinguishing between immediate and long-term needs
- Convening appropriate and effective planning teams
- Communicating effectively with the public regarding key decisions, options, and rationales
- Practicing a positive outlook, remaining confident that the effort is worth it
- Considering options that will result in a more disaster-resilient community, including previously untried opportunities
- Maintaining a timeline for projects and initiatives while continually assessing the progress and addressing shortfalls and stop points
- Shoring up or restoring morale and confidence among those shouldering the burden of recovery
- Securing, monitoring, and accounting for funding
- Praising, recognizing, and rewarding efforts throughout all ranks and all sectors of the community
- Celebrating milestones

When elected officials or government staff close the door on possibilities, they repress the kinds of creative solutions and local commitment that might otherwise arise. Politicians must possess and demonstrate the enthusiasm and determination to see it through and pass on their passion to those laboring through the recovery process. That process begins with effective communication between government and the public.

Communication

In a disaster situation, people become hungry for news. Government and the media represent the two most common sources for information, although increasingly the Internet serves as a means to secure information as well. Government, though, plays a particularly important role in disseminating correct information so that people can make decisions.

After Hurricane Gustav churned along the Louisiana coast on September 1, 2008, local and state officials reached out to inform people about the damage and when they could return home. Officials went on numerous television and radio stations, streamed video on the Internet, provided sign-language interpretation, and released public statements. Because of Hurricane Katrina, officials in Jefferson Parish had preestablished reentry procedures. Their policy allowed key businesses to return. Meanwhile, short-term recovery crews turned to debris removal and utility restoration. When government plans for recovery, businesses will be open to provide food, health care, and pharmacy supplies along roads free of obstructions. People will be able to return to their homes, begin private property cleanup, contact insurance agents, and initiate repairs for power, communications, water, and sewage. Citizens rely on government to lead efforts and provide information so they can reestablish a normal routine.

Communication thus represents one of the most important activities that a local government can undertake after a disaster. Communication may include a wide range of informational needs from factual statements to rumor control. In this section, we examine some basic guidelines for handling recovery communications.

Communications matter because how government handles information influences how people think about, believe, trust, and ultimately follow governmental leaders and staff. A four-stage model may be used (Gillingham and Noizet 2007). First, it is important to think through how the public and the media view the situation. By working from their perspective, government may be able to anticipate informational needs. Second, it is important that government be among the first to put forth a message in order to provide accurate information before others. The media are prone to speculation, in part because they must fill air time. Sending out timely messages can stem miscommunication and confusion over such speculation. Third, communicators must be frank and direct in communicating with the public. If the public finds out that government has not been forthcoming, it will lose confidence in local leaders. It is important to tell the public everything that it needs to know in a clear and straightforward manner. Speaking to people in terms they understand works best. Being direct and honest about what is and is not known is also a good strategy, as is promising to "find out" and then delivering that information or update in a rapid manner. Fourth, people always come first. Communicators must sincerely believe and express concern when telling the public that they matter.

Communication strategies must be diverse and potentially widespread. Avenues for communicating with the public might include:

- A city's Web site and links from other Web sites that residents routinely connect to (For example, the New Orleans *Times-Picayune* offered neighborhood blogs after Hurricanes Katrina, Rita, and Gustav.)

- Newspapers, radio, and television (For example, governmental leaders could write a weekly column outlining recovery plans and initiatives in progress.)
- Public meetings, disaster recovery centers, worship locations, library events, county fairs, sporting events, and civic association meetings
- Webcasts and blogs, which can be monitored to identify public concerns
- Flyers, handouts, brochures, and similar materials posted in public locations (grocery stores, banks, health-care centers, pharmacies, businesses) and disseminated in utility bills and other items routinely mailed to residents
- Communications that are diverse in terms of languages locally spoken or signed and that consider the recipients' abilities to read or see the proffered materials

Communication also includes dealing with difficult subjects that people may not want to hear. From James Lee Witt (Witt and Morgan 2002, 222), "Make sure that everyone knows all the bad news as soon as you know it, so you can disarm the danger and start getting people focused on the opportunities." In particular, this means addressing inaccurate information that tends to be passed as rumors. The best way to manage rumor dissemination is through direct, diverse, and forthright means of communication. A rumor control center, phone number, or Web site may be set up to manage incorrect information. Flyers and Web sites can offer "frequently asked questions" (FAQs) relevant to specific topics. Information should be distributed through as many outlets as possible. By diversifying those outlets, it is more likely that accurate information will be spread through social networks, thereby reducing rumor transmission.

Recovery Challenges and Opportunities

A number of challenges and opportunities will develop as a consequence of the disaster, including the ways in which the event impacted city staff, the need for new legislation, and the consequences of the event or recovery actions for elected officials. We turn to these issues next.

Impact on Staff

After the Loma Prieta earthquake, the Santa Cruz city manager (Wilson 1991) wrote that employee turnover emerged as a considerable problem. At the time, the city employed 620 full-time individuals. The city's typical annual turnover of 11% rose to 26% in the year following the earthquake. Clearly, losing one-fourth of the city's staff represents a considerable potential disruption of public services. What could lead to such loss of human resources? Normal turnover accounts for some, when people leave for other jobs or better opportunities. However, the burden of managing the recovery falls on local government, which is borne by elected officials and city staff. In addition to normal operations, disaster operations add additional and sometimes unfamiliar tasks to a workload. Local government officials and staff will also have to deal with a stressed-out public eager to return to normal. It would not be surprising to discover significant turnover among a staff dealing with such a situation.

As noted in Chapter 10 (Social Psychological Recovery), local government also needs to be concerned with the mental and physical safety of those involved in disaster recovery work. Several studies after September 11 looked at the 100,000+ who worked at the World Trade Center site. At the one-year mark, 13% reported posttraumatic stress disorder (PTSD) symptoms. At the three-year mark, 10% of sanitation and construction workers presented mental-health concerns. PTSD was higher among those who took on work outside of their normal profession, suggesting that local government bears responsibility to train staff and officials for what they might encounter in new roles. Police officers reported a relatively low PTSD rate of 6.2%, while unaffiliated volunteers indicated a much higher rate of 21.2%. Those most at risk for PTSD, three years after the event, were construction, engineering, and sanitation workers and unaffiliated volunteers (Perrin et al. 2007).

To care for the community and to lead it through recovery, governmental officials and supervisors must pay close attention to the impacts of events on their staff. Because city staff feel a sense of responsibility to the public, they may put their own needs aside to help their community. The burden may become immense, and those managing the recovery need to pay attention to those carrying this load. Suggestions for assisting employees through a disaster can be found in Chapter 8.

Mitigation Opportunities

Historically, citizens "bear the brunt of human suffering and financial loss in disasters," while "local officials pay insufficient attention to policies to limit vulnerability" (Burby 2006, 171). Most local governments use the response and recovery time to enact new and stronger codes, policies, and procedures. For example, governments will often strengthen building codes designed to reduce future damage. While comprehensive and mitigation planning remain the single best ways for public officials to address vulnerability, the recovery time period also offers chances to build a more disaster-resilient community. Toward that end, government has the opportunity to pass new policies that safeguard or provide for (Schwab et al. 1998):

- *Floodplain management*: Strategies might include requiring set-backs, elevations, or relocations. In areas that experience flooding, pilings or columns can be required rather than fill. Businesses that manufacture hazardous materials can be disallowed in areas with flooding risks.
- *Annexation*: A jurisdiction might consider annexing an area to control development in the area and reduce risks to existing homes and businesses.
- *Building codes*: Public officials might require that new codes be established that exceed state building codes. Code enforcement can be made a priority; this is particularly important, as codes are established at state levels, but compliance at the local level remains problematic in many areas (Schwab et al. 1998).
- *Development regulations*: New developments and newly built businesses may feature open space, permeable surfaces, congregate or individual safe rooms, and features specific for local hazards, such as flood elevations, hurricane clamps, or seismic retrofits.
- *Environmental reviews*: Communities might require environmental reviews in areas that impinge on sensitive locations, habitats, and other areas prior to new development or before allowing rebuilding. Coastal areas may emphasize protection of coastal wetlands, sand dunes, and habitats.
- *Zoning changes*: Zoning dictates what kinds of structures can be built in a given location. Zoning can manage residential and commercial construction and can require specific changes. Density transfers, which trade off the number of homes versus the open space, can be negotiated for builders and developers that introduce mitigation features.
- *Affordable housing*: As described in Chapter 7 (Housing), the city of Watsonville passed an ordinance requiring that 25% of all new construction must be affordable housing.
- *Accessible housing*: Per the Americans with Disabilities Act, new construction must meet certain standards for accessibility. In a postdisaster context, public officials may want to exceed standards to produce an environment that supports people with disabilities as well as senior citizens.
- *Navigable communities*: Communities can choose to exceed minimal features to design travel routes for a variety of users in cars, wheelchairs, bicycles, service animals, strollers, and on foot.
- *Setbacks*: Setbacks specify how far a building must be from the sidewalk, street, or some other environmental feature. Setbacks can be used, for example, to create more green space or a wildfire buffer between houses and vegetation.

- *District overlays*: As described in Chapter 8 (Business Recovery), public officials might want to establish a particular geographic location for special design features, amenities, and tax incentives.

The recovery period provides opportunities to enhance quality of life for residents and to reduce the future effects of disasters. The window of opportunity that opens will close fairly quickly in the face of building pressures to return to normal. Effective governmental leaders lay the groundwork for the above suggestions in advance through recovery planning (see Chapter 3) and then move quickly to enact legislation and policies.

Political Fallout

The people and organizations most likely to be blamed for problems in a disaster are those most active, visible, and responsible for specific activities. Public officials fall into these categories and bear the burden of failures. FEMA was criticized for a "sluggish" response after Hurricane Hugo in 1989 (Sylves 2006, 43). After Hurricane Andrew struck Florida in 1992, the governor "initially refused to make the request" for federal aid, and President Bush suffered politically. President Clinton and his advisors learned from those errors and followed the basic rules: "act fast … send it all … [because local and state officials are reluctant to admit they need help] … and explain and console" (Sylves 2006, 43).

After Hurricane Katrina, both the White House and a bipartisan committee in the U.S. House of Representatives conducted investigations. The White House assessed federal actions but did not address state and local responses; the congressional report assessed a broad array of issues (Menzel 2006). The White House report included 125 recommendations. Of particular interest, the White House report indicated that government officials were not familiar with the National Response Plan (now the National Response Framework), which included an emergency support function (ESF) on recovery. The report also found a "systemic failure" (Menzel 2006, 810) of federal, state, and local governments. The bipartisan House report, titled *Failure of Initiative*, identified governmental leadership failures at all levels of government.

The political damage was significant, with elected officials either choosing not to run for office again or facing falling ratings in the polls. Years later, those in positions of authority still faced critique as other storms moved toward the Louisiana coast. The political fallout has been significant: "Politicians and administrators may pay a high price for failing to deal with the disaster adequately or simply for appearing ineffectual in the days and weeks after" (Waugh 2006, 10–11).

Although Hurricane Katrina is considered by many to be a catastrophic event that undermined regional capacities to respond, the event nonetheless became a political watershed moment in how government must respond to disasters of any size or kind. As one author wrote, "Elected officials and policy makers at all levels of government must take a broader, more comprehensive view of the problem.... Well-meaning intentions by individuals, agencies and nonprofits to rise to the occasion are not sufficient" (Menzel 2006, 812). The hurricanes of 2005, including Katrina and Rita, "raise serious questions concerning the capacities of local, state, and federal governments to deal with major hazards and disasters. Obviously, we are not prepared to deal with catastrophic events, including a terrorist attack or an avian influenza pandemic" (Waugh 2006, 11). The White House, congressional, and Governmental Accountability Office reports, coupled with evidence amassed by researchers, make it clear that "for the officials who failed to address the hazards and/or failed to respond adequately, there may be serious political costs" (Waugh 2006, 23).

Key Governmental Resources

Clearly, the challenges facing local government in a disaster are significant, and leadership is critical. A number of resources exist to support government through the crisis. Those resources include emergency management staff, creative financing, legal and accounting staff, the private sector, community recovery committees, governmental partners, and additional education and training.

Emergency Management Staff

Emergency managers work in and operate out of **emergency operations centers** (EOCs; see Photo 11.2). The EOC serves as the "central hub for coordinating disaster response. Key activities within EOCs include coordination of tasks, policy making, operations, information, dispersal of public information, and hosting visitors" (Neal 2003, 35; 2005). EOCs must be close to local government operations in order to facilitate key activities, but they must also remain free from risks due to area hazards. Historically, emergency management staff and EOCs have been underused in recovery capacities. In this section, we examine their value starting with ensuring that the facilities will be available after the disaster.

In Smith County, Texas, officials decided to build a "first-responder facility" for use by 9-1-1 communications and emergency managers that would withstand local hazards (FEMA 2003). Local government built a 15,000-square-foot building with "a roof and exterior walls hardened to resist tornadic forces, a lobby designed to minimize blast effects, multiple security

PHOTO 11.2 The Harrison County Emergency Operations Center in Gulfport, Mississippi, operated during Hurricane Katrina. (Photo by Mark Wolfe/FEMA News Photo.)

access levels" and places for officials and the media (FEMA 2003, 3). Exterior walls could withstand a three-second gust of wind at a speed of 250 miles per hour and a lumber projectile 2′ × 4′ traveling at 100 miles per hour. Local codes require buildings to be able to withstand a three-second burst at 90 miles per hour; therefore, the EOC represents a considerable upgrade in survivability. The roof used a steel-truss system that can withstand "uplift pressures of 360 pounds per square foot" (FEMA 2003, 12). Doors and windows are bulletproof. Smith County's efforts demonstrate a key feature necessary for an EOC and sustained response and recovery efforts: survivability.

FEMA recommends six key features for EOCs:

1. *Facility features*: How should the EOC be laid out? How should the space be arranged to facilitate communications and key activities?
2. *Survivability*: Can the EOC withstand the local hazard?
3. *Security*: Are personnel and equipment protected from natural, technological, and terrorist hazards?
4. *Sustainability*: Can the EOC continue despite power interruptions and other utility failures?
5. *Interoperability*: How well does the EOC communicate and work with local, state, and federal partners; equipment and communications resources; and policies and procedures?
6. *Flexibility*: Can the EOC respond to a range of events from small to catastrophic?

The EOC "represents the location where key officials assemble to gather information and make decisions regarding the disaster response" (Neal 2003, 36). Internal design must thus consider seating in order to facilitate communications in an area free from congestion and noise. Separate rooms are often provided for general office work, critical communications, and operational activities. The operations room, one of several key spaces within an EOC, is usually where officials coordinate with emergency managers. This space may be in the area where the key functions are taking place or, ideally, be adjacent to the area but free from what can be a noisy environment. EOCs may also have sleeping and shower facilities, kitchen units, and water and power/generator sources (Neal 2005). Exterior areas usually provide parking for emergency vehicles of various kinds. Additional office areas may allow for other staff or to expand the number of organizations and agencies necessary to help with relief and recovery efforts. Jurisdictions with resources may be able to provide televised coverage of the events underway, radio rooms, radar imagery, computer stations, and other critical resources. A number of organizations and agencies may participate, including the American Red Cross, amateur radio, Salvation Army, police, fire, emergency medical services, public health, public works and sanitation, and others tasked with specific areas under an emergency operations plan.

It is critical that the EOC survives the disaster so that it can provide resources during response and a place to convene meetings and provide personnel throughout the recovery. The EOC is where key decisions are made that influence recovery. Government leaders must be present during those decisions and must continue to involve emergency managers in the recovery effort.

Emergency management staff members are historically underused during long-term recovery. Quite often, recovery falls on the shoulders of local governmental leaders and long-term recovery committees, while emergency management turns back to emergency preparedness and response matters. This is unfortunate, because emergency management professionals understand how important it is to link recovery to mitigation, work with the public, and manage local risks. Their expertise and insights are required in both short- and long-term recovery to build disaster resistance to future events. Too often, recoveries become politicized and spurn the contributions of emergency managers.

To foster a truly resilient recovery requires the integral participation of emergency management staff. Because they may bear multiple burdens at this point in managing overlapping life cycles and hazardous events, they should be provided with sufficient support staff. This may require hiring additional people, establishing memoranda of understanding with other jurisdictions, or redirecting staff to provide assistance. The recovery time period is not the time to learn a new game without the best players in town.

Financing Recovery

Santa Cruz city manager Richard Wilson observed (1991, 49), "Your earliest recovery concern will be to maintain the best possible financial position for your organization." Santa Cruz lost 10% of the city's sales tax in the downtown area. It enacted a half-cent sales tax that went for six years to generate $15 million, but it barely passed 52% to 48%. All of it was to be allocated to fund recovery, and it would still be $5 million less than what was needed. Disasters also have the potential to undermine the tax base, a problem that happened in Baytown, Texas, during the 1980s, when floods destroyed taxable properties (Settle 1985). Destruction of the tax base leads to loss of governmental income needed for recovery.

The financing process for recovery can begin far in advance if public officials choose to plan for long-term recovery. For most recoveries, a wide array of financing mechanisms will be tapped (see Table 11.1). In some states, a **rainy-day fund** or catastrophe fund sets aside money to be used in the event of a disaster (Kunreuther and Linnerooth-Bayer 2003). Governments that fail to assess possible losses, design mitigation measures, and set aside funds may find themselves in trouble. By transferring rainy day or contingency funds (recommended as 3%–7% of the city budget) to response and recovery needs, the jurisdiction may be able to rebound better (Settle 1985).

Insurance may also provide a financial buffer against losses and help jump-start rebuilding. Local communities may seek a sales tax increase or design a **capital campaign** to raise money for specific projects. A capital campaign typically designates specific projects for potential funding and then places the item on the ballot for voter approval. The campaign is then usually funded by an increase in taxes or special fees. Fees can be placed on items like gasoline, car rentals, hotels, vehicle registration fees, or other reliable sources of revenue (Settle 1985). Another option may be municipal bonds, which usually require voter approval. Bonds were used in Phoenix, Arizona, in 1979 to finance $353 million in flood control and other city issues (Settle 1985). As described in Chapter 8, the Main Street program may be an option for funding (see Photo 11.3).

For most communities, though, financing recovery occurs during the postdisaster time period. The process begins with conducting damage assessments to estimate losses. Damage assessments are then routed through the governor's office and on to FEMA and the desk of the president. Should conditions warrant, the president can authorize spending for a variety of projects. Funds for emergency measures, loans and grants for households, loans for businesses, and funds for public facilities and infrastructure may be released. Specific programs, such as the Public Assistance (PA) program, are described more fully in Chapter 15. A brief example of FEMA's PA program can be viewed in Box 11.2. However, public officials should never

TABLE 11.1   Financing Recovery

Mechanism	Advantages and Disadvantages
Rainy-day fund	Sets aside funds for future events; likely to experience pressure for use in a wide variety of events
Insurance	May provide immediate funds; may not cover all hazards
FEMA public assistance	Only available under a presidential disaster declaration; provides for up to 75% of the costs, with a 25% match from local and state government; funds are used to repair public facilities (see Chapter 15 for more details)
Fees and special taxes	Can be attached to recurrently purchased or used items, such as hotels, rental cars, gasoline, cigarettes, alcohol, and similar items
Municipal bonds	Used as a form of debt financing that usually needs voter approval
Sales tax	Current sales tax depends on the ability of the business sector to bounce back; new or additional sales taxes can be dedicated specifically to recovery if the increase is supported by taxpayers
Capital-improvement campaign	May take time to design, approve, and implement; if connected to preexisting campaign and planning, could provide expedited projects and funds
Grants	Grant proposal must be written, and funded projects must be consistent with what the agency or foundation is willing or able to fund (see Chapter 15 for grant-writing guidance); Hazard Mitigation Grants and Community Development Block Grants are two common postdisaster recovery grants; urban-renewal funds may represent another option
Donations	May include cash or in-kind donations; must include accountability for donor intent; can provide flexible means to support unique or unmet needs (see Chapter 12 for more details)

assume that a declaration is automatic or that FEMA will release all forms of funding possible (Setttle 1985).

Local government may also need to apply for grants from federal agencies and private foundations. Typically, the federal government directs a local government toward funds that may be available. It is up to the local government to apply for these grants. Usually, granting agencies and foundations have specific parameters under which the grants may be secured and used. Consequently, while communities are still struggling to get basics back to normal, a grant-writing team will have to be established to pursue aggressively any funds that may be available. If the disaster affects a large regional area, jurisdictions may compete with each other for funds or may need to develop joint applications. Additional guidance on writing grants can be found in Chapter 15.

PHOTO 11.3 Community residents from Waveland, Mississippi, meet to discuss a downtown revitalization project under the Hancock County Main Street Program. (Photo by Jennifer Smits/FEMA News Photo.)

BOX 11.2 FUNDING RECOVERY

In 2005, Hurricane Katrina seriously impaired facilities of the New Orleans Police Department (NOPD). Police headquarters was flooded. Seven of eight police stations sustained roof and flooding damage. By the third anniversary of the storm, one continued to operate in an undamaged facility, one was in a FEMA trailer, two were in temporary locations, and four were operating in damaged facilities. One crime lab was flooded, as well as the Special Operations Department, the NOPD Training Academy, the Mounted and Canine Facility, and the Central Evidence and Property Department. The latter two remained in FEMA trailers at the three-year mark while others had relocated to temporary locations.

To aid in the recovery of the New Orleans police system, a number of partners worked cooperatively. First, FEMA reimbursed overtime to the NOPD and replaced damaged equipment, vehicles, computers, and other crucially needed resources. The crime lab was moved to a temporary location at the University of New Orleans through assistance from FEMA and the attorney general's office. The Youth Study Center will be replaced eventually, as the replacement was determined to cost less than repairs. FEMA obligated at least $273 million to help the criminal justice system recover through its Public Assistance Program. Still, the recovery of the local justice system has taken far longer than hoped. Local police remain working in temporary locations, including FEMA trailers. Crime, particularly homicides, is up. Hurricane Katrina and the levee failures devastated criminal justice facilities.

Source: Federal Emergency Management Agency

Donations can also help with expenses at the local levels. Most donations filter into voluntary and faith-based organizations to help needy clients. However, donations can also be used to establish joint programs that fit local need. For example, after the Loma Prieta earthquake, the City of Watsonville established programs using grants and donations to support residential reconstruction.

Legal and Accounting Staff

Just as the emergency management office represents the best recovery expertise, the legal and accounting staff members contribute knowledge to the recovery process as well. Although rebuilding may seem like a bricks-and-mortar type of activity, recovery activities must be handled legally and financed with accountability. As described in Chapter 4, for example, legal staff must develop and manage contracts for debris management. The different kinds of contracts require expertise and monitoring. Further, as the recovery proceeds, the legal staff may need to initiate proceedings that allow city staff onto private property. Or, demolitions may be necessary. Legal staff must be consulted in order to follow proper legal requirements for doing so. As the city passes new ordinances for how the rebuilding is to commence, legal opinion needs to ensure that the proceeding is indeed under the authority of the local government and does not overstep boundaries, set inappropriate precedents, or hinder what is intended. Legal counsel will also be helpful with interpreting the many regulations now impinging on funds and proceedings, including those from the Environmental Protection Agency, FEMA, the Department of Housing and Urban Development, and other key partners.

In many disasters, the accounting staff represents the single most valuable office. In order to qualify for federal assistance and the 75%/25% match available through FEMA's Public Assistance programs (see Chapter 15), accounting staff must help document expenditures, manage grants, handle financial donations, and disperse funds appropriately. Careful records must be kept for some time, which is a task that also falls on the accounting staff. As experienced by the New Orleans Health Department after Hurricane Katrina, "filing for reimbursement for certain losses through FEMA is extensive and has tested the city's ability to work together with other levels of government on fiscal matters" (Stephens 2007, 224). Consequently, in preparing a recovery plan, it is also necessary to include the accounting staff in any planning, training, and exercising. The accounting staff helps keep the recovery moving along financially and safeguards local interests by ensuring compliance with federal regulations.

The Private Sector

Local government must support the private sector during the recovery period for several reasons. First, businesses generate tax revenues that continue to fund local government. Reestablishing those businesses helps sustain governmental abilities to pay staff, fund programs, and deal with the costs of not only routine, but disaster-related expenses. The private sector can also generate substantial support for local recovery.

Many large industries and corporations have well-established foundations that provide grants to worthy causes. Businesses donate generously in times of disaster as well. After the 2008 Midwest floods, for example, John Deere donated $1 million to the American Red Cross. Employers also offer matching programs when employees make donations. In addition to cash, the private sector may also donate in-kind donations. After Hurricane Andrew, American beer companies shut down beer production and sent canned water to Florida survivors. Fast-food companies routinely donate pizza, tacos, burgers, and sandwiches to shelters, meetings, first responders, and emergency operating centers. The private sector can thus represent a potential source of financial support.

As seen in Box 11.3, the federal government provided an additional tax benefit to the private sector after Hurricane Katrina. By donating leave and medical time, businesses converted time into cash and sent funds to worthy causes. Businesses may also decide to lend staff to good causes. After Hurricane Katrina, many local governments, agencies, universities, and businesses allowed employees to go to the Gulf Coast. Their volunteer efforts provided police and fire resources, counseling, health care, debris removal, utility restoration, and more.

Building strong partnerships between the private sector and local government prior to disaster can help build a more disaster-resilient recovery effort. By including the private sector, the recovery effort will be more robust. Through linking private-sector recovery to other areas such as housing, environmental quality, and infrastructure, a more holistic recovery can result. Including the private sector in recovery efforts helps to maintain these critical employers, the taxes they generate, and the employees who live in the affected area.

BOX 11.3 DONATING LEAVE TO DISASTER CHARITIES

"The IRS is encouraging employers to establish Hurricane Katrina Relief leave donation programs and is providing special tax treatment to support such programs. Under a leave donation program, employees can elect to forgo their vacation, sick or personal leave in exchange for the employer making cash payments to a qualified tax-exempt organization providing relief for victims of Hurricane Katrina" (IRS. 2005. Hurricane Katrina relief leave donation program. IR-2005-113. http://www.irs.gov/newsroom/article/0,,id=148114,00.html).

Scott Mezistrano, senior manager for government relations, American Payroll Association: "The American Payroll Association applauds IRS'[s] reinstating the tax-preferred treatment for workers who donate their accrued leave for their employers to pass on to organizations helping victims of Hurricane Katrina. This encourages employee donations because everyone gets an immediate break on their income, social security, and Medicare taxes. It doesn't matter whether or not the worker itemizes deductions on the personal income tax return because the donated leave is never added to the W-2. Many employers of APA members are implementing leave donation plans. Most importantly, this will support immediate assistance to the hurricane victims" (IRS. 2005. Partners spread the word on leave-donation program. IR-2005-113. http://www.irs.gov/irs/article/0,,id=149191,00.html).

Long-Term Recovery Committees

As described in several chapters (especially Chapter 14), the long-term recovery committee (LTRC), or its equivalent, may serve as a crucial resource. The LTRC may take several forms. Government leaders and officials may convene formal groups to conduct recovery planning. FEMA may provide funds to hire a consultant to lead the local community through the process. Or, the LTRC may arise out of local social, civic, and faith-based service organizations. Regardless of the form, the LTRC brings that critical mass of social capital directly to bear on recovery matters. Connecting with, resourcing, and relying on the LTRC can benefit local government.

In Santa Cruz, California, several types of recovery organizations and efforts emerged. Congressional Representative Leon Panetta convened Saturday meetings where local, state, and federal officials could meet and work through problems. Vision Santa Cruz targeted the downtown but enjoyed membership across the community. A broader recovery group tackled specific issues. The Housing Recovery Task Force, for example, eventually spun off into short- and long-term housing committees. Housing efforts were led by city staff supported by local social workers and elected officials. In Santa Cruz, a broadly based community pulled together, made the commitment to recovery, and leveraged both governmental and volunteer resources.

Recovery committees may also convene solely for the purposes of planning, as described in Chapter 3. Activities might include establishing a vision for sectors to be rebuilt and a set of principles that guide reconstruction. Specific sectors are then usually addressed separately, including housing, transportation, utilities, environmental issues, historic preservation, and the business sector. The purpose of this type of recovery committee is specifically to lay out the strategy for rebuilding. Subcommittees may spin off to accomplish projects, or the committee may pass its plan along to a new group for implementation.

Local government can play a role in identifying potential leaders, convening an initial planning group (see Chapter 3 for a list of suggested members), and developing a strategy for involving and informing the public. Governmental leaders and city staff must work closely with such a group to ensure consistency with existing or newly revised plans, codes, and ordinances. Government may also provide locations for meetings, resources for communicating with the broader community, and staff to support committee tasks such as mapping, research, funding, engineering consultation, and other necessary skills and expertise.

Recovery committees nearly always include a wide representation from the social service, civic organization, and faith-based sectors. These linking organizations connect local government to additional resources, including funds, volunteers, and the affected population. As described further in Chapter 14, recovery is usually not possible for all members of the community without the support of these organizations. For single parents, people with disabilities, and low-income households, recovery may simply not take place. Involving these partners is thus a crucial component of any recovery initiative launched by local government.

Governmental Partners

In 1993, the U.S. Congress required the National Academy of Public Administration to examine governmental capacity to respond to disasters. The request occurred in the aftermath of Hurricane Andrew and recommended major changes. In particular, the report indicates that "state and local governments must be able not only to effectively manage small and medium disasters on their own but also to function effectively as part of an intergovernmental team when an event warrants a presidential disaster declaration and federal intervention" (NAPA 1993, 81). However, as noted earlier in this chapter, the report also indicated that local government finds the federal emergency management process confusing and in continual flux. Further, the report noted that local "emergency management organizations and officials generally are at the mercy of the state and federal government for much of their budgets, planning and reporting requirements, and staffing determinations" and often feel they receive mixed messages about preparedness, planning, response, and recovery.

State capacity, and local jurisdictions as well, "differ markedly in their capacity to respond to disasters and to work in partnership with federal agencies" (NAPA 1993, 81). In turn, the federal government finds it difficult to ascertain which areas require considerable assistance and which can stand on their own. When federal assistance does arrive, it may be critiqued as not being locally sensitive or contextually appropriate. Thus, from both the local and federal perspectives, there are intergovernmental problems and issues that require greater coordination and communication.

Nonetheless, government bears the responsibility to serve as a liaison between the citizens and the collective resources available at local, state, and federal levels. Local government in particular must liaise with state and federal partners as a means to facilitate damage assessment; planning; repairs to public facilities, infrastructure, and utilities; and economic well-being. Throughout the 1990s and to the present day, a number of initiatives took place designed to build that relationship. The Emergency Management Institute (EMI), the training arm of FEMA, designed and offered dozens of courses to local and state officials. For example, course E210 brings elected officials and staff into EMI for a 4.5-day recovery training experience.

The bipartisan congressional committee report on Hurricane Katrina titled "A Failure of Initiative" indicated that efforts between many governmental levels failed (see link in Resources section). In particular, the report claimed that there was no "unified strategy" between governmental levels to communicate with the public. A total breakdown in communications occurred. The committee also indicated that local and state officials failed to maintain order. Although the report concurred that everyone tried, efforts failed collectively, particularly between levels of government.

It is incumbent upon governmental officials, as part of their public responsibility, to secure appropriate education and training. Local officials must become knowledgeable about disasters, state and federal policies, and leadership in disaster situations. Local officials will be tasked with working in concert with state and federal partners who can provide considerable levels of support throughout the recovery, from physical resources to extensive financing.

Education and Training

To offer the most effective recovery possible for damaged communities, it is essential that public officials, city staff, and recovery leaders (including emergency managers) rely on sound information and guidance. Disaster recovery is often a rapid-learning-curve experience, with too much information thrown at those who must lead recovery. The postdisaster recovery time is not the best time to learn "on the job." Consequently, congratulations to those of you reading this text in an effort to avoid such a situation. Additional sources of insight, education, and training can be found in a variety of places:

- Numerous universities and colleges now offer graduate and undergraduate programs including degrees, certificates, and minors in emergency management. The strongest programs typically organize around or include the life cycle of emergency management, including courses on recovery. The best programs provide faculty with research backgrounds and practical expertise on specific subjects. Public officials may choose to send staff to these programs to either acquire college credit or to audit the recovery course. FEMA's Higher Education Project provides links to a wide set of programs available across the nation. Information is available at http://www.training.fema.gov/EMIweb/edu/collegelist/.

- FEMA also provides residence courses at its Emergency Management Institute in Emmittsburg, Maryland. Courses on recovery, leadership, and other topics can be taken on the EMI campus. Information is available at http://training.fema.gov/EMICourses/.

- FEMA's Independent Study courses may offer the most convenient source of immediate information. Topics include volunteer organizations, public assistance, debris management, and more. Courses are free, and most can be downloaded at http://training.fema.gov/IS/crslist.asp.

- Professional organizations routinely offer conferences and training sessions. Organizations such as the International Association of Emergency Managers, the National Hurricane Conference, and others can be sources of information, networking, and support for public officials and emergency management staff. By paying the dues and conference fees for city staff to attend these events, local government can build capacity among its emergency and nonemergency staff.

- A wide number of professional journals contain useful articles and should be consulted, as they offer objective, scientific recommendations regarding emergency management and disaster recovery. Several are available free online, including the *International Journal of Mass Emergencies and Disasters* and the *Australian Journal of Emergency Management* (both include authors from many nations) or through subscription fees such as *Natural Hazards Review, Environmental Hazards, Risk Analysis, Disaster Prevention* and *Management, Disasters, Natural Hazards,* and the *Journal of Emergency Management.*

Summary

Government bears the responsibility to coordinate and move recovery forward. By using a creative, flexible, problem-solving approach to recovery, governmental leaders can more readily identify and address recovery challenges. Anticipated challenges will include the impact on city staff, financing, a push for a return to normal, and massive needs across the economic, social, and infrastructural sectors of the community. During crisis, citizens will expect government to provide leadership and solutions. The political will to respond must be generated and sustained through what can become a tedious and difficult recovery. Failure to do so will result in recoveries that languish and political fallout for the careers of both elected and employed officials.

Government can also mitigate future risks by rebuilding smart. Initial efforts that government must commence include reconsideration of building codes to enhance survivability, financing from a wide range of partners, recovery planning, and working closely with the public. Historically, emergency management staff have not been sufficiently used during recovery, yet they represent crucial human resources able to inform and assist elected and appointed officials and city staff. Governmental leaders must ensure the survivability of emergency management agencies and integrate the staff into recovery efforts. Other personnel will prove crucial as well, including legal and accounting staff. Government officials must ensure that they are well-trained and informed about disaster-recovery processes in order to provide effective leadership. Additional chapters in this text are recommended for information on the governmental role in recovery planning (Chapter 3), financing projects (Chapter 15), and community involvement (Chapters 13 and 14).

Study Guide

Summary Questions

1. What are the implications of the emergent-norm perspective for recovery planning?
2. Describe key governmental roles that must be taken to support the public and governmental functioning after a disaster.
3. What is the role of the EOC and emergency management staff after a disaster? How might these resources be used during the long-term recovery period?

4. How might a disaster affect various staff offices within local government? What can local government do to prepare for the impact of a long-term recovery effort on governmental employees?
5. What kinds of financing can be identified for recovery?
6. What do governmental leaders need to know about recovery? Where can they obtain that information?

Discussion Questions

1. Discuss the pros and cons of a bureaucratic versus an emergent-norm approach. (You may also want to review Chapter 2.)
2. What kind of EOC is there in your community? Can you arrange to visit and tour the facility? What kinds of rooms, resources, and staffing does it have?
3. Which locations do you believe could benefit from "hardening" of the facilities in your community: police, fire, ambulances, or other first responder locations? How about the local EOC? Should such mitigation efforts extend further into the community? For example, should local government strengthen codes to ensure that nursing homes can withstand local hazards? Should schools in tornado areas have safe rooms? How might a local government fund such an activity?
4. Search your local government Web site. What can you find about emergency management? Is there anything available on long-term recovery plans?
5. Has your community ever gone through a disaster recovery? How about a community in your state? Research the event and identify the key actions taken by public officials. What actions seemed to move the recovery forward?
6. Browse through the list of FEMA's independent-study courses (free of charge for U.S. citizens). What would be your first choice? Consider the Professional Development Series as a good starting point. A link can be found in the Resources section.

Key Terms

Bureaucratic authority
Capital campaign
Charismatic authority
Emergency operations center (EOC)
Emergent-norm theory
Emergent Human Resources Model (EHRM)
Leadership
Legal-rational authority

Political will
Rainy-day fund

References

Burby, R. J. 2006. Hurricane Katrina and the paradoxes of government disaster policy: Bringing about wise governmental decisions for hazardous areas. *The ANNALS of the American Academy of Political and Social Science* 604: 171–191.

Dynes, R. R. 1993. Disaster reduction: The importance of adequate assumptions about social organization. *Sociological Spectrum* 6: 24–25.

Dynes, R. R., and E. L. Quarantelli. 1968. Group behavior under stress: A required convergence of organizational and collective behavior perspectives. *Sociology and Social Research* 52: 416–429.

Edwards, F. L., and D. C. Goodrich. 2007. Organizing for emergency management. In *Emergency management: Principles and practice for local government*, ed. W. L. Waugh and K. Tierney. Washington, DC: International City/County Management Association.

FEMA. 2003. Hardened first responder facility. Washington, DC: Federal Emergency Management Agency.

Gillingham, D., and J. Noizet. 2007. A response model for the public relations management of a critical incident. *Disaster Prevention and Management* 16 (4): 545–550.

Kunreuther, H. C., and J. Linnerooth-Bayer. 2003. The financial management of catastrophic flood risks in emerging-economy countries. *Risk Analysis* 23 (3): 627–639.

Menzel, D. C. 2006. The Katrina aftermath: A failure of federalism or leadership? *Public Administration Review* 66 (6): 808–812.

NAPA. 1993. Coping with catastrophe: Building an emergency management system to meet people's needs in natural and man-made disasters. Washington, DC: National Academy of Public Administration.

Natural Hazards Center. 2005. *Holistic disaster recovery*. Boulder, CO: Natural Hazards Center and Public Entity Risk Institute.

Neal, D. M. 2003. Design characteristics of emergency operating centers. *Journal of Emergency Management* 1 (2): 35–38.

———. 2005. Four case studies of emergency operations centers. *Journal of Emergency Management* 3 (1): 29–32.

Neal, D. M., and B. D. Phillips. 1995. Effective emergency management: Reconsidering the bureaucratic approach. *Disasters: The Journal of Disaster Studies and Management* 19 (4): 327–337.

Neal, D. M., and G. Webb. 2006. Structural barriers to implementing the National Incident Management System. In *Learning from Catastrophe: Quick Response Research in the Wake of Hurricane Katrina*, ed. C. Bvec. 263–284. Boulder: University of Colorado.

Perrin, M. A., L. DiGrande, K. Wheeler, L. Thorpe, M. Farfel, and R. Brackbill. 2007. Differences in PTSD prevalence and associated risk factors among World Trade Center disaster rescue and recovery workers. *The American Journal of Psychiatry* 164 (9): 1385–1394.

Schwab, J., K. C. Topping, C. C. Eadie, R. E. Deyle, and R. A. Smith. 1998. *Planning for post-disaster recovery and reconstruction*. Chicago: American Planning Association.

Settle, A. K. 1985. Financing disaster mitigation, preparedness, response, and recovery. *Public Administration Review* 45: 101–106.

Stephens, K. U. 2007. Staying financially afloat in the wake of a public health crisis. *Journal of Public Health Management Practice* 13 (2): 223–224.

Sylves, R. T. 2006. President Bush and Hurricane Katrina: A presidential leadership study. *The ANNALS of the American Academy of Political and Social Science* 604 (26): 26–56.

Tierney, K. J., M. K. Lindell, and R. W. Perry. 2001. *Facing the unexpected*. Washington, DC: Joseph Henry Press.

Waugh, W. L. 2000. *Living with hazards dealing with disasters*. Armonk, NY: M.E. Sharpe.

———. 2006. The political costs of failure in the Katrina and Rita disasters. *The Annals of the American Academy of Political and Social Science* 604 (10): 10–25.

Wilson, R. C. 1991. *The Loma Prieta quake: What one city learned*. Washington DC: International City Management Association.

Witt, J. L., and J. Morgan. 2002. *Stronger in the broken places: Nine lessons for turning crisis into triumph*. New York: Times Books.

Wolensky, R. P., and K. C. Wolensky. 1990. Local government's problem with disaster management. *Policy Studies Review* 9 (4): 703–725.

Resources

- Australian Emergency Management is currently at http://www.ema.gov.au/agd/ema/emainternet.nsf/Page/Communities_Natural_Disasters_Australian_Government_Role_in_National_Natural_Disasters. Accessed August 4, 2008.
- EOC Assessment help can be obtained at http://www.fema.gov/library, search for EOC Assessment Checklist. Accessed August 29, 2008.
- FEMA acronyms related to the field of emergency management and federal assistance can currently be found at http://www.fema.gov/plan/prepare/faat.shtm. Accessed August 4, 2008.
- FEMA Independent Study courses are available through Internet downloads or CD-ROMs. A long list of such courses can currently be viewed at http://training.fema.gov/IS/crslist.asp.
  - A recommended course is IS-240, Leadership and Influence available at http://training.fema.gov/EMIWeb/downloads/is240.pdf. Accessed August 12,2008.
  - The Incident Command System can be learned through IS-100, available at http://training.fema.gov/EMIWeb/IS/IS100A.asp. Accessed August 12, 2008.
- FEMA's Emergency Management Institute (EMI) offers on-campus courses for local government. Lists and schedules for EMI courses can currently be found at http://training.fema.gov/EMICourses/EMICourse.asp. Accessed August 4, 2008. Course E210 Recovery from Disaster: The Local Government Role is one such course. E581

Emergency Management Operations for Tribal Governments is also available.

- FEMA's web page for governmental resources related to recovery can currently be found at http://www.fema.gov/government/recovery.shtm. Accessed August 4, 2008.
- International City/County Management Association has resources for governmental authorities handling various dimensions of disaster response and recovery. Their website can be found at http://www.icma.org. Accessed August 4, 2008.
- National Response Framework information is currently found at http://www.dhs.gov/xgovt/. Accessed August 4, 2008.
- New Zealand Ministry of Civil Defence and Emergency Management can currently be viewed at http://www.civildefence.govt.nz/mem-website.nsf. Accessed September 17, 2008.
- U.S. Congressional report on Hurricane Katrina can be found at http://katrina.house.gov/. Accessed September 1, 2008.

Section III

Recovery Resources

Chapter **12**

Donations

Learning Objectives

After reading this chapter, you should be able to:

- Explain why donations can be a "second disaster" due to unexpected forms of convergence
- Understand the importance of public education surrounding appropriate disaster donations
- Identify the benefits and challenges associated with disaster donations
- Understand, honor, and work with the reasons why people donate money and items in disaster situations
- List which donations are best in particular situations
- Outline key parts of a donations management strategy
- Explain basic principles for working with donors, donations, and partnering organizations
- Outline strategies for effective management and distribution of donations
- Link donations management to the longer recovery period, when donations are most needed
- Appreciate the importance and value of financial accountability for donations

Introduction

Our hearts go out to those affected by disasters. As we watch the television, grateful that it is not our home or neighborhood, we can see that people have lost everything to the tornado, flood, hurricane, or earthquake. Surely they need our help—and our American values lean us toward doing all that we can for those impacted by the unexpected. We dig deeply into our closets, cupboards, garages, and even our bank accounts, and we send whatever we have. We roll up our sleeves and donate blood. We join in with others and fill grocery bags to the brim, drop off canned goods at radio and television drives, and send truckloads of goods to the impacted area.

In this chapter we will learn that Americans have generous hearts—sometimes too generous. As this chapter reveals, **unsolicited donations**—much like the problem of spontaneous volunteers reported in Chapter 13—can result in significant problems. We will learn what to donate, when we should send it, and how to manage such **donations**. Ultimately, this chapter is about donating the right thing at the right time for the right reasons so that the generosity seen so frequently in disasters results in the intended outcomes: helping those in need. First, we will look at two situations where donations required creative management. The first scenario comes from Bridge Creek, Oklahoma, where teachers and volunteers organized a **distribution center** after an F5 tornado. Our second scenario centers on September 11, a unique situation in which the donations you might expect to send were not needed and where massive amounts of funds went into creative programs for long-term recovery efforts.

The Bridge Creek SuperCenter

In Oklahoma, the date May 3 (1999) immediately brings images of widespread devastation to mind. Massive supercell tornados sent highly destructive F5 and F4 tornados across the state in multiple paths, resulting in the largest single-day outbreak in the state's history (NOAA 1999). Forty people died and 675 sustained injuries. Well over 2,000 homes and apartments were destroyed, with 7,000+ damaged by winds that exceeded 318 mph. Bridge Creek is located in an unincorporated area of Grady County, southwest of Oklahoma City. This rural community includes agricultural production, home-based businesses, and small towns. Residents also drive into Oklahoma City and the metro area for work. Thirty-five percent of the residents lived below the poverty level at the time of the tornado, with 35% of the school children eating at school through the free or reduced-cost lunch program. Presumably, the extensive damage would require an outpouring of assistance.

PHOTO 12.1   Stacks of baby clothing await use at a Hurricane Katrina shelter. (Photo by Andrea Booher/FEMA News Photo.)

And in it came: shoes, canned goods, bedding, toys, school supplies, furniture, and more (for an example, see Photo 12.1). Within a few days, the donations had increased so much that the unincorporated community faced a challenge of where to store, organize, and distribute donated items. Bridge Creek is fortunate, though, in having a strong school system with effective faculty and administrative leaders, along with a willing faith-based sector able to step up and spontaneously handle the situation.

Bridge Creek's middle school gym had initially been used as a place for triage and first aid as injured persons awaited transportation to medical facilities. Two days after the tornado outbreak, though, donations had begun to arrive. By May 8, the gymnasium and adjacent rooms overflowed. Sixteen semitrailer trucks of donated goods were parked outside awaiting handling. Secretarial and teaching staff organized the gym into a donations distribution center, dubbing it the Bridge Creek "SuperCenter." A nearby store provided shopping carts. Those affected by the storm arrived to shop in a gym abundantly filled with shoes, clothes, toys, food, and more. A nearby church assisted with additional storage, organizing, and distribution throughout the area.

September 11

In contrast to other disasters, September 11 represents a departure from what the public thought would be needed. Volunteers turned out en masse, as described in Chapter 13, but organizations working the disaster often could not use them—the same problem occurred with donated goods. Think about it. At the Pentagon near Washington, DC, in New York City, and in Shanksville, Pennsylvania, where United Airlines Flight 93 crashed, the needs of those affected were different.

Blood drives began all over the nation, but blood supplies were fairly quickly overrun. The situation in each location meant that people died or survived with traumatic injuries, typically with burns. The need for blood was minimal, as was the need for medical personnel rushing to the scene or to hospitals to help care for the injured. In most medical facilities, existing staff and disaster plans handled those who arrived. Yet, massive donations inundated those at the disaster sites, prompting those who had to manage the unexpected items term them as "rebel food and renegade supplies" (Kendra and Wachtendorf 2002). In the aftermath of a terrorist attack, some wondered if the food might contain biological agents or other contaminants (Kendra and Wachtendorf 2002).

Long-term recovery needs demanded something other than used clothing and canned goods. September 11 represented a psychic injury, an attack on the feelings of safety that we all assumed prior to the attack. The event was also a collective trauma for the public, especially for the families who lost loved ones or who struggled to survive with serious injuries. Consequently, the single most valuable donation after September 11 would prove to be the one resource most commonly needed in all disasters: financial contributions.

Within a few months after the attack, nearly $2 billion had been donated, a massive amount not previously seen in other disasters (Steinberg and Rooney 2005). The Center on Philanthropy at Indiana University conducted a survey of giving, finding that 74.4% of a representative sample of Americans donated money, food, clothing, blood, or volunteer hours, a percentage confirmed by a Wirthlin Worldwide poll (Independent Sector 2001). Wirthlin Worldwide discovered that 58% of the representative sample they surveyed gave money, 13% gave blood donations, and 11% volunteered. According to Steinberg and Rooney (2005, 18), the average household donated $133.72 and 17 hours of volunteer time.

Many organizations set up programs to distribute funds received for survivors and the families of those affected. What would you do with a billion dollars, especially if you knew that psychological needs for bereavement, physical rehabilitation, and loss of a family income would cause problems perhaps for many years to come? The American Red Cross (ARC) established the Liberty Disaster Relief Fund to help survivors and the families of those affected. Using approximately $1.1 billion in donated funds, interest income, materials, and services, the Red Cross had offered a wide range of programs and support by June 30, 2006 (ARC 2006). In addition to the

14 million meals and snacks, shelters, service delivery sites, mental-health contacts, and other services provided immediately afterward, the American Red Cross organized recovery efforts to deliver a wide variety of services. As you read through the list below, think about the ways in which this disaster illuminates a wide range of needs that are not covered by unsolicited donations such as used clothing or canned goods:

- Funeral services as well as memorial urns with ashes taken from Ground Zero for families who never recovered the remains of their loved ones
- Financial assistance for surgeries, including limb amputations, skin transplants, physical and occupational therapy, and pain medication
- Assistance to cleanup workers and families who experienced mental and physical health problems from working at the sites of the attacks (see related material in Chapter 4, Debris Management, which alludes to the World Trade Center "cough")
- Support for families to relocate either temporarily or permanently when their homes were damaged or destroyed from debris, lack of access, or structural failures
- Financial and mental-health assistance for those who lost jobs, from stockbrokers to janitors
- Case-management services to 6,780 families and individuals, including clinical case management for health services to many injured persons
- Assistance to 1,983 families and individuals to attend memorial services
- Family group-therapy services in multiple languages and facilitated by professional therapists
- A client assistance center that offered information, referrals, and problem solving
- Payment for cleaning up the contaminated homes, including distribution of air purifiers and special vacuums—many of which were delivered directly to seniors and those with disabilities
- Programs—through the Red Cross and other nonprofits that received recovery grants—in multiple languages: English, Spanish, Korean, Chinese, Vietnamese, and the many other languages spoken in New York City alone (list generated from ARC 2006)

Understanding Why People Donate in Disaster Situations

Clearly, people are generous in times of disaster. They contribute time, money, and items from their personal households, hoping to make a difference. Why do people donate after a disaster? This section examines the varying reasons for why such massive efforts and amounts appear in the aftermath of disaster.

Motivations for Giving

Why do people give money, food, clothing, their time, and more in disasters? Dr. Russell Dynes (1994), cofounder of the Disaster Research Center at the University of Delaware, describes several different types of selfless or altruistic behavior. First, there is **individual altruism**, which means that people give "time, money and energy" to worthy causes. Individual altruists include the many volunteers we see doing good works within the community on a regular basis. A second kind of **collective altruism** arises from a broader social arrangement where we as a community take care of others. For example, entitlement programs provide for homeless persons, veterans, children, the elderly, and others. Most of the time we assume that individual and collective altruism provide for most people in need.

The form of altruism that concerns us in this chapter is **situational altruism**. With disasters, we seem to assume that new, unmet needs have developed—and we assume we need to fill those needs (Dynes 1994). The media play a role in this newly defined altruism by giving us images of those in need. Because the media may overplay or selectively demonstrate the need, we may get the idea that needs are massive, the area has been devastated, and people have become desperate. This selective media portrayal makes us think that we must act.

Other studies indicate that we give because it provides a feeling of solidarity with others, particularly evident after a terrorist attack. Donating may actually be a therapeutic act, subconsciously helping us to restore a collective sense of well-being. We donate also because we feel sympathetic toward those impacted by the unexpected, those innocent victims of unusual weather events, hazardous-materials spills, or assaults from outside. Donating also provides that "warm glow" that makes us feel that we have made a difference in the lives of others, reinforcing our sense of connection to a larger community. When disaster strikes, we donate because we feel it gives us a little more control over events otherwise outside our control. Interestingly, we may also donate because of social pressure or guilt (Andreoni 1990), perhaps because we were the lucky ones who emerged unscathed.

Donor Profiles

Who gives? Only a few studies have looked at the question of who donates in a disaster context. One study found that middle- and high-income households were, understandably, more likely to give financial contributions than other homes after September 11 (Steinberg and Rooney 2005). Interestingly, those who had volunteered in the previous year and those with some college education donated more hours. People who regularly attended worship services were also more likely to volunteer at higher levels (Steinberg and Rooney 2005).

The Wirthlin Worldwide survey mentioned earlier indicates that Americans under the age of 35 were more likely than others to donate blood. African-American women were the single group most likely to have volunteered immediately after September 11 (Independent Sector 2001). Some of those volunteer activities occurred locally, such as religious services, prayer and candlelight vigils, and other community or neighborhood activities (Independent Sector 2001).

But in reality, after disasters, many people donate far too much "stuff." The generosity of individual households, well-meaning groups and organizations, local businesses and large corporations, and the media mean that too many unsolicited items—especially used clothing and canned goods (Neal 1994)—flow into a disaster area, presenting a range of challenges. This chapter will likely surprise you and change your own behavior. Ideally, you will spread the word so that we can donate appropriately and ensure that such altruism extends into the recovery period.

Challenges Associated with Donations

In this section, we examine some of the problems associated with donations. First, we look at the challenge of various forms of what is called "**convergence**," when unexpected people and "stuff" arrive on the scene (see Figure 12.1). The people part will be covered in more detail in Chapter 13 (Community Resources). Next, we will deal with the practical problems associated with convergence.

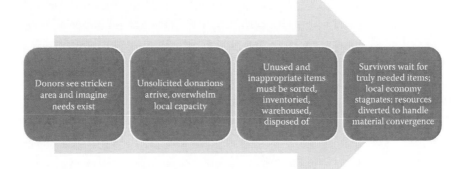

FIGURE 12.1 The problem of unsolicited donations.

Convergence

By now you will have realized that donations can help or hinder response and recovery efforts. Surprised? Many people are, but once they learn why unsolicited donations become problematic, they tend to respond well. The purpose of this section is to ensure that you become one of the many altruistic individuals who help appropriately.

The behavior associated with inappropriate donations is termed *convergence*, defined as the inflow of materials and people into a disaster site (Fritz and Mathewson 1956). It may seem counterintuitive that, when danger is present, we move toward a disaster site rather than away from it. However, the altruism and even curiosity of people overcomes the urge to stay away. Several forms of convergence may occur.

For example, **personal convergence** will occur through those arriving by foot or by vehicle (Fritz and Mathewson 1956). Such convergence may arise from those who are trying to rescue those at risk, the media, parents seeking their children, family members rushing to check on loved ones, or simply sightseers. They become the first to clog up transportation arteries and prevent needed help and supplies from arriving. After the 1982 Coalinga earthquake, for example, officials had to clear the airspace over the damaged area out of fear that media helicopters would collide and cause further problems.

A second form of convergence is called **substitute convergence**, or "messages, inquiries, offers of assistance and donations of material goods" (Fritz and Mathewson 1956, 3). Apparently, when people cannot get to the site, they seek other means for making a contribution. Two forms of substitute convergence develop. The first is **informational convergence**, which occurs when people try to offer a variety of goods and services to help the area. To summarize, the flow that you would expect to see is that people may first try to get to the area. If they cannot get there, they offer aid. Because local officials may be desperately busy with search and rescue as well as attempts to secure property and lives from further damage, they may not be able to respond to these kind offers. It seems apparent, then, that if people cannot get their offer into the area, they may just go ahead and send it anyway. This form of substitute convergence is called **material convergence**, defined as the "actual movement of supplies and equipment," also known as unofficial donations (Fritz and Mathewson 1956, 4) or unsolicited goods—referred to by voluntary organizations that handle it as "stuff" or, more frequently, as the **second disaster**.

Practical Dilemmas

Voluntary agencies and emergency management officials involved in multiple disasters report common problems with donations management. Imagine that you are the shelter manager when a truckload of iceberg lettuce or fresh orange juice arrives unannounced at midnight and you have one refrigerator for the entire shelter. Where will you put such perishable goods? Have you planned an inventory process so that you know what you have, where you put it, and when you will use it? Do you have forms prepared to accept and acknowledge the donation? Major donors such as corporations surely will want such a receipt for tax purposes.

Or, imagine that it is day two after a major hurricane. As you help to coordinate debris removal, pickup trucks loaded with unsolicited clothing and canned goods begin to arrive in the community. Well-meaning individuals, who have collected these items and driven hundreds of miles, want to know where to put the items sent by caring members of their communities. After Hurricane Andrew, daily rains dampened and mildewed piles of unused clothing that rotted in the hot, humid Florida climate. People had dropped off clothing, sometimes in the middle of the night, at tent cities, shelter locations, the local library, and even at local businesses. Within a few weeks, the smell had become so intense that the military mobilized to remove piled clothing with small bulldozers (Neal 1994). Over at the local shelters, volunteers filled up 88 Red Cross emergency response vehicles (ERVs), which can serve up to 2,000 meals at a time, with hot food cooked at a school cafeteria. If you were preparing that many meals, would you rather open industrial-sized cans of food or small, two-person serving sizes? How much time would it take? Could you be certain that food dropped off was cooked in sanitary conditions and would not cause illness?

OK, so you have a lot of perishable and canned foods and bottled water on hand now and lots of used clothing. Imagine your surprise when the clothing turns out to be inappropriate for the climate or geographic area. After the 1985 Mexico City earthquake, donations of high heels were sent to presumably needy Mexican women wading through fallen structures. After Hurricane Andrew, researchers spotted winter coats and flannel shirts (Neal 1994). What are you going to do with all the stuff? The next major challenge thus becomes sorting, organizing, inventorying, and distributing these items. Who is going to do that work? Will you need to swing volunteers away from shelters, debris clearance, case management, or other important activities to handle the trucks that keep coming in?

Next, now that materiel convergence is underway and trucks are arriving with perishable food, canned goods, used clothing, and the occasional major pieces of furniture, appliances, and boxes of household goods, where are you going to put them? Your task will be to figure out where to store items for the short term so that they can be sent out to those in need. We will talk more about this shortly. But the larger problem that arises will be where and how to store items for long-term use. People displaced by disaster may not be able to use those appliances and household items for months, perhaps years. Where are you going to put these things so that they do go to good use? What will it cost to store them in a warehouse, storage center, or other location? Will they be exposed to weather, heat and humidity, or insects and rodents? And, how will you ensure that they move into the hands of those in need in 18 months? Take a look at Box 12.1 to see how they handled the situation in Oklahoma.

BOX 12.1   OKLAHOMA: MAY 3, 1999, TORNADO OUTBREAK

When tornados cut wide swaths across Oklahoma and destroyed well over 5,000 homes, the state VOAD (Voluntary Organizations in Active Disasters) and those experienced from the attack on the Murrah Federal Building put their experience to work. Less than 48 hours after the outbreak, the state VOAD convened on a Wednesday in Oklahoma City, with dozens of local, state, and national organizations in attendance. The Seventh Day Adventist Disaster Services volunteered to organize a multiagency warehouse in a donated facility, which was formerly a massive food warehouse. The facility, located just off of I-35, proved ideal with a large parking area, docks for trucks, large spaces to sort and store items, and office spaces with electrical power. The state office of emergency management established a phone bank to handle incoming donations and briefed the media on appropriate donations.

By Friday, the warehouse had nearly filled to capacity. The Adventists coordinated with several other organizations to handle the influx of largely unsolicited items. A local Housing and Urban Development (HUD) office provided staff to inventory the donations on spreadsheets. They did so as payback, because they had benefited from volunteerism after surviving the Murrah Federal Building attack. Americorps youth volunteers sorted items into aisles of diapers, canned goods, furniture, clothing, and more. They did so cautiously, uncovering knives and even a loaded weapon in the boxes that had been dropped off. The American Red Cross provided a list of agencies and organizations working the disaster, along with contact information. HUD then faxed the lists of items out to various agencies for distribution to clients. Goodwill set up distribution centers within their stores so that disaster victims could come in and shop for what they needed. As one emergency manager said, "We have a can of green beans for every single American family to eat tonight." A few months later, much remained. Second Harvest Food Bank handled excessive food donations. Goodwill baled massive amounts of unused clothing and stored it for over a year to honor donor intent.

Look at a short list of just *some* of the items that came in during the first week—bearing in mind that while many items were needed and appreciated, the task of managing the amounts of material required considerable effort. Most of these items are listed in "pallet" sizes. A pallet is a flat,wooden structure that must be lifted and moved about by a forklift. In the first example, where 40 pallets of baby diapers arrived in the first few days, one pallet may have contained up to 4,000 diapers. Thus in the first few days alone, you would have to find space and then distribute 40 pallets × 4,000 diapers = 160,000 diapers.

- 40 pallets of baby diapers
- 42 pallets of orange juice (and hundreds more of other beverages)
- 22 pallets of applesauce
- 20 pallets of pork
- 10 pallets of chili
- 252 pallets of cereal (with additional cases not on pallets)
- Thousands of cases and dozens of pallets of paper and plastic products
- 325 pallets of toothpaste
- Trailer truckloads full of water

In contrast, what items went out the door first in Oklahoma City?

- Appliances
- Baby wipes, diapers, beds, mattresses, car seats, formula
- Bedding, box springs, sheets
- Individual cases of food, towels, juices, cereal, cleaning supplies— all sent to separate shelters, churches, and schools that then distributed the items to individual families.

In short, the pallets and cases had to be sorted; inventoried; broken down into manageable amounts for individual families; and then coordinated with dozens of relief organizations, faith-based groups, and community agencies—and still there was a lot left over.

Donations during the Recovery Period

It is true that donations are sorely needed after disaster. Donating what is truly needed, though, is the best thing to do. Donations can provide immediate relief, which is the time period when most people tend to donate. However, the recovery period represents the time frame when most resources are needed rather than the short-term response period. Rebuilding a home may take from 3 to 18 months or, in the case of catastrophic disasters, even longer. Reconstruction on a large apartment building or on public housing may take years, especially given a lack of federal assistance to larger apartment dwellings (Comerio 1997).

Because of the long time period for rebuilding, it will be necessary to either store items until needed or find ways to secure those items when families are ready to move back home. Unfortunately, by the time families return home, media attention has typically turned to other events, and public interest has waned. Reconstruction after Hurricane Katrina will continue for many years to come. In 2008, many blocks in both Louisiana and Mississippi still had only one house rebuilt. Yet when the topic arises in discussions, people are often surprised that New Orleans has not yet recovered. Massive rebuilding donations, including material resources and volunteer time, will be needed for some time (see Photo 12.2).

Families and households with insurance will be among the first to recover, and will do so even more quickly with FEMA loans or grants. Lower-income households and those who are under- or uninsured will require longer to recover. Providing key donations at the right times will expedite the recovery process. But what is needed? First, needed household items are likely to include major appliances as well as furniture like beds, dressers, tables, and chairs. Donors are far less likely to be able to part with or ship large items in good condition; consequently, money is the best thing to send so that an appropriate agency can purchase the items or offer a gift card or voucher to a household.

Second, agencies and organizations helping with the rebuilding process will need a wide variety of supplies. To rebuild a home requires lumber, sheetrock, paint, nails, roofing materials, doors, cabinetry, plumbing, and electrical supplies, to name just some! Organizations that set up rebuilding projects may also require locations and materials to support volunteers, ranging from food to bedding to laundry supplies. They will also require basic office supplies and support to pay communication and construction bills. Providing funds may also help with transporting volunteers from their home locations to and around the work site.

Third, survivor needs will continue for some time. Seasonal needs may occur, for example, when children return to school and require uniforms, supplies, and books. Holidays and birthdays represent opportunities to give gifts to families beset with financial difficulty due to the disaster. Psychological trauma and medical care may also linger, thus providing a means for families and households to restore their well-being should be considered by donors.

In short, the long-term recovery needs of survivors and those who serve them requires securing resources, possibly for years. Those resources, preferably financial ones, must be safeguarded and used by trustworthy disaster agencies and organizations so that they will be maximized for the greatest and broadest benefits.

Why Financial Donations Are Best

Why is money better? First, despite what you may see on television, the area surrounding a disaster site is usually intact and functioning. Tornados, for example, may impact only a segment of a city, leaving the large areas intact. Thus, if we send money directly to reputable relief organizations, they can

PHOTO 12.2 Members of the Disaster Medical Assistance Team (DMAT) sort through donated clothing at the New Orleans airport on September 4, 2005. (Photo by Micael Rieger/FEMA News Photo.)

use the money to revitalize the local economy. By sending clothing, food, and other materials, we may actually hinder economic recovery.

Second, imagine that you are a disaster victim. If all of your clothes were destroyed, you would need specific sizes and types of clothing. For example, you would need clothing that you could wear to go back to work—which may be very job specific, such as those working in the medical field, construction, commercial fishing, or in professional offices. You may need medical scrubs, heavy work boots, water-resistant clothing, and attire suitable for secretarial or receptionist work. Most people, well-intentioned though they may be, clean out unwanted clothing from their closets and send it to disaster sites. Money, offered through relief organizations directly to victims, can be used to purchase the specific clothing needed to return to work.

Third, it is psychologically important for a survivor to wear clothing that is new, clean, and appropriate for their climate and culture. If you do not have traditional Islamic clothing in your closet to donate, then maybe giving money to a Muslim relief organization can help replace lost clothing. Similarly, the heavy coats mentioned earlier that were donated for Hurricane Andrew obviously went unused, when lightweight, moisture-wicking clothing would have been better. And, that clothing could have been pur-chased in Miami and delivered directly to Homestead and Florida City and the agricultural labor camps. Think also about teenagers who have lost their clothing. Wouldn't the teenagers that you know prefer to have clothing that fits well, allows them to blend in rather than stand out as a "victim," and enables them to return to school feeling good about themselves?

Fourth, it is a lot easier to move money around. It can be donated through credit cards on Web-based systems, transmitted via electronic delivery, and stored easily in an organization's bank account. Funds needed for a hearing aid in Houston and a wheelchair in Memphis can be delivered within sec-onds—meaning that a survivor does not have to wait for critically needed sup-plies. Money can ease the pain and trauma of survivors in appropriate ways.

Finally, and perhaps most important, money can buy the things that you do not have in your closets or cupboards. People can lose everything in disasters, including hearing aids, dentures, wheelchairs (which can be very specialized and expensive) and other assistive devices, telecommunications devices for those who are deaf, medical prescriptions (which those surviving on Medicare and Medicaid cannot afford to replace), specific infant formulas, medical equipment including feeding tubes and insulin supplies, and even appropriate kinds of food. For example, people may need to replace food appropriate for their diet, including sugar-free, gluten-free, and nondairy items.

When we hear that organizations prefer money, we may become discouraged because our own pockets lack the same thing. However, a creative group can raise money to send, even if it is a small amount (Bennett and Kottasz 2000). For example, instead of sending donated items and clothing, try the following:

- Set up a garage or yard sale and send the money to a disaster organization
- Sell items on E-Bay
- Sell used clothing to a rag company and donate the money to a wor-thy organization
- Hold a raffle with items donated by local businesses
- Request food from donors, cook it, and hold a fund-raiser picnic
- Contact nondisaster agencies that may not be getting the donations they usually receive due to attention diverted to the disaster situa-tion and help replenish their stores

To summarize, donating or raising money instead of sending what we think the survivors may need is always the best. To do so, review the wide array of disaster organizations (http://www.nvoad.org provides an extensive list) and determine which you think would best represent your wishes and serve victims effectively. (See Box 12.2 on finding a trustworthy charity.)

BOX 12.2   HOW TO FIND A TRUSTWORTHY CHARITY

The Federal Trade Commission provides a set of suggestions on how to find an organization that you would trust with your money. Among their suggestions:

- Request written information about the charity's mission and how it will use your donation.
- Ask for proof that your donation is tax deductible.
- Look at the charity's financial profile at GuideStar www.guidestar. org, the BBB Wise Giving Alliance at www.give.org, or the American Institute of Philanthropy at www.charitywatch.org.
- Check with others who have donated to the same organization.
- Check with recipients of the funds from the organization to see what their experience has been.
- Ask how much of your donation will go to the survivors and how much goes to the organization's administrative costs.
- Do not give cash. Checks are best and provide proof for your annual taxes.
- Do not give in to high-pressure solicitations.
- Check with the state attorney general to see if your state requires charities to be registered or licensed.
- If necessary, you can file a complaint with the FTC, www.ftc.gov, or call toll-free at 1-877-382-4357; TTY 1-866-653-4261.

Source: Adapted from the Federal Trade Commission, "Charitable Donations: Give or Take?" http://www.ftc.gov/bcp/edu/pubs/consumer/telemarketing/tel01.shtm

Donations Management Planning

As you now know, unsolicited donations of used clothing and canned goods can clog response and recovery systems and weigh down organizations trying to assist affected households. You probably now understand why many officials and experts refer to donations as the "second disaster." NVOAD and FEMA observed this problem and initiated a series of meetings in response. In 1990, a FEMA task force developed a draft policy recommending a central telephone number with database support. However, at the 1991 NVOAD annual meeting, FEMA representatives informed participating organizations that it appeared the federal government did not have legislative authority to accept either material or financial donations (NVOAD 2007).

One year later, Hurricane Andrew slammed into Florida, resulting in "thousands of tractor trailer loads of donated goods" (NVOAD 2007). FEMA's hotline took 8,000 calls from people trying to sell goods; the NVOAD member Adventist Community Services, however, took up to 30,000 calls

for direct donations. The groundwork was laid for involving voluntary organizations more directly in the donations management process, with FEMA
support. FEMA consequently established a Donations Steering Committee
with wide voluntary-agency participation including NVOAD, the National
Emergency Management Agency, and the National Coordinating Council
on Emergency Management as well as state and national agency representatives. They agreed to develop a donations management plan, to have a VOAD
representative facilitate donations coordination, and to have NVOAD assist
in training, public education, and consultation. NVOAD set up a permanent
donations committee within its organizational structure (NVOAD 2007).
These efforts have transformed donations management.

Ten Key Principles

In 2002, at the National Leadership Forum on Disaster Volunteerism,
participating agencies developed ten key principles based on an emerging
National Donations Management Strategy. These principles outline how a
state should work to design and implement a plan for handling unsolicited
items and for encouraging appropriate contributions (FEMA n.d., FEMA
and NVOAD 1999).

1. *Early coordination.* Because we know that unsolicited donations will
   arrive, we can anticipate and plan for that behavioral response. To
   do so, the key organizations must gather and outline a strategy for
   handling the overly abundant arrivals. Ideally, the plan will outline
   (a) who is to do what and (b) how the donations will flow into the
   homes of those in need. Preplanning can also serve to educate the
   public and the media about appropriate donations, a topic that will
   come up later in this chapter.
2. *Anticipate convergence.* Donations management plans should assume
   that unsolicited items will arrive. Knowing that such items will arrive
   means that a system can be put into place, including phone centers,
   database inventory systems, and preidentification of warehousing as
   well as interorganizational and intergovernmental coordination of
   legal, financial, and ethical issues. Having a system in place to manage donations means that inappropriate donations might be mini-
   mized and appropriate donations could be leveraged to jump-start the
   recovery.
3. *Transportation of donations.* Disasters have a tendency to disrupt
   transportation, with downed trees blocking roads, access limited
   by police and other authorities, and roads and bridges impacted
   or damaged. Earthquakes, for example, can damage railways, airports, and ports, which could hinder the delivery of necessary donations. Consequently, those writing up the plan should work with

transportation agencies, highway departments, and authorities who will clear roadways and permit access.

4. *Establish lines of authority.* As indicated by Figure 12.2, state and local officials are designated as those with the authority to manage donations. The state may request and receive assistance from FEMA and NVOAD agencies experienced with donations management. Ideally, the state and local authorities will have appointed a **donations management team** with a **donations management coordinator**, a **donations coordination center**, and a process through which donations—both solicited and unsolicited—will flow. Specific roles are outlined next (adapted from FEMA n.d., FEMA 2007).

   • *Donations management team.* A team of broadly based partners will bring together expertise and information to ensure that all affected agencies and organizations work together to deliver resources.

   • *Donations management coordinator.* A **donations management coordinator** may be preselected by the state or local authorities, or volunteer from an experienced organization such as Adventist Community Services (ACS). During Katrina, the ACS staffed eight **multiagency warehouses** across multiple states. The coordinator will work with all agencies and organizations to educate the media about appropriate donations, manage phone banks, activate a donations coordination center, open a multiagency warehouse, and ensure that resources flow through a predesignated system.

   • *Donations coordination center (DCC).* The DCC will serve as a location for handling administrative matters related to donations,

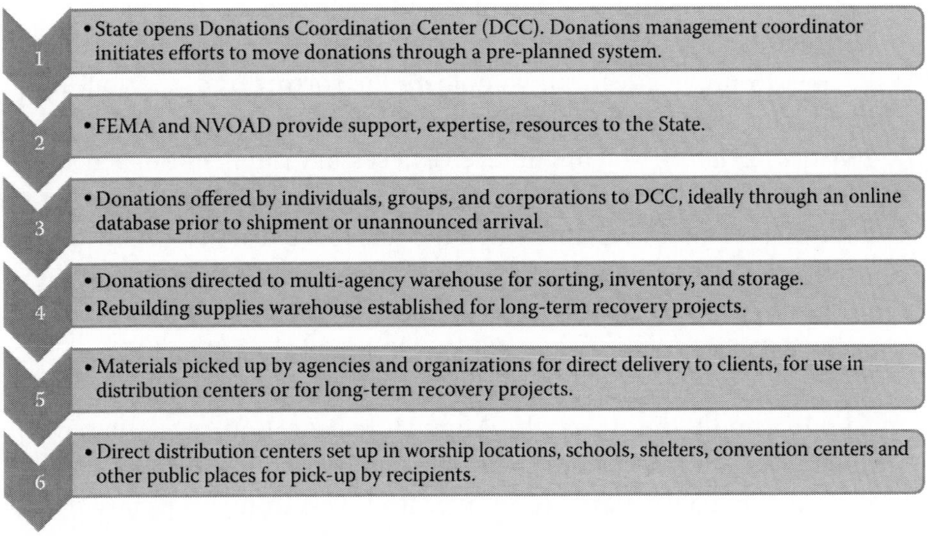

1 • State opens Donations Coordination Center (DCC). Donations management coordinator initiates efforts to move donations through a pre-planned system.

2 • FEMA and NVOAD provide support, expertise, resources to the State.

3 • Donations offered by individuals, groups, and corporations to DCC, ideally through an online database prior to shipment or unannounced arrival.

4 • Donations directed to multi-agency warehouse for sorting, inventory, and storage.
• Rebuilding supplies warehouse established for long-term recovery projects.

5 • Materials picked up by agencies and organizations for direct delivery to clients, for use in distribution centers or for long-term recovery projects.

6 • Direct distribution centers set up in worship locations, schools, shelters, convention centers and other public places for pick-up by recipients.

FIGURE 12.2   Donations management flow.

such as the phone bank and support staff necessary to move resources through the system.

- *Multiagency warehouse.* Typically, an empty location will serve as a location for the items that arrive. Ideally, agencies and organizations will access the inventory through an online database and match up available resources with client and organizational needs (see Photo 12.3).
- *Distribution centers.* These locations will serve as places where survivors and agencies can pick up needed items. Worship centers, fairgrounds, schools, and other locations may suffice, as can Goodwill, Salvation Army, and Second Harvest food-bank stores. Distribution centers may offer a general package of items, such as several days' worth of food, used toys, and clothing, or they may allow survivors to browse and select.

5. *External assistance.* Because the federal government cannot directly accept donations and money, FEMA works as a partner in the donations process by providing expertise and assistance. As described in Chapter 13 (Community Resources), a FEMA voluntary agency liaison (VAL) serves in a pivotal informational role by helping NVOAD and others pull together responsible organizations in need of donations for their clients.

6. *Leverage local capacity.* Local voluntary agencies, who know local resources and people best, can provide useful insights for how to best work with the public, the media, and the clients. Local agencies know neighborhoods that may have been affected and may even have lists of clients they know to be in need, particularly seniors, persons with disabilities, and the medically dependent. Local agencies, faith-based organizations, and community-based organizations may be able to provide leaders, volunteers for sorting and distributing items, and locations for distribution centers.

7. *Practice flexibility.* You might receive necessary shipments of generators, or you might get three truckloads of lettuce. Being ready for anything requires flexibility when the unexpected arrives in the distribution center or multiagency warehouse. Local leaders may need to think creatively with how to thank well-intentioned donors and then deal with a wide variety of items to honor donor intent.

8. *Teamwork matters.* After disasters, it may take a wide array of partners to handle the materials. After Hurricane Katrina, a massive multiagency warehouse opened, with assistance from many partners. A National Guard troop, recently back from Iraq, provided logistical support. An Islamic trucking company moved materials around. Adventist Community Services volunteers provided expert

PHOTO 12.3 Interfaith Disaster Task Force of South Mississippi loads donated sheetrock. Voluntary organizations will help a local homeowner. Local organizations made up to 300 orders daily for such supplies. (Photo by Sally Mendzela/ FEMA News Photo.)

leadership based on past disasters. By working as a team, they made it possible to handle an overwhelming amount of materials.

9. *Encourage cash.* As described earlier, financial donations are always best. Donations management plans should emphasize this in all

media and public-education materials, and such plans should preestablish donations hotlines, Web sites, procedures for **accountability**, and receipts and bank accounts for documenting and moving the money as needed. For suggestions on fundraising, see Box 12.3.

BOX 12.3   FAITH COMMUNITIES AND DONATION MANAGEMENT

DISASTER TIP SHEETS FOR NYC RELIGIOUS LEADERS

Faith Communities & Donations Management

Appeals for donations and support are part of the fabric of disaster recovery. You may be relying on donations to support your disaster recovery program, or you may be asked to provide guidance to your congregants on how best to support a recovery operation outside your area. Managing material and financial support can allow you to make significant contributions to your community, but it is also very challenging. You can help ensure your success by educating yourself about best practices. This tip sheet will help.

Fundraising
- **General Principles Related to Fundraising**
  - Make fundraising the focal point of your plan. Most organizations prefer financial donations because they can purchase services and supplies specifically needed and can help stimulate the local economy in disaster affected areas. Donated goods entail processing and storage costs and should be solicited carefully to ensure you receive what you need in a timely and efficient manner (see tips below).
  - There is power in numbers. Work through your networks to develop interfaith and community-wide disaster missions and fundraising strategies that avoid duplication of services and make your message more powerful.
  - Make sure your house of worship or network has a clear disaster mission and program that is meeting a particular need.
  - Make sure your accounting practices are transparent and well documented. You need to be able to defend the way you are spending your money and distributing goods.
  - **Don't spend too soon. Save money for long term recovery.** There are numerous pressures at the beginning of a disaster operation to raise and spend money quickly.
  - Communicate clearly what you need and what you intend to do with money. If you are raising money for recovery work within your own community, will funds go directly to your house of worship? A particular program?

- **Organizations and Consortiums That Will Be Doing Disaster-Related Fundraising**
  - Non-profit Organizations with established disaster programs (many of them faith-based)
  - Social Service organizations, to provide disaster-related case-work services and direct assistance
  - New organizations that emerge as a result of a disaster
  - NYDIS, to support the Unmet Needs Roundtable and other disaster-related programs
  - The Human Services Council, to support the coordination of NYC social service organizations providing disaster assistance
  - Community foundations and local governments may set up funds for a particular purpose. Your house of worship and faith-based disaster program, if engaged in disaster recovery, may be eligible to apply for these funds

- **Supporting Other Organizations' Programs**
  Your house of worship may want to support other disaster relief organizations/initiatives as a congregation or you may need to provide guidance to individual members wanting to donate:
  - Follow the same principals outlined above. Think about how you would like to receive assistance: The National Voluntary Organizations Active in Disaster (NVOAD) publication "When Disaster Strikes" provides good guidance: **www.nvoad.org/disaster**.
  - If you are raising funds to donate to efforts, know who you're giving to, what the money is used for, what percentage goes to administrative overhead, etc.
  - These two links provide good information on the work of disaster organizations: **www.nvoad.org/disaster** (domestic); **www.interaction.org** (international).

TAKE NOTE:
- **Plan carefully before engaging in fundraising activities. Fundraising efforts that are mismanaged run the risk of tarnishing the reputation of your house of worship and its ability to support ongoing programs.**
- **Make material donations that are appropriate to the situation.**

Continued on reverse

BUILDING PARTNERSHIPS FOR READINESS, RESPONSE, AND RECOVERY

Material Donations
- Be careful how you ask for items. General press releases to broad audiences WILL result in an influx of goods. And once the spigot is open, it is virtually impossible to turn it off.
- Make targeted appeals that are very specific. Include:
  - Exact quantity and type of goods needed
  - Shipping and warehousing requirements
  - Time constraints
- If you are a service provider and intend to provide items/services to clients, think about:
  - Is consistency important to you? Do you want all your clients to receive the same items? What will you do with those that aren't consistent with your plans?
  - If you will accept donations such as vacations or scholarships, how will you decide which clients will be offered such donations?
- How will you handle offers of goods you don't want or need?
- How will you manage goods that come to your house of worship unsolicited? Even with good messaging, you will receive unsolicited goods, especially if you have a visible presence in the community. Think about:
  - Food – There are a number of safety and legal issues around using donated food items. Work with organizations such as City Harvest and The Food Bank for New York City that have experience working with perishable and nonperishable foods: **www.cityharvest.org** and **www.foodbanknyc.org**. The U.S. Department of Agriculture also has excellent food safety information: **www.fsis.usda.gov**.
  - Coordinate with other organizations who are also receiving goods through the New York City Voluntary Organizations Active in Disaster (NYCVOAD). You may be able to share warehouse space, exchange goods, or get volunteer support for processing donated items. Contact NYCVOAD at 212.669.6100.

NYC Disaster Donations & Fundraising Systems
- **Unsolicited Donations Warehouses**
  - Governments discourage the public to send unsolicited goods to a disaster scene, for the reasons listed above. However, even with clear public messages that discourage donated goods, people feel compelled to donate goods after disasters. Often, truckloads of goods will come in from neighboring cities.
  - In order to house and distribute these goods, states and localities open donated goods warehouses. In New York, the State Emergency Management Office (SEMO) is responsible for identifying and running these sites. SEMO works closely with the New York City Office of Emergency Management (NYC OEM), which manages the distribution of goods.
  - Faith-based disaster programs such as those run by Adventist Community Services, The Salvation Army, and World Vision play major roles in managing and staffing these warehouses.
  - Your religious organization can tap into this source of goods through NYCVOAD. Priority for distributing goods is usually:
    1) Victims and recovery workers
    2) Organizations supporting recovery work
    3) Nonprofit organizations that can use these items for other programs
- **City or State-Wide Hotlines/Websites**
  - Local and state governments and designated non-profits will provide ways, such as hotlines and websites, for the public to donate funds and offer in-kind goods that are specifically needed. Subscribe to NYDISNET for the latest information or call 311.

RESOURCES
- State Emergency Management Office (SEMO), **www.semo.state.ny.us**, 518.292.2200
- NYC Office of Emergency Management (NYC OEM), **www.oem.nyc.gov**, Call 311
- Adventist Community Services, **www.communityservices.org**, 301.680.6438
- The Salvation Army of Greater New York, **www.salvationarmy-newyork.org**, 212.337.7200
- World Vision, **www.worldvision.org/worldvision/wvususfo.nsf/stable/newyork**, 1.888.511.6548

NEW YORK DISASTER INTERFAITH SERVICES
22 Cortlandt Street, 20th Floor, New York, NY 10007 ■ Tel 212.669.6100 ■ Fax 212.669.6101 ■ www.NYDIS.org
BUILDING PARTNERSHIPS FOR READINESS, RESPONSE, AND RECOVERY

Source: New York Disaster Interfaith Services. With permission.

10. *Phone banks.* People need to know how to donate. Thus, setting up a phone bank with people trained in talking to the public about donations opportunities is key. Those answering the phones should be able to explain to donors how their money will be handled, how to obtain a receipt, and tax-deduction criteria. Telecommunications staff should be trained on how to explain why material donations may not be the best option. Phone banks should be linked directly to an online inventory system so that donations are immediately accessible to participating agencies and organizations. FEMA recently partnered with others to establish AidMatrix, an online portal for donations management. The AidMatrix Foundation Web site allows donors to make online contributions to a wide variety of charitable organizations.

Educating about Donations

Any donations management plan must have an educational component. The general goal is to inform the public and the media about appropriate ways to donate and to explain why money is the best form of donation. A goal more specific to this text is to help people understand that items will be needed during the recovery period. Thus an educational plan must educate, motivate, and inspire donors to act responsibly and with an eye on long-term needs.

- *The media.* After September 11, reporters requested shovels and gloves for those working at the World Trade Center with the expected result, but what was really needed were steel-plated boots in appropriate sizes. Working with the media starts with getting to know reporters and broadcasters in your area. Because journalists are always looking for stories, they will likely be open to new stories. Letting them know that a donations coordination center, a multiagency warehouse, or a distribution center will open provides them with a visual backdrop for their stories. However, caution must be taken to educate the journalist about the possible impact of that visual imagery—that donors will assume donations are needed. Thus, the donations management team and the donations center coordinator should meet with media representatives to show them photos of prior donations disasters and explain why money and other appropriate materials are best. Prewritten press releases and informational items for news Web sites can be helpful as well. A list of bulleted talking points can help a reporter tired from days of on-air communications to stay on message, and that same list can be easily reproduced in newspapers and on Web sites. Never make it hard for a journalist to get information or access to the story.
- *The public.* The media can provide one means for educating the public, but there are other strategies as well. Before a disaster, it may be hard to get the public's attention, but giving talks at community, faith-based, and voluntary organizations may be a good starting point. Photos and videos of past donations inundations can go a long way to alerting the public. Organizations may even have a plan in place to provide

volunteers in a disaster, and the organization could be tapped to designate a donations leader. Those same organizations could immediately launch an appropriate donations drive by working in concert with the donations coordination center. When a disaster is imminent, the donations management team and coordinator should be ready to disseminate information via the media, email, Web sites, and other means. Getting out the phone bank number is the first item of business, so that people can be directed to the proper place for information and giving. The first message should be "no used clothing" followed immediately by a list of appropriate donations, why these types of donations are needed, and how donors can give. However, when asking for material contributions, it is best to exercise caution. As one experienced multiagency warehouse manager put it, the best way to donate items—if you must—is to "sort, size, box, label, palletize, and shrink-wrap." The public also includes elected officials, who may not have experience with disasters. Well-meaning mayors and city council members should tell the public to bring donations. However, the donations management team must work closely with elected officials to ensure that they do not bring on a second disaster; if they do, it might be appropriate to invite them to sort whatever arrives.

Donations Accountability

One final area that remains to be covered concerns what happens to the donations that we give. People may hesitate to give money because they do not know exactly what will happen with their dollars. Giving clothing and canned goods seems to make more sense because we assume it will feed and clothe people, even though it may not. Several areas of concern for how donations are managed include organizational stewardship of your dollars, dealing with fraud, and ensuring that people indeed qualify for a donation. We turn to these concerns next.

Accountability and Stewardship

What concerns most donors—and what should concern reputable disaster organizations—is how our money is taken care of and leveraged, the main ideas behind stewardship. To be a good steward means that you would take care of what has been entrusted to you, ensuring that donations are used for their intended purpose.

People become upset, for example, when they learn that organizations use funds to pay high salaries to executive officers, order lavish meals, travel in style, or expend the funds to run the office. In 2008, investigative stories by ABC News uncovered allegations of misuse of funds donated to organizations serving war-injured veterans. Such stories undermine our confidence in donating money to any organization. And, when disaster organizations go online or on television asking for money, we have a tendency to think they are only in it for the money. Despite our willingness to help, we seem to have a healthy skepticism about sending funds.

The American Red Cross has come under fire a number of times when elected officials and the public think that this long-time disaster organization may not be getting the money out either fast enough or in sufficient amounts. The truth is that it takes time to identify specific needs and set up appropriate programs that use resources wisely, a time span that can prove frustrating when you know that people are hurting. A good example comes from the Anniversary Travel program after September 11.

The American Red Cross used Liberty Funds to transport families to the anniversary events in New York City, Washington, DC, and Shanksville, Pennsylvania, to remember their loved ones. The program was called the September 11 Memorial Travel Program. Families that qualified were offered up to four days and three nights of transportation, hotel, food, and related expenses. Other organizations helped out as well, which meant that, to serve as good stewards, case managers had to work with other organizations to avoid "duplication of benefits" (ARC 2006). For example, the Department of Defense provided funds, and both United and American Airlines provided travel. A significant amount of time was spent coordinating organizations, airlines, and families. In the end, though, 1,983 families and individuals received help to go to the memorial events. By taking the time to serve as good stewards—despite what might seem like bureaucracy and tedious case-by-base examination—funds remained to help others through additional programs.

Another example of nonfinancial donations stems from the example given earlier about Oklahoma City. Massive donations resulted in mountains of clothing. The local Goodwill baled the clothing and stored it for over a year to ensure that anyone remaining in need could go and get the items required. Doing so took staff time and used up storage space that could have been set aside for other projects. But being accountable to donor intent emerged as the single highest priority and ensured the good reputation of disaster organizations in the community. Though the bulk of the used clothing could not eventually go to disaster victims, the spirit of the donations was honored, which is the essence of organizational accountability.

Qualifying for Donations

How do you decide who "deserves" a donation? A number of challenges may arise when determining qualification, such as:

- Should all survivors be treated equally, or should aid be based on income, amount of damage, or other factors?
- How does geographic location play into aid? Should those living in rural Iowa receive the same amount as those living in areas with a high cost of living such as California or New York City?
- What credentials should be used to determine who receives aid? If a tornado destroyed your home, how can you prove that you lived there without identification or other papers?
- Should undocumented workers receive the same benefits from all organizations? Should there be differences between federal and charitable organization aid?
- How much does family size influence the amount that is received?
- How do you determine what is truly needed? Psychological and emotional trauma, for example, may not be apparent. Should funds be set aside for when those needs arise? Medical problems may go on for some time as well. How do you determine what medical problems should remain eligible for assistance over the long term?
- How long can you staff a program with either paid employees or volunteers? When should you end a program? Should some households be carried beyond the deadline? Under what circumstances?
- In some areas of the country, some persons refuse aid out of pride or independence. Should you respect their wishes or, knowing that they will eventually need some form of aid, should you set funds aside for their need?
- Should some families receive priority, such as single parents, seniors, persons with disabilities?
- Should degree of damage be the determining factor in what amount a family or household receives?
- Should monetary donations be used to pay for storage facilities for unused items? For how long?

In the case of September 11, the American Red Cross (ARC) faced these difficult decisions—particularly because of the massive amounts of donated funds that became available. In the ARC Family Gift Program, which extended from the attack through December 2004, the ARC provided 3,572 families and individuals with an average gift of $58,567 (ARC 2006). Amounts were determined based on how much it would cost to "run an individual household, including rent or mortgage payments, food, utilities and funeral expenses." Food amounts were based on the number of people in the family, and the ARC used a formula based on information from the Bureau of Labor Statistics to determine a maximum amount based on family size and geographic location (New York City is far more expensive than rural Kansas). Could they have given more? The ARC was bounded in part by the Internal Revenue Service, which indicated that amounts should not offer "significantly greater assistance to individuals in a better position to provide for themselves than to individuals with fewer financial resources."

A supplemental gift program offered by the ARC gave $55,000 to 3,056 families and individuals. Eligibility was determined by caseworkers specifically to award the money to the families of those who died or had experienced a major injury. In a unique program, the ARC gave an average gift of $20,926 to 563 families and individuals who were affected but would not be eligible for the supplemental gift, including fiancés, same-sex partners, and others who depended on or were connected to someone lost in the attack.

Summary

In times of disaster, Americans are generous with volunteer time, money, and donated items. Unsolicited donations tend to be problematic, as these materials converge unannounced on sites already beset by disaster. Often called the "second disaster," donations can overwhelm an area and divert critical staff to handle items. Many items go unused, particularly used clothing and shoes. All items must be sorted, separated into usable and unusable piles, organized for use, and transported to distribution sites or stored for long time periods. Most donated items tend to focus on the immediate perceived need, and long-term recovery needs, like building materials, often go unmet. Money is usually the best donation to make, as it can be easily moved around electronically for immediate use or stored for future needs. Money can help jump-start a locally damaged economy, and it be applied to specific items such as medications, wheelchairs, or hearing aids. A donations management plan and team must be put into place to coordinate donated items. The team and a coordinator must anticipate that convergence will occur and be ready to handle the unexpected items that will arrive. The donations management team should act before, during, and after disaster to educate the media, the public, and elected officials about what items should be donated, as well as when and where. The team will also need to establish a means to account for donations if it hopes to be a good steward of the items and funds entrusted to its care. A system establishing eligibility to receive donations must be developed to ensure fair and appropriate use.

Study Guide

Summary Questions

1. Why is it important to be accountable to donors?
2. Why do people donate unsolicited items other than money?
3. Why are unsolicited donations a problem?

4. What are the differences between donations coordination centers, distribution centers, and multiagency warehouses?
5. Who should be on a disaster management team?
6. Define the different forms of convergence.
7. Distinguish between the different kinds of altruism.

Discussion Questions

1. As noted earlier, the American Red Cross (ARC) gave an average gift of $20,926 to 563 families and individuals who were affected but would not be eligible for the ARC supplemental gift of approximately $55,000, including fiancés, same-sex partners, and others who depended or were connected to someone lost in the attack. Was that amount too much, not enough, or just right?
2. What concerns would you have about a monetary donation you might want to make?
3. Why are donations referred to as the "second disaster"?
4. What kinds of items are needed for long-term recovery? Why aren't these kinds of items easily available as a donation? What might you want to do to help a community obtain these types of donations?

Key Terms

Accountability
Collective altruism
Convergence
  Informational convergence
  Material convergence
  Personal convergence
  Substitute convergence
Distribution center
Donations
Donations coordination center
Donations management coordinator
Donations management team
Donor intent
Individual altruism
Multiagency warehouse
Situational altruism
The "second disaster"
Unsolicited donations

References

Andreoni, J. 1990. Impure altruism and donations to public goods: A theory of warm-glow giving. *The Economic Journal* 100: 464–477.

ARC. 2006. September 11 recovery program. American Red Cross. http://www.redcross.org/general/0,1082,0_152_1392,00.html.

Bennett, R., and R. Kottasz. 2000. Emergency fund-raising for disaster relief. *Disaster Prevention and Management* 9: 352–359.

Comerio, M. C. 1997. Housing issues after disasters. *Journal of Contingencies and Crisis Management* 5: 166–178.

Dynes, R. R. 1994. Situational altruism: Toward an explanation of pathologies in disaster assistance. Preliminary paper 201. Newark: University of Delaware, Disaster Research Center.

FEMA. 2007. Volunteer and donations management support annex (draft). Federal Emergency Management Agency. http://www.fema.gov/pdf/emergency/nrf/nrf-support-vol.pdf.

FEMA. n.d. Volunteer and donations management. Federal Emergency Management Agency. http://training.fema.gov/emiweb/edu/docs/Volunteer%20and%20Donations%20Mgmt%20Information%20Overview.ppt.

FEMA and NVOAD. 1999. When disaster strikes. Federal Emergency Management Agency and National Voluntary Organizations Active in Disaster. http://www.nvoad.org/disaster.php.

Fritz, C. E., and J. H. Mathewson. 1956. Convergence behavior: A disaster control problem. Special report prepared for the Committee on Disaster Studies. National Academy of Sciences, National Research Council.

Independent Sector/Wirthlin Worldwide Report. 2001. A survey of charitable giving after September 11. http://www.independentsector.org/PDFs/Sept11_giving.pdf, accessed January 26, 2009.

Kendra, J., and T. Wachtendorf. 2002. Rebel food … renegade supplies: Convergence after the World Center attack. Paper presented at the 97th annual meeting of the American Sociological Association, Chicago.

Neal, D. M. 1993. Flooded with relief: Issues of effective donations distribution. In *Crosstraining: Light the torch*, 179–182. Proceedings of the 17th Annual Conference of Floodplain Managers. Boulder, CO: Natural Hazards Center.

Neal, D. M. 1994. The consequences of excessive unrequested donations: The case of Hurricane Andrew. *Disaster Management* 66 (1): 23–28.

NOAA. 1999. The Great Plains outbreak of May 3, 1999. http://www.srh.noaa.gov/oun/storms/19990503/, accessed January 26, 2009.

NVOAD. 2007. Donated goods in disaster response. National Voluntary Organizations Active in Disaster. http://www.nvoad.org/history5.php.

Steinberg, K. S., and P. M. Rooney. 2005. America gives. *Nonprofit and Voluntary Sector Quarterly* 34: 110–135.

Walker, P., B. Wisner, J. Leaning, and L. Minear. Smoke and mirrors: Deficiencies in disaster funding. *BMJ* 330: 247–250.

Resources

- Central United States Earthquake Consortium offers donations guidance at its weblink, http://www.cusec.org/plans-a-programs/outreach-a-education/28-public-outreach/86-disaster-donations-get-the-facts-before-you-donate-.html. Accessed September 15, 2008.

- FEMA's AidMatrix Network can be viewed at http://www.aidma-trixnetwork.org/fema/. Accessed September 15, 2008.
- FEMA's donations management annex for the National Response Framework can be viewed at http://www.fema.gov/pdf/emergency/nrf/nrf-support-vol.pdf. Accessed September 15, 2008.

Chapter **13**

Community Resources

Learning Objectives

After reading this chapter, you should be able to:

- Identify reasons why the community can be a valuable resource during disaster recovery
- Situate the notion of community involvement in the democratic tradition
- Understand participation as a reflection of civic culture and responsibility
- Define various kinds of social capital that can be accumulated and applied during the disaster recovery process
- Explain strategies that can engage the community
- Address barriers that may prevent participation of community members
- Describe various means to facilitate participation of community members
- Understand participatory action strategies designed to enhance community involvement

Introduction

Disasters cannot be defined as disasters unless they cause a human impact. As defined in Chapter 1, a disaster disrupts functioning across the **community** (Quarantelli 1998). Schools and businesses close, people stop their daily routines, residents lose their housing, and a wide variety of organizations move forward to help. Efforts will be launched to regroup and function again as a community. Children will need to return to school. Household routines must be reestablished, in temporary sites or in new, permanent locations. Businesses, public facilities, and hospitals will need the power back on and employees to go back to work. People living in the affected areas will be motivated to restore their daily lives to normal. The purpose of this chapter is to show how this motivation can be turned into an asset for recovery. Such an effort is currently underway in the nation of New Zealand.

Recovery in New Zealand

In 2002, New Zealand passed the Civil Defence Emergency Management Act. The law was designed to "build resilient New Zealand communities" through emphasizing sustainable approaches and holistic frameworks (MCDEM 2005a). Recovery planning efforts involve "central and local government, emergency services, lifeline utilities, businesses and volunteer agencies" (MCDEM 2005a, 3). As their theme, the Ministry of Civil Defence and Emergency Management (MCDEM) has adopted "Resilient New Zealand—Communities understanding and managing their hazards" (MCDEM 2005a, 4).

The Ministry of CDEM (2005a, 5) strategy is based on the idea that people and their organizations:

- Are well-informed about the direct and indirect consequences of hazards
- Recognise the need to plan for recovery, even where risks are reduced
- Understand the ways in which they rely on others and jointly pre-plan for recovery involving the social, economic, built and natural environments
- Act to ensure effective recovery arrangements are in place
- Take immediate post-event response and recovery actions which limit the repercussions of the event on society and the economy
- Integrate recovery considerations into everyday decision-making processes
- Are involved in pre-event planning about how they can use disasters as opportunities to reduce risks for their communities and local economy in the future

New Zealand's forward-thinking approach involves the community in an integrated and holistic recovery effort. Using a systems approach, the community lies at the heart of the effort to address holistic concerns in the natural, social, built, and economic environments. New Zealand has determined that "community involvement in the decision-making process following a disaster is essential" (MCDEM 2005a, 7). Involvement is considered essential because of the complexity of recovery, which "can have long lasting effects on the community and will usually be costly in financial and resource terms" (MCDEM 2005b, 7; see Figure 13.1).

Increasing community involvement takes several forms in New Zealand. For example, pre-event preparedness activities include community members and help in building relationships with community leaders. Ministry of CDEM officials promote and encourage the participation of community members in recovery planning and activities, seek ideas from residents, and offer community awards after disasters.

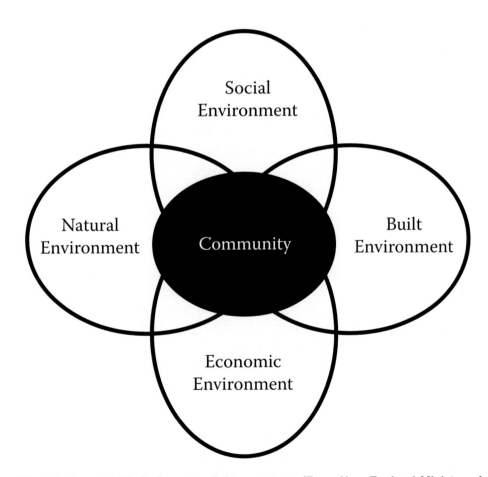

FIGURE 13.1   A holistic framework for recovery. (From New Zealand Ministry of Civil Defence and Emergency Management. With permission.)

The New Zealand initiative is enacted through the creation of CDEM groups. A local group recovery manager is appointed to bring people together for planning purposes, ideally before disaster occurs. The local group recovery manager is tasked to communicate with and involve **stakeholders** across the community. Predisaster, a CDEM group builds relationships and networks across the community by working with existing groups (for example, cultural, humanitarian, civic, and religious organizations) that connect to residents. A local recovery committee might be formed to design mechanisms and set priorities for restoring the community (Ministry of CDEM 2005b).

After a disaster, the CDEM group may open a recovery center to help with launching the restoration activities. Again, local organizations are involved as a means to connect to those affected: social welfare groups, women's organizations, community support groups, and tribal and cultural groups. Key tasks include (MCDEM 2005b, 31):

- Work within existing community structures
- Recruit additional representatives of the wider community into recovery activity if needed
- Establish strategies for uniting the community behind the agreed objectives
- Provide one-stop shops for advice, information and assistance during recovery
- Use established mechanisms for sharing information and reporting local initiatives, e.g., regular community meetings and local newsletters
- Recognise and use local knowledge for improvements to physical and social environments
- Include specific sector representation where significant loss has occurred
- Use civic and religious organizations

In short, recovery efforts in New Zealand, either before or after disaster, invest heavily in community participation. Because all disasters are experienced locally, engaging local residents in the recovery process means that people who care the most about the decisions are involved and informed. They bring local knowledge and contextually appropriate insights and ideas to the planning table. Without their support, recovery efforts may fail. As the Maori say in New Zealand: *he tangata, he tangata, he tangata* (it's the people, it's the people, it's the people).

Defining Community

What or who is the community? A community can be defined by several criteria, including geographical location, shared experience, and common interests (Boughton 1998). Geographic locations can occur in areas as small as a neighborhood or as large as a major metropolitan area. Shared experiences develop within similarities that can be based on ethnic identity, professional interests, or recreational hobbies. Sector-based groups can also define community when combined with geographic location and shared interests (Boughton 1998). For example, the South Florida economy depends heavily on agriculture, and communities of farm workers live in permanent and temporary residences.

Shared Locations

Geographically, communities enjoy a shared location where they can interact and build relationships, usually on the basis of shared interests (Boughton 1998). Communities of senior citizens, called *naturally occurring retirement communities* or NORCs, develop when people retire to a similar geographic location. In the same way, a community of similarly aged neighbors can appear when young couples purchase homes in a newly constructed development and remain in the area over time.

University alumni feel a sense of community when watching sporting events on television or especially when returning to campus. Annual homecoming events reflect that tie to a geographic location, an emotional connection that is enhanced through shared experiences from college days.

Shared Experiences

A combination of cultural interests or historic patterns of race relations can also spur the creation of community through shared experience (Boughton 1998). As seen in Chapter 5 (Environmental Recovery), the town of Princeville developed as a consequence of the end of the Civil War and patterns of local segregation. Princeville grew because people developed shared bonds when they forged a new town out of a swamp, a heritage they held onto despite repetitive flooding. The ties to the land and to their ancestors were strong.

It is not unusual for new immigrant groups to live near each other as a means to provide support through shared language and values. Along the Gulf Coast, for example, a number of Vietnamese-American families live and work in close proximity in the shrimp and fishing industries. After Hurricane Katrina, those strong bonds remained as they returned to familiar locations and restarted their livelihoods. Geographic locations provide economic bases for communities to develop, which subsequently foster shared experiences. People develop strong ties as a result.

Communities may also form out of political, social, or recreational interests (Marsh and Buckle 2001). A running or cycling club will gather for training or recreational purposes, actively recruit new members, and conduct fund-raisers for a good cause. EMILY's List (Early Money is Like Yeast) formed through the connections of highly placed women in the national political arena. Its efforts resulted in nominating Geraldine Ferraro in 1984 as the first woman to run for vice-president.

Disaster fosters a broadened and heightened sense of community across shared locations. Disaster tends to bring people together across lines that may routinely divide people geographically. To help those affected, we reach out from within our familiar neighborhoods and regions to connect and help. The shared experience of September 11 prompted such a response, as seen in the public-service announcements where people from across the nation faced the camera and said, "I am a New Yorker."

Sector-Based Communities

Communities that span sectors are also located geographically and share common experiences (Boughton 1998). The Silicon Valley may be such an area, where computer sophistication and high-tech interests tend to be concentrated within a younger set of professionals. As another example, sports teams also reflect sector-based communities and are tied to geographic locations. Fans who follow their teams, wear their colors and symbols, and delight in championships share in the experience. Bumper stickers that read "I bleed scarlet and gray" demonstrate sector affiliation.

Sector-based groups may also emerge as a means for survival. It appears, for example, that domestic violence may increase after disaster (Jenkins and Phillips 2008; see also Box 10.1 in Chapter 10). To evacuate women and children at risk from New Orleans required a dedicated commitment from shelter staff that put themselves at personal risk. Due to the limited postdisaster housing availability, some women felt compelled to return to violent offenders. Under such circumstances, a modern-day "underground railroad" may help women and their children to escape to a safer, undisclosed location. Sector-based communities that span geographical locations make that possible.

As another example, many voluntary organizations help with the recovery. At the first meetings of the voluntary organizations active in disaster (VOAD), interfaith, or unmet-needs committees (for more detail, see Chapter 14, Voluntary Organizations), a sector-based community immediately begins to work together. Most of those present bring extensive years of experience to the area, and they usually have well-established relationships with each other. The first meeting is not unlike a family reunion as old friends reconnect, remember former disasters, and talk about what will work in the present circumstance.

The Myth of a Single Community

Although the term *community* suggests a single, large group of people, the reality is that we actually belong to a "mosaic of communities" for which we feel a sense of connection and belonging (Marsh and Buckle 2001, 5). Communities also contain considerable internal diversity. Couples that marry despite different alma mater affiliations put on bumper stickers that read "The House Divided." People of similar ages sharing a given location will vote along a spectrum of political affiliations. And it is certainly understandable that people may feel a limited sense of belonging to what is presumably their community.

Communities diverge, converge, and experience change; they are not static (Marsh and Buckle 2001). People move into and out of communities, and some drop their membership or may even be expelled, disbarred, or terminated. Disasters can disrupt as well as build community, as we learn from Box 13.1 about Hurricane Katrina. Communities are diverse and dynamic. Community richness brings a wide variety of resources for the postdisaster recovery effort.

BOX 13.1   HURRICANE KATRINA

The repopulation of New Orleans demonstrates the potential impact of disasters on community, with about 72% of the population back three years after Hurricane Katrina (GNOCDC 2008), but with a different demographic composition than before. It appears that repopulation slowed in the first months of 2008, especially in Orleans and St. Tammany parishes. Let us look at some of the issues.

First, why aren't people back? It is nearly impossible to rebuild from afar. Where have people from Louisiana and Mississippi gone as a result of the storm? No definitive studies can document the diaspora or dispersion, as it is called, but there are some indicators. Applicants for federal assistance remain dispersed across the United States through July 2008. People have temporarily, or perhaps permanently, relocated to nearly every state in the nation.

Second, what are the "new" demographics that influence public debate? As one example, Latino workers have entered the area in search of work, although precise numbers remain unknown. Approximately 75% are unaccompanied men, and 25% are women. It is not clear how long they will stay in the area, although reports suggest that their presence may be temporary (Fussell 2007). Their new presence, coupled with the absence of familiar community members, has led to much public discussion about whether the cultural character of the city may be changing. There is also concern that those with resources, including insurance and savings, have been able to return at a faster rate than others with limited income. Some neighborhoods lag behind in rebuilding, including the Lower Ninth Ward populated historically by African Americans for multiple generations.

The effect on the community and the unique character of the affected areas will not be known for some time, but it remains a concern to those with a strong sense of identity tied to the damaged region. As noted in Chapter 10 (Social Psychological Recovery), social networks that are an important part of community affiliation help us to cope with disaster effects. Faculty involved in efforts to help their students at Tulane University observed "emotional and psychological trauma suffered by the people who were displaced, suffered physical losses, endured family separations, and lost their generations-old lifestyle" (Kahn et al. 2007, 200).

The Value of Community Involvement for Disaster Recovery

At this point in the text, it should be clear that disaster recovery can take some time, that there are limits on funding, and that few locales plan for recovery. It is also true that, as time goes on, people, staff, and officials wear out from the often multiyear and seemingly nonstop nature of recovery. A number of good reasons thus exist for involving the community, including (Scillio 2001/2002):

- Developing support for various options and initiatives that evolve
- Informing the public so that it knows what is happening and why
- Finding out what the various communities think about options and projects
- Ensuring that stakeholders understand and influence the hard decisions that must be made
- Understanding the context in which various communities live their lives and how their realities must be considered when making recovery decisions
- Soliciting help and labor for projects
- Changing behaviors so that they buy into mitigation measures that reduce their risks

Social Capital

We involve the public in disaster recovery because it brings something to the process called **social capital** (Nakagawa and Shaw 2004). Researchers Nakagawa and Shaw, both with the United Nations Center for Regional Development, discovered that communities rich in social capital reported faster recoveries and higher levels of satisfaction. They defined social capital as "the function of mutual trust, social networks of both individuals and groups, and social norms such as obligation and willingness toward mutually beneficial collective action" (2004, 10). The basic idea is that engaging the community accumulates assets that can be directed toward the recovery.

Types of Social Capital

Several types of social capital can be amassed, including **bonding**, **bridging**, **linking**, **structural**, and **cognitive** capital (Nakagawa and Shaw 2004; Uphoff 2000; Woolcock 2000). Let us examine and define each kind.

Bonding social capital brings valuable connections between similar people to the table. The support and commitment that develops through social relationships, such as among neighbors, can potentially be directed toward a neighborhood recovery project. People who care about each other demonstrate shared bonds that can be leveraged to a higher level of effort. Bonding social capital is usually described as the type that occurs between people with similar characteristics, for example, people who work in the same area, live within an historic or culturally situated neighborhood, or belong to the same faith traditions.

Bridging social capital forms across people from different backgrounds. For example, people who live in a geographic region may share bonds and networks that bridge racial and ethnic differences. Bridging social capital probably forms because of ties that occur on the basis of other similarities. For example, such a resource could accumulate in an ethnically diverse neighborhood among people of similar income levels or professions (Nakagawa and Shaw 2004).

Linking social capital develops between communities and organizational representatives (Woolcock 2000). Relationships between a neighborhood parent–teacher organization and a school demonstrate linking social capital. Likewise, links between business owners, the chamber of commerce, and city hall might produce social capital as they work collectively toward recovery.

Structural social capital reflects elements of the social structure, including roles and status. Roles are behaviors that we play out, which are often attached to status. A status is a position that we occupy in society. For example, the status of "student" requires a role behavior that is studious and committed. People within our communities bring their status to the disaster recovery effort, which can be quite helpful. A banker may be able to secure funding or build a financial coalition. A janitor can suggest the best places to mitigate continual problems and alleviate future problems. A homemaker can bring organizational skills and dedication to protection of the family. The status that we occupy within our local communities can help expedite recovery.

Cognitive social capital means that people can bring perspectives and attitudes from their communities that promote recovery (Woolcock 2000). Cultural values that encourage cooperation, dedication to a common good, and volunteerism bring in people with a mindset already focused on accomplishing broadly beneficial goals. As described in Chapter 10, maintaining a psychologically positive outlook helps people to heal. That kind of mindset is a critical recovery resource.

If recovery leaders manage social capital well, they can amass a broader base of resources and hasten recovery to everyone's benefit (Nakagawa and Shaw 2004). Massive efforts to sandbag communities along the Mississippi River in 2008 clearly demonstrated that people can and will turn out, engage in strenuous labor, and work alongside neighbors to save a building (see Photo 13.1). As described in Chapter 14 (Voluntary Organizations), it is often difficult to stem volunteerism, particularly during the response stage. Harnessing those energies can and will make a difference for community-based recovery efforts. For strategies on how to retain and utilize response-time volunteers, see Chapter 14.

Community Engagement

How should officials and leaders engage communities? There is some evidence that the type of participation matters (Beierle and Cayford 2002). Less intensive formats, such as public meetings and advisory committees, experience somewhat less success. Formats that involve negotiations and mediations result in much higher levels of success. It appears that intensity makes a difference in success, particularly in formats that involve people participating actively in discussion.

PHOTO 13.1 Communities will turn out for even the most strenuous work. In Columbus Junction, Iowa, volunteers try to save a local restaurant during the 2008 floods. (Photo by Greg Henshall/FEMA News Photo.)

Thus, engagement can range across a continuum from no participation or limited **consultation** to high levels of involvement (Scillio 2001/2002). Based on how much recovery leaders are willing to involve the public, the amount of control or influence that community members have can vary from low to high. Public engagement fosters **political efficacy**, which means that people feel they can effect change. Consequently, people who lead the disaster recovery process should actively engage affected communities to maximize success. This section reviews strategies for doing so by examining leadership, barriers to participation, and strategies for enhancing involvement.

Characteristics of Effective Recovery Leaders

Working with the community may require adoption of new skills or finding people with the required skills. Engaging community members may mean that a leader has to set aside his or her agenda and preferred models and use alternatives. Think back, for example, on the last meeting that you attended. What style or format did the meeting rely on? Was it a formal, structured event with a strict agenda? (See Box 13.2 for a list of other options.) Did the leader use parliamentary procedure? Or was it an informal event where people spoke their minds? Did the leader ask everyone's opinion to ensure that everyone was heard?

**BOX 13.2   OPTIONS FOR ENHANCING
COMMUNITY PARTICIPATION**

What might work in your community to bring in people to the disaster recovery process? What kinds of interactions or meetings do you like or prefer to avoid? Based on a reading of the participatory literature, it might be worthwhile to consider these options (based in part on Natural Hazards Center 2005; Stringer 1999; Picou et al. 1992; Picou 2000; Pisaniello et al. 2002):

- Focus groups
- Talking circles (Picou et al. 1992; Picou 2000)
- Informal gatherings
- Workshops
- Charettes (structured planning events that work through a series of steps)
- Issue presentations
- Field trips
- Online chats, forums, and blogs
- Radio call-in shows
- Surveys to find those who remain silent and obtain their views
- Web-camera presentations and video streaming
- Facebook, Myspace, Twitter and similar social networking spaces

Experts in **community engagement** suggest that effective leaders embody a particular set of skills. First and foremost, a skilled recovery leader dedicated to engaging the community must listen. Doing so requires that leaders monitor how much they say as well as when and how they say it. Because the purpose of community engagement is to get people to participate, a talkative leader mutes the potential contributions of stakeholders. The role of a leader is therefore that of a facilitator who assists people in working through a decision-making process. Leaders should not be overbearing; they should be enabling. Ultimately, this requires a different kind of leadership that is a "deeply democratic and constructive way of making public decisions" (Chrislip 2002, xiv).

Effective, community-oriented leaders also value what people know from within the context of their lives. Leaders value people's opinions, no matter how much they may disagree. Doing so is particularly important in the early stages of a community engagement process. Quite often, people who feel comfortable speaking up will do so first, while others watch. If leaders cut off those initial offerings, those who are watching may not participate further. Equally true, though, is that leaders must work to ensure that those who speak up first do not take over the process. Effective leaders work to seek out a variety of opinions and perspectives, including comments from those who may feel intimidated or who lack confidence.

Strategies include listening attentively (Burby 2001; Stringer 1999). One technique for doing so is to focus on the person who is speaking and then summarize the key points to ensure that understanding took place. Leaders should use words that are understood by all, avoiding technical terms that may confuse those present. Good leaders also interpret difficult items so that a wide variety of people can understand and appreciate why something is important. Historical issues, for example, may not be on the front burner for people living in temporary housing. Taking the time to talk through the issues and what they might mean for a community increases the likelihood of support.

In the early stages, then, leaders should focus on how things are to be done and set a tone that inspires trust. Leaders should be constantly reflexive, thinking through how they are being perceived and how the process is going. Two types of leaders may be needed: **process leaders** and **content leaders** (Chrislip 2002). A process leader focuses on how the effort transpires and pays attention to integrating everyone fully into the discussions. The process leader keeps people moving forward in an appropriate and timely manner but without marginalizing those present. Content leaders concentrate on the substance of the initiative and insure that the key tasks are discussed in detail sufficient to develop good recovery plans and projects.

Leaders should start where people are, in the context in which they are currently situated, rather than where the leader thinks the people should be

(Stringer 1999). Leaders may want to talk about rerouting transportation to enhance business recovery, but stakeholders may be more concerned with how they get to work. By integrating what stakeholders deem most relevant to their lives, leaders can then expand and connect their concerns to broader recovery issues.

Effective leaders also present a truthful, sincere demeanor when interacting with stakeholders. To move through a recovery process requires trust, which is based on credibility. Lying or misleading people, or giving out information that proves to be inaccurate, undermines credibility. Rumors or inaccurate statements should be corrected immediately and widely. Leaders should also behave in ways that are socially and culturally appropriate (Stringer 1999). For example, in some Native American cultures it is not appropriate to make direct eye contact. Handshakes also vary by culture, as does the "personal space" distance that is deemed acceptable between people. By understanding these behavioral norms, leaders can enhance their relationships within and across the community. In short, leaders must accept people as they are.

Relationships matter in the process of engaging the community. Effective recovery leaders form collaborative teams, which requires that they lead as fellow citizens rather than as superiors (Chrislip 2002). Recovery leaders dedicated to community engagement do not need to be the center of attention. Rather, they must focus on both process and content. Good leaders get people to participate, keep them participating, and enable them to feel good about the experience.

Challenges and Barriers

At this point in your life, you have undoubtedly been to many meetings that have not worked or suffered through a committee meeting that never seemed to end or never reached its goal. A number of barriers exist that prevent successful community engagement and participation. In this section, we review some of the more typical barriers and reveal strategies for reducing their impact.

Information Dissemination

In order to participate, you have to hear about the meeting. People beset by the challenges of recovery may not learn of meetings because their daily schedules have changed. Power may be out for some time, preventing people from hearing television or radio announcements. In southern Dade County, where power was out for a month after Hurricane Andrew, officials lofted large, color-coded balloons to designate places for food, shelter, and first aid. Thus, the first task of recovery leaders seeking to involve the community is to reach them. A wide variety of methods should be used to get the word out:

- Disseminate information over television (including closed captioning), radio, and newspapers in multiple languages, sign interpretation, and Braille.
- Offer flyers door to door (employ Scout troops to do so) and make sure that they can be understood by people who may be blind, illiterate, or non-English speaking.
- Pass out flyers at public events like softball or soccer games.
- Use home health agencies and organizations like Meals on Wheels to get information to hard-to-reach individuals.
- Put messages up on bulletin boards, kiosks, and in places where people must go: aid stations, shelters, grocery stores, pharmacies, emergency rooms, and social service and health-care settings.
- Ask other organizations that regularly connect with people to pass on the message, such as weekly worship services, civic clubs, senior centers, and professional organizations.
- Use personal encouragement methods to get people to pass the word and attend. Ask leaders of local civic and faith-based organizations to personally ask their membership to attend.
- Send information home through children in school systems. Drop off flyers at day-care centers.
- Ask voluntary organizations working in the area to inform their clients.
- Contact the local case managers working with survivors to invite their clients.
- Host a Web site, send out email, and offer text-messaging services.
- List upcoming meetings on grocery-store bags.
- Set up a hotline to answer questions. Include an automated section announcing upcoming meetings, but be sure to offer a quick link to a real person.
- Pass out fans and relief items at outdoor events, listing times and places of upcoming meetings.
- Hold an outdoor festival or fair to distribute and collect information (Andrews 2001).
- Ask community leaders who know different languages, including American Sign Language, to invite the participation of those who speak that language. Ensure that translation will be offered at the meeting in those languages.

In general, diverse information-dissemination efforts diversify participation. By maximizing efforts to let people know of meetings, the social capital that can be brought to the table increases. More importantly, the recovery efforts will reflect the needs, interests, and support of a wider set of stakeholders and result in a better recovery across the community.

Issues of Daily Life

Two dimensions of daily life may interfere with participation, including routine activities and disaster-related daily life. We have spent considerable time in this book discussing how disasters disrupt routines. Recall, for example, Chapter 7 (Housing). The mental and physical energies required for application, relocation, and rebuilding are immense. People may move a half-dozen times before finally landing in permanent housing. That kind of disruption and exhaustion may reduce people's capacities and interests in participating. Public employees, who are also citizens, are likely to be exhausted by dealing with a stressed-out public and feel unable to go to yet another meeting.

Similarly, getting back to a regular schedule may also interfere. People work different shifts and schedules. Someone who works the night or swing shift may not be able to participate at all. People who travel as part of their work may be present erratically. Parents, especially single parents who work multiple part-time jobs, may not have any control over their free time. People may have to spend considerably longer time commuting to new workplaces, solving transportation problems, and returning to temporary housing.

A related issue is child care. Parents who do not have access to reliable child care—those who cannot afford it, or who do not have access to a reputable, trustworthy form of child care offered by the organizers of the meeting—may be unable to attend or participate. Some parents may be available only when their children are in school, while others may need to leave early to put their children to bed. Addressing these types of diverse work and parenting barriers may enhance community participation. Including others depends on understanding the context in which they live.

Local Participation

In the 1980s, a new virus claimed lives among the Navajo and others across New Mexico and Arizona. Seeking answers, the Centers for Disease Control (CDC) interviewed the Navajo people. The CDC left with what seemed like local superstition: when it rains, the mice increase and run across your clothing. This causes bad luck and people die. While the explanation seemed like a myth, the answer was there: Mice were spreading what came to be known as the Hanta virus (Stoecker 2005). While the Navajo answered the questions truthfully, failure to really understand the cultural context undermined abilities to involve those at risk in a meaningful way.

Local knowledge can provide insights. Such local information is often overlooked and can cause significant consequences for those involved. "Lives were lost by ignoring community knowledge and were saved by treating that knowledge as legitimate" (Stoecker 2005, 54). By working with locally affected populations, we may be able to generate new insights, develop bridging capital, and generate more-appropriate recommendations. We must understand the context of people's lives. When we make that effort, relationships build and participation increases (Krajeski and Peterson 2008).

Emergency Management Australia, the equivalent of our FEMA, adopted a series of principles for including culturally and linguistically diverse participants (Mitchell 2003; see also Photo 13.2). Knowing your community is the first step, which requires that we identify community residents, build partnerships, maintain effective communication, offer education and training, and monitor the process. In an exemplary model for getting to know the community, firefighters took action in the Broadmeadows community of Australia. Firefighters discovered that the local migrant community seemed to fear them. By researching the community, they discovered a large number of immigrants from Turkey. To build trust and enhance communication, five firefighters learned about the Turkish language and culture. They formed a partnership with local schools and media and held information sessions for senior citizens. Fewer fires resulted, and residents purchased smoke detectors. For ideas on how to learn more about your community, see Box 13.3.

It is imperative that we work to include those who might otherwise be overlooked, "She brought to the recovery ... the necessary ingredients for

PHOTO 13.2 Inclusive practices invite more people into the process. FEMA provides community relations specialists and interpreters for Vietnamese Americans in Biloxi, Mississippi, after Hurricane Katrina. (Photo by Mark Wolfe/FEMA News Photo.)

BOX 13.3   KNOW YOUR COMMUNITY

The U.S. Census provides initial insights into local populations. To find such information, do the following steps (as of July 2008):

- On the Internet, go to http://www.census.gov, which will take you to the U.S. Census.
- Look on the right-hand side and note the boxes under the words "Population Finder."
  - Enter your city, town, county, or zip code. Depending on the size of your community, you may need to select the next-largest geographic area that includes your location. Select "Go."
- The census will now present you with information on your community. Notice that there are a series of options posted on the left-hand side of the Web page. Select "People," where you can probably find some combination of information on (some communities may not have all of this information available):
  - Age and sex
  - Disability
  - Education
  - Employment
  - Income
  - Origin and language
  - Poverty
  - Race and ethnicity
  - Relationships
  - Veterans

You should bear in mind that the census misses some groups likely to be present in your community. For example, the census undercounts people who are homeless and may not include many recent immigrants. Undocumented workers may have avoided census workers during data-collection times. In short, the census is a starting point. To find the populations least likely to be included, check with these local sources:

- Faith-based organizations
- Social-service providers
- Emergency rooms
- Ethnic-related grocery stores and restaurants
- Missions and food banks

And listen. Listen to voices in the stores where you shop. Listen for other languages, accents and dialects. Look around as well. Do you see sign language in use? People using wheelchairs or other devices? Culturally specific clothing? Senior citizens arriving in vans from congregate-care facilities? Take note of the people who might experience difficulties in learning about or attending community participation meetings and make room.

doing the job well: deep caring for the people; the trust of a community that did not take well to strangers or officials; the street smarts to run the system; and finally, incredible intuition" (Krajeski and Peterson 2008, p. 208). For suggestions on how to be more inclusive, see Box 13.4.

Motivating Participation

To motivate people to participate, we must address the barriers that prevent them from doing so. The following is a series of suggestions that may increase participation by the community:

- *Provide reliable, trustworthy child care.* After disaster, organizations such as the Church of the Brethren can provide trained child-care workers who have undergone criminal-background checks. Other local organizations may be willing to provide help, including a local day-care center, a faith-based preschool, or even a local gym that offers sitting services.
- *Offer meals.* By reducing the time that people must put into cooking and cleaning, you free their time to participate. Organize a meeting around mealtime. Ask a local faith-based organization, civic club, Scout troop, or other unit to host that meal and use its facility.
- *Hold meetings at different times.* People who work different shifts cannot participate easily. By varying the meeting time or by holding multiple meetings on the same topic, you can increase the amount of participation and acquire more social capital.
- *Hold meetings where people live and work.* You do not always have to hold a meeting in a formal location. Use recreational facilities around town. Consider meeting in the laundry room of a public-housing unit. Gather people in the senior center. Go to a large employer during break time or cosponsor a training period. Host an informal gathering at the local coffee shop.
- *Use regular events to your advantage.* People must buy food. Set up a table at the local grocery store with meeting information and ask people to fill out surveys, sit and talk for a few minutes, or join a focus group. Collect information at the local food banks and missions. People impacted by disasters may increasingly use these services. People who were already homeless before the disaster were affected as well, and they now endure even more difficult conditions and have fallen further back in line for housing. Their experiences and opinions matter too.
- *Rely on local organizations.* Many people attend regular worship services. Put a survey in the weekly bulletin. Many civic clubs require weekly attendance. Send them forms for obtaining citizen input.

BOX 13.4   ENVIRONMENTAL JUSTICE PUBLIC PARTICIPATION CHECKLIST

The items below have been excerpted from the EPA checklist and modified for the purposes of this chapter. For a more detailed list, please visit http://www.epa.gov/epaoswer/hazwaste/permit/pubpart/appendd.txt.

- Obtain senior-level support among agency heads and public officials.
- Practice honesty and integrity throughout the process.
- Recognize community/indigenous knowledge.
- Encourage active community participation.
- Utilize cross-cultural formats and exchanges.
- Provide opportunities for stakeholders to offer input into decisions.
- Identify individuals who can represent various stakeholder interests.
- Use consultation and phone or written contacts.
- Consider information-gathering techniques that include modifications for minority and low-income communities; consider language and cultural barriers, technical background, literacy, access to respondents, privacy issues, and preferred types of communications.
- Involve stakeholders early in the policy-making process, beginning in the planning and development stages and continuing through implementation and oversight.
- Develop cosponsoring/coplanning relationships with community organizations, providing resources for their needs.
- Regionalize materials to ensure cultural sensitivity and relevance. Make information readily accessible (handicap access, Braille, etc.) and understandable. Executive summaries and fact sheets should be prepared in layman's language. Whenever practicable and appropriate, translate targeted documents for limited English-speaking populations.
- Make information available in a timely manner.
- Establish site-specific community advisory boards where there is sufficient and sustained interest. Schedule meetings and public hearings to make them accessible and user friendly. Consider time frames that do not conflict with work schedules, rush hours, dinner hours, and other community commitments that may decrease attendance.
- Consider locations and facilities that are local, convenient, and located on neutral turf.
- Ensure that the facility meets American with Disabilities Act requirements for equal access. Provide assistance for hearing-impaired individuals. Whenever practical and appropriate, provide translators for limited English-speaking communities.
- Advertise the meeting and its proposed agenda in a timely manner in the print and electronic media. Provide a phone number and address for communities to find out about pending meetings and

issues, to enter concerns, or to seek participation or alter meeting agendas.
- Create an atmosphere of equal participation (avoid a "panel of experts" or "head table" scenario).
- Develop a mechanism to provide communities with feedback about the actions being considered after community meetings.
- Utilize, as appropriate, historically black colleges and universities (HBCU) and minority institutes (MI), Hispanic-serving colleges and universities (HSCU), and Indian centers to network and form community links.
- Provide "open microphone" formats during meetings to allow community members to ask questions and identify issues from the community.

Source: U.S. Environmental Protection Agency. http://www.epa.gov/compliance/environmentaljustice/index.html.

Deliver those same forms through home health agencies or organizations like Meals on Wheels.
- *Employ current technologies.* Use the local Web site to set up a way to inform the public and solicit its feedback. Provide regular, daily updates with critical information to keep people coming back. Establish an e-mail distribution list with a daily or weekly message updating residents on the recovery process. Link to other Web sites across the community.
- *Be inclusive.* Make the meeting location, leadership, and topics of interest relevant to a range of people. Invite a diverse set of participants by reaching out to various communities through recognized, credible leaders.
- *Translate meetings.* Be sure to recognize and include translation services for the entire community. Area universities may be able to offer students with relevant language skills, perhaps in exchange for academic credit. Contact international student organizations, language clubs, and non-English radio/television stations for help.
- *Accommodate.* Be sure that meetings and information collection and distribution points allow for people with disabilities to participate. Understand that a range of disabilities may deter participation, but that the perspective from that person ensures a more equitable recovery outcome. Work with area organizations and advocates to reach out, include, and accommodate people using assistive devices, motorized wheelchairs and scooters, and service animals to be a part of the process. Advertise the accommodations widely to heighten participation.

Yes, the list of strategies to enhance participation may be daunting. But the outcome is worthwhile. "If emergency managers make the right choices in involving citizens ... they can overcome many of the barriers that have contributed to limited success in the past" (Burby 2001, 45).

Participatory Strategies

Experts have concluded that the majority of public meetings tend to be one-way events, at which information is delivered and the public is invited to comment. However, this consultation approach has been critiqued as a way to limit public involvement. Consultation approaches will "leave the professionals largely in control" of decisions that will influence people's lives for generations (Fordham 1998). Participatory strategies, conversely, truly engage community residents into the process of identifying the problem, working through related issues, designing and implementing solutions, and then evaluating the outcomes.

Disaster researcher Dr. Maureen Fordham, from Northumbria University in the United Kingdom, advises that "participation should occur early within the decision-making process, before major choices have been made and options foreclosed" (Fordham 1998, 31). American researcher Dr. Ray Burby, from the University of North Carolina at Chapel Hill, conducted research that confirmed Fordham's point: "Local governments that involved citizens early adopted 85 percent more mitigation measures than those that initiated citizen involvement at a later stage" (Burby 2001, 47).

The key characteristics of participation that enhance effective outcomes include (Stringer 1999):

- High levels of individual involvement
- Active involvement of people in relevant, meaningful work
- Supportive environments that encourage participation, particularly among those lacking experience or confidence in public settings
- Creating activities that participants can take on
- Actively involving people directly rather than through a representative

In the next sections, we will explore some popular strategies for truly **participatory processes**. Ideally, efforts will result in "a sense of community" (Stringer 1999, 11). As found during such an effort in Australia, "Community involvement in the process of emergency risk management or the process of planning is more likely to engender ownership and influence behaviour" (Pisaniello et al. 2002, 30). Although the process may seem time consuming, a 15-month risk mitigation process in Berri, Australia, resulted in the identification of 120 strategies. The community completed an astounding 84 of those projects (Pisaniello et al. 2002). Researchers and practitioners reported that the effort generated tremendous good will. Elected officials realized that people were interested and willing to be involved, and citizens realized that officials would listen. Publicity from their success inspired other communities across the region as well.

The Australian examples demonstrate that we must move beyond community consultation, where we ask people what they think through one-way surveys or feedback mechanisms (Betts 2003). The notion of local participation is so widely valued that it became one of the guiding principles for the United Nations' International Decade for Natural Disaster Reduction in the 1990s (Betts 2003).

From Consultation to Participation

In contrast to consultation, where recovery leaders elicit feedback or suggestions, a participatory process invites the stakeholders into active decision making. Participatory strategies are believed to work during the disaster recovery period due to some basic principles. First, a wider group of people can bring more ideas to the planning table. Second, engaging people in active participation tends to build a greater sense of community. Third, participation can help leaders to accumulate, inventory, and apply the various types of social capital in the community. Fourth, when local residents participate, they gain a greater sense of "ownership" of the recovery process (Natural Hazards Center 2005). When people feel they own the means for recovery, they are more likely to understand the challenges and to support difficult decisions.

Participatory processes require collaboration, defined as working together toward a common goal. Collaboration helps to foster bridging social capital, which can bring people and recovery leaders together (Chrislip 2002). By convening collaborative events and meetings, people from different neighborhoods, occupations, ethnic groups, ages, and perspectives can help build a comprehensive recovery plan that addresses a fuller range of needs. Doing so should help reduce inequitable outcomes and foster a holistic recovery that works across the affected communities.

Collaboration also meshes well with the reasons for why this country was founded: to restore power to the people. As collaborative leadership author David Chrislip (2002) writes, "Citizens are responsible for the problems of the community and the solutions that address them." Collaboration moves beyond consultation to engage actively a full set of stakeholders whose lives will be affected by the process. Strategies for collaboration in a disaster context are addressed in Box 13.5.

The Participatory Action Approach

Participatory action (PA) is known by a number of names, including action science, collaborative learning, and collaborative leadership. Although

---

BOX 13.5   WORKING WITH WOMEN AT RISK

In 2003, a dedicated core of academics and practitioners designed a step-wise guide for conducting vulnerability assessments. The document, titled *Working with Women at Risk*, is available free of charge at the Gender and Disaster Network (www.gdnonline.org) in both English and Spanish. Dr. Elaine Enarson and Lourdes Meyreles led a team effort to design procedures for teaching local women how to conduct their own research, write up the findings, and design action projects.

This grass roots focus brings local women, with their local knowledge, to a series of workshops that teach them action research skills. The women form teams to go out and conduct interviews with local residents about area risks. Together, the women analyze the information in a series of workshops. New insights about local risks often emerge, as well as ideas about how to reduce those risks.

Working with Women at Risk provides written explanations, forms, and sample agendas to guide emergency managers, social-service organizations, citizen groups, and neighborhood associations through the vulnerability assessment. These tools can be modified for use in a recovery context and for a wide variety of groups. The inclusion of historically marginalized populations is a particular strength of this participatory action guide.

Source: For additional information, see Enarson et al. (2003)

---

relatively new to emergency management and disaster recovery, the perspectives and strategies that participatory action provides offer useful tools to engage the community.

Participatory action has been used in a wide variety of settings, including social services, voluntary organizations, planning departments, academic institutions, educational settings, and more (Greenwood and Levin 1998). PA resonates well with the notion of collaboration and engagement. Its features include (Greenwood and Levin 1998; McNiff, Lomax, and Whitehead 1996; Smith 1997; Stringer 1999):

- Direct involvement of the stakeholders, defined as people most likely to be affected by and vested in the outcome
- Collaboration among a wide variety of stakeholders
- Problem solving
- An equitable, democratic process that brings people into the problem solving and empowers the stakeholders
- Efforts to maximize the involvement of everyone affected
- Broad inclusion of social, economic, cultural, and political issues as well as those directly relevant to the recovery
- An outcome tied to action

Through participatory action, people connect ideas to change. Participatory action thus requires **praxis**, defined as "informed, committed action that gives rise to knowledge rather than just successful action" (McNiff, Lomax, and Whitehead 1996, 8). Praxis results in the adoption of and commitment to new ideas, including holistic strategies, green rebuilding, and integrating mitigation into recovery. Praxis requires participants to be self-reflexive, by working through what they think and feel about a recovery effort and then acting to research options and decide on action (Reason 1994).

For the purposes of disaster recovery, PA allows for stakeholders "to have meaningful influence (control) on how decisions are made, how resources are used, and how information is produced and distributed" (Smith 1997, 178). Several different approaches to PA can be adopted, a topic that we turn to next. The first offers a stepwise approach to walk people through the process, followed by a less formal option that works equally well. Communities and recovery leaders should select an approach that works best for their locale.

A Stepwise Approach to Participatory Action

PA models that rely on stepwise movement guide participants through a research process designed to root out problems and solutions. A first step is usually to codevelop the agenda, including recovery stages, goals, and strategies. By cogenerating the process, people are more likely to understand what needs to be done and be more willing to participate (Stringer 1999). The key is to involve stakeholders in deciding how these options might work (or not) for their local context. The goal is to involve people in every aspect of the process to maximize and leverage local knowledge and social capital.

For example, the Action-Research Routine Model by Stringer (1999) walks stakeholders through three steps: look, think and act. In the first step, collaborators look at the situation by gathering information and data. Options include interviews, observations, and document analysis. Participants might conduct their own research, hire a local researcher to do the work, or ask a researcher to provide guidance (Stoecker 2005; Stringer 1999). For a disaster recovery process, that might mean interviewing local residents about new building codes, their willingness to rebuild green, or their concerns about historical and cultural resources. Observations could include counting the numbers and types of vehicles on roads and bridges before deciding on new transportation routing. Document analysis might analyze historical records to identify previous hazards to develop a range of appropriate mitigation solutions.

Step two walks participants through the implications of the information obtained in step one. By doing so, it is possible to identify goals and objectives for projects. Here, the value of broadly based participation emerges. A set of recovery planners might not think of the needs of senior citizens, people with disabilities, or single parents or about historic structures, environmental resources, or local landfills. The fuller set of people present in a participatory action effort pays off with the bridging social capital that they bring in. In step three, people act. They usually develop a plan, prioritize their initiatives, and implement projects. Ultimately, a stepwise PA approach leads to action and change.

As a final part in step three, participants design an evaluation plan to see how they are doing. They might set benchmarks or develop satisfaction surveys to see how they are doing. Most PA experts concur that the evaluation phase is very important, as it helps participants to know whether the effort worked and made a difference (Stoecker 2005). Evaluations can also serve to refocus and reenergize efforts that have derailed or become sidetracked.

The Highlander Folk School Approach

The Highlander Folk School formed in the 1930s in rural Tennessee. Myles Horton, the founder of Highlander, did so after observing that real life required the involvement of people to address their own problems. Highlander became involved in the struggles of coal miners, the labor movement, and the civil rights movement, based on a philosophy that "the problems of the poor must emerge from the poor themselves" (Adams and Horton 1975).

Highlander's approach is simple: bring people together and give them time and space to identify the problems and solutions that work for them. A typical Highlander workshop convenes people in the hills of New Market, Tennessee, where participants sit in a circle of handmade rocking chairs. The facilitator asks two simple questions, "What is the problem" and "What do you want to do about it?" The facilitator, following the principles for effective leadership described earlier, stays out of the discussion and allows participants to work through the issues.

Does the Highlander approach work? In 1955, a group of people from Alabama went to the school to talk about segregation. After the discussion moved to solutions, Horton asked the second question. One woman replied that responding to segregation was very dangerous and felt that it would be impossible to do so. A short time later, Horton learned that this reticent woman had indeed refused to stand up for her rights. As Horton describes it, Rosa Parks sat down for her rights on a bus in Montgomery, Alabama, and would not give up her seat to a white person. Her case resulted in a Supreme Court decision that ended bus segregation. Parks became known as the mother of the modern civil rights movement.

You have certainly heard of Mrs. Parks, but have you heard of Highlander or Myles Horton? He earned a Nobel Peace Prize nomination in 1983 but is not as well known as the people who left Highlander workshops to change their communities. Horton would probably add, "You can do a lot of good in the world if you don't care who gets the credit for it," the essence of effective leadership in a participatory process (Adams and Horton 1975). Highlander embodies the notion that leadership can be found within the community if we create a place for it to emerge.

Summary

Communities provide valuable resources for recovery efforts. Within any given geographic area there may be multiple kinds of communities to which people belong. Within and across those communities, recovery leaders can find, build, and apply key resources. Those resources include varying kinds of social capital. Bonding social capital develops through relationships and shared bonds, usually between people of similar characteristics. Bridging social capital forms across differences such as occupations within a given work sector. Linking social capital arises out of relationships between communities and organizations. Structural social capital comes from positions that people occupy and can use to generate resources. Cognitive social capital provides attitudes and perspectives that offer insights and new ideas.

Recovery leaders need to engage community capital by working effectively with and for community members. Effective leaders will set aside their own agendas and work to build consensus within and across communities. Good leadership enables social capital to accumulate. In order to leverage the capital found in communities, leaders need to overcome barriers that prevent community participation. By being intentionally and broadly inclusive, the range of participants, along with their resources and their insights, deepens. Effective engagement strategies generally include high levels of participation in contrast to consultation. Participatory processes invite stakeholders to engage actively in problem identification and solution.

Study Guide

Summary Questions

1. How can community be defined and characterized? What dimensions of community connect people?
2. Why is community not a static concept?
3. How do disasters affect communities? Think of both positive and negative impacts.
4. How are the various forms of social capital defined? How are those various kinds of social capital usable during a disaster recovery process?
5. Why should communities become engaged in the discovery process? What is their value?
6. What is the difference between consultation and engagement?

7. How is participatory action different from simply asking people what they think?
8. What are the benefits of participatory strategies for the practice of emergency management and disaster recovery? What lessons can be learned from the Australian examples?

Discussion Questions

1. What kinds of communities do you belong to and why?
2. What kinds of populations are there in your community? Look at www.census.gov for information on the demographic profile where you live. Check the yellow pages for social, political, and recreational communities.
3. Where could you find various kinds of social capital in your community? Can you observe social capital being used already in local, nondisaster projects?
4. What could the loss of social capital mean for the communities in New Orleans? For a greater understanding of those communities, look at the neighborhood data provided by the Greater New Orleans Community Data Center at http://www.gnocdc.org.
5. What forms of public participation occur routinely in your community? Visit your community's Web site or call city hall and ask. Are the forms of participation consultative, or are they truly participatory?
6. What barriers might exist to engaging people in your community? What resources exist locally to overcome those barriers?
7. How could people in your community best be engaged in a communitywide disaster-recovery process?

Key Terms

Consultation
Content leader
Community
Community engagement
Participatory process
   Participatory action
Political efficacy
Praxis
Process leader
Social capital
   Bonding
   Bridging
   Cognitive

Linking
Structural
Stakeholder

References

Adams, F., and M. Horton. 1975. *Unearthing seeds of fire: The idea of highlander.* Winston-Salem, NC: John F. Blair.

Andrews, J. H. 2001. Safe in the 'hood: Earthquake preparedness in midcity Los Angeles. *Natural Hazards Review* 2 (1): 2–11.

Beierle, T. C., and J. Cayford. 2002. *Democracy in Practice: Public Participation in Environmental Decisions.* Washington, DC: Resources for the Future.

Betts, R. 2003. The missing links in community warning systems: Findings from two Victorian community warning system projects. *Australian Journal of Emergency Management* 18 (3): 37–45.

Boughton, G. 1998. The community: Central to emergency risk management. *Australian Journal of Emergency Management* 13 (2): 2–5.

Burby, R. J. 2001. Involving citizens in hazard mitigation planning: Making the right choices. *Australian Journal of Emergency Management* 16 (3): 45–51.

Chrislip, D. 2002. *The collaborative leadership fieldbook.* San Francisco: Jossey-Bass.

Enarson, E., L. Meyreles, M. González, B. Hearn Morrow, A. Mullings, and A. Soares. 2003. *Working with women at risk.* Miami: Florida International University International Hurricane Center.

Fordham, M. 1998. Participatory planning for flood mitigation: Models and approaches. *Australian Journal of Emergency Management* 13 (4): 27–34.

Fussell, E. 2007. Mexican Mobile Consultate survey. New Orleans.

GNOCDC. 2008. May 2008 population estimate confirms decelerated growth in first quarter of 2008. New Orleans: Greater New Orleans Community Data Center.

Greenwood, D., and M. Levin. 1998. *Introduction to action research: Social research for social change.* Thousand Oaks, CA: Sage.

Jenkins, P., and B. D. Phillips. 2008. Battered women, catastrophe, and the context of safety after Hurricane Katrina. *NWSA Journal.* 20/3: 541–555.

Kahn, M. J., R. J. Markert, J. E. Johnson, D. Owens, and N. K. Krane. 2007. Psychiatric issues and answers following Hurricane Katrina. *Academic Psychiatry* 31: 200–204.

Krajeski, R. L., and K. J. Peterson. 2008. But she's a woman and this is a man's job: Lessons for participatory research and participatory recovery. In *women and disasters: From theory to practice,* ed. B. D. Phillips and B. H. Morrow. Philadelphia: Xlibris and International Research Committee on Disasters.

Marsh, G., and P. Buckle. 2001. Community: The concept of community in the risk and emergency management context. *Australian Journal of Emergency Management* 16 (1): 5–7.

McNiff, J., P. Lomax, and J. Whitehead. 1996. *You and your action research project.* London: Routledge.

Ministry of CDEM. 2005a. Focus on recovery: A holistic framework for recovery in New Zealand. Wellington, New Zealand: Ministry of Civil Defence and Emergency Management.

———. 2005b. Recovery management. Wellington, New Zealand: Ministry of Civil Defence and Emergency Management.

Mitchell, L. 2003. Guidelines for emergency managers working with culturally and linguistically diverse communities. *Australian Journal of Emergency Management* 18 (1): 13–24.

Nakagawa, Y., and R. Shaw. 2004. Social capital: A missing link to disaster recovery. *International Journal of Mass Emergencies and Disasters* 22 (1): 5–34.

Natural Hazards Center. 2005. *Holistic disaster recovery: Ideas for building local sustainability after a natural disaster*, 2nd ed. Boulder, CO: Natural Hazards Center.

Picou, J. S., D. A. Gill, C. L. Dyer, and E. W. Curry. 1992. Disruption and stress in an Alaskan fishing community: Initial and continued impacts of the Exxon Valdez spill. *Organization and Environment* 6 (3): 235–257.

Picou, J. S. 2000. The talking circle as sociological practice: Cultural transformation of chronic disaster impacts. *Sociological Practice* 2 (2): 77–97.

Pisaniello, J., J. McKay, G. Reedman, L. Mitchell, and M. Stephensen. 2002. Effectively involving an Australian rural community in a risk management process: A "community partnerships" approach. *Australian Journal of Emergency Management* 17 (2): 30–39.

Quarantelli, E. L. 1998. *What is a disaster?* London: Routledge.

Reason, P. 1994. Three approaches to participative inquiry. In *Handbook of Qualitative Research*, ed. N. Denzin and Y. Lincoln. Newbury Park, CA: Sage.

Scillio, M. 2001/2002. Working with the community in emergency risk management. *Australian Journal of Emergency Management* 16 (4): 59–61.

Smith, S. E. 1997. *Nurtured by knowledge: Learning to do participatory action-research*. Ottawa, Canada: Apex Press.

Stoecker, R. 2005. *Research methods for community change*. Thousand Oaks, CA: Sage.

Stringer, E. T. 1999. *Action Research*, 2nd ed. Newbury Park, CA: Sage.

Uphoff, N. 2000. Understanding social capital: Learning from the analysis and experience of participation. In *Social capital: A multifaceted perspective*, ed. P. Dasgupta and I. Serageldin. Washington, DC: The World Bank.

Woolcock, M. 2000. Social capital in theory and practice. http://poverty.worldbank.org/library/view/12045/. Accessed June 14, 2008.

Resources

- Center for Disease Control Community Engagement Principles http://www.cdc.gov/phppo/pce/ (Access date July 22, 2008).
- Church of the Brethren Children's Disaster Services, http://www.brethren.org/genbd/BDM/CDSindex.html
- Emergency Management Australia, http://www.ema.gov.au. To find the "Guidelines for Culturally and Linguistically Diverse Communities" click on Community Information (Access date July 22, 2008).
- EPA Public Participation Manual http://www.epa.gov/osw/hazard/tsd/permit/pubpart/
- Highlander Folk School website can be found at http://www.highlandercenter.org/.

- New Zealand CDEM groups, visit http://www.civildefence.govt.nz/memwebsite.nsf. Accessed July 23, 2008.
- Participatory action links can be found at Goshen College website, http://www.goshen.edu/soan/soan96p.html (Access date July 22, 2008).
- United Nations International Decade for Natural Disaster Reduction is now named the International Strategy for Disaster Reduction. Resources can be found here http://www.unisdr.org/
- Urban neighborhood involvement, see Jill Andrews, "Safe in the 'Hood: earthquake preparedness in MidCity Los Angeles" (complete reference can be found in the bibliography).

Chapter **14**

Voluntary Organizations

Learning Objectives

After reading this chapter, you should be able to:

- Understand the benefits and challenges associated with volunteers working during disaster recovery
- Specify the conditions that influence volunteerism
- Identify the types of voluntary organizations operating in disaster
- Explain how to develop voluntary capacity prior to a disaster event
- Recognize the ways that volunteers and voluntary organizations contribute to disaster recovery
- Outline the challenges associated with volunteer participation
- Spell out strategies for addressing the challenges of volunteer participation
- Summarize effective dimensions of a volunteer management program during the disaster recovery period
- Identify organizations and organizational forms through which volunteers flow
- Point out connections between federal partners and voluntary organizations

Introduction

Most people, seeing horrific images on television, volunteer during the immediate response period. Yet, search and rescue ends within days, shelters usually close fairly quickly, and media attention wanes. However, as previous chapters have demonstrated, debris removal and rebuilding can take years. Thus, the extended recovery period represents the time when most volunteer efforts are needed. Volunteers can help with many of these initiatives, from rebuilding neighborhoods to planting trees and cleaning up public areas like parks and schools. Volunteers bring in seemingly boundless energy to gut, demolish, frame, roof, sheetrock, paint, repair, and help communities recover (see Photo 14.1). Recovery would not be possible without volunteers and **voluntary organizations**. Local leaders must harness that initial response-time energy and retain people's interest and commitment for the long haul.

Volunteers may represent the single most valuable resource for disaster recovery. They arrive with hot meals, warm hugs, and high levels of enthusiasm for all types of hard, sweaty work. Their unlimited compassion promotes healing within a stricken community. In addition, many voluntary organizations offer decades of disaster-related experience, equipment, work

PHOTO 14.1   Mennonite Disaster Service volunteers work on a home in New Iberia, Louisiana. (Photo by Andi Dube/Mennonite Disaster Service. With permission.)

teams, and more to help your family and neighborhood recover. The challenge for local recovery leaders is to organize and leverage these amazing energies to move the recovery process forward. This chapter outlines the value and benefits of volunteers along with the associated challenges and recommended strategies for effective volunteer management.

We can always count on our fellow citizens to show up when we need them. No single scenario can capture this phenomenon, one that occurs over and over and over. Even in the most dangerous situations, volunteers converge on a disaster scene. After September 11, more than 30,000 volunteers spontaneously showed up, along with over 55,000 American Red Cross volunteers. Despite concerns for their lives, Canadian volunteers participated in managing a Severe Acute Respiratory syndrome (SARS) virus medical crisis (Clizbe 2004). When Hurricane Katrina evacuees outnumbered available shelters by the tens of thousands, civic organizations, faith-based groups, and entire communities opened places of worship, convention centers, formerly closed military bases, and their own homes to displaced residents. Their caring efforts have continued throughout the recovery period across the Gulf Coast. Both September 11 and Hurricane Katrina represent different kinds of volunteer needs and opportunities.

September 11

After September 11, massive numbers of **unaffiliated volunteers** sought opportunities to help their fellow citizens. What was unique about September 11, though, was that it was not a typical disaster. Although residents experienced damage to their homes, the majority of the effort required cleanup of potentially toxic materials inside homes—not a task for unskilled labor. Working on the debris pile also required expertise and care due to its relevance as a crime scene with human remains. Families who lost loved ones required spiritual care, and in some cases, children who were orphaned needed professional social services. Continuing services for families often involved medical and psychological health care, both of which are the province of skilled professionals. Working across the anger that erupted over religious issues required practiced clergy and counselors. Thus, it became both difficult and frustrating to try and volunteer for the September 11 disaster. People who tried to volunteer sometimes reported leaving frustrated, upset at what they deemed a lack of organization—not realizing that "this one was different."

Hurricane Katrina

The same could be said to be true of Hurricane Katrina, that "this one was different." Getting into the flooded areas of Orleans, St. Bernard, and

Plaquemine Parishes took months. Deciding where to rebuild, given the real possibility of future losses in floodplains, took time. Deciding where to set up projects in isolated neighborhoods across the cities and parishes required that organizations spread out. The hurricane also impacted people in Mississippi, Alabama, and, indirectly, across dozens of other states, which spread organizations thin. This recovery, in contrast to others, would roll out slowly. Because of the nearly complete devastation across the Gulf Coast, skilled and unskilled volunteers would be needed for an estimated five to ten years for:

- Cleanup, demolition, and reconstruction of housing, schools, worship centers, and recreational areas
- Support for transportation, counseling, and recreation in trailer parks and to those displaced across dozens of states
- Medical, dental, psychological, and other health services due to nearly complete destruction of the medical sector in the damaged parishes of Louisiana
- Damage to environmentally sensitive areas and species, not to mention devastation of landscaping in public parks, homes, schools, and other areas
- Rebuilding social services in every area, including support to victims of domestic violence and to families now living apart or doubled or tripled up due to the devastation
- Loss of income due to job loss, use of savings, and loss of personal material resources
- Spiritual care arising from heavy damage within the faith-based sector, including loss of facilities and displacement of staff and clergy
- Transitional services to families moving into and out of temporary housing and on to permanent housing
- Transportation for those dependent on public transportation within urban areas or upon paratransit and other services for seniors and persons with disabilities
- Advocacy and case management for those whose needs were not met fully by federal, state, or local services

September 11 stands as an event that generated extensive spontaneous volunteers for a situation that required specialized skills within a specified area. Hurricane Katrina represents the opposite: elongated time for an exceptionally large set of needs across a massive area. These two events collectively provide a glimpse of the kinds of volunteers and organizations that will be needed after a disaster. We are fortunate that people do volunteer. In the next section, we find out why.

Why People Volunteer

Why do people volunteer? Certainly, a wide variety of reasons can be identified. Some people feel called by a higher power or purpose; others simply want to be of service to others in time of need. Some act because they are returning a favor, while others see themselves as banking goodwill for a future withdrawal.

People volunteer because they are raised to be of service to others. **Altruism**, the act of giving to others, represents a core value of American society, a reflection of who we are and how we raise our children. Volunteerism and benevolent action go back to the earliest days in the history of this nation. As symbolized by the first Thanksgiving and demonstrated through the men and women who volunteered for the American Revolution, Americans step up time and time again, no matter the personal cost.

Altruism is a common behavioral response to disasters. While the media seem to dwell on negative myths such as looting, the truth is that crime rates drop and prosocial behavior increases after disaster, including events as massive as Hurricane Katrina (Rodriguez, Trainor, and Quarantelli 2006; see also Box 14.1). We can count on our fellow citizens to come to our aid after disaster.

BOX 14.1   TURNING POINTS IN U.S. DISASTER VOLUNTEER WORK

Disasters tend to produce turning points in how we handle response and recovery. Major disasters in particular generate both changes and challenges. Organizations that have adapted to these events and circumstances have improved service delivery to the benefit of all. FEMA's course on voluntary agencies identifies these key moments in time (see also the References and the Resources section):

- The Johnstown Flood of 1889 caused the Conemaugh River in Pennsylvania to overflow, rupturing the South Fork Dam. Over 2,000 Americans died, and 20,000 faced meager food supplies. The American Red Cross responded to the crisis with "mass care," including food and water, medical care, and mass shelters—the organization's largest effort to that date.
- A few years later, in 1900, a massive hurricane and storm surges rolled over Galveston Island off the Texas coast. Over 6,000 people died, with another 10,000 left without homes. The American Red Cross and Salvation Army arrived to provide food, tent shelters, spiritual care, and clothing.
- In what must have seemed like an unending list of major disasters, the San Francisco earthquake and resulting fires left 250,000 homeless in 1906. Extensive volunteer effort produced Red Cross

tent cities, a special train run by the Volunteers of America to save orphaned children, and citizen-based emergent groups that fed and clothed survivors. The U.S. Army helped as well.

- Those who remember the flooding from levee failures after Hurricane Katrina or the Midwest flooding in 1993 might be surprised to discover that the Mississippi River caused similar widespread destruction in 1927. To respond, the American Red Cross established 154 shelters for hundreds of thousands of survivors. African-American families were brutalized—men were used as human sand bags to stop the flood waters—and the Tuskegee Institute volunteered to "promote interracial cooperation" (FEMA 1999, 2–10; Barry 1997).

- Hurricane Camille in 1969 represents perhaps the most significant turning point in voluntary-agency participation. Camille came ashore as a Category 5 storm and tore apart the Mississippi coastline. Voluntary agencies rushed to help, but realized that their efforts lacked coordination. To improve, they created an umbrella organization called National Voluntary Organizations Active in Disaster (NVOAD, more later in this chapter).

- Since Camille, the voluntary-agency sector has become increasingly coordinated, with organizations focused on various disaster-related specialties. After Hurricane Hugo in 1989, agencies worked together to handle the massive problems generated by donated items (Chapter 12) and unaffiliated volunteers (as discussed in this chapter). In the Midwest floods of 1993, NVOAD agencies launched a formal Donations Coordination Center. Further, they expanded their efforts to aid those with unmet needs by working more closely with FEMA and creating unmet-needs committees. NVOAD partners created guidelines, handbooks, and training. By the time that Hurricane Marilyn damaged the Caribbean in 1995, efforts had become even more specialized. For example, a specific organization, Adventist Community Services, assumed responsibility for establishing donations warehouses, an effort they continue to this day. Today, NVOAD ranks as the leading coordinating entity among disaster organizations and demonstrates how specialized and focused voluntary agencies can be in disaster situations. For more information, visit the NVOAD Web site at www.nvoad.org.

Sources: FEMA 1999; Barry 1997

Further, in a democracy, involvement matters. It is up to each of us to engage proactively in the democratic process to build, invigorate, challenge, and renew government at all levels. Through our actions, we create a place where we want to live, work, and enjoy our neighborhoods and communities. Since the earliest days of this nation, individual action through groups and organizations has built a strong culture of **civic involvement**, the process of participating in building a strong community.

In the 1800s, an extensive set of social-movement organizations evolved, from antislavery societies to organizations seeking reform in mental health. Those organizations laid a foundation for a series of efforts dedicated to serving the broader society. Civic involvement, addressing concerns of persons who were blind or deaf and health issues such as the elimination of polio, gave birth to organizations such as the Lions, Rotary, and Kiwanis. The mid-twentieth century observed massive efforts for social and political change through the civil rights, women's, environmental, and disability rights movements. Concern over poverty launched the Peace Corps and Americorps. Those trying to support and involve the elderly created retired-senior volunteer programs. **Faith-based organizations** (FBOs), recognizing that disasters touched the lives of the poor, minorities, and seniors more than others, designed disaster-specific programs (FEMA 1999).

Each presidential administration has organized some type of volunteer effort, some tied directly to disasters. Most recently, community emergency response teams (CERTs) have developed across the nation. Each presidential effort has opened new doors, created new possibilities, and built upon a sturdy core of involved citizens. Today, a broad array of agencies and organizations can be counted on to step up in time of disaster whether they are community-based, civic, or disaster-specific.

Studies suggest that faith is also a reason for why people volunteer, particularly in disaster situations (Ross 1980; Ross and Smith 1974). In disasters, voluntary service allows people to act on their beliefs. Faith-based organizations, such as Lutheran Disaster Services, Presbyterian Disaster Assistance, or the Mennonite Disaster Service (see Photo 14.2), arise out of various faith traditions and offer an organizational framework for volunteer activity (Nelson and Dynes 1976). Congregations that suffer more extensive damages are more likely to generate long-term volunteers (Smith 1978). Faith traditions that emphasize community involvement and benevolence tend to turn out more volunteers as well (Smith 1978). Faith-based organizations are often viewed by communities in recovery as the key pieces that allowed them to survive and return home. Two-thirds of the national members of the **National Voluntary Organizations Active in Disaster** (NVOAD) come from the faith-based sector.

People also reap benefits from volunteering. After September 11, spontaneous volunteers reported that they felt empowered and healed by their volunteer effort. In a situation where the terrorist attack felt personalized, volunteering helped people generate positive energy for themselves and others. Volunteers reported feeling more connected to others and experienced heightened levels of solidarity within and across their communities (Lowe and Fothergill 2003). Similarly, an Australian bushfire generated feelings

PHOTO 14.2   Volunteers from First Presbyterian Church in Stillwater, Oklahoma, put sheetrock on the home of a New Orleans family. (Photo by Larry Caldwell. With permission.)

of sympathy and a personal obligation to help others (Amato, Ho, and Partridge 1984). History shows that we have been raised to volunteer based on multiple civic, religious, and social beliefs.

Benefits and Challenges of Volunteers and Voluntary Organizations

As seen in Box 14.2, experienced voluntary organizations can provide a wide range of benefits. Many organizations, such as the American Red Cross, Church World Service, or the Southern Baptist Convention, have helped disaster victims for decades. Their experience means that they can size up a situation quickly and mobilize key resources necessary for the tasks at hand, from simple home repairs to rebuilding entire neighborhoods. Organizations link to large numbers of volunteers, which saves local communities from having to find and organize volunteer labor.

Over the past decades, experienced disaster organizations have evolved an even more specialized division of labor. They come together in initial organizing meetings, such as the **unmet-needs committee** or **long-term recovery committee** (described later in this chapter), and immediately set about

BOX 14.2 BENEFITS OF EXPERIENCED VOLUNTARY ORGANIZATIONS IN DISASTER SITUATIONS

- Can generate large amounts of needed items in a short amount of time.
- Can organize large efforts to feed, shelter, sort, and distribute donations.
- Always bring enthusiastic groups of work teams in to rebuild.
- Can catch those who would otherwise fall through the cracks of federal assistance, particularly low-income families, and enable them to return home.
- Can offer a wide variety of expertise, skills, and knowledge from working in previous disasters.
- Many enjoy well-established, long-term relationships in working with each other and on a wide variety of disasters.
- Will work on disaster sites whether there is a presidential disaster declaration or not.
- Are known and trusted by the public.
- Are less bureaucratic than government.
- Tend to use donations and donated resources to the fullest extent possible.
- Typically work in concert and collaboration with federal, state, and local agencies and organizations.
- Can offer specific and crucial services such as day care, roofing, warehousing, mobile showers and cooking facilities, case management, and donations-management services that government may not be able to provide.

Often referred to as the "first to arrive and last to leave," experienced disaster voluntary organizations can be counted on to deliver critically needed assistance.

Source: FEMA (1999)

their work. You can count on organizations like the Adventists to open and organize donations warehouses, on the Mennonites to rebuild homes of the poor, or the Salvation Army to show up with mobile canteens. These initial organizing meetings feel almost like reunions, where the "family" catches up since the last disaster, compares this one to others, and sets out to heal the damaged community.

Challenges also emerge as well, particularly in massive or widespread events. Catastrophic contexts like Hurricane Katrina bring major logistical challenges. Rather than setting up in one community, it was necessary to decide where to place scarce resources over an area the size of the United Kingdom. The challenges included transporting volunteers, providing training, ensuring their safety, arranging for building supplies, housing and feeding, working with local government to ensure code compliance, obtaining building permits, and passing inspections for new construction.

Consider also the type of hazard and how it affects volunteering. The type of disaster usually does not matter—a destroyed house is a home that just needs to be rebuilt. But new types of disasters bring new challenges. September 11 and the Oklahoma City bombing meant that organizations did not rebuild, but offered psychological support, spiritual care, programs for orphans, and community outreach. Future events, such as pandemics or even cyber warfare, may require a reconsideration of tasks and efforts as well. Volunteer management thus emerges as one of the greatest challenges not only for organizations, but for the communities that host them. These challenges will be addressed throughout this chapter.

Types of Volunteers and Voluntary Organizations

There are two main types of individual volunteers: **affiliated volunteers**, trained through disaster organizations, and those arriving as unaffiliated, **spontaneous unplanned volunteers** or SUVs (NVOAD n.d.). Ideally, communities will have trained a cadre of volunteers to show up at appropriate times with the right skills for the right jobs (discussed later in this chapter). However, the truth is that thousands of volunteers may show up at the worst time for the right reasons. After Hurricane Andrew, for example, busloads of volunteers showed up in southern Florida unannounced, assuming that they would be put to work. Lacking training for hazardous conditions, as well as equipment such as gloves, boots, and other critical items, many volunteers went unused while local organizations scrambled to use their labor (Neal 1993, 1994).

Affiliated Volunteers

The first type, the affiliated volunteers, are permanent disaster volunteers, defined as "those who have some disaster training and carry a designated title which facilitates the role-playing expectations prior to and during the disaster" (Britton 1991, 395). Permanent disaster volunteers link local communities to external resources and can be counted on to offer the exact kind of effort that is needed.

Organizations provide training to their volunteers, saving the local community the effort of having to do so. American Red Cross volunteers, for example, go through increasingly specialized training to assist with disaster response and recovery. From making and delivering meals to rebuilding blocks of homes, volunteers must undergo appropriate training in order to be as helpful as possible.

For something as significant as mental-health outreach within the Red Cross, volunteers are specially screened, prepared, and credentialed.

Other organizations may bring in a wide variety of skilled and unskilled labor. Skilled labor may come from professional organizations or unions, such as electricians and plumbers. Unskilled labor may include those simply willing to join the organization and raise a hammer to help. Unskilled labor can be trained on the job, under the supervision of experienced work team leaders and within the organizing framework of an established disaster voluntary organization. Affiliated volunteers are the best types of resources, as they can step in immediately to help and usually arrive with their own support resources. Communities are well advised to encourage their development prior to disaster.

Unaffiliated Volunteers

Large events produce new insights, and after September 11, it was clear that the nation needed a plan to manage spontaneous unplanned volunteers (SUVs), or unaffiliated volunteers. Although they mean well, their arrival can add new problems. For example, where do they sleep and get meals? How do they get around? Do they have the proper training for the jobs that need to be done? Imagine this from the perspective of the eager volunteer. For example: "Why aren't they using me?" "Don't they care that I care?" "Who is in charge of this?" "There's so much need, why aren't we being put to good use?"

There are two main options for local recovery managers to handle SUVs: rapid, on-site training (preferably preplanned) and registering them for future use. In 2003, NVOAD worked with the Points of Light Foundation to create a Volunteer Management Committee. Their recommendations, included later in the Volunteer Management section of this chapter, recommend creation of a **Volunteer Coordination Team** (VCT) (NVOAD n.d.).

Disaster Voluntary Organizations

Decades of disaster experience have generated many experienced disaster-specific organizations that arrive at a site, set up, and start to work. Many of them are faith-based organizations, such as the Mennonite Disaster Service, Adventist Disaster Response, and Presbyterian Disaster Assistance. These organizations will tap into work teams from member congregations that can come for a week or longer. Others, including the American Red Cross, offer over a century of experience with an ability to expand numbers of trained volunteers into the thousands within days of an event.

More broadly, umbrella organizations such as the National Voluntary Organizations Active in Disaster (NVOAD) bring networks of disaster voluntary organizations along with experienced staff; networks to federal agencies; links among their members at the national, state, and even local levels; and decades of experience troubleshooting volunteer efforts. Related organizations, such as the Medical Reserve Corps and the Veterinary Medical Assistance Teams (VMAT), bring specific expertise into a community after a disaster.

A review of some organizations still working on the Gulf Coast Katrina recovery reveals these contributions and talents:

- The Adventist Community Services (ACS) disaster-response teams organized warehouses and assisted in distributing donations across the affected areas. In a good example of interorganizational coordination, they worked with the Aid Matrix Foundation to develop a Web-based inventory system that allowed other organizations to access and order donated items (ACS 2006).
- The Episcopal Relief and Development (ERD 2004) program partnered with the Diocese of Louisiana and Grace Community Services to help African-American families in New Orleans. The Jericho Road Episcopal Housing Initiative created plans to build affordable homes. ERD expects to work on the Gulf Coast for up to five years.
- The Mennonite Disaster Service (MDS) established long-term facilities along the Gulf Coast, including Alabama, Mississippi, and Louisiana. MDS set up mobile homes to house and feed volunteers. This FBO also provides individual case management to its clients and works in concert with NVOAD and other faith partners. Typically, MDS works on the homes of low-income households, especially those of senior citizens, people with disabilities, and single parents. MDS will remain in an area for years to complete the job.
- The Lutheran Disaster Response organized Camp Noah for children affected by disasters and has provided camping opportunities for Katrina kids. Children from kindergarten through sixth grade participate. Trained counselors and mental-health professionals support children working through the trauma of the disaster in an environment away from the debris reminders, in a fun setting that provides beneficial stress relief and counseling.

Disaster voluntary organizations and permanent disaster volunteers thus represent the backbone of disaster recovery. These organizations must be identified and accessed in order to leverage the resources they offer (Britton 1991). Other types of organizations exist that bring additional resources, a topic we turn to next.

Community-Based Organizations (CBOs)

Each community will have varying kinds and levels of **community-based organizations** (CBOs). CBOs include organizations like the United Way and Goodwill as well as others, including advocacy and social-service organizations for senior citizens, persons with disabilities, children, and the homeless. Community-based organizations know the local context and their clients exceptionally well. Involving local CBOs in the recovery process can help outside voluntary organizations negotiate local social, political, and economic issues. Local organizations know exactly what their clients need to recover and where they are located.

It should be recognized, though, that CBOs may face their own challenges postdisaster. External aid may help bolster their abilities to deliver services. Outside organizations may wish to rebuild offices or provide volunteer caseworkers, counselors, and others with proper credentials to the local CBOs. Local CBOs may also experience burnout over the years that follow the disaster by trying to provide support to a negatively impacted clientele. Local caseworkers typically care a great deal about their clients, and the burden of trying to meet routine needs, let alone those generated by disaster, can exhaust local staff and resources.

Civic Clubs and Organizations

After a disaster, many local and national **civic clubs** and organizations may want to help as well. Organizations such as the Lions, Elks, Moose, and Rotary as well as the local Business and Professional Women's organization (BPW) and others may be able to offer financial support, referrals, labor, and resources. Civic clubs bring social networks with resources. Some specialize, an organizational feature that can be tapped into for unmet needs. Part of the Lions Club mission is eyesight aid. For Hurricane Katrina, the Bayou Lions Club in Alabama used funds from the Lions Club International Foundation (LCIF) to test the eyesight of 325 persons and provided 107 with glasses. Using disaster relief funds, the Biloxi Lions Club built the Lions Sea and Sun Camp for children who are blind and visually impaired, the only post-Katrina park on the Gulf Coast for people with disabilities. Lions Clubs across the nation organized other fund-raising and donations drives as well, beyond their primary focus on eyesight and blindness. Civic clubs and organizations work locally, but with extensive networks of support from across the nation and even around the world.

Emergent Organizations

It is not unusual for new organizations to appear after a disaster, usually in response to unmet needs. Some surface to assist those in trouble, others develop to point out a particular problem and seek a remedy (Parr 1970). Emergent organizations are usually characterized by a new structure, as they have never existed before. Emergence also involves new tasks that are taken on to address the concerns, such as when an emergent organization tries to assist the elderly (Dynes 1974). After the Loma Prieta earthquake in 1989, a number of new organizations appeared. One such organization called itself the Comite de Diecisiete de Octubre (the October 17th Committee) to represent issues affecting the Latino community.

After Hurricane Andrew occurred in 1992, concerned women organized Women Will Rebuild. This organization grew out of concerns that women's issues and capacities were not recognized or funded by the primary fund-raising group, We Will Rebuild. Women Will Rebuild sought increased representation of women's, children's, and family interests on the We Will Rebuild agenda. Their efforts resulted in families and children and domestic violence committees and increased funding for social services and affordable housing (Enarson and Morrow 1998). Clearly, a wide variety of organizations provide useful resources that can be tapped into during the disaster recovery period, a topic that we turn to next.

Contributions of Voluntary Organizations during Disaster Recovery

Put yourself in the position of a family that has just lost its home. You are a young family, with two small children. Your home has been destroyed. Perhaps you are a renter. If so, do you have renter's insurance to replace household items like the baby's crib, pots and pans for cooking, and your washer and dryer? Where will you stay while your apartment is rebuilt? Maybe you can send your family to another state to live with relatives, but how will you pay travel expenses to get them there?

Maybe you are in your first home. You were able to put down a little bit of money for it, but you do not have a lot of equity built up from making mortgage payments just yet—so you cannot borrow against it. You earn just enough money so that you cannot get a FEMA grant, but you can get a small loan. Combined with your insurance, though, it is going to be difficult to rebuild that home while also paying on your mortgage and loan. You are staying in a FEMA trailer in the meantime, and your commute to work has doubled in distance. Now, you cannot spend as much time with your partner and children, who are very stressed out by the experience. Looking at the debris seems overwhelming, let alone trying to rebuild the home. Where do you start? How do you get a permit? A contractor? What happens when you cannot afford all the labor and materials that you need? And, because the disaster was so widespread, your parents or other family members move in with you. Where can you turn?

Voluntary agencies and organizations help with unmet needs generated by the disaster. Voluntary agencies can provide a wide set of services to get you and your community through this. If you are an individual or a recovery manager, knowing what these agencies can bring and which organization to turn to represents useful information. In this section, we review what services and resources voluntary organizations typically bring. Throughout this chapter, pay attention to the names of particular organizations and what they do, as each offers specific services for you, your family, and your community. Services typically fall into three general time periods: immediate needs, short-term recovery, and long-term recovery (the following sections are based in part on Phillips and Jenkins, 2009).

Immediate Needs

Some organizations maintain a capacity to respond immediately when disaster strikes. The most visible organizations are usually the American Red Cross (ARC) and the Salvation Army. The ARC provides "mass care," which includes shelters, food, showers and restrooms, mental-health outreach, individual case management, first aid, and vouchers for clothing and basic household needs (beds, appliances, first month's rent in some cases, food). All ARC services are provided free of charge, typically through volunteers from the immediate or surrounding community—your neighbors active in service to you.

The Salvation Army establishes tents or locations with centralized services that include food, clothing, and help with reestablishing individual households. Along with the emergency response vehicles (ERVs) of the American Red Cross, the Salvation Army sends out mobile vans to distribute hot meals and beverages and also conducts individual assistance.

The American Baptist Men Disaster Relief Ministry rolls in large kitchens to feed thousands of people on-site, including survivors, first responders, and relief workers. Among the most appreciated services, the Baptist Men may also build or bring in mobile shower facilities, sometimes offering the first opportunities for a refreshing hot shower. In recent events, voluntary organizations have begun to fund or provide medical and dental services. Sometimes national organizations provide funds to local clinics or mobile units to reach out to those in need; at other times, they may assist in bringing external resources into the community.

Imagine the situation of Greensburg, Kansas, for example, which was almost completely destroyed by an EF5 tornado in May 2007. Where do you go for immediate health-care needs? Driving to another city to secure those services means losing a day of work on rebuilding your home, taking the kids out of school, or losing a day of wages from your job. Providing medical and dental services helps to maintain the educational, economical, and social well-being of the family as well as its physical health.

Although search and rescue by voluntary organizations is not typical among the usual disaster organizations, this is emerging as a new function. Organizations that train dogs to do search and rescue have been used increasingly, with the understanding that such work can be dangerous and must involve experienced, well-trained work teams. After Hurricane Katrina, though, local faith-based groups actually went to the coast to rescue people from their rooftops and porches. In New Orleans, a minister from a deaf church waded through floodwaters to find missing parishioners. Though we should note the obvious danger of these efforts, the compassion and willingness of volunteers to be there for us in the worst of times demands appreciation. As another illustration, FBOs (such as the Salvation Army) will also support families with the expense of funeral services.

As witnessed in Hurricane Katrina, families became separated during the evacuation, often finding themselves thousands of miles away from each other. Voluntary organizations put together reunification services. These efforts included establishing Web sites for missing persons, searching through other shelters for missing family members, driving people to reunions, and providing safe spaces for lost children. The Traveler's Aid Society offered assistance to families in need of transportation. Angel Flights flew the displaced back into the arms of their family members or other safe locations. After Katrina, voluntary organizations became the linking mechanisms that brought families back together again.

Short-Term Recovery

In the immediate days and weeks that follow basic response activities, voluntary organizations may participate in a wide variety of activities. Amish and Mennonite volunteers associated with the Mennonite Disaster Service often show up with chain saws to cut trees and move debris to the roadside. This early cleanup effort offered by organizations can also include pulling damaged items out of homes, washing plates and clothing, finding lost possessions, and beginning the initial work to prepare a site for eventual rebuilding. When families feel overwhelmed by just the thought of how to retrieve household items amid the muck and demolition piles, volunteers can ease the burden and provide a guiding direction.

Volunteers may also participate in damage assessment (see Chapter 2) to estimate the type and amount of losses (which can feed into insurance claims or federal declarations, see Chapter 1). Damage assessment may include debris estimation (see Chapter 4) and identification of the most damaged properties. This information identifies the areas that were hardest hit, the types of housing that were damaged, and the locations most likely to be in need of assistance. At this stage, local, state, and national voluntary organizations usually convene a meeting of interested organizations. At that meeting, often organized by the state or national VOAD, organizations bring up issues, review damage assessments, share information, describe what they can offer, and scope out the range and type of work they will provide.

Experienced disaster organizations can provide valuable suggestions. Local organizations or organizations new to disaster can learn from what the experienced organizations bring to the community—but outside volunteers also need a local perspective. Local organizations can provide those insights. The short-term recovery period also emerges as the best time to organize fund-raising drives. National organizations may receive millions of dollars in donations, which they can use to restore and rebuild. Thus, the network of donors that outside organizations bring in may prove the most useful service of all, especially in an area with economic damage and job displacement.

At this point, voluntary organizations begin to expand their support to families beginning to recover. Families describe the recovery process as frustrating and overwhelming, standing in long lines, or trying to fill out applications either on the phone or online. Imagine yourself in this situation, with two small children to care for and a house in ruins. What is your priority today? In order to access recovery assistance, you need to know where to go and what to say, and you hope that the information and person assisting you speaks your language and understands how your disability affects your recovery efforts.

Specific organizations can help. The Church of the Brethren, for example, provides a carefully developed child-care center. The Brethren's Children's Disaster Services trains volunteers through a 27-hour training workshop, coupled with careful reference and criminal background checks. With such a service in place, you may feel free to pursue recovery assistance, confident that your children are safe in an environment that offers child-care workers experienced in disaster trauma.

Where do you turn next? Voluntary organizations are usually involved in individual and family case-management efforts, as described in Chapter 7 (Housing). Case management involves the direct, face-to-face relationship between a case worker and an individual or family (called the client) to plan out their recovery. The case worker becomes a guide for the client and, often, advocates for his or her interests. As mentioned in Chapter 7, UMCOR and FEMA have partnered to create case-management forms and processes. Their efforts provide evidence that massive events generate organizational learning and specialization.

Voluntary organizations also bring a focus on those most affected by disasters, namely vulnerable populations. Specific groups affected locally may vary. Recent immigrants may prove to be the most vulnerable—unaware of services, unsure of what is available to assist them, or unable to speak the language effectively. Senior citizens may also benefit from attention brought by voluntary organizations, particularly the elderly living alone or with medical conditions limiting their ability to participate in recovery processes. In other areas, vulnerable individuals may be single parents with children who need advocacy, rebuilding, or child care. Some voluntary organizations also recognize the needs of persons with disabilities, such as building ramps, and encourage the participation of volunteers with disabilities while advocating for their interests.

Finally, as detailed in Chapter 12, voluntary organizations handle massive amounts of (over)generously donated items. The Adventist Community Services often establishes warehouses to hold items. Without the help of such voluntary organizations, states and cities can be overwhelmed by donations, and many items might go unused.

Long-Term Recovery

Although there is no clear line between short- and long-term recovery, the rebuilding phase is certainly a visible indicator that long-term recovery has commenced. Many homes and even entire communities would not revive without the support, resources, labor, and compassion of volunteers and voluntary organizations. Rebuilding requires more than volunteer labor, though. During a meeting of the unmet-needs committee, for example, a particular family's situation may be presented. Their needs could range from an entire house to simple repairs. While a single organization may take on the challenge of rebuilding an entire home, it can also offer to restore certain elements, such as a roof or painting.

In order to be ready, organizations must either accumulate building supplies or tap into a reliable source for such supplies. Sometimes a local **emergent group** will play the role of local resource manager. After the 1999 tornados in Oklahoma, a builder's association emerged and assisted with acquiring, storing, and distributing supplies to voluntary organizations. An organization like the Presbyterian Disaster Assistance might arrive to help with roofing, get a referral to someone in need of roofing from the unmet-needs committee, and then secure shingles from the emergent building-supplies group. Single organizations may also use donated funds to purchase building materials, or local construction companies may even donate wood, drywall, and other items. Volunteer work teams require a coordinated inter-organizational effort to get the job done.

If you have never built your own home or worked on a construction crew, you might not think about the value of bringing in experienced work teams. To do so, you would need to know the nature of the job in advance and ensure that scheduled work crews arrive with the right mix of skilled and unskilled labor. Painting is a fairly simple procedure, and you can learn to put up drywall fairly quickly. However, plumbing and electrical work require proper training and certification. A voluntary organization might be lucky enough to have such persons volunteer, but it may also need to hire someone to do that kind of work, a good example of why donated money is valuable. In some cases, unions may send volunteer teams of electricians and plumbers to an area to assist. Project directors hold responsibility for working with the family, coordinating the work teams, meeting local building codes, and passing city inspections. Along the Gulf Coast, rebuilding projects require massive numbers of both skilled and unskilled volunteers. Experienced disaster voluntary organizations thus provide an established network of skilled and unskilled labor proven effective over and over.

Some organizations bring in their own cooks and set up their own facilities, trying to have a low impact on the community's resources. Others may partner with local denominations or community-based organizations to host the valuable volunteers. In Santa Cruz, California, after the 1989 earthquake, a housing recovery committee was led by city employees but supported by local social-service agencies and private health-care providers. Together, they created unique temporary housing opportunities (see Chapter 7) and secured funding for various outreach efforts. One such outreach provided for city staff to assist mobile-home residents with restoring appliances and stabilizing trailers to resist additional earthquakes. The majority of the people assisted were elderly women living alone. Outreach may also include counseling services that involve networks and partnerships among experienced organizations. As we learned after September 11, the health, psychological, and family-support services needed to recover from both physical and emotional trauma can go on for a long time (see Chapter 10). After September 11, the Church World Services (CWS) Emergency Response Program sent qualified volunteers to New York City. The Church of the Brethren donated space and equipment to CWS to set up locations for stress counseling.

Disasters threaten the economic well-being of a community, as seen in Chapter 8. As if losing your home is not bad enough, add in losing the ability to earn a living to feed your family, pay the mortgage, or manage new costs from the disaster. In Chapter 15 we will look at how the federal government assists those unemployed by disaster; nevertheless, it is important to remember that voluntary organizations also help with economic opportunities. Aid may take several forms, from hiring local people to work on rebuilding projects or managing local cases to providing microloans or grants to jump-start economic recovery.

As homes near completion, voluntary organizations may assist with transitional support from temporary to permanent housing. The Salvation Army, for example, gathers used pots and pans, bedding, and basic furniture for that purpose. Other organizations rally to support the family during transition as well. A family may be offered a house blessing and receive gifts donated by volunteers: quilts, baby items, prayer shawls, backpacks of school supplies, photos of the rebuilding process, and religious materials appropriate to the family's faith. In Watsonville, California, ecumenical house blessings were offered after the Loma Prieta earthquake to celebrate the family's new home, with such homilies based on the family's cultural heritage. In one blessing organized by the Watsonville Area Interfaith Disaster Relief, representatives came from many FBOs to enjoy a Latino breakfast of *churros* (donuts), café, chocolate, and other *postres* (pastries). In short, voluntary organizations help people reestablish their households.

The uniqueness of disaster impact may also compel voluntary organizations to move beyond their normal missions. After Katrina, for example, voluntary efforts extended to the educational sector by cleaning up schools, organizing library drives, and providing volunteer teachers. Another unusual service that developed from Katrina included satellite services for people of different faiths. All of the denominations in New Orleans and many along the Gulf Coast suffered terrible destruction. Pastors, rabbis, and their staffs were displaced along with their congregations. Thus, an important source of community solidarity and support during crisis was lost as well. Faith-based and other voluntary organizations assisted the locally damaged denominations by funding outreach vans, paying travel expenses of religious leaders, and helping to reunite lost congregations. Many faith-based organizations set about rebuilding worship centers and locations, and some of these efforts continued for years after the hurricane (see Box 14.3).

**BOX 14.3   CONTRIBUTIONS OF VOLUNTARY
ORGANIZATIONS AFTER DISASTER**

- Immediately after
  - Mass care (food, shelter, water, clothing)
  - Individual assistance
  - Mobile showers
  - Medical and dental services
  - Search and rescue
  - Funeral services
  - Reunification programs
  - Transportation assistance
- Short-term recovery (may continue through long-term phase as well)
  - Clean up
  - Provide guidance
  - Damage assessment
  - Convene interested organizations
  - Fund-raising and network of donors
  - Child-care center
  - Case management

- Needs assessment
- A focus on vulnerable populations
- Donations management
  - Long-term recovery
    - Rebuilding assistance
    - Amassing building supplies
    - Experienced work teams—skilled and unskilled labor
    - Work-team leadership and coordination
    - Key partnerships
    - Outreach
    - Counseling services
    - Economic development and opportunities
    - Transitional support for temporary and permanent housing
    - Reestablishing permanent households
    - Community support—educational sector, faith-based sector

Source: Based in part on Phillips and Jenkins (2009)

The Federal Government and Voluntary Agencies

Voluntary agencies must be involved in disaster recovery, as they serve as a critical means by which many families can return home. Although care must be taken to ensure proper separation of church and state, the federal government does work closely with voluntary agencies. This occurs through several means, such as the NVOAD and a FEMA representative called the **voluntary agency liaison** (VAL).

The VAL provides extremely important information to agencies about what is happening with federal efforts, representing a crucial link between the federal effort and agencies reaching out directly to survivors. FEMA's roles for the VAL include (FEMA 1999, 4–20):

- Providing information and lists of contacts
- Coconvening a voluntary-agency coordination meeting, often the start of an unmet-needs committee
- Providing telephone, fax, or other communication tools
- Coordinating with other ESF (emergency support function) officers to represent and explain voluntary-agency roles and contributions
- Transmitting information about local mitigation issues, such as rebuilding in floodplains
- Setting up an emergency referral system to the volunteer agencies

The FEMA VAL links voluntary agencies (whether associated with NVOAD or not) into the federal response effort. The VAL specifically integrates agencies into federal response under a presidential disaster declaration. If the National Response Framework is implemented, FEMA will set up a joint field office (JFO) with areas set aside for each **emergency support function** (ESF). ESF #6 includes voluntary agencies. Each agency can work out of the JFO and have access to information, telephones, cell phones, computers, paper, mapping services, and other resources.

FEMA has worked cooperatively with NVOAD since FEMA's inception in 1979 under President Carter. FEMA participates in the annual NVOAD conference. Under President Clinton and FEMA director James Lee Witt, a NVOAD representative was named to FEMA's advisory board. Under the National Response Framework, NVOAD agencies provide support when catastrophic events occur. FEMA is an important partner in helping to bring in and support voluntary agencies after disaster. Organizations may arise within the community or out of the FEMA support, coupled with guidance from NVOAD (see Box 14.4). These kinds of partnerships enable communities to maximize their volunteer capacity, which is the topic of the next section.

BOX 14.4   ORGANIZATIONAL STRUCTURES FOR LONG-TERM RECOVERY

The National Voluntary Organizations Active in Disaster (NVOAD) identifies three main types of umbrella structures that can operate locally to design and guide volunteer efforts. These include a Long-Term Recovery Committee (LTRC), an Interfaith Committee, and a Voluntary Organization Active in Disaster (VOAD). Although NVOAD indicates that each structure serves a separate purpose, in reality, local communities may use the terms interchangeably, and the functions of each may overlap. VOADs may develop at the local or state level. Their focus is to foster cooperation, coordination, communication, and collaboration among those responding and participating in the recovery. VOADs offer training, opportunities to meet, and—in many locations as well as nationally—established partnerships with federal agencies. VOADs specifically support the LTRC.

A Long-Term Recovery Committee includes representatives from a wide set of disaster and local organizations with a goal of coordinating services to families. The LTRC focuses on unmet needs of local households and tries to streamline services to these families, who are now clients of the LTRC process. In some locations, the LTRC is simply called the Unmet-Needs Committee.

An Interfaith Committee may also form, with faith-based organizations at its heart. The Interfaith may also join the LTRC and work in concert on projects and with clients who have unmet needs. The Interfaith may choose to conduct casework or to establish specific types of services, such as stress management, reconstruction, fund-raising, or to focus on particular at-risk populations, including senior citizens. Interfaith may arise out of existing alliances among religious groups or may appear newly on the scene after disaster. The New York Disaster Interfaith Services (NYDIS) was originally formed as a result of September 11 and continues its work to this day with those displaced by Hurricane Katrina. NYDIS offers advocacy for underserved populations, disaster planning and training, and disaster response/recovery support for caseworkers, clergy, and caregivers.

Source: NVOAD, Long-Term Recovery Manual

http://www.nvoad.org

Volunteer Management

Ideally, a community or volunteer center will organize and train volunteers before disaster strikes. This can be accomplished using any number of different strategies. A local faith-based group might connect with its national disaster organization, seek training, and practice on local projects prior to a long-distance volunteer effort. A local volunteer center might incorporate disaster training into regular, nondisaster instruction so as to prepare a cadre of persons able to step up when needed.

ARC Disaster Action Teams stand by in communities across the nation, specifically for shelter, mass care, and case management. All state governors have implemented the federal Citizen Corps programs (FEMA n.d.) by assigning a state coordinator. Congress has provided some funding to the states for development of Citizen Corps programs, including Neighborhood Watch, Community Emergency Response Teams (CERTs), Volunteers in Police Service, and the Medical Reserve Corps. Calling upon or building up the capacities of these organizations can develop a ready cadre of experienced, enthusiastic volunteers prior to an event.

Further, local and state groups may want to further develop or initiate their own Voluntary Organizations Active in Disaster (VOAD). These organizations can provide monthly training by bringing in various experts. Often the unanticipated benefit of such groups is to build a network of people who know each other, share similar training and dedication, and are willing to work with each other under difficult situations. After the May 3, 1999, tornado outbreak across Oklahoma, the OK VOAD met within 48 hours of the events. A variety of local, state, and national organizations had arrived. Because the framework already existed for outsiders to step in, the state VOAD was able to convene the interested parties, divide up the tasks, and expedite the disaster recovery. In a state that suffered terrible damage to its housing stock as well as the loss of more than 5,000 vehicles, the disaster recovery was jump-started by the existence of a trained, knowledgeable VOAD.

Recall from the earlier part of this chapter that thousands of unaffiliated volunteers may show up unannounced, wanting to help. While many may be able to do so, the reality is that thousands may also be turned away out of safety concerns, because they lack training, or because the local community has not prepared for their arrival. Local recovery leaders would be well advised to tap a local community-based or disaster organization to prepare for the arrival of unaffiliated volunteers. Ideally, they will include a strategy to retain these volunteers for the long process of recovery. NVOAD recommends that locals establish a volunteer reception center and a "Go Kit," as outlined in Box 14.5. The following sections explain various strategies for managing volunteers.

BOX 14.5   THE VOLUNTEER RECEPTION CENTER "GO KIT"

- Materials to register unaffiliated volunteers with contact information usable in the next two years: name, address, phone, fax, e-mail, age, and parent/guardian contact information
- Interview/intake forms to assess volunteer skills and make appropriate assignments: languages spoken, specific skills, previous training, job preference, location preference
- Safety training and deployment where possible (see NVOAD 2003 for additional suggestions to use volunteers during the response time period)
- Job-specific training for the various types of activities, including the recovery activities that will come at a later time, emphasizing that the greatest need is during the recovery
- Equipment and resources to set up and supply areas for registration, training, and breaks
- Public information about anticipated recovery needs and ways to volunteer
- A list of local, state, regional, and national disaster voluntary organizations that offer training and opportunities to participate in the recovery
- A formal thank-you for arriving to help and an invitation to return extended from city officials and community leaders
- Contact information for volunteers to use in the future prior to their return

The Volunteer Reception Center, during the response period, should compile registrations and assessment forms for the unaffiliated volunteers and—when time permits—enter this information into a database (NVOAD n.d.). Efforts to match unaffiliated volunteers with compatible organizations working in the recovery period can maximize the use of these well-meaning individuals seeking to help your community. Once the initial response period ends, organize local volunteers to write thank-you letters to the unaffiliated volunteers, encouraging them to contact an appropriate disaster organization, take training, and return to help.

Source: **Based on NVOAD (n.d.), but modified for the recovery time period by the author**

Volunteer Centers

Local communities may wish to use existing or to establish new volunteer centers to coordinate efforts. Volunteer centers first began in Minneapolis in 1919 as a response to World War I (Points of Light Foundation 2007). Known then as volunteer bureaus, the idea spread across the United States, with an Association of Volunteer Bureaus forming in the 1950s. Volunteer efforts garnered the attention and support of most U.S. presidents, who supplemented and designed additional programs. By 1986, 380 volunteer centers were in place, with an estimated half million volunteers in 100,000 private organizations and agencies.

The Volunteer Center National Network, part of the Points of Light Foundation, was established to foster such efforts. Volunteer Centers organize, train, and encourage volunteering and organize projects. Links among volunteer centers and other agencies maximize the potential resources available for recovery purposes. Local volunteer centers may be available in or near your area.

Finally, placing volunteers matters as well. Ideally, a local community will have a cadre of trained, affiliated volunteers. But, the community should also anticipate that unaffiliated volunteers will also appear. If the community has taken care to record its contact information and backgrounds or interests, proper placement can be made. Knowing that volunteering makes a difference to the volunteer and to the community, it is important to have a good match between what the individual volunteer offers and what the community needs (Clizbe 2004).

A good starting point is to list the tasks, sort them into manageable categories, and then assign task leaders to the categories (like cleanup, demolition, construction, outreach, and even secretarial, administrative, and errand running). Then, task leaders could review the available volunteers and try to match the backgrounds to the tasks at hand. A homemaker, for example, might bring excellent organizational skills as well as experience in child care. A football team could be brought in to carry debris to the curb and move construction materials. Scout troops can deliver water, distribute educational materials, and develop play programs for kids in trailer parks.

Training and Placement of Volunteers

Ideally, volunteers will be trained prior to a disaster, and records will be kept carefully so that a community or organization can easily contact and involve these valuable human resources. Organizations should provide knowledgeable instructors, accessible materials and locations, well-tested materials, opportunities to practice, testing, and completion certificates (Clizbe 2004). Training should include psychological instruction to prepare the volunteer to deal with traumatized families, devastated landscapes, and demanding physical labor (Paton 1996, 1994).

A first principle of training is that consistent standards should be used (Clizbe 2004). Applying this to the recovery context, volunteers might be trained in basic demolition, including separation of recyclable and reusable materials. Volunteers could arrive in any community across the nation to sort construction and demolition materials. Imagine as well that volunteers receive increasingly complex training. They start with basic demolition and then work their way up to mudding and taping sheetrock and then to shingling a roof.

To ensure that volunteers leave training with the right skills, they should be taught and supervised by qualified instructors and field supervisors. During the recovery period, careful attention must be directed to the work teams involved in construction, including electrical and plumbing work. All dimensions of the rebuilding process are governed by building codes and permitting processes. If volunteer teams do the work incorrectly, it has to be torn out, redone, and reapproved by a city inspector—which delays the recovery process. Getting it right the first time depends on quality instruction and careful oversight.

Training should be done in a format that is as accessible as possible (Clizbe 2004), including offering training in the languages spoken in the community. Prospective volunteers work at different time periods and take care of family members; consequently, they need flexible training opportunities. Thus, an organization might offer training on weekends, evenings, and even over the Internet (video streaming, podcasts, online courses). Further, ensuring that persons with disabilities can take training means that:

- Materials and training sites must be accessible per ADA requirements, and service animals must be accommodated.
- Appropriate translation, such as American Sign Language, should be offered.
- Enhanced materials may be needed, including larger print or Braille.
- Care should be taken to ensure that persons who are hard of hearing, such as senior citizens, can hear the training and join the volunteer team.

Next, while many skills are taught via observation and experience, the procedures and any associated materials should be well-developed and tested in advance of the training (Clizbe 2004). Providing a means to test and credential volunteers is a good idea, because you do want the building to pass inspection, right? This may mean facing the unpleasant task of not passing someone in a particular skill. After all, not everyone should conduct case management with traumatized survivors. In these cases, a caring volunteer coordination team would find an appropriate location and job for the willing citizen trainee.

Students from Hesston College's Disaster Management Program in Kansas practiced their skills before volunteering for the Mennonite Disaster Service efforts on the Gulf Coast. At Hesston, students first built a child's playhouse using the construction techniques they would employ to help Hurricane Katrina families (see Photo 14.3). Once on the coast, they worked to respond, rebuild, and restore residential areas. Their efforts also represent another principle for training: peer support; it is always easier to work in coordinated, collaborative teams, especially when tackling something as massive as a rebuild (Clizbe 2004).

**PHOTO 14.3   Hesston College student secures a roof with hurricane clips to miti-
gate future damage. (Photo by Hesston College. With permission.)**

Housing and Feeding Volunteers

Now that you have trained and placed volunteers, where are you going to put them? Look around your own community and see where you might house potentially thousands of outsiders. Is there a community center that has floor space for cots and sleeping bags? Does it have cooking and shower facilities? Who will do the cooking (see Photo 14.4)? How will you provide for laundry service?

In past disasters, a variety of ways to house and feed volunteers have been used successfully. Those options include:

- *Encouraging outside organizations to arrive self-contained.* The Mennonite Disaster Service, for example, typically brings in or purchases trailers to house its volunteers. In Pass Christian, Mississippi, MDS volunteers stayed in two double-wide trailers, with a single-wide used for cooking, case management, administrative activities, daily meetings, and debriefings. In other locations, MDS has placed volunteers in rented buildings. Often, local communities will provide space free of charge to such experienced organizations.
- *Providing a tent city for volunteers.* In some locations, it may be necessary to set up a campground, preferably using an existing facility,

PHOTO 14.4 Presbyterian Disaster Assistance volunteers from Stillwater, Oklahoma, put together meals for their work team. (Photo by Larry Caldwell. With permission.)

to host volunteers. When this is done, it is important to ensure that shelter is available should severe weather arise. Tent cities may also become extremely uncomfortable in extreme weather temperatures. Inclement weather, particularly rain, can quickly turn a tent city into a swamp. In long-term recoveries, strong and sturdy facilities should be established rather than temporary settings.

- *Using existing facilities.* Local resources may include a church retreat facility, a scouting encampment with permanent buildings, or even a closed military base. With local support, these may turn out to be ideal locations, although they do require consideration of the cost of utilities and other amenities. Volunteers can be asked to donate a certain amount per day to cover the cost of their housing and food, or donations can be used for expenses.

- *Hosting volunteers.* Local denominations may want to host outside volunteers in their fellowship halls or other facilities. Presbyterian churches in the New Orleans area have opened their facilities to outside organizations. When the external work crews arrive, they have been provided with floor space, cots, blankets, laundry service, t-shirts, and cooking facilities. At Parkway Presbyterian Church near New Orleans, outside work teams brought in or purchased locally their own food and prepared it. Though volunteers had to walk a block to use shower facilities, the local church provided daily laundry along with clean towels and clean t-shirts. Local families may also be willing to take in volunteers, although this can usually be done only for limited amounts of time.

Housing matters. Taking care of the physical comfort of volunteers can increase their energy, renew their commitment, and bring them back again. Poor facilities or poor provisions can diminish their eagerness to help, increase their stress, and deplete volunteer capacity. Perhaps even more important than housing is food. Having good cooks along for the volunteer journey can be its own reward. Not eating well or eating food of poor nutritional value can lead to more than complaints; it can result in not feeling well, lost energies, poor concentration, and even injuries and illness.

Risk Management for Voluntary Organizations and Volunteers

The Public Entity Risk Institute (PERI) defines risk as "any uncertainty about a future event that threatens your organization's ability to accomplish its mission" (PERI 2007a). Risk management is the process that identifies potential threats to the organization, such as injuries to volunteers or harm to others caused by volunteers. For organizations working with volunteers in disaster situations, risk management might include screening volunteers, checking on the motor vehicle records of drivers, creating training materials, and purchasing insurance (PERI 2007b).

Nearly every state has some type of volunteer act, sometimes referred to as "good samaritan laws." However, the laws vary considerably across the states, a problem that was addressed nationally in the 1990s by the Volunteer Protection Act of 1997 (VPA or Public Law 105-19). The law specifically applies to 501(c)3 organizations. The Volunteer Protection Act protects volunteers if they are "acting within the scope" of their responsibilities, were "properly licensed, certified or authorized to act," if the harm was not "willful, criminal or reckless misconduct or gross negligence," and if the harm was not caused by someone "operating a motor vehicle, vessel, or aircraft" (PERI 2007c).

Voluntary organizations may wish to purchase insurance to provide for the health and safety of their volunteers. Options can include purchasing insurance with limits, such as health-care policies that specify a certain amount for a particular injury, such as a maximum payout of $2,500 for a broken limb (PERI 2007c). An organization may also require that volunteers sign a waiver or release that they will not hold the organization responsible for injury. Or, an organization may ask that volunteers provide proof of insurance and a physician's approval. Requiring or providing vaccinations for tetanus, influenza, and other viral illnesses is advisable (Clizbe 2004). Some insurance providers also offer special, one-time policies that cover emergency transport home from a given location. The main point is that health problems do occur to volunteers, whether it is stepping on a nail, developing a respiratory infection, an emergency appendectomy, or something as severe as a traumatic injury. Wise organizations anticipate taking care of their volunteers.

Some research finds that healthy, well-adjusted individuals may be more likely than others to volunteer. Volunteering also enhances feelings of well-being, including happiness, overall satisfaction, and the absence of depression (Thoits and Hewitt 2001). However, it may also be true that permanent disaster volunteers may experience more significant costs (Britton 1991). They are more likely than other types of volunteers to be exposed to hazardous materials, to be injured with equipment, or to return home with lingering images of traumatized communities. Local communities may want to provide counseling for their volunteers to ensure that they return home with a positive outcome and are not psychologically harmed in any way.

Work may be physically or psychologically demanding. NVOAD (n.d.) recommends that volunteers do a few things to manage their mental and physical health:

- Manage use of caffeine, alcohol, tobacco, and sugar
- Set up limits to work hours, including shifts

- Develop a plan for the work to be done and assess it daily to ensure that it is manageable

Although these items may seem obvious, in a disaster context they may be overlooked. It is easy to turn to comfort foods (soda, chips, burgers) instead of healthier options like fruits, vegetables, and healthy beverages. And, in the urge to finish a job, people may grow fatigued; in such instances, injuries usually increase. In extremely hot climates, volunteers should be advised to drink water and sports drinks that replace electrolytes and minerals lost through excessive perspiration. Such a simple act can reduce significantly the possibility of heat exhaustion and heat stroke. A work-team member should be tasked with ensuring group safety by adhering to basic guidelines for physical and mental health, including drinking fluids at regular intervals and taking rest breaks.

Simply providing an outlet for volunteers can help with the stresses associated with volunteering. Opportunities can vary from informal to formal means of supporting volunteers. Work teams with young people may want to use local recreational areas for swimming, ball games, or other outdoor activities. A local community center might want to host a dance, offer card playing, or bring in a local band. These informal, fun means of providing stress relief can reduce anxiety felt by those trying to finish a difficult job in arduous conditions. Working within a disaster zone can also be depressing, and although volunteers provide valuable support to families going through the process, it can also be dispiriting to listen to others' stories (Pennebaker 1997).

More formal means for enhancing volunteer safety may include providing personal protective equipment and training. Areas affected by flooding may suffer chemical and other potentially toxic spills. Residues left in the soil and construction materials may be harmful to volunteers. After Katrina, for example, many voluntary organizations required that volunteers wear masks, gloves, and even entire body suits to protect them from the potentially hazardous environment. Volunteer work crews can also be encouraged to hold nightly or weekly discussion or debriefing sessions. Faith-based organizations often do this routinely as part of their devotional services, which may include discussion of the painful realities they observe. Local counselors, clergy, or mental-health professionals may be brought in to help the volunteers process what they have seen and experienced. Not doing so may result in harmful internalization of negative images, causing lingering sadness or even depression.

Volunteer Recognition and Rewards

While it may be true that volunteering reaps its own reward by empowering, healing, and making people feel good about themselves, it is also true that good work merits a reward. Volunteer recognition can vary, depending on what the local community has to offer. Formal rewards might include t-shirts, certificates, or even plaques for exceptional effort. A local community or volunteer center might organize a thank-you meal or an end-of-the-week party. Tying food and festivities into local culture can make the reward especially meaningful and fun. Volunteer work crews from the outside can be hosted or adopted by local denominations or community or civic groups for housing, group meals, cultural activities, pool parties, or other fun ways to recognize and reward volunteers.

Informal rewards might include something as simple as a thank you, either written or spoken, or a personal visit to a work site by homeowners, volunteer task leaders, or local officials. A local volunteer could be tasked to take photos of the volunteer effort and post them on a Web site to visibly demonstrate local appreciation. Billboards can be erected too.

Summary

Volunteerism tends to be quite high after a disaster event, particularly during the response period. Good emergency managers, elected officials, and recovery leaders will tap into that altruistic energy. Two types of volunteers are usually available. Unaffiliated volunteers are the ones who show up, well-intentioned, and want to help. It is more difficult to weave these kinds of volunteers into recovery efforts. Thus it is recommended that recovery leaders work to design volunteer management programs that recruit, train, and organize affiliated volunteers. A wide set of organizations can provide links to those volunteers. Many religious groups have disaster organizations and cadres of experienced, capable individuals. After a disaster, these faith-based organizations will extend their services into both short- and long-term recovery efforts. Community-based organizations, civic organizations, and newly appearing emergent groups may also offer resources and people.

Communities would be well advised to establish volunteer centers and hire or recruit a volunteer coordinator. Volunteer centers can recruit, train, and manage volunteers. The centers can also schedule projects in a reasonable timeline that coincides with the availability of various volunteer groups and their skill sets. Housing, feeding, and provision of a safe working environment for arriving volunteers may also fall under the responsibilities of the volunteer coordinator and center.

When a presidential disaster is declared, FEMA may make a voluntary-agency liaison available to assist with linking disaster organizations to specific needs. Several organizational forms may develop, with or without a disaster declaration, including a Long-Term Recovery Committee, an **Interfaith** Committee, or an Unmet-Needs Committee. Volunteers and voluntary organizations represent critical assets for recovery, especially for projects that rebuild housing for seniors, people with disabilities, single parents, and others at risk for losing their homes.

Study Guide

Summary Questions

1. Why do people volunteer? What is altruism?
2. What kinds of benefits and challenges are associated with volunteers after disaster?
3. What are the differences between affiliated and unaffiliated volunteers?
4. Distinguish between faith-based disaster organizations, community-based organizations, civic organizations, and emergent groups. What is the value of each for disaster recovery?
5. What kinds of contributions do voluntary organizations make during immediate response, short-term recovery, and long-term recovery?
6. What kinds of project personnel would be needed for a team rebuilding a house?
7. What should be included in a volunteer training program?
8. What is the role of the federal government regarding volunteers?
9. Why should a volunteer center be established?

Discussion Questions

1. What would you do if 1,000 unaffiliated volunteers showed up in your community to help with a disaster?
2. What kinds of volunteer work would you like to do in a disaster-recovery setting?
3. Is there a volunteer center in your community? What kinds of volunteerism go through it?
4. Are there any disaster organizations in your community that involve volunteers? What kinds of work do they do? Do they offer training?
5. Research the Web sites of disaster organizations to see what they did in recent disasters. What kinds of funding and staffing did they provide? What were their specific contributions? How many volunteers did they send? Where did they house them?
6. Examine Web sites, yellow pages, and other sources to identify the range of community-based, faith-based, and civic organizations located in your community. If you were to organize them into a disaster recovery effort, what would you ask them to do? How can you best tap into their resources?

Key Terms

Affiliated volunteers
Altruism
Civic club
Civic involvement
Community-based organization (CBO)
Emergency Support Function #6 (ESF #6)
Emergent group
Faith-based organization (FBO)
Interfaith
Long-Term Recovery Committee (LTRC)
National Voluntary Organizations Active in Disaster (NVOAD)
Spontaneous unplanned volunteers (SUVs)
Unaffiliated volunteers
Unmet-Needs Committee
Voluntary-agency liaison (VAL)
Voluntary organization
Volunteer coordination team (VCT)

References

ACS. 2006. Adventists respond to Katrina and Rita. Adventist Community Services. http://www.communityservices.org.

Amato, P., R. Ho, and S. Partridge. 1984. Responsibility attribution and helping behaviour in the Ash Wednesday bushfires. *Australian Journal of Psychology* 36 (2): 191–203.

Barry, J. 1997. *Rising tide: The great Mississippi flood of 1927 and how it changed America.* New York: Simon and Schuster.

Britton, N. 1991. Permanent disaster volunteers. *Nonprofit and voluntary sector quarterly* 20 (4): 395–415.

Clizbe, J. 2004. Challenges in managing volunteers during bioterrorism response. *Biosecurity and Bioterrorism: Biodefense Strategy, Practice, and Science* 2 (4): 294–300.

Dynes, R. 1974. *Organized behavior in disaster.* Newark: University of Delaware, Disaster Research Center.

Enarson, E., and B. Morrow. 1998. Women will rebuild Miami: A case study of feminist response to disaster. In *The gendered terrain of disaster*, ed. E. Enarson and B. Morrow, 185–200. Miami: International Hurricane Center.

Episcopal Relief and Development. 2006. Hurricane Katrina response: One year report. http://www.er-d.org.

FEMA. 1999. The role of voluntary agencies in emergency management. Independent Study 288 (IS-288). Federal Emergency Management Agency. http://training.fema.gov/EMIWeb/IS/IS288.asp.

FEMA. No date. Citizen Corps: A guide for local officials. Federal Emergency Management Agency. http://www.citizencorps.gov/pdf/council.pdf.

Lowe, S., and A. Fothergill. 2003. A need to help: Emergent volunteer behavior after September 11th. In *Beyond September 11th: An account of post-disaster research*, ed. J. Monday, 293–314. Boulder, CO: Natural Hazards Research and Applications Information Center.

NVOAD. No date. Managing spontaneous volunteers in times of disaster: The synergy of structure and good intentions. National Voluntary Organizations Active in Disaster. http://www.pointsoflight.org/programs/disaster/.

Neal, D. 1993. Flooded with relief: Issues of effective donations distribution. In *Cross training: Light the torch*. Proceedings of the 1993 National Floodplain Conference, 179–182. Boulder, CO: Natural Hazards Center.

Neal, D. 1994. Consequences of excessive donations in disaster: The case of Hurricane Andrew. *Disaster Management* 6 (1): 23–28.

Nelson, L. D., and Dynes, R. 1976. The impact of devotionalism and attendance on ordinary and emergency helping behavior. *Journal for the Scientific Study of Religion* 15: 47–59.

Parr, A. 1970. Organizational response to community crises and group emergence. *American Behavioral Scientist* 13: 423–429.

Paton, D. 1994. Disaster relief work: An example of training effectiveness. *Journal of Traumatic Stress* 7 (2): 275–288.

Paton, D. 1996. Training disaster workers: Promoting well-being and operational effectiveness. *Disaster Prevention and Management* 5 (5): 11–18.

Pennebaker, J. 1997. *Opening up*. New York: Guildford Press.

Phillips, B., and P. Jenkins. 2009. The roles of faith-based organizations after Hurricane Katrina. In *Meeting the needs of children, families, and communities post-disaster: Lessons learned from Hurricane Katrina and its aftermath*, ed. K. Kilmer, V. Gil-Rivas, R. Tedeschi, and L. G. Calhoun. Washington, D.C.: American Psychological Association. Forthcoming.

PERI. 2007a. Risk management basics. Public Entity Risk Institute. http://www.riskinstitute.org/peri/index.php?option=com_bookmarks&task=detail&id=576.

PERI. 2007b. Protecting your nonprofit and the board. Public Entity Risk Institute. http://www.riskinstitute.org/peri/index.php?option=com_bookmarks&task=detail&id=570.

PERI. 2007c. Understanding the volunteer protection act. Public Entity Risk Institute. http://www.riskinstitute.org/peri/index.php?option=com_bookmarks&task=detail&id=584.

Rodriguez, H., J. Trainor, and E. L. Quarantelli. 2006. Rising to the challenges of a catastrophe: The emergent and prosocial behavior following Hurricane Katrina. *Annals of the American Academy of Political and Social Science* 604: 82–101.

Ross, A. 1980. The emergence of organizational sets in three ecumenical disaster recovery organizations. *Human Relations* 33: 23–29.

Ross, A., and S. Smith. 1974. The emergence of an organizational and an organization set: A study of an interfaith disaster recovery group. Preliminary Paper 16. University of Delaware, Disaster Research Center.

Smith, M. H. 1978. American religious organizations in disaster: A study of congregational response to disaster. *Mass Emergencies* 3: 133–142.

Sutton, J. 2003. A complex organizational adaptation to the World Trade Center disaster: An analysis of faith-based organizations. In *Beyond September 11th: An account of post-disaster research*, ed. J. Monday, 405–428. Boulder, CO: Natural Hazards Applications and Information Research Center.

Thoits, P., and L. Hewitt. 2001. Volunteer work and well-being. *Journal of Health and Social Behavior* 42 (2): 115–131.

Resources

- American Red Cross Disaster Services Training samples can be currently viewed at http://www.redcross.org/flash/course01_v01/.
- Church of the Brethren Children's Disaster Services, http://www.brethren.org/genbd/BDM/CDSindex.html
- FEMA Independent Study Courses on volunteers, http://training.fema.gov/IS/crslist.asp.
- Lions Clubs International Foundation (Katrina) http://www.lions-katrina.org/what_lions_are_doing.php
- Lutheran Disaster Services Camp Noah, http://www.campnoah.org
- National Response Framework annex for volunteer and donations management can be viewed at http://www.redcross.org/flash/course01_v01/.
- National Response Framework ESF6 can be viewed at http://www.fema.gov/emergency/nrf/.
- National Voluntary Organizations Active in Disaster, http://www.nvoad.org. Links to most of the organizations mentioned in this chapter can be found at this website. Additional materials, including long term recovery manuals, are available via free download.
- Points of Light Foundation Voluntary Center National Network http://www.pointsoflight.org/centers/

Chapter **15**

Financing Recovery

Learning Objectives

After reading this chapter, you should be able to:

- Identify places to secure funding for recovery projects, including federal, state, local, foundational, corporate, and other private sources
- Explain how to contact prospective funders
- Describe how grant proposals are put together
- Portray the skills, abilities, and characteristics of an effective grant writer
- Understand the reasons for grant management and accountability
- Identify commonly available federal grant opportunities after disaster
- Search for nongovernmental sources to fund disaster projects

Introduction

The purpose of this chapter is multifold. First, recovery projects can take extensive amounts of time, energy, and particularly funding. Postdisaster recovery funding is available, but it may take considerable effort to identify the proper sources, design projects, develop **proposals** to secure the funding, task staff with project management, and implement the funded project. Funding could come from federal, state, or local programs, as well as from private sources, including corporations, foundations, organizations, and individuals. It is likely that an extensive effort will have to be made to identify and develop funding, particularly for creative, forward-thinking projects not covered by existing programs.

The purpose of this chapter is to encourage readers to think comprehensively about the possibilities of recovery funding. Toward that end, the chapter begins with the key skill necessary to secure funding: **grant writing**. Developing a proposal that an agency would like to fund is a skill required of emergency managers, government staff, and others involved in recovery.

The next section of the chapter revisits, in more depth, some of the key programs that provide funding. To illustrate, we look into traditional (FEMA) federal funding for public and individual assistance as well as **grants** that can come from other agencies such as HUD's Community Development Block Grant (CDBG). Because federal funding is not automatic, and requires a presidential disaster declaration, it may be that a given community will not secure the federal support necessary to cover all recovery expenses, projects, and possibilities. Further, federal funding may not allow for upgrades, improvements, or other changes, as much of the funding specifies that the money must be spent to restore something to what it was before the disaster. In short, federal funding is unlikely to cover all needs. It is probably going to be necessary to secure nonfederal funds through writing grant proposals.

Grant Writing

A grant is a set amount of money given in response to a written proposal. Writing a proposal for funding is thus the first step that must be undertaken. In this section we review the basic skills necessary to produce a quality proposal worthy of being funded, along with useful strategies for moving the proposal from ideas to implementation. The sections that follow describe general grant-writing strategies that could be used for a variety of funders. It should be noted that funders often vary in how they want materials submitted to them. Thus, although these general strategies should help you to get started, it is also important to understand what a particular funder wants you to do.

General Funding Sources

Funding for recovery can generally be secured from a variety of sources, including:

- *The federal government.* While a presidential declaration automatically triggers specific kinds of grants, loans, and funds, there are also numerous agencies that require submissions through existing or disaster-related programs. The degree of competition can vary significantly among these funders and programs.

- *Corporations.* Many major corporations include some type of funding mechanism, often through a company foundation, as part of giving back to the community. Usually a community needs to contact the corporation's foundation or go to its Web site to identify what it is willing to fund. Corporations may provide submission guidelines and forms on their Web sites, or it may be necessary to contact the corporation to secure these important items.
- *Foundations.* Public and private foundations may offer funds too. A foundation could be set up by a wealthy family, a set of benefactors, a political partnership, a service organization, or an individual. Foundations may operate at the national, regional, state, or local level. Accordingly, the foundation may fund only at that level. Foundations usually have specific projects they are willing to fund. Free materials on grant writing, including webinars, and links to funders can be found at the Foundation Center, http://foundationcenter.org/.
- *Disaster funds.* Many organizations and communities find themselves beneficiaries of funds donated during time of disaster. They may set up specific program guidelines that others can apply to for funding or may seek to collaborate with partners on projects.

Finding Disaster Recovery Grants

If a presidential declaration is secured, FEMA will work with state and local officials to explain funding opportunities. Those same federal officials can provide guidance on how to develop an appropriate project proposal in order to secure funds. It is critically important that writers follow the guidelines precisely to avoid rejection. Beyond the direct contact afforded through a presidential declaration, proposal writers can contact a FEMA regional office to identify prospective funding sources.

In addition, a number of specific Web sites link to potentially relevant disaster recovery grants as well as to nonrecovery grants. (All of the Web sites in the following list were last accessed on October 27, 2008):

- *Catalog of Federal Domestic Assistance (CFDA).* The CFDA Web site at www.cfda.gov offers access to a database of federal assistance that may include items relevant to recovery. State and local governments as well as tribal governments, nonprofit organizations, groups, and individuals may be eligible. CFDA provides a useful guide to writing grant proposals at http://12.46.245.173/pls/portal30/CATALOG.GRANT_PROPOSAL_DYN.show.

- *FEMA*. At the FEMA Web site, http://www.fema.gov/government/ grant/administration.shtm, there are links to grants administration, information about grant opportunities, grant application forms and information, grant administration forms and circulars, and program-specific information. Emergency personnel, governments, individuals, and nonprofits can also search for grants at http://www.fema.gov/government/grant/index.shtm.
- *Federal Register*. **Disaster Federal Register Notices** (DFRN) can be found at the www.gpoaccess.gov/fr. The *Federal Register* publishes news and other items daily on its Web site. The DFRN for Hurricane Katrina included notification of the presidential disaster declaration allowing for funds to be drawn from:

The following Catalog of Federal Domestic Assistance Numbers (CFDA) are to be used for reporting and drawing funds: 97.030, Community Disaster Loans; 97.031, Cora Brown Fund Program; 97.032, Crisis Counseling; 97.033, Disaster Legal Services Program; 97.034, Disaster Unemployment Assistance (DUA); 97.046, Fire Management Assistance; 97.048, Individuals and Households Housing; 97.049, Individuals and Households Disaster Housing Operations; 97.050 Individuals and Households Program—Other Needs, 97.036, Public Assistance Grants; 97.039, Hazard Mitigation Grant Program.

Source: http://www.fema.gov/news/dfrn.fema?id=4547

- *Grants.gov*. The federal government provides www.grants.gov as a centralized location to find and apply for grants from 26 federal agencies. You can search for grants by keyword, **Funding Opportunity Number** (FON, a unique number assigned to a grant), **Catalog of Federal Domestic Assistance** (CFDA) number, or by category, agency, or through advanced searches. E-mail subscriptions of new grant postings can be secured. The site also offers a quarterly newsletter titled "Succeed." It may be necessary to identify grant opportunities in advance of deadlines. For example, the Severe Repetitive Loss Grant Program for fiscal year 2009 required that proposals be submitted by December 19, 2008 (FON DHS-09-FEMA-110-001). DHS and FEMA expected to provide up to 75 awards from an estimated total program funding of $160,000,000.
- *U.S. Department of Homeland Security*. DHS provides primarily funds for "planning, equipment, training and exercise needs" for port security, critical infrastructure protection, regional and local mass transit systems (buses, trucking, rail), equipment and training for first responders, and homeland security grants. Although not recovery-specific, these grants could merit higher rankings in a

postdisaster context in order to enhance disaster resilience. Grants are also available to harden facilities, as described in Chapter 11 (Public Sector Recovery).

- *State emergency management agencies.* State agencies and governments may make funds available to beleaguered communities. Staying in touch with officials and liaisons can help to identify potential sources of funding. Most funds usually are made available after a disaster event. State legislatures may establish disaster-specific funds.

- *One-time grant competitions.* In specific disasters, the federal government may make funds available; thus it is important to stay alert for such disaster recovery opportunities. For example, in September 2006, DHS and FEMA offered an Alternative Housing Pilot Program (CFDA #97.087). Public Law 109-234, also known as the Emergency Supplemental Appropriation, provided $400 million to identify and evaluate alternative forms of FEMA Disaster Housing. Funds were available only to Gulf Coast States including Florida, Alabama, Mississippi, Louisiana, and Texas.

Proposal Writing Skills and Abilities

First among the necessary grant-writing skills is the ability to write effectively. A proposal author must be able to convince the funder that: (1) the project is appropriate for the funds requested; (2) the project team is capable of completing the task; (3) there is a compelling reason to fund the project; and (4) the proposal stands out among others that were submitted for limited funds. A second skill is the ability to stay focused on proposal requirements. For example, most grant proposals require preset formats with sections and points that must be addressed carefully. A third skill requires the writer to produce a quality proposal on time. Most agencies have specific deadlines that must be adhered to. Federal agencies usually may have a set time period after a disaster in which the proposal can be submitted. Nondisaster agencies that might fund projects often specify times as well as dates. Missing the time deadline by as much as one second usually results in automatic rejection by the agency.

Agencies, corporations, foundations, and others award grants for specific reasons. Foremost, the proposal must be consistent with what the agency wants to fund. Proposal writers should never ask for or try to convince the agency to fund something outside the scope of its mission or program.

Next, the proposal must be meritorious. This means that, in a competitive grant situation, the proposal must stand out above others. Meritorious proposals include specific qualities: clarity of ideas, an identifiable impact, a manageable project, a reasonable timeline, measurable outcomes, appropriate assessment procedures, and a qualified team. The writing within the proposal convinces reviewers to recommend funding.

Proposal writers should also be persistent. First-time submissions are often rejected. Going back to a funder a second, third, or even a fourth time is not unusual, particularly for corporations and foundations. All potential funders will provide some level of written guidance before submission. Many will provide reviews of the proposal so that a grant writer can fine-tune the proposal for the next round of submissions. Successful grant writing, which embodies the skills identified here, is usually referred to as **grantsmanship**.

Contacting Prospective Funders

Procedures for contacting prospective funders vary by funder. In the aftermath of a disaster, FEMA and other government officials may contact state and local authorities to inform them of prospective opportunities. For grants outside of that context, it will be necessary to contact prospective funders. Doing so begins with first researching the prospective funder. By looking at their Web sites or other materials, you can identify how they prefer initial contact. Some funders will permit phone calls or direct office visits. Others accept only a letter of inquiry or an e-mail. Still others will require that you submit an abstract or concept paper of your proposal so that they can verify that it qualifies.

It is important to bear in mind that funders may be receiving hundreds or even thousands of proposals. They have chosen the "first contact" approach to handle those inquiries and to sort through the requests efficiently. Follow their preferences. It would be unusual for you to send a complete proposal to a prospective funder during initial contacts. Therefore, before you e-mail or call, be sure to have your general idea scoped out and be sure it is consistent with the funder's mission. Doing so will help you to convince the prospective funder that you have a good idea and can conduct the project in a professional capacity.

Parts of the Proposal

Proposal requirements vary by funder. It is of the utmost importance that you follow the directions explicitly. Funders and reviewers will be looking at how you have written the proposal, and the easier you make it for them to follow what you have written, the better the final result is likely to be. Most funders specify sections that they want to see in a proposal. Be sure to use those sections as headings and subheadings. Typically, the sections fall into these general categories, but you should verify exactly what the funder wants:

- **Introduction**. The opening paragraph matters, because this is where you engage or "hook" the reader into your idea. The first sentence should be explicit and state exactly what you seek, such as, "This proposal seeks funding to restore affordable housing for senior citizens through a sound partnership among local, state, and national voluntary agencies." Additional sentences should go on to address why that is important and how the funds will be leveraged to make a difference. The introduction is usually fairly short, often less than one page. Remember, the reviewers and funders of your proposal will want to get to the substance of what you propose. Be succinct.

- **Significance**. The next section helps you to sell the proposal. You will want to point out why the idea and the project matters and will want to appeal directly to the funding agency. For example, write about why rebuilding affordable housing for seniors matters, "to ensure continued independence and financial well-being among those at risk for housing loss and/or homelessness." In this section, you should connect carefully to the mission of the organization. To illustrate, perhaps the agency specifically funds senior citizens or has concerns about affordable housing. Tap into those missions and build your argument that the project is appropriate for agency funding.

- **Project Goals and Objectives**. The next section typically outlines general goals and objectives. Goals are more general, such as "to replace the number of affordable senior housing units damaged by the storm." Objectives are specific, measurable outcomes. Objective 1 might be "to rebuild 17 affordable senior housing units." Objective 2 might be "to ensure that senior housing units are accessible according to Americans with Disabilities Act standards." Another goal might be "to rebuild senior housing using local, state, and national organizations." Objective 1 might be "to convene all available agencies and organizations in a Senior Housing Task Force." The remainder of the section should outline specifically how you will tackle all of the objectives. Strategies for doing so must be sound, convincing, and feasible. It would be important to address concerns that the funder might raise, such as how or why the units were destroyed in the first place and how the proposal would prevent that from happening again. Again, these concerns can be linked into goals and objectives. A third goal, then, could be "to mitigate the disaster risk experienced with affordable senior housing." Objective 1 would be "to elevate senior housing structures 3 feet above the anticipated 300-year floodplain." Objective 2 should anticipate the problems caused by elevations, including such as "include ramps for wheelchairs and/or lifts that permit access by seniors with disabilities." The value of the abstract or concept paper now becomes clear: By having the agency review your ideas, you can identify concerns it may have and develop a project designed to address questions and enhance funding potential.

- **The Budget**. All proposals require carefully prepared budgets. Many agencies will have their own forms for your use, or they may allow you to develop your own. There are two key components to the budget. The first is the itemization of specific needs. Although you don't have to list every paper clip or nail, you do need to generally list office or building supplies. Costs should be realistic, because an unrealistic budget may red-flag a proposal and result in questions or elimination. By talking to the agency before submission, it may be possible to get a ballpark figure for a proposal, or at least a budget limit. The second component is usually the budget justification. This is a written explanation of why you need the paper clips or nails. Though it may seem obvious that you need particular supplies for a particular project, never assume that the reviewer or agency understands what you are proposing. Explain everything.

- **Evaluation**. Although an agency may not require evaluation, it is always a good idea to include an evaluation or assessment component. In this section, explain how you will measure your project's effectiveness. You could do so with benchmarks that measure success. For a rebuilding project, perhaps you expect to have the project pass 95% of its first local code inspections for plumbing and wiring. Or, you could include an evaluation by asking building partners to assess their level of satisfaction and to identify problems that occurred in the rebuilding process. Another strategy could be to include periodic reviews and input from the target population, in this case, senior citizens. A mechanism to roll that feedback back into project management should be included. Evaluations help inform the project and tend to convince the funder that there will be appropriate oversight and accountability of funds. The evaluation component can also feed into the final project report that the funder is likely to require. Finally, you can use those evaluations to convince future funders that you did a great job and deserve additional grants.

- **Timeline**. Most funders will specify a funding period for the start and end of a grant. Consequently, it is a good idea to write a realistic timeline of what will happen and at what point in time. It is usually a good idea to build in some time for untoward events that can disrupt a project. A new storm could impede progress, such as when Hurricanes Gustav and Ike slowed down work on the Gulf Coast in 2008. Rebuilding projects in particular tend to succumb to the vagaries of weather. Extreme heat becomes dangerous for roofing projects, for example. Delays have a tendency to snowball. When a portion of a project cannot be completed, it slows other parts. If a roof cannot be put on, then the interior work slows. Construction crews must be scheduled for particular tasks. If they are not available due to delays, the timeline suffers. Establish a reasonable timeline.

- **Staffing**. One of the more critical portions of the proposal concerns the staffing for the project. In this section, you should describe your human resources and note their credentials and capabilities. Discuss the experience the staff has and how they will work together to make the project happen. Include job titles and descriptions and, where possible, identify the people who will fill in those positions. An organizational chart and description that depicts how the team will work together may help sell reviewers on project management.

- **Additional Forms**. Many agencies, especially federal funders, require completion of extensive forms. Failure to comply with the requirement will result in rejection of your proposal. Although the forms may be tedious and even confusing, they must be completed. Federal forms are not optional.

Submitting the Proposal

There are a number of rules that good grant writers keep in mind when working on a proposal. The best advice is to work on the proposal as far ahead of the submission deadline as possible. By waiting until the last minute, you will undermine your chance for success. Identify the deadline and establish a writing timeline. Keep on time so that there is no last-minute rush to submit, to find a missing form, or to secure a letter of commitment from a partner.

A number of agencies kindly offer checklists for submissions. If they do not, develop one that identifies the parts of the proposal that are required, the forms, the format for the budget, and the deadlines. Post the checklist at eye level next to your workstation and stay on target for your deadlines. Be sure to include key details such as the font, font size, and any number of copies that must be submitted.

Many agencies now require electronic submissions (see Photo 15.1). It is important to learn this system well in advance of the deadline. Submission day is not the time you want to discover that you need a login and password, or have to download software, or that the upload takes a long time. In some competitions, the number of submissions slows the electronic submission system. Consequently, submit the proposal the day before where at all possible. Some agencies may require hard copies. Overnight delivery is not always guaranteed from all locations, nor is on-time delivery. If the delivery company presents your proposal to the person who time-stamps your proposal, it needs to be there before the deadline. Even if the delivery person is

PHOTO 15.1 An Emergency Management Institute workshop instructs partici-pants about electronic grant opportunities. (Photo by Lauren Hobart/FEMA News Photo.)

standing in line at 5 p.m., if the time stamp says 5:01, the proposal will be rejected. And, of course, be sure you have the correct address on the pack-age. Within large bureaucracies, be sure the proposal is submitted to the right directorate, division, or office.

Details matter with proposals. Grant writing requires that you must cross all the t's and dot all the i's if you want to succeed. Never, ever submit a first draft. Always follow the directions. Dedicate yourself to the substance of the project. Be sure that the project is feasible and that you have presented a sound argument to support your proposal. Then, sit back and wait. Do not contact the funder. Wait until the funder responds.

The Review Process

The review process for your proposal will vary by agency. In some disaster agencies, it may be as straightforward as having a staff member verify that you are in compliance, that the budget is realistic, and that the project is doable. If so, it may simply release the funds. In many other instances, fed-eral agencies, corporations, and foundations bring in experts to review your proposal. Typically, the reviewers have a set of guidelines that they must keep in mind as they read through your work. You will be assessed vis-à-vis those criteria and may be awarded points. Proposals with higher points typically get funded. The hard work you put into following the guidelines and crafting your proposal have now paid off.

The federal government typically funds no more than four out of every ten proposals. Some agencies fund far fewer. Many foundations have even higher rates of rejection. Political administrations also change priorities, so you may find that what a previous administration funded is now not a top priority. Get used to rejection and do not take it personally. Try, try again. Secure copies of the reviews and attend to the critiques to improve your proposal for the next round of submissions.

Grants Management

Congratulations! You are funded! Now it is time to call your team together, set up budgets and accounting procedures, and launch the projects. Several Web sites provide forms and necessary materials for use in managing federal grants. Most federal agencies will require that grants be submitted through the www.grants.gov Web site described earlier in this chapter. Useful links from that site include:

- *Federal forms*: Forms that have been developed through the Office of Management and Budget (OMB) can be found at www.whitehouse. gov/omb/grants/grants_forms.html. Forms include Financial Status Report forms (long and short) for reimbursement, the Federal Cash Transactions Report, the Performance Progress Report, and relevant disclosure forms relating to subjects such as lobbying activities.
- *Software*: The software necessary to work with Grants.gov is available free on the Web site at http://www.grants.gov/agencies/grantors_help_resou.jsp#animated.
- *Training materials*: Animated tutorials, downloads, and archived webcasts are available at http://www.grants.gov/agencies/grantors_help_resou.jsp#animated.
- *A glossary*: Grant terms can be confusing. A list of terms and definitions can be located at the www.grants.gov Web site, http://www.grants.gov/help/glossary.jsp.

Grants management requires proper supervision of the project and monitoring of the budget. A project manager and financial and administrative support team members should be in place. A kickoff meeting should be called to get everyone on the team together to review the project deliverables (housing, reports, etc.) and the timeline. Monthly or weekly updates on the project and budget should be made and reviewed. As the project nears completion, assessment measures should be implemented, and a final report should be crafted.

Traditional Federal Recovery Resources

A wide set of programs exists to help those affected through the recovery process. Some of the funds and programs listed in this section are made specifically to individuals, and others go to states, nonprofit organizations, or other entities. Unless otherwise noted, additional information can be found at www.cfda.gov by inserting the CFDA number into the Web site's search engine. Also, unless otherwise noted, the quotes given below to illustrate the programs can be found under the CFDA number. These programs represent a selective sampling of what may be available. Presidential administrations may change programs, initiatives, and funding; thus it is important to stay alert to opportunities that may arise or to programs that may change. Readers should also refer to specific chapters for additional ideas and programs that finance recovery.

Public Assistance

FEMA, under a presidential disaster declaration, can assist state government agencies, local governments, tribal organizations and governments, and nonprofit institutions (with restrictions) to engage in public assistance projects. Eligible private or nonprofit institutions may include educational facilities, hospitals, rehabilitation facilities, utilities, and other critical facilities used by the public. These facilities might include museums, zoos, libraries, shelters for the homeless, sites that provide work for people with disabilities, food programs, day-care and adult-care centers, and other locations such as community centers that primarily serve the public. Public assistance (PA) programs are usually designed to restore a facility to functional condition and do not usually involve improvements unless the improvement provides future safeguards. An example of an appropriate improvement might include floodplain management measures.

An extensive list of publicly used facilities—including roads, bridges, water control facilities (dams, levees, reservoirs, drainage, irrigation, pumping, shore protection), buildings, equipment, utilities, parks, recreational areas, beaches, trees, and ground cover—is potentially eligible if the damage is caused by disaster. Restrictions may apply. Should a presidential declaration be issued, FEMA will work with eligible jurisdictions to identify and scope out projects. Specific FEMA personnel may be assigned to work with the jurisdiction as they move from initial application to a kickoff meeting and through project completion.

PA falls into three types of work: debris removal, emergency protective measures, and permanent restoration. Relocations may also be funded, including demolition, land acquisition, new construction, and infrastructure, such as roads and utilities. Reasonable costs, which are confirmed by FEMA, must be used. As described in Chapter 4 (Debris Management), several kinds of contracts may be let for specific work. FEMA will provide up to 75% of the costs of a project that is matched by another 25% from the state or the affected area; donated labor may be considered as part of the match. The PA program is extensive and requires that those involved become conversant with the procedures that are involved. FEMA offers multiple ways to learn about the PA program, including Emergency Management Institute (EMI) and independent study courses (see Resources section at the end of this chapter).

Individual Assistance

FEMA, under a presidential declaration, will offer various programs to assist individuals and households. A variety of assistance options can be secured from FEMA, as described in other chapters. An overview of the basic housing and nonhousing needs that are covered by the Individual Assistance (IA) program can be viewed in Box 15.1.

BOX 15.1   FEMA'S INDIVIDUAL ASSISTANCE PROGRAM

FEMA, under a presidential disaster declaration, may offer the following (verbatim):

Housing Needs

- Temporary Housing (a place to live for a limited period of time): Money is available to rent a different place to live, or a government provided housing unit when rental properties are not available.
- Repair: Money is available to homeowners to repair damage from the disaster to their primary residence that is not covered by insurance. The goal is to make the damaged home safe, sanitary, and functional.
- Replacement: Money is available to homeowners to replace their home destroyed in the disaster that is not covered by insurance. The goal is to help the homeowner with the cost of replacing their destroyed home.
- Permanent Housing Construction: Direct assistance or money for the construction of a home. This type of help occurs only in insular areas or remote locations specified by FEMA.

Other than Housing Needs

Money is available for necessary expenses and serious needs caused by the disaster. This includes:

- Disaster-related medical and dental costs.
- Disaster-related funeral and burial cost.
- Clothing; household items (room furnishings, appliances); tools (specialized or protective clothing and equipment) required for your job; necessary educational materials (computers, school books, supplies).
- Fuels for primary heat source (heating oil, gas).
- Clean-up items (wet/dry vacuum, dehumidifier).
- Disaster damaged vehicle.
- Moving and storage expenses related to the disaster (moving and storing property to avoid additional disaster damage while disaster-related repairs are being made to the home).
- Other necessary expenses or serious needs as determined by FEMA.
- Other expenses that are authorized by law.

Source: Federal Emergency Management Agency, http://www.fema.gov/assistance/process/assistance.shtm.

Note: Items are subject to change. The FEMA Web site and officials should be consulted regarding eligible expenses.

Some disasters generate need beyond the traditional 18 months of individual assistance that FEMA offers. Recovery leaders must remain alert to possibilities to extend coverage or to the availability of new programs that are offered by the federal government. For example, HUD has periodically become involved in disaster housing, and increasingly so in recent years. After the 2005 hurricanes, it became clear that people would not return home perhaps for many years. Consequently, FEMA transferred its rental assistance program to HUD. The effort emerged out of a new Disaster Housing Assistance Program (DHAP). The program was established through a partnership with public housing authorities across the United States. Ultimately, nearly 600 such authorities are expected to participate. The effort is to be supplemented with case management for job training and other appropriate forms of postdisaster counseling. As another example, HUD funded $5.2 million for federally recognized tribes to house families made homeless in the 2007 California wildfires. Funding was extended through Indian Housing Block Grants and Indian Community Development Block Grants, among others. More information about each of these examples is available at www.hud.gov.

Community Development Block Grants (e.g., CFDA 14.218)

Community Development Block Grants (CDBGs) are administered by HUD. Although these CDBG grants are usually obtained outside of disasters, they have been made available or expedited after a disaster. Grants are designed to provide "decent housing and sustainable living environments" for low-income individuals and households. Projects are designed to expand economic opportunities, including revitalization of impoverished areas and expansion of community services. Funds can be used to acquire or rehabilitate property and for public facilities improvements. Jurisdictions can contract with nonprofit organizations in the community to implement the plans. After the 2008 Midwest floods, HUD gave $100 million to Iowa, Indiana, and Wisconsin through this program. Funds were to go toward unmet needs, particularly housing, business, and infrastructure issues. The funds became available after Congress appropriated $300 million to HUD for such unmet needs.

Hazard Mitigation Grant Program (CFDA 97.039)

FEMA's Hazard Mitigation Grant Program (HMGP) offers funding for either public or private property (see Photo 15.2). Mitigation is hazard-specific, such as elevating or acquiring homes in areas prone to flooding. Seismic retrofit is also a possibility, as is assistance with high-wind hazards. FEMA also assists communities in developing model codes and building guides for the recovery process. HMGP funds are dispersed to states, which administer the programs. FEMA provides oversight to ensure compliance with funding requirements, environmental laws, and regulations. Funding is based on a percentage of funds provided under a presidential declaration for public and individual assistance. States benefit by having mitigation plans in place. For states with such a plan, FEMA can provide 15% of the first $2 billion of "aggregate amounts of disaster assistance." FEMA will pay up to 75% of the cost of a project, with the state and affected area making up the rest. For additional information and success stories, see the FEMA Mitigation Directorate, Hazard Mitigation Grant Program at http://www.fema.gov/about/divisions/mitigation.shtm.

Community Disaster Loans (CFDA 97.030)

Jurisdictions may apply for loans if a disaster has been declared. Funds may be used to replenish "substantial loss of tax and other revenue." Funds can be obtained to financially support governmental functions. The total request cannot exceed 25% of the jurisdiction's annual budget or $5 million. More information is available at http://www.fema.gov/government/grant/fs_cdl.shtm. Funds are distributed to the localities affected.

PHOTO 15.2 Nearly 700 applications for the Hazard Mitigation Grant Program (HMGP) arrive at a FEMA Long-Term Recovery Office. (Photo by Alonzo E. Scott, Jr./FEMA News Photo.)

Cora Brown Fund (CFDA 97.031)

The Cora Brown Fund provides funds to help those with unmet needs. Individuals do not apply for these funds. Rather, FEMA will work with disaster organizations and agencies to identify those needs. After Hurricane

Katrina, the Katrina Aid Today program, developed in part by the United Methodist Committee on Relief (see Chapter 7), received funds to help with case management needs. FEMA gave out the $25.4 million in a two-phase process specifically for use in Mississippi. The two-phase process applied funds to help close cases in the Katrina Aid Today program. In phase two, the funds were dedicated to families experiencing health problems in FEMA-funded hotels or motels and to families still remaining from phase one. Phase two also involved the Department of Housing and Urban Development and the Disaster Housing Assistance Program as part of a federal–voluntary organization partnership. Other Katrina Aid Today partners included Boat People SOS, Catholic Charities USA, Episcopal Relief and Development, Lutheran Disaster Response, the National Disability Rights Network, Odyssey House of Louisiana, the Society of St. Vincent DePaul, the Salvation Army and Volunteers of America (FEMA 2008). The program helped storm survivors in 32 states.

Crisis Counseling (CFDA 97.032)

Funds for crisis counseling can be obtained for "assisting disaster survivors in understanding their current situations and reactions, mitigating additional stress, assisting survivors in reviewing their options, promoting the use or development of coping strategies, providing emotional support and encouraging linkages with other individuals and agencies who may help survivors recover to their pre-disaster level of functioning." Funds can be secured from two separate programs: immediate services and regular services. The latter program provides funding for up to nine months of counseling. Benefits are made to individuals through the state affected.

Disaster Legal Services (CFDA 97.033)

Disaster legal assistance is provided free through FEMA. Services can include legal advice, counseling, and representation. This program specifically assists low-income individuals, families, and groups in need of legal advice. Benefits are distributed to individuals through the state affected.

Disaster Unemployment Assistance (CFDA 97.034)

People experiencing disaster-related job loss may benefit from the Disaster Unemployment Assistance Program. Funds are used for "individuals, project administrative costs to States, oversight payments to Department of Labor (DOL), and technical assistance." Program benefits are paid to individuals after documentation of eligibility and can be received on a weekly basis.

Crop Disaster Program (CFDA 10.073)

Farmers may be eligible for federal assistance when crops sustain damage from adverse weather, insects, or disease. Certain eligibility requirements must be met for different implementations of this program, such as having previously obtained coverage of losses under the Noninsured Crop Disaster Assistance Program, or being in compliance with specific federal provisions. The program is managed by the U.S. Department of Agriculture's Farm Service Agency. Careful calculations regarding crop yields and production losses must be made prior to an award. Losses for both quantity of yield and quality of product may be possible. USDA also provides other programs, including the Emergency Conservation Program, the Disaster Debt Set-Aside Program, and the Emergency Loan Program. More information is available at www.usda.gov.

Flood Mitigation Assistance Program (CFDA 97.029)

Mitigation assistance can be obtained for areas covered under the National Flood Insurance Program to states and localities. Funds can be obtained from three types of programs. Planning grants enable communities to assess and design appropriate efforts to reduce repetitive structural losses. Project grants allow for implementation of mitigation measures. Technical assistance grants bring expertise into the affected area. Funding amounts vary for each program and are subject to change annually. Funds go to states and localities. The Repetitive Flood Claims Program (97.092) also assists with reducing or eliminating risk to structures that have sustained flood damage in one or more events, specifically for those that do not meet the Flood Mitigation Assistance Program.

National Flood Insurance Program (CFDA 97.022)

The National Flood Insurance Program (NFIP) supports about 20,000 communities in reducing flood damage. The NFIP program has three elements: flood insurance, floodplain management, and flood hazard mapping. Citizens benefit from the program through their ability to acquire federally backed flood insurance. The additional program strategies reduce potential damage through floodplain management and mapping. Overall, the NFIP is designed to protect residents and business owners while supporting the broader community to reduce its long-term recovery needs. FEMA funds this program. Additional information can be found at http://www.fema.gov/about/programs/nfip/index.shtm.

Severe Repetitive Loss Program (CFDA 98.110)

For properties under the NFIP, funding may be secured to address situations of severe repetitive losses. Funding will go to state emergency management agencies or those responsible for floodplain management. Options for correcting situations of repeat losses include acquiring or relocating, elevations, conversion of properties to open space, and dry flood-proofing for historic structures. Severe repetitive loss locations are pre-identified by FEMA prior to qualification for funding. FEMA will pay for up to 75% of the costs for appropriate actions with a matching 25% from the state.

Infrastructure Protection Program

Forward-thinking jurisdictions, especially those subject to terrorist attack, can apply for infrastructure protection grants. Funds go to states, localities, and U.S. territories for preparedness activities. Although not specific to recovery, the funds can ultimately result in strengthening key infrastructure against attack, thus reducing the time needed for long-term recovery. Funds are subject to change annually. Additional funds may be possible under other Department of Homeland Security Grants (DHS 2008). In fiscal year 2008, DHS provided the following funds across the nation:

- Transit Security Grant Program, $350,108,572
- Freight Rail Security Grant Program, $4,991,429
- Intercity Passenger Rail (Amtrak), $25,000,000
- Port Security Grant Program, $388,600,000
- Intercity Bus Security Grant Program, $11,172,250
- Trucking Security Program, $15,544,000
- Buffer Zone Protection Program, $48,575,000

National Dam Safety Program (CFDA 97.041)

As with the Infrastructure Protection Program, this grant program helps mitigate disaster. If dams are strengthened prior to an event, the recovery time will lessen. Money goes directly to a state for nonfederal dams. Two types of programs can be funded. Primary assistance grants are for designing and implementing dam safety programs, including structural mitigation as well as inspection programs. States that successfully implement the primary assistance grants are then eligible for advanced assistance grants. The goal of both programs is life safety.

National Earthquake Hazards Reduction Program (CFDA 97.082)

Similarly, the National Earthquake Hazards Reduction Program (NEHRP) addresses earthquake safety. NEHRP offers funding to "develop mitigation, preparedness and response plans, prepare inventories and conduct seismic safety inspection of critical structures and lifelines, update building and zoning codes and ordinances to enhance seismic safety, increase earthquake awareness and education, and encourage the development of multi-State groups for such purposes." Funding goes directly to states.

Emergency Management Institute (CFDA 97.026, 97.027, 97.028)

As recommended in Chapter 11 (Public Sector Recovery), officials should take advantage of opportunities to gain education and training. The Emergency Management Institute (EMI) of FEMA offers such training, including a 4.5-day seminar on recovery. Funds can pay for first responders, emergency management staff, and other individuals to attend.

There are many more types of federal grants that may become available after disaster. By working with federal partners, those opportunities can be maximized.

Foundation Grants

For disaster situations that do not receive presidential declarations and for areas that remain underfunded or unaddressed, recovery committees may wish to seek grants from nonfederal sources. Most major corporations establish foundations for philanthropic giving. Wealthy patrons may also establish private foundations. Foundations may specify exactly what they are willing to fund, including the geographic region.

Several Web sites can link you to prospective funders. The Foundation Center (www.foundationcenter.org) offers extensive resources and links, training materials, and information on up to 600 granting agencies. A fee may be charged for some of the training and resources. The Foundation Center has also made its Web site materials accessible to people with disabilities. In 2008, the Foundation Center launched a Web page on Hurricane Katrina designed to inform people about the approximately $1 billion in donations and grants made to various projects. The page can be accessed at http://fconline.foundationcenter.org/maps/katrina/. The Council on Foundations in Washington, D.C., also offers guidance on how grantors should make funds available, which provides insights on how grantees might craft their proposals.

Online searches by topic can also yield good leads to grants. For example, the Disability Funders Network, though not a granting organization, provides useful links, grant-writing guidelines, and an online list of prospective donors at www.disabilityfunders.org.

Finally, it may be very useful to connect to a college or university in your area. Most institutions in higher education include a grant-writing office with people expert in searching for appropriate grants. State universities also maintain high-level administrative offices with research professionals who want to link their faculty to both research and applied project opportunities.

According to the *Philanthropy News Digest*, an online publication of the Foundation Center, a number of foundations and corporations had already begun to contribute to Hurricane Ike (September 2008), which devastated Galveston Island, Texas, and damaged other portions of the state as well as locales within Louisiana. Giving came from major corporations likely to contribute to rebuilding efforts, including Lowe's and Home Depot. Such corporations may give outright or may ask for specific proposals. Locally owned stores and franchises of major corporations may offer several thousand dollars for a project, or it may be possible to apply to the entire corporation's foundation for more significant amounts. Most major oil, discount, delivery, banking, credit card, and insurance companies (among others) also maintain foundation links on their Web sites.

For example, Home Depot provides funds through its Local Initiatives Support Corporation, which donated $100,000 to help local, community volunteer efforts with cleanup after Hurricane Gustav. Similarly, Home Depot has the Homer Fund for employees who go through a disaster. Lowe's has established an in-store matching-contribution program. United Parcel Service (UPS) gave funds directly to national and regional American Red Cross units as well as in-kind support for Hurricane Gustav. These kinds of funds are typically available immediately after a disaster. However, foundations may also offer additional funding as the recovery rolls out.

Foundations may also be associated with specific topics or organizational affiliations. For example:

- The American Psychiatric Foundation offered a Disaster Recovery Fund for Psychiatrists to help professionals assist patients affected by the 2005 hurricanes (http://pn.psychiatryonline.org/cgi/content/full/41/2/2).
- The Ford Foundation was established in 1936 by Edsel Ford to serve human welfare. It provides extensive grants to a wide variety of community improvement efforts. The foundation funded Dillard University in New Orleans with $400,000 to help with rebuilding, environmental, and health issues and clean-up after Hurricane Katrina.

- Islamic Relief funded a $30,000 grant to the Interfaith Ministries of Greater Houston for Katrina relief work. Half of the grant went to the Office of Disaster Preparedness and Response to help make 300 faith communities more disaster resistant (www.irw.org/katrina/texas).
- The Humane Society of the United States provided Hurricane Katrina grants to help rebuild facilities across the Gulf Coast, including animal shelters, rescue facilities, preservation offices, search and rescue efforts, and rehabilitation centers (www.hsus.org).
- The Lilly Endowment in Indianapolis (Eli Lilly is a pharmaceutical company) gave a $2.5-million grant to the Salvation Army for the 2008 Midwest Floods (Moore 2008).
- The Oklahoma City Community Foundation managed grants and donations from individuals, local companies, the Tides Foundation, and the mayor's office. Funds were used for multiple programs. At the ten-year mark, the foundation was providing scholarship funds to children of those lost or affected by the bombing (Council on Foundations 2008).
- A wide set of faith-based and voluntary organizations may provide grants to community-based partnerships. Contact should be made through national disaster organizational offices (see suggestions throughout this text for specific topics).
- Specific disasters and opportunities may attract individual donors. Proposals may be made to individuals regarding elements of projects, such as green initiatives or culturally specific projects such as the Musicians' Village in New Orleans, which was supported by private individuals and Habitat for Humanity volunteers.
- It may be necessary to pull together grants from multiple funders. The Princeville Heritage Trail (see Photo 15.3) was constructed from matching funds. Lowe's Charitable and Educational Foundation gave $165,750, which was matched by the North Carolina Parks and Recreation Trust Fund.

Search engines, research offices, professional networks of colleagues, and others can lead you to grants. Should disaster strike your community, contact other jurisdictions that have been through similar events and ask where they secured funding. Work with state and federal partners to identify prospective funding. Assign staff to write and manage grants. Be creative and thorough in identifying prospective funders. Keep trying, and remember that you may have to submit your proposal more than once to secure the grant. Rejection does not necessarily mean failure.

PHOTO 15.3 The Princeville Heritage Trail. (Photo by Brenda Phillips.)

Summary

Financing recovery may include federal, state, local, and private sources. Grant writing emerges as a critical strength to tap into among staff and volunteers. Grants may be secured for disaster recovery from the federal government under a presidential disaster declaration. Lacking such a declaration, federal funds from agencies may still be available under relevant funding programs, such as low-income housing, environmental restoration, or downtown revitalization. Grant writing requires specific skills, including the ability to organize material into a coherent project proposal. Grantsmanship also requires effective communication and writing skills.

Extensive federal programs may be made available for disaster recovery. Jurisdictions and organizations seeking those funds should work closely with state and federal partners to identify and secure appropriate funds. Grants must be managed carefully to ensure compliance with federal requirements. Other grant opportunities may be found through private corporations, foundations, and individuals. Such opportunities may include disaster-specific funding or related opportunities.

Study Guide

Summary Questions

1. What is the difference between a grant and a proposal?
2. What are the main elements of a grant proposal? What should go into each section?
3. Describe the kinds of skills that a successful grant writer will need.
4. Where can you find resources for financial management of federal grants?
5. Distinguish between public and individual assistance grants.
6. What kinds of funding should a community try to secure if a presidential disaster declaration is not received?

Discussion Questions

1. What kinds of limitations are there on federal grants?
2. Search the Web for a recent disaster. Which private foundations and corporations provided funds and for what kinds of projects?
3. Are there local, regional, or state foundations in your area? Are they private foundations or corporate?
4. What kinds of major corporations offer grants in your area? What are they interested in funding?
5. What skills do you have for writing grant proposals? Should you take additional courses at EMI, look at online training options, or take college writing courses?

Key Terms

Catalog of Federal Domestic Assistance (CFDA)
Disaster Federal Register Notice
Federal Register (FR)
Funding Opportunity Number (FON)
Grant
Grantsmanship
Grant writing
Proposal

References

Council on Foundations. 2008. *We were there: The role of philanthropy in national disasters.* Washington DC: Council on Foundations.
DHS. 2008. Overview: FY 2008 infrastructure protection activities. Washington DC: Department of Homeland Security.

FEMA. 2008. FEMA provides $25.4 million to continue case management in Mississippi. FEMA press release 1604-666, August 13. http://www.fema.gov/news/newsrelease. fema?id=45409.

Foundation Center. 2008. Corporate donations begin to roll in for Hurricane Ike recovery efforts. *Philanthropy News Digest* September 17. http://foundationcenter.org/pnd/news/story.jhtml?id=227700028.

Moore, C. 2008. Donations for Midwest floods reach $16.3 million. *The Chronicle of Philanthropy News* Updates June 25. http://philanthropy.com/news/index. php?id=5046.

Resources

- FEMA offers free Independent Study courses at their website for the Public Assistance process. Select IS 630 and IS 631. Available at http://training.fema.gov/IS/crslist.asp. Accessed September 18, 2008.
- U.S. Department of Homeland Security, Financial Management Guide for grants is available at http://www.dhs.gov/xlibrary/assets/Grants_FinancialManagementGuide.pdf. Accessed September 18, 2008.
- U.S. Department of Homeland Security, FY 2008 Overview of Grants. Available at http://www.dhs.gov/xlibrary/assets/grant-program-overview-fy2008.pdf. Accessed September 18, 2008.

Glossary

accessibility	The ability to move about to take care of families, return to work, and launch both personal and community efforts.
accountability	Assurance that donated funds are used for their intended purpose by an agency.
affiliated volunteers	People associated with a disaster-relief organization; they are usually trained or experienced.
air-curtain incineration	A debris management procedure that involves digging a pit and installing a blower unit to feed air to a fire; smoke and small particles are trapped and collected.
anxiety	A psychological reaction that may include phobias, worry, fear, or panic attacks.

blaming	The act of holding another responsible for the impact of a disaster.
bonding social capital	Connections that form between people with similar backgrounds and similar objectives.
bridging social capital	Connections that form between people with different backgrounds, such as occupations, but with similar objectives.
bureaucratic authority	Power vested in a position within an agency or governmental office.
business continuity planning	Efforts taken to ensure that critical operations can continue after disaster.
capital campaign	An effort designed to convince taxpayers to support new taxes or bonds that finance various measures, such as recovery efforts.
capital-infusion model	Brings in outside aid through government or the assistance of voluntary organizations.
case management	Technique used by social workers to move individuals and families through a decision-making process toward recovery.
Catalog of Federal Domestic Assistance (CFDA)	A federal Web site that lists grants, eligibility, and application information.
charismatic authority	Power that arises from the personality of an individual and his or her ability to convince others or to attract followers.
chipper	Device used to chop up brush from downed limbs and trees.
civic club	An organization dedicated to public service.
civic involvement	The process of contributing to the public good through volunteerism.

cognitive social capital	Perspectives, ideas, and attitudes that people bring to a recovery process.
collective altruism	Arises from a broader social arrangement, where the community takes the initiative to care for others.
collective loss	The experience of losing a set of important relationships that spans a community.
community	A group of people who share a sense of belonging that may include geographical location, shared experience, and common interests.
community-based organization (CBO)	An entity located within a given geographic location that links to specific populations or resources.
community engagement	Efforts to ensure that stakeholders likely to be affected by a decision are included in the decision-making process.
compassion fatigue	Psychological exhaustion and possibly other traumas as a result of attempting to help others.
comprehensive emergency management	Includes the four phases of preparedness, response, mitigation, and recovery; used to organize activities of emergency managers.
comprehensive planning	An effort to scope out how a community might grow and develop; such efforts may include elements of disaster planning.
construction and demolition (C&D) debris	Material that results from rebuilding, including discarded lumber and building supplies.
consultation	Asking the public for a reaction or opinion.

content leader	The person responsible for ensuring that the substance of a meeting is discussed.
convergence	The arrival of unsolicited items and volunteers at a disaster scene.
cultural resource	Tangible or intangible item such as a building, monument, or art.
cyber-commuting	Employees work via computers at home to temporarily relocate into cyberspace.
debriefing	A meeting in which people express sentiments about their disaster experience and process those emotions.
debris	Material that occurs as a result of the disaster, including that directly generated through the event and indirectly through response and recovery activities.
debris management	Efforts to reduce, recycle, and reuse materials in an attempt to handle materials correctly according to environmental regulations.
depression	A mood disorder that might include sadness, sleeplessness, and feelings of guilt, lack of energy, or difficulty concentrating.
direct loss	Damage sustained by a business as a result of a disaster event.
disaster	An event that disrupts the structure and functioning of a community, causing closures and altering daily routines.
Disaster Federal Register Notice (DFRN)	Information given by the federal government regarding a disaster declaration.
Disaster Recovery Center (DRC)	The federal government's one-stop shop for federal aid applications and assistance.

disaster resilience	The ability to rebound from a disaster event with less damage and a shorter recovery period.
displacement	The temporary relocation of a business or household resulting from a disaster.
distribution center	A location where survivors can pick up donated items.
district overlay	A special set of design considerations for a business in order to enhance environmental quality, reduce risks through mitigation measures, or feature historic elements.
donations	Items and funds given for the purpose of providing relief to disaster victims.
donations coordination center	The location where a donations management team works to ensure that items are inventoried, stored in warehouses, or sent to distribution centers.
donations-management coordinator	The lead person responsible for managing solicited and unsolicited contributions.
donor intent	What the person giving the item or money wants done with the contribution.
downtime	The amount of time that a business cannot operate.
ecological footprint	A calculation of an activity's impact on the Earth and its resources.
economic vitality	The ability to survive and rebound from disaster. A disaster-recovery process that integrates economic interests can help people recover lost income and launch recoveries.

emergency declaration	Issued by the president to allow federal funds to be used for emergency measures such as road clearance or sandbagging.
emergency operations center (EOC)	A location where emergency managers handle response operations and work with officials to make decisions that affect recovery.
emergency shelter	Short-term location that houses residents displaced by a disaster.
emergent group	Group brought together as a result of unmet needs in a disaster context.
Emergent Human Resources Model (EHRM)	A management model that emphasizes flexibility and problem solving over bureaucratic rules and regulations.
Emergent-norm theory	New behavior or activities that appear in reaction to a disaster event.
environmental conservation	Actions taken to set aside or save habitat, vegetation, watersheds, and other environmentally sensitive areas.
environmental impact statement	A written assessment of the potential effects of an action on a specific physical location.
environmental justice	A social movement that has pointed out how some groups fare worse in disasters or bear higher environmental risks.
environmental protection	Actions taken, such as laws and regulations limiting release of pollutants, to prevent further harm.
environmental quality	An element of recovery that focuses on how to protect natural resources and change how we impact our environment.

environmental restoration	Efforts taken to put back what has been damaged, usually through human impact, including the effects of technological disaster or human encroachment.
equity	Fairness among groups and populations experiencing recovery such as different generations, racial and ethnic groups, and people with disabilities.
faith-based organization (FBO)	An entity connected to a faith tradition that provides support, resources, and volunteers in disaster situations.
Federal Emergency Management Agency (FEMA)	Federal agency tasked with disaster mitigation, preparedness, response, and recovery planning.
***Federal Register* (FR)**	Official journal of the federal government in which the Disaster Federal Register Notice is posted.
feminist theory	A theoretical framework that involves several strands of thinking and poses solutions regarding the concerns and issues of women in disaster situations.
flexibility	The ability of an interconnected system of parts to demonstrate resilience, robustness, and adaptability.
funding opportunity number (FON)	A unique number assigned to a federal grant.
grant	Money given to fund a project.
grantsmanship	The ability to write a successful grant proposal.
grant writing	The act of crafting a grant proposal to secure money.
grinder	Device used to handle large amounts of debris; requires a large area to stockpile the resulting mulch.

hazard-mitigation planning	A process that involves the community in deciding priorities for risk-reduction efforts.
heritage tourism	Visits by tourists to locations that offer cultural or historic meaningfulness.
high-hazard dam	A dam at risk for failure.
historic district	An area that qualifies for special recognition under the National Register of Historic Places.
historic property	Any prehistoric or historic district, site, building, structure, or object that is eligible for the National Register of Historic Places.
holistic recovery	An approach that considers how all elements of a recovery interconnect.
home-based business	A business enterprise located in a dwelling.
indirect losses	Losses caused as the by-product of a disaster, such as utility interruption, that causes a business to cease operations.
individual altruism	A personal act of giving.
individual assistance	A FEMA program that helps individuals and households recover from disaster, including housing assistance and other programs.
informational convergence	Occurs when people try to offer a variety of goods and services to help an area recover from disaster.
infrastructure	The built environment, including bridges, ports, roads, railways, and airports.
interconnectedness	A linkage of two or more systems.
interfaith	An effort of religious organizations to address unmet needs.

joint field office	A temporary location set up by FEMA to coordinate activities, usually under the National Response Framework.
landfill	An area set aside for disaster debris, garbage, and other refuse that must be managed in accordance with environmental regulations.
land-use planning	Decisions made by a jurisdiction regarding how land will be used, such as for commercial, industrial, or residential purposes.
leadership	The ability to provide guidance and support that moves a community through a recovery process.
legal-rational authority	Power that is vested as a result of election as an official representative.
limited-intervention model	A recovery approach in which insurance provides relief funds along with some government assistance.
linking social capital	Social assets developed by communities and organizational representatives.
long-term recovery	A process that involves a wide variety of activities directed toward restoring businesses, homes, infrastructure, utilities, the environment, and other community elements.
long-term recovery committee (LTRC)	An organization dedicated specifically to recovery that spans multiple organizations, usually in a given geographic location affected by a disaster.

market model	The real estate market determines who gets housing, with recovery heavily dependent on the financial resources of the individual.
material convergence	Movement of supplies and equipment.
micro-loan	A small loan given to help a business start or survive disruption.
mitigation	Measures taken to reduce risks, including structural measures like levees or nonstructural measures like insurance.
multiagency warehouse	A place where donations are stored for use by relief organizations.
National Disaster Housing Plan	A plan regarding how to provide postdisaster housing.
National Disaster Housing Strategy	A strategy to establish principles for housing disaster victims developed by FEMA.
National Priority List	An EPA list of locations needing federal action or support due to hazardous waste.
National Register of Historic Places	A list of eligible cultural and historic resources that meet specific criteria.
National Response Framework	The federal plan to respond to major disaster events; includes more than a dozen emergency-support functional plans and several key annexes for specific issues.
National Voluntary Organizations Active in Disaster (NVOAD)	A national umbrella organization that includes multiple faith-based organizations and other disaster organizations designed to address unmet needs and provide widespread relief and recovery resources.
natural disaster	A result of natural forces, including weather or ground movement.

nonstructural mitigation	Building codes, land-use planning, insurance, and similar measures that reduce risk.
notice of intent	Notice issued when the federal government expects to take some action that will affect human or environmental systems.
ordinance	A policy that is passed governing specific measures to be taken after a disaster, such as emergency road clearance, measures to safeguard environmental areas, or restrictions on floodplain development.
outreach	Efforts to extend services to a client or community affected by disaster.
participatory action	A strategy to ensure that the community becomes engaged in the decision-making process by linking reflective thought to action.
participatory recovery	An approach to recovery that integrates citizens and leaders to maximize stakeholder participation.
permanent housing	No more moves are necessary; a final location has been obtained, and a household routine has been reestablished.
personal convergence	Volunteers arriving by foot or by vehicle at a disaster site.
physical disaster loan	Offered to businesses of all sizes by the Small Business Administration after a disaster.
place	A location that offers meaningful connections to those who live or lived there.
planning	Determining how recovery will be accomplished.
political efficacy	A feeling or belief that an individual can effect political change

political will
Determination by elected officials and others in positions of authority to ensure that a recovery will be conducted and funded properly.

postdisaster planning
Principles, goals, and objectives for all elements that must be restored after a disaster.

posttraumatic stress disorder
A form of anxiety that may produce flashbacks, nightmares, or other symptoms.

praxis
Action as the result of reflective thought.

predisaster planning
Procedures intended to reduce the effects of a disaster and determine the means by which a community will restore lost capacities.

preliminary damage assessment
An inventory of losses sustained after a disaster and a necessary first step to secure a presidential disaster declaration.

preparedness
Activities designed to ensure that a jurisdiction or household is ready for a disaster event: planning, education, and training.

presidential disaster declaration
After a location becomes overwhelmed by a disaster event and requires federal assistance, a request is made through the governor and issued by the U.S. president.

process leader
The person responsible for ensuring that specified stages or steps occur in a decision-making or planning process.

proposal
A set of ideas designed to secure funding from a granting agency.

quality of life
A key element of a holistic recovery that focuses on how people prefer to live and what kind of community they want to live in.

rainy-day fund   A set-aside of money for a future disaster event.

rebuilding green   Selection of energy-efficient and other means to reduce the future impact of human use on limited natural resources.

reconstruction   The physical act of rebuilding.

recovery   A process that involves communities and officials in a series of steps and stages through which households and businesses move at varying rates toward reestablishing normal routines.

recycling   Efforts to convert debris into other usable items.

redevelopment model   A process in which national-level agencies will lead and fund the recovery to rebuild the community.

reduction   Efforts to decrease the amount of debris that must be managed. See debris management.

rehabilitation   Actions taken to improve a prior state.

relocation/buyouts   A federal strategy that offers fair market value for a home in order to relocate residents out of a hazardous area such as a floodplain.

remedy   The EPA term for an action such placement of a site on the National Priority List.

residential care   A psychological treatment location or facility where patients stay as residents.

response   Activities taken to save lives.

restitution   Funds or other compensation given to plaintiffs during legal disputes as a consequence of an event.

restoration	A return to a prior state, such as restoration of utilities to functioning order or an historic property to its meaningful origins.
reuse	Efforts to retrieve materials for rebuilding, for example, the historic features of a building.
scoping	The process by which the EPA works to identify issues and concerns of the public surrounding a federal action or environmental concern.
secondary trauma	A social worker or similar professional begins to experience the emotions and symptoms of clients.
short-term recovery	Activities that lay a foundation for long-term recovery, including planning, utility restoration, and debris management.
situational altruism	Donations based on need following a disaster.
social capital	The intangible assets that people bring to a recovery process through their labor, ideas, and other resources.
sociopolitical ecology theory	A focus on interactions within a social system.
spontaneous unplanned volunteers (SUVs)	Unaffiliated volunteers who arrive unannounced and usually without training.
stakeholders	Those who benefit or lose the most from the impact of recovery planning and the implementation of recovery projects.
State Historic Preservation Office	The state entity that offers support and guidance on historic properties.

structural mitigation	Actions that affect the built environment, including seismic retrofit, levee construction, and hardening of key facilities to reduce risk.
structural social capital	Elements of the social structure, including roles and statuses.
substitute convergence	Messages, inquiries, offers of assistance, and donations of material goods.
Superfund	The money set aside for sites on the National Priority List.
sustainability	An approach to recovery that ensures continued survival of key elements present in a given location.
systems theory	A focus on the interaction of three key systems (built, human, and physical environments) and how a misfit results in disaster.
technological disaster	An event that occurs as a result of hazardous materials, nuclear accidents, oil spills, or other events outside of nature.
temporary housing	A location between temporary shelter and permanent housing, in which a household routine is established but is not permanent.
temporary shelter	A location where displaced disaster victims have basic needs met.
terrorism	A deliberate act by humans to instill fear and cause destruction and disruption.
therapy	Treatment for a psychological reaction to a disaster.
the "second disaster"	The arrival of unsolicited donations that may interfere with response capacities.

trauma	The consequence of exposure to a disaster; symptoms include depression and anxiety.
Tribal Historic Preservation Office	The tribal entity that offers support and guidance on historic properties.
unaffiliated volunteers	Volunteers without a link to an experienced disaster organization.
unmet needs	Items that emerge when needs "fall through the cracks" of federal aid or when unanticipated issues arise.
unmet-needs committee	A group that tries to find ways to address the problems of those who do not meet federal program guidelines or who lack sufficient means to recover.
unsolicited donations	Items that are not requested and may not be needed.
utility	A provider of critical resources, such as water, telephone, or power.
visioning process	A meeting in which people discuss their ideas and dreams for a restored community, thereby laying the foundation for recovery planning.
voluntary agency liaison (VAL)	The FEMA personnel assigned to link federal efforts to disaster organizations.
volunteer coordination team (VCT)	A group that attempts to manage unaffiliated volunteers and affiliated volunteers and leverages its capacity to fulfill recovery needs.
vulnerability theory	Concentrates on human lives, with a focus on those at highest risk and most vulnerable to injury, death, economic disruption, and property loss.
xeriscaping	The use of native plants that reduce water use and survive local climate variation.

Index

M

N

T